GLENCOE FRENCH ①

Student and Parent Resources
Bon voyage! Florida Edition

Features of Your
Florida Student Edition

- **Bon voyage!** is fully correlated to the **Sunshine State Standards**. Correlations to these standards are located on the Sunshine State Standards pages and throughout the book at point of use.

- **FCAT Reading and Writing Practice** and study tips are included within each chapter to help students prepare for the **FCAT** while learning French.

- Dinah Zike's **Foldables™** Study Organizers are included at the beginning of the Student Edition to help all types of learners organize and retain information.

- **Bon voyage!** includes a series of **National Geographic** photographs called **Reflets**. Each of the four **Reflets** sections features stunning photography that examines the traditional and modern aspects of life in a variety of French-speaking countries.

Student and Parent Resources

Bon voyage! Florida Edition

Additional **Student Resources**

Florida Passport to Success Notebook provides notetaking and study skills to help students organize and internalize new information, allowing them to become more effective communicators in the French language. Reading Tips are also provided to take the mystery out of reading and give students the tools they need to become more effective readers.

Interactive Conversations CD-ROM gives students extra practice listening and speaking in French. After watching a video conversation, students can play the role of one of the characters, recording their part of the conversation on the computer. Students can then play back the conversation and listen to their own voices embedded in the video.

StudentWorks™ Plus CD-ROM provides an all-in-one interactive Student Edition with access to the student workbook. **StudentWorks™ Plus** includes the full audio program to enhance students' listening and speaking skills.

Bon voyage! Video Program exposes students to the linguistic and cultural diversity of the French-speaking world.

Log on to www.glencoe.com

Glencoe French Online provides Self-Check Quizzes, eGames, and online postcards to reinforce the vocabulary, grammar, and culture that students learn in class. It also provides an opportunity for students to explore the French language and Francophone cultures beyond the textbook with Web Explore, World News Online, and WebQuest.

GLENCOE FRENCH ①

Bon voyage!

FLORIDA EDITION

WITH FEATURES BY

NATIONAL GEOGRAPHIC

Conrad J. Schmitt • Katia Brillié Lutz

McGraw Hill Glencoe

New York, New York   Columbus, Ohio   Chicago, Illinois   Peoria, Illinois   Woodland Hills, California

About the Authors

Conrad J. Schmitt

Conrad J. Schmitt received his B.A. degree magna cum laude from Montclair State University. He received his M.A. from Middlebury College. He did additional graduate work at New York University.

Mr. Schmitt has taught Spanish and French at all levels—from elementary school to university graduate courses. He served as Coordinator of Foreign Languages for the Hackensack, New Jersey, public schools. He also taught Methods of Teaching a Foreign Language at the Graduate School of Education, Rutgers University. Mr. Schmitt was Editor-in-Chief of Foreign Languages and ESL/EFL materials for the School Division of McGraw-Hill and McGraw-Hill International Book Company.

Mr. Schmitt has authored or co-authored more than one hundred books, all published by Glencoe/McGraw-Hill or by McGraw-Hill. He has addressed teacher groups and given workshops in all states of the United States and has lectured and presented seminars throughout the Far East, Latin America, and Canada. In addition, Mr. Schmitt has traveled extensively throughout France, French-speaking Canada, North Africa, French-speaking West Africa, the French Antilles, and Haiti.

Katia Brillié Lutz

Katia Brillié Lutz has her **Baccalauréat** in Mathematics and Science from the Lycée Molière in Paris and her **Licence ès Lettres** in languages from the Sorbonne. She was a Fulbright scholar at Mount Holyoke College.

Ms. Lutz has taught French language at Yale University and French language and literature at Southern Connecticut State College. She also taught French at the United Nations in New York City.

Ms. Lutz was Executive Editor of French at Macmillan Publishing Company. She also served as Senior Editor at Harcourt Brace Jovanovich and Holt Rinehart and Winston. She was a news translator and announcer for the BBC Overseas Language Services in London.

Ms. Lutz is the author of many language textbooks at all levels of instruction.

Send all inquiries to:
Glencoe/McGraw-Hill
8787 Orion Place
Columbus, OH 43240-4027

ISBN-13: 978-0-07-874793-9
ISBN-10: 0-07-874793-7

Printed in the United States of America.

2 3 4 5 6 7 8 9 10   058/055   12 11 10 09 08 07

Teacher Reviewers

We wish to express our appreciation to the numerous individuals throughout the United States and the French-speaking world who have advised us in the development of these teaching materials. Special thanks are extended to the people whose names appear below.

Anne-Marie Baumis
Bayside, NY

Claude Benaiteau
Austin, TX

Sr. M. Elayne Bockey, SND
St. Wendelin High School
Fostoria, OH

Linda Burnette
Rockville Junior/Senior
High School
Rockville, IN

Linda Butt
Loyola Blakefield
Towson, MD

Betty Clough
Austin, TX

Yolande Helm
Ohio University
Athens, OH

Jan Hofts
Northwest High School
Indianapolis, IN

Kathleen A. Houchens
The Ohio State University
Columbus, OH

Dominique Keith
Lake Forest, CA

Raelene Noll
Delmar, NY

Nancy Price
Fort Atkinson High School
Fort Atkinson, WI

Sally Price
Marysville-Pilchuck
High School
Marysville, WA

Bonita Sanders
Eisenhower High School
New Berlin, WI

Deana Schiffer
Hewlett High School
Hewlett, NY

Julia Sheppard
Delaware City Schools
Delaware, OH

James Toolan
Tuxedo High School
Tuxedo, NY

Mary Webster
Romeo High School
Romeo, MI

Marian Welch
Austin ISD
Austin, TX

Richard Wixom
Miller Middle School
Lake Katrine, NY

Brian Zailian
Tamalpais High School
Mill Valley, CA

For the Parent or Guardian

We are excited that your child has decided to study French. Foreign language study provides many benefits for students in addition to the ability to communicate in another language. Students who study another language improve their first language skills. They become more aware of the world around them and they learn to appreciate diversity.

You can help your child be successful in his or her study of French even if you are not familiar with that language. Encourage your child to talk to you about the places where French is spoken. Engage in conversations about current events in those places. The section of their Glencoe French book called **Le monde francophone** on pages xxi–xxxv may serve as a reference for you and your child. In addition, you will find information about the geography of the French-speaking world and links to foreign newspapers at **glencoe.com**.

The methodology employed in the Glencoe French books is logical and leads students step by step through their study of the language. Consistent instruction and practice are essential for learning a foreign language. You can help by encouraging your child to review vocabulary each day. As he or she progresses through the text, you will want to use the study tips on pages H51–H67 to help your child learn French. If you have Internet access, encourage your child to practice using the activities, games, and practice quizzes at **glencoe.com**.

Table des matières

Leçons préliminaires

Objectifs
In these preliminary lessons you will learn to:

- ✔ greet people
- ✔ say good-bye to people
- ✔ ask people how they are
- ✔ ask and tell names
- ✔ express simple courtesies
- ✔ find out and tell the days of the week
- ✔ find out and tell the months of the year
- ✔ count from 1 to 30
- ✔ find out and tell the time

CHAPITRE ① Une amie et un ami

Objectifs

In this chapter you will learn to:

✔ *ask or tell what someone is like*

✔ *ask or tell where someone is from*

✔ *ask or tell who someone is*

✔ *describe yourself or someone else*

✔ *talk about students from France and Martinique*

Standards and Study Tips

CHAPITRE ② Les cours et les profs

🪻 *Standards and Study Tips*

Objectifs

In this chapter you will learn to:

✔ describe people and things

✔ talk about more than one person or thing

✔ tell what subjects you take in school and express some opinions about them

✔ speak to people formally and informally

✔ talk about French-speaking people in the United States

CHAPITRE ③ Pendant et après les cours

⚜ *Standards and Study Tips*

Objectifs

In this chapter you will learn to:

✔ *talk about what you do in school*

✔ *talk about what you and your friends do after school*

✔ *identify and shop for school supplies*

✔ *talk about what you don't do*

✔ *tell what you and others like and don't like to do*

✔ *discuss schools in France*

CHAPITRE 4 La famille et la maison

Standards and Study Tips

Objectifs

In this chapter you will learn to:

✔ talk about your family

✔ describe your home and neighborhood

✔ tell your age and find out someone else's age

✔ tell what belongs to you and others

✔ describe more people and things

✔ talk about families and homes in French-speaking countries

Timothy Fuller

CHAPITRE (5) Au café et au restaurant

Standards and Study Tips

Objectifs

In this chapter you will learn to:

✔ *order food or a beverage at a café or restaurant*

✔ *tell where you and others go*

✔ *tell what you and others are going to do*

✔ *give locations*

✔ *tell what belongs to you and others*

✔ *describe more activities*

✔ *compare eating habits in the United States and in the French-speaking world*

(tl)Explorer/Photo Researchers, (tr b)Larry Hamill

CHAPITRE ⑥ La nourriture et les courses

🏴 *Standards and Study Tips*

Objectifs

In this chapter you will learn to:

✔ *identify more foods*

✔ *shop for food*

✔ *tell what you or others are doing*

✔ *ask for the quantity you want*

✔ *talk about what you or others don't have*

✔ *tell what you or others are able to do or want to do*

✔ *talk about French food-shopping customs*

CHAPITRE ⑦ Les vêtements

🌴 **Standards and Study Tips**

Objectifs

In this chapter you will learn to:

✔ identify and describe articles of clothing

✔ state color and size preferences

✔ shop for clothing

✔ describe people's activities

✔ compare people and things

✔ express opinions and make observations

✔ discuss clothes and clothes shopping in the French-speaking world

Owen Franken/Stock Boston

CHAPITRE (8) L'aéroport et l'avion

Objectifs

In this chapter you will learn to:

✔ check in for a flight

✔ talk about some services aboard the plane

✔ talk about more activities

✔ ask more questions

✔ talk about people and things as a group

✔ discuss air travel in France

🏴 *Standards and Study Tips*

CHAPITRE 9

Objectifs

In this chapter you will learn to:

✔ *purchase a train ticket and request information about arrival and departure*

✔ *use expressions related to train travel*

✔ *talk about people's activities*

✔ *point out people or things*

✔ *discuss an interesting train trip in French-speaking Africa*

La gare et le train

🔻 *Standards and Study Tips*

MONTREUX

CHAPITRE ⑩ Les sports

Standards and Study Tips

Objectifs

In this chapter you will learn to:

✔ *talk about team sports and other physical activities*

✔ *describe past actions and events*

✔ *ask people questions*

✔ *discuss what sports are popular in Canada and in French-speaking Africa*

Tim De Waele/CORBIS

CHAPITRE L'été et l'hiver

Standards and Study Tips

Objectifs

In this chapter you will learn to:

✔ *describe summer and winter weather*

✔ *talk about summer activities and sports*

✔ *talk about winter sports*

✔ *discuss past actions and events*

✔ *make negative statements*

✔ *talk about a ski trip in Québec*

CHAPITRE ⑫ La routine quotidienne

⚜ *Standards and Study Tips*

Objectifs

In this chapter you will learn to:

✔ *describe your personal grooming habits*

✔ *talk about your daily routine*

✔ *talk about your family life*

✔ *tell some things you do for yourself*

✔ *talk about daily activities in the past*

✔ *discuss a French family's daily routine*

(tl tr)Timothy Fuller, (b)Curt Fischer

CHAPITRE Les loisirs culturels

🌸 *Standards and Study Tips*

Objectifs

In this chapter you will learn to:

✔ *discuss movies, plays, and museums*

✔ *tell what you know and whom you know*

✔ *tell what happens to you or someone else*

✔ *refer to people and things already mentioned*

✔ *talk about some cultural activities in Paris*

CHAPITRE 14 La santé et la médecine

Standards and Study Tips

Objectifs

In this chapter you will learn to:

✔ *explain a minor illness to a doctor*

✔ *have a prescription filled at a pharmacy*

✔ *tell for whom something is done*

✔ *talk about some more activities*

✔ *give commands*

✔ *refer to people, places, and things already mentioned*

✔ *discuss medical services in France*

Timothy Fuller

Literary Companion

Video Companion

Handbook

Guide to Symbols

Throughout **Bon voyage!** you will see these symbols, or icons. They will tell you how to best use the particular part of the chapter or activity they accompany. Following is a key to help you understand these symbols.

 Audio Link This icon indicates material in the chapter that is recorded on compact disk.

 Recycling This icon indicates sections that review previously introduced material.

 Paired Activity This icon indicates sections that you can practice orally with a partner.

 Group Activity This icon indicates sections that you can practice together in groups.

 Encore Plus This icon indicates additional practice activities that review knowledge from current chapters.

 Allez-y! This icon indicates the end of new material in each section and the beginning of the recombination section at the end of the chapter.

 Literary Companion This icon appears in the review lessons to let you know that you are prepared to read the literature selection indicated if you wish.

 **Interactive CD-ROM** This icon indicates that the material is also on an Interactive CD-ROM.

Le monde francophone

The French geographer Onésime Reclus first coined the word *francophonie* in 1880 to designate geographical entities where French was spoken. Today, *la francophonie* refers to the collective body of over one hundred million people all over the world who speak French, exclusively or in part, in their daily lives. The term *francophonie* refers to the diverse official organizations, governments, and countries that promote the use of French in economic, political, diplomatic, and cultural exchanges. Politically, French remains the second most important language in the world. In some Francophone nations, French is the official language (France), or the co-official language (Cameroon); in others, it is spoken by a minority who share a common cultural heritage (Andorra). The French language is present in Europe, Africa, the Americas, and Oceania.

Le monde

LE MONDE FRANCOPHONE

Le monde

The areas in color indicate the vast Francophone world.

La Mer des Antilles

OCÉAN GLACIAL ARCTIQUE

Mer de Beaufort

Baie de Baffin

Baie d'Hudson

Mer de Bering

Golfe de l'Alaska

CANADA

Mer du Labrado

AMÉRIQUE DU NORD

ÉTATS-UNIS

OCÉAN ATLANTIQUE

MEXIQUE

Golfe du Mexique

OCÉAN PACIFIQUE

Mer des Caraïbes

VENEZUELA

GUYANA

SURINAME

GUYANE FRANÇAISE

COLOMBIE

ÉQUATEUR

PÉROU

AMÉRIQUE DU SUD

BRÉSIL

BOLIVIE

PARAGUAY

SAMOA

TONGA

URUGUAY

CHILI

ARGENTINE

Golfe du Mexique

BAHAMAS

CUBA

ÎLES TURKS ET CAÏCOS (G.B)

OCÉAN ATLANTIQUE

MEXIQUE

HAÏTI

RÉPUBLIQUE DOMINICAINE

ÎLES VIERGES (E.-U. et G.B.)

ANTIGUA-ET-BARBUDA

BELIZE

JAMAÏQUE

PORTO RICO (E.-U.)

ST KITTS-ET-NEVIS

GUADELOUPE (FR.)

GUATEMALA

HONDURAS

Mer des Caraïbes (Antilles)

DOMINIQUE

MARTINIQUE (FR.)

SAINTE-LUCIE

SALVADOR

SAINT-VINCENT-ET-GRENADINES

BARBADE

NICARAGUA

ARUBA

ANTILLES NÉERLANDAISES

GRENADE

TRINITÉ-ET-TOBAGO

COSTA RICA

PANAMA

VENEZUELA

OCÉAN PACIFIQUE

COLOMBIE

GUYANA

GUYANE FRANÇAISE

SURINAME

OCÉAN GLACIAL ARCTIQUE

Mer du Groenland | Mer de Norvège | Mer de Barents | Mer de Kara | Mer des Laptev

ISLANDE

Mer du Nord

EUROPE

ASIE

RUSSIE

Mer d'Okhotsk

KAZAKHSTAN

MONGOLIE

GÉORGIE
ARMÉNIE
TURQUIE
OUZBÉKISTAN | KIRGHIZISTAN
TURKMÉNISTAN | TADJIKISTAN

CORÉE DU NORD | Mer du Japon | JAPON

CHINE

CORÉE DU SUD

MAROC

LIBAN SYRIE
Mer Méditerranée
AZERBAIDJAN
ISRAËL
IRAK
JORDANIE

IRAN | AFGHANISTAN

Mer de Chine orientale

TUNISIE

ALGÉRIE

LIBYE

ÉGYPTE

KOWEÏT

PAKISTAN

NÉPAL

BHOUTAN

TAÏWAN

SAHARA OCCIDENTAL
MAURITANIE

BAHREÏN
QATAR
ARABIE SAOUDITE
EMIRATS ARABES UNIS

INDE

BANGLADESH

MYANMAR

MARSHALL

MALI | NIGER | TCHAD

SOUDAN

OMAN

LAOS

Mer de Chine méridionale

SÉNÉGAL
GAMBIE
GUINÉE-BISSAU
GUINÉE
SIERRA LEONE
LIBERIA
CÔTE D'IVOIRE

BURKINA FASO

NIGERIA

AFRIQUE

ÉRYTHRÉE

YÉMEN

DJIBOUTI

Golfe du Bengale

THAÏLANDE

VIÊT NAM

PHILIPPINES

ÉTATS FÉDÉRÉS DE MICRONÉSIE

GHANA
BÉNIN
TOGO

ÉTHIOPIE

SRI LANKA

CAMBODGE

BRUNEI

PALAU

KIRIBATI

SÃO TOMÉ ET PRINCIPE
GUINÉE ÉQUATORIALE

CAMEROUN

RÉPUBLIQUE CENTRAFRICAINE

SOMALIE

MALAISIE

GABON
CONGO

OUGANDA
RWANDA
RÉP. DÉM. DU CONGO
BURUNDI

KENYA

MALDIVES

INDONÉSIE

PAPOUASIE-NOUVELLE-GUINÉE

NAURU

ÎLES SALOMON

ÎLES SEYCHELLES

OCÉAN INDIEN

TUVALU

TANZANIE

WALLIS-ET-FUTUNA

ANGOLA

MALAWI
ZAMBIE

COMORES

Mer de Corail

VANUATU

FIDJI

MOZAMBIQUE

MADAGASCAR

ÎLE MAURICE

NAMIBIE

ZIMBABWE

OCÉAN ATLANTIQUE

BOTSWANA

RÉUNION

AUSTRALIE

NOUVELLE-CALÉDONIE

AFRIQUE DU SUD

SWAZILAND
LESOTHO

Mer de Tasman

NOUVELLE-ZÉLANDE

ANTARCTIQUE

L'Europe

NORVÈGE | FINLANDE

SUÈDE

IRLANDE | GRANDE-BRETAGNE | DANEMARK

ESTONIE

LETTONIE

RUSSIE

LITUANIE
RUSSIE

PAYS-BAS

BÉLARUS
BIÉLORUSSIE

OCÉAN ATLANTIQUE

BELGIQUE
LUXEMBOURG

ALLEMAGNE

POLOGNE

PARIS

RÉPUBLIQUE TCHÈQUE

UKRAINE

FRANCE

SUISSE

AUTRICHE

SLOVAQUIE

HONGRIE

MOLDAVIE

SLOVÉNIE
CROATIE

ROUMANIE

PORTUGAL

ESPAGNE

MONACO

BOSNIE-HERZÉGOVINE
MONTÉNÉGRO

SERBIE
YOUGOSLAVIE

GÉORGIE

ITALIE

Mer Noire

ALBANIE

BULGARIE

MACÉDOINE

GIBRALTAR (Brit.)

Mer Méditerranée

GRÈCE

TURQUIE

AFRIQUE

MALTE

CHYPRE

SYRIE

LIBAN

La francophonie

L'Afrique

Le Bénin

CAPITAL
Porto-Novo

POPULATION
7,041,000

FUN FACT
Benin has one of the most popular tourist attractions in all of West Africa—the fishing village of Ganvié built on stilts in the middle of a lagoon not far from the capital, Porto-Novo.

Le Burkina Faso

CAPITAL
Ouagadougou

POPULATION
13,228,000

FUN FACT
Burkina Faso is known for its friendly people. Villagers are fond of allowing foreigners to live in their homes and take part in village life.

L'Algérie

CAPITAL
Algiers

POPULATION
32,818,000

FUN FACT
Algeria is called "the geographic giant" of the Maghreb. It is four times the size of France. Most of the country lies in the Sahara desert.

Le Burundi

CAPITAL
Bujumbura

POPULATION
6,096,000

FUN FACT
Burundi was first under German control. It then became Ruanda-Urundi under Belgian control. It became independent in 1962.

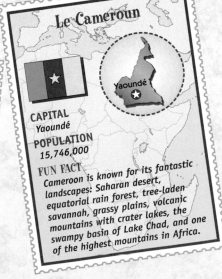

Le Cameroun

CAPITAL
Yaoundé

POPULATION
15,746,000

FUN FACT
Cameroon is known for its fantastic landscapes: Saharan desert, equatorial rain forest, tree-laden savannah, grassy plains, volcanic mountains with crater lakes, the swampy basin of Lake Chad, and one of the highest mountains in Africa.

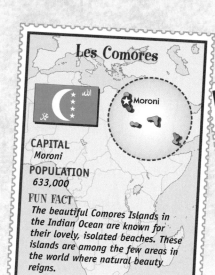

Les Comores

CAPITAL
Moroni

POPULATION
633,000

FUN FACT
The beautiful Comores Islands in the Indian Ocean are known for their lovely, isolated beaches. These islands are among the few areas in the world where natural beauty reigns.

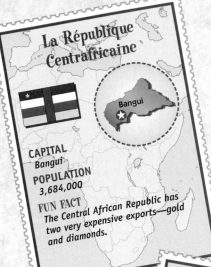

La République Centrafricaine

CAPITAL
Bangui

POPULATION
3,684,000

FUN FACT
The Central African Republic has two very expensive exports—gold and diamonds.

La Côte d'Ivoire

CAPITAL
Yamoussoukro

POPULATION
16,962,000

FUN FACT
The Ivory Coast's principal city, Abidjan, is West Africa's most cosmopolitan city and is often referred to as the "Paris of West Africa."

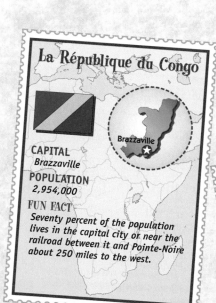

La République du Congo

CAPITAL
Brazzaville

POPULATION
2,954,000

FUN FACT
Seventy percent of the population lives in the capital city or near the railroad between it and Pointe-Noire about 250 miles to the west.

La République Démocratique du Congo

CAPITAL
Kinshasa

POPULATION
56,625,000

FUN FACT
The population of the Democratic Republic of the Congo is made up of six major ethnic groups which are divided into over 250 subgroups.

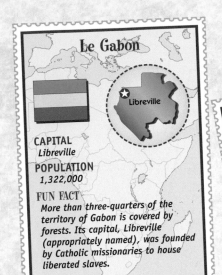

Le Gabon

CAPITAL
Libreville

POPULATION
1,322,000

FUN FACT
More than three-quarters of the territory of Gabon is covered by forests. Its capital, Libreville (appropriately named), was founded by Catholic missionaries to house liberated slaves.

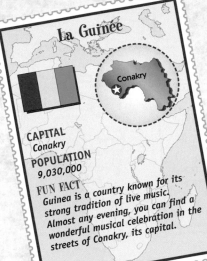

La Guinée

CAPITAL
Conakry

POPULATION
9,030,000

FUN FACT
Guinea is a country known for its strong tradition of live music. Almost any evening, you can find a wonderful musical celebration in the streets of Conakry, its capital.

Djibouti

CAPITAL
Djibouti

POPULATION
457,000

FUN FACT
Djibouti is the name of both the republic and its capital. Its position at the entrance to the Red Sea makes it one of the most important seaports in Africa.

Madagascar

CAPITAL
Antananarivo

POPULATION
16,980,000

FUN FACT
Madagascar is a beautiful and, in some areas, rocky volcanic island in the Indian Ocean.

Le Mali

CAPITAL
Bamako

POPULATION
11,626,000

FUN FACT
Mali is the home of Timbuktu, which was and still is the terminus of a camel caravan route across the Sahara, linking Arabia with West Africa since ancient times.

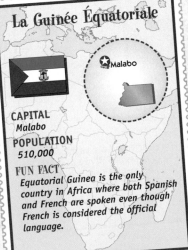

La Guinée Équatoriale

CAPITAL
Malabo

POPULATION
510,000

FUN FACT
Equatorial Guinea is the only country in Africa where both Spanish and French are spoken even though French is considered the official language.

L'île Maurice

CAPITAL
Port Louis

POPULATION
1,210,000

FUN FACT
Mauritius is a volcanic island in the Indian Ocean known for its natural beauty.

La Mauritanie

CAPITAL
Nouakchott

POPULATION
2,913,000

FUN FACT
Mauritania is a bridge between the Maghreb in the North and sub-Saharan Africa in the South.

Le Niger

CAPITAL
Niamey

POPULATION
11,059,000

FUN FACT
Niger is a starkly dramatic country with its desert terrain. The capital, Niamey, on the fringe of the Sahara, is a city of modern buildings and wide boulevards—where many times you will see camels walking.

Le Maroc

CAPITAL
Rabat

POPULATION
31,689,000

FUN FACT
Morocco is a country of many beautiful, fascinating cities, such as Casablanca, Tangiers, Fez, and Marrakech.

Les Seychelles

CAPITAL
Victoria

POPULATION
86,000

FUN FACT
The Republic of the Seychelles is made up of more than one hundred islands and is a vacationer's paradise. The Seychelles attract people from all over the world.

Le Tchad

CAPITAL
N'Djamena

POPULATION
9,253,000

FUN FACT
Chad has a lake in the southwest of the country that doubles in size during the rainy season.

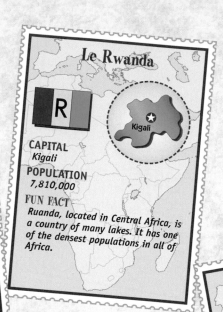

Le Rwanda

CAPITAL
Kigali

POPULATION
7,810,000

FUN FACT
Ruanda, located in Central Africa, is a country of many lakes. It has one of the densest populations in all of Africa.

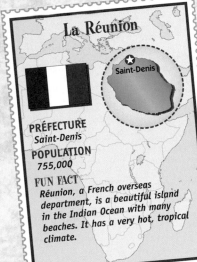

La Réunion

PRÉFECTURE
Saint-Denis

POPULATION
755,000

FUN FACT
Réunion, a French overseas department, is a beautiful island in the Indian Ocean with many beaches. It has a very hot, tropical climate.

Le Sénégal

CAPITAL
Dakar

POPULATION
10,580,000

FUN FACT
Senegal is a country that has a fabulous mix of Afro-French characteristics. More visitors go to Senegal than to any other Western African country.

Le Togo

CAPITAL
Lomé

POPULATION
5,429,000

FUN FACT
Togo is a pencil-thin strip of land whose capital, Lomé, has some of the most beautiful beaches just a block or two from the heart of town.

La Tunisie

CAPITAL
Tunis

POPULATION
9,925,000

FUN FACT
Tunisia contains Roman archaeological sites second only to Rome itself.

L'Amérique du Nord et du Sud

La Guadeloupe

PRÉFECTURE
Basse-Terre

POPULATION
440,000

FUN FACT
Guadeloupe, a French overseas department in the Caribbean, is made up of two major islands in addition to some smaller ones. It is known for its jungle highlands and beautiful seaside resorts.

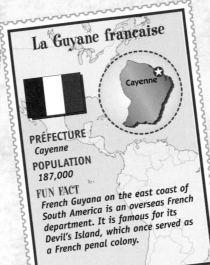

La Guyane française

PRÉFECTURE
Cayenne

POPULATION
187,000

FUN FACT
French Guyana on the east coast of South America is an overseas French department. It is famous for its Devil's Island, which once served as a French penal colony.

Haïti

CAPITAL
Port-au-Prince

POPULATION
7,528,000

FUN FACT
Haiti shares the island of Hispaniola with the Dominican Republic. Its friendly people are known for their musical and artistic talents. Haitian primitive art is sought after in art galleries around the world.

La province de Québec

CAPITAL
Québec

POPULATION
7,040,000

FUN FACT
Quebec is the oldest and largest of Canada's provinces. About 90 percent of Quebec's inhabitants are French-speaking.

La Martinique

PRÉFECTURE
Fort-de-France

POPULATION
426,000

FUN FACT
Martinique, like Guadeloupe, is a French overseas department in the Caribbean Sea. It is a highly developed island famous for its beautiful, exotic flowers—orchids, hibiscus, and flamingo flowers.

Saint-Pierre-et-Miquelon

PRÉFECTURE
Saint-Pierre

POPULATION
7,000

FUN FACT
Saint-Pierre and Miquelon are French-speaking islands in the Atlantic Ocean, south of Newfoundland. Many residents work in the cod-fishing industry.

L'Europe

La Belgique

CAPITAL
Bruxelles

POPULATION
10,289,000

FUN FACT
Belgium is a rather small country but one of the world's most densely populated. Belgium has two distinct cultures—Flemish in the North and French in the South.

La principauté d'Andorre

CAPITAL
Andorre-la-Vieille

POPULATION
69,000

FUN FACT
Andorra is a co-principality governed by France's president and a Spanish bishop.

La France

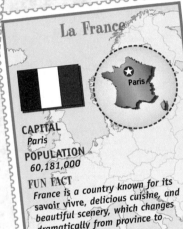

CAPITAL
Paris

POPULATION
60,181,000

FUN FACT
France is a country known for its savoir vivre, delicious cuisine, and beautiful scenery, which changes dramatically from province to province.

Le grand-duché de Luxembourg

CAPITAL
Luxembourg

POPULATION
454,000

FUN FACT
Luxembourg is smaller than the state of Rhode Island. The native Luxembourgers all speak three languages fluently: Luxembourgish, German, and French.

La principauté de Monaco

CAPITAL
Monaco

POPULATION
32,000

FUN FACT
Monaco is one of the world's smallest sovereign states. It is located on a horseshoe-shaped strip of land bathed by the Mediterranean on one side and shielded by alpine peaks on the other.

La Suisse

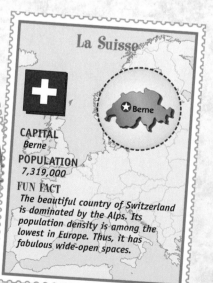

CAPITAL
Berne

POPULATION
7,319,000

FUN FACT
The beautiful country of Switzerland is dominated by the Alps. Its population density is among the lowest in Europe. Thus, it has fabulous wide-open spaces.

L'Océanie

La Nouvelle-Calédonie

CAPITAL
Nouméa

POPULATION
211,000

FUN FACT
New Caledonia is a French overseas territory in the South Pacific. It is made up of one large island and numerous small, beautiful coral islands.

Vanuatu

CAPITAL
Port-Vila

POPULATION
199,000

FUN FACT
The republic of Vanuatu is an archipelago in the South Pacific, made up of forty islands of volcanic origin. Some of the volcanoes are still active.

La Polynésie française

CAPITAL
Papeete

POPULATION
270,000

FUN FACT
French Polynesia is a French overseas territory made up of approximately 130 islands. The islands are known for their volcanic mountains, tropical climate, and beautiful bays and coves.

Wallis-et-Futuna

CAPITAL
Mata-Utu

POPULATION
16,000

FUN FACT
Wallis-et-Futuna is a French overseas territory in the South Pacific. The mountainous islands of the archipelago are surrounded by coral reefs.

La France

ANGLETERRE

Mer du Nord

PAYS-BAS

BELGIQUE

ALLEMAGNE

Manche

Calais

Lille

Nord-Pas-de-Calais

LUXEMBOURG

Le Havre

Haute-Normandie

Amiens

Picardie

Caen

Rouen

Brest

Basse-Normandie

Seine

Paris

Île-de-France

Châlons-en-Champagne

Metz

Marne

Meuse

Lorraine

Bretagne

Rennes

Champagne-Ardenne

Strasbourg

Rhin

Le Mans

Orléans

Alsace

Pays de la Loire

Tours

Loire

Centre

Nantes

Bourgogne

Besançon

Dijon

Franche-Comté

Poitiers

SUISSE

OCÉAN
ATLANTIQUE

Poitou-Charentes

Moulins

Limoges

Clermont-Ferrand

Limousin

Lyon

Saône

Bordeaux

Auvergne

Rhône-Alpes

Garonne

Grenoble

Aquitaine

Rhône

ITALIE

Biarritz

Midi-Pyrénées

Montpellier

Provence-Alpes-Côte d'Azur

Monaco

Toulouse

Nice

Languedoc-Roussillon

Marseille

MONACO

ANDORRE

ESPAGNE

Corse

Mer Méditerranée

Paris

Le Canada

OCÉAN GLACIAL ARCTIQUE

ALASKA (ÉTATS-UNIS)

YUKON
Whitehorse

COLOMBIE-BRITANNIQUE
Victoria

TERRITOIRES DU NORD-OUEST
Yellowknife

ALBERTA
Edmonton

SASKATCHEWAN
Regina

MANITOBA
Winnipeg

NUNAVUT

GROENLAND (DANEMARK)

Baie D'Hudson

Iqaluit

ÉTATS-UNIS

ONTARIO

Toronto

Ottawa

Montréal

Québec

QUÉBEC

Mer du Labrador

TERRE-NEUVE

OCÉAN ATLANTIQUE

Fredericton

NOUVEAU-BRUNSWICK

ÎLE-DU-PRINCE-ÉDOUARD

Charlottetown

Halifax

NOUVELLE-ÉCOSSE

ST-PIERRE-ET-MIQUELON (FR.)

St-John's

OCÉAN ATLANTIQUE

EUROPE

ASIE

Mer Méditerranée

Alger
Tunis
TUNISIE
Tripoli
Rabat
MAROC
Le Caire
ÉGYPTE
LIBYE
ALGÉRIE

SAHARA
OCCIDENTAL
(MAROC)

MAURITANIE
Nouakchott

MALI
NIGER
TCHAD
SOUDAN
Khartoum
ÉRYTHRÉE
Asmara

Dakar
SÉNÉGAL
Banjul
GAMBIE
Bamako
BURKINA
FASO
Niamey
N'Djamena
Bissau
GUINÉE-BISSEAU
Ouagadougou
DJIBOUTI
Djibouti
Conakry
GUINÉE
BÉNIN
NIGERIA
Addis
Ababa
ÉTHIOPIE
SIERRA
LEONE
CÔTE
D'IVOIRE
GHANA
TOGO
Abuja
Freetown
Yamoussoukro
Monrovia
LIBERIA
Lomé
Accra
Porto-
Novo
CAMEROUN
Bangui
RÉPUBLIQUE
CENTRAFRICAINE
OUGANDA
KENYA
SOMALIE
Mogadishu
Malabo
Yaoundé
Kampala
GUINÉE ÉQUATORIALE
SÃO TOMÉ
ET PRINCIPE
São Tomé
Libreville
CONGO
GABON
Brazzaville
RÉPUBLIQUE
DÉMOCRATIQUE
DU CONGO
RWANDA
Kigali
BURUNDI
Bujumbura
Nairobi
CABINDA
(ANGOLA)
Kinshasa
TANZANIE
Dodoma
Luanda
ANGOLA
MALAWI
Lilongwe
Moroni
COMORES
ZAMBIE
Lusaka
MOZAMBIQUE
MADAGASCAR
Antananarivo
Harare
ZIMBABWE
NAMIBIE
BOTSWANA
Windhoek
Gaborone
Maputo
Pretoria
Mbabane
SWAZILAND
Bloemfontein
LESOTHO
Maseru
AFRIQUE
DU SUD
Le Cap

OCÉAN
ATLANTIQUE

Why Learn French?

The Francophone World

Culture Knowing French will open doors to you around the world. As you study the language, you will also come to understand and appreciate the way of life, customs, values, and cultures of people from many different countries. Look at the map on page xxii to see the areas of the world in which French is spoken, either as a first or second language. You might be surprised to see that people speak French in places as close to home as Haiti, Martinique, Quebec, and Louisiana.

Learning French can be fun and will bring you a sense of accomplishment. You'll be really pleased when you are able to carry on a conversation with a French-speaking person in French. You will also be able to read French literature, keep up with current events in French magazines and newspapers, and understand French films without relying on subtitles. The French language will be a source of enrichment for the rest of your life.

Career Opportunities

Business Your knowledge of French will also be an asset to you in a variety of careers. Many French companies are multinational and have branches around the world, including the United States. Some of the fields in which French companies excel are: clothing and fashion, cosmetics, tourism, agriculture, the automotive and aerospace industries, and technology.

Research France is also a world leader in high-energy physics research and medical genetics. Did you know that French and English are the two major languages of the Internet? French can help you in almost any career path you choose.

Language Link

Another benefit to learning French is that it will improve your English. Once you know another language, you can make comparisons between the two and gain a greater understanding of how languages function. As a result, your use of English will be more effective. You'll also come across many French words that are used in English. Just a few examples are: **rouge, chaise longue, chic, crêpe, à la mode, omelette, chargé d'affaires, déjà vu, détente,** and **laisser faire.** French will also be helpful if you decide to learn yet another language. Once you learn a second language, the learning process for acquiring other languages becomes much easier.

French is a beautiful, rich language that is spoken on many continents. Many people use French on a daily basis as their second language. Whatever your motivation is for choosing to study it, French will expand your horizons and increase your job opportunities. **Vive la langue française! Et bon voyage!**

L'alphabet français

a *a*mis

b *b*ébé

c *c*irque

d *d*eux

e *l*eçon

f *f*enêtre

g *g*iraffe

h *h*uit

i *i*gloo

j *j*eu

k *k*ilo

l *l*ivre

m *m*aison

n *n*ez

o *o*live

p *p*ain

q *q*uatre

r *r*eine

s *s*oupe

t *t*able

u *u*nivers

v *v*iolette

w *w*agon

x e*x*tra

y *y*eux

z *z*èbre

READING IN A NEW LANGUAGE

Following are skills and strategies that can help you understand what you read in a language you have just begun to learn. *Reading and Succeeding* will help you build skills and strategies that will make it easier to understand what you are reading in your exciting new language.

The strategies you use frequently depend on the purpose of your reading. You do not read a textbook or questions on the FCAT the same way you read a novel or a magazine article. You read a textbook for information. You read a novel or magazine article for fun.

In the early stages of second-language learning, your vocabulary is, of course, very limited in comparison to the vast number of words you already know in English. The material presented to you to read in the early stages must accommodate this reality. Your limited knowledge of the language does not have to deter you from enjoying what you are reading. Most of what you read, however, will come from your textbook, since original novels and magazine articles are not written for people who have limited exposure to the language.

As you develop your reading ability in French you will encounter basically two types of readings.

Intensive Readings

These readings are short. They are very controlled, using only language you have already learned. You should find these readings easy and enjoyable. If you find them difficult it means you have not sufficiently learned the material presented in the chapter of the textbook. The vast majority of these informative readings will introduce you to the fascinating cultures of the French-speaking world.

A very important aspect of reading in French is to give you things to "talk about" in the language. The more you read, speak, and use the language, the more proficient you will become. Whenever you finish reading one of the intensive reading selections, you should be able to talk about it; that is, you should be able to retell it in your own words.

Extensive Readings

Since it is unrealistic to assume that you will never encounter new words as you branch out and read material in French, you will also be presented with extensive readings. The goal of these extensive readings is to help you develop the tools and skills you need in order to read at some future date an original novel or magazine article. They do indeed contain some words and structures that are unfamiliar to you. In this *Reading and Succeeding* section, you will learn to develop many skills that will enable you to read such material with relative ease.

USE *READING AND SUCCEEDING* TO HELP YOU:

- **adjust the way you read to fit the type of material you are reading**
- **identify new words and build your vocabulary**
- **use specific reading strategies to better understand what you read**
- **improve your ability to speak by developing strategies that enable you to retell orally what you have read**
- **use critical thinking strategies to think more deeply about what you read**

Identifying New Words and Building Vocabulary

What do you do when you come across a word you do not know as you read? Do you skip the word and keep reading? You might if you are reading for fun. If it hinders your ability to understand, however, you might miss something important. When you come to a word you don't know, try the following strategies to figure out what the word means.

• Reading Aloud

In the early stages of learning a second language a good strategy is to sit by yourself and read the selection aloud. This can help you understand the reading because you once again hear words that you have already practiced orally in class. Hearing them as you read them can help reinforce meaning.

• Identifying Cognates

As you read you will come across many cognates. Cognates are words that look alike in both English and French. Not only do they look alike but they mean the same thing. Recognizing cognates is a great reading strategy. Examples of cognates are:

| classe | septembre | cinéma | télévision | voyage | sociable |
| dîner | sculpteur | chocolat | Américain | bloquer | sandales |

• Identifying Roots and Base Words

The main part of a word is called its root. From a root, many new words can be formed. When you see a new word, identify its root. It can help you pronounce the word and figure out its meaning.

For example, if you know the word **important,** there is no problem determining the meaning of **importance.** The verb **importer** becomes a bit more problematic, but with some intelligent guessing you can get its meaning. You know it has something to do with importance so it means *it is important,* and by extension it can even carry the meaning *to matter.*

• Prefixes

A prefix is a word part added to the beginning of a root or base word. French as well as English has prefixes. Prefixes can change, or even reverse, the meaning of a word. For example, the prefixes **in-, im-,** and **des-** mean *not.*

egal/in**égal**   possible/**im**possible   habiller/**dés**habiller

Reading and Succeeding

Using Syntax

Like all languages, French has rules for the way words are arranged in sentences. The way a sentence is organized is called its syntax. English and French syntax are similar in many ways. In a simple English or French statement, someone or something (the subject) does something (the predicate or verb) to or with another person or thing (the object). The order is the same in both languages (subject, verb, object). However, when a pronoun replaces a direct or indirect object, the syntax of the sentence differs in the two languages. Also, in English an adjective always come before the noun it modifies, while in French the adjective usually follows the noun. Adverbs, also, may be placed differently. You will notice, too, that French has more ways to form questions.

READING PRACTICE

English states: *John sees it.*
French states: *John it sees.*

English states: *John shows it to me*
French states: *John me it shows.*

English states: *the smart student*
French states: *the student smart*

English states: *He can do better.*
French states: *He can better do.*

Taking into account that French and English syntax vary is one of the many important reasons why, when you read, you should think in French and not try to translate what you are reading into English. Reading in French will then have a natural flow and follow exactly the way you learned it. Trying to translate it into English confuses the matter and serves no purpose.

Using Context Clues

This is a very important reading strategy in a second language. You can often figure out the meaning of an unfamiliar word by looking at it in context (the words and sentences that surround it). Let's look at the following example.

READING PRACTICE

The glump ate it all up and flew away.

You have no idea what a *glump* is. Right? But from the rest of the sentence you can figure out that it's a bird. Why? Because it flew away and you know that birds fly. In this way you guessed at the meaning of an unknown word using context. Although you know it is a bird, you cannot determine the specific meaning such as a robin, a wren, or a sparrow. In many cases it does not matter because that degree of specificity is not necessary for comprehension. Let's look at another example:

The glump ate it all up and phlumped.

In this case you do not know the meaning of two key words in the same sentence—*glump* and *phlumped.* This makes it impossible to guess the meaning and this is what can happen when you try to read something in a second language that is beyond your proficiency level. This makes reading a frustrating experience. For this reason all the readings in your textbook control the language to keep it within your reach. Remember, if you have studied the vocabulary in your book, this will not happen.

Understanding What You Read

Try using some of the following strategies before, during, and after reading to understand and remember what you read.

Previewing

When you preview a piece of writing, you are looking for a general idea of what to expect from it. Before you read, try the following.
- Look at the title and any illustrations that are included.
- Read the headings, subheadings, and anything in bold letters.
- Skim over the passage to see how it is organized. Is it divided into many parts? Is it a long poem or short story?
- Look at the graphics—pictures, maps, or diagrams.
- Set a purpose for your reading. Are you reading to learn something new? Are you reading to find specific information?

Using What You Know

Believe it or not, you already know quite a bit about what you are going to read. Your own knowledge and personal experience can help you create meaning in what you read. There is, however, a big difference in reading the information in your French textbook. You already have some knowledge about what you are reading from a United States oriented base. What you will be reading about takes place in a French-speaking environment and thus you will be adding an exciting new dimension to what you already know. Comparing and contrasting are important critical skills to put to use when reading material about a culture other than your own. This skill will be discussed later.

Visualizing

Creating pictures in your mind about what you are reading—called visualizing—will help you understand and remember what you read. With the assistance of the many accompanying photos, try to visualize the people, streets, cities, homes, etc., you are reading about.

Identifying Sequence

When you discover the logical order of events or ideas, you are identifying sequence. Look for clues and signal words that will help you find how information is organized. Some signal words are **au début, d'abord, avant, ensuite, puis, après, plus tard, enfin, pour finir, finalement.**

Determining the Main Idea

When you look for the main idea of a selection, you look for the most important idea. The examples, reasons, and details that further explain the main idea are called supporting details.

Reviewing

When you review in school, you go over what you learned the day before so that the information is clear in your mind. Reviewing when you read does the same thing. Take time now and then to pause and review what you have read. Think about the main ideas and organize them for yourself so you can recall them later. Filling in study aids such as graphic organizers can help you review.

Monitoring Your Comprehension

As you read, check your understanding by summarizing. Pause from time to time and state the main ideas of what you have just read. Answer the questions: **Qui?** *(Who?)* **Quoi?** *(What?)* **Où?** *(Where?)* **Quand?** *(When?)* **Comment?** *(How?)* **Pourquoi?** *(Why?)*. Summarizing tests your comprehension because you state key points in your own words. Remember something you read earlier: reading in French empowers your ability to speak by developing strategies that enable you to retell orally what you have read.

Thinking About Your Reading

Sometimes it is important to think more deeply about what you read so you can get the most out of what the author says. These critical thinking skills will help you go beyond what the words say and understand the meaning of your reading.

Compare and Contrast

To compare and contrast shows the similarities and differences among people, things, and ideas. Your reading experience in French will show you many things that are similar and many others that are different depending upon the culture groups and social mores.

As you go over these culturally oriented readings, try to visualize what you are reading. Then think about the information. Think about what you know about the topic and then determine if the information you are reading is similar, somewhat different, or very different from what you know.

Continue to think about it. In this case you may have to think about it in English. Determine if you find the similarities or the differences interesting. Would you like to experience what you are reading about? Analyzing the information in this way will most certainly help you remember what you have read.

- Signal words and phrases that indicate similarity are **semblable, même, similaire, comparable, de la même façon, égal.**
- Signal words and phrases that indicate differences are **différent, d'autre part, par ailleurs, cependant, toutefois, par contre, au contraire, néanmoins.**

Cause and Effect

Just about everything that happens in life is the cause or the effect of some other event or action. Writers use cause-and-effect structure to explore the reasons for something happening and to examine the results of previous events. This structure helps answer the question that everybody is always asking: Why? Cause-and-effect structure is about explaining things.

- Signal words and phrases are **donc, parce que, par conséquent, pour cette raison.**

Using Reference Materials

In the early stages of second-language learning you will not be able to use certain types of reference materials that are helpful to you in English. For example, you could not look up a word in a French dictionary as you would not be able to understand many of the words used in the definition.

You can, however, make use of the glossary that appears at the end of your textbook. A glossary includes only words that are included in the textbook. Rather than give you a French definition, the glossary gives you the English equivalent of the word. If you have to use the glossary very frequently it indicates to you that you have not studied the vocabulary sufficiently in each of your lessons. A strategy to use before beginning a reading selection in any given lesson is to quickly skim the vocabulary in the **Mots 1** and **Mots 2** sections of the lesson.

Enjoy reading as you take **un bon voyage.**

Dear Student,

Foldables are interactive study organizers that you can make yourself. They are a wonderful resource to help you organize and retain information. Foldables have many purposes. You can use them to remember vocabulary words or to organize more in-depth information on any given topic, such as keeping track of what you know about a particular country.

You can write general information, such as titles, vocabulary words, concepts, questions, main ideas, and dates, on the front tabs of your Foldables. You view this general information every time you look at a Foldable. This helps you focus on and remember key points without the distraction of additional text. You can write specific information—supporting ideas, thoughts, answers to questions, research information, empirical data, class notes, observations, and definitions—under the tabs. Think of different ways in which Foldables can be used. Soon you will find that you can make your own Foldables for study guides and projects. Foldables with flaps or tabs create study guides that you can use to check what you know about the general information on the front of tabs. Use Foldables without tabs for projects that require information to be presented for others to view quickly. The more you make and use graphic organizers, the faster you will become able to produce them.

To store your Foldables, turn one-gallon freezer bags into student portfolios which can be collected and stored in the classroom. You can also carry your portfolios in your notebooks if you place strips of two-inch clear tape along one side and punch three holes through the taped edge. Write your name along the top of the plastic portfolio with a permanent marker and cover the writing with two-inch clear tape to keep it from wearing off. Cut the bottom corners off the bag so it won't hold air and will stack and store easily. The following figures illustrate the basic folds that are referred to throughout the following section of this book.

Good luck!

Dinah Zike

www.dinah.com

Category Book

Les nombres Use this *category book* organizer as you learn dates and numbers.

Step 1 **Fold** a sheet of paper (8½" x 11") in half like a *hot dog*.

Step 2 On one side, **cut** every third line. This usually results in ten tabs. Do this with three sheets of paper to make three books.

Step 3 **Write** one Arabic number on the outside of each of the tabs. On the inside write out the respective number. As you learn more numbers, use *category books* to categorize numbers in this way.

OTHER SUGGESTIONS FOR A *CATEGORY BOOK* FOLDABLE

You may wish to use *category book* foldables to help remember numbers. As you learn numbers, make two *category book* foldables. One will have the numerals on the outside and the numbers written out on the inside. The other will have the numbers written out on the outside and the numerals on the inside. This is a good way for you to practice your numbers on your own. You may also wish to make one foldable containing even numbers and one containing odd numbers.

A *category book* foldable may be used to help you remember the names of school subjects. Use pictures, numbers, or a few French words you already know to describe the subject on the outside of the foldable. You will write the name of the subject in French on the inside. Then show your descriptions to a partner and have the partner come up with the name of the subject in French. You may also use this foldable to group school subjects by discipline.

A *category book* foldable may be useful to you as you are learning terms related to computers, faxes, or telephones. Write the name of the machine in French on the outside of the foldable. On the inside, write instructions for how to use it and terms related to it in French.

Forward-Backward Book

Les saisons Use this *forward-backward book* to compare and contrast two seasons of your choice.

Step 1 **Stack** three sheets of paper. On the top sheet, trace a large circle.

Step 2 With the papers still stacked, **cut out** the circles.

Step 3 **Staple** the paper circles together along the left-hand side to create a circular booklet.

Step 4 **Write** the name of a season on the cover and on the page that opens to the right list the months of the year in that particular season. On the following page draw a picture to illustrate the season.

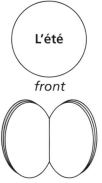

L'été

front

inside

Step 5 **Turn the book upside down** and write the name of a season on the cover. On the page that opens to the right list the months of the year in that particular season. On the following page draw a picture to illustrate the season.

back L'hiver

inside

OTHER SUGGESTIONS FOR A *FORWARD-BACKWARD BOOK* FOLDABLE

You may wish to use a *forward-backward book* foldable to organize summer and winter activities. You may use titles such as *the beach* and *skiing* in French. On the inside, list activities that go with each on the right-hand page as well as illustrating a scene on the opposite page. To give information for the second category, turn the book upside down.

It may be helpful to use a *forward-backward book* foldable to organize the food groups. You could use the name of a food group in the target language (meat, vegetables, fruit, etc.) as the title. On the inside, list as many foods in this food group as you can on the right-hand page and illustrate these foods on the opposite page. Give the same information for a second food group by reversing the book.

Pocket Book

La géographie Use this *pocket book* organizer in your ongoing study of all the countries in the French-speaking world.

Step 1 **Fold** a sheet of paper (8½" x 11") in half like a *hamburger.*

Step 2 **Open** the folded paper and fold one of the long sides up two inches to form a pocket. Refold the *hamburger* fold so that the newly formed pockets are on the inside.

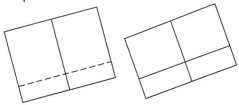

Step 3 **Glue** the outer edges of the two-inch fold with a small amount of glue.

Step 4 **Make a multipaged booklet** by gluing six pockets side-by-side. Glue a cover around the multipaged *pocket book.*

Step 5 **Label** five pockets with the following geographical areas: **l'Europe, l'Afrique, l'Océanie, l'Amérique (du Nord et du Sud),** and **les Antilles françaises.** Use index cards inside the pockets to record information each time you learn something new about a specific country. Be sure to include the name of the country (in French, of course) and its capital.

OTHER SUGGESTIONS FOR A *POCKET BOOK* FOLDABLE

You may wish to use a *pocket book* foldable to organize masculine and feminine nouns or singular and plural forms. You can make an index card to put in the correct pocket each time you learn a new word.

A *pocket book* foldable may be used to organize information about several subjects. For example, to organize information about traveling, label four pockets with topics such as *the train station, the train, the airport, the airplane* in French. Make cards for all the words and phrases you know that go with each topic.

If you wish to organize what you are learning about important people, works of art, festivals, and other cultural information in countries that speak French, a *pocket book* foldable may be helpful. You can make a card for each person, work of art, or event that you study, and you can add cards and even add categories as you continue to learn about cultures that speak French.

Vocabulary Book

Synonymes et antonymes Use this *vocabulary book* to practice your vocabulary through the use of synonyms and antonyms.

Step 1 **Fold** a sheet of notebook paper in half like a *hot dog*.

Step 2 On one side, **cut** every third line. This usually results in ten tabs. Do this with two sheets of paper to make two books.

Step 3 **Label** the tops of the *vocabulary books* with the word **Synonymes** on one and **Antonymes** on the other. As you learn new vocabulary in each unit, try to categorize words in this manner. Remember also to think of words you have previously learned to fill in your books.

OTHER SUGGESTIONS FOR A *VOCABULARY BOOK* FOLDABLE

You may wish to use a *vocabulary book* foldable to help you remember words related to illness and going to the doctor or hospital. Come up with categories to write on the outside such as *a cold, the flu, at the doctor's office, at the pharmacy, at the hospital,* etc. On the inside, write as many terms and phrases as you can think of which relate to that category.

You can use a *vocabulary book* foldable to help remember any verb conjugation in French. Write the infinitive at the top. If you know several tenses of a verb, you should also write what tense or tenses are being practiced. On the outside of the foldable, write the pronouns, and on the inside, write the corresponding verb form. You can use this as a quick study and review tool for any verb. At a more advanced level, you may wish to write many verbs down the outside and entire conjugations on the inside.

You may wish to use a *vocabulary book* foldable to help organize different kinds of clothing. Come up with categories in French to list on the outside, such as *dressy, casual, men's, women's, both,* etc. On the inside, list as many articles of clothing fitting the category as you can in French.

You can use *vocabulary book* foldables to practice adjective forms. Create two *vocabulary book* foldables, one for singular forms and the other for plural forms. On the singular book, write either masculine or feminine singular adjective forms on the outside and the other forms on the inside. To make this more challenging, write a mix of masculine and feminine forms on the outside, with the corresponding form on the inside. Repeat this process on the second book for the plural forms.

Tab Book

Les questions Use this *tab book* to practice asking and answering questions.

Step 1 **Fold** a sheet of paper (8½" x 11") like a *hot dog* but fold it so that one side is one inch longer than the other.

Step 2 On the shorter side only, **cut** five equal tabs. On the front of each tab, **write** a question word you have learned. For example, you may wish to write the following.

Step 3 On the bottom edge, **write** any sentence you would like.

Anne est élève dans un lycée à Paris.

Step 4 Under each flap, **write** the word from your sentence that answers the question on the front of the flap.

OTHER SUGGESTIONS FOR A *TAB BOOK* FOLDABLE

You may also use a *tab book* foldable to practice verb conjugations. You would need to make six tabs instead of five. Write a verb and a tense on the bottom edge and write the pronouns on the front of each tab. Under each flap, write the corresponding verb form.

You may wish to use a *tab book* foldable to practice new vocabulary words. Leave extra space on the bottom edge. Choose five or six vocabulary words and write each one on a tab. You may also make multiple *tab book* foldables to practice more words. Under each flap, write a definition or translation of the word. If you can, write an original definition in French. At a more beginning level, you may wish to illustrate the word or write the word in English. Use the bottom edge to write one or more original sentences using all of the words on the tabs.

Miniature Matchbook

Les descriptions Use this *miniature matchbook* to help you communicate in an interesting and more descriptive way.

Step 1 **Fold** a sheet of paper (8½" x 11") in half like a *hot dog*.

Step 2 **Cut** the sheet in half along the fold line.

Step 3 **Fold** the two long strips in half like *hot dogs,* leaving one side ½" shorter than the other side.

Step 4 **Fold** the ½" tab over the shorter side on each strip.

Step 5 **Cut** each of the two strips in half forming four halves. Then cut each half into thirds, making twelve miniature matchbooks.

Step 6 **Glue** the twelve small matchbooks inside a *hamburger* fold (three rows of four each).

Step 7 On the front of each matchbook, **write** a subject you are going to tell or write about, for example, **l'école**. Open up the tab and list any words you think you could use to make your discussion more interesting. You can add topics and words as you continue with your study of French. If you glue several sections together, this foldable will "grow."

OTHER SUGGESTIONS FOR A *MINIATURE MATCHBOOK* FOLDABLE

You may use a *miniature matchbook* foldable to test each other on your knowledge of the vocabulary. Work in pairs with each partner making a blank *miniature matchbook* foldable. Each partner writes a topic related to the subjects you have just studied on the front of each matchbook. You may use categories of vocabulary, verbs you have recently learned to conjugate, or the subject of a reading. Your partner then writes as much as he or she can about that topic under the flap. This can alert you if you need to go back and review a topic.

A *miniature matchbook* foldable may help you organize and remember information you have read. After doing a cultural or literary reading, write down a concept presented in the reading on the front of each matchbook. Open up each tab and write down supporting details that support the idea.

Single Picture Frame

Dessiner et écrire Use this *single picture frame* book to help you illustrate the stories you write.

Step 1 **Fold** a sheet of paper (8½" x 11") in half like a *hamburger*.

Step 2 **Open** the *hamburger* and gently roll one side of the *hamburger* toward the valley. Try not to crease the roll.

Step 3 **Cut** a rectangle out of the middle of the rolled side of paper, leaving a ½" border and forming a frame.

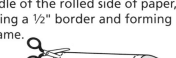

Step 4 **Fold** another sheet of paper (8½" x 11") in half like a *hamburger*.

Step 5 **Apply** glue to the picture frame and place inside the *hamburger* fold.

Variation:
- Place a picture behind the frame and glue the edges of the frame to the other side of the *hamburger* fold. This locks the picture in place.
- Cut out only three sides of the rolled rectangle. This forms a window with a cover that opens and closes.

OTHER SUGGESTIONS FOR A *SINGLE PICTURE FRAME* FOLDABLE

You may wish to write about a shopping trip using a *single picture frame* foldable. Before you begin, organize what you will say by drawing your path through the shops at the market, through the supermarket, or through the mall. You can then write about the shopping trip using your drawings as a guide.

Work in small groups. Each student should create a *single picture frame* foldable with a picture glued into it. You may either cut out a magazine picture or draw your own, although it should be fairly complex. Then give your foldable to another member of the group who will write sentences about what is in the picture and what people in the picture are doing. That student will pass it on to a third student who will write sentences about what is not in the picture and what people in the picture are not doing. The foldables can be passed to additional students to see if they can add more sentences.

Minibook

Mon autobiographie Use this *minibook* organizer to write and illustrate your autobiography. Before you begin to write, think about the many things concerning yourself that you have the ability to write about in French. On the left pages, draw the events of your life in chronological order. On the right, write about your drawings.

Step 1 **Fold** a sheet of paper (8½" x 11") in half like a *hot dog*.

Step 2 **Fold** it in half again like a *hamburger*.

Step 3 Then **fold** in half again, forming eights.

Step 4 **Open** the fold and **cut** the eight sections apart.

Step 5 **Place** all eight sections in a stack and fold in half like a hamburger.

Step 6 **Staple** along the center fold line. **Glue** the front and back sheets into a construction paper cover.

OTHER SUGGESTIONS FOR A *MINIBOOK* FOLDABLE

Work in pairs to practice new verbs and verb forms using a *minibook* foldable. Illustrate different verbs on the left pages. If it is not clear what pronoun is required, you should write the pronoun under the drawing, for instance to differentiate between *we* and *they*. Then trade *minibooks* and write sentences to go with each picture on the right pages, using the new verb and the pronoun illustrated or indicated.

A *minibook* foldable can be used to help practice vocabulary about the family and house as well as possessive adjectives and the verb *to have* in French. Draw your family members and the rooms of your house on the left pages. If you have several brothers or sisters, several cousins, and several aunts or uncles, you should draw each group on one page. On the right page, write sentences about the drawings, telling how many brothers you have, for example. Add additional sentences describing the family members and rooms using possessive adjectives.

Paper File Folder

Les émotions Use this *paper file folder* organizer to keep track of happenings or events that cause you to feel a certain way.

Step 1 **Fold** four sheets of paper (8½" x 11") in half like a *hamburger*. Leave one side one inch longer than the other side.

Step 2 On each sheet, **fold** the one-inch tab over the short side, forming an envelope-like fold.

Step 3 **Place** the four sheets side-by-side, then move each fold so that the tabs are exposed.

Step 4 Moving left to right, **cut** staggered tabs in each fold, 2⅛" wide. Fold the tabs upward.

Step 5 **Glue** the ends of the folders together. On each tab, write an emotion you sometimes feel. Pay attention to when it is that you feel happy, sad, nervous, etc. Describe the situation in French and file it in the correct pocket.

OTHER SUGGESTIONS FOR A *PAPER FILE FOLDER* FOLDABLE

You may use a *paper file folder* organizer to keep track of verbs and verb forms. You should make a folder for each type of regular verb and for each type of irregular verb. Write the conjugations for some important verbs in each category and file them in the *paper file folder* organizer. Add new tenses to the existing cards and new verbs as you learn them.

A *paper file folder* organizer can be useful for keeping notes on the cultural information that you will learn. You may wish to make categories for different types of cultural information and add index cards to them as you learn new facts and concepts about the target cultures.

Envelope Fold

Une ville spéciale Use this *envelope fold* to make a hidden picture or to write secret clues about a city in the French-speaking world you would like to visit.

Step 1 **Fold** a sheet of paper into a *taco,* forming a square. Cut off the leftover piece.

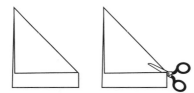

Step 2 **Open** the folded *taco* and refold it the opposite way, forming another *taco* and an X-fold pattern.

Step 3 **Open** the *taco fold* and fold the corners toward the center point of the X, forming a small square.

Step 4 **Trace** this square onto another sheet of paper. Cut and glue it to the inside of the envelope. Pictures can be drawn under the tabs.

Step 5 Use this foldable to **draw** a picture of the city you would like to visit. Or if you prefer, **write** clues about the city and have your classmates raise one tab at a time until they can guess what city the picture represents. Number the tabs in the order in which they are to be opened.

OTHER SUGGESTIONS FOR AN *ENVELOPE FOLD* FOLDABLE

An *envelope fold* can be useful for practicing vocabulary related to airports, trains, hotels, or driving. Draw a scene that depicts many of the vocabulary words. Then write on each of the four flaps the new words that are represented under that flap. You could also give the picture to a partner and have the partner fill in the words.

You may want to use an *envelope fold* to review a selection you have read. Depict a scene from the selection on the paper covered by the tabs. Number the tabs in the order they are to be opened and have a partner open the tabs one at a time to guess what scene is illustrated. The partner should then write a description of the scenes.

Large Sentence Strips

Le présent et le passé Use these *large sentence strips* to help you compare and contrast activities in the past and in the present.

Step 1 Take two sheets of paper (8½" x 11") and **fold** into *hamburgers.* Cut along the fold lines, making four half sheets. (Use as many half sheets as necessary for additional pages to your book.)

Step 2 **Fold** each half sheet in half like a *hot dog.*

Step 3 Place the folds side-by-side and **staple** them together on the left side.

Step 4 About one inch from the stapled edge, **cut** the front page of each folded section up to the mountain top. These cuts form flaps that can be raised and lowered.

Step 5 To make a half-cover, use a sheet of construction paper one inch longer than the book. **Glue** the back of the last sheet to the construction paper strip, leaving one inch on the left side to fold over and cover the original staples. Staple this half-cover in place.

Step 6 With a friend, **write** sentences on the front of the flap, either in the present tense or in the past tense. Then switch your books of sentence strips and write the opposite tense inside under the flaps.

OTHER SUGGESTIONS FOR A *LARGE SENTENCE STRIPS* FOLDABLE

You may work in pairs to use *large sentence strips* to practice using direct and/or indirect object pronouns. On the front of each flap, write full sentences which have direct or indirect objects or both. Then trade sentence strips. You and your partner will each write sentences under the flaps replacing the direct or indirect objects with object pronouns.

Large sentence strips can help you contrast summer and winter activities. On the front of each flap, write sentences about activities that you do in either summer or winter. Under each flap, you should write that in the other season you do not do that activity, and you should tell what you do instead. This may be done as an individual or a partner activity.

You may use *large sentence strips* to practice using verbs that can be used reflexively and nonreflexively. Write a sentence using a reflexive verb on the outside of each flap. Under the flap, write a sentence using the same verb nonreflexively.

Project Board With Tabs

Les loisirs culturels Use this *project board with tabs* to display a visual about your favorite movie or video. Be sure to make it as attractive as possible to help convince others to see it.

Step 1 **Draw** a large illustration, a series of small illustrations, or write on the front of a sheet of paper.

Step 2 **Pinch** and slightly fold the sheet of paper at the point where a tab is desired on the illustrated piece of paper. Cut into the paper on the fold. Cut straight in, then cut up to form an "L." When the paper is unfolded, it will form a tab with the illustration on the front.

Step 3 After all tabs have been cut, **glue** this front sheet onto a second sheet of paper. Place glue around all four edges and in the middle, away from tabs.

Step 4 **Write** or draw under the tabs. If the project is made as a bulletin board using butcher paper, tape or glue smaller sheets of paper under the tabs.

Think of favorite scenes from a movie or cultural event that you enjoyed and draw them on the front of the tabs. Underneath the tabs write a description of the scene or tell why you liked that part of the movie. It might be fun to not put a title on the project board and just hang it up and let classmates guess the name of the movie you are describing.

OTHER SUGGESTIONS FOR A *PROJECT BOARD WITH TABS* FOLDABLE

A *project board with tabs* may be used to describe games, hobbies, or sports. Illustrate a game or one aspect of that game on the outside of the tab and write a description of your drawing under the tab. You may also wish to illustrate a series of important events in a particular game that you watched or participated in recently. You may wish to work together.

You may describe a visit to a museum or park using a *project board with tabs*. You may wish to sketch your favorite paintings, or write titles and artists, on the outside of the tab and describe them on the inside. To describe a park, you may illustrate what you did at the park or your favorite features of the park.

You may wish to use a *project board with tabs* to practice the use of object pronouns. Draw a series of scenes involving two or more people on the outside of the tabs. Write sentences using object pronouns describing the people's conversations or interactions under the tabs.

Sentence Strip Holder

La révision Use this *sentence strip holder* to practice your vocabulary, your verbs, or anything else you might feel you need extra help with.

Step 1 **Fold** a sheet of paper (8½" x 11") in half like a *hamburger*.

Step 2 **Open** the *hamburger* and fold the two outer edges toward the valley. This forms a shutter fold.

Step 3 **Fold** one of the inside edges of the shutter back to the outside fold. This fold forms a floppy L.

Step 4 **Glue** the floppy L tab down to the base so that it forms a strong straight L tab.

Step 5 **Glue** the other shutter side to the front of this L tab. This forms a tent that is the backboard for the flashcards or student work to be displayed.

Step 6 **Fold** the edge of the L up ¼" to ½" to form a lip that will keep the sentence strips from slipping off the holder.

Vocabulary and spelling words can be stored inside the "tent" formed by this fold.

OTHER SUGGESTIONS FOR A *SENTENCE STRIP HOLDER* FOLDABLE

You may wish to practice new or irregular verbs using a *sentence strip holder*. Work in pairs. Make flash cards showing the infinitives of the verbs to practice in French. You should each take half of the cards and take turns setting one verb on the *sentence strip holder*. One partner will then say as many sentences as possible using different forms of that verb, and the other will write down the subject and conjugated verb form (or just the verb form) for each sentence. Partners should check to make sure each verb form is spelled correctly. You can repeat this activity for each verb.

You may practice restaurant and food vocabulary working in small groups and using a *sentence strip holder*. Groups may make flash cards containing the names of local restaurants that everyone will be familiar with, making sure to include different types of restaurants. Put the cards up on the *sentence strip holder* one at a time. Each student will spend several minutes writing about a typical trip to that restaurant. After writing about each restaurant on the list, share a few of your favorite stories with the group.

Expand your view of the French-speaking world.

Glencoe's **Le monde francophone** will take you to the many places where you will be able to use your French.

Maps, facts, and figures will serve as a valuable resource for you throughout your journey.

Start your journey into language and culture.

Objectives let you know what you will be able to do at the end of the chapter.

Opening photo provides a cultural backdrop for the chapter.

CHAPITRE
II

L'été et l'hiver

Objectifs
In this chapter you will learn to:

- describe summer and winter weather
- talk about summer activities and sports
- talk about winter sports
- discuss past actions and events
- make negative statements
- talk about a ski trip in Quebec

Maurice Utrillo Montmartre sous la neige

354

French Online
To interact with your online edition of
Bon voyage! go to: glencoe.com.

Fine Art related to the chapter enriches your cultural knowledge and serves as a springboard for discussion.

Continue to explore French language and culture online at glencoe.com.

Prepare for success with the Sunshine State Standards.

Stay on target with the Standards you will address in each chapter.

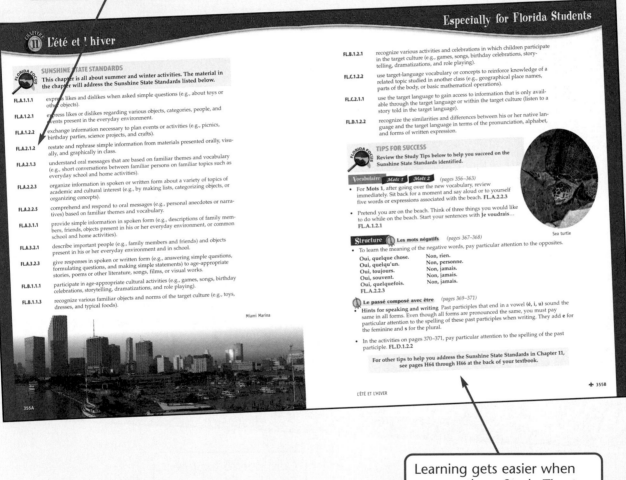

Learning gets easier when you use these Study Tips to guide you through each chapter.

Talk about the chapter theme with your new vocabulary.

Use StudentWorks to access your book, the practice activities, and the audio recordings on any computer.

Vocabulary is introduced and practiced in two manageable sections.

Recorded presentation ensures proper pronunciation.

Photos and illustrations aid comprehension and vocabulary acquisition.

New words are used in a meaningful context.

Practice and master new vocabulary.

Historiette enables you to tell and retell a story, using your new words.

Realia adds interest to the lesson. You can see the language you are learning in real-life contexts.

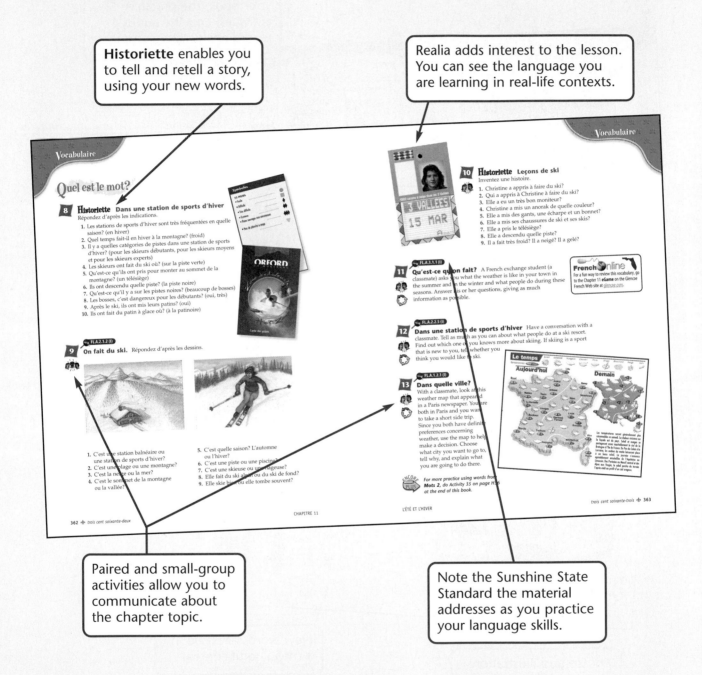

Paired and small-group activities allow you to communicate about the chapter topic.

Note the Sunshine State Standard the material addresses as you practice your language skills.

Learn grammar within the context of the chapter theme.

New structures are presented in simple terms with familiar vocabulary.

You will build confidence as you complete activities that progress from easy to more challenging.

Immediate reinforcement shows you how structure works to build meaning.

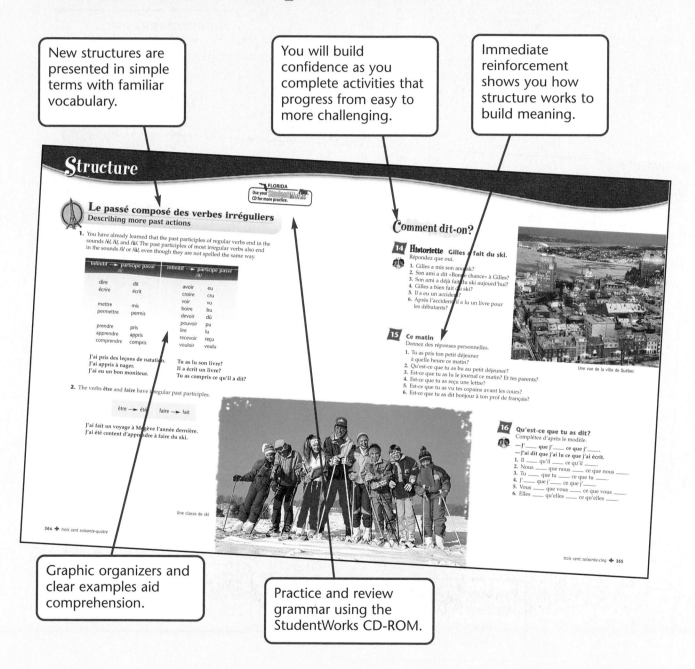

Structure

FLORIDA
Use your StudentWorks Plus CD for more practice.

Le passé composé des verbes irréguliers
Describing more past actions

1. You have already learned that the past participles of regular verbs end in the sounds /é/, /i/, and /ü/. The past participles of most irregular verbs also end in the sounds /i/ or /ü/, even though they are not spelled the same way.

Infinitif	participe passé /i/	Infinitif	participe passé /ü/
dire	dit	avoir	eu
écrire	écrit	croire	cru
		voir	vu
mettre	mis	boire	bu
permettre	permis	devoir	dû
		pouvoir	pu
prendre	pris	lire	lu
apprendre	appris	recevoir	reçu
comprendre	compris	vouloir	voulu

J'ai pris des leçons de natation.
J'ai appris à nager.
J'ai eu un bon moniteur.

Tu as lu son livre?
Il a écrit un livre?
Tu as compris ce qu'il a dit?

2. The verbs **être** and **faire** have irregular past participles.

être → été   faire → fait

J'ai fait un voyage à Megève l'année dernière.
J'ai été content d'apprendre à faire du ski.

Une classe de ski

364 ✤ trois cent soixante-quatre

Comment dit-on?

14 Historiette Gilles a fait du ski.
Répondez que oui.
1. Gilles a mis son anorak?
2. Son ami a dit «Bonne chance» à Gilles?
3. Son ami a déjà fait du ski aujourd'hui?
4. Gilles a bien fait du ski?
5. Il a eu un accident?
6. Après l'accident il a lu un livre pour les débutants?

15 Ce matin
Donnez des réponses personnelles.
1. Tu as pris ton petit déjeuner à quelle heure ce matin?
2. Qu'est-ce que tu as bu au petit déjeuner?
3. Est-ce que tu as lu le journal ce matin? Et tes parents?
4. Est-ce que tu as reçu une lettre?
5. Est-ce que tu as vu tes copains avant les cours?
6. Est-ce que tu as dit bonjour à ton prof de français?

Une vue de la ville de Québec

16 Qu'est-ce que tu as dit?
Complétez d'après le modèle.
—J'___ que j'___ ce que j'___.
—J'ai dit que j'ai lu ce que j'ai écrit.
1. Il ___ qu'il ___ ce qu'il ___.
2. Nous ___ que nous ___ ce que nous ___.
3. Tu ___ que tu ___ ce que tu ___.
4. J'___ que j'___ ce que j'___.
5. Vous ___ que vous ___ ce que vous ___.
6. Elles ___ qu'elles ___ ce qu'elles ___.

trois cent cinq ✤ 365

Graphic organizers and clear examples aid comprehension.

Practice and review grammar using the StudentWorks CD-ROM.

Build on what you already know.

Use your new vocabulary as you practice the new structure points.

Rappelez-vous que... links what you already know to the new structure being presented.

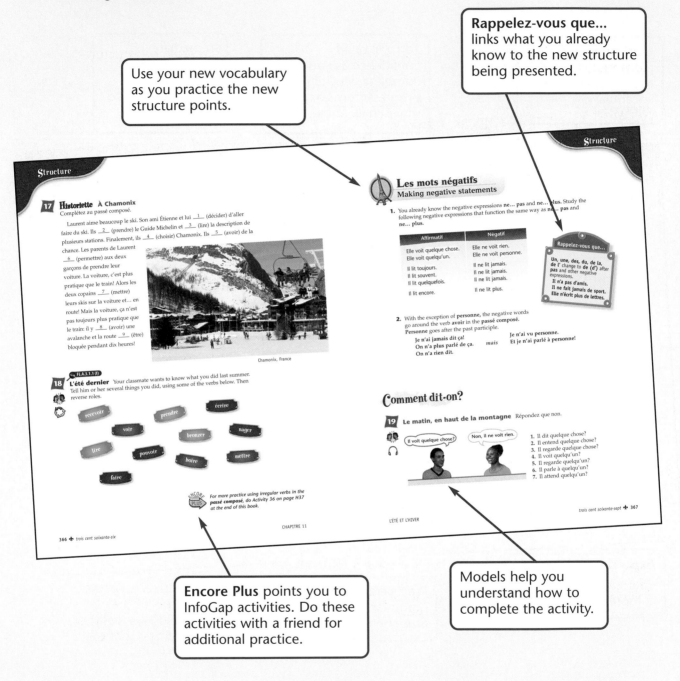

Encore Plus points you to InfoGap activities. Do these activities with a friend for additional practice.

Models help you understand how to complete the activity.

Engage classmates in real conversation.

You can watch and participate in the Interactive Conversation on CD-ROM.

Apply newly learned vocabulary and structures to real-life situations.

Expand your knowledge about the chapter theme online with Web Explore.

You will have a sense of accomplishment when you are able to comprehend the conversation.

Listen to speakers from diverse areas of the French-speaking world to improve pronunciation.

Heighten your cultural awareness.

Reading strategies help to develop your reading skills.

Recorded reading on CD provides options for addressing various skills and learning styles.

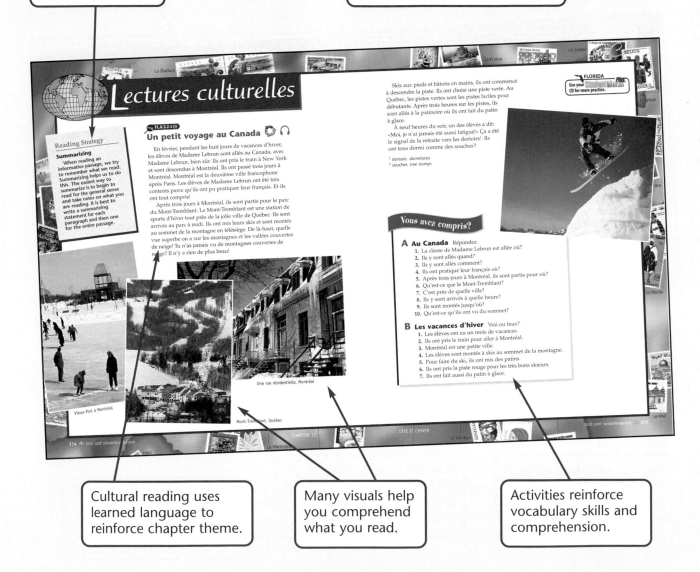

Cultural reading uses learned language to reinforce chapter theme.

Many visuals help you comprehend what you read.

Activities reinforce vocabulary skills and comprehension.

Enrich your cultural knowledge.

Optional cultural readings reinforce the chapter theme.

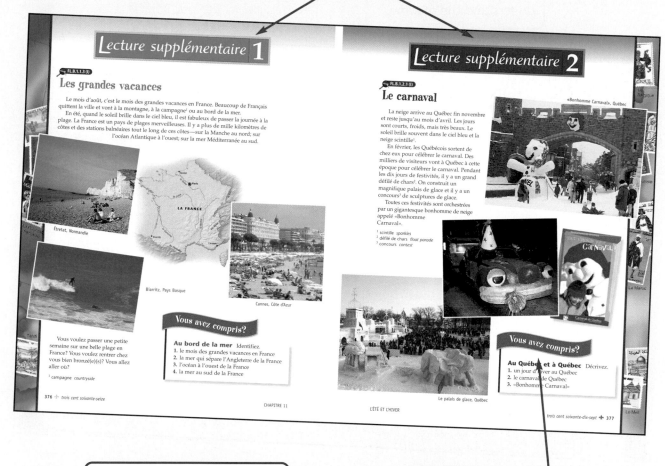

Lecture supplémentaire 1

FL.B.1.1.3 (I)

Les grandes vacances

Le mois d'août, c'est le mois des grandes vacances en France. Beaucoup de Français quittent la ville et vont à la montagne, à la campagne[1] ou au bord de la mer.

En été, quand le soleil brille dans le ciel bleu, il est fabuleux de passer la journée à la plage. La France est un pays de plages merveilleuses. Il y a plus de mille kilomètres de côtes et des stations balnéaires tout le long de ces côtes—sur la Manche au nord; sur l'océan Atlantique à l'ouest; sur la mer Méditerranée au sud.

Étretat, Normandie

LA FRANCE

Biarritz, Pays Basque

Cannes, Côte d'Azur

Vous voulez passer une petite semaine sur une belle plage en France? Vous voulez rentrer chez vous bien bronzé(e)(s)? Vous allez aller où?

[1] campagne *countryside*

Vous avez compris?

Au bord de la mer Identifiez.
1. le mois des grandes vacances en France
2. la mer qui sépare l'Angleterre de la France
3. l'océan à l'ouest de la France
4. la mer au sud de la France

376 ✦ *trois cent soixante-seize*

CHAPITRE 11

Lecture supplémentaire 2

FL.B.1.2.1 (I)

Le carnaval

«Bonhomme Carnaval», Québec

La neige arrive au Québec fin novembre et reste jusqu'au mois d'avril. Les jours sont courts, froids, mais très beaux. Le soleil brille souvent dans le ciel bleu et la neige scintille[1].

En février, les Québécois sortent de chez eux pour célébrer le carnaval. Des milliers de visiteurs vont à Québec à cette époque pour célébrer le carnaval. Pendant les dix jours de festivités, il y a un grand défilé de chars[2]. On construit un magnifique palais de glace et il y a un concours[3] de sculptures de glace.

Toutes ces festivités sont orchestrées par un gigantesque bonhomme de neige appelé «Bonhomme Carnaval».

[1] scintille *sparkles*
[2] défilé de chars *float parade*
[3] concours *contest*

Carnaval!

Vous avez compris?

Au Québec et à Québec Décrivez.
1. un jour d'hiver au Québec
2. le carnaval de Québec
3. «Bonhomme Carnaval»

Le palais de glace, Québec

L'ÉTÉ ET L'HIVER

trois cent soixante-dix-sept ✦ 377

Optional readings further expand your understanding of the French-speaking world.

Questions follow each selection to check comprehension and to expand upon the topic.

Connect with other disciplines.

Introduction to the Connexions provides the background for you to understand the reading.

CONNEXIONS

FL.C.1.2.2 (I)   FL.C.2.1.1 (I)

Les Beaux-Arts

La peinture

One may know a great deal or just a little about art. But almost everyone has at least some interest in art. How often have we heard, "I may not know anything about art, but I certainly know what I like"?

There is no doubt that France has produced many of the world's greatest artists. Do you recognize the names of these famous French artists: Renoir, Monet, Manet, Degas, Seurat, Boudin, Gauguin?

In 1874, two of these painters, Monet and Renoir, were among a group of artists who held a famous exhibition of their works in Paris. The critics laughed at their works and called the artists "Impressionists" to mock one of Monet's paintings entitled *Impression, soleil levant*. Today, paintings by the Impressionists are among the most admired works in the history of art.

Claude Monet *La pie*

Claude Monet *La route sous la neige à Honfleur*

Les impressionnistes

On dit que les impressionnistes sont les peintres de la vie moderne. Ils ont peint la vie quotidienne¹ des gens (personnes) simples. Pour eux, tous les sujets sont bons. Ils ont peint des parcs, des gares, des usines². Beaucoup de peintres impressionnistes ont préféré quitter leur atelier³ pour aller peindre en plein air. Les scènes d'été et les scènes d'hiver sont des sujets favoris de plusieurs impressionnistes.

Voici deux tableaux de paysages d'hiver de Claude Monet—*La pie* et *La route sous la neige à Honfleur*.

¹ vie quotidienne *daily life*
² usines *factories*
³ atelier *studio*

Voici maintenant des scènes de plage. Eugène Boudin a peint *La plage de Trouville*.

Ce tableau *Sur la plage* a été peint par l'ami de Monet, Édouard Manet.

Georges Seurat a peint *Les baigneurs à Asnières*. Asnières est dans la banlieue⁴ parisienne sur la Seine. Au fond, on voit les cheminées des usines de Clichy. Il fait très chaud et les ouvriers⁵ font un petit plongeon dans la Seine.

⁴ banlieue *suburbs*
⁵ ouvriers *workers*

Eugène Boudin *La plage de Trouville*

Édouard Manet *Sur la plage*

Georges Seurat *Les baigneurs à Asnières*

Vous avez compris?

A Un peu de géographie
Find all the places mentioned where these artists painted.

FL.A.3.2.3 (I)

B Mon tableau favori Pick your favorite painting, describe it, and explain why it is your favorite.

trois cent soixante-dix-neuf ✦ 379

378 ✦ *trois cent soixante-dix-huit*   CHAPITRE 11   L'ÉTÉ ET L'HIVER

You further your knowledge of other disciplines—in French!

It's your turn! Apply what you have learned.

Use your new skills to communicate in meaningful, open-ended activities.

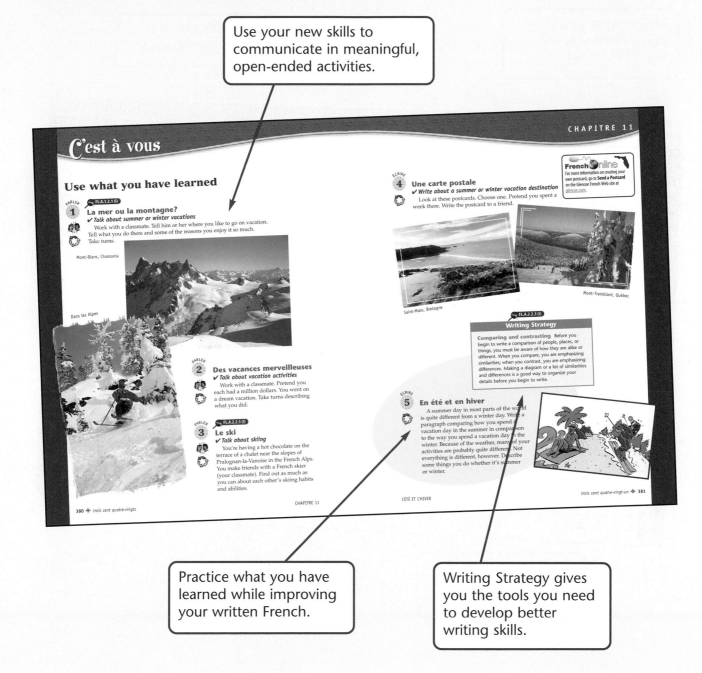

Practice what you have learned while improving your written French.

Writing Strategy gives you the tools you need to develop better writing skills.

Check your progress.

Review what you have learned and prepare for your chapter test.

Take a Self-Check Quiz online at glencoe.com.

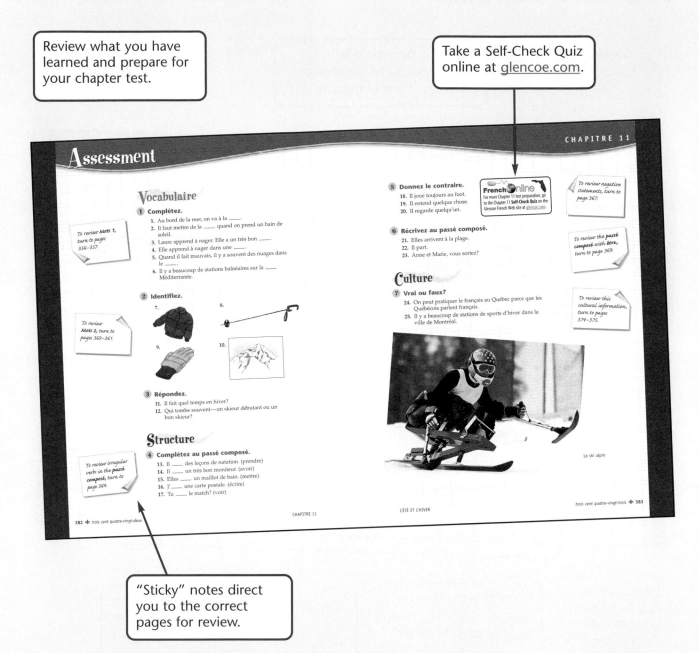

"Sticky" notes direct you to the correct pages for review.

Prepare for success on the FCAT.

Multiple-choice questions have you select the best answer from the choices provided.

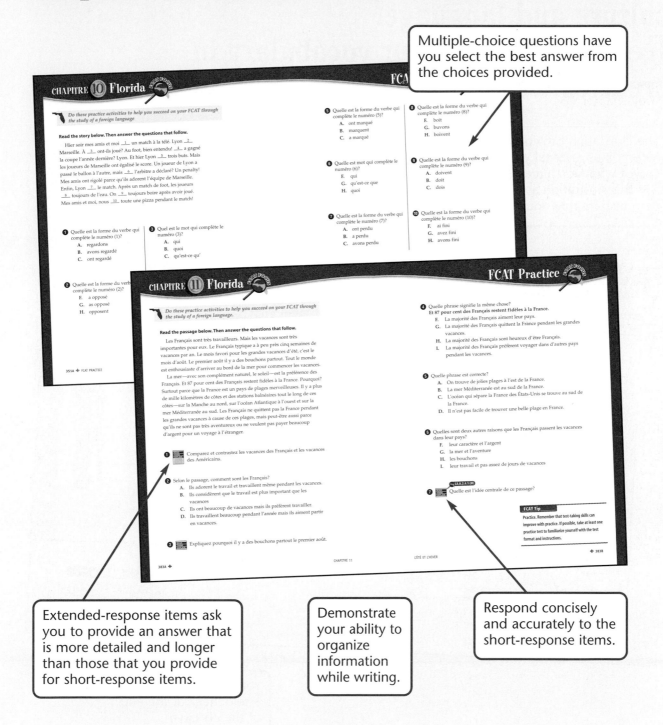

Extended-response items ask you to provide an answer that is more detailed and longer than those that you provide for short-response items.

Demonstrate your ability to organize information while writing.

Respond concisely and accurately to the short-response items.

Go beyond the text to learn more about culture and language.
Review and use your vocabulary in creative ways.

The illustration provided at the end of each chapter recombines material you have learned to remind you of what you already know how to say in French. Use this illustration as a prompt to allow you to demonstrate how much you know how to say or write.

Vocabulary is categorized to help recall.

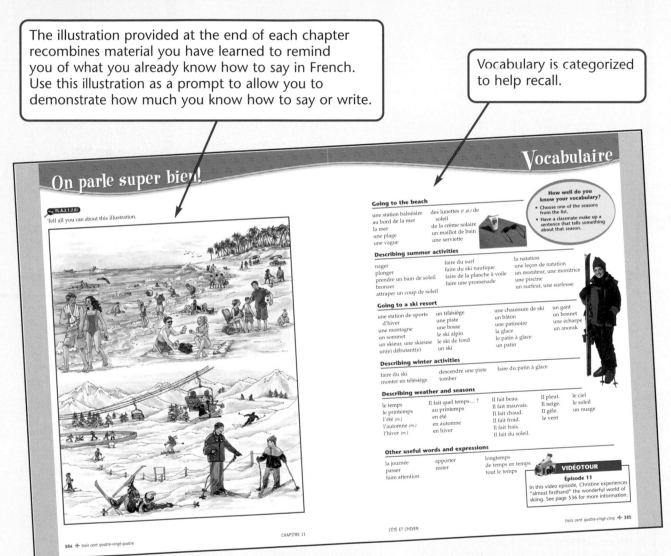

You can use the list as a self-check at the end of the chapter.

Cultivate an appreciation of the diverse Francophone world with National Geographic Reflets.

Explore the diversity of the French-speaking world.

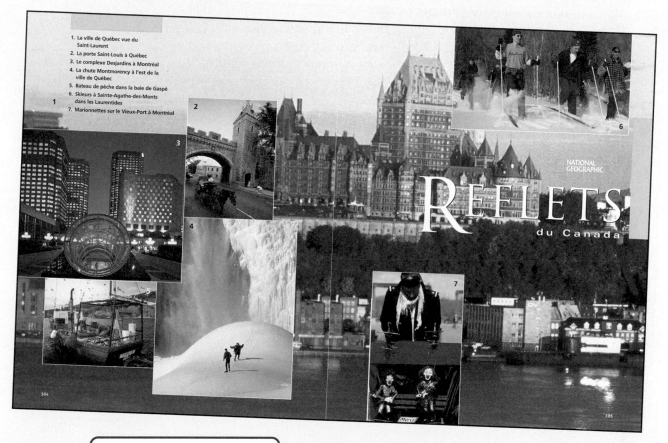

1. La ville de Québec vue du Saint-Laurent
2. La porte Saint-Louis à Québec
3. Le complexe Desjardins à Montréal
4. La chute Montmorency à l'est de la ville de Québec
5. Bateau de pêche dans la baie de Gaspé
6. Skieurs à Sainte-Agathe-des-Monts dans les Laurentides
7. Marionnettes sur le Vieux-Port à Montréal

NATIONAL GEOGRAPHIC

REFLETS du Canada

Stunning **National Geographic** photography illustrates the variety of the Francophone world.

Enhance your appreciation of literature and culture.

Literary Companion gives you another opportunity to apply your reading skills in French.

Literary selections present another view of Francophone culture.

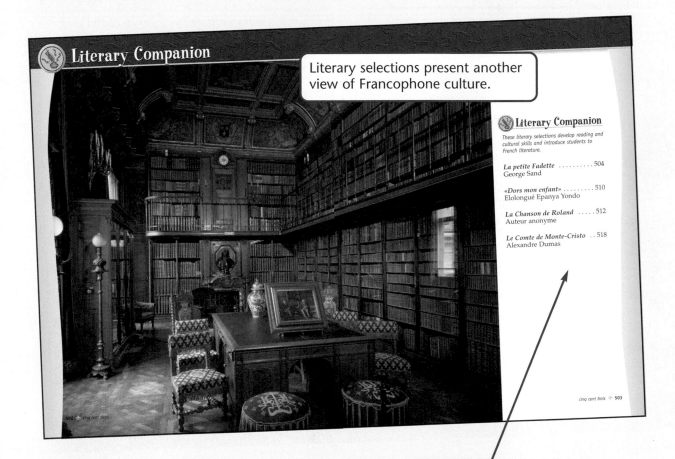

Literary Companion

These literary selections develop reading and cultural skills and introduce students to French literature.

cinq cent trois 503

502 cinq cent deux

Level-appropriate literature selections make reading fun.

Go on a tour of the French-speaking world with the Bon voyage! Video Program.

The **Bon voyage! Video Program,** filmed in various French-speaking countries, lets you experience the diversity of the French-speaking world while reinforcing the language you have learned and improving your listening and viewing skills.

You will love seeing the adventures and mishaps of the **Bon voyage!** video characters.

Video Companion

Using video in the classroom

The use of video in the classroom can be a wonderful asset to the World Languages teacher and a most beneficial learning tool for the language student. Video enables students to experience whatever it is they are learning in their textbook in a real-life setting. With each lesson, they are able to take a vicarious field trip. They see people interacting at home, at school, at the market, etc., in an authentic milieu. Students sitting in a classroom can see real people going about their real life in real places. They may experience the target culture in many countries. The cultural benefits are limitless.

Developing listening and viewing skills In addition to its tremendous cultural value, video, when properly used, gives students much needed practice in developing good listening and viewing skills. Video allows students to look for numerous clues that are evident in a tone of voice, facial expressions, and gestures. Through video students can see and hear the diversity of the target culture and, as discerning viewers and listeners, compare and contrast the French-speaking cultures to each other and to their own culture. Video introduces a dimension into classroom instruction that no other medium—teachers, overhead, text, Audio CDs—can provide.

Reinforcing learned language Video that is properly developed for classroom use has speakers reincorporate the language students have learned in a given lesson. In keeping with reality, however, speakers introduce some new words, expressions, and structures because students functioning in a real-life situation would not know every word native speakers use with them in a live conversation. The lively and interactive nature of video allows students to use their listening and viewing skills to comprehend new language in addition to seeing and hearing the language they have learned come to life.

Getting the most out of video The intrinsic benefit of video is often lost when students are allowed to read the scripted material before viewing. In many cases, students will have come to understand language used by the speakers in the video by means of reading comprehension, thus negating the inherent benefits of video as a tool to develop listening and viewing skills. Because today's students are so accustomed to the medium of video as a tool for entertainment and learning, a well-written and well-produced video program will help them develop real-life language skills and confidence in those skills in an enjoyable way.

On Location!

Je suis Manu. Je suis algérien.

Je suis Christine. Je suis de Fort-de-France, à la Martinique.

Je suis Vincent. Je suis de Paris.

Je suis Chloé. Je suis de Lyon, en France.

Je suis Amadou. Je suis malien.

524 cinq cent vingt-quatre   VIDEO COMPANION

You will visit places where you will hear different accents, dialects, and languages. The **Bon voyage! Video Program** will take you on an exciting tour of the French-speaking world.

Guide to FCAT Success

CHAPITRE 11 L'été et l'hiver

Especially for Florida Students

FLORIDA FOCUS

TIPS FOR SUCCESS
Review the Study Tips below to help you succeed on the Sunshine State Standards identified.

Vocabulaire *Mots 1* *Mots 2* *(pages 356–363)*
- For **Mots 1**, after going over the new vocabulary, review immediately. Sit back for a moment and say aloud or to yourself five words or expressions associated with the beach. **FL.A.2.2.3**
- Pretend you are on the beach. Think of three things you would like to do while on the beach. Start your sentences with **Je voudrais**… **FL.A.1.2.1**

Structure 11 **Les mots négatifs** *(pages 367–368)*
- To learn the meaning of the negative words, pay particular attention to the opposites.

Oui, quelque chose.	Non, rien.
Oui, quelqu'un.	Non, personne.
Oui, toujours.	Non, jamais.

Sea turtle

> In the beginning of **each chapter** there is a list of the Sunshine State Standards covered in the chapter.

> **Standardized Test Practice** pages will help you succeed on your FCAT through the study of French.

CHAPITRE 11 Florida FCAT FOCUS

Do these practice activities to help you succeed on your FCAT through the study of a foreign language.

Read the passage below. Then answer the questions that follow.

Les Français sont très travailleurs. Mais les vacances sont très importantes pour eux. Le Français typique a à peu près cinq semaines de vacances par an. Le mois favori pour les grandes vacances d'été, c'est le mois d'août. Le premier août il y a des bouchons partout. Tout le monde est enthousiaste d'arriver au bord de la mer pour commencer les vacances.

La mer—avec son complément naturel, le soleil—est la préférence des Français. Et 87 pour cent des Français restent fidèles à la France. Pourquoi? Surtout parce que la France est un pays de plages merveilleuses. Il y a plus de mille kilomètres de côtes et des stations balnéaires tout le long de ces côtes—sur la Manche au nord, sur l'océan Atlantique à l'ouest et sur la mer Méditerranée au sud. Les Français ne quittent pas la France pendant les grandes vacances à cause de ces plages, mais peut-être aussi parce qu'ils ne sont pas très aventureux ou ne veulent pas payer beaucoup d'argent pour un voyage à l'étranger.

1 Comparez et contrastez les vacances des Français et les vacances des Américains.

2 Selon le passage, comment sont les Français?
- A. Ils adorent le travail et travaillent même pendant les vacances.
- B. Ils considèrent que le travail est plus important que les vacances
- C. Ils ont beaucoup de vacances mais ils préfèrent travailler.
- D. Ils travaillent beaucoup pendant l'année mais ils aiment partir en vacances.

3 Expliquez pourquoi il y a des bouchons partout le premier août.

FCAT Practice FCAT FOCUS

4 Quelle phrase signifie la même chose?
Et 87 pour cent des Français restent fidèles à la France.
- F. La majorité des Français aiment leur pays.
- G. La majorité des Français quittent la France pendant les grandes vacances.
- H. La majorité des Français sont heureux d'être Français.
- I. La majorité des Français préfèrent voyager dans d'autres pays pendant les vacances.

5 Quelle phrase est correcte?
- A. On trouve de jolies plages à l'est de la France.
- B. La mer Méditerranée est au sud de la France.
- C. L'océan qui sépare la France des États-Unis se trouve au sud de la France.
- D. Il n'est pas facile de trouver une belle plage en France.

6 Quelles sont deux autres raisons que les Français passent les vacances dans leur pays?
- F. leur caractère et l'argent
- G. la mer et l'aventure
- H. les bouchons
- I. leur travail et pas assez de jours de vacances

7 LA.2.4.1 (M) Quelle est l'idée centrale de ce passage?

FCAT Tip
Practice. Remember that test-taking skills can improve with practice. If possible, take at least one practice test to familiarize yourself with the test format and instructions.

How should I prepare for the FCAT?

Have you ever heard the saying "Practice makes perfect"? When preparing for the FCAT, the best thing to do is practice. Solving example questions ahead of time will help you prepare and become more comfortable with the different types of question-and-answer formats that appear on the test. Depending on your grade and the subject matter of the test, questions have any of several different formats.

Multiple Choice

Multiple-choice items are worth one point each. These questions require you to choose the **best** answer from three or four possible choices. Answer choices are lettered with "A, B, C, D" or "F, G, H, I." Choose your answer by filling in the correct bubble.

1 Quel est un bon titre pour cette histoire?

A. Dans une petite boutique

B. Annie fait du shopping

C. Des vêtements pour l'école

D. Les vêtements et les chaussures

 FCAT TIPS

Read Carefully Be sure you understand the question before you read the answer choices. Make special note of words like NOT or EXCEPT. Read and consider all the answer choices before you mark your answer sheet.

When in Doubt If you don't know the answer to a multiple-choice question, try to eliminate as many incorrect answers as possible. Mark your best guess from the remaining answers before moving on to the next question.

Mark Your Answer Sheet Carefully Be sure to fill in the answer bubbles completely. Do not make any stray marks around answer spaces.

Short Response

Short-response items are worth zero to two points depending on your answer. These questions ask you to respond in your own words in a concise manner. Spend about five minutes answering each short-response question.

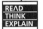

1 Décrivez la maison de la famille Marin.

Les Marin habitent dans une assez grande maison au centre-ville à Tours. La maison a quatre chambres à coucher, trois salles de bains, deux salles de séjour et une grande cuisine. Il y a un beau jardin avec beaucoup de jolies fleurs et deux grands arbres.

FCAT TIPS

Show All Your Work For "Read, Think, Explain" questions, show all your work on your answer sheet.

Write Clearly Write your explanations neatly in clear, concise language. Use only the space provided in the answer book.

Double-Check Your Answer When you have answered each question, reread your answer to make sure it is reasonable and that it is the *best* answer to the question.

Practice Remember that test-taking skills can improve with practice. If possible, take at least one practice test to familiarize yourself with the test format and instructions.

Get Enough Sleep Do not "cram" the night before the test. It can confuse you and make you tired.

Pay Attention Listen carefully to the instructions from the teacher and carefully read the directions and each question.

Extended Response

Extended-response items are worth zero to four points depending on your answer. These questions require you to provide a longer, more detailed response. Allow ten to fifteen minutes to answer each extended-response question.

1 Comparez et contrastez les courses en France et aux États-Unis.

READ
THINK
EXPLAIN

En France les gens préfèrent aller d'un petit magasin à un autre pour faire les courses. Par exemple, on va à la boulangerie pour acheter du pain et à la boucherie pour acheter de la viande. Les Français achètent les fruits et les légumes à l'épicerie ou au marché. Aux États-Unis les Américains font les courses dans un supermarché ou un hypermarché où on peut trouver toutes sortes de choses. Ils ne préfèrent pas aller aux beaucoup de magasins pour faire les courses.

FCAT TIPS

Keep Your Cool Stay focused during the test and don't rush, even if you notice that other students are finishing the test early.

List and Organize First For extended-response "Read, Think, Explain" questions, spend a few minutes listing and organizing the main points that you plan to discuss.

Keep Track of Time Allow about five minutes to answer short-response questions and about ten to fifteen minutes to answer extended-response questions.

Bon voyage! Level 1

Bold page numbers indicate in-depth coverage of Benchmark.

1. Engage in conversation in French to express feeling and ideas and exchange opinions.

Benchmark(s)	Page(s)
FL.A.1.1.1 express likes and dislikes when asked simple questions (e.g., about toys or other objects).	**56, 92, 93, 95, 193, 197, 226,** 252, 271, **389, 393, 434,** 435
FL.A.1.1.2 greet others and exchange essential personal information (e.g., home address, telephone number, place of origin, and general health).	**2, 5, 6, 7, 14,** 31, **32,** 32, 33, **35, 42,** 62, **74, 142, 471**
FL.A.1.1.3 use appropriate gestures and expressions (i.e., body language) to complete or enhance verbal messages.	**57, 488**
FL.A.1.2.1 express likes or dislikes regarding various objects, categories, people, and events present in the everyday environment.	**29, 53, 74, 95, 157, 165, 200, 223,** 230, **242, 316, 331, 341, 359, 363, 380, 435**
FL.A.1.2.2 exchange information necessary to plan events or activities (e.g., picnics, birthday parties, science projects, and crafts).	**137, 205, 212, 213, 253, 284, 309,** 349, **359, 393, 439, 449,** 456, **471**
FL.A.1.3.4 use repetition, rephrasing, and gestures effectively to assist in communicating spoken messages.	**335, 336, 338**

2. Demonstrate understanding of spoken and written French on a variety of topics.

Benchmark(s)	Page(s)
FL.A.2.1.2 restate and rephrase simple information from materials presented orally, visually, and graphically in class.	**31, 46,** 57, **78, 85, 100, 108, 136, 140, 163, 182, 188, 216, 239, 246, 263, 280, 288, 299, 320, 327, 352, 362, 384, 407, 428, 460, 492**
FL.A.2.1.3 understand oral messages that are based on familiar themes and vocabulary (e.g., short conversations between familiar persons on familiar topics such as everyday school and home activities).	30, **34, 66, 93, 121, 128, 165, 170, 234, 248, 276, 308, 334, 340, 349, 372, 386, 410, 415, 416, 425, 448, 480, 481, 494**
FL.A.2.1.4 listen and read in the target language and respond through role playing, drawing, or singing.	**8, 9, 65, 171, 178, 439, 449**
FL.A.2.2.1 give and understand written and verbal instructions, using known, verbal patterns in the target language.	**284, 309, 476, 477, 488**
FL.A.2.2.3 organize information in spoken or written form about a variety of topics of academic and cultural interest (e.g., by making lists, categorizing objects, or organizing concepts).	56, **67, 88, 105,** 192, **205,** 253, **285, 317, 349, 381, 393, 425, 439,** 455, **457**
FL.A.2.2.5 comprehend and respond to oral messages (e.g., personal anecdotes or narratives) based on familiar themes and vocabulary.	33, **42, 53,** 62, **91, 223, 227, 235, 267, 274, 277, 284, 295, 302, 316, 334, 336, 348, 363, 371, 373, 380, 393, 415, 424, 441, 456, 467, 471, 481**

Bold page numbers indicate in-depth coverage of benchmark.

3. Present information and ideas to an audience through speaking and writing in French.

Benchmark(s)	Page(s)
FL.A.3.1.1 provide simple information in spoken form (e.g., descriptions of family members, friends, objects present in his or her everyday environment, or common school and home activities).	**21**, 32, **33, 35, 42, 60, 63, 67, 94, 97, 105, 115,** 121, **125, 127, 147, 161, 165, 169, 195, 203, 212, 227, 229, 231, 242, 267, 271, 339, 348, 363, 366, 368, 403, 407, 412, 415, 417, 424, 447, 456, 471, 473, 497**
FL.A.3.2.1 describe important people (e.g., family members and friends) and objects present in his or her everyday environment and in school.	**25,** 29, **46, 52, 75, 78, 105, 108, 119, 124, 137, 140, 147, 182, 231,** 243, **246, 273, 288, 307, 331, 352, 371,** 407, **428, 460**
FL.A.3.2.3 give responses in spoken or written form (e.g., answering simple questions, formulating questions, and making simple statements) to age-appropriate stories, poems or other literature, songs, films, or visual works.	**13, 36, 37, 38, 39, 43, 57, 68, 71, 98, 99, 115, 119, 130, 131, 136, 156, 161, 165, 179, 183, 193, 222, 278, 279, 310, 311, 317, 342, 343, 344, 345, 374, 375, 379, 407, 411, 415, 447,** 457, **488, 506, 507, 508, 509, 510, 511, 514, 515, 516, 517, 520, 521, 522, 523**

Florida Keys

Bold page numbers indicate in-depth coverage of benchmark.

4. Demonstrate understanding of social interaction patterns within French culture(s) through participation in cultural activities.

Benchmark(s)	Page(s)
FL.B.1.1.1 participate in age-appropriate cultural activities (e.g., games, songs, birthday celebrations, storytelling, dramatizations, and role playing).	**89, 104, 157, 178, 235, 242, 253, 263, 277, 305, 348, 359, 371, 373**
FL.B.1.1.2 recognize patterns of social behavior or social interaction in various settings (e.g., school, family, or immediate community).	3, 4, 7, **65, 160, 174, 199, 204, 206, 207, 208, 209, 418, 419,** 448, **450, 451, 482, 483,** 485
FL.B.1.1.3 recognize various familiar objects and norms of the target culture (e.g., toys, dresses, and typical foods).	9, **157, 160, 161, 175, 189, 236, 237, 238,** 251, **327, 341, 342, 343, 376, 452, 453**
FL.B.1.2.1 recognize various activities and celebrations in which children participate in the target culture (e.g., games, songs, birthday celebrations, storytelling, dramatizations, and role playing).	114, **377, 452, 453**

5. Apply knowledge of French language and culture(s) to further knowledge of other disciplines.

Benchmark(s)	Page(s)
FL.C.1.1.1 use simple vocabulary and phrases to identify familiar objects and concepts from other disciplines.	**25, 40, 41,** 56, **72, 73, 102, 103, 176, 177, 210, 211, 422, 423,** 438
FL.C.1.1.2 participate in an activity in the target-language class that is based on a concept taught in a content class (e.g., shapes or relationships).	71, **97, 177**
FL.C.1.2.1 participate in activities in the language class designed to integrate content-area concepts (e.g., mathematical calculations or cause-and-effect relationships) into target-language instruction (e.g., about countries or cultures).	**176, 177, 240, 241, 282, 283,** 305, **314, 315, 439, 487**
FL.C.1.2.2 use target-language vocabulary or concepts to reinforce knowledge of a related topic studied in another class (e.g., geographical place names, parts of the body, or basic mathematical operations).	38, **39, 40, 41,** 118, 132, **134, 135, 176,** 280, 311, **346, 347, 378, 379, 454, 455, 486, 487**
FL.C.2.1.1 use the target language to gain access to information that is only available through the target language or within the target culture (listen to a story told in the target language).	36, **37,** 70, **134, 135, 206, 207,** 281, **312, 313, 344, 345, 378, 379, 450, 451, 506, 507, 508, 509, 510, 511, 514, 515, 516, 517, 520, 521, 522, 523**

Bold page numbers indicate in-depth coverage of benchmark.

6. Analyze and use different patterns of communication and social interaction appropriate to the setting.

Benchmark(s)		Page(s)
FL.D.1.1.1	know examples of word borrowing from one language to another.	36, **39, 102, 103,** 137
FL.D.1.1.2	use simple vocabulary and short phrases in the target language.	**10, 11, 13, 24, 25, 31, 43, 52, 56, 114, 156, 166, 195, 222, 243, 269, 299, 333**
FL.D.1.2.1	identify examples and understand the significance of true and false cognates (i.e., words derived from a common original form).	19, 23, **72, 73,** 83, 113, 141, **191,** 331, **347, 423, 454,** 465, **485**
FL.D.1.2.2	recognize the similarities and differences between his or her native language and the target language in terms of the pronunciation, alphabet, and forms of written expression.	12, **35,** 67, **97,** 133, 171, **277,** 393, **467,** 484
FL.D.2.1.1	know the similarities and differences between the patterns of behavior of the target culture related to recreation, celebration, holidays, customs, and the patterns of behavior of the local culture.	**96,** 100, 101, **172, 173,** 340, 342, 343, **420, 421**
FL.D.2.1.2	recognize that there are similarities and differences between objects from the target culture and objects from the local culture (e.g., inside dwellings).	130, 131, 132
FL.D.2.2.1	distinguish the similarities and differences between the patterns of behavior of the target culture related to recreation, holidays, celebrations and the patterns of behavior of the local culture.	**349, 482, 483**
FL.D.2.2.2	recognize forms of the target language evident in the local culture (e.g., signs, symbols, advertisements, packages, displays, murals, songs, and rhymes).	**136,** 176, 177, 193, **210, 211,** 213, **243, 267, 315**

7. Demonstrate knowledge of use of the French language within and beyond the school setting.

FL.E.1.2.1	know that many people in the United States use languages other than English on a daily basis.	**68, 69**
FL.E.1.2.2	demonstrate an awareness of employment possibilities (and other applications) for those who are able to master the target language.	**274,** 489

Leçons préliminaires

Bienvenue

Objectifs

In these preliminary lessons you will learn to:

- ✔ greet people
- ✔ say good-bye to people
- ✔ ask people how they are
- ✔ ask and tell names
- ✔ express simple courtesies
- ✔ find out and tell the days of the week
- ✔ find out and tell the months of the year
- ✔ count from 1 to 30
- ✔ find out and tell the time

Miss Melissa Kingston
7 Elm St-et-Hudson, NY 10533
Ardsley-on-Hudson
États-Unis d'Amérique

1. Karim Ashour, Tunis, Tunisie
2. Yvonne Senghor, Abidjan, Côte d'Ivoire
3. Jacques Ferrand, Montréal, Canada
4. Thérèse Nguyen, Lyon, France
5. Yves Clémenceau, Fort-de-France, Martinique
6. Ahmed Rashid, Paris, France
7. Vincent Daudet, Rouen, France
8. Élodie Lutz, Strasbourg, France
9. Marie Robert, Marseille, France

Bienvenue

SUNSHINE STATE STANDARDS

In these preliminary lessons, you will begin to communicate in spoken French. You will learn to greet others, say good-bye, ask and tell names, express yourself politely, use calendar terms, count, and tell time. The material in this **Bienvenue** section will address the Sunshine State Standards listed below.

FL.A.1.1.2   greet others and exchange essential personal information (e.g., home address, telephone number, place of origin, and general health).

FL.A.2.1.4   listen and read in the target language and respond through role playing, drawing, or singing.

FL.A.3.2.3   give responses in spoken or written form (e.g., answering simple questions, formulating questions, and making simple statements) to age-appropriate stories, poems or other literature, songs, films, or visual works.

FL.B.1.1.2   recognize patterns of social behavior or social interaction in various settings (e.g., school, family, or immediate community).

FL.B.1.1.3   recognize various familiar objects and norms of the target culture (e.g., toys, dresses, and typical foods).

FL.D.1.1.2   use simple vocabulary and short phrases in the target language.

FL.D.1.2.2   recognize the similarities and differences between his or her native language and the target language in terms of the pronunciation, alphabet, and forms of written expression.

Tampa, Florida

TIPS FOR SUCCESS

Bottlenose dolphins

Introduction

The Study Tips in each chapter are designed to help you achieve success as you embark on the adventure of learning another language. There are many ways to learn new information. You may find some of these suggestions more useful than others, depending upon which style of learning works best for you. Before you begin, it is important to understand how we acquire language.

Receptive Skills

Each day of your life you receive a great deal of information through the use of language. In order to obtain (get, receive) this information, it is necessary to understand the language being used. It is necessary to understand the language in two different ways. First you must be able to understand what people are saying when they speak to you. This is referred to as oral or listening comprehension. Oral comprehension or listening comprehension is the ability to understand the spoken language.

You must also be able to understand what you read. This is referred to as reading comprehension. Reading comprehension is the ability to understand the written language.

Listening comprehension and reading comprehension are called the *receptive skills*. They are receptive skills because as you listen to what someone else says or read what someone else has written you receive information without having to produce any language yourself.

It is usually very easy to understand your native language. It is a bit more problematic to understand a second language that is new to you. As a beginner, you are still learning the sounds of the new language, and you recognize only a few words. Throughout **Bon voyage!,** we will give you hints or suggestions to help you understand when people are speaking to you in French or when you are reading in French.

Productive Skills

There are two productive skills in language. These two skills are speaking and writing. They are called productive skills because it is you who has to produce the language when you say or write something. When you speak or write, you have control over the language and which words you use. If you don't know how to say something, you don't have to say it. With the receptive skills, on the other hand, someone else produces the language that you listen to or read, and you have no control over the words they use.

There's no doubt that you can easily speak your native language. You can write, too, even though you may sometimes make errors in spelling or punctuation. In French, there's not a lot you can say or write as a beginner. You can only talk or write about those topics you have learned in French class.

In each chapter of **Bon voyage!,** you will learn how to say and write new words. For example, in the preliminary lessons, you learn how to greet people and bid farewell. It won't be long before you'll be able to talk about many things in French. **Bon voyage!**

For tips to help you address the Sunshine State Standards, see the Study Tips for each respective chapter on pages H53 through H67 at the back of your textbook.

Préliminaire A

Bonjour!

Greeting people

When someone wants to know how you are doing and asks **Ça va?**, there are several different answers you can give.

Ça va.
Bien, merci.
Ça va très bien.
Pas mal, merci.

FL.A.1.1.2 (I)

1 Salut!

Get up from your desk. Walk around the classroom. Say hello to each classmate you meet.

FL.A.1.1.2 (I)

2 Ça va?

Work with a classmate. Greet one another and find out how things are going.

More greetings 🎧

1. Salut! is an informal greeting that you can use with people your own age. When you greet an older person, you may use the following expressions.

Bonjour, monsieur.

Bonjour, madame.

Bonjour, mademoiselle.

2. Note that the titles **monsieur, madame,** and **mademoiselle** are almost always used without the last name of the person.

3 FL.B.1.1.2 (M)
Bonjour!

Draw some figures on the board. Some will represent friends your own age and others will represent older people. Greet each of the figures on the board properly.

4 FL.B.1.1.2 (M)
Salutations

Look at these photographs of young people in France and Martinique. As they greet one another they do some things that are different from what we do when we greet each other. What do you notice in the photographs?

Préliminaire B Au revoir!

Saying good-bye 🎧

Au revoir, madame.

Au revoir, Christine.

Ciao, Thomas. À tout à l'heure.

Ciao, Charlotte.

1. A very common expression to use when saying good-bye to someone is **Au revoir.**

2. If you plan to see the person again soon, you can say **À bientôt!** If you plan to see the person very soon, you can say **À tout à l'heure.** If you plan to see the person the next day, you can say **À demain.**

3. An informal expression you often hear is **Ciao.** It comes from Italian and is used in many parts of Europe.

1 Ciao!

Go over to a classmate and say good-bye to him or her.

2 À bientôt!

Work with a classmate. Say **Ciao** to each other and let one another know when you will be getting together again.

FL.B.1.1.2 (M)

3 Au revoir!

Say good-bye to your French teacher. Use **monsieur, madame,** or **mademoiselle,** as appropriate. Then say good-bye to a friend. Use a different expression with each person.

Conversation

Salut, Julie. Ça va?

Salut, Rémi.

Ça va. Et toi?

Pas mal, merci.

Au revoir.

Au revoir. À bientôt!

FL.A.1.1.2 (I)

4 Salut!

Work with a classmate. Have a conversation in French. Say as much as you can to each other.

FL.A.1.1.2 (I)

5 Bonjour!

Work with a classmate. One of you will pretend to be an older person. Have a conversation. Say as much as you can to each other.

Finding out a person's name 🎧

When you want to find out the name of a person who is about the same age as you, you can ask **Tu t'appelles comment?** However, you would not use this expression with an older person. You will learn the more formal forms at a later time.

FL.A.1.1.2 (I)

1 Tu t'appelles comment?

Get up from your desk. Walk around the room. Find out several of your classmates' names. Let them know your name, too.

Conversation

FL.A.1.1.2 (I)

2 Salut!

Have a conversation with a classmate. Find out each other's name, how things are going, and say good-bye to each other.

FL.B.1.1.2 (M)

3 Je m'appelle...

Look at this photograph of young French people introducing each other. Are they doing something that you probably would not do? What is it?

Ordering food politely 🎧

Expressions of politeness are always appreciated. The following are the French expressions for "please," "thank you," and "you're welcome."

Formal	Informal
S'il vous plaît.	S'il te plaît.
Merci (madame).	Merci.
Je vous en prie.	Je t'en prie.

FL.A.2.1.4 (I)

1 La politesse

With a classmate, practice reading the preceding conversation aloud. Be as animated and as polite as you can.

FL.A.2.1.4 (I) **FL.B.1.1.3 (M)**

2 Une limonade, s'il vous plaît.

You are at a café in Canada. Order the following things. Your partner will be the server. Be polite when you order.

1.

un sandwich

2.

un coca

3.

une limonade

4.

un café

5.

une pizza

6.

une saucisse de Francfort,
un hot-dog

7.

une crêpe

Préliminaire E

Telling the days of the week 🎧

To find out and give the day of the week, you say:

C'est quel jour aujourd'hui?
(Aujourd'hui), c'est lundi.
Demain, c'est mardi.

LUNDI	MARDI	MERCREDI	JEUDI	VENDREDI	SAMEDI	DIMANCHE
1	2	3	4	5	6	7
8	9	10	11	12	13	14

FL.D.1.1.2 (I)

1 **C'est quel jour?**

 Answer the following questions in French.

1. C'est quel jour aujourd'hui?
2. Et demain? C'est quel jour?

Telling the months 🎧

janvier	mai	septembre
février	juin	octobre
mars	juillet	novembre
avril	août	décembre

Les nombres de 1 à 30

1 un	7 sept	13 treize	19 dix-neuf	25 vingt-cinq
2 deux	8 huit	14 quatorze	20 vingt	26 vingt-six
3 trois	9 neuf	15 quinze	21 vingt et un	27 vingt-sept
4 quatre	10 dix	16 seize	22 vingt-deux	28 vingt-huit
5 cinq	11 onze	17 dix-sept	23 vingt-trois	29 vingt-neuf
6 six	12 douze	18 dix-huit	24 vingt-quatre	30 trente

Finding out and giving the date

> **Quelle est la date aujourd'hui?**

> **(C'est) le trente et un août.**

	A O Û T						
	LUNDI	MARDI	MERCREDI	JEUDI	VENDREDI	SAMEDI	DIMANCHE
	1	2	3	4	5	6	7
	8	9	10	11	12	13	14
	15	16	17	18	19	20	21
	22	23	24	25	26	27	28
	29	30	(31)				

Premier is used for the first day of the month.
For other days you use **deux, trois, quatre,** etc.

> **le premier août**
> **le deux septembre**

FL.D.1.1.2 (I)

2 La date, s'il vous plaît.

Answer the following questions in French.

1. Quelle est la date aujourd'hui?
2. Et demain?

le 6 janvier

le 14 juillet à Paris

FL.D.1.1.2 (I)

3 En quel mois?

Each of you will stand up in class and give the date of your birthday in French. Listen carefully and keep a record of how many of you were born in the same month. Then tell in French in which month the greatest number of students were born. In which month were the fewest born?

FL.D.1.2.2 (M)

Telling time 🎧

1. To find out the time, you ask:

Il est quelle heure?

2. To give the time on the hour, you say:

1 h
Il est une heure.

2 h
Il est deux heures.

10 h
Il est dix heures.

12 h
Il est midi.

12 h
Il est minuit.

3. To give the time after the hour, you say:

1 h 05
Il est une heure cinq.

3 h 10
Il est trois heures dix.

4 h 25
Il est quatre heures vingt-cinq.

4. To give the time before the hour, you say:

4 h 50
Il est cinq heures moins dix.

5 h 40
Il est six heures moins vingt.

9 h 35
Il est dix heures moins vingt-cinq.

5. To express time on the quarter hour and half hour, you say:

2 h 15
Il est deux heures et quart.

6 h 45
Il est sept heures moins le quart.

6 h 30
Il est six heures et demie.

6. If you need to specify whether it is A.M. or P.M., you can use the following expressions.

Il est six heures du matin.

Il est quatre heures de l'après-midi.

Il est onze heures du soir.

FL.A.3.2.3 (I)   FL.D.1.1.2 (I)

1 ## Il est quelle heure?

Look at each clock and give the time.

1.

2.

3.

4.

5.

6.

Préliminaire F

Conversation

> **Salut, Julie. Il est quelle heure, s'il te plaît?**

> **Il est trois heures vingt.**

> **Trois heures vingt! Déjà? Zut! Au revoir!**

> **Au revoir, Vincent. À bientôt!**

 FL.A.1.1.2 (I)

2 ## Ciao!

Work with a classmate. Greet each other. Find out the time and react as if you have to get going.

 FL.A.1.1.2 (I)

3 ## Il est quelle heure, s'il te plaît?

Get up from your desk and walk around the room. Go up to a classmate. Greet the person quickly and ask the time. Show your classmate a piece of paper with a time on it. He or she will give you the time.

Greeting people

Salut!	Ça va?	Bien.
Bonjour!	Pas mal.	Très bien.

Giving titles

Monsieur	Madame	Mademoiselle

Saying good-bye

Au revoir.	À bientôt.
Ciao!	À demain.
À tout à l'heure.	

Finding out a person's name

Tu t'appelles comment?
Je m'appelle…

How well do you know your vocabulary?

- Choose an expression from the list to begin a conversation.
- Have a classmate respond.
- Take turns.

Being courteous

S'il te plaît.	Je t'en prie.
S'il vous plaît.	Je vous en prie.
Merci.	

Telling the days of the week

C'est quel jour?	jeudi	samedi	aujourd'hui
lundi	vendredi	dimanche	demain
mardi			
mercredi			

Telling the months of the year

Quelle est la date?	avril	août	novembre
janvier	mai	septembre	décembre
février	juin	octobre	
mars	juillet		

Telling time

Il est quelle heure?	Il est midi.
Il est ____ heure(s).	Il est minuit.
du matin	
de l'après-midi	
du soir	

VOCABULAIRE

POSTES 99 RF Bonne Fête Maman
Polynésie Française

Une amie et un ami

Objectifs

In this chapter you will learn to:

✔ ask or tell what someone is like

✔ ask or tell where someone is from

✔ ask or tell who someone is

✔ describe yourself or someone else

✔ talk about students from France and Martinique

Victor Gabriel Gilbert *Enfants jouant au cerceau*

French Online
To interact with your online edition of
Bon voyage! go to: glencoe.com.

SUNSHINE STATE STANDARDS

This chapter is all about friends and how to describe them. The material in the chapter will address the Sunshine State Standards listed below.

FL.A.1.1.2 greet others and exchange essential personal information (e.g., home address, telephone number, place of origin, and general health).

FL.A.1.2.1 express likes or dislikes regarding various objects, categories, people, and events present in the everyday environment.

FL.A.2.1.2 restate and rephrase simple information from materials presented orally, visually, and graphically in class.

FL.A.2.1.3 understand oral messages that are based on familiar themes and vocabulary (e.g., short conversations between familiar persons on familiar topics such as everyday school and home activities).

FL.A.2.2.5 comprehend and respond to oral messages (e.g., personal anecdotes or narratives) based on familiar themes and vocabulary.

FL.A.3.1.1 provide simple information in spoken form (e.g., descriptions of family members, friends, objects present in his or her everyday environment, or common school and home activities).

FL.A.3.2.1 describe important people (e.g., family members and friends) and objects present in his or her everyday environment and in school.

FL.A.3.2.3 give responses in spoken or written form (e.g., answering simple questions, formulating questions, and making simple statements) to age-appropriate stories, poems or other literature, songs, films, or visual works.

FL.C.1.1.1 use simple vocabulary and phrases to identify familiar objects and concepts from other disciplines.

FL.C.1.2.2 use target-language vocabulary or concepts to reinforce knowledge of a related topic studied in another class (e.g., geographical place names, parts of the body, or basic mathematical operations).

FL.C.2.1.1 use the target language to gain access to information that is only available through the target language or within the target culture (listen to a story told in the target language).

FL.D.1.1.1 know examples of word borrowing from one language to another.

FL.D.1.1.2 use simple vocabulary and short phrases in the target language.

FL.D.1.2.1 identify examples and understand the significance of true and false cognates (i.e., words derived from a common original form).

FL.D.1.2.2 recognize the similarities and differences between his or her native language and the target language in terms of the pronunciation, alphabet, and forms of written expression.

Seaside, Florida

TIPS FOR SUCCESS

Review the Study Tips below to help you succeed on the Sunshine Standards identified.

Great egret

Vocabulaire · Mots 1 · Mots 2 *(pages 18–25)*

- Read the words as you look at the illustrations. This will help you visualize and better understand the meaning of your new vocabulary. **FL.A.2.1.2**

- Use your technology (audio program, StudentWorks™ Plus, etc.) to listen to a variety of speakers to practice your vocabulary. This will introduce you to different accents of native speakers. In addition, the more you listen to your new words, the more you will be able to reproduce them. **FL.D.1.2.2**

- After doing any activity that says **Historiette**, read all the answers aloud. Each time you do this, you will be telling a story in French. It's an excellent way to keep using the material you are learning and will help you with your own pronunciation and comprehension. **FL.A.3.1.1; FL.A.3.2.1**

Structure · Les adjectifs *(page 28)*

- What letter do you delete from the feminine form? Remember that you delete the **e** that follows the consonant when referring to a male. Do adjectives in English change depending on whether you are referring to a male or a female? Sometimes comparing aspects of the target language with a language you know helps you retain a concept better. **FL.D.1.2.2**

- As you do the activities, don't try to use words you don't know in French. For example, you may want to talk about someone who is very outgoing, but you don't know a French equivalent for *outgoing*. Give the message using what you do know. For example, you can say: **Jean n'est pas timide, pas du tout.** You can also say: **Marie, elle est timide? Non, pas du tout. Marie n'est pas timide.** Using **ne . . . pas** with a word you know, you can convey the meaning you wish even though you do not know the precise word. **FL.D.1.1.2**

- Listen to your classmates as they respond to the structure activities. Remember, the more you hear a form, the more readily you will be able to use it. **FL.A.2.1.3**

Lectures culturelles · Un garçon et une fille *(pages 36–37)*

- The Reading Strategy on page 36 talks about cognates and how they help you guess the meanings of words you do not know. For example, you read: **Jean est un garçon français. Il est très intelligent, très capable.** You have probably never seen or used the word **capable** in French. However, you can guess its meaning because it is a cognate of the English word *capable*. **FL.D.1.2.1**

> **For other tips to help you address the Sunshine State Standards in Chapter 1, see pages H53 and H54 at the back of your textbook.**

CORBIS

Vocabulaire

Comment est la fille?

brune

amusante

petite

grande

C'est qui?
C'est Julie Lacroix.
Julie est française.

Elle est d'où, Julie?
Julie est de Paris.

Larry Hamill

Comment est le garçon? 🎧

brun

petit

amusant

grand

C'est qui?
C'est Olivier Charpentier.
Olivier est français aussi.

Il est d'où, Olivier?
Il est de Nice.

FL.D.1.2.1 (M)

Note 🎧

Many words in French and English look alike even though they are pronounced differently. These words are called "cognates." You can use the following cognates to describe people.

américain   intelligent
blond   intéressant
patient

Here are some words used to express degree.

Il est amusant.
Il est assez amusant.
Il est très amusant.
Il est vraiment amusant.

Quel est le mot?

1 Historiette Une fille française

Inventez une histoire. *(Make up a story.)*

1. Sophie est française ou américaine?
2. Elle est de Paris ou de New York?
3. Elle est brune ou blonde?
4. Elle est amusante?
5. Elle est grande ou petite?

Sophie Legrand

2 Historiette Un garçon français

Inventez une histoire. *(Make up a story.)*

1. Christophe est américain ou français?
2. Il est de Lyon ou de Houston?
3. Il est brun ou blond?
4. Il est amusant?
5. Il est très intelligent?
6. Il est assez patient?

Christophe Gaudin

Bill

Henri

3 Un Français ou un Américain?

Répondez d'après les photos.
(Answer according to the photos.)

1. Qui est américain?
2. Qui est français?
3. Qui est de Paris?
4. Qui est de Los Angeles?
5. Qui est blond?
6. Qui est brun?

FL.A.3.1.1 (I)

4 **Il est... ? Elle est... ?** Look at the following people and say two things about each of them. Then, find out who they are. They are all famous.

5 **C'est qui?** Think of a student in the class. A classmate will ask you questions about the person and try to guess who it is. Take turns.

 *For more practice using words from **Mots 1**, do Activity 1 on page H2 at the end of this book.*

(tl)Pacha/CORBIS, (tr)Bettmann/CORBIS, (bl)Mitchell Gerber/CORBIS, (br)Christie's Images/CORBIS

Vocabulaire

Mots 2

Une sœur et un frère 🎧

le frère

la sœur

une amie

un ami

Voilà Nathalie et Luc Simonet.
Nathalie est la sœur de Luc.
Luc est le frère de Nathalie.

Voilà Philippe.
Philippe n'est pas le frère de Nathalie.
Philippe est un ami de Nathalie.

Une école et un collège 🎧

une école
américaine

WESTERVILLE NORTH

OPEN HOUSE
SEPT 14
7 PM

une élève

Carol est élève dans une école américaine.

un collège français

un élève

Bruno est élève dans un collège français.
Un collège est une école secondaire en France.

(tl tr bc)Larry Hamill, (bl)John Evans, (br)Dale Durfee/Getty Images

Bonjour, tout le monde!
Je m'appelle Mark.
Je suis américain.
Je suis de Californie.
Je suis un ami de Mae.

Mae est une amie de Mark.
Mae est très sympathique.
Mark est très sympa aussi.

FL.D.1.2.1 (M)

Note

You can also use the following cognates to describe people.

dynamique	égoïste
énergique	enthousiaste
populaire	sociable
timide	

Les nombres de 30 à 60

30 trente	35 trente-cinq	40 quarante
31 trente et un	36 trente-six	50 cinquante
32 trente-deux	37 trente-sept	60 soixante
33 trente-trois	38 trente-huit	
34 trente-quatre	39 trente-neuf	

(l)John Evans, (r)file photo

Quel est le mot?

6 **Historiette** **Une élève française** Choisissez la bonne réponse. *(Choose the right answer.)*

1. _____ est française.
   a. Céline Dupont   **b.** Thomas Duhamel
2. Céline est élève dans _____.
   a. une école américaine   **b.** un collège français
3. Elle est _____.
   a. de Paris   **b.** de Miami
4. Céline est _____ de Karim.
   a. un ami   **b.** une amie
5. Karim est _____ de Céline.
   a. un ami   **b.** un élève
6. David est _____ de Céline.
   a. la sœur   **b.** le frère
7. Céline est _____ de David.
   a. le frère   **b.** la sœur

FL.D.1.1.2 (I)

7 **Qui est d'où?** Répondez d'après la carte. *(Answer according to the map.)*

1. Qui est de Bordeaux?
2. D'où est Maïa?
3. Et Olivia, elle est d'où?
4. Et Ahmed, il est d'où?

Maïa

Ahmed

Strasbourg

Paris

Bordeaux

Cannes

Paul

Olivia

8 **FL.D.1.1.2 (I)**

Historiette **David Williams, un garçon américain**

Inventez une histoire. *(Make up a story.)*

1. Qui est américain, David Williams ou Serge Legrand?
2. D'où est David Williams? Il est de New York ou de Paris?
3. Il est de quelle nationalité? Il est français ou américain?
4. David est élève dans un collège français ou dans une école américaine?
5. Comment est David? Il est timide ou sociable?

9 **Historiette** **Sophie est vraiment amusante.** Complétez. *(Complete.)*

Sophie Bellecour est de Lyon. Elle est ___1___.
Elle n'est pas américaine. Sophie est blonde. Elle
n'est pas ___2___. Elle n'est pas timide. Pas du tout!
Elle est très ___3___. Elle est très sympa aussi.
Elle est ___4___ dans un collège à Lyon.

Lyon, France

Pascal Denjean

10 **FL.A.3.2.1 (I)**

Pascal Denjean Here is a photo of Pascal
Denjean. He is a student from Bordeaux.
Say a few things about Pascal.

11 **FL.A.3.2.1 (I)**

Élodie Denjean The blonde
girl in the photo is Élodie Denjean.
She is Pascal's sister. She is also a
student in Bordeaux. Say a few
things about Élodie.

Élodie Denjean

12 **Jeu** **FL.C.1.1.1 (I)**

Un nombre secret Think of a number
between 1 and 60. Your partner tries to guess the number you
have in mind. Use a hand gesture to indicate whether the
number you are thinking of is higher or lower. Continue until
your partner guesses the correct number. Take turns.

ENCORE PLUS *For more practice using words from **Mots 2**,
do Activity 2 on page H3 at the end of this book.*

Structure

Les articles au singulier
Talking about a person or a thing

1. A noun is the name of a person, place, or thing. In French, every noun has a gender, either masculine or feminine. Except for people, you cannot tell what the gender of a noun is by just looking at it. You need other clues.

2. Many words that accompany nouns can indicate gender. They are called "gender markers." **Une** and **un** are gender markers. They are indefinite articles and correspond to *a (an)* in English. **Une** accompanies a feminine noun and **un** accompanies a masculine noun.

LES ARTICLES INDÉFINIS

Féminin	Masculin
une amie	un ami
une sœur	un frère
une école	un collège

3. **Le, la,** and **l'** are definite articles and often correspond to *the* in English.

LES ARTICLES DÉFINIS

Féminin	Masculin
la fille	le garçon
la sœur	le frère
l'amie	l'ami

Attention!

Note that the definite articles **le** and **la** are shortened to **l'** when they accompany a noun that begins with a vowel. When pronounced, the vowel sound is dropped. This is called "elision."

la amie → l'amie
le ami → l'ami

The **n** of the indefinite article **un** is pronounced when it accompanies a noun beginning with a vowel. This is called "liaison."

un͜n ami   un͜n élève

Une sœur et un frère

Comment dit-on?

13 **Historiette** **Olivier et Marie** Complétez avec **un** ou **une**. *(Complete with* un *or* une.*)*

Olivier est ___1___ garçon très sympa. Olivier est ___2___ ami de Christophe. Christophe est ___3___ élève très intelligent. Il est élève dans ___4___ école secondaire à New York.

Marie est ___5___ amie de Christophe. Marie est ___6___ élève intelligente aussi. Marie est ___7___ fille vraiment amusante.

14 **Historiette** **Brendan Jones et Sabine Morel**
Complétez avec **le, la** ou **l'**. *(Complete with* le, la, *or* l'.*)*

___1___ garçon, Brendan Jones, est américain, mais ___2___ fille, Sabine Morel, n'est pas américaine. Elle est française. Sabine est ___3___ amie de Ludovic Girard et ___4___ sœur de Luc Morel. Brendan n'est pas ___5___ ami de Sabine; il est de Miami et Sabine est de Strasbourg. Brendan est ___6___ ami de Karen Miller et ___7___ frère de Melissa Jones. Brendan est élève et Sabine est élève aussi.

___8___ école de Brendan est à Miami. ___9___ collège de Sabine est à Strasbourg.

Strasbourg, France

UNE AMIE ET UN AMI

L'accord des adjectifs
Describing a person or a thing

1. An adjective is a word that describes a noun. The highlighted words in the following sentences are adjectives.

> **La fille est blonde. Le garçon est blond aussi.**
> **Jeanne est française. Vincent aussi est français.**

2. In French, an adjective must agree with the noun it describes or modifies. Adjectives that end in a consonant such as **blond** and **français** have two forms in the singular. Study the following.

Féminin	Masculin
La fille est blonde.	Le garçon est blond.
La fille est française.	Le garçon est français.
La fille est brune.	Le garçon est brun.
La fille est intelligente.	Le garçon est intelligent.
L'école est grande.	Le collège est grand.

3. Adjectives that end in **e,** such as **énergique** and **sympathique,** are both feminine and masculine.

Féminin	Masculin
Charlotte est très énergique.	Nicolas est très énergique.
Elle est sympathique.	Il est sympathique.

La fille est blonde. Le garçon est brun.

Attention!

When a final consonant is followed by an e, you pronounce the consonant. When a word ends in a consonant, you don't pronounce it.

petite   petit
française français
intéressante intéressant

French Online

For a fun way to review this grammar point and the Chapter 1 vocabulary, go to the **eGame** on the Glencoe French Web site at glencoe.com.

Comment dit-on?

FL.A.3.2.1 (M)

15 **Historiette** **Chloé et Adrien Chancel** Répondez d'après le dessin. *(Answer according to the illustration.)*

1. Chloé est française ou américaine?
2. Elle est blonde ou brune?
3. Elle est grande ou petite?
4. Elle est amusante?
5. Adrien est le frère de Chloé?
6. Adrien est blond ou brun?
7. Il est grand ou petit?
8. Il est amusant?
9. Chloé est élève dans un collège français ou dans une école américaine?
10. Et le frère de Chloé, il est élève dans un collège français ou dans une école américaine?

16 **Historiette** **Maïa, Emmanuel et moi** Complétez. *(Complete.)*

1. Maïa est une amie _____ et _____. (amusant, sympathique)
2. Emmanuel est le frère de Maïa. Il est _____ aussi. Il est _____ et très _____! (sympathique, amusant, sociable)
3. Maïa est _____. (français)
4. Et moi, je m'appelle _____ *(your name)*. Je suis _____. Je ne suis pas _____. (américain, français)
5. Je suis élève dans une école _____ _____. (secondaire, américain)
6. Je ne suis pas élève dans un collège _____. (français)

17 **Jeu** **Devinez.** You often hear French teenagers talk about their friends' younger siblings and say something like: «**Oh, la petite sœur de Corinne, elle est vraiment casse-pieds!**» (literally, *a foot-breaker*). Can you guess what expression we use in English?

FL.A.1.2.1 (I)

18 **Un ami idéal ou une amie idéale**

What are some qualities an ideal friend would have? With a classmate, discuss what you think an ideal friend is like.

FL.A.2.1.3 (M)

19 **C'est qui?** Work with a classmate. Say three things that describe someone in the class. First your partner will tell you whether you're describing a boy or a girl. Then, he or she will guess who it is. Take turns.

—brun, grand, amusant
—C'est un garçon. C'est Marc.

Le verbe être au singulier
Identifying people and things

1. The verb *to be* in French is **être.** Study the following forms.

ÊTRE	
je	suis
tu	es
il	est
elle	est

2. You use **je** to talk about yourself.

You use **tu** to address a friend.

You use **il** to talk about a boy or a man.

You use **elle** to talk about a girl or a woman.

3. You also use **il/elle** when referring to things.

Le collège? Il est grand.
L'école? Elle est petite.

Comment dit-on?

FL.D.1.1.2 (I)

20 **Historiette** **Sylvie Latour** Voici une photo de Sylvie Latour. Décrivez Sylvie d'après les indications. *(Here is a photo of Sylvie Latour. Describe Sylvie using the cues.)*

1. canadienne
2. blonde
3. amusante et intelligente
4. sociable
5. de Montréal

FL.A.2.1.2 (I)

21 **En France** Répétez la conversation. *(Repeat the conversation.)*

> Salut! Tu es l'ami américain de Sandrine Valois, n'est-ce pas?

> Oui, je m'appelle Matt, Matt Porter.

> Tu es de New York?

> Oui, je suis de New York.

FL.A.2.1.2 (I)

22 **Historiette** **Matt Porter** Parlez de Matt. *(Say all you can about Matt.)*

FL.A.1.1.2 (M)

23 **Pardon!** Répondez d'après le modèle. *(Answer according to the model.)*

> Je suis de Paris.

> Pardon, tu es d'où?

1. Je suis de Nice.
2. Je suis d'Antibes.
3. Je suis de Lille.
4. Je suis de Strasbourg.

UNE AMIE ET UN AMI

(t)Peter McCabe/The Image Works, (b)Monika Graff/The Image Works

FL.A.1.1.2 (M)

24

Je suis... Donnez des réponses personnelles. (*Give your own answers.*)

Je m'appelle __1__ (*name*). Je suis de __2__ (*place*). Je suis __3__ (*nationality*). Je suis __4__ (*occupation*).

FL.A.1.1.2 (I)

25

Une interview Posez des questions à un(e) ami(e).
(*Ask a friend the following questions.*)

1. Tu es français(e) ou américain(e)?
2. Tu es d'où?
3. Tu es élève dans une école secondaire?
4. Tu es sociable ou timide?

FL.A.3.1.1 (M)

26

Rémi Voici une photo de Rémi Tonon. Il est de Nîmes. Posez des questions à Rémi d'après le modèle. (*Ask Rémi questions according to the model. Your partner will answer as Rémi.*)

français ➔
—Rémi, tu es français?
—Oui, je suis français.

1. de Nîmes
2. élève dans un collège de Nîmes
3. sociable
4. intelligent

Rémi Tonon

27

Historiette **Antoine Delcourt** Complétez. (*Complete.*)

Voici Antoine Delcourt. Il __1__ français. Il est de Marseille. Moi aussi, je __2__ de Marseille. Marseille __3__ un port important en France. Antoine __4__ élève dans un collège à Marseille. Le collège est assez grand.

Et toi, tu __5__ français(e) ou américain(e)? Tu __6__ d'où? Tu __7__ élève dans une école secondaire? L'école __8__ petite?

Marseille, France

(t)Larry Hamill, (b)Claudie/Sunset, (inset)Wayne Rowe

La négation
Making a sentence negative

To make a sentence negative in French, you put **ne... pas** around the verb.
Note that **ne** becomes **n'** before a vowel.

Affirmatif	Négatif
Je suis américain.	Je ne suis pas français.
Tu es amusant.	Tu n'es pas timide.
Il est sociable.	Il n'est pas égoïste.
Elle est de Lyon.	Elle n'est pas de Paris.

Comment dit-on?

Lycée Henri IV, Paris

28 **Non, Justine n'est pas américaine.**
Mettez à la forme négative. (*Change to the negative.*)

1. Justine est américaine.
2. Elle est de San Francisco.
3. Et moi, je suis français(e).
4. Je suis de Paris.
5. Je suis élève dans un collège à Paris.

29 **FL.A.1.1.2 (M)**

Tu es français(e)? Donnez des réponses
personnelles. (*Give your own answers.*)

1. Tu es français(e)?   3. Tu es timide?
2. Tu es de Lyon?   4. Tu es l'ami(e) de Justine?

30 **FL.A.2.2.5 (M)**   **FL.A.3.1.1 (I)**

Un petit ami ou une petite amie A classmate will
pretend that he or she has a new boyfriend or girlfriend.
Ask as many questions as you can to find out who it is.

For more practice using the verb *être*, do Activity 3 on page H4 at the end of this book.

Vous êtes sur le bon chemin. Allez-y!

Owen Franken/CORBIS

Conversation

Il est d'où, Luc?

Sophie: Luc, tu es de Paris, non?

Luc: Non. Je ne suis pas de Paris.

Sophie: Tu es d'où, alors?

Luc: Je suis de Cannes.

Sophie: Tu es de Cannes… sur la Côte d'Azur?

Luc: Oui.

Sophie: C'est super, la Côte d'Azur!

Vous avez compris?

Répondez. *(Answer.)*

1. Luc est de Paris?
2. Il est d'où?
3. Où est Cannes?
4. Comment est la Côte d'Azur?

(t)Travelpix/FPG, (b)Larry Hamill

Parlons un peu plus

A **Au café** You've just met a student your own age at a café in Antibes, near Cannes. Have a conversation to get to know each other better.

B **Jeu** **Tu es... !**
Play a guessing game. Think of someone in the class. Pretend you are this person and describe yourself. Your classmates have to guess who you are.

Antibes, France

Prononciation

L'accent tonique 🎧

1. In English, you stress certain syllables more than others. In French, you pronounce each syllable evenly. Compare the following pairs of English and French words.

timid / **timide**   *patient* / **patient**
popular / **populaire**   *American* / **américain**
sociable / **sociable**

2. Repeat the following sentences. Notice how each word is linked to the next so that the sentence sounds like one long word.

Élisabeth est l'amie de Nathalie.
Paul est le frère de Nathalie.
Il est très sympathique.

Le Québec

FL.D.1.1.1 (M)

Reading Strategy

Cognates

Words that look alike and have similar meanings in French and English are called "cognates." Look for cognates whenever you read in French. Recognizing cognates can help you figure out the meaning of many words in French and will help you understand what you read.

FL.A.3.2.3 (I) FL.C.2.1.1 (I)

Un garçon et une fille

Un Parisien

Nicolas Martin est français. Il est de Paris, la capitale de la France. Nicolas est un garçon sympa. Il est très intelligent aussi. Nicolas est élève dans un lycée à Paris, le lycée Henri IV. Un lycée est aussi une école secondaire en France, mais après[1] le collège. Le lycée Henri IV à Paris est une école excellente.

[1] après *after*

Lycée Henri IV, Paris

La Polynésie française

Tahiti

FUTUNA RF

Haïti

La Martinique

Une Martiniquaise

Valérie Boucher est française aussi. Elle est de Fort-de-France, la ville[2] principale de la Martinique. La Martinique est une île[3] française dans la mer des Caraïbes (la mer des Antilles). Valérie est élève dans un lycée à Fort-de-France—le lycée Bellevue. Le lycée Bellevue est une école excellente.

[2] ville *city*   [3] île *island*

Fort-de-France, Martinique

Vous avez compris?

A Un Parisien Répondez. *(Answer.)*

1. Nicolas Martin est de quelle nationalité?
2. Il est d'où?
3. Quelle est la capitale de la France?
4. Comment est Nicolas?
5. Il est élève où?

B Une Martiniquaise Vrai ou faux? *(True or false?)*

1. Valérie Boucher est espagnole.
2. Elle est de Pointe-à-Pitre.
3. La Martinique est une île portugaise.
4. Valérie est élève dans une école américaine.

*L*ecture supplémentaire 1

FL.A.3.2.3 (I)   FL.C.1.2.2 (M)

Le français en Afrique

Bonjour! Je m'appelle Diane Koffi. Je suis d'Abidjan. Abidjan est la ville principale de la Côte d'Ivoire. La Côte d'Ivoire est un pays[1] d'Afrique Occidentale[2]. C'est un pays francophone[3].

Moi, je m'appelle Karim Ashour. Je suis tunisien. Je suis de Tunis, la capitale de la Tunisie. La Tunisie est un pays nord-africain sur la mer Méditerranée. La langue officielle de la Tunisie est l'arabe. Le français est la deuxième[4] langue.

[1] pays *country*
[2] Occidentale *Western*
[3] francophone *French-speaking*
[4] deuxième *second*

Abidjan, Côte d'Ivoire

Tunis, Tunisie

Vous avez compris?

A Diane Complétez. *(Complete.)*
1. Diane Koffi est d'_____.
2. Abidjan est la ville principale de la _____.
3. La Côte d'Ivoire est un pays d'_____ Occidentale.

B Karim Vrai ou faux? *(True or false?)*
1. Karim Ashour est une fille.
2. Karim est algérien.
3. Karim est de Tunis.
4. Tunis est la capitale de la Tunisie.
5. La Tunisie est en Europe.
6. La langue officielle de la Tunisie est le français.

FL.A.3.2.3 (I)   **FL.C.1.2.2 (I)**

Un artiste français

Henri de Toulouse-Lautrec est un peintre français. Il est d'Albi, une petite ville dans le sud de la France. La famille d'Henri est noble et assez riche.

Le jeune Henri est très petit. Il est boiteux[1]. Le petit garçon souffre de beaucoup de[2] fractures. Mais le jeune Henri possède un grand talent. Il adore la peinture[3].

Un sujet favori de Toulouse-Lautrec est la vie[4] parisienne.

Un autre sujet favori de Toulouse-Lautrec est le cirque. Le clown est très amusant, n'est-ce pas?

[1] boiteux *lame*   [3] peinture *painting*
[2] beaucoup de *many*   [4] vie *life*

Vous avez compris?

A Un peintre français
Répondez. *(Answer.)*
1. Qui est Toulouse-Lautrec?
2. Il est d'où?
3. Comment est la famille Toulouse-Lautrec?
4. Comment est le jeune Henri?
5. Il souffre de beaucoup de fractures?
6. Il adore la peinture?
7. Il adore le cirque?

FL.D.1.1.1 (I)

B Stratégie de lecture
Trouvez les mots apparentés dans la lecture.
(Find the following cognates in the reading.)

1. family   5. possess
2. talent   6. favorite
3. rich   7. circus
4. subject   8. painter

Albi, France

CONNEXIONS

FL.C.1.1.1 (I)   FL.C.1.2.2 (I)

Les sciences sociales

La géographie

Geography is the study of the earth. It deals with all the earth's features, such as mountains, rivers, and seas. It is also the study of where people live and how the earth's features affect their lives. It is a subject that has interested human beings since the earliest of times.

Look at the map of France. Notice how many geographical terms you are able to recognize in French. See how easy it is to read about geography in French.

L'ANGLETERRE
L'ALLEMAGNE
Lille · LA BELGIQUE
LE LUXEMBOURG
la Seine
Paris (la capitale)
Strasbourg
le Rhin
Orléans
la Loire
LA FRANCE
LA SUISSE
l'océan Atlantique
Limoges
Lyon
le Rhône
les Alpes
Bordeaux
L'ITALIE
la Garonne
Albi
Nîmes · Avignon   Nice
Toulouse   Cannes
MONACO
Marseille   Toulon
les Pyrénées
le nord
L'ESPAGNE
l'ouest — l'est
la mer Méditerranée
le sud

Le Rhône à Avignon

La Seine à Paris

La France

Villes

La France est en Europe. La France est un pays important dans le monde[1]. La capitale, Paris, est une ville culturelle. Lille, dans le nord, est une ville industrielle. Marseille, dans le sud, est un port important sur la mer Méditerranée.

Fleuves

Il y a[2] cinq fleuves[3] en France. La Seine passe à Paris. La Seine est un fleuve très calme. La Loire est un fleuve très long. Le Rhin forme une frontière naturelle entre la France et l'Allemagne. Le Rhône est un fleuve important: c'est une grande source d'énergie électrique. La Garonne est un fleuve assez violent.

[1] monde *world*   [2] Il y a *There are*   [3] fleuves *rivers*

Musée du Louvre, Paris

La Loire à Orléans

Vous avez compris?

Un peu de géographie
Vrai ou faux? *(True or false?)*

1. La France est un continent.
2. Paris est une ville industrielle.
3. Lille est dans le sud de la France.
4. Marseille est un port.
5. La Seine est un fleuve violent.
6. La Loire est un fleuve très long.
7. Un fleuve forme une frontière naturelle entre la France et l'Allemagne.

C'est à vous

Use what you have learned

PARLER 1

  FL.A.2.2.5 (I) FL.A.3.1.1 (I)

Un ami

✔ *Describe a male friend and answer questions about him*

Work with a classmate. Here's a picture of Vincent Terrier, a friend of yours from Paris, France. Say as much as you can about him. Answer any questions your partner may have about Vincent.

PARLER 2

  FL.A.1.1.2 (I)

Une élève

✔ *Ask a female friend questions and tell her about yourself*

Jeanne Marin (a classmate) is a new girl in your school. She is from Montreal, Canada. You want to get to know her better and help her feel at home. Find out as much as you can about her. Tell Jeanne about yourself, too.

Jeanne Marin

PARLER 3

  FL.A.3.1.1 (I)

Dis donc, c'est qui?

✔ *Ask someone questions about another person*

You and a friend (a classmate) are at a sidewalk café in Saint-Tropez, on the French Riviera. You see an attractive girl or boy sitting a few tables away. It just so happens that your friend knows the person. Ask your friend as many questions as you can to find out about the boy or girl you're interested in.

Saint-Tropez, France

French Online
For information on creating your own postcard, go to **Send a Postcard** on the Glencoe French Web site at glencoe.com.

ÉCRIRE

FL.A.3.2.3 (I)

4 Un ami français

✔ *Write a postcard to a friend about yourself*

Here's a postcard you just received from a new pen pal. First read his message. Then answer it. Give Christophe similar information about yourself.

Notre-Dame

PARIS

Salut !

Je m'appelle Christophe Legrand. Je suis de Paris, la capitale de la France. Je suis français. Je suis élève dans un collège à Paris – le collège Eugène Delacroix. C'est un collège excellent.

Je suis brun et assez grand. Je suis très sociable. Je ne suis pas timide. Pas du tout !

À bientôt,

Christophe

Writing Strategy

Freewriting One of the easiest ways to begin any kind of personal writing is simply to begin—to let your thoughts flow and write the first thing that comes to mind. Sometimes as you think of one word, another word you know will come to mind. If you get stuck, take several minutes to think of another word or phrase you have already learned. Brainstorming and freewriting are often methods for generating ideas when writing about yourself.

ÉCRIRE

FL.D.1.1.2 (I)

5 Moi

On a piece of paper, write down as much as you can about yourself in French. Your teacher will collect the descriptions and choose students to read them to the class. You'll all try to guess who's being described.

Assessment

Vocabulaire

To review **Mots 1,** turn to pages 18–19.

1 **Répondez d'après la photo.**
(Answer according to the photo.)

1. Jeanne est française ou américaine?
2. Elle est de Paris ou de Boston?
3. Elle est blonde ou brune?

To review **Mots 2,** turn to pages 22–23.

2 **Choisissez.** *(Choose.)*

4. Guillaume est _____ dans un collège français.
   a. ami   b. élève
5. Guillaume est _____ de Françoise.
   a. le frère   b. la sœur

Paris, France

French ⬤**nline**

For more Chapter 1 test preparation go to the Chapter 1 **Self-Check Quiz** on the Glencoe French Web site at glencoe.com.

Structure

To review these gender markers, turn to page 26.

3 **Complétez avec «un» ou «une».**
(Complete with un *or* une.*)*

6. Sylvie est élève dans _____ collège français.
7. Sylvie est _____ fille très sympa.
8. Paul est _____ ami de Sylvie.
9. Paul est _____ garçon sympa aussi.

4 **Complétez avec «le», «la» ou «l'».**
(Complete with le, la, *or* l'.*)*

10. _____ fille, Sylvie, est de Lyon.
11. Jean-Pierre est _____ frère de Sylvie.
12. _____ école de Sylvie est grande.

To review agreement of adjectives, turn to page 28.

5 **Complétez.** *(Complete.)*

13. C'est une école assez _____. (petit)
14. Martine est une fille très _____. (dynamique)
15. Le garçon _____ est amusant. (américain)
16. Robert est un élève _____. (intelligent)

6 **Complétez avec «être».** *(Complete with* être.*)*

17. Dominique, tu _____ français?
18. Oui, je _____ de Bordeaux.
19. La fille blonde, elle _____ américaine?
20. Non, elle _____ canadienne.

To review the verb **être,** turn to page 30.

7 **Répondez au négatif.** *(Answer in the negative.)*

21. Alain Gérard est américain?
22. Il est timide?
23. Alain est le frère de Julie?

To review making a sentence negative, turn to page 33.

Culture

8 **Choisissez.** *(Choose.)*

24. Un lycée est _____ secondaire en France.
    a. un collège   **b.** un élève   **c.** une école
25. La ville principale de la Martinique est _____.
    a. Bellevue   **b.** Fort-de-France   **c.** Paris

To review this cultural information, turn to pages 36–37.

Grand-Rivière, Martinique

J. Brun/Explorer

Do these practice activities to help you succeed on your FCAT through the study of a foreign language.

Read the story below. Then answer the questions that follow.

Jacqueline est française. Elle est élève dans un collège à Paris. Un collège est une école secondaire en France. Jacqueline est brune. Elle est petite. Elle n'est pas timide. Pas du tout! Elle est très sociable. Elle est très sympa aussi. Elle est la sœur de Paul. Paul est élève aussi dans un collège à Paris.

David est élève dans une école américaine. Il n'est pas français. Il est américain. Il est de la Floride. David est blond. Il est grand. David est un garçon sympa. Il est amusant. Il est très intelligent aussi.

❶ Dans l'histoire, l'auteur utilise quels mots pour présenter une description de l'apparence de Jacqueline?

    A. française, brune

    B. brune, petite

    C. sœur, élève

    D. timide, française

❷ Dans l'histoire, l'auteur utilise quels mots pour présenter une description de la personnalité de David?

    F. sympa, amusant

    G. français, américain

    H. brun, timide

    I. blond, intelligent

❸ READ THINK EXPLAIN L'histoire contraste Jacqueline avec David. Quelle est une différence?

4 **READ THINK EXPLAIN** Quelle est la différence entre **un collège** en français et *college* en anglais?

5 Quelle phrase indique que David est un bon élève?
- **A.** Il est américain.
- **B.** Il est grand.
- **C.** Il est très intelligent.
- **D.** Il est blond.

6 L'histoire indique que Jacqueline n'est pas une amie de David. Pourquoi pas?
- **F.** David est élève dans l'école où Jacqueline est élève aussi.
- **G.** David est de la Floride et Jacqueline est de Paris.
- **H.** Jacqueline est brune et David est blond.
- **I.** Jacqueline est la sœur de Paul.

LA.A.2.4.1 (M)

7 Choisissez un bon titre pour l'histoire.
- **A.** Deux amis
- **B.** Écoles en Europe
- **C.** Frères et sœurs
- **D.** Élèves en France et en Amérique

FCAT Tip

Learn how to answer each kind of question. FCAT reading tests have three types of questions: multiple choice, short response, and extended response.

On parle super bien!

Tell all you can about this illustration.

Identifying a person or thing

un garçon	un frère
une fille	une sœur
un ami	une école
une amie	un collège
un(e) élève	être

Describing a person

petit(e)	sympa(thique)
grand(e)	timide
brun(e)	énergique
blond(e)	égoïste
amusant(e)	dynamique
patient(e)	populaire
intelligent(e)	sociable
intéressant(e)	enthousiaste

Stating nationality

français(e)
américain(e)

Finding out information

Qui?	C'est qui?
D'où?	De quelle nationalité?
Comment?	

Expressing degrees

assez
très
vraiment

Other useful words

voilà
aussi
secondaire

How well do you know your vocabulary?

- Choose five words that describe a good friend.
- Use these words to write several sentences about him or her.

VIDÉOTOUR

Épisode 1

In this video episode, Vincent and Chloé, each hoping to get a great shot of **le Sacré-Cœur**, bump into each other on the steps below the church. See page 526 for more information.

Les cours et les profs

Objectifs

In this chapter you will learn to:

✓ *describe people and things*

✓ *talk about more than one person or thing*

✓ *tell what subjects you take in school and express some opinions about them*

✓ *speak to people formally and informally*

✓ *talk about French-speaking people in the United States*

Pierre Bonnard *Écriture de fille*

French nline
To interact with your online edition of
Bon voyage! go to: glencoe.com.

FLORIDA FOCUS

SUNSHINE STATE STANDARDS

This chapter is all about courses in school and teachers. The material in the chapter will address the Sunshine State Standards listed below.

FL.A.1.1.1 express likes and dislikes when asked simple questions (e.g., about toys or other objects).

FL.A.1.1.2 greet others and exchange essential personal information (e.g., home address, telephone number, place of origin, and general health).

FL.A.1.1.3 use appropriate gestures and expressions (i.e., body language) to complete or enhance verbal messages.

FL.A.1.2.1 express likes or dislikes regarding various objects, categories, people, and events present in the everyday environment.

FL.A.2.1.2 restate and rephrase simple information from materials presented orally, visually, and graphically in class.

FL.A.2.1.3 understand oral messages that are based on familiar themes and vocabulary (e.g., short conversations between familiar persons on familiar topics such as everyday school and home activities).

FL.A.2.1.4 listen and read in the target language and respond through role playing, drawing, or singing.

FL.A.2.2.3 organize information in spoken or written form about a variety of topics of academic and cultural interest (e.g., by making lists, categorizing objects, or organizing concepts).

FL.A.2.2.5 comprehend and respond to oral messages (e.g., personal anecdotes or narratives) based on familiar themes and vocabulary.

FL.A.3.1.1 provide simple information in spoken form (e.g., descriptions of family members, friends, objects present in his or her everyday environment, or common school and home activities).

FL.A.3.2.1 describe important people (e.g., family members and friends) and objects present in his or her everyday environment and in school.

FL.A.3.2.3 give responses in spoken or written form (e.g., answering simple questions, formulating questions, and making simple statements) to age-appropriate stories, poems or other literature, songs, films, or visual works.

FL.B.1.1.2 recognize patterns of social behavior or social interaction in various settings (e.g., school, family, or immediate community).

FL.C.1.1.1 use simple vocabulary and phrases to identify familiar objects and concepts from other disciplines.

South Beach, Miami Beach, Florida

FL.C.1.1.2   participate in an activity in the target-language class that is based on a concept taught in a content class (e.g., shapes or relationships).

FL.C.2.1.1   use the target language to gain access to information that is only available through the target language or within the target culture (listen to a story told in the target language).

FL.D.1.1.2   use simple vocabulary and short phrases in the target language.

FL.D.1.2.1   identify examples and understand the significance of true and false cognates (i.e., words derived from a common original form).

FL.D.1.2.2   recognize the similarities and differences between his or her native language and the target language in terms of the pronunciation, alphabet, and forms of written expression.

FL.E.1.2.1   know that many people in the United States use languages other than English on a daily basis.

TIPS FOR SUCCESS

Review the Study Tips below to help you succeed on the Sunshine State Standards identified.

Vocabulaire   Mots 1   Mots 2   *(pages 50–57)*

Yellowtail snappers

- **Hint for speaking** Listen to your teacher pronounce new words or phrases and then repeat them several times. Once you know how to pronounce the words, read the words in your book. If you try to read a word in French before ever having pronounced it, the spelling will most probably interfere with your pronunciation. Always try to listen, repeat, and then read. **FL.A.2.1.2**

- The vocabulary in **Mots 2** should be very easy to recognize and learn because many words are cognates. A cognate is a word that looks alike in both English and French and has the same meaning in both languages. In the early lessons of **Bon voyage!** we have used many cognates to help you acquire a substantial vocabulary quickly and easily. However, be careful with the pronunciation of cognates. Even though they look alike and mean the same thing in both languages, they can be pronounced very differently. **FL.D.1.2.1**

 ### Lectures culturelles   **Le français aux États-Unis** *(pages 68–69)*

- Read the Reading Strategy at the beginning of the **Lecture culturelle**. Look at the title of the reading on page 68. It lets you know immediately the general topic you'll be reading about.

- Read the three subtitles or heads in the passage. They give you a more specific idea of what you'll be reading. Without having read the reading selection, you now have some understanding of what the reading is about. This will make comprehension much easier. **FL.B.1.1.2**

> **For other tips to help you address the Sunshine State Standards in Chapter 2, see pages H54 through H56 at the back of your textbook.**

Vocabulaire

Mots 1

Les élèves et les profs 🎧

les professeurs (les profs)

la prof   le prof

les amies, les copines

les amis, les copains

Karine et Stéphanie sont françaises.
Pierre et Alexandre sont français aussi.

Les quatre copains sont de Rouen.
Ils sont élèves dans le même lycée.
Ils sont tous très sympathiques.

50 ⚜ *cinquante*

Catherine et Bernard Desjeux

CHAPITRE 2

Comment sont les cours? 🎧

la salle de classe

la classe

les élèves

Le cours de français est facile.
La prof n'est pas trop stricte. Juste un peu.

Mais les cours de sciences sont vraiment difficiles. Toi, tu es d'accord ou pas?

Non, je ne suis pas d'accord. Pour moi, les cours de sciences sont très faciles.

Quel est le mot?

Rennes, France

Des lycéens de Rennes

FL.D.1.1.2 (I)

1 Historiette
Deux copines françaises
Inventez une histoire. (*Make up a story.*)

1. Léa et Touria sont françaises ou américaines?
2. Elles sont copines?
3. Elles sont de Rennes?
4. Elles sont élèves dans le même lycée?
5. Le lycée est à Rennes?
6. Elles sont dans la salle de classe?

FL.D.1.1.2 (I)

2 Historiette
Deux copains français
Inventez une histoire. (*Make up a story.*)

1. Paul et Jamal sont français ou américains?
2. Ils sont copains?
3. Ils sont amusants?
4. Ils sont sympathiques?
5. Ils sont de Rennes?
6. Ils sont élèves dans le même lycée?

French Online
To learn more about French schools, do the Chapter 2 **WebQuest** activity on the Glencoe French Web site at glencoe.com.

FL.A.3.2.1 (I)

3 Le cours de français
Donnez des réponses personnelles. (*Give your own answers.*)

1. Qui est le/la prof de français?
2. Il/Elle est sympa?
3. Il/Elle est strict(e)?
4. Il/Elle est de quelle nationalité?
5. Le cours de français est facile ou difficile?
6. Pour toi, les cours de sciences sont faciles ou difficiles?

(t)Marge/Sunset, (b)Timothy Fuller

FL.A.1.2.1 (I) **FL.A.2.2.5 (I)**

4 **Le prof idéal ou la prof idéale** Work with a classmate. Share ideas as to what you look for in an ideal teacher. Let your classmate know whether you agree with him or her. You may want to use some of the following words.

 intéressant sympathique patient strict

 intelligent amusant enthousiaste dynamique

Un cours de français aux États-Unis

 For more practice using words from Mots 1, do Activity 4 on page H5 at the end of this book.

Vocabulaire

Mots 2

Les matières

Les sciences naturelles
la biologie
la chimie
la physique

Les mathématiques (Les maths)
l'algèbre
la géométrie
la trigonométrie
le calcul

Les langues
le français
l'italien
l'espagnol
l'allemand
l'anglais
le latin

Les sciences sociales
l'histoire
la géographie
l'économie

D'autres matières
la littérature
l'informatique
la gymnastique
la musique
le dessin

Curt Fischer

En cours de français

> Salut les copains!
> Nous sommes américains.
> Nous sommes de New York.
> Et vous, vous êtes américains
> aussi, n'est-ce pas?

> Nous sommes tous très
> forts en français!

> C'est pas vrai!
> Vous êtes très mauvais!

M. Boursier est le prof de français.
Maintenant, nous sommes en
   cours de français.

Les nombres de 70 à 100

70 soixante-dix	80 quatre-vingts	90 quatre-vingt-dix
71 soixante et onze	81 quatre-vingt-un	91 quatre-vingt-onze
72 soixante-douze	82 quatre-vingt-deux	92 quatre-vingt-douze
73 soixante-treize	83 quatre-vingt-trois	93 quatre-vingt-treize
74 soixante-quatorze	84 quatre-vingt-quatre	94 quatre-vingt-quatorze
75 soixante-quinze	85 quatre-vingt-cinq	95 quatre-vingt-quinze
76 soixante-seize	86 quatre-vingt-six	96 quatre-vingt-seize
77 soixante-dix-sept	87 quatre-vingt-sept	97 quatre-vingt-dix-sept
78 soixante-dix-huit	88 quatre-vingt-huit	98 quatre-vingt-dix-huit
79 soixante-dix-neuf	89 quatre-vingt-neuf	99 quatre-vingt-dix-neuf
		100 cent

John Evans

Vocabulaire

Quel est le mot?

Un cours de chimie à Paris

FL.A.2.2.3 (M)

5 Sciences ou langues? Vrai ou faux?
(True or false?)

1. La chimie est une science.
2. L'histoire et la géographie sont des mathématiques.
3. Le calcul est une langue.
4. Le latin et l'espagnol sont des langues.
5. Pour vous, le français est un cours obligatoire.

FL.A.1.1.1 (I)

6 Des cours faciles et difficiles Donnez des
réponses personnelles. *(Give your own answers.)*

1. Le cours de français est facile ou difficile?
2. Pour toi, quels sont les cours faciles?
3. Quels sont les cours difficiles?
4. Tu es fort(e) en français?
5. Tu es fort(e) en sciences?
6. Tu es très fort(e) en quelle matière?
7. Tu es assez mauvais(e) en quelle matière?

FL.D.1.1.2 (I)

7 Historiette Des élèves américains
Inventez une histoire. *(Make up a story.)*

1. Les élèves sont de quelle nationalité?
2. Ils sont élèves dans une école secondaire américaine?
3. Ils sont en cours de français?
4. Le cours de français est facile ou difficile?
5. Les élèves sont forts en français?

FL.C.1.1.1 (M)

8 C'est quel cours? Identifiez le cours. *(Identify the course.)*

1. la littérature, la grammaire anglaise
2. la conversation, la culture française
3. un poème, une pièce de théâtre, une fable
4. un microbe, un animal, une plante, un microscope
5. un cercle, un rectangle, un triangle, un parallélogramme
6. un piano, un violon, un concert, un opéra
7. les montagnes, les villes, les villages, les capitales, les océans
8. la peinture, la sculpture, les statues, les artistes
9. une disquette, un moniteur, un microprocesseur, un bit

FL.A.3.2.3 (I)

9 **Comment est la classe?** With a classmate, look at the illustration. Take turns asking each other questions about it. Use the following question words: **qui, où, quel cours, à quelle heure, comment.**

LUGAGNE-DELPON Olivier
257 r Lecourbe 15e.................01 45 58 96 30
LUGAGNE DELPON Paul
4 r Chevert 7e.................01 44 05 55 31
LUGAGNE-DELPONT Véronique
15 r Marie et Louise 10e.................01 43 41 37 85
LUGAN Benoît
34 pl Marché St-Honoré 1e.......01 42 97 55 05
» **Bernard et Gabrielle**
5 bd Grenelle 15e.................01 45 75 47 83
» **Bruno et Stéphanie** Bat A2
64 r Compans 19e.................01 40 18 13 57
» **Hermann**
11 r Vasco de Gama 15e.............01 45 55 44 35
» **Jacques** 75 av Ledru Rollin 12e......01 43 47 84 57

FL.A.2.1.2 (M)

10 **Le numéro de téléphone** Look at this page from the Paris phone book with a classmate. Give a telephone number. Your classmate will tell whose number it is. Then reverse roles.

FL.A.1.1.3 (I)

11 **Jeu** **Quelle matière?** Work with a classmate. Think of a school subject and use whatever means necessary (voice, hands, drawings) to help your partner guess which subject it is.

Un cours de dessin à Paris

*For more practice using words from **Mots 2**, do Activity 5 on page H6 at the end of this book.*

Larry Hamill

Structure

Le pluriel: articles, noms et adjectifs
Talking about more than one person or thing

1. The articles you know (**un/une, le/la/l'**) are singular markers. The plural forms of these articles are plural markers. Study the following.

LES ARTICLES INDÉFINIS

Masculin		Féminin	
Singulier	**Pluriel**	**Singulier**	**Pluriel**
un garçon	des garçons	une fille	des filles
un_ami	des_amis	une amie	des_amies
un collège	des collèges	une école	des_écoles

LES ARTICLES DÉFINIS

Masculin		Féminin	
Singulier	**Pluriel**	**Singulier**	**Pluriel**
le garçon	les garçons	la fille	les filles
l'ami	les_amis	l'amie	les_amies
le collège	les collèges	l'école	les_écoles

2. In French, you form the plural of most nouns by adding an **s.** This **s,** however, is not pronounced. It is the article **les** or **des** that lets you know the noun is plural: **un prof → des profs; la prof → les profs.**

3. When a noun is plural, any adjective that describes or modifies it must also be in the plural. You form the plural of most adjectives in French by adding an **s.** The **s** is not pronounced.

Singulier	Pluriel
La classe est petite.	Les classes sont petites.
La prof est patiente.	Les profs sont patientes.
Le lycée est grand.	Les lycées sont grands.
Le prof est intéressant.	Les profs sont intéressants.

Note: You do not add an **s** if the word already ends in **s.**
    un cours   **des cours**

Comment dit-on?

12 **Ils sont comment?** Mettez au pluriel.
(Put in the plural.)

—Le garçon est blond.
—Les garçons sont blonds.
1. La fille est blonde.
2. Le garçon est brun.
3. La sœur de Valentin est amusante.
4. Le frère de Stéphane est égoïste.
5. Le prof est intéressant.
6. Le cours est assez difficile.
7. La salle de classe est petite.
8. L'ami de Paul est vraiment sympathique.
9. L'élève est très intelligent.
10. L'ami de Valérie est amusant.

Deux lycéennes de Yerres, France

13 **Pour toi...** Citez... *(Name . . .)*

Pour moi, deux matières très intéressantes sont ＿＿ et ＿＿.
1. deux matières très intéressantes
2. deux cours très intéressants
3. deux écoles excellentes
4. deux élèves sociables
5. deux professeurs stricts
6. deux filles très intelligentes
7. deux garçons très sympas
8. deux élèves fort(e)s en géographie
9. deux élèves assez mauvais(es) en musique

Larry Hamill

14 **En commun** Inventez des points communs.
(Make up what these people have in common.)

Caroline et Marie →
Elles sont amusantes, fortes en algèbre…

1. Laurent et Christian
2. Isabelle et Sandrine
3. Romain et Christophe
4. Marine et Nathalie
5. Loïc et Mathias

 FL.A.3.1.1 (I)

15 **Comme moi** Work with a classmate. Tell your partner
what you and your friends have in common. Your partner
will agree or disagree.

Sue et Jennifer sont
sociables… comme moi.

Moi, je ne suis pas
d'accord. Elles ne sont
pas sociables du tout!

Les vrais amis sont amis pour la vie

 # Le verbe être au pluriel
Talking about more than one

1. You have already learned the singular forms of the verb **être.** Now study
the plural forms.

ÊTRE

Singulier	Pluriel
je suis	nous sommes
tu es	vous_z êtes
il/elle est	ils/elles sont

2.

Nous sommes amis.

Vous êtes amusants.

You use **nous** when referring to
   yourself and another person or
   other people.

You use **vous** when talking to two or
   more people.

Ils sont sympas.

Ils sont sympas.

You use **ils** when referring to two or more males
   or to a group of males and females.

Elles sont copines.

You use **elles** when referring to two
   or more females.

Savez-vous que... ?

You also use **ils/elles**
when referring to things.
**Les cours? Ils sont très
faciles.**
**Les salles? Elles sont
petites.**

Structure

Comment dit-on?

FL.A.2.2.5 (M)

16 **Vous êtes d'où?** Répétez la conversation. *(Repeat the conversation.)*

FL.A.2.2.5 (M)

17 **Historiette** **Ils sont américains.** Complétez d'après la conversation. *(Complete according to the conversation.)*

Les deux garçons __1__ américains. Ils ne __2__ pas de New York. Ils __3__ de Boston. Boston __4__ une grande ville américaine.

Les deux filles ne __5__ pas américaines. Elles __6__ françaises. Elles __7__ de Toulouse. Toulouse __8__ une grande ville française.

FL.A.1.1.2 (M)

18 **À vous** Répondez en utilisant **nous**. *(Choose a partner and answer for both of you using* nous.*)*

1. Vous êtes américain(e)s?
2. Vous êtes d'où?
3. Vous êtes élèves dans une école secondaire?
4. Vous êtes dans la classe de quel professeur?
5. Vous êtes fort(e)s en français?

 For more practice using the verb **être**, *do Activity 6 on page H7 at the end of this book.*

19 **Des questions** Posez des questions et répondez d'après le modèle. *(Ask and answer questions according to the model.)*

américaine / française ⟶
—**Vous êtes américaines ou françaises?**
—**Nous sommes françaises.**

1. martiniquaise / américaine
2. petit / grand
3. sociable / timide
4. brune / blonde

20 **Historiette** **L'ami de Christophe**
Complétez en utilisant **être.** *(Complete with* être.*)*

Je __1__ un ami de Christophe. Christophe __2__ très sympa et très amusant. Nous __3__ français, Christophe et moi. Nous __4__ de Cancale, un petit village breton (en Bretagne). Cancale __5__ vraiment très pittoresque.

Nous __6__ élèves dans un collège. Où __7__ le collège? À Dinard. Tous les deux, nous __8__ forts en anglais. La prof d'anglais, Mlle Fielding, __9__ anglaise. Elle __10__ de Liverpool. Elle __11__ assez stricte et le cours d'anglais n'__12__ pas facile. Mais les élèves de Mlle Fielding __13__ très intelligents!

Dinard, Bretagne

21 **Vous êtes américains?** Complétez la conversation. *(Complete the conversation.)*

—Vous __1__ américains, n'est-ce pas?
—Oui, nous __2__ américains. Nous __3__ de __4__.
—Vous __5__ élèves dans une école secondaire?
—Oui, et nous __6__ très forts en français.
—Vraiment? Qui __7__ le/la prof de français?
—C'est __8__.
—Il/Elle __9__ comment?
—Il/Elle __10__ __11__.

French Online
For a fun way to review the verb **être,**
go to the Chapter 2 **eGame** on the
Glencoe French Web site at glencoe.com.

FL.A.3.1.1 (I)

22 **Tous les deux** Work with a classmate. Discuss things you have in common.

—**Nous sommes sympathiques, intelligent(e)s, fort(e)s en…**

Tu et vous
Talking to people formally or informally

1. As you already know, there are two ways to say *you* in French: **tu** and **vous.** You use **tu** when talking to a friend, a person your own age, or a family member.

Éric, tu es trop timide!

Maman, tu es d'accord?

2. You use **vous** when talking to two or more people.

Vous deux, vous êtes d'accord?

3. You also use **vous** when talking to an older person, a person whom you do not know very well, or anyone to whom you wish to show respect.

Monsieur, s'il vous plaît! Vous êtes le professeur de musique?

Comment dit-on?

(tl)Zephyr Images/Sunset, (tc)Sierpinski/DIAF, (tr)Robert Fried Photography, (bl)Sylwa Villerot/DIAF, (bc)Stuart Cohen/The Image Works, (br)Robert Fried Photography

FL.A.2.1.4 (I) **FL.B.1.1.2 (I)**

23 **Vous êtes français?** Regardez les photos et posez la question.
(Ask the people in the photographs if they are French.)

1.

2.

3.

4.

5.

6.

24 **D'autres questions** Ask the same people other questions.
You may want to use some of the following words or expressions:
d'où, de quelle nationalité, d'accord, patient, fort en.

Vous êtes sur le bon chemin. Allez-y!

Conversation

Quel prof? Interactive Conversations

Paul: Vous êtes dans la classe de Mme Martin?

Anne: Non, nous sommes dans la classe de M. Lepic.

Paul: M. Lepic?

Anne: Ben oui, le prof de maths.

Paul: Ah oui. Comment il est?

Anne: Un peu strict, mais sympa.

Paul: Oui, mais toi et Samuel, vous êtes forts en maths.

Anne: Ben, toi aussi.

Paul: Moi? Je suis très mauvais en maths. Je suis complètement nul!

Vous avez compris?

Répondez. *(Answer.)*

1. Anne et Samuel sont dans la classe de Mme Martin?
2. Ils sont dans la classe de quel professeur?
3. Qui est M. Lepic?
4. Il est comment?
5. Samuel et Anne sont forts en maths?
6. Et Paul, il est fort en maths?

Larry Hamill

Parlons un peu plus

FL.A.2.2.3 (I)   FL.A.3.1.1 (I)

A

D'accord ou pas? Make a chart like the one below. List all your classes and rate them. Then compare your chart with that of a classmate.

—Pour moi, le cours de français n'est pas difficile. Tu es d'accord?

—Oui, je suis d'accord. / Non, je ne suis pas d'accord. Pour moi, le cours de français est très difficile.

Cours	Pas difficile	Assez difficile	Très difficile
le français	✓		
l'algèbre			✓

B **Jeu**   **Quel cours?** Work with a classmate. He or she gives you one word about a class. Guess what class it is. If you're wrong, your partner will give you another hint until you can guess the class. Take turns.

FL.D.1.2.2 (M)

Prononciation

Les consonnes finales 🎧

1. In French, you do not usually pronounce the final consonant you see at the end of a word. Repeat the following.

peti**t**   gran**d**   intéressan**t**   françai**s**
amusan**t**   intelligen**t**   patien**t**   blon**d**

2. You also do not pronounce the final **s** you add to a word to make it plural. This is why a singular noun and its plural sound alike. Repeat the following pairs of words and then the sentences.

un copain ⟶ des copains   une copine ⟶ des copines
le garçon ⟶ les garçons   la fille ⟶ les filles

Tous les copains de Vincent sont sympathiques.
Les cours de maths sont très difficiles.

intelligent

Lectures culturelles

FLORIDA

Use your **StudentWorks** *Plus*
CD for more practice.

Reading Strategy

Using titles

Always look at titles and subtitles before you begin to read. They will help you figure out what a reading selection is about. Having an idea of what a reading is about will help you guess the meaning of unfamiliar words and therefore understand better as you read.

Deux copains haïtiens

Une plage près de Port-au-Prince, Haïti

FL.A.3.2.3 (I) **FL.E.1.2.1 (I)**

Le français aux États-Unis

L'influence haïtienne

Bonjour! Nous sommes Abélard Jean-Baptiste et Nicole Jolicœur. Nous sommes élèves dans une école secondaire à Miami. Et pour nous, le cours de français est vraiment très facile! Pour nous, le français n'est pas une langue étrangère[1]. Nous sommes haïtiens. Nous sommes de Port-au-Prince, la capitale d'Haïti. En Haïti, il y a[2] deux langues—le français et le créole. Le créole est une langue à base de français, d'espagnol et de divers dialectes africains.

L'influence canadienne

Et nous? Nous sommes Antonine Gagnon et Donald Maillet. Nous sommes de Montpelier dans le Vermont. Comme beaucoup de personnes de la Nouvelle-Angleterre[3], nous sommes d'origine canadienne. Et pour nous, le français n'est pas une langue étrangère. Le français est la langue maternelle des Canadiens français.

Deux amis de Montpelier

[1] étrangère *foreign*
[2] il y a *there are*
[3] Nouvelle-Angleterre *New England*

Tahiti

Haïti

La Martinique

L'influence «cajun»

Bonjour! Ici Alice Richard et Pierre Doucet. Nous sommes de Louisiane. Nous sommes cajuns. Nous les Cajuns, nous sommes des descendants des Acadiens. Les Acadiens sont les Français expulsés[4] de l'est du Canada par les Anglais.

L'influence cajun est assez forte en Louisiane. Il y a même[5] deux langues officielles en Louisiane—l'anglais et le français.

[4] expulsés *expelled*   [5] même *even*

Deux élèves de Louisiane

Vous avez compris?

A Les Haïtiens
Répondez. *(Answer.)*
1. Abélard Jean-Baptiste et Nicole Jolicœur sont d'où?
2. Pour Abélard et Nicole, le français est facile?
3. Ils sont de quelle nationalité?
4. Le créole est à base de quelles langues?

B Les descendants des Canadiens français Répondez. *(Answer.)*
1. D'où sont Antonine et Donald?
2. Montpelier est dans quel état?
3. Il y a beaucoup de personnes d'origine canadienne en Nouvelle-Angleterre?
4. Quelle est la langue maternelle des Canadiens français?

C Les Cajuns Répondez. *(Answer.)*
1. Qui sont les Cajuns?
2. Quelles sont les deux langues officielles en Louisiane?

FL.C.2.1.1 (I)

La scolarité en France

Le collège en France est une école secondaire. Les élèves sont des collégiens. Le collège est obligatoire pour quatre ans.

Après[1] le collège, le lycée est aussi une école secondaire, mais pour trois ans. Les élèves sont des lycéens. Il y a[2] deux diplômes d'études secondaires—un diplôme professionnel après deux ans et le baccalauréat après trois ans. Le baccalauréat ou «le bac» est nécessaire pour entrer à l'université.

Voici l'emploi du temps de Louise Belleroche. Elle est en troisième, l'équivalent de *ninth grade*. Il y a combien de[3] cours en troisième en France?

[1] Après   *After*   [2] Il y a   *There are*   [3] combien de   *how many*

Vous avez compris?

A **La scolarité** Vrai ou faux?
(True or false?)
1. En France un collège est une petite université.
2. Le collège n'est pas obligatoire.
3. Le lycée est une école secondaire.
4. Le «bac» est un diplôme universitaire.
5. Le «bac» est nécessaire pour entrer à l'université.

B **L'emploi du temps de Louise** Répondez. *(Answer.)*
1. Il y a combien de cours?
2. Le cours de maths est quels jours? À quelle heure?
3. Et le cours d'anglais?
4. Et le cours de français?
5. Et le cours de biologie?
6. Et le cours d'histoire/géographie?
7. Et le cours de dessin?

Lycée Pasteur, Neuilly, France

La Belgique

(tl)Larry Hamill, (tr)Stephane Cande/Mission/Wallis Phototheque, (b)Robert Holmes/CORBIS

FL.A.3.2.3 (I)

Un message

Salut! Je m'appelle Nicolas Vidal. Je suis de Versailles, une ville[1] dans la banlieue[2] parisienne. Je suis élève dans un lycée. Mais maintenant, je ne suis pas à Versailles. Je suis à Biarritz avec la famille de Guillaume Cartier. Guillaume et moi, nous sommes copains. Nous sommes élèves dans le même lycée. Mais maintenant, pas de profs, pas de cours! Nous sommes libres[3]! Nous sommes en vacances à Biarritz. Biarritz est une petite ville très pittoresque à la frontière espagnole. Pour moi, les vacances, c'est toujours super. Tu es d'accord?

[1] ville *town*   [2] banlieue *suburbs*   [3] libres *free*

Biarritz, France

La Tunisie

Versailles, France

...aroc

Vous avez compris?

A Deux copains Répondez. *(Answer.)*
1. D'où est Nicolas?
2. Où est Versailles?
3. Où est Nicolas maintenant?
4. Il est à Biarritz avec qui?
5. Les deux garçons sont copains?
6. Les deux copains sont en vacances? Où?

FL.C.1.1.2 (M)

B Un peu de géographie
Vrai ou faux? *(True or false?)*
1. Versailles est sur la Côte d'Azur.
2. Versailles est dans la banlieue parisienne.
3. Biarritz est aussi dans la banlieue parisienne.
4. Biarritz est à la frontière espagnole.
5. Biarritz est en Espagne.
6. Biarritz est en France.

Le Mali

CONNEXIONS

Les sciences naturelles

La biologie, la physique et la chimie

Sciences are an important part of the school curriculum. If you like science, it would be fun to be able to read some scientific material in French. You will see how easy it is. It's easy because you already have some background in science from your science courses. In addition, many scientific terms are cognates.

La biologie

La biologie est l'étude des organismes vivants. En biologie, il y a trois catégories importantes: l'anatomie, la zoologie et la botanique. L'anatomie est l'étude du corps humain. La zoologie est l'étude des animaux et la botanique est l'étude des plantes.

La botanique est l'étude des plantes.

La zoologie est l'étude des animaux.

(t)Jean-Paul Garcin/DIAF, (b)Art Wolfe/Getty

La physique et la chimie

La physique est l'étude de la matière et de l'énergie. La chimie est l'étude des caractéristiques des éléments.

Les savants

Dans un laboratoire, le savant (le biologiste, le chimiste ou le physicien) observe et analyse des phénomènes scientifiques. Le biologiste, par exemple, observe et analyse des microbes[1], des cellules, des bactéries et des virus à l'aide d'un microscope.

[1] microbes *germs*

Une biologiste

Vous avez compris?

A Des termes scientifiques

Préparez une liste. *(Make a list of scientific terms you recognize in the reading.)*

B C'est quelle science? Répondez. *(Answer.)*

1. l'étude des animaux
2. l'étude des plantes
3. l'étude de la matière et de l'énergie
4. l'étude du corps humain

C Stratégie de lecture Note that the words in each of the following groups are all related to one another. If you know the meaning of one word, you can guess the meanings of the others. Can you figure them all out?

1. la biologie, un(e) biologiste, biologique
2. analyser, une analyse, analytique
3. un microbe, microbien
4. une bactérie, bactérien
5. un virus, viral

Des élèves dans un laboratoire à Paris

LES COURS ET LES PROFS

C'est à vous

Use what you have learned

L'école internationale de Paris

FL.A.1.1.2 (I)

Nous
✔ *Describe yourself and someone else*

Work with a classmate. You are at an international student gathering in France. You and your partner introduce yourselves to the other students. Try to get to know one another better. You may use the following as a guide:

- say who you are
- give your nationality
- tell where you're from
- give the name of your school
- describe some of your strengths or weaknesses

FL.A.1.2.1 (I)

L'école idéale
✔ *Talk about school*

Work with a classmate. Describe what for each of you is an ideal school. Say as much as you can about the teachers, classes, and students. Determine whether or not you share the same opinions.

Lycée Janson de Sailly, Paris

Larry Hamill

ÉCRIRE 3

🔍 **FL.A.3.2.1 (I)**

Un message
✔ Write about your classes and friends

You answer an e-mail message from a student in France who wants to know about your life in the United States. Give him or her as many details as possible about your classes and your friends.

Collège de Montois, Noyen-sur-Seine

Writing Strategy

Keeping a journal There are many kinds of journals you can keep, each having a different purpose. One type of journal is the kind in which you write about daily events and record your thoughts and impressions about these events. It's almost like "thinking aloud." By keeping such a journal, you may find that you discover something new that you were not aware of.

ÉCRIRE 4

🔍 **FL.A.3.2.1 (I)**

Les cours et les professeurs

You've been in school for about a month. You've had a chance to get to know what your courses are like and to become familiar with your teachers. Create a journal entry about school. Try to write about your classes, the days and times of each, what the class is like, who the teacher is, and what he or she is like. When you have finished, reread your journal entry. Did you discover anything about your courses or your teachers that you hadn't thought of before?

LES COURS ET LES PROFS

Larry Hamill

Assessment

French Online

For more Chapter 2 test preparation, go to the Chapter 2 **Self-Check Quiz** on the Glencoe French Web site at glencoe.com.

Vocabulaire

To review **Mots 1**, turn to pages 50–51.

1 **Choisissez.** *(Choose.)*

1. Christophe et Julien sont amis. Ils sont _____.
   a. frères   **b.** sœurs   **c.** copains

2. Les deux garçons sont _____ dans un lycée français.
   a. élèves   **b.** profs   **c.** cours

3. Le cours de français n'est pas difficile. Le cours de français est _____.
   a. strict   **b.** facile   **c.** comique

4. La prof n'est pas très stricte. Juste _____.
   a. difficile   **b.** d'accord   **c.** un peu

To review **Mots 2**, turn to pages 54–55.

2 **Vrai ou faux?** *(True or false?)*

5. L'algèbre et la musique sont des sciences naturelles.

6. L'économie est une langue.

7. Pour les élèves américains, l'anglais est un cours obligatoire.

8. L'allemand est une science sociale.

Structure

To review plural articles, nouns, and adjectives, turn to page 58.

3 **Mettez au pluriel.** *(Put in the plural.)*

9. Le copain de Lucie est amusant.
   _____ copain__ de Lucie sont amusant__.

10. La sœur de Monique est intelligente.
    _____ sœur__ de Monique sont intelligente__.

11. L'ami de Frédéric est français.
    _____ ami__ de Frédéric sont français__.

12. Le prof de biologie est strict.
    _____ prof__ de biologie sont strict__.

13. La fille brune est américaine.
    _____ fille__ brune__ sont américaine__.

4 **Complétez avec «être».**
(Complete with être.*)*

To review the verb
être, *turn to
page 60.*

14. Nous ____ élèves dans une école
secondaire américaine.

15. Ils ____ élèves dans un lycée français.

16. Vous ____ élèves où?

17. Les élèves de Madame Fauvet ____ intelligents.

18. Qui ____ le prof de géométrie?

Culture

To review this
cultural information,
turn to pages 68–69.

5 **Choisissez.** *(Choose.)*

19. En Haïti, il y a deux langues—le français et ____.

    a. l'anglais   **b.** le créole   **c.** l'espagnol

20. Il y a beaucoup d'influence «cajun» en ____.

    a. Nouvelle-Angleterre   **b.** Haïti   **c.** Louisiane

La Nouvelle-Orléans, Louisiane

Do these practice activities to help you succeed on your FCAT through the study of a foreign language.

Read the story below. Then answer the questions that follow.

Jean et Anne __1__ élèves dans le même lycée à Marseille. Ils sont __2__ en chimie. Mme Dupont est la prof de chimie. Elle est assez __3__. Le frère de Mme Dupont est le prof d'anglais. Il est __4__ aussi. __5__ profs sont patients. Les salles de classe de chimie et d'anglais sont __6__. __7__ ne sont pas grandes!

Jean:	Le cours de chimie est très facile. Anne, __8__ __9__ d'accord?
Anne:	Oui, je __10__ d'accord.
Jean:	Nous __11__ vraiment intelligents!
Anne:	Mme Dupont, __12__ __13__ la prof de musique aussi?
Mme Dupont:	Non, je suis très __14__ en musique!

❶ Quelle est la forme du verbe qui complète le numéro (1)?

    A. est

    B. sont

    C. sommes

❷ Quel est le mot qui complète le numéro (2)?

    F. fort

    G. fortes

    H. forts

❸ Quel est le mot qui complète le numéro (3)?

    A. patient

    B. patiente

    C. patientes

❹ Quel est le mot qui complète le numéro (4)?

    F. patient

    G. patiente

    H. patients

❺ Quel est le mot qui complète le numéro (5)?

    A. Le

    B. La

    C. Les

❻ Quel est le mot qui complète le numéro (6)?

    F. petit

    G. petite

    H. petites

7 Quel est le mot qui complète le numéro (7)?

    A. Elle

    B. Ils

    C. Elles

8 Quel est le mot qui complète le numéro (8)?

    F. tu

    G. vous

    H. ils

9 Quelle est la forme du verbe qui complète le numéro (9)?

    A. est

    B. es

    C. êtes

10 Quelle est la forme du verbe qui complète le numéro (10)?

    F. est

    G. sommes

    H. suis

11 Quelle est la forme du verbe qui complète le numéro (11)?

    A. sont

    B. sommes

    C. êtes

12 Quel est le mot qui complète le numéro (12)?

    F. tu

    G. vous

    H. nous

13 Quelle est la forme du verbe qui complète le numéro (13)?

    A. es

    B. est

    C. êtes

14 Quel est le mot qui complète le numéro (14)?

    F. mauvais

    G. mauvaise

    H. mauvaises

FCAT Tip

Read the directions carefully. Ask your teacher to explain any directions you do not understand.

On parle super bien!

FL.A.2.1.2 (I)   FL.A.3.2.1 (I)

Tell all you can about this illustration.

Identifying a person or thing

un professeur	une copine	un cours
un(e) prof	un lycée	une classe
un copain	une salle de classe	une matière

Identifying school subjects

les sciences naturelles	les langues *(f. pl.)*	les sciences sociales	d'autres matières
la biologie	le français	l'histoire *(f.)*	la littérature
la chimie	l'espagnol *(m.)*	la géographie	l'informatique *(f.)*
la physique	l'italien *(m.)*	l'économie *(f.)*	la gymnastique
les mathématiques,	l'allemand *(m.)*		la musique
les maths *(f. pl.)*	l'anglais *(m.)*		le dessin
l'algèbre *(f.)*	le latin		
la géométrie			
la trigonométrie			
le calcul			

Describing teachers, students, and courses

facile	strict(e)	fort(e)
difficile	intéressant(e)	mauvais(e)

Agreeing and disagreeing

Tu es d'accord?
Oui, je suis d'accord.
Non, je ne suis pas d'accord.
C'est vrai.
Ce n'est pas vrai. C'est pas vrai.

Other useful words and expressions

en cours de (français, maths, etc.)
même
tous
trop
juste un peu

How well do you know your vocabulary?

- Choose your favorite school subject. Choose words to describe this subject.
- Use these words to describe the subject and your teacher.

VIDÉOTOUR

Épisode 2

In this video episode, you will see Vincent at the lycée Louis-le-Grand, interviewing students about their teachers and courses. See page 527 for more information.

(t)Larry Hamill, (b)Curt Fischer

Pendant et après les cours

Objectifs

In this chapter you will learn to:

✔ *talk about what you do in school*

✔ *talk about what you and your friends do after school*

✔ *identify and shop for school supplies*

✔ *talk about what you don't do*

✔ *tell what you and others like and don't like to do*

✔ *discuss schools in France*

FÊTE DU TIMBRE

LA POSTE 2000

RF

0,46 €

Pierre Auguste Renoir *La lecture*

French Online
To interact with your online edition of
Bon voyage! go to: glencoe.com.

Musée Du Louvre, Paris/SuperStock

PRIORITAIRE PRIOR

PAR AVION / AIR M

CHAPITRE ③ Pendant et après les cours

SUNSHINE STATE STANDARDS

This chapter is all about activities that French students engage in during school and after. The material in the chapter will address the Sunshine State Standards listed below.

FL.A.1.1.1	express likes and dislikes when asked simple questions (e.g., about toys or other objects).
FL.A.1.2.1	express likes or dislikes regarding various objects, categories, people, and events present in the everyday environment.
FL.A.2.1.2	restate and rephrase simple information from materials presented orally, visually, and graphically in class.
FL.A.2.1.3	understand oral messages that are based on familiar themes and vocabulary (e.g., short conversations between familiar persons on familiar topics such as everyday school and home activities).
FL.A.2.2.3	organize information in spoken or written form about a variety of topics of academic and cultural interest (e.g., by making lists, categorizing objects, or organizing concepts).
FL.A.2.2.5	comprehend and respond to oral messages (e.g., personal anecdotes or narratives) based on familiar themes and vocabulary.
FL.A.3.1.1	provide simple information in spoken form (e.g., descriptions of family members, friends, objects present in his or her everyday environment, or common school and home activities).
FL.A.3.2.1	describe important people (e.g., family members and friends) and objects present in his or her everyday environment and in school.
FL.A.3.2.3	give responses in spoken or written form (e.g., answering simple questions, formulating questions, and making simple statements) to age-appropriate stories, poems or other literature, songs, films, or visual works.
FL.B.1.1.1	participate in age-appropriate cultural activities (e.g., games, songs, birthday celebrations, storytelling, dramatizations, and role playing).
FL.C.1.1.1	use simple vocabulary and phrases to identify familiar objects and concepts from other disciplines.
FL.C.1.1.2	participate in an activity in the target-language class that is based on a concept taught in a content class (e.g., shapes or relationships).
FL.D.1.1.1	know examples of word borrowing from one language to another.
FL.D.1.2.1	identify examples and understand the significance of true and false cognates (i.e., words derived from a common original form).

A pier at sunset

Getty Images

Especially for Florida Students

FL.D.1.2.2   recognize the similarities and differences between his or her native language and the target language in terms of the pronunciation, alphabet, and forms of written expression.

FL.D.2.1.1   know the similarities and differences between the patterns of behavior of the target culture related to recreation, celebration, holidays, customs, and the patterns of behavior of the local culture.

 TIPS FOR SUCCESS

Review the Study Tips below to help you succeed on the Sunshine State Standards identified.

Vocabulaire *Mots 1* *Mots 2*   *(pages 82–89)*

Conch, a type of mollusk

- Look at each photo or illustration carefully.

- Read the labels. What does each word refer to?

- Each word is then used in a meaningful context in a complete sentence. Repeat the individual words and then the sentences.

- Note that in Activity 4 on page 85, the answer to the question word **qu'est-ce que (qu')** is always a thing. Therefore you should be able to guess at the meaning of this question word. Does it mean *who or what?*

- On page 86, after you have practiced your new words, cover up the words as you look at the drawing or photo of each classroom item. See how many you remember. If you don't remember many, you'll have to practice the words some more. **FL.A.2.2.3**

- **Hint** Always pay careful attention to both the pronunciation and the spelling of your new words. You have now seen more than one form of certain verbs. For example: **Ils jouent. Il joue. Ils regardent. Il regarde.** Have you noticed that there is no difference in pronunciation between **regardent** and **regarde** even though they are written differently? Think about whether there are any words in English that were written differently and pronounced the same. **FL.D.1.2.2**

 Lectures culturelles   **Une journée avec Jacqueline** *(pages 98–99)*

- Look at the photos. These photos let you know the reading is about:
  a. shopping for clothes
  b. going to school
  c. making a meal

- Skim the reading selection and look for the important information such as:
  - Who's the story about?
  - Where does she live and go to school?
  - What are her school hours?
  FL.A.2.1.2; FL.A.3.2.3

- Factual recall is an important reading skill. First, find the facts in the reading and then commit them to memory. Activity B tells you what factual information to look for. **FL.A.3.2.3**

> **For other tips to help you address the Sunshine State Standards in Chapter 3, see pages H56 and H57 at the back of your textbook.**

PENDANT ET APRÈS LES COURS

Getty Images

Vocabulaire

Une journée à l'école 🎧

une maison

une rue

quitter

Patrick habite près de Paris.
Il habite rue Saint-Paul.
Patrick quitte la maison.

arriver

Le matin, Patrick arrive à l'école.
À quelle heure?
Il arrive à l'école à huit heures.
Il passe la journée à l'école.

parler

un CD

écouter

Le prof parle.
Les élèves écoutent bien.
Les élèves étudient.

Les élèves regardent une vidéo (un DVD).
Deux élèves écoutent des CD.

Larry Hamill

la main

Moi, je n'aime pas du tout les examens. Je déteste les examens.

Sophie lève la main.
Elle pose une question.

FL.D.1.2.1 (M)

Note

The expression **passer un examen** is an example of a false cognate (**un faux ami**). It means "to take an exam," not "to pass an exam."

Vincent passe un examen.
Il n'aime pas les examens.

la cantine

Les élèves déjeunent à la cantine.
Ils déjeunent à midi (12 h).

jouer

la cour

Pendant la récré(ation) les élèves
   jouent dans la cour.
Il y a beaucoup d'élèves dans la cour.
Ils rigolent.
Ils parlent entre les cours.

Note

The popular word **rigoler** means "to joke around."
Tu rigoles! means "You don't mean it!" or "You're joking!"

Quel est le mot?

1 Historiette Un élève parisien

Inventez une histoire. *(Make up a story.)*

1. Fabien est de Paris?
2. Il habite rue Jacob?
3. Il quitte la maison à quelle heure?
4. Il passe la journée où?
5. Il déjeune à la cantine?

2 Toujours des questions Répondez.

(Answer.)

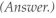

Le matin, les élèves arrivent à l'école à huit heures.

1. Qui arrive à l'école?
2. Ils arrivent où?
3. Ils arrivent à quelle heure?
4. Ils arrivent à l'école le matin ou à midi?

Les élèves déjeunent à la cantine à midi.

5. Qui déjeune?
6. Les élèves déjeunent où?
7. Ils déjeunent à la cantine à quelle heure?

Un lycéen français

3 Historiette En classe Complétez.

(Complete.)

En classe la prof __1__ (parle) et les élèves __2__ (écoute). Anne est une élève excellente. Elle __3__ (étudie) beaucoup. Sophie est dans la même classe. Elle __4__ (lève) la main et __5__ (pose) une question.

Vincent __6__ (passe) un examen. Les examens sont difficiles. Vincent n'__7__ (aime) pas les examens. Il __8__ (déteste) les examens.

4 Pardon! Préparez une petite conversation d'après le modèle.
(Prepare a short conversation according to the model.)

Sandrine regarde un DVD.

Pardon? Qu'est-ce qu'elle regarde?

1. Sandrine regarde une vidéo.
2. Sandrine écoute un CD.
3. Sandrine lève la main.
4. Sandrine pose une question.
5. Sandrine passe un examen.
6. Sandrine adore les vidéos.

5 Historiette Dans la cour Répondez. *(Answer.)*

1. Les élèves sont dans la cour?
2. Ils sont dans la cour pendant la récréation?
3. Ils parlent entre les cours?
4. Ils jouent où?
5. Ils rigolent avec les copains?
6. Ils déjeunent dans la cour?

 FL.A.2.1.2 (I)

6 En classe With a classmate, look at the illustration. Take turns saying as much as you can about it.

*For more practice using words from **Mots 1**, do Activity 7 on page H8 at the end of this book.*

Vocabulaire

Mots 2

Des fournitures scolaires 🎧

un bloc-notes

Graph paper

un sac à dos

un classeur

une feuille de papier

sheet of paper

un stylo-bille

une règle

un feutre

un cahier

un crayon

un livre

une calculatrice

Qu'est-ce que c'est?
C'est un cahier.

une gomme

eraser

Après les cours 🎧

> Le sac à dos, c'est combien, s'il vous plaît?

> Vingt dollars cinquante.

la caisse

payer

un magasin

Lucette travaille après les cours.
Elle travaille dans une papeterie.
Combien d'heures par semaine?
Dix heures.

Sylvain regarde un sac à dos.
Il demande combien coûte le sac à dos.
Il achète le sac à dos.
Il paie à la caisse.

Les nombres de 100 à 1 000

100	cent	400	quatre cents
101	cent un	500	cinq cents
102	cent deux	600	six cents
200	deux cents	700	sept cents
220	deux cent vingt	800	huit cents
300	trois cents	900	neuf cents
350	trois cent cinquante	1000	mille

Après les cours, Patrick ne travaille pas.
Il rentre à la maison l'après-midi.
Il rentre chez lui.

Il écoute la radio.
Il parle un peu au téléphone.

Larry Hamill

Quel est le mot?

FL.A.2.2.3 (I)

7 **Des fournitures scolaires** Préparez une liste de fournitures scolaires. (*Make a list of school supplies.*)

8 **Historiette** **Loïc est français.**
Répondez d'après l'indication.
(*Answer according to the cues.*)

1. Loïc est français ou américain? (français)
2. Il habite où? (près de Paris)
3. Il travaille après les cours? (non)
4. Il rentre chez lui après les cours? (oui)
5. Qu'est-ce qu'il écoute? (la radio)
6. Qu'est-ce qu'il regarde? (une vidéo)
7. Il parle au téléphone? (oui)
8. Avec qui? (les copains)

9 **Historiette** **Dans une papeterie** Inventez une histoire.
(*Make up a story.*)

1. Catherine est canadienne?
2. Elle travaille après les cours?
3. Elle travaille combien d'heures par semaine?
4. Elle travaille dans une papeterie?
5. Où est la papeterie?
6. Qu'est-ce qu'il y a dans une papeterie?
7. Il y a beaucoup d'élèves dans la papeterie?
8. Un garçon paie à la caisse?
9. Un cahier coûte combien?

French Online
For a fun way to review this vocabulary, go to the Chapter 3 **eGame** on the Glencoe French Web site at glencoe.com.

Une papeterie,
Montréal, Canada

10 **Historiette** **À la papeterie** Choisissez la bonne réponse. *(Choose the correct completion.)*

1. Sandrine ____ dans une papeterie.
   a. étudie b. habite c. travaille
2. Elle ____ à un client au téléphone.
   a. écoute b. parle c. paie
3. Les élèves ____ des fournitures scolaires dans la papeterie.
   a. travaillent b. rentrent c. regardent
4. Un garçon ____ un cahier.
   a. regarde b. joue c. rentre
5. Il ____ une calculatrice pour le cours de maths.
   a. passe b. quitte c. achète
6. La calculatrice ____ six dollars canadiens.
   a. paie b. habite c. coûte
7. Le garçon ____ à la caisse.
   a. quitte b. coûte c. paie

FL.B.1.1.1 (I)

11 **Pour la rentrée des classes** Work with a classmate. It's back-to-school time and you're buying the school supplies below. Take turns being the customer and the salesperson.

12 **Jeu** **Qu'est-ce que c'est?** Work with a classmate. Have your partner close his or her eyes. Hand your partner a school supply. Have your partner guess what it is. Take turns.

For more practice using words from **Mots 2**, do Activity 8 on page H9 at the end of this book.

§tructure

Les verbes réguliers en -er au présent
Talking about people's activities

1. A word that expresses an action or a state is a verb. **Parler** (*to speak*), **écouter** (*to listen to*), and **aimer** (*to like*) are verbs in the infinitive form. They are called regular verbs because they all follow a regular pattern. Their infinitives end in **-er.**

2. French verbs change endings with each subject. To form the stem to which the endings are added, you drop the **-er** from the infinitive.

Infinitive	Stem
parler	parl-
écouter	écout-
aimer	aim-

3. You add the ending for each subject to the stem. Note that, although the endings for the **je, tu, il,** and **ils** forms are spelled differently, they are pronounced the same.

	PARLER	AIMER
je `parl` -e	je parle	j' aime
tu `parl` -es	tu parles	tu aimes
il/elle `parl` -e	il/elle parle	il/elle aime
nous `parl` -ons	nous parlons	nous‿aimons
vous `parl` -ez	vous parlez	vous‿aimez
ils/elles `parl` -ent	ils/elles parlent	ils‿/elles‿aiment

4. You will see and hear the word **on** a great deal. **On** has several meanings, such as "we," "they," and "people." **On** always takes the **il/elle** form of the verb. In spoken French, people use **on** more often than **nous.**

> On parle français en France.
> On travaille beaucoup.
> On‿arrive à l'école le matin.

Attention!

There is elision when **je** or **ne** is followed by a verb that begins with a vowel or silent **h.**
J'habite à Paris. **Je n'habite pas à Lyon.**
J'aime les maths. **Je n'aime pas les sciences.**

There is a liaison with all plural subject pronouns and a verb that begins with a vowel or silent **h.** The **s** on the pronoun is pronounced as a **z.**
nous‿étudions   vous‿aimez   ils‿habitent

Comment dit-on?

13 Historiette Un Américain

Un cours de français aux États-Unis

Inventez une histoire. *(Make up a story.)*

1. Kevin est français ou américain?
2. Il habite à Paris ou à Chicago?
3. Il parle anglais ou français?
4. Il étudie quelle langue?
5. Il parle beaucoup en classe?
6. Il travaille bien à l'école?

14 Historiette Les élèves ou les profs? Suivez le modèle. *(Follow the model.)*

—**Qui arrive à l'école le matin?**

—**Les élèves et les profs arrivent à l'école.**

1. Qui parle en classe?
2. Qui écoute quand le prof parle?
3. Qui écoute des CD?
4. Qui passe des examens?
5. Qui étudie beaucoup?
6. Qui lève la main?
7. Qui pose des questions?
8. Qui rigole dans la cour?

FL.A.2.2.5 (I)

15 Aux États-Unis Un(e) élève français(e) pose des questions à un(e) élève américain(e). *(You are a French student. Ask a classmate about life in the United States.)*

> On arrive à l'école à quelle heure?

> On arrive à l'école à huit heures.

1. On arrive à l'école à quelle heure?
2. On quitte l'école à quelle heure?
3. On travaille beaucoup à l'école?
4. On aime beaucoup les examens?
5. On travaille après les cours?
6. On achète des CD?
7. On regarde la télé?
8. On parle au téléphone?

16 **Tu parles français?** Répétez la conversation. *(Repeat the conversation.)*

Sue: Tu n'es pas français, toi?
Luc: Non, je ne suis pas français.
Sue: Mais tu parles français!
Luc: Bien sûr que je parle français.
Sue: Et comment ça, si tu n'es pas français?
Luc: Mais je suis belge.
Sue: Ah, c'est vrai. On parle français en Belgique.

FL.A.1.1.1 (I)

17 **Historiette** **À votre tour!** Donnez des réponses personnelles. *(Give your own answers.)*

1. Tu habites dans quelle ville?
2. Tu quittes la maison à quelle heure le matin?
3. Tu arrives à l'école à quelle heure?
4. Est-ce que tu parles français avec les copains?
5. Tu aimes quelles matières?
6. Tu aimes quels profs?
7. Tu détestes quelles matières?
8. Tu travailles après les cours?
9. Tu parles beaucoup avec les copains au téléphone?
10. Tu regardes la télé?

Bruxelles, Belgique

18 **Pardon?** Posez des questions d'après le modèle. *(Ask questions according to the model.)*

Nous écoutons des CD.

Pardon? Qu'est-ce que vous écoutez?

1. Nous détestons les examens.
2. Nous regardons la télé.
3. Nous regardons des magazines.
4. Nous écoutons la radio.
5. Nous aimons l'école.
6. Nous étudions l'espagnol.

FL.A.1.1.1 (I)

19 **Nous tous** Donnez des réponses personnelles en utilisant **nous.** (*Give answers about you and your classmates. Use* nous.)

1. Vous arrivez à l'école à quelle heure le matin?
2. Vous quittez l'école à quelle heure l'après-midi?
3. Vous passez combien d'heures à l'école?
4. Vous aimez les cours?
5. Vous écoutez bien quand le professeur parle en classe?
6. Vous aimez ou vous détestez les examens?

20 **Historiette** **À l'école** Complétez. (*Complete.*)

Nous __1__ (arriver) à l'école à sept heures et demie. Et vous, vous __2__ (arriver) à quelle heure? Avant les cours, j'__3__ (aimer) parler un peu avec les copains. On __4__ (rigoler). Mais en classe, non! On __5__ (travailler) beaucoup. Moi, j'__6__ (écouter) bien quand les profs __7__ (parler). Et toi, tu __8__ (travailler) beaucoup aussi? Tu __9__ (passer) des examens? Tu __10__ (aimer) les examens ou pas?

FL.A.2.1.3 (I)

21 **Une journée typique** Work with a classmate. Tell each other about a typical school day. Find out what activities you have in common.

FL.A.2.1.3 (I)

22 **Tu travailles ou pas?** Get together in small groups and find out who works after school in your group. Find out where, how many hours a week, etc. Here are some words you may want to use.

un restaurant

un fast-food

une station-service

un magasin

un supermarché

 ENCORE PLUS For more practice using **-er** verbs in the present, do Activity 9 on page H10 at the end of this book.

La négation des articles indéfinis
Talking about what you don't do

In the negative, the indefinite articles **un, une,** and **des** change to **de** (or **d'**).

Affirmatif	Négatif
Julie regarde un CD.	Éric ne regarde pas de CD.
Julie regarde une vidéo.	Éric ne regarde pas de vidéo.
Julie regarde des photos.	Éric ne regarde pas de photos.

Attention!

Note the elision with **de.**
Je suis content: pas d'examen aujourd'hui!

Comment dit-on?

23 **En classe** Répondez que non. *(Answer with* non.*)*

1. Tu écoutes un CD?
2. Tu regardes une vidéo?
3. Tu poses des questions?
4. Tu écoutes des cassettes?
5. Tu passes un examen aujourd'hui?

24 **Historiette** **Dans une papeterie**
Répondez d'après les indications. *(Answer according to the cues.)*

1. René est dans une papeterie? (oui)
2. Il regarde un feutre et un cahier? (oui)
3. Il achète un stylo-bille? (non)
4. Il achète un feutre? (oui)
5. Il achète un DVD? (non)
6. Il achète une vidéo? (oui)

FL.A.3.1.1 (I)

25 **J'achète ou je n'achète pas.** Work with a classmate. Take turns telling what you buy or don't buy.

Beryl Goldberg

Verbe + infinitif
Discussing likes and dislikes

1. In French when the verbs **aimer, adorer,** and **détester** are followed by another verb, the second verb is in the infinitive form.

> **Il aime rigoler.**
> **J'adore écouter la radio.**
> **On déteste travailler.**

2. In a negative sentence, the **ne… pas** goes around the first verb.

> **Vous n'aimez pas travailler?**

Comment dit-on?

 FL.A.1.1.1 (I)

26 **Tu aimes travailler?** Posez les questions suivantes à un copain ou une copine. *(Ask a classmate the following questions.)*

—**Tu aimes travailler?**
—**Oui. J'aime travailler./**
  Non. Je n'aime pas travailler.

1. Tu aimes regarder la télé?
2. Tu aimes écouter la musique?
3. Tu aimes étudier?
4. Tu aimes rigoler?
5. Tu aimes parler au téléphone?

 FL.A.1.2.1 (I)

27 **On aime ou on n'aime pas!** Work with a classmate. Tell some things you like and don't like to do.

Vous êtes sur le bon chemin. Allez-y!

Conversation

FL.D.2.1.1 (I)

Un élève français aux États-Unis

Carol: En France, tu arrives à quelle heure à l'école le matin?

Cédric: Moi, j'arrive à l'école vers sept heures et demie.

Carol: Et les cours commencent à quelle heure?

Cédric: À huit heures. J'aime parler un peu avec les copains avant la classe.

Carol: Et tu quittes l'école à trois heures?

Cédric: À trois heures! Tu rigoles! En France on quitte l'école à cinq heures.

Carol: À cinq heures! C'est pas vrai!

Cédric: Si, c'est vrai.

Vous avez compris?

Répondez. (*Answer.*)

1. En France, Cédric arrive à l'école à quelle heure?
2. Cédric parle avec une amie américaine ou française?
3. Les cours de Cédric commencent à quelle heure?
4. Cédric quitte l'école à quelle heure?
5. Et Carol, elle quitte l'école à quelle heure?

(t)Larry Hamill, (b)John Evans

Parlons un peu plus

A **FL.A.3.1.1 (I)**

Comparaisons With a classmate, look at the illustrations. Then compare your own daily school habits with those of the students in the illustrations.

 1.   2.   3.   4.   5.

B **Jeu** **FL.C.1.1.2 (I)**

Les nombres Give some numbers in a mathematical pattern but leave one out. Your partner will guess what the missing number is. Take turns. Use the model as a guide.

—**deux cents, quatre cents, _____, huit cents**
—**six cents**

Prononciation **FL.D.1.2.2 (I)**

Les sons /é/ et /è/ 🎧

élève

1. There is an important difference in the way French and English vowels are pronounced. When you say the French word **des,** your mouth is tense, in one position. You can repeat the sound /é/ many times without moving your mouth at all. But when you pronounce the English word *day*, your mouth is relaxed and you actually say two vowel sounds.

2. Listen to the word **élève.** It has two distinct vowel sounds. The sound /é/ is "closed" and the sound /è/ is "open." This describes the positions of the mouth for each sound. Repeat the following.

   Le son /é/: **la télé**   **l'école**   **la journée**   **parler**   **écoutez**
   Le son /è/: **après**   **la cassette**   **vous êtes**   **le collège**

   Après l'école, les élèves aiment écouter des cassettes.
   Elles aiment regarder la télé.

Lectures culturelles

(l)John Evans, (c)Hartmut Krinitz/Hemisphères Images, (r)Robert Fried Photography

FL.A.3.2.3 (I)

Une journée avec Jacqueline

Jacqueline est une élève française. Elle habite rue Jacob à Paris. La rue Jacob est dans le Quartier latin, tout près de¹ la Sorbonne. La Sorbonne est une université célèbre² à Paris. Le Quartier latin est un quartier très fréquenté par les étudiants d'université et les lycéens.

¹ tout près de *very near*
² célèbre *famous*

Une librairie, boulevard Saint-Michel, Paris

La Sorbonne, Paris

NÉSIE FR

La Polynésie française

Bonne Fête Maman

Tahiti

FUTUNA RF

Haïti

La Martinique

Jacqueline est élève au lycée Louis-le-Grand. Le matin, elle quitte la maison à sept heures et demie. Les cours commencent à huit heures. Jacqueline passe la journée au lycée. Comme tous[3] les lycéens, Jacqueline travaille beaucoup, à Louis-le-Grand et à la maison. À la récréation, Jacqueline retrouve[4] des copains dans la cour. Ils parlent et ils rigolent un peu. À midi, ils déjeunent à la cantine. Ils ne rentrent pas à la maison pour déjeuner.

Jacqueline quitte le lycée à cinq heures de l'après-midi. Et vous, vous quittez l'école à quelle heure?

[3] Comme tous *Like all*
[4] retrouve *meets, gets together with*

Lycée Louis-le-Grand, Paris

Vous avez compris?

French Online
To investigate how French students spend their time away from school, go to the Chapter 3 **WebQuest** on the Glencoe French Web site at glencoe.com and do the activity about French community centers (MJC).

A Une élève française Répondez. (*Answer.*)
1. Qui est Jacqueline?
2. Elle habite où?
3. Jacqueline quitte la maison à quelle heure?
4. Les cours commencent à quelle heure?
5. Elle retrouve des copains où?
6. À midi, elle rentre chez elle pour déjeuner?
7. Elle déjeune avec qui?
8. Elle quitte le lycée à quelle heure?

B Paris Trouvez les informations dans la lecture.
(*Find the information in the reading.*)
1. la rue où Jacqueline habite
2. le nom d'une université célèbre à Paris
3. un quartier de Paris fréquenté par les étudiants et les lycéens
4. le nom du lycée de Jacqueline

FL.A.2.1.2 (I) **FL.D.2.1.1 (M)**

Qui travaille?

Le centre commercial «Place de la Cathédrale»

Antoine est canadien. Il est québécois. Il est de Montréal, la deuxième ville francophone du monde après Paris. Après les cours, il travaille dans une papeterie pour gagner un peu d'argent[1]. Il travaille dix heures par semaine. La papeterie où il travaille est dans le centre commercial[2] «Place de la Cathédrale». C'est un très grand centre commercial souterrain[3].

Un restaurant fast-food, Montréal

Aux États-Unis et au Québec aussi, un grand nombre d'élèves travaillent après les cours. Ils travaillent dans un magasin, dans un supermarché ou dans un restaurant fast-food (de restauration rapide). Ils gagnent de l'argent pour acheter des CD, une pizza, un blue jean. En France, non. Très peu de collégiens ou de lycéens travaillent après les cours. C'est assez rare. Certains travaillent, mais seulement pendant les vacances. Mais… ils sont à l'école jusqu'à cinq heures de l'après-midi!

[1] gagner un peu d'argent *to earn a little money*
[2] centre commercial *mall*
[3] souterrain *underground*

Vous avez compris?

Au Québec Exprimez d'une autre façon.
(*Express another way.*)
1. Antoine est *du Canada*.
2. Montréal est la *seconde* ville francophone du monde.
3. Antoine travaille après *l'école*.
4. C'est un *immense* centre commercial.
5. Aux États-Unis, *beaucoup* d'élèves travaillent.
6. *Pas beaucoup* de lycéens français travaillent après les cours.

GRaffiti

RESTO-CITÉ

• SITUÉ AU CŒUR DE LA VILLE ET DE LA VIE DES GENS DE QUÉBEC

• FINE CUISINE DU MARCHÉ ITALO-FRANÇAISE

• DÉJEUNER-DÎNER LE DIMANCHE
• DÉCOR CHALEUREUX, VERRIÈRE ET SALON PRIVÉ

• STATIONNEMENT

Tahiti

FUTUNA RF

(t)Guido Cozzi/Agence ANA, (c)Beryl Goldberg

FL.D.2.1.1 (M)

Un groupe de rap–Manau

Quand les collégiens ou les lycéens français rentrent à la maison l'après-midi, qu'est-ce qu'ils écoutent? Eh bien, ils écoutent la même musique que les élèves américains. Ils écoutent du rap, par exemple.

Manau, c'est un groupe de rap très populaire chez les collégiens français. Et Manau n'est pas un groupe de rap ordinaire. C'est un groupe de rap «celtique». Les instruments de musique sont la cornemuse[1], le violon, la harpe… Les chansons[2] de Manau parlent de mythes et légendes celtes avec des druides et des dolmens.

Les deux garçons du groupe, Cédric et Martial, sont copains. Le musicien, c'est Cédric: Cédric est le compositeur de la musique. Et le texte, c'est Martial: Martial est l'auteur des paroles[3].

Les deux garçons sont de la région parisienne. Mais les mères[4] de Cédric et Martial sont de Bretagne. Comme beaucoup de Bretons, elles sont d'origine celtique. Le nom du premier[5] album de Manau? *Panique Celtique!*

[1] cornemuse *bagpipes*
[2] chansons *songs*
[3] paroles *words*
[4] mères *mothers*
[5] premier *first*

French Online
For more information about music in the Francophone world, go to **Web Explore** on the Glencoe French Web site at glencoe.com.

Un dolmen près de Carnac, Bretagne

Vous avez compris?

Un groupe de rap Vrai ou faux? *(True or false?)*
1. Les collégiens français n'écoutent pas la même musique que les élèves américains.
2. Manau, c'est un groupe de rap ordinaire.
3. Les chansons de Manau parlent de l'école.
4. Cédric et Martial sont de Bretagne.

CONNEXIONS

FL.C.1.1.1 (I) **FL.D.1.1.1 (I)**

La technologie

L'ordinateur

Some years ago computers began to revolutionize the way people conduct their lives. They have changed the way we view the world. Computers have a place in our homes, in our schools, and in the world of business.

If you are interested in computers, you may want to familiarize yourself with some basic computer vocabulary in French. Then read the information about computers on the next page.

un ordinateur

un écran

une souris

un CD-ROM

un clavier

une disquette

une imprimante

L'ordinateur travaille!

Le hardware et le software

Un ordinateur exécute très rapidement les instructions d'un programme. Le hardware, c'est la partie électronique de l'ordinateur. Le software, c'est la partie programmation de l'ordinateur. Les logiciels sont des programmes. Un programme ou un logiciel est un groupe d'instructions. Un document est un fichier. L'ordinateur stocke des données[1]. On sauvegarde les documents importants sur une disquette ou un CD.

Internet

Quand on est connecté à Internet par cable ou satellite, la connexion est pratiquement instantanée. Les satellites transmettent l'information vingt fois plus vite que le modem. Et l'ADSL transmet l'information de cinquante à cent cinquante fois plus vite que le modem. De jour en jour, grâce aux progrès de la technologie, les communications deviennent[2] plus faciles et plus rapides. C'est un fait, le monde[3] entier est connecté! Le nombre des sites est infini. On télécharge[4] des informations sur l'histoire, l'économie, l'art, la musique et toutes sortes de domaines intéressants. Quand on navigue sur Internet, on est capable d'envoyer[5] un e-mail, parler avec des amis sur d'autres continents… Il n'y a pas de limites!

[1] données *data*   [4] télécharge *download*
[2] deviennent *become*   [5] envoyer *to send*
[3] monde *world*

Vous avez compris?

A En français, s'il vous plaît. Trouvez les mots suivants dans la lecture. (*Find the following words in the reading.*)

1. hardware
2. software
3. program
4. file
5. modem
6. surf the net
7. e-mail
8. connection
9. site
10. save

B Une page Web Look at the monitor on page 102. This is the World Languages home page at **glencoe.com**. Scroll down the list of products until you find your French textbook. Click on it and go to **World News Online**. Find an article related to computer technology and tell the class the article's title or topic.

Ed Taylor Studio/FPG

C'est à vous

Use what you have learned

PARLER 1

 FL.B.1.1.1 (I)

Dans une papeterie
✔ *Identify and shop for school supplies*

With a classmate, take turns playing the parts of a student and a salesperson in a stationery store. Here are a few exchanges you may want to use.

—Où sont les _____, s'il vous plaît?

—Là-bas.

—Merci.

—_____, c'est combien?

—_____ euros.

—On paie à la caisse?

—Non, ici.

Une papeterie, Évry, France

Larry Hamill

PARLER

2 Au café
✔ **Talk about school life in the United States**

You're seated at a café in Provins. You're chatting with a French student (your partner). He or she has some questions about school life in the United States. Have a conversation. Be sure to answer his or her questions.

ÉCRIRE

3 Une journée typique
✔ **Write about a typical school day**

You can now go back to the e-mail you sent your new friend on page 75 and add more details about what a typical school day is like in the United States.

Un café, Provins, France

D'où?

À quelle heure?

Comment?

Où?

Qui?

Writing Strategy

Preparing for an interview An interview is one way to gather information for a story or a report. A good interviewer should think about what he or she hopes to learn from the interview and prepare the questions ahead of time. The interview questions should be open-ended. Open-ended questions cannot be answered by "yes" or "no." They give the person being interviewed more opportunity to "open up" and speak freely.

PARLER
ÉCRIRE

FL.A.2.2.3 (I)

4 Interview avec Charles Bauchart

Your first assignment for the school newspaper is to write an article about a new exchange student, Charles Bauchart, from Fort-de-France in Martinique. To prepare for your interview with him, write down as many questions as you can. Ask him about himself, his school, and his friends in Martinique. After you have prepared your questions, conduct the interview with a partner who plays the role of Charles. Write down your partner's answers. Then organize your notes and write your article.

PENDANT ET APRÈS LES COURS

Larry Hamill

Assessment

French Online

For more Chapter 3 test preparation, go to the Chapter 3 **Self-Check Quiz** on the Glencoe French Web site at glencoe.com.

Vocabulaire

1 Choisissez. *(Choose.)*

To review **Mots 1,** turn to pages 82–83.

1. Sandrine _____ la maison à sept heures et demie.
   a. quitte   **b.** arrive   **c.** habite
2. Les élèves passent _____ à l'école.
   a. la cantine   **b.** la prof   **c.** la journée
3. Leïla pose une _____.
   a. rue   **b.** question   **c.** maison
4. Vincent _____ des cassettes.
   a. écoute   **b.** quitte   **c.** passe
5. Le prof _____ et les élèves écoutent bien.
   a. travaille   **b.** regarde   **c.** parle

2 Identifiez. *(Identify.)*

To review **Mots 2,** turn to pages 86–87.

6.   7.   8.

9.   10.

Structure

3 Complétez. *(Complete.)*

To review **-er** verbs in the present tense, turn to page 90.

11. Les élèves _____ à l'école le matin. (arriver)
12. Nous _____ entre les cours. (parler)
13. Je _____ à la cantine avec les copains. (déjeuner)
14. Luc _____ la télé après les cours. (regarder)
15. Tu _____ beaucoup à la maison? (travailler)
16. On _____ français en France. (parler)

4 Mettez à la forme négative.
(Make each sentence negative.)

17. Sandrine achète un crayon à la papeterie.
18. Elle regarde une calculatrice.
19. Ils achètent des livres.
20. Les élèves passent un examen aujourd'hui.

To review indefinite articles in the negative, turn to page 94.

5 Choisissez. *(Choose.)*

21. On aime _____ la télé.
   a. regardent   **b.** regarder   **c.** regarde
22. Je déteste _____.
   a. travailler   **b.** travaille   **c.** travaillons

To review the use of verbs with infinitives, turn to page 95.

Culture

6 Vrai ou faux? *(True or false?)*

Une rue du Quartier latin, Paris

To review this cultural information, turn to pages 98–99.

23. La Sorbonne est une université célèbre à Paris.
24. La Sorbonne est dans le Quartier latin.
25. En France, les élèves quittent le lycée à trois heures de l'après-midi.

Do these practice activities to help you succeed on your FCAT through the study of a foreign language.

Read the passage below. Then answer the questions that follow.

Aux États-Unis les élèves quittent l'école à trois heures. Beaucoup d'élèves travaillent après les cours. Ils travaillent, par exemple, dans un magasin, dans un supermarché ou dans un restaurant fast-food. Avec l'argent, ils achètent des CD, de la pizza et des jeans. Ils aiment aussi le cinéma.

En France, au contraire, il est rare que les lycéens travaillent après les cours. Ils quittent l'école à cinq heures de l'après-midi. Les lycéens français travaillent beaucoup mais pas dans un restaurant fast-food. Ils travaillent au lycée.

Tous les élèves achètent des fournitures scolaires—des classeurs, des cahiers, des crayons, des feuilles de papier et des stylos. Ils passent la journée à l'école. Ils écoutent les profs et ils étudient beaucoup. Ils n'aiment pas du tout passer les examens! Ils aiment rigoler dans la cour!

① Pourquoi les élèves américains travaillent-ils après les cours?
- **A.** pour passer les examens
- **B.** pour acheter des choses avec l'argent
- **C.** parce qu'ils aiment travailler
- **D.** parce qu'ils étudient beaucoup

② Quelle phrase est correcte?
- **F.** Les élèves américains ne travaillent pas après l'école.
- **G.** Les élèves français quittent l'école à trois heures.
- **H.** Les élèves français travaillent rarement après l'école.
- **I.** Les élèves américains n'aiment pas acheter de CD.

3 Pourquoi les lycéens français ne travaillent-ils pas après les cours?

    A. parce que le travail est difficile

    B. parce qu'ils quittent l'école à cinq heures

    C. parce qu'ils achètent des fournitures scolaires

    D. parce qu'ils détestent l'argent

4 READ THINK EXPLAIN Quelles sont des différences et des similarités entre les lycéens américains et les lycéens français?

LA.A.2.4.1 (M)

5 Quel est un bon titre pour cette histoire?

    F. Les lycéens américains

    G. Les lycéens français

    H. Les lycéens américains et français

    I. Une journée à l'école

6 Pendant la classe de français les élèves

    A. rigolent et jouent.

    B. écoutent le professeur.

    C. achètent des cahiers.

    D. quittent l'école.

FCAT Tip

Read the passages and questions very carefully. You may look back at a passage as often as you like.

On parle super bien!

Tell all you can about this illustration.

Vocabulaire

Getting to school

une maison	habiter
une rue	arriver
quitter	

Discussing classroom activities

passer la journée	étudier
parler	lever la main
écouter	poser une question
regarder	passer un examen

Discussing recess and lunch activities

la récré(ation)	jouer
la cour	rigoler
la cantine	déjeuner

Discussing afterschool activities

rentrer à la maison	parler au téléphone
écouter la radio	travailler

How well do you know your vocabulary?

- Identify the words and expressions that describe what you do at school and after school. Make two lists.
- Use as many words as you can from one of your lists to write a story about either your school activities or what you do after school.

Identifying school supplies

Qu'est-ce que c'est?	un stylo-bille	une calculatrice
des fournitures *(f. pl.)*	un feutre	une feuille de papier
scolaires	une gomme	un sac à dos
un cahier	une règle	une cassette
un bloc-notes	un livre	une vidéo, un DVD
un crayon	un classeur	un CD

Shopping for school supplies

un magasin	acheter	coûter
une papeterie	payer	C'est combien?
la caisse	demander	Ça coûte combien?

Other useful words and expressions

aimer	combien de (d')	beaucoup de (d')
détester		
après		
pendant		
entre		
chez		
le matin		
l'après-midi		
À quelle heure?		

VIDÉOTOUR

Épisode 3

In this video episode, you will join Amadou and Christine after school. See page 528 for more information.

La famille et la maison

Objectifs

In this chapter you will learn to:

✓ *talk about your family*

✓ *describe your home and neighborhood*

✓ *tell your age and find out someone else's age*

✓ *tell what belongs to you and others*

✓ *describe more people and things*

✓ *talk about families and homes in French-speaking countries*

Pierre Auguste Renoir *Madame Charpentier et ses enfants*

French Online
To interact with your online edition of
Bon voyage! go to: glencoe.com.

SUNSHINE STATE STANDARDS

This chapter is all about the family and their homes. The material in the chapter will address the Sunshine State Standards listed below.

FL.A.1.1.2 greet others and exchange essential personal information (e.g., home address, telephone number, place of origin, and general health).

FL.A.1.2.2 exchange information necessary to plan events or activities (e.g., picnics, birthday parties, science projects, and crafts).

FL.A.2.1.2 restate and rephrase simple information from materials presented orally, visually, and graphically in class.

FL.A.2.1.3 understand oral messages that are based on familiar themes and vocabulary (e.g., short conversations between familiar persons on familiar topics such as everyday school and home activities).

FL.A.3.1.1 provide simple information in spoken form (e.g., descriptions of family members, friends, objects present in his or her everyday environment, or common school and home activities).

FL.A.3.2.1 describe important people (e.g., family members and friends) and objects present in his or her everyday environment and in school.

FL.A.3.2.3 give responses in spoken or written form (e.g., answering simple questions, formulating questions, and making simple statements) to age-appropriate stories, poems or other literature, songs, films, or visual works.

FL.B.1.2.1 recognize various activities and celebrations in which children participate in the target culture (e.g., games, songs, birthday celebrations, storytelling, dramatizations, and role playing).

FL.C.1.2.2 use target-language vocabulary or concepts to reinforce knowledge of a related topic studied in another class (e.g., geographical place names, parts of the body, or basic mathematical operations).

FL.C.2.1.1 use the target language to gain access to information that is only available through the target language or within the target culture (listen to a story told in the target language).

Kennedy Space Center

Getty Images

FL.D.1.1.1   know examples of word borrowing from one language to another.

FL.D.1.1.2   use simple vocabulary and short phrases in the target language.

FL.D.1.2.1   identify examples and understand the significance of true and false cognates (i.e., words derived from a common original form).

FL.D.1.2.2   recognize the similarities and differences between his or her native language and the target language in terms of the pronunciation, alphabet, and forms of written expression.

FL.D.2.1.2   recognize that there are similarities and differences between objects from the target culture and objects from the local culture (e.g., inside dwellings).

FL.D.2.2.2   recognize forms of the target language evident in the local culture (e.g., signs, symbols, advertisements, packages, displays, murals, songs, and rhymes).

TIPS FOR SUCCESS

Review the Study Tips below to help you succeed on the Sunshine State Standards identified.

Vocabulaire — Mots 1 — Mots 2   *(pages 112–120)*

- Activity 4 on page 115 helps you with productive skills. Remember that when you speak or write about yourself, you must always use the masculine form if you are a male and the feminine form if you are a female. **FL.D.1.2.2**

- After you have learned the new words in **Mots 2**, look at each illustration, cover up the sentences, and say as much as you can about the illustration. If you can describe the illustration, you know your vocabulary. If you cannot describe it, you have to study some more. **FL.A.3.2.3**

- **Hint** Read or say aloud all the answers to the **Historiette** activities to give you practice in telling coherent stories in French. **FL.A.3.1.1**

Florida panther

C'est à vous   *(pages 136–137)*

- In Activity 5 on page 137, you are going to write about your house or a house of your dreams.
- Picture the house.
- In French, think of or write a list of words you can use to identify parts of the house.
- In French, think about or write a list of words you can use to describe a house or rooms of a house.
- Organize your story. Divide the house into parts, such as living area, sleeping area, first floor, second floor. You may even want to make a drawing of your house. Write a few sentences about each area.
- Put the sentences in a logical order.
- Add a few sentences to describe the area around your house. **FL.D.1.1.2; FL.D.2.1.2**

> **For other tips to help you address the Sunshine State Standards in Chapter 4, see pages H57 and H58 at the back of your textbook.**

Vocabulaire

Mots 1

FLORIDA
Use your **StudentWorks** *Plus*
CD for more practice.

La famille Morel 🎧

le mari — la femme

Marc   Anne

les parents

le père — — la mère

le fils —

la fille

les enfants

le frère   la sœur

Luc   Juliette

les petits-enfants   les grands-parents

le petit-fils   la grand-mère

la petite-fille   le grand-père

Luc   Juliette   Thérèse   André

Médor

le chien

Voici la famille Morel.
M. et Mme Morel ont deux enfants—un fils et une fille.
Les Morel ont un chien.
Leur chien est adorable.
La famille Morel n'a pas de chat.

Lucie

le chat

112 ❧ *cent douze*

(b)PhotoDisc, (others)Larry Hamill

CHAPITRE 4

L'anniversaire de Marie

> **Tu as quel âge, Marie?**

> une bougie un gâteau un cadeau

> **Moi? J'ai quinze ans. Aujourd'hui, c'est mon anniversaire.**

C'est quand, l'anniversaire de Marie?
C'est le deux août.
Tout le monde a un cadeau pour Marie.
Il y a beaucoup de cadeaux.

Marie donne une fête pour son anniversaire.
Elle invite ses amis et ses cousins.

FL.D.1.2.1 (M)

Note 🎧

In French, some of the words for family members are cognates. Can you guess who these family members are?

une tante	un oncle
une cousine	un cousin
une nièce	un neveu

Here are some words for other family members.

une belle-mère *stepmother*
un beau-père *stepfather*
une demi-sœur *half sister*
un demi-frère *half brother*

Timothy Fuller

Quel est le mot?

1 **Historiette** La famille Senghor
Inventez une histoire. *(Make up a story.)*

1. Madame Senghor est la femme de Monsieur Senghor?
2. Monsieur Senghor est le mari de Madame Senghor?
3. La famille Senghor est française?
4. M. et Mme Senghor ont deux enfants? Ils ont un fils et une fille?
5. Les enfants ont quel âge?
6. Quelle est la date de l'anniversaire de la fille?
7. Il y a combien de personnes dans la famille Senghor?
8. Les Senghor ont un chien ou un chat?

Marie et Blaise Senghor habitent à Paris.

FL.B.1.2.1 (M)

2 **Historiette** L'anniversaire de Francine Répondez
d'après les indications. *(Answer according to the cues.)*

1. Elle a quel âge, Francine? (quinze ans)
2. C'est quand, son anniversaire? (aujourd'hui)
3. Quelle est la date aujourd'hui? (le deux août)
4. Qu'est-ce que Francine donne pour son anniversaire? (une fête)
5. Elle invite qui à la fête? (ses amis et ses cousins)
6. Qu'est-ce que tout le monde a pour Francine? (beaucoup de cadeaux)
7. Il y a un gâteau pour Francine? (oui)
8. Le gâteau a des bougies? (oui, quinze)

FL.D.1.1.2 (I)

3 **La famille** Complétez. *(Complete.)*

1. Le frère de mon père est mon _____.
2. La sœur de mon père est ma _____.
3. Le frère de ma mère est mon _____.
4. La sœur de ma mère est ma _____.
5. Le fils de mon oncle et de ma tante est mon _____.
6. La fille de mon oncle et de ma tante est ma _____.
7. Le père de ma mère est mon _____.
8. Et la mère de mon père est ma _____.

Ma grand-mère habite à Paris.

4 **Moi** Donnez des réponses personnelles.
(Give your own answers.)

1. Moi, je suis _____ de mes grands-parents.
   a. le petit-fils   **b.** la petite-fille
2. Je suis _____ de mes parents.
   a. le fils   **b.** la fille
3. Je suis _____ de mon oncle.
   a. le neveu   **b.** la nièce
4. Je suis _____ de mes cousins.
   a. le cousin   **b.** la cousine

Une noce à la campagne

5 FL.A.3.2.3 (I)

Une famille This country wedding, *Une noce à la campagne,* was painted by le Douanier Rousseau in 1905. Give the people names and decide who they are in relation to one another.

6 FL.A.3.1.1 (I)

Une fête d'anniversaire
With a classmate describe some things that take place at a typical birthday party. You may want to use some of the following words.

 arriver

 écouter

 danser

 inviter

 donner

préparer

 regarder

ENCORE
PLUS

For more practice using words from **Mots 1**, *do Activity 10 on page H11 at the end of this book.*

Vocabulaire

Mots 2

La maison 🎧

une vieille maison

une fleur

un arbre

un garage

une voiture

un jardin

une terrasse

La vieille maison est très belle.
Il y a un jardin autour de la maison.
De la terrasse on a une vue du jardin.

L'immeuble 🎧

un immeuble

un appartement

un quartier

le troisième étage

le deuxième étage

le premier étage

le rez-de-chaussée

une station de métro

un balcon

une entrée

un code:
B0275

Le balcon donne sur la rue.
Les Briand ont un très joli appartement.
Il est dans un très beau quartier de Paris.
Leur immeuble est (tout) près d'une station de métro.
L'immeuble n'est pas loin d'une station de métro.

Attention! Il y a
un nouveau code!

Les voisins sont dans la cour.

Les Briand montent toujours en ascenseur.
Ils montent au troisième étage.

Les pièces de la maison 🎧

Larry Hamill

Quel est le mot?

La maison de Claude Monet, Giverny

FL.C.1.2.2 (M)

7 **Historiette** **La maison de Monet** Répondez que **oui**. (*Answer* oui.)

1. Monet est un artiste célèbre?
2. Il a une jolie maison?
3. Sa maison est grande?
4. Il y a un jardin autour de sa maison?
5. C'est un très beau jardin?
6. Il y a des arbres et des fleurs dans le jardin?

French Online

To investigate French painters, go to **Web Explore** on the Glencoe French Web site at glencoe.com.

8 **Historiette** **L'appartement des Lapeyre**

Inventez une histoire. (*Make up a story.*)

1. La famille Lapeyre a un appartement dans un vieil immeuble à Paris?
2. Leur appartement est dans un beau quartier de Paris?
3. L'appartement est au rez-de-chaussée ou au troisième étage?
4. Leur balcon donne sur la rue ou sur la cour?
5. Il y a six pièces dans l'appartement de la famille Lapeyre?
6. Quelles pièces?
7. Les Lapeyre montent toujours à pied ou en ascenseur?
8. L'immeuble est près d'une station de métro ou loin d'une station de métro?
9. Il y a un code pour entrer dans l'immeuble?

9 **Quelle pièce?** Choisissez la bonne réponse. (*Choose the correct answer.*)

1. On regarde la télé dans _____.
   a. la salle de bains **b.** la salle à manger **c.** la salle de séjour
2. On prépare le dîner dans _____.
   a. la salle à manger **b.** la cuisine **c.** la chambre à coucher
3. On parle avec ses voisins dans _____.
   a. la salle de bains **b.** la cour **c.** la chambre à coucher
4. On dîne dans _____.
   a. la salle à manger **b.** la salle de séjour **c.** la chambre à coucher
5. On a une belle vue _____.
   a. du balcon **b.** de l'étage **c.** de l'ascenseur

FL.A.3.2.1 (I)

10 Historiette **Chez moi** Donnez des réponses personnelles.
(Give your own answers.)

1. Tu habites quelle rue?
2. Tu habites dans un appartement ou dans une maison privée?
3. Il y a combien de pièces dans l'appartement ou la maison?
4. Il y a combien de chambres à coucher?
5. Il y a un jardin ou un balcon?
6. La maison ou l'immeuble a un garage?
7. Il y a une voiture dans le garage?

FL.A.3.2.3 (I)

11 Quelle maison pour nous? Work with a classmate. Your families plan to spend a month in France. Read the following real estate ads and discuss which house or apartment is good for your family.

Appartement

dans un bel immeuble, cinq pièces, deux chambres à coucher, une grande cuisine moderne, bien situé au centre-ville, près d'une station de métro

Très jolie villa

avec jardin et terrasse, vue sur l'océan, huit pièces, quatre chambres à coucher, garage pour deux voitures, située dans une rue très calme, loin de la ville

Petit bungalow

dans un vieux quartier, beaucoup de charme, trois pièces, une chambre à coucher, vingt minutes de la ville de Caen

*For more practice using words from **Mots 2**, do Activity 11 on page H12 at the end of this book.*

Structure

Le verbe avoir au présent
Telling what you and others have

1. Study the following forms of the irregular verb **avoir** (to have).

AVOIR	
j' ai	nous_z avons
tu as	vous_z avez
il/elle/on_n a	ils_z/elles_z ont

2. You also use the verb **avoir** to express age.

Tu as quel âge?
Moi? J'ai quatorze ans.

3. The expression **il y a** means "there is" or "there are."

Il y a un jardin autour de la maison.
Il n'y a pas de fleurs dans le jardin.

Rappelez-vous que...

Un, une, and **des** become de (d') after a negative.
J'ai une sœur mais Marc n'a pas de sœur.

Comment dit-on?

12 **Historiette** **Les Binand**
Inventez une histoire.
(Make up a story.)

1. Suzanne Binand a un frère?
2. Guillaume a une sœur?
3. Monsieur et Madame Binand ont deux enfants?
4. La famille Binand a un appartement à Paris?
5. Ils ont un chat?

Deux amis, Narbonne, France

FL.A.2.1.3 (I)

13 **Tu as un frère?** Répétez la conversation. (*Repeat the conversation.*)

Flore: Tu as un frère?
Rémi: Non, je n'ai pas de frère, mais j'ai une sœur.
Flore: Tu as une sœur? Elle a quel âge?
Rémi: Elle a quatorze ans.
Flore: Et toi, tu as quel âge?
Rémi: Moi, j'ai seize ans.
Flore: Et… vous avez un chien?
Rémi: Non, on n'a pas de chien. Mais on a un petit chat.

FL.A.2.1.3 (I)

14 **Rémi** Complétez d'après la conversation. (*Complete according to the conversation.*)

1. Rémi n'____ pas ____ frère.
2. Il ____ une sœur.
3. Sa sœur ____ quatorze ans.
4. Rémi ____ seize ans.
5. Rémi et sa sœur n'____ pas ____ chien.
6. Mais ils ____ un petit chat adorable.

FL.A.3.1.1 (M)

15 **Historiette** **Ma famille** Donnez des réponses personnelles. (*Give your own answers.*)

1. Tu as des frères? Tu as combien de frères?
2. Tu as des sœurs? Tu as combien de sœurs?
3. Tu as un chien ou un chat?
4. Tu as des amis?
5. Tu as des cousins?
6. Tu as combien de cousins?
7. Tu as une grande famille ou une petite famille?
8. Tu as quel âge?

Un père et son fils

LA FAMILLE ET LA MAISON

(t)Michelle Chaplow, (b)Zephyr Images/Sunset

16 **Dans mon sac à dos** Préparez une conversation d'après le modèle. (*Make up a conversation according to the model.*)

—Tu as des livres dans ton sac à dos?
—Oui, j'ai des livres dans mon sac à dos. /
Non, je n'ai pas de livres dans mon sac à dos.

17 **Qu'est-ce que vous avez?** Préparez une conversation d'après le modèle. (*Make up a conversation according to the model.*)

une maison ou un appartement →
—Vous avez une maison ou un appartement?
—Nous avons _____.

1. une grande famille ou une petite famille
2. une grande voiture ou une petite voiture
3. un chien ou un chat
4. un PC ou un Mac

French Online

For a fun way to review the verb **avoir**, go to the Chapter 4 **eGame** on the Glencoe French Web site at glencoe.com.

18 **Historiette** **La famille Ghez** Complétez avec **avoir**. (*Complete with* avoir.)

La famille Ghez __1__ un bel appartement à Nice. Leur appartement __2__ six pièces. Leur appartement __3__ un balcon. Le balcon donne sur la mer Méditerranée. Du balcon les Ghez __4__ une très belle vue sur la mer.

Il y a quatre personnes dans la famille Ghez. Halima a dix-sept ans et son frère, Ahmed, __5__ quinze ans. Halima et Ahmed __6__ un petit chat adorable.

Et toi, tu __7__ un chien ou un chat? Tu __8__ une petite ou une grande famille? Vous __9__ un appartement ou une maison?

Moi, j'__10__ quinze ans et j'__11__ un chien adorable. J'adore mon petit chien.

Les adjectifs possessifs
Telling what belongs to you and others

1. You use a possessive adjective to show possession or ownership. Like other adjectives, a possessive adjective must agree with the noun it modifies.

2. The adjectives **mon** (*my*), **ton** (*your*), and **son** (*his/her*) each have three forms. The adjectives **notre** (*our*), **votre** (*your*), and **leur** (*their*) each have two forms.

SINGULIER		PLURIEL	
Masculin	**Féminin**	**Masculin**	**Féminin**
mon frère	ma sœur	mes frères	mes sœurs
ton frère	ta sœur	tes frères	tes sœurs
son frère	sa sœur	ses frères	ses sœurs
notre frère	notre sœur	nos frères	nos sœurs
votre frère	votre sœur	vos frères	vos sœurs
leur frère	leur sœur	leurs frères	leurs sœurs

3. **Son, sa,** and **ses** can mean "his" or "her." The adjective agrees with the item owned, not the owner.

   C'est le chien de Paul.   **C'est son chien.**
   C'est le chien de Marie.   **C'est son chien.**

4. You use **mon, ton,** or **son** before a feminine singular noun that begins with a vowel or silent **h.**

   son‿amie et mon‿amie

Une famille d'origine marocaine, Saint-André, France

Attention!

Liaison occurs with **mon, ton,** and **son,** as well as with all plural possessive adjectives.

mon‿oncle	**nos‿amis**
ton‿ami	**vos‿amis**
son‿école	**leurs‿amis**

Michelle Chaplow

Structure

Comment dit-on?

FL.A.3.2.1 (I)

19 Historiette Ta famille et chez toi Donnez des réponses personnelles. (*Give your own answers.*)

1. Où est ta maison ou ton appartement?
2. Ta maison ou ton appartement a combien de pièces?
3. Ta maison est grande ou petite? Ton appartement est grand ou petit?
4. C'est quand, ton anniversaire? Tu as quel âge?
5. Quel âge a ton frère, si tu as un frère?
6. Quel âge a ta sœur, si tu as une sœur?

Un beau chalet, Suisse

20 J'ai une question pour toi.
Suivez le modèle. (*Follow the model.*)

—Où est __ta__ maison?
—Ma maison est dans la rue Jacob.

1. Qui est _____ amie?
2. Qui est _____ ami?
3. Où habitent _____ grands-parents?
4. _____ frère a quel âge?
5. _____ sœur a quel âge?
6. Où est _____ maison ou _____ appartement?
7. Tu aimes _____ cours de français?
8. _____ prof est sympa?

21 Oui! Suivez le modèle. (*Follow the model.*)

—Le frère de Marine est dans sa chambre?
—Oui, son frère est dans sa chambre.

1. Le père de Marine est dans la cuisine?
2. La sœur de Marine est blonde?
3. La sœur de Thomas est à Paris?
4. La maison de Thomas est jolie?
5. L'appartement de Marine est beau?
6. Les cousins de Thomas sont élèves?
7. Les grands-parents de Thomas ont un chien?

124 ❖ *cent vingt-quatre*
Pawel Wysocki/Hémisphères Images

CHAPITRE 4

FL.A.3.1.1 (I)

22 **Historiette** **Notre école**
Donnez des réponses personnelles.
(Give your own answers.)

1. Votre école est grande ou petite?
2. Votre école est près ou loin de votre maison?
3. Votre école a combien d'élèves?
4. Vos cours sont faciles ou difficiles?
5. Vos profs sont intéressants ou pas?
6. Vos classes sont grandes ou petites?

La Techno Parade, Paris

23 **Historiette** **Leur maison**
Complétez. *(Complete.)*

Fabien et Christophe sont frères. Ils sont dans __1__ chambre. Ils écoutent __2__ disques. __3__ collection de CD est surtout de la techno. __4__ amies, Catherine et Émilie, aiment aussi la techno. Fabien et Christophe, __5__ deux amies et __6__ copains écoutent souvent de la techno. Mais __7__ parents n'aiment pas du tout la techno.

 FL.A.3.1.1 (I)

24 **Votre famille** Draw your own family tree and say as many things as you can about your family to your classmates.

 *For more practice using **avoir** and possessive adjectives, do Activity 12 on page H13 at the end of this book.*

Structure

D'autres adjectifs
Describing more people and things

1. Most French adjectives follow the noun. Some common ones, such as **petit** and **grand,** come before the noun. The adjectives **beau** *(beautiful)*, **nouveau** *(new)*, and **vieux** *(old)* also come before the noun. These adjectives have several forms. Pay careful attention to both the spelling and the pronunciation of these adjectives.

SINGULIER

Féminin	Masculin (Voyelle)	Masculin (Consonne)
une belle maison	un bel appartement	un beau quartier
une nouvelle maison	un nouvel appartement	un nouveau quartier
une vieille maison	un vieil appartement	un vieux quartier

PLURIEL

Féminin	Masculin (Voyelle)	Masculin (Consonne)
de belles maisons	de beaux‿appartements	de beaux quartiers
de nouvelles maisons	de nouveaux‿appartements	de nouveaux quartiers
de vieilles maisons	de vieux‿appartements	de vieux quartiers

2. In formal French, **de** is used instead of **des** with a plural adjective that precedes the noun. In informal French, people use **des.**

Attention!

Liaison occurs with **beaux, nouveaux,** and **vieux** when they come before a word beginning with a vowel or silent **h.** The **x** is pronounced as a **z.**

> mes nouveaux‿amis
> les vieux‿appartements

De belles maisons, Montréal, Canada

Comment dit-on?

25 **Historiette** **Le bel appartement des Texier** Complétez. *(Complete.)*

1. Les Texier ont un _____ appartement dans un _____ immeuble dans un _____ quartier de la ville. (beau, vieux, beau)
2. Il y a de _____ et de _____ quartiers à Montréal. (nouveau, vieux)
3. L'appartement des Texier a de très _____ pièces. (beau)
4. Il a de _____ pièces et un très _____ balcon. (grand, beau)
5. De l'appartement il y a une très _____ vue sur la ville. (beau)
6. Les Texier ont une _____ voiture. (nouveau)
7. Leur _____ voiture est _____. (nouveau, beau)

Attention!

You have just learned that the plural of **beau** and **nouveau** is spelled with an **x**. Almost all words in French that end in **(e)au** or **eu** are spelled with **x**, not **s**, in the plural.

un cadeau	des cadeaux
un beau château	de beaux châteaux
mon neveu	mes neveux

Mettez au pluriel. *(Write in the plural.)*

1. Il a un très beau cadeau pour son neveu.
   Il a de très _____ _____ pour ses _____.
2. Le beau gâteau est aussi pour son neveu.
   Les _____ _____ sont aussi pour ses _____.
3. Il visite un beau château avec son neveu.
   Il visite de _____ _____ avec ses _____.

FL.A.3.1.1 (I)

26 **Comme qui?** Work with a classmate. Take turns saying whom you and your family members take after. You may wish to use the following words.

Je suis intelligent(e) comme ma mère.
Mon frère est enthousiaste comme notre père.

petit

amusant   blond   sympa

grand   beau   brun

Vous êtes sur le bon chemin. Allez-y!

Conversation

Ma nouvelle adresse

Vincent: Tu as ma nouvelle adresse?
Charlotte: Ta nouvelle adresse? Non! Tu habites où maintenant?
Vincent: 21, avenue de la Bourdonnais.
Charlotte: Ah, avenue de la Bourdonnais. C'est dans le 7ᵉ tout près de la tour Eiffel, non?
Vincent: Oui. De notre balcon on a une très belle vue sur la tour Eiffel.
Charlotte: Génial!

Vous avez compris?

Répondez. *(Answer.)*

1. Vincent parle à qui?
2. Charlotte a la nouvelle adresse de Vincent?
3. Quelle est sa nouvelle adresse?
4. Où est l'avenue de la Bourdonnais?
5. Est-ce que l'appartement de Vincent a un balcon?
6. De son balcon il a une vue sur la tour Eiffel?

Larry Hamill

Parlons un peu plus

A **Appartement ou maison?** Work with a classmate. Pretend you live in Rouen. One of you lives in a house, the other lives in an apartment. Decide who lives where. Then describe your house or apartment.

B **Jeu** **Qui est qui?** Work with a classmate. Write down the first names of some of your family members. Exchange lists and then ask each other who's who.

C'est qui, Paul?

C'est mon oncle. C'est le frère de ma mère.

Prononciation

Le son /ã/ 🎧

1. There are three nasal vowel sounds in French: /ã/ as in **cent,** /õ/ as in **sont,** and /ẽ/ as in **cinq.** They are called "nasal" because some air passes through the nose when they are pronounced. In this chapter, you will practice only the sound /ã/ as in **cent.**

2. Repeat the following. Notice that there is no /n/ sound after the nasal vowel.

Jean	cent	grand	amusant
français	parent	fantastique	

Voilà les grands-parents, les parents et les enfants.
Jean-François est fantastique. Il est français, grand, amusant.

les parents et les enfants

(l)file photo, (r)Ken Karp

Lectures culturelles

Où habitent les Français?

Maisons et appartements

Beaucoup de Français qui habitent en ville habitent dans un appartement. Il y a des appartements de toutes sortes: des studios, de petits appartements, de grands appartements. Pour les gens qui n'ont pas beaucoup d'argent il y a des H.L.M.[1] (Habitations à Loyer Modéré). Les H.L.M. sont généralement à l'extérieur des villes, à la périphérie ou en banlieue[2]. En banlieue, il y a aussi de petites maisons individuelles—des pavillons.

[1] H.L.M. *low-income housing*
[2] en banlieue *in the suburbs*

Reading Strategy

Visualizing

As you are reading, try to visualize or make a mental picture of what is being described. Allow your mind to freely develop an image. This will help you remember what you read. It may also help you identify with what you are reading.

FLORIDA
Use your StudentWorks™ Plus
CD for more practice.

Des H.L.M.

Des pavillons de la banlieue parisienne

Tahiti

Haïti

La Martinique

La famille Duval

Les Duval habitent à Paris. Leur appartement est dans un vieil immeuble dans le premier arrondissement. Les Duval habitent dans un très beau quartier.

L'immeuble où habitent les Duval a six étages. Les Duval habitent au cinquième. Ils ont un appartement de quatre pièces: une salle de séjour, une salle à manger et deux chambres à coucher. Il y a aussi, bien sûr, une cuisine, une salle de bains, des toilettes et même une petite entrée. La salle de séjour et la salle à manger donnent sur la rue. La cuisine et les chambres à coucher donnent sur la cour. De leur balcon, les Duval ont une très belle vue sur le musée du Louvre.

Un bel appartement à Paris

Vous avez compris?

A Le logement Vrai ou faux? *(True or false?)*
1. Beaucoup de Français habitent dans des appartements.
2. Il y a beaucoup de maisons individuelles dans les villes françaises.
3. Les H.L.M. sont pour les gens qui n'ont pas beaucoup d'argent, qui ne sont pas très riches.
4. Les H.L.M. sont toujours au centre-ville.
5. Il y a des pavillons en banlieue.

B La famille Duval Répondez. *(Answer.)*
1. Où habitent les Duval?
2. Où est leur appartement?
3. Il y a combien d'étages dans l'immeuble?
4. Ils habitent au cinquième?
5. Quelles pièces donnent sur la rue?
6. Quelles pièces donnent sur la cour?
7. Du balcon de l'appartement, il y a une vue sur quel musée parisien?

FL.C.1.2.2 (M) FL.D.2.1.2 (M)

Le logement dans d'autres pays

Une maison avec un toit de chaume, Sénégal

En Afrique

Dans les grandes villes modernes de l'Afrique Occidentale comme Abidjan ou Dakar il y a beaucoup de grands immeubles où les Ivoiriens et les Sénégalais habitent dans de très beaux appartements de grand standing. Mais dans les petits villages de la brousse¹, les gens habitent dans des petites maisons avec un toit de chaume. Voilà une maison typique de la brousse.

À la Martinique

La Martinique est une belle île francophone dans la mer des Antilles (la mer des Caraïbes). La Martinique est un département français d'outre-mer². Beaucoup de Martiniquais habitent dans des maisons en bois³. Les couleurs des maisons martiniquaises sont très belles.

¹ brousse *bush*
² d'outre-mer *overseas*
³ en bois *wooden*

Dakar, Sénégal

Vous avez compris?

Le monde francophone Donnez les informations suivantes. (*Give the following information.*)

1. deux grandes villes africaines
2. une région rurale dans beaucoup de pays africains
3. un département français d'outre-mer
4. une île où il y a beaucoup de maisons multicolores en bois

Une maison en bois, Pointe-à-Pitre, Guadeloupe

FL.D.1.2.2 (M)

Les noms de famille

En France les noms de famille ont des origines très variées. Certains évoquent une caractéristique physique: **Legrand, Lebrun, Petit.**

D'autres sont des noms de profession.

Médecin   Boucher   Charpentier

D'autres sont des noms d'endroits.

Lacour

Dujardin

Delarue

D'autres encore sont des termes géographiques.

Dumont

Duval

Dubois

Quel est votre nom de famille?
Il signifie quelque chose de spécial?

Vous avez compris?

Noms de famille américains Can you think of some American family names for each of the above categories? Can you think of any other categories for American family names?

La Belgique

La Tunisie

Le Maroc

Le Mali

CONNEXIONS

FL.C.1.2.2 (I)   FL.C.2.1.1 (I)

Les Beaux-Arts

Art et histoire

Art and history are often closely connected. Looking at a beautiful painting brings us much enjoyment. It can also teach us a great deal about the period in which the artist produced it. A portrait, for example, shows us how people looked and dressed at the time.

Today many families keep a photo album. Prior to the invention of photography many families had a portrait done. This was particularly true of the royal families, and King Louis XVI and his queen, Marie-Antoinette, were no exception.

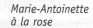
Marie-Antoinette à la rose

La portraitiste de Marie-Antoinette

Élisabeth Vigée-Lebrun est née[1] à Paris en 1775 (mille sept cent soixante-quinze). Elle étudie l'art auprès de son père, l'artiste Louis Vigée. La jeune Élisabeth a beaucoup de talent et en très peu de temps[2] elle a du succès. Élisabeth Vigée-Lebrun est la portraitiste de Marie-Antoinette.

Marie-Antoinette

Voici un portrait de Marie-Antoinette avec ses quatre enfants. La reine est une mère dévouée. Elle adore ses enfants.

[1] née *born*
[2] en très peu de temps *in a short time*

Marie-Antoinette et ses enfants

Versailles

La famille royale habite dans le grand palais à Versailles. Mais Marie-Antoinette n'aime pas beaucoup la vie[3] au grand palais. Elle a un petit palais—le Petit Trianon. Pas loin du Petit Trianon Marie-Antoinette a un petit hameau où elle aime passer du temps. Le hameau est un petit village avec des maisonnettes (petites maisons) avec un toit de chaume. Là, Marie-Antoinette aime passer du temps avec les gens[4] simples.

La Révolution

Pendant la Révolution la famille royale est séparée et emprisonnée. Louis XVI et Marie-Antoinette sont guillotinés. *Les adieux de Louis XVI* est un tableau de l'artiste J.-J. Hauer de l'époque révolutionnaire.

[3] vie *life*   [4] gens *folks, people*

Le hameau de Marie-Antoinette

Les adieux de Louis XVI

Vous avez compris?

La famille royale Donnez les informations suivantes. *(Give the following information.)*

1. le nom de la portraitiste de Marie-Antoinette
2. le nom du mari de Marie-Antoinette
3. la résidence officielle de la famille royale
4. le nom du petit palais de Marie-Antoinette
5. la destinée de la famille royale

C'est à vous

Use what you have learned

FL.A.2.1.2 (I)   **FL.D.2.2.2 (I)**

1 Belle résidence
✔ *Describe a home or apartment*

You are trying to sell one of the apartments or houses listed in the ads. Say as much as you can to convince your client (your classmate) to buy one.

Région PAMIERS : (09) **NID D'AIGLE** rénové, cuisine campagnarde, séjour-salon cheminée 65 m², bureau, 4 chambres, salle de bains, wc. Tout confort. Grande dépendance. Site isolé avec très bel environnement.

CHAUSSON IMMOBILIER IMMO *Plus*
• 33, av. de Foix - 09120 VARILHE
Tél. : **05.61.60.79.80** - Fax : 05.61.60.86

Près VARILHES : (09) **MAISON** campagne, 5 pièces, salle d'eau, wc, grandes dépendances (bergerie, étable, chai) aménageables. Cour, jardin. Proximité toutes commodités.

FL.A.3.2.3 (I)

2 L'immeuble
✔ *Talk about families and where they live*

With a classmate, look at the apartment building. A different family lives on each floor. University students live in the garrets under the roof. Give each family and student a name. Say as much as you can about them and their lodgings.

Dans station thermale des **PYRÉNÉES** : près station de ski, **MAISON** de maître, 12 pièces, bon état, maison de gardien, garage, boxes à chevaux. Terrain 8 ha. Situation exceptionnelle.

ÉCRIRE
3

FL.A.1.2.2 (I) FL.D.1.1.1 (M)

Quinze ans
✔ *Invite a friend to a birthday party*

A good friend will soon be fifteen. Write an invitation to his or her birthday party. You may wish to use the well-known French expression R.S.V.P.— **Répondez, s'il vous plaît.**

ÉCRIRE
4

FL.A.3.2.1 (I)

Ma famille et moi
✔ *Describe yourself and your family*

You plan to spend next year as an exchange student in Toulouse, France. You have to write a letter about yourself and your family to the agency in your community that selects the exchange students. Your letter must be in French. Make your description as complete as possible.

Writing Strategy

Ordering details There are several ways to order details when writing. The one you choose depends upon your purpose for writing. When describing a physical place, it is sometimes best to use spatial ordering. This means describing things as they actually appear—from left to right, from back to front, from top to bottom, or any other logical order that works.

ÉCRIRE
5

La maison de mes rêves

Write a description of your dream house. Be as complete as you can.

To investigate French real estate sites and find a house or apartment in Paris for your family, do the Chapter 4 **WebQuest** activity on the Glencoe French Web site at glencoe.com.

Un château à Rocamadour, France

LA FAMILLE ET LA MAISON

Travelpix/FPG

Assessment

Vocabulaire

1 Complétez. *(Complete.)*

To review **Mots 1**, turn to pages 112–113.

1. Mes parents sont ma ____ et mon ____.
2. Les parents de mes parents sont mes ____.
3. La sœur de ma mère est ma ____.
4. Le frère de mon père est mon ____.
5. Les enfants de mes oncles et de mes tantes sont mes ____ et mes ____.

2 Identifiez. *(Identify.)*

To review **Mots 2**, turn to pages 116–117.

Structure

To review the verb **avoir**, turn to page 120.

3 Complétez avec «avoir». *(Complete with* avoir.*)*

11. J'____ une petite famille.
12. Marc aussi ____ une petite famille.
13. Sa sœur ____ seize ans.
14. Les parents de Marc et sa sœur ____ un appartement à Paris.
15. Vous ____ une maison ou un appartement?
16. Et toi, tu ____ une petite ou une grande famille?

4 Choisissez. *(Choose.)*

17. Où est la voiture de Serge? _____ voiture est dans le garage?

   a. Sa   **b.** Son   **c.** Ses

18. Où est _____ maison?

   a. ta   **b.** ton   **c.** tes

19. _____ anniversaire est le 4 novembre.

   a. Ma   **b.** Mon   **c.** Mes

20. Paul et Marc sont les frères de Sandrine? Oui, ce sont _____ frères.

   a. leurs   **b.** son   **c.** ses

To review possessive adjectives, turn to page 123.

5 Complétez. *(Complete.)*

21. Il y a de très _____ maisons dans notre _____ quartier. (vieux, beau)

22. Nous avons un _____ appartement avec de _____ pièces. (nouveau, beau)

To review these adjectives, turn to page 126.

Culture

6 Vrai ou faux? *(True or false?)*

23. Les pavillons sont de petites maisons en banlieue.

24. Les H.L.M. sont généralement à l'extérieur des villes.

25. Beaucoup de Français qui habitent en ville habitent dans une maison privée.

To review this cultural information, turn to pages 130–131.

French Online
For more Chapter 4 test preparation, go to the Chapter 4 **Self-Check Quiz** on the Glencoe French Web site at glencoe.com.

Des H.L.M.

Curt Fischer

CHAPITRE ④ Florida

Do these practice activities to help you succeed on your FCAT through the study of a foreign language.

Read the story below. Then answer the questions that follow.

Les Marin sont une famille française. Ils habitent à Tours, une assez petite ville en France. Leur maison est au centre-ville dans un beau quartier de la ville. Leurs voisins sont très sympathiques. La maison est assez grande. Elle a quatre chambres à coucher, deux salles de séjour, trois salles de bains et une grande cuisine. La famille a trois enfants—une fille, Amandine, et deux fils, Jacques et Christophe. Amandine a onze ans, Jacques a neuf ans et Christophe a six ans. Ils aiment beaucoup jouer ensemble dans le beau jardin de la maison. Le jardin a beaucoup de jolies fleurs et deux grands arbres. Le chat, Pompon, aime jouer dans le jardin avec les enfants. Ils adorent Pompon. Amandine et Christophe sont très énergiques. Ils jouent beaucoup. Jacques n'est pas énergique. Il est assez timide. Il aime écouter de la musique dans sa chambre à coucher.

Aujourd'hui, c'est l'anniversaire de leur grand-mère. Elle a quatre-vingts ans! Tout le monde arrive à l'appartement de la grand-mère pour célébrer son anniversaire. Les enfants donnent une vidéo et une photo à leur grand-mère. Elle est très heureuse. La famille déjeune au restaurant ensemble. Amandine pose beaucoup de questions à sa grand-mère. Elle adore parler avec sa grand-mère. La famille passe une journée amusante ensemble. Plus tard ils quittent l'appartement de la grand-mère et ils rentrent à la maison.

LA.A.2.4.1. (M)

❶ Quel est un bon titre pour cette histoire?

    A. L'anniversaire d'Amandine

    B. Pompon, le chat dynamique

    C. Une famille française

    D. Un cadeau pour Jacques

2 Quelle est une activité possible pour Jacques?

    F. parler avec tout le monde

    G. écouter la radio

    H. rigoler avec des copains

    I. travailler au restaurant

3 READ THINK EXPLAIN Décrivez la famille Marin.

4 READ THINK EXPLAIN Décrivez la maison de la famille Marin.

5 READ THINK EXPLAIN Quelles sont des différences entre la maison des Marin et votre maison?

6 Quel mot décrit Amandine?

    A. patiente

    B. timide

    C. égoïste

    D. dynamique

7 Qu'est-ce que les enfants donnent à leur grand-mère?

    F. des fleurs

    G. un chat

    H. des cadeaux

    I. un restaurant

FCAT Tip

Answer the questions you are sure about first. If a question seems too difficult, skip it and go back to it later.

On parle super bien!

Tell all you can about this illustration.

Vocabulaire

Identifying family members

la famille	le frère	la petite-fille
les parents *(m. pl.)*	la sœur	l'oncle
le père	les grands-parents	la tante
la mère	*(m. pl.)*	le neveu
le mari	le grand-père	la nièce
la femme	la grand-mère	le/la cousin(e)
le fils	les petits-enfants	un chat
la fille	*(m. pl.)*	un chien
l'enfant *(m. et f.)*	le petit-fils	

Talking about family affairs or events

un anniversaire	donner
un cadeau	inviter
un gâteau	avoir… ans
une bougie	Quel âge… ?
une fête	

FL.D.1.2.1 (M)

How well do you know your vocabulary?

- Find the sixteen cognates.
- Use as many of them as you can to write a story.

Identifying the rooms of a house

une pièce	une chambre à coucher
une salle de séjour	une salle de bains
une cuisine	des toilettes *(f. pl.)*
une salle à manger	

Talking about a home and the neighborhood

une maison	un garage	un code	(tout) près de
un appartement	une voiture	une cour	loin de
un immeuble	un balcon	un(e) voisin(e)	donner sur
un quartier	une vue	beau, belle	monter
une station de métro	le rez-de-chaussée	nouveau, nouvelle	à pied
une terrasse	un étage	vieux, vieille	en ascenseur
un jardin	un escalier	premier, première	
un arbre	un ascenseur	deuxième	
une fleur	une entrée	troisième	

Other useful words and expressions

une journée	il y a
tout le monde	C'est (pas) rigolo.
autour de (d')	

VIDÉOTOUR

Épisode 4

In this video episode, you will accompany Christine and Madame Séguin on a trip to Giverny. See page 529 for more information.

Révision

FL.A.1.1.2 (I)

Conversation

Un anniversaire

Sandrine: Bonjour, Christophe. Ça va?

Christophe: Oui, ça va. Et toi?

Sandrine: Pas mal. Qu'est-ce que tu as dans ton sac?

Christophe: J'ai un cadeau pour ma sœur. C'est son anniversaire aujourd'hui.

Sandrine: Ta sœur Mélanie? Elle a quel âge?

Christophe: Elle a seize ans. Et Sandrine, tu as ma nouvelle adresse?

Sandrine: Ta nouvelle adresse? Tu n'habites pas rue de l'Odéon?

Christophe: Non, maintenant on habite dans le 5e, tout près de la station de métro Maubert-Mutualité.

Le boulevard Haussmann, Paris

La station de métro Maubert-Mutualité

Vous avez compris?

Répondez. (*Answer.*)

1. Sandrine parle à qui?
2. Qu'est-ce qu'il y a dans son sac?
3. C'est l'anniversaire de qui?
4. C'est quand, son anniversaire?
5. Elle a quel âge?
6. Qui a une nouvelle adresse?
7. Il habite où maintenant?
8. Il habite près de quelle station de métro?

Structure

Les verbes au présent

1. Review the forms of regular **-er** verbs.

PARLER	je parle, tu parles, il/elle/on parle, nous parlons, vous parlez, ils/elles parlent
AIMER	j'aime, tu aimes, il/elle/on‿aime, nous‿aimons, vous‿aimez, ils‿/elles‿aiment

2. Review the irregular verbs you have learned so far.

ÊTRE	je suis, tu es, il/elle/on‿est, nous sommes, vous‿êtes, ils/elles sont
AVOIR	j'ai, tu as, il/elle/on‿a, nous‿avons, vous‿avez, ils‿/elles‿ont

3. Review the placement of **ne (n')… pas** when expressing a negative idea.

Je ne travaille pas.
Il n'habite pas à Paris.

1 **Historiette** **Flore habite à Paris.**
Inventez une histoire. *(Make up a story.)*

1. Flore habite à Paris?
2. Elle quitte la maison à quelle heure le matin?
3. Et toi, tu habites où?
4. Le matin, tu arrives à l'école à quelle heure?
5. Tu parles français ou anglais à l'école?
6. Et Flore, qu'est-ce qu'elle parle?
7. Flore quitte le collège à cinq heures de l'après-midi?
8. Tes copains et toi, vous quittez l'école à quelle heure?
9. Vous travaillez après les cours?
10. Les élèves français travaillent après les cours?

2 Historiette Une famille
Complétez. *(Complete.)*

1. Bonjour. Moi, je ____ français. Je ____ de Paris. (être)
2. Ma famille n'____ pas très grande. Nous ____ quatre. (être)
3. J'____ une sœur. (avoir)
4. Ma sœur ____ dix ans et moi, j'____ dix-sept ans. (avoir)
5. Et vous, vous ____ quel âge? (avoir)
6. Vous ____ américain(e) ou français(e)? (être)

Une famille française avec leur chat

Les articles et les adjectifs

1. Review the following forms of the indefinite and definite articles.

   un garçon   **une fille**
   des copains   **des_z écoles**

   le garçon   **la fille**   **l'ami(e)**
   les copains **les_z écoles** **les_z ami(e)s**

2. Adjectives that end in a consonant have four forms.

   Le garçon est brun.   **Les garçons sont bruns.**
   La fille est brune.   **Les filles sont brunes.**

3. Adjectives that end in **e** have only two forms, singular and plural.

   un ami sympathique   **des amis sympathiques**
   une amie sympathique   **des amies sympathiques**

Deux copains sympathiques à Paris

3 **Historiette** **La famille de Valentin** Complétez avec **un, une** ou **des.** (*Complete with* un, une, *or* des.)

Valentin a une grande famille. Il a __1__ père et __2__ mère.
Il a __3__ frères et __4__ sœurs? Oui, il a trois frères et quatre
sœurs. Il a aussi sept cousins, mais __5__ seule cousine. Il a __6__
chien, Tifou, et __7__ chat, Pompon.

Valentin et sa famille habitent dans __8__ grande maison à
Pontchartrain. Valentin est élève dans __9__ lycée de la région.
Valentin est __10__ élève excellent.

4 **C'est qui?** Complétez avec **le, la, l'** ou **les.**
(*Complete with* le, la, l', *or* les.)

1. Guillaume est _____ ami de Loïc.
2. Joanne est _____ sœur de Guillaume.
3. Mais Joanne n'est pas _____ amie de Loïc.
4. Justine et Mélanie sont _____ amies de Joanne et Guillaume.
5. Marc et Jean-Paul aussi sont _____ amis de Joanne et Guillaume.
6. Guillaume est _____ frère de Joanne et Christelle.
7. Christelle est _____ cousine de Loïc.

5   **Sa sœur aussi** Répondez d'après le modèle.
(Answer according to the model.)

—**Il est très intelligent.**
—**Sa sœur aussi est très intelligente.**

1. Il est content.   4. Il est énergique.
2. Il est amusant.   5. Il est très intéressant.
3. Il est sympathique.   6. Il est brun.

Les adjectifs possessifs

1. Review the forms of the possessive adjectives. The adjectives
mon, ton, and **son** have three forms.

mon appartement	ma maison	mes appartements	mes maisons
ton appartement	ta maison	tes appartements	tes maisons
son appartement	sa maison	ses appartements	ses maisons

2. The adjectives **notre, votre,** and **leur** have two forms—singular
and plural.

notre appartement	notre maison	nos appartements	nos maisons
votre appartement	votre maison	vos appartements	vos maisons
leur appartement	leur maison	leurs appartements	leurs maisons

3. Remember that you use **mon, ton, son** before a feminine singular
noun that begins with a vowel or silent **h: mon adresse,
mon amie.**

La salle à manger de
la maison de Monet
à Giverny

6 **Qui?** Complétez. *(Complete.)*

Julien a un frère, Paul, et une sœur, Magali. __1__ parents ont donc trois enfants. __2__ trois enfants sont Julien, __3__ frère et __4__ sœur.

—Julien, __5__ frère a quel âge?

—Euh… __6__ frère a quinze ans et __7__ sœur a neuf ans.

—Julien et Paul, comment est __8__ prof de musique?

—Qui? __9__ prof de musique? Il est très sympa. Beaucoup de __10__ profs sont sympas.

École nationale de musique et de danse, Yerres

FL.A.3.2.1 (I)

7 **Un(e) ami(e)** Work with a classmate. Each of you will tell about a friend. Describe your friend, some things he or she does, and where he or she lives.

FL.A.3.1.1 (I)

8 **Une conversation** Have a conversation with a classmate. Talk about your school, classes, family, and house.

 LITERARY COMPANION *You may wish to read the adaptation of* La petite Fadette, *a novel by George Sand, on pages 504–509. The activities for this reading will help you continue to practice your reading comprehension skills.*

Larry Hamill

Florida

La géographie de la Floride

La Floride est une péninsule. Il y a de l'eau sur trois côtés. À l'est, c'est l'océan Atlantique, à l'ouest le golfe du Mexique et au sud le détroit de Floride. Au nord se trouvent[1] l'Alabama et la Géorgie.

En Floride il y a soixante-sept comtés. La capitale, c'est Tallahassee. Tallahassee se trouve dans le *panhandle* de la Floride. Dans l'état il y a beaucoup de grandes villes cosmopolites telles que Miami, Tampa, Orlando et Jacksonville.

[1]se trouvent *are*

Le relief de la Floride est assez plat. Il n'y a pas de montagnes mais au centre, il y a des régions où il y a des collines[2]. Dans le sud, il y a des marais[3] qui s'appellent les Everglades. Le lac Okeechobee est un très grand lac qui alimente[4] les marais.

Le climat de l'état est très doux et agréable. Il y a presque[5] toujours du soleil. Dans le sud, il fait chaud pendant toute l'année. Dans le nord, il fait frais, et de temps en temps[6] il fait même[7] froid.

[2]collines *hills*
[3]marais *marshland*
[4]alimente *feeds*
[5]presque *almost*
[6]de temps en temps
    once in a while
[7]même *even*

Everglades

Focus on Florida

Étude de mots

A. Choisissez la définition.

1. de l'eau
2. une péninsule
3. un comté
4. le relief
5. une région

a. un terrain avec de l'eau sur trois côtés
b. une zone
c. la forme de la surface de la terre
d. une division politique d'un état
e. ce qu'il y a dans un lac, une mer, un océan

B. Choisissez le contraire.

1. l'ouest
2. le nord
3. plat
4. petit
5. froid
6. beaucoup de

a. grand
b. le sud
c. chaud
d. peu de
e. montagneux
f. l'est

Compréhension

A. Répondez.

1. La Floride est dans le nord ou le sud des États-Unis?
2. La Floride est une île ou une péninsule?
3. Il y a combien de comtés en Floride?
4. Tu habites quel comté?
5. Quelle est la capitale de la Floride?
6. Quelles sont trois grandes villes en Floride?

Des cyprès

B. Décrivez le climat en Floride.

C. Corrigez.

1. La Floride est un comté.

2. Dade est un état.

3. La capitale de la Floride est Miami.

4. Une montagne est haute et une colline est très haute.

5. L'eau du golfe du Mexique alimente les marais.

D. Choisissez.

une ville   un état   un comté   la capitale

1. Tampa est _____ dans l'ouest de la Floride sur le golfe du Mexique.

2. Tallahassee est _____ de la Floride.

3. Orange est _____ très grand.

4. L'Alabama est _____ au nord de la Floride.

E. Discutez.

Vous êtes de quelle région de la Floride? Décrivez la terre et le climat de la région.

Miami Beach

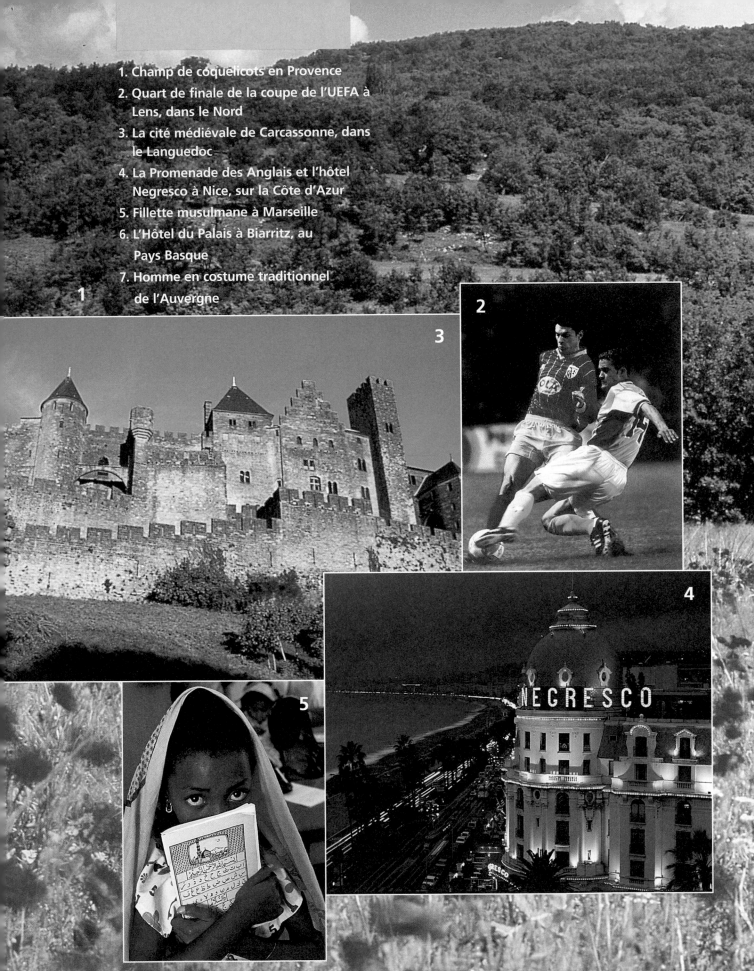

1. Champ de coquelicots en Provence
2. Quart de finale de la coupe de l'UEFA à Lens, dans le Nord
3. La cité médiévale de Carcassonne, dans le Languedoc
4. La Promenade des Anglais et l'hôtel Negresco à Nice, sur la Côte d'Azur
5. Fillette musulmane à Marseille
6. L'Hôtel du Palais à Biarritz, au Pays Basque
7. Homme en costume traditionnel de l'Auvergne

NATIONAL GEOGRAPHIC

REFLETS
de la France

8. Paons dans le parc du château de Valençay, dans la vallée de la Loire
9. Fillette en costume traditionnel au festival d'Obernai, en Alsace
10. Le Mont-Saint-Michel, en Normandie
11. Un TGV (un Train à Grande Vitesse)
12. Coureurs cyclistes du Tour de France à Vitré, en Bretagne
13. Rosace de la cathédrale Notre-Dame de Reims, en Champagne
14. Jeune écolier et cycliste, en Normandie

NATIONAL GEOGRAPHIC

REFLETS
de la France

14

Au café et au restaurant

Objectifs

In this chapter you will learn to:

✔ *order food or a beverage at a café or restaurant*

✔ *tell where you and others go*

✔ *tell what you and others are going to do*

✔ *give locations*

✔ *tell what belongs to you and others*

✔ *describe more activities*

✔ *compare eating habits in the United States and in the French-speaking world*

Vincent Van Gogh *Terrasse du café le soir*

French Online

To interact with your online edition of
Bon voyage! go to: glencoe.com.

VISIT FLORIDA

SUNSHINE STATE STANDARDS

This chapter is all about ordering foods at a café or restaurant. The material in the chapter will address the Sunshine State Standards listed below.

FL.A.1.2.1 express likes or dislikes regarding various objects, categories, people, and events present in the everyday environment.

FL.A.2.1.2 restate and rephrase simple information from materials presented orally, visually, and graphically in class.

FL.A.2.1.3 understand oral messages that are based on familiar themes and vocabulary (e.g., short conversations between familiar persons on familiar topics such as everyday school and home activities).

FL.A.2.1.4 listen and read in the target language and respond through role playing, drawing, or singing.

FL.A.3.1.1 provide simple information in spoken form (e.g., descriptions of family members, friends, objects present in his or her everyday environment, or common school and home activities).

FL.A.3.2.1 describe important people (e.g., family members and friends) and objects present in his or her everyday environment and in school.

FL.A.3.2.3 give responses in spoken or written form (e.g., answering simple questions, formulating questions, and making simple statements) to age-appropriate stories, poems or other literature, songs, films, or visual works.

FL.B.1.1.1 participate in age-appropriate cultural activities (e.g., games, songs, birthday celebrations, storytelling, dramatizations, and role playing).

FL.B.1.1.2 recognize patterns of social behavior or social interaction in various settings (e.g., school, family, or immediate community).

FL.B.1.1.3 recognize various familiar objects and norms of the target culture (e.g., toys, dresses, and typical foods).

FL.C.1.1.2 participate in an activity in the target-language class that is based on a concept taught in a content class (e.g., shapes or relationships).

FL.C.1.2.2 use target-language vocabulary or concepts to reinforce knowledge of a related topic studied in another class (e.g., geographical place names, parts of the body, or basic mathematical operations).

FL.D.1.1.2 use simple vocabulary and short phrases in the target language.

FL.D.1.2.2 recognize the similarities and differences between his or her native language and the target language in terms of the pronunciation, alphabet, and forms of written expression.

Fort Jefferson, Dry Tortugas National Park

FL.D.2.1.1 know the similarities and differences between the patterns of behavior of the target culture related to recreation, celebration, holidays, customs, and the patterns of behavior of the local culture.

FL.D.2.2.2 recognize forms of the target language evident in the local culture (e.g., signs, symbols, advertisements, packages, displays, murals, songs, and rhymes).

TIPS FOR SUCCESS

Review the Study Tips below to help you succeed on the Sunshine State Standards identified.

Vocabulaire **Mots 1** **Mots 2** *(pages 154–161)*

Roseate spoonbill

- It can be fun to study with a classmate. You can do the following.

  - Ask one another questions in French about the illustrations.
  - Have a contest. See who can give more French words describing the illustrations in a three-minute period.
  - Tell your friend which of the items you would order if you were at a café.

- Activity 1 on page 156 helps you reinforce the meaning of the important question words:

où	au café
qui	Chantal, le serveur
qu'est-ce que	une table libre, une boisson
quand	après les cours

- Act out Activity 4 on page 157 with a classmate. The more you practice speaking French together, the more you'll be able to communicate. **FL.A.2.1.2; FL.A.3.2.3; FL.B.1.1.1**

Conversation *(page 170)*

Listen carefully to the conversation. You can listen to your teacher or use the CD-ROM. Listen more than once. Each time listen for a different bit of information.

Where are Claire and Loïc?
What do they order?
Why is there a possible disagreement?
FL.A.2.1.3

Lectures culturelles **Au restaurant? Vraiment?** *(pages 172–173)*

- Making comparisons while reading is an important reading comprehension skill. In this reading, you learned about a cultural difference that's quite interesting. What is it? You may want to share this information with family or friends who don't know any French.

- Finding the main idea is another important reading comprehension skill. As you read, look for the main idea in the second paragraph. What is it? What is the main idea in the third paragraph? **FL.D.2.1.1**

> **For other tips to help you address the Sunshine State Standards in Chapter 5, see pages H58 and H59 at the back of your textbook.**

Vocabulaire

Mots 1

À la terrasse d'un café 🎧

CAFÉ DE LA PAIX

une serveuse

trouver une table

une table libre

une table occupée

Karim va au café avec Maïa.
Les deux copains y vont ensemble.
Ils trouvent une table libre.

un serveur

la carte

Le serveur arrive.
Il donne la carte à Karim.
Maïa regarde la carte.

Vous désirez?

Un coca, s'il vous plaît.

Et pour moi, une limonade.

Karim prend un coca.
Maïa prend une limonade.
Ils commandent une boisson (une consommation).

un café (un express)

un citron pressé

un crème

un jus de pomme

un jus d'orange

des tartines de
pain beurré

un croissant

une omelette
nature

une omelette aux
fines herbes

un sandwich
au jambon

un croque-monsieur

un sandwich
au fromage

une salade
verte

des frites

une soupe
à l'oignon

une saucisse de Francfort,
un hot-dog

une crêpe

une glace
au chocolat

une glace
à la vanille

AU CAFÉ ET AU RESTAURANT

(orange juice, apple juice)Timothy Fuller, (fries)Aaron Haupt, (others)John Evans

Quel est le mot?

1 **Historiette** **On va au café.**
Répondez d'après les indications.
(Answer according to the cues.)

1. Pierre va où? (au café)
2. Il va au café avec qui? (Chantal)
3. Ils vont au café quand? (après les cours)
4. Les deux copains y vont ensemble? (oui)
5. Qu'est-ce qu'ils trouvent?
   (une table libre)
6. Qui arrive? (le serveur)
7. Il donne la carte à qui? (à Chantal)
8. Qu'est-ce que les amis commandent?
   (une boisson)
9. Chantal prend une limonade? (oui)
10. Qu'est-ce que Pierre prend? (un coca)

Un café, Nice

FL.D.1.1.2 (I)

2 **Tu as faim ou soif?** Suivez les modèles.
(Follow the models.)

une salade ——→
Moi, j'ai faim. Je voudrais quelque chose à manger.

un coca ——→
Moi, j'ai soif. Je voudrais quelque chose à boire.

1. un citron pressé
2. un petit crème
3. une omelette nature
4. une limonade
5. une glace à la vanille
6. un jus d'orange
7. un croque-monsieur
8. une crêpe

FL.A.3.2.3 (I)

3 **Historiette** **Un beau café**
Répondez d'après le dessin.
(Answer according to the illustration.)

1. C'est la terrasse d'un café ou l'intérieur
   d'un café?
2. Il y a beaucoup de tables occupées?
3. Il y a une table libre?
4. Qui travaille dans le café?
5. Magali a soif. Qu'est-ce qu'elle commande?
6. Rémi a faim. Qu'est-ce qu'il commande?

4 **À la terrasse d'un café** Suivez le modèle.
(Follow the model.)

Client: Monsieur, s'il vous plaît!
Serveur: Oui, vous désirez?
Client: Une glace au chocolat, s'il vous plaît.

1. 2. 3.

4.

5. 6. 7.

5 **J'aime ça.** Work with a classmate. Tell what snack foods and beverages you like or don't like.

6 **Au café** Work in small groups. You're in a café in Honfleur, in Normandy. One of you will be the server. Have a conversation from the time you enter the café until you leave. You will get a table, order, and talk about your friends, family, and school. The server will have to interrupt once in a while.

Honfleur, Normandie

7 **Jeu** **Devinette** French people often tell you: **J'ai une faim de loup!** Can you guess whether it means they are very hungry or not? You also hear: **Elle mange comme un oiseau.** Can you guess whether it means she eats a lot or very little? Are there similar expressions in English? What are they?

*For more practice using words from **Mots 1**, do Activity 13 on page H14 at the end of this book.*

Gérard Gsell/DIAF

Vocabulaire

Le couvert 🎧

une tasse

une nappe

une assiette

un verre

une serviette

une fourchette

une cuillère

un couteau

Au restaurant 🎧

Alexandre va au restaurant.
Il ne va pas au restaurant tout seul.
Il y va avec des copains.
Ils n'y vont pas en voiture.
Ils ne prennent pas le bus.
Ils y vont à pied.

Vous aimez votre steak comment?

À point, s'il vous plaît.

Monsieur, s'il vous plaît! Je n'ai pas de serviette.

Alexandre prend un steak frites.

saignant

à point

bien cuit

L'addition, s'il vous plaît.

Alexandre n'invite pas ses copains.
Chacun paie pour soi.

un pourboire

de l'argent

Note 🎧

Here are some common time expressions. They range from "always" to "very seldom."

Au café...
Il y va **toujours.**
Il y va **souvent.**
Il y va **quelquefois.**
Il y va **très peu.**

Le service est compris.
Mais Alexandre laisse tout de même un petit pourboire.
Il laisse un peu d'argent pour le serveur.

Les trois repas de la journée 🎧

le petit déjeuner

On prend le petit déjeuner
le matin.

le déjeuner

On déjeune entre midi
et deux heures.

le dîner

On dîne le soir.

(l)John Evans, (c r)Aaron Haupt

Vocabulaire

Quel est le mot?

FL.B.1.1.2 (I)   FL.B.1.1.3 (I)

8 Historiette Au restaurant Inventez une histoire. *(Make up a story.)*

1. Laurène va au restaurant?
2. Elle prend le bus pour aller au restaurant?
3. Elle a faim?
4. Elle regarde la carte?
5. Elle commande un steak frites?
6. Elle aime son steak comment?
7. Pour le dessert, elle prend une glace? À quel parfum? Au chocolat ou à la vanille?
8. Après le déjeuner, Laurène demande l'addition?
9. Le service est compris ou pas?
10. Laurène laisse un pourboire pour le serveur?
11. Elle laisse un peu d'argent ou beaucoup d'argent?

Laurène regarde la carte.

Un serveur

FL.B.1.1.2 (I)   FL.B.1.1.3 (I)

9 Historiette Un dîner au resto Choisissez. *(Choose.)*

1. Loïc ne va pas au restaurant _____. Il y va avec des copains.
   - **a.** ensemble
   - **b.** au cinquième
   - **c.** tout seul
2. Ils n'y vont pas en voiture. Ils ne prennent pas le métro. Ils y vont _____.
   - **a.** ensemble
   - **b.** à pied
   - **c.** après les cours
3. Loïc _____ un steak frites.
   - **a.** prend
   - **b.** laisse
   - **c.** prépare
4. Après le dîner, Loïc demande _____.
   - **a.** la carte
   - **b.** le pourboire
   - **c.** l'addition
5. Dans les restaurants en France, le service est _____.
   - **a.** occupé
   - **b.** compris
   - **c.** libre
6. Le service est excellent et Loïc _____ un pourboire.
   - **a.** laisse
   - **b.** prend
   - **c.** commande
7. Mais Loïc n'invite pas ses copains. _____ paie pour soi.
   - **a.** L'addition
   - **b.** Chacun
   - **c.** Le serveur

(t)Timothy Fuller, (b)Curt Fischer

FL.B.1.1.3 (I)

10 **Madame, s'il vous plaît!** Demandez à la serveuse.
(Tell the server what you need.)

Une serviette, s'il vous plaît, madame!

 1.   2.   3.   4.   5.

French **Online**

For more information about cafés and restaurants in Paris, go to **Web Explore** on the Glencoe French Web site at glencoe.com. You may also want to do the Chapter 5 **WebQuest** activity at this site.

FL.B.1.1.3 (I)

11 **Les repas** Vrai ou faux? *(True or false?)*

1. On dîne le matin.
2. En France, on déjeune entre midi et deux heures.
3. On prend une tartine et un grand crème pour le dîner.
4. On prend un croque-monsieur pour le déjeuner.
5. On prend une soupe à l'oignon pour le dessert.
6. Une fourchette, c'est pour la soupe.
7. Une assiette, c'est pour le café.
8. Une nappe, c'est pour la soupe.

FL.A.3.2.3 (I)

12 **Au restaurant** Work with a classmate. Take turns asking each other questions about the illustration. Answer each other's questions.

French **Online**

For a fun way to review the Chapter 5 vocabulary, go to **eGames** on the Glencoe French Web site at glencoe.com.

FL.A.3.1.1 (I)

13 **Qu'est-ce que tu manges?** With a classmate, take turns finding out what each of you eats for breakfast and lunch.

For more practice using words from ***Mots 2****, do Activity 14 on page H15 at the end of this book.*

Structure

Le verbe aller au présent
Telling and finding out where people go

1. The verb **aller** *(to go)* is an irregular verb. Study the following forms.

ALLER	
je vais	nous‿allons
tu vas	vous‿allez
il/elle/on va	ils/elles vont

Je vais au café, mais mes parents vont au restaurant.
Tu vas au restaurant avec des copains?
Vous y allez en bus?

Savez-vous que... ?

The expression **On y va!** means "Let's get going." As a question, it means "Should we go?"

2. If you do not mention the place you are going to, you must put the word **y** before the verb **aller**. Y refers to a place already mentioned. **Aller** cannot stand alone.

Tu vas au café?
Oui, j'y vais et Laurent y va aussi.

3. As you already know, the verb **aller** is also used to express how you feel.

Ça va?	**Oui, ça va bien, merci.**
Comment tu vas?	**Très bien, merci. Et toi?**
Vous allez bien?	**Oui, je vais bien, merci. Et vous?**

Café de Flore, Paris

Comment dit-on?

FL.A.2.1.2 (I)

14

Au restaurant! Répétez la conversation avec un copain ou une copine.
(Repeat the conversation with a classmate.)

Salut, Paul! Ça va?

Ça va, et toi? — *Ça va. Tu vas où, là?*

CAFÉ DE FLORE
Je vais au Café de Flore.

Tu y vas tout seul?

Oui. On y va ensemble? — *Pourquoi pas!*

FL.A.2.1.2 (I)

15

On va au Flore. Complétez d'après la conversation.
(Complete according to the conversation.)

1. Marie _____ bien.
2. Où _____ Paul?
3. Il _____ au Café de Flore.
4. Il n'y _____ pas tout seul.
5. Son amie Marie y _____ aussi.
6. Les deux copains y _____ ensemble.
7. Ils n'y _____ pas en voiture.
8. Ils y _____ à pied.

16 **Historiette** **Oui, j'y vais.** Donnez des réponses personnelles.
(Give your own answers.)

1. Tu vas souvent ou très peu au restaurant?
2. Tu y vas seul(e) ou avec ta famille?
3. Tu vas quelquefois dans un restaurant chinois ou italien?
4. Tu vas toujours dans le même restaurant?
5. Tu vas quelquefois au restaurant avec des copains?

17 **Historiette** **À l'école** Donnez des réponses personnelles.
(Give your own answers.)

1. Tes copains et toi, vous allez à l'école?
2. Vous allez à quelle école?
3. Vous allez à l'école à quelle heure?
4. Vous y allez comment—à pied, en car scolaire ou en voiture?
5. Après les cours, vous allez au café?

Honfleur, Normandie

18 **On dîne au restaurant.** Complétez la conversation avec **aller**. *(Complete the conversation with aller.)*

Anne: Ce soir, je dîne au restaurant.
Jean: Ah oui? Où est-ce que tu __1__?
Anne: Au Vieux Honfleur.
Jean: Excellente idée! On y __2__ ensemble.
Anne: Mais, euh… je n'y __3__ pas toute seule.
Jean: Ah bon, tu y __4__ avec qui?
Anne: Euh… avec Olivier.
Jean: Vous y __5__ à quelle heure?
Anne: Mais tu es bien indiscret!

Aller + infinitif
Telling what's going to happen

1. You use **aller** + an infinitive to express what is going to take place in the near future.

> **Demain on va avoir un examen.**
> **Les élèves vont étudier.**
> **Je vais passer l'examen.**
> **L'examen va être difficile, c'est sûr!**

2. To make a sentence negative, you put **ne... pas** around the conjugated form of **aller**.

> **Tu ne vas pas aller au café?**
> **Moi, je ne vais pas regarder la télé.**

Comment dit-on?

19 **Ce soir!** Donnez des réponses personnelles. *(Give your own answers.)*

1. Ce soir, tu vas regarder la télé?
2. Tu vas téléphoner à un copain ou une copine?
3. Tu vas préparer le dîner?
4. Tu vas aller en classe?
5. Tu vas inviter tes professeurs au restaurant?

FL.A.2.1.3 (I)

20 **Absurdités** Mettez à la forme négative.
(Make the sentences negative.)

1. Nous allons en classe pendant le week-end.
2. Les chiens et les chats vont à l'école.
3. Demain le prof de maths va parler français.
4. Vous allez déjeuner pendant le cours de géographie.
5. Ce soir, je vais parler au téléphone avec Elvis Presley.

FL.A.1.2.1 (I) **FL.A.3.1.1 (I)** ◯

21 **Quand?** Work with a classmate. Tell each other some things you like to do. Then tell when you are going to do them—**ce soir, demain, demain matin, la semaine prochaine.**

Les contractions avec à et de
Expressing direction and possession

1. The preposition **à** can mean "to," "in," or "at." **À** is contracted with **le** and **les** to form one word—**au, aux.** Note that liaison occurs when **aux** is followed by a vowel.

à + le	= au	Je vais au lycée.
à + les	= aux	Le prof parle aux_z élèves.
à + la	= à la	Tu vas à la cantine?
à + l'	= à l'	Vous allez à l'école à pied?

Savez-vous que... ?

À is used in many food expressions.

une soupe à l'oignon
une omelette aux fines herbes

2. The preposition **de** can mean "of," "from," or "about." **De** contracts with **le** and **les** to form one word—**du, des.** Liaison occurs when **des** is followed by a vowel.

de + le	= du	Il y a une belle vue du balcon.
de + les	= des	On parle toujours des_z amis.
de + la	= de la	Il arrive de la cantine.
de + l'	= de l'	Je rentre de l'école.

3. The preposition **de** also indicates possession or ownership.

> **Le lycée de Vincent est à Paris.**
> **C'est la voiture du professeur de Vincent.**
> **Minou est le chat des voisins de Vincent.**

Comment dit-on?

FL.D.1.1.2 (I)

22 **Tu vas où?** Donnez des réponses personnelles. *(Give your own answers.)*

1. Quel est le nom de ton école?
2. Tu vas à l'école à quelle heure?
3. Tu vas au cours de français le matin ou l'après-midi?
4. Tu vas au cours d'anglais à quelle heure?
5. Tu aimes parler aux profs?
6. Tu aimes parler des profs aussi?
7. Tu habites près de l'école ou loin de l'école?
8. Tu rentres de l'école à quelle heure?
9. Comment est-ce que tu rentres de l'école?

23 **Historiette** **Je n'y vais pas.** Complétez avec **à.** (*Complete with* à.)

Ce soir, je ne vais pas __1__ (le concert). Je ne vais pas __2__ (le parc). Je ne vais pas __3__ (le collège). Je ne vais pas __4__ (le restaurant). Je ne vais pas parler __5__ (les copains). Je ne vais pas __6__ (l'anniversaire) de Julie. Je vais aller où, alors? Je vais rentrer __7__ (la maison). Pourquoi? Je suis fatigué(e)!

24 **Au café** Suivez le modèle. (*Follow the model.*)

une tarte aux fruits / une tarte aux pommes ➞
—Qu'est-ce que tu vas prendre?
—Je vais prendre une tarte.
—Une tarte aux fruits ou une tarte aux pommes?
—Oh, je vais prendre une tarte ____.
1. un sandwich au jambon / un sandwich au fromage
2. une omelette au fromage / une omelette aux fines herbes
3. une soupe à la tomate / une soupe à l'oignon
4. une glace au chocolat / une glace à la vanille
5. une crêpe au chocolat / une crêpe aux fruits

25 **Le dîner des copains** Combinez d'après le modèle. (*Combine according to the model.*)

c'est la voiture / les parents de Vincent ➞
C'est la voiture des parents de Vincent.
1. je vais à la table / les amis de Marc
2. ils sont à la terrasse / le café
3. nous regardons la carte / le restaurant
4. c'est le coca / l'amie de Marc
5. voilà le pourboire / la serveuse

Cellia Saubry *Coin de rue*

AU CAFÉ ET AU RESTAURANT

Le verbe prendre au présent
Describing more activities

1. The verb **prendre,** "to take," also means "to have" when used with foods. It is an irregular verb. Pay particular attention to both its spelling and pronunciation.

PRENDRE			
je	prends	nous	prenons
tu	prends	vous	prenez
il/elle/on	prend	ils/elles	prennent

Je prends le car scolaire pour aller à l'école.
Les voisins ne prennent pas l'ascenseur.
Je vais prendre un coca.

2. The verbs **apprendre** *(to learn)* and **comprendre** *(to understand)* are conjugated the same way as **prendre.**

On apprend beaucoup à l'école.
Vous comprenez le français, n'est-ce pas?

Les deux amis apprennent l'anglais.

Comment dit-on?

26 **Historiette** **Alexandre** Inventez une histoire.
(Make up a story.)

1. Alexandre prend le car scolaire pour aller à l'école?
2. En classe, il prend des notes quand le professeur parle?
3. Il comprend bien le français?
4. Il apprend beaucoup de choses au cours de français?

Ils prennent leur petit déjeuner.

FL.A.3.1.1 (I)

27 **À l'école** Donnez des réponses personnelles. *(Give your own answers.)*

1. Tu prends ton petit déjeuner à la maison ou à la cafétéria de l'école?
2. À l'école, tu prends l'escalier ou l'ascenseur pour monter au premier étage?
3. À la cafétéria de l'école, qu'est-ce que tu prends quand tu as soif?
4. Qu'est-ce que tu prends quand tu as faim?

28 **Toujours à l'école** Répondez. *(Answer.)*

1. La majorité des élèves prennent le car scolaire pour aller à l'école?
2. Les élèves prennent l'escalier ou l'ascenseur pour monter au premier étage?
3. En cours de français, tout le monde comprend bien quand le professeur parle?
4. Vous apprenez beaucoup de choses en cours de français?

29 **Au pluriel!** Mettez au pluriel. *(Make the sentences plural.)*

1. Je prends le car scolaire pour aller à l'école.
2. Je prends l'ascenseur pour monter au quatrième étage.
3. Tu prends le bus, le métro ou la voiture?
4. Tu prends beaucoup de notes en classe?
5. L'élève est très intelligent et il apprend beaucoup de choses.
6. Elle comprend bien la leçon.
7. Son copain prend un coca au café.
8. Et moi, je prends une glace au chocolat.

*For more practice using the verbs **aller** and **prendre**, do Activity 15 on page H16 at the end of this book.*

Vous êtes sur le bon chemin. Allez-y!

Conversation

Au restaurant Interactive Conversations

Claire: Tu as faim?

Loïc: Oui. J'ai hyper faim! Je vais prendre un bon steak frites.

Serveur: Vous désirez?

Loïc: Un steak frites, s'il vous plaît. Saignant.

Serveur: Et pour vous, mademoiselle?

Claire: Ben, un steak aussi, mais pas de frites. Une salade verte.

Serveur: Et vous aimez votre steak comment?

Claire: À point, s'il vous plaît.
(Après le dîner)

Loïc: L'addition, s'il vous plaît!

Serveur: Oui, monsieur, j'arrive!

Claire: On laisse quelque chose? Il est sympa, le serveur.

Loïc: Oh, écoute, le service est compris.

Vous avez compris?

Répondez. *(Answer.)*

1. Où sont Claire et Loïc?
2. Loïc a faim?
3. Qu'est-ce qu'il va prendre?
4. Et Claire, qu'est-ce qu'elle va prendre?
5. Qu'est-ce qu'elle commande avec le steak?
6. Claire et Loïc prennent leur steak comment?
7. Après le dîner, qui demande l'addition?
8. À votre avis *(In your opinion)*, est-ce qu'ils vont laisser un pourboire?

Parlons un peu plus

FL.A.2.1.4 (I)

 On commande? You and your friend are at a restaurant. Look at the menu and try to decide what to order. Then order. Another one of your classmates will be the server.

sandwichs

Jambon blanc, beurre, cornichons, salade verte, carottes rapées
Jambon de pays, beurre, cornichons

Plateaux repas

Le végétarien (avocat, melon, quiche, tomate, concombre, brie, fruit)
Le frenchie (charcuterie, jambon de pays, taboulé, tomate, concombre, brie, fruit)

salades

Salade grecque (concombre, tomate, oignon, feta, olives, huile d'olive)
Salade du jardin (salade, tomate, melon, jambon de pays, roquefort)
Salade fraicheur (salade, avocat, melon, carottes rapées, emmenthal)

Dessert

Flan noix de coco

Glaces

Profitez de la visite des jardins du PALAIS DE LA BERBIE pour une halte à

l'espace détente

LES JARDINS DE LA FONTAINE

salades
Plateaux repas
glaces

FL.D.1.2.2 (M)

Prononciation

Le son /r/ 🎧

The French sound **/r/** is very different from the American /r/. When you say **/r/,** the back of your tongue should almost completely block the air going through the back of your throat. Repeat the following words and sentences.

le verre	toujours	la voiture	le pourboire
la carte	la tartine	la cuillère	la fourchette
pour	les crêpes	le serveur	le croque-monsieur
boire	les frites	le croissant	

Le serveur arrive avec un verre de jus d'orange.
Je voudrais laisser un pourboire pour la serveuse.

verre

Lectures culturelles

FL.D.2.1.1. (I)

Au restaurant? Vraiment?

Ce soir, Valentin va dîner dans un petit restaurant du coin[1]. Il invite ses deux amis Ahmed et Julie. Ils vont aller tous ensemble au restaurant.

Les copains arrivent au restaurant. Ils trouvent une table libre et ils prennent leur place. Tango prend sa place aussi, sous[2] la table. Sous la table? Oui. Mais qui est Tango? C'est le chien de Julie. Il est très bien élevé[3], Tango. Julie ne laisse pas Tango seul à la maison. Tango accompagne Julie partout, même au restaurant. Pourquoi pas? Un chien bien élevé est toujours le bienvenu[4]!

[1] du coin *local*
[2] sous *under*
[3] bien élevé *well-behaved*
[4] le bienvenu *welcome*

Haïti

La Martinique

Le serveur arrive. Les amis regardent la carte et ils commandent. Après le dîner, Valentin demande l'addition. Le serveur arrive et donne l'addition à Valentin. Valentin regarde l'addition et paie. D'habitude chacun paie pour soi, mais aujourd'hui, c'est exceptionnel. Valentin paie pour tout le monde parce qu'il invite ses copains. En France, «inviter», c'est «payer»!

Vous avez compris?

A Valentin va au restaurant? Vrai ou faux? *(True or false?)*

1. Valentin va au restaurant tout seul.
2. Les copains entrent dans le restaurant et demandent une table au serveur.
3. Tango est un chien bien élevé.
4. Tango aussi va au restaurant.
5. Ahmed et Julie demandent l'addition.
6. Les trois amis paient l'addition.

B Des différences culturelles In this reading, there are some interesting cultural differences between France and the United States. What are they?

FL.B.1.1.2 (I)

Les repas en France

La façon de manger en France change assez vite[1]. Pour le petit déjeuner, ça ne change pas vraiment; on prend toujours le petit déjeuner à la maison. C'est toujours un petit déjeuner rapide et frugal: une tartine de pain beurré et un bol de café, de thé ou de chocolat. Quelquefois, les enfants mangent des céréales.

On déjeune entre midi et deux heures. Mais le déjeuner n'est plus[2] le repas principal parce que les enfants déjeunent à la cantine de l'école. Les parents déjeunent à la cafétéria de leur entreprise[3] ou dans un restaurant près de l'entreprise.

Le dîner est maintenant le repas principal pour beaucoup de Français. Un des parents (ou les deux) prépare le dîner dans la cuisine et la famille dîne ensemble. Souvent on mange des produits surgelés[4]. En France, il y a des plats surgelés excellents. Le dîner est un moment important pour la famille; c'est le seul moment de la journée où on est ensemble.

[1] vite *fast*
[2] n'est plus *is no longer*
[3] entreprise *firm*
[4] surgelés *frozen*

Un restaurant aux Champs-Élysées

Vous avez compris?

Les repas Répondez. *(Answer.)*
1. En France, comment est le petit déjeuner?
2. Qu'est-ce qu'on prend pour le petit déjeuner?
3. On déjeune à quelle heure?
4. On déjeune où?
5. Quel est le repas principal?
6. Qu'est-ce qu'on prépare souvent pour le dîner?
7. Le dîner est un moment important pour la famille? Pourquoi?

Un dîner en famille

FL.B.1.1.3 (I)

Les goûts changent.

Beaucoup de Français sont de vrais gourmets. Ils aiment manger bien. La cuisine française est excellente. Elle est célèbre dans le monde entier. Les Français continuent à apprécier leur cuisine mais ils apprécient aussi les plats d'autres pays[1]. La cuisine asiatique est très populaire: la cuisine chinoise, la cuisine thaïlandaise et aussi la cuisine vietnamienne. En France, il y a beaucoup de restaurants vietnamiens. La cuisine vietnamienne ressemble un peu à la cuisine chinoise. Il y a aussi beaucoup de restaurants algériens, tunisiens et marocains où la spécialité est toujours le couscous.

Comme aux États-Unis, il existe en France des chaînes de restaurants et des chaînes de fast-food. Certaines sont américaines, d'autres sont européennes. Elles sont françaises ou belges, par exemple, comme *Léon de Bruxelles*. Sa spécialité: les moules[2] frites, c'est-à-dire[3] des moules avec toutes sortes de sauces et des frites. C'est un plat traditionnel en Belgique.

Et la pizza? La pizza est très appréciée en France! Tout le monde aime la pizza!

[1] pays *countries*
[2] moules *mussels*
[3] c'est-à-dire *that is to say*

Au restaurant *Léon de Bruxelles*

> **Les aliments préférés des jeunes de 7 à 14 ans sont:**
> le steak frites (51%), les hamburgers (51%), la pizza (49%), les gâteaux (37%), les spaghettis ou raviolis (32%), les sandwichs (17%).
> 71% des Français indiquent qu'ils préfèrent la cuisine française aux cuisines étrangères.

PIZZA VESUVIO

25, RUE QUENTIN-BAUCHARD
75008 PARIS
☎ 01 47 23 60 26
Fax 01 47 23 63 24

Vous avez compris?

Au restaurant en France Vrai ou faux? *(True or false?)*
1. Les Français aiment manger bien.
2. Les Français n'apprécient pas leur cuisine.
3. La cuisine asiatique est très populaire en France.
4. Les restaurants asiatiques en France sont toujours des restaurants chinois.
5. Le couscous est une spécialité vietnamienne.
6. *Léon de Bruxelles* est une chaîne de restaurants belge en France.
7. Les Français n'aiment pas du tout la pizza.

La Belgique

a Tunisie

Le Maroc

Le Mali

CONNEXIONS

Les mathématiques

L'arithmétique

When we go shopping or out to eat, it is often necessary to do some arithmetic. We either have to add up the bill ourselves or check the figures someone else has done for us. In a café or restaurant we may want to figure out what we should leave for a tip, even if **le service est compris.**

We almost never do arithmetic in a foreign language. We normally do arithmetic in the language in which we learned it. However, it is fun to know some basic arithmetical terms in case we have to discuss a problem concerning a bill, for example, with a French-speaking person.

Before we learn some of these arithmetical terms in French, let's look at some differences in numbers. Note how the numbers 1 and 7 are written in French.

Note also that the thousands are indicated by a space or a period and the decimals are indicated by a comma.

```
1 000  2 000  3 000  4 000
1.000  2.000  3.000  4.000
        210,75
```

1   7

FL.C.1.1.1 (I)   FL.C.1.2.2 (I)

L'arithmétique

additionner	+	soustraire	−
multiplier	×	diviser	÷

Pour additionner:
   Deux plus deux, ça fait quatre.
   $2 + 2 = 4$
Pour soustraire:
   Quatre moins deux, ça fait deux.
   $4 - 2 = 2$
Pour multiplier:
   Deux fois deux, ça fait quatre.
   $2 \times 2 = 4$
Pour diviser:
   Quatre divisé par deux, ça fait deux.
   $4 \div 2 = 2$
Dix pour cent (%) de 200 euros, c'est 20 euros.

Vous avez compris?

FL.C.1.1.1 (I)   FL.C.1.1.2 (I)

A **Ça fait combien?** Faites les opérations suivantes à voix haute. *(Solve the following problems aloud.)*

1. $2 + 2 =$ **5.** $4 \times 4 =$

2. $14 + 6 =$ **6.** $8 \times 3 =$

3. $30 - 8 =$ **7.** $27 \div 9 =$

4. $20 - 4 =$ **8.** $80 \div 10 =$

FL.C.1.2.1 (I)   FL.D.2.2.2 (M)

B **L'addition, s'il vous plaît!** You went out to a restaurant with three friends. This is your bill. Do the following.

1. Add up to see if the total is correct.

2. Add 10 percent, even though the tip is included.

3. Calculate how much each of you owes.

C **Comment compter sur ses doigts** Here are three different ways people count on their fingers. Which one is yours? With a classmate, choose a way that is not yours and show each other numbers. Take turns figuring out which number it is.

```
LE BAR À HUÎTRES
112, Bd du Montparnasse
75014 PARIS
TEL: 01 . 43 . 20 . 71 . 01

        6 Thomas
----------------------------------
Tbl 16/1      Fct 9919       Cts 5
          25 Jul  20:19
         *** Réimprimée ***
----------------------------------

3 Salade de Thon          25.00
1 M. FRAICH               19.00
3 Terrine Volaille        23.00
3 SOLE MEUNIÈRE           78.00
1 Tout café                3.00
1 Café Colombie            2.00
1 Café Crème               3.00

      T. V. A.  19.6%
      Service   15%
      Total du   153.00


Toute l'équipe
Bar À Huîtres Montparnasse
vous remercie de votre visite.
À BIENTÔT
```

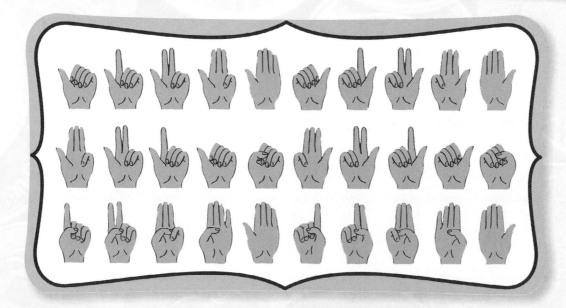

C'est à vous

Use what you have learned

PARLER 1 **FL.A.2.1.4 (I)**

Au café

✔ *Order something to eat or drink in a café*

Work with a classmate. One of you is the customer and the other is the server. You order from the menu provided.

BUFFET CHAUD

CROQUE-POILÂNE

SUPER CROQUE-POILÂNE
(Jambon, fromage, tomate, œuf au plat)

CROQUE-MONSIEUR
CROQUE-MADAME   OMELETTE JAMBON
                      ou FROMAGE

HOT-DOG FROMAGE   OMELETTE MIXTE *(Jambon, fromage)*

SAUCISSES FRITES *(2 saucisses)*   1/4 POULET FRITES

ŒUFS AU PLAT JAMBON   JAMBON DE PARIS FRITES

OMELETTE ou ŒUFS PLAT QUICHE MAISON
NATURE   LASAGNES, SALADE

PARLER 2 **FL.B.1.1.1 (I)**

À la terrasse des Deux Magots

✔ *Talk about school and teachers as you order food and drinks*

Work in groups of three or four. You're all friends sitting on the **terrasse** of the famous café **Les Deux Magots** in Paris, watching the world go by. You talk about many things—school, teachers, friends, etc. One of you will play the role of the server. You have to interrupt the conversation once in a while to take the orders and serve.

3 La carte

✔ *Plan a menu*

Write a menu in French for your school cafeteria.

Élodie prend le déjeuner
à la cantine.

Writing Strategy

Visualizing Many writers have a mental picture of what they want to write before they actually begin to write. The mental picture helps organize what they want to say. It also helps them visualize what they want to describe in their writing. Closing your eyes and visualizing what you want to write can make the writing experience more pleasant. When writing in a foreign language, you also have to restrict your mental picture to what you know how to say.

 FL.A.3.2.3 (I)

4 Un restaurant

You have been asked to write a short article about a visit to a restaurant. Look at this illustration. Pretend this is the mental picture you have of the restaurant you are going to write about. Look at it for several minutes and then write a paragraph about it.

Assessment

French Online

For more Chapter 5 test preparation, go to the Chapter 5 **Self-Check Quiz** on the Glencoe French Web site at glencoe.com.

Vocabulaire

1 **Choisissez.** *(Choose.)*

To review **Mots 1,** turn to pages 154–155.

1. Après les cours, Michel et Chantal vont au _____.
   a. café   **b.** ensemble

2. Ils trouvent _____ à la terrasse.
   a. une table libre   **b.** une tartine

3. Le serveur _____ la carte à Chantal.
   a. regarde   **b.** donne

4. Chantal a soif. Elle commande quelque chose à _____.
   a. manger   **b.** boire

5. Michel a faim. Il prend _____.
   a. un jus d'orange   **b.** une tartine de pain beurré

Deux amis au café

2 **Choisissez.** *(Choose.)*

To review **Mots 2,** turn to pages 158–159.

6. À midi, Henri va _____ au restaurant.
   a. dîner   **b.** déjeuner   **c.** payer

7. Il _____ le métro.
   a. prend   **b.** commande   **c.** laisse

8. Henri aime son steak _____.
   a. à pied   **b.** à point   **c.** ensemble

9. Après le déjeuner, Henri _____ l'addition.
   a. demande   **b.** invite   **c.** laisse

10. Dans les restaurants en France _____ est compris.
    a. le verre   **b.** l'addition   **c.** le service

Structure

3 Complétez avec «aller».
(Complete with the verb aller.*)*

11. Nous _____ à l'école en voiture?
12. Laurent, tu _____ au café?
13. Vous _____ bien, madame?

Au centre de Paris, près de l'Opéra
Angle 14, rue Favart - 9, rue d'Amboise
75002 - Paris - France
Tél : 01 42 96 36 89 - Fax : 01 47 03 97 31
Métro - Richelieu-Drouot

To review the verb **aller,** turn to page 162.

4 Choisissez. *(Choose.)*

14. Je vais _____ au café avec mes copains.
   a. déjeune   **b.** déjeuner
15. Ils vont _____ un pourboire pour le serveur.
   a. laisser   **b.** laissent

To review the use of **aller** + an infinitive, turn to page 165.

5 Complétez avec «à» ou «de».
(Complete with à *or* de.*)*

16. Les amis vont _____ café.
17. Vincent rentre _____ école à cinq heures.
18. C'est la voiture _____ père de Marie.
19. Le prof donne un examen _____ élèves.

To review the forms of **à** and **de**, turn to page 166.

6 Complétez avec «prendre».
(Complete with the verb prendre.*)*

20. Les copains _____ le métro.
21. Vous _____ le petit déjeuner à la maison?
22. Pour monter à l'appartement, on _____ l'ascenseur.
23. Tu _____ un sandwich à midi?

To review the verb **prendre,** turn to page 168.

Culture

7 Complétez. *(Complete.)*

24. Les copains _____ une table libre au restaurant.
25. Claire paie pour tout le monde. Elle _____ ses copains.

To review this cultural information, turn to pages 172–173.

Do these practice activities to help you succeed on your FCAT through the study of a foreign language.

Read the story below. Then answer the questions that follow.

Ce soir Julien et son copain Jean-Luc dînent au restaurant. À quelle heure est-ce qu'ils vont au restaurant? Vers huit heures, parce qu'en général on dîne au restaurant entre huit et dix heures en France. Le serveur arrive et donne la carte aux copains. Qu'est-ce qu'ils vont commander? Julien va prendre une omelette aux fines herbes avec une salade verte. Jean-Luc, qui a très faim, va prendre un steak frites. Il commande toujours son steak à point. Il pense que le steak bien cuit, c'est pour les Américains. Mais quand le steak arrive, il est bien cuit! Jean-Luc est furieux. Et Julien n'est pas content; il n'a pas de fourchette. Ils commandent de la glace au chocolat comme dessert mais le serveur apporte de la glace à la vanille! Julien paie l'addition. Le service est compris mais, à votre avis, est-ce qu'il laisse un pourboire pour le serveur?

① Pourquoi le dîner au restaurant est-il un désastre?

    A. parce que le serveur ne demande pas «Vous désirez?»

    B. parce que le service n'est pas bon

    C. parce que le service est compris

    D. parce que Julien ne laisse pas de pourboire

② READ THINK EXPLAIN Écrivez une liste de choses que les copains commandent.

③ READ THINK EXPLAIN Identifiez les problèmes dans ce restaurant.

4 Quelle phrase est correcte?

    F. On dîne à la même heure en France et aux États-Unis.

    G. Les Américains préfèrent souvent le steak bien cuit.

    H. Dans ce restaurant le service n'est pas compris.

    I. Julien laisse probablement un pourboire pour le serveur.

5 Pourquoi Julien paie-t-il l'addition?

    A. parce qu'il est plus riche que Jean-Luc

    B. parce qu'il ne laisse pas de pourboire

    C. parce qu'il invite son copain

    D. parce que chacun paie pour soi

LA.A. 2.4.1 (M)

6 Quel est un bon titre pour cette histoire?

    F. Julien et son copain

    G. Un repas

    H. On va au café

    I. Une mauvaise expérience

7 Que signifie «le service est compris»?

    A. Le service est bon.

    B. Le serveur paie l'addition.

    C. Le pourboire est inclus.

    D. On va laisser un pourboire.

FCAT Tip

Think positively. Some questions may seem hard, but others will be easy.

On parle super bien!

Tell all you can about this illustration.

Vocabulaire

Getting along in a café or restaurant

un café	la carte	inviter	avoir soif
la terrasse d'un café	l'addition (f.)	payer	Vous désirez?
une table	l'argent (m.)	laisser	je voudrais
occupée	le pourboire	prendre	quelque chose
libre	aller	déjeuner	à manger
un serveur	trouver une table	dîner	à boire
une serveuse	commander	avoir faim	Le service est compris.

Identifying snacks and beverages

une boisson	un jus d'orange	un steak	une saucisse de
une consommation	une tartine de pain	saignant	Francfort, un
un coca	beurré	à point	hot-dog
une limonade	un croissant	bien cuit	une salade verte
un café	un sandwich	des frites (f. pl.)	une glace
un express	au jambon	une soupe à l'oignon	À quel parfum?
un crème	au fromage	une omelette	au chocolat
un citron pressé	un croque-monsieur	nature	à la vanille
un jus de pomme		aux fines herbes	une crêpe

Identifying a place setting

le couvert	une fourchette	une assiette
un verre	un couteau	une nappe
une tasse	une cuillère	une serviette

FL.A.3.2.3 (I)

How well do you know your vocabulary?
- Choose words for specific foods you enjoy.
- Create a menu using these words.

Identifying meals

un repas
le petit déjeuner
le déjeuner
le dîner

Other useful words and expressions

tout(e) seul(e)	quelquefois
toujours	peu
souvent	

VIDÉOTOUR

Épisode 5
In this video episode, you will join Chloé and Christine at a café. See page 530 for more information.

6

La nourriture et les courses

Objectifs

In this chapter you will learn to:

✔ *identify more foods*

✔ *shop for food*

✔ *tell what you or others are doing*

✔ *ask for the quantity you want*

✔ *talk about what you or others don't have*

✔ *tell what you or others are able to do or want to do*

✔ *talk about French food-shopping customs*

Paul Cézanne *Nature morte au panier*

French Online
To interact with your online edition of
Bon voyage! go to: glencoe.com.

SUNSHINE STATE STANDARDS

This chapter is all about shopping for food. The material in the chapter will address the Sunshine State Standards listed below.

FL.A.1.1.1   express likes and dislikes when asked simple questions (e.g., about toys or other objects).

FL.A.1.2.1   express likes or dislikes regarding various objects, categories, people, and events present in the everyday environment.

FL.A.1.2.2   exchange information necessary to plan events or activities (e.g., picnics, birthday parties, science projects, and crafts).

FL.A.2.1.2   restate and rephrase simple information from materials presented orally, visually, and graphically in class.

FL.A.2.2.3   organize information in spoken or written form about a variety of topics of academic and cultural interest (e.g., by making lists, categorizing objects, or organizing concepts).

FL.A.3.1.1   provide simple information in spoken form (e.g., descriptions of family members, friends, objects present in his or her everyday environment, or common school and home activities).

FL.A.3.2.3   give responses in spoken or written form (e.g., answering simple questions, formulating questions, and making simple statements) to age-appropriate stories, poems or other literature, songs, films, or visual works.

FL.B.1.1.2   recognize patterns of social behavior or social interaction in various settings (e.g., school, family, or immediate community).

FL.B.1.1.3   recognize various familiar objects and norms of the target culture (e.g., toys, dresses, and typical foods).

FL.C.1.1.1   use simple vocabulary and phrases to identify familiar objects and concepts from other disciplines.

FL.C.2.1.1   use the target language to gain access to information that is only available through the target language or within the target culture (listen to a story told in the target language).

FL.D.1.1.2   use simple vocabulary and short phrases in the target language.

FL.D.1.2.1   identify examples and understand the significance of true and false cognates (i.e., words derived from a common original form).

FL.D.2.2.2   recognize forms of the target language evident in the local culture (e.g., signs, symbols, advertisements, packages, displays, murals, songs, and rhymes).

Big Lagoon State Park

TIPS FOR SUCCESS

Review the Study Tips below to help you succeed on the Sunshine State Standards identified.

Vocabulaire *Mots 1* *Mots 2* *(pages 186–193)*

Hibiscus

- Try to use your French as often as possible. When you see a food item at home or in a store that is labeled in French, say the French word to yourself. You'll learn to identify many more food items as you continue with your study of French.

- As you complete the activities, answer each question orally before you write the answers for homework. Try reading your written responses aloud for Activities 2 and 3 on page 188. Activity 2 reviews the question words **qui, qu'est-ce que, quand, où.**

- On your own, review the foods you have learned by putting them with an appropriate package or container. For example:

  un paquet de fromage
  un paquet de six tranches de jambon
  un pot de confiture
  un paquet de légumes surgelés
  FL.D.1.1.2

Structure Le partitif et l'article défini *(pages 196–197)*

- Always try to make what you are learning as simple as possible. If you're talking about something in general, you use **le, la, les**. If you're talking about "some" or "any," you use **du, de la,** or **des**.

- When doing Activities 18 and 19, pay particular attention to the contrast between the general sense and the partitive. You want to buy some (partitive) of the things you like (in general). **FL.A.2.2.3**

Conversation *(page 204)*

- Intonation is the melody of a language. Intonation is produced by the rise and fall of the voice. Each language has its own intonation patterns. English intonation is very different from French intonation. Pay special attention to the rise and fall of the speakers' voices as you listen to the conversations on the CD or CD-ROM.

- Try to imitate the native speakers' intonation as accurately as possible. If you do, you'll sound much more French. Don't be inhibited. Pretend you are acting while you imitate the intonation. **FL.D.1.2.2**

> **For other tips to help you address the Sunshine State Standards in Chapter 6, see pages H59 through H61 at the back of your textbook.**

Vocabulaire

Mots 1

À la boulangerie-pâtisserie

un gâteau

une tarte aux pommes

du pain

un pain complet

une baguette

un croissant

À la crémerie

de la crème

du lait

un œuf

du fromage

un yaourt

du beurre

À la boucherie

un poulet

du porc

de la viande

du bœuf

de l'agneau

À la poissonnerie

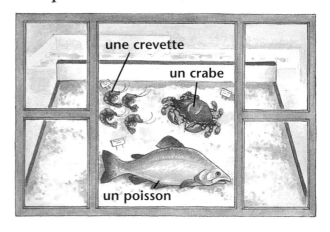

une crevette

un crabe

un poisson

À la charcuterie

du saucisson

du jambon

À l'épicerie

de l'huile

du vinaigre

du poivre

du sel

un sac

Paul fait les courses.
Il va à la boulangerie.
Il va chercher du pain.

Je voudrais une baguette, s'il vous plaît.

Ah, je regrette, il n'y a plus de baguettes.

Paul est à la boulangerie.
Il veut acheter une baguette.
Il n'y a plus de baguettes.

Bon, alors un pain complet.

Et avec ça?

C'est tout, merci.

Il ne peut pas acheter de baguette.
Il achète un pain complet.

Quel est le mot?

1 **Historiette** **À la crémerie** Inventez une histoire. *(Make up a story.)*

1. Madame Cadet va chercher du beurre. Elle va à la crémerie ou à la boucherie?
2. Elle veut acheter aussi du lait. Elle va à la crémerie?
3. Elle veut des œufs aussi?
4. Elle peut acheter du fromage à la crémerie?
5. Elle va acheter des yaourts pour le dessert?

2 **Historiette** **On fait les courses.** Répondez d'après les indications. *(Answer according to the cues.)*

1. Qui fait les courses? (Élodie)
2. Elle fait les courses quand? (le samedi matin)
3. Elle a un sac? (oui)
4. Elle va au supermarché? (non)
5. Elle va où? (à la boulangerie)
6. Qu'est-ce qu'elle va acheter à la boulangerie? (du pain)
7. Elle veut une baguette? (oui)
8. Il n'y a plus de baguettes? (non)
9. Alors, qu'est-ce qu'elle achète? (un pain complet)

Une crémerie, Montgeron, France

French Online
For a fun way to review this vocabulary, go to the Chapter 6 **eGame** on the Glencoe French Web site at glencoe.com.

3 **À l'épicerie** Complétez d'après la photo. *(Complete according to the photo.)*

On va acheter du __1__, des __2__, de la __3__, du __4__, de l'__5__, du __6__ et du __7__.

4 **FL.B.1.1.3 (I)**

On va où? Complétez. *(Complete.)*

1. Pour acheter un poulet, du bœuf, du porc et de l'agneau, on va _____.
2. Pour acheter du lait, on va _____.
3. Pour acheter des croissants et un gâteau, on va _____.
4. Pour acheter de la viande, on va _____.
5. Pour acheter du saucisson et du jambon, on va _____.
6. Pour acheter de la crème et des œufs, on va _____.
7. Pour acheter du poisson et des crevettes, on va _____.
8. Pour acheter des yaourts, on va _____.
9. Pour acheter une tarte aux pommes, on va _____.
10. Pour acheter des crabes, on va _____.

Une poissonnerie, Paris

5 **FL.B.1.1.3 (I)**

Les courses You're living in Arles with a French family. You offered to do the grocery shopping. Your host gives you this list. Find out from your French brother or sister (your partner) where you go for each item.

des crevettes et des crabes
du saucisson
4 tartes aux pommes
2 baguettes
un poulet
du fromage (du camembert)
du lait
un gâteau au chocolat

 *For more practice using words from **Mots 1**, do Activity 16 on page H17 at the end of this book.*

Vocabulaire

Mots 2

Au marché 🎧

Il est bon, mon melon!

la marchande

Elle est bonne, ma salade!

une salade

une pomme de terre

des haricots verts

le marchand

une poire

une pomme

des fraises

C'est combien, les carottes?

Un euro le kilo.

Alors, un kilo, s'il vous plaît.

Vous voulez autre chose?

Oui, une livre de tomates et c'est tout.

Alors ça fait deux euros cinquante.

Ariane est au marché.
Elle veut acheter des légumes.
Elle va chez la marchande de fruits et légumes.

> un kilo = 1 000 (mille) grammes
> une livre = 500 (cinq cents) grammes

190 *cent quatre-vingt-dix*

CHAPITRE 6

Julien et son frère sont
   au supermarché.
Julien veut acheter de
   l'eau minérale et du lait.
Il achète une bouteille d'eau
   minérale et un litre de lait.

FL.D.1.2.1 (I)

Note 🎧
Many words for foods in French
are cognates.

un fruit   une carotte
une banane   une tomate
une orange   un oignon

un paquet de légumes surgelés

un pot de moutarde

un litre de lait

250 grammes de beurre

une boîte de petits pois
une boîte de conserve

une tranche de jambon

une bouteille d'eau minérale

un pot de confiture

une douzaine d'œufs

Quel est le mot?

FL.A.2.2.3 (M)

6 **Fruit(s) ou légume(s)?** Identifiez d'après le modèle.
(Identify according to the model.)

C'est une pomme. C'est un fruit.

1.

2.

3.

4.

5.

6.

7.

8.

7 **Historiette** **Mathilde va au marché.** Complétez. *(Complete.)*

Mathilde veut préparer une grande salade. Elle va au marché. Elle va chez
la __1__. Elle achète une __2__, des __3__ et des __4__. La marchande demande:
«Vous voulez autre chose?» Mathilde répond: «Non, merci, __5__.» Elle donne
de l'argent à la __6__.

8 **Historiette** **Martin va au supermarché.** Complétez. *(Complete.)*

Martin veut acheter de la moutarde, de l'eau minérale, une boîte de petits
pois et un paquet de légumes surgelés. Pour acheter tout ça, il va au
supermarché. Au supermarché, il prend un chariot. Il achète deux __1__ d'eau
minérale, un __2__ de carottes surgelées et trois __3__ de sardines. Et autre
chose aussi—un __4__ de moutarde. Martin va à la caisse. Ça __5__ combien,
les bouteilles d'eau minérale, le paquet de carottes surgelées, les __6__ de
sardines et le __7__ de moutarde? Ça fait onze euros cinquante.

FL.D.2.2.2 (M)

9 **C'est combien, s'il vous plaît?** Conversez d'après le modèle.
(Make up a conversation according to the model.)

—C'est combien, la boîte de petits pois?
—Un euro quatorze.

1.

2.

3.

4.

5.

6.

 FL.A.1.1.1 (I)

10 **Pourquoi pas?** Conversez d'après le modèle.
(Make up a conversation according to the model.)

Tu veux des épinards?

Des épinards? Non.

Pourquoi?

Parce que je n'aime pas ça.

1. Tu veux du saucisson?
2. Tu veux des fraises?
3. Tu veux des haricots verts?
4. Tu veux des petits pois?
5. Tu veux de la confiture de fraises?
6. Tu veux du poisson?

eau minérale
jambon
fraises
œufs
lait
beurre
frites surgelées

FL.A.3.2.3 (I)

11 **À l'épicerie** You're in a grocery store in Paris. You want to buy the items on the list. Tell the clerk (your partner) how much you want of each item and find out how much it costs.

For more practice using words from **Mots 2,** *do Activity 17 on page H18 at the end of this book.*

Structure

Le verbe faire au présent
Telling and finding out what people do

1. The verb **faire** (*to do, to make*) is an irregular verb. Study the following forms.

FAIRE			
je	fais	nous	faisons
tu	fais	vous	faites
il/elle/on	fait	ils/elles	font

2. You will use the verb **faire** a great deal in French. **Faire** is used in many expressions that take a different verb in English. Such expressions that cannot be translated directly from one language to another are called "idiomatic expressions." **Faire les courses** (*to go grocery shopping*) and **faire ses devoirs** (*to do homework*) are examples of idiomatic expressions. The following are some others.

> **Maman prépare un bon dîner. Elle aime beaucoup faire la cuisine.**
> **Les copains vont faire un pique-nique.**
> **Moi, je fais de l'allemand et ma sœur fait de l'espagnol.**

Comment dit-on?

12 **On fait les courses.**
Répétez la conversation.
(*Repeat the conversation.*)

Éric: Salut, Anne! Ça va?
Anne: Ça va. Qu'est-ce que tu fais?
Éric: Je fais les courses.
Anne: Ben, moi aussi. Je vais au marché de la rue Dejean. On fait nos courses ensemble?
Éric: Merci, mais j'ai beaucoup de choses différentes à acheter. Je vais aller au supermarché.
Anne: Ben, je vais avec toi. C'est dans la même direction.
Éric: D'accord.

Rue Dejean, Paris

13 **Qu'est-ce qu'ils font?** Complétez et répondez d'après la conversation. *(Complete and answer according to the conversation.)*

1. Qu'est-ce qu'il ____, Éric?
2. Qu'est-ce qu'elle ____, Anne?
3. Qu'est-ce qu'ils ____, Anne et Éric?
4. Est-ce qu'ils ____ les courses ensemble?

FL.D.1.1.2 (I)

14 **Et toi?** Donnez des réponses personnelles. *(Give your own answers.)*

1. Tu fais quelquefois la cuisine chez toi?
2. Tu fais tes études dans un lycée français ou dans une école secondaire américaine?
3. Tu fais tes devoirs devant la télévision?
4. Tu fais du français?

15 **À chacun son travail** Suivez le modèle. *(Follow the model.)*

> Moi, je fais le dîner. Et vous deux, qu'est-ce que vous faites?

> Nous aussi, on fait le dîner.

1. Moi, je fais les courses.
2. Moi, je fais la cuisine.
3. Moi, je fais le déjeuner.
4. Moi, je fais les sandwichs.
5. Moi, je fais le gâteau.

16 **Historiette** **Mon copain Hugo** Complétez. *(Complete.)*

Hugo et moi, on est copains. Il est très intelligent. Hugo __1__ du russe. Moi aussi, je __2__ du russe. Nous __3__ du russe ensemble. Hugo et moi, nous __4__ quelquefois nos devoirs ensemble.

Hugo et son amie Marie __5__ de l'histoire avec Madame Delcourt. Qu'est-ce qu'ils __6__ au cours d'histoire? Ils apprennent beaucoup de nouvelles choses. Vous __7__ du français, n'est-ce pas? Vous __8__ du français avec qui?

FL.A.3.1.1 (I)

17 **Nous sommes gentils.** Get together with a classmate. Discuss the things you do to help around the house. Decide who is the most helpful.

 For more practice using the verb faire, do Activity 18 on page H19 at the end of this book.

Le partitif et l'article défini
Talking about all or some

1. In French, you use the definite article **(le, la, l', les)** when talking about something in a general sense.

Les enfants aiment le lait.	*Children like milk.*
Je déteste les œufs.	*I hate eggs.*
Je n'aime pas la salade.	*I don't like lettuce.*

2. The partitive expresses an unspecified amount. English uses "some," "any," or no word at all to express the partitive.

Do you have (any) toast?
Yes, I do. Would you like (some) jam with your toast?

3. In French, you use **de** + the definite article to express the partitive. Remember that **de** contracts with **le** and **les** to form one word, **du** and **des**.

de + le = du	Tu as du lait et du beurre?
de + les = des	Je vais acheter des fruits et des légumes.
de + la = de la	Je voudrais de la crème.
de + l' = de l'	Je voudrais de l'eau.

4. Study the following chart. It contrasts the use of a noun in the general sense with the partitive.

General Sense	Partitive
J'aime le poulet.	Je voudrais du poulet.
J'aime la viande.	Je voudrais de la viande.
J'aime l'eau minérale.	Je voudrais de l'eau minérale.
J'aime les pommes.	Je voudrais des pommes.

Note that verbs indicating likes and dislikes are followed by the definite article. All other verbs are followed by the partitive.

Il déteste la viande.	**Elle va acheter de la viande.**
J'adore le fromage.	**Tu prends du fromage?**

Comment dit-on?

 FL.A.1.1.1 (I)

18 **Qu'est-ce que je vais acheter?** Répondez d'après le modèle.
(Answer according to the model.)

> Tu veux des fruits?

> Oui, je vais acheter des fruits. J'aime les fruits.

1. Tu veux du pain?
2. Tu veux du fromage?
3. Tu veux des bananes?
4. Tu veux de la glace?

19 **J'aime tout!** Conversez d'après le modèle.
(Make up a conversation according to the model.)

la crème ⟶
—J'aime beaucoup la crème.
—D'accord. Je vais chercher de la crème.

1. le saucisson   3. l'eau minérale   5. le jambon
2. le lait   4. la limonade   6. les pommes

20 **Historiette** **Des provisions** Complétez. *(Complete.)*

Au marché, Jean-Marc achète __1__ pain, __2__ jambon, __3__ fromage, __4__ fraises et __5__ crème. Il va préparer __6__ sandwichs au jambon et au fromage. Pour le dessert, il va préparer __7__ fraises avec __8__ crème.

21 **Historiette** **Des différences** Complétez. *(Complete.)*

Isabelle Marquet a une sœur, Sophie. Quand les deux sœurs vont au restaurant, Isabelle commande toujours __1__ poisson. Elle aime bien __2__ poisson. Mais Sophie n'aime pas du tout __3__ poisson. Elle aime __4__ viande et elle commande toujours __5__ viande. Elle commande toujours __6__ bœuf. Et elle aime son bœuf à point, pas bien cuit!

Le partitif au négatif
Expressing what people don't have

1. All forms of the partitive, **du, de la, de l'**, and **des**, change to **de (d')** after a negative.

Affirmatif		Négatif	
Je veux {	du pain. de la crème. de l'eau. des carottes.	Je ne veux pas {	de pain. de crème. d'eau. de carottes.

Note that the same is true after **ne... plus.**

Je ne mange plus de viande.

2. Remember that the definite article does not change in the negative.

J'aime les carottes. Je n'aime pas les carottes.

Comment dit-on?

22 **Non, merci.** Conversez d'après le modèle.
(Make up a conversation according to the model.)

de l'eau ⟶
—**Vous voulez de l'eau?**
—**Non, merci. Pas d'eau pour moi.**

1. du pain	3. du porc	5. du lait
2. de l'agneau	4. des crevettes	6. de la limonade

23 **Qu'est-ce que tu as?** Conversez d'après le modèle.
(Make up a conversation according to the model.)

des livres ⟶
—**Tu as des livres?**
—**Non, je n'ai pas de livres. / Oui, j'ai des livres.**

1. un ami	3. un chat	5. des frères
2. une amie	4. des cousines	6. des sœurs

FL.B.1.1.2 (I)

24 **Je voudrais...** Conversez d'après le modèle.
(Make up a conversation according to the model.)

Je voudrais du jambon, s'il vous plaît.

Je regrette, mais il n'y a plus de jambon.

1. Je voudrais de l'eau minérale, s'il vous plaît.
2. Je voudrais de la glace à la vanille, s'il vous plaît.
3. Je voudrais des croissants, s'il vous plaît.
4. Je voudrais des fraises, s'il vous plaît.
5. Je voudrais du fromage, s'il vous plaît.

25 **Juliette fait les courses.** Répondez d'après le modèle.
(Answer according to the model.)

—**Elle va acheter du poisson à la boucherie?**
—**Non, elle ne va pas acheter de poisson à la boucherie. Elle va acheter de la viande.**

1. Elle va acheter du pain à la boucherie?
2. Elle va acheter du fromage à la boulangerie?
3. Elle va acheter des légumes à la charcuterie?
4. Elle va acheter de la viande à la crémerie?
5. Elle va acheter des œufs chez le marchand de fruits et légumes?

Une charcuterie, Conques, France

26 **Je n'aime pas ça!**
Répondez d'après le modèle.
(Answer according to the model.)

—**Tu as de la confiture?**
—**Non, je n'ai pas de confiture. Je n'aime pas la confiture.**

1. Tu as du saucisson?
2. Tu as du fromage?
3. Tu as du café?
4. Tu as de la limonade?
5. Tu as des épinards?
6. Tu as des sardines?

27 **Historiette** **Au supermarché** Complétez. *(Complete.)*

Quand je vais au supermarché, je n'achète pas __1__ fruits. Je n'aime pas __2__ fruits du supermarché. J'achète __3__ fruits au marché, chez le marchand de fruits et légumes. Je n'achète pas __4__ café au supermarché. Je n'achète pas __5__ viande. Je n'achète pas __6__ légumes, pas __7__ oignons. Qu'est-ce que j'achète au supermarché? J'achète seulement __8__ boîtes de conserve, __9__ bouteilles d'eau minérale, __10__ sel, __11__ poivre, __12__ vinaigre et __13__ huile.

28 **Dans le frigidaire** Work with a classmate. Ask him or her for something you'd like to eat or drink. Your partner will check to see whether or not it's in the refrigerator. Use the model as a guide.

—**Tu as de la glace au chocolat? J'adore la glace au chocolat.**

—**Je regrette, il n'y a plus de glace au chocolat.**

FL.A.1.2.1 (I)

29 **Un sandwich extraordinaire** Work with a classmate. Discuss what would be a great sandwich. You may (or may not) want to use some of the following ingredients.

du beurre de cacahouète

de la mayonnaise

du chocolat

de la gelée de raisin

des cornichons

des sardines

Attention!

Pay special attention to the spelling and pronunciation of the following adjectives that double the consonant in the feminine.

FÉMININ	MASCULIN
bonne(s)	bon(s)
canadienne(s)	canadien(s)
gentille(s)	gentil(s)
quelle(s)	quel(s)

Complétez. *(Complete.)*

1. Tu fais de la _____ cuisine? (bon)
2. Tu fais de _____ sandwichs? (bon)
3. Tu as des amis _____ et _____? (canadien, vietnamien)
4. Tu as des amies _____? (tunisien)
5. Tu aimes les filles qui sont _____? (gentil)
6. Tu aimes _____ profs? (quel)

Les verbes pouvoir et vouloir
Telling what one can do or wants to do

1. Study the forms of the verbs **pouvoir** *(to be able to)* and **vouloir** *(to want)*.

POUVOIR	VOULOIR
je peux	je veux
tu peux	tu veux
il/elle/on peut	il/elle/on veut
nous pouvons	nous voulons
vous pouvez	vous voulez
ils/elles peuvent	ils/elles veulent

Savez-vous que... ?

Je voudrais is a polite form of **je veux.** It means "I would like."

Je voudrais une livre de haricots verts, s'il vous plaît.

Michel ne peut pas aller au marché à pied.
Il veut acheter des légumes et des fruits.
Vous voulez manger maintenant?
Vous pouvez si vous voulez.

2. In the negative, you put **ne... pas** around the verbs **pouvoir** and **vouloir**.

Je ne veux pas manger de frites.
Ils ne peuvent pas aller au restaurant ce soir.

Comment dit-on?

30 **Je veux bien, mais je ne peux pas.** Conversez d'après
le modèle. *(Make up a conversation according to the model.)*

—**Tu veux aller au restaurant?**
—**Je veux bien, mais je ne peux pas.**

1. Tu veux aller au café?
2. Tu veux dîner avec Caroline?
3. Tu veux travailler après l'école?
4. Ta sœur veut faire les courses?

5. Elle veut aller au marché?
6. Elle veut préparer le dîner?
7. Elle veut inviter des amis?

Un marché, Saint-Rémy-de-Provence, France

31 **Si vous voulez, vous pouvez.** Conversez d'après le modèle.
(Make up a conversation according to the model.)

Nous voulons travailler.

Si vous voulez travailler, vous pouvez travailler.

1. Nous voulons manger maintenant.
2. Nous voulons inviter des amis.
3. Nous voulons aller au restaurant.
4. Nous voulons commander de la pizza.
5. Nous voulons regarder le film.
6. Nous voulons écouter nos CD.

32 **Historiette** **Pas assez d'argent** Complétez avec **pouvoir** ou **vouloir.** (*Complete with* pouvoir *or* vouloir.)

Pierre et son frère ont faim. Ils __1__ aller dans un restaurant où ils __2__ dîner rapidement. Ils __3__ commander deux hamburgers chacun, mais ils ne __4__ pas. Pierre insiste, mais son frère ne __5__ pas: «Pas question! On n'a pas assez d'argent! Tu __6__ commander seulement un hamburger aujourd'hui.»

33 **Qui peut préparer le dîner?** Complétez. (*Complete.*)

Marie: Je voudrais bien faire le dîner ce soir, mais vraiment, je ne __1__ (pouvoir) pas.
Julien: Tu ne __2__ (pouvoir) pas? Pourquoi?
Marie: Je __3__ (être) très fatiguée! Je __4__ (être) vraiment crevée.
Julien: On __5__ (pouvoir) aller au restaurant, si tu __6__ (vouloir).
Marie: Oh, je ne __7__ (vouloir) pas aller au restaurant ce soir.
Julien: On __8__ (pouvoir) faire des sandwichs.
Marie: Oui, ou… toi, tu __9__ (pouvoir) faire le dîner.
Julien: Je __10__ (vouloir) bien, mais ce n'__11__ (être) pas une très bonne idée.
Marie: Pourquoi?
Julien: Parce que je __12__ (faire) très mal la cuisine!

French Online

For more information about foods, food shopping, and markets in the Francophone world, go to **Web Explore** on the Glencoe French Web site at glencoe.com. You may also want to do the **WebQuest** activity at this site.

FL.A.3.1.1 (I)

34 **Pourquoi pas?** Work with a classmate. Tell each other some things you or you and your friends want to do but can't. When possible, give reasons.

ENCORE PLUS For more practice using the verbs **pouvoir** and **vouloir**, do Activity 19 on page H20 at the end of this book.

Vous êtes sur le bon chemin. Allez-y!

Conversation

FL.B.1.1.2 (I)

Au marché

Marchand: Et maintenant, je suis à vous, madame. Comment allez-vous ce matin?

Mme Brun: Très bien, merci. Et vous?

Marchand: Oh, comme ci, comme ça! Enfin… Qu'est-ce que vous désirez aujourd'hui?

Mme Brun: Je voudrais des haricots verts et des carottes. C'est combien, les haricots verts?

Marchand: Quatre euros le kilo. Et ils sont bons!

Mme Brun: Alors, un kilo, s'il vous plaît, et une livre de carottes.

Marchand: Et avec ça, madame?

Mme Brun: C'est tout, merci. Ça fait combien?

Marchand: Alors, un kilo de haricots verts, une livre de carottes… Ça fait quatre euros cinquante.

Mme Brun: Voilà, monsieur.

Marchand: Merci, madame. Et à samedi prochain.

Vous avez compris?

Répondez. *(Answer.)*

1. Mme Brun fait ses courses?
2. Le marchand va bien?
3. Mme Brun fait ses courses au supermarché?
4. Elle parle au marchand de légumes?
5. Qu'est-ce qu'elle veut acheter?
6. Elle veut des haricots verts?
7. Ça fait combien, les haricots verts et les carottes?

Parlons un peu plus

Qu'est-ce qu'on va manger?
Work with a classmate. Prepare a menu in French for tomorrow's meals—**le petit déjeuner, le déjeuner et le dîner.** Based on your menus, prepare a shopping list. Be sure to include the quantities you need.

Une poissonnerie, Abidjan, Côte d'Ivoire

Prononciation

Les sons /œ́/ et /œ̀/

1. Listen to the difference in the vowel sounds in **peut** and **peuvent.** The sound /œ́/ in **peut** is a closed vowel sound and the sound /œ̀/ in **peuvent** is an open vowel sound. Repeat the following words with the sound /œ́/.

   il peut   il veut   des œufs   deux

2. Repeat the following words with the sound /œ̀/.

   ils peuvent   ils veulent   un œuf
   leur sœur   du beurre

3. Now repeat the following pairs of words. Be sure to distinguish between the two vowel sounds.

   il peut / ils peuvent
   il veut / ils veulent

4. Now repeat the following sentences.

   Elle veut faire les courses, mais ils ne veulent pas.
   Elle veut du beurre et des œufs.
   Leur sœur est sérieuse.

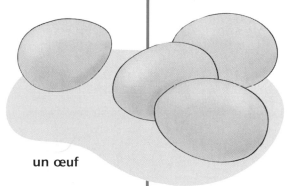

un œuf

des œufs

Lectures culturelles

FL.B.1.1.2 (I)　FL.C.2.1.1 (I)

Les courses

Reading Strategy

Guessing meaning from context

It's easy to understand words you have already studied. There are also ways to understand words you are not familiar with. One way is to use the context—the way these words are used in the sentence or reading—to help you guess the meanings of those words you don't know.

C'est aujourd'hui mardi. À dix heures du matin, comme tous les matins, excepté le lundi quand les magasins sont fermés[1], Mme Lelong quitte son appartement. Elle a son sac et elle va faire les courses. Elle fait les courses dans différents petits magasins. Elle achète du pain tous les jours. Elle va à la boulangerie où elle achète une baguette. Si elle veut de la viande, elle va à la boucherie. Si elle veut du poisson, elle peut aller à la poissonnerie, mais elle est très loin. Pour un pot de confiture ou une bouteille d'eau minérale, l'épicerie n'est pas loin.

Après le déjeuner, si elle n'a pas assez de pain pour le soir, elle peut acheter une autre baguette. Mais pas avant 16 heures. Les petits magasins sont fermés tous les jours de 13 heures à 16 heures, et bien sûr le dimanche!

[1] fermés *closed*

La Polynésie française

Bonne Fête Maman

Une boulangerie-pâtisserie, Paris

Un marchand de fruits, Paris

Haïti

La Martinique

Une boulangerie, Paris

Une boucherie, Domme, France

Les Français aiment bien aller chez les petits commerçants du quartier—l'épicier, le boucher, le boulanger, etc. Leurs prix sont un peu plus chers² qu'au supermarché, mais la qualité de leurs produits est très bonne. Il y a aussi le côté humain³. Les Français aiment bavarder (converser) un peu avec le marchand ou la marchande. On trouve ça sympa.

² Leurs prix sont un peu plus chers *Their prices are a little more expensive*
³ côté humain *human dimension*

Vous avez compris?

A Madame Lelong Répondez. *(Answer.)*
  1. Mme Lelong quitte son appartement à quelle heure?
  2. Qu'est-ce qu'elle prend pour faire ses courses?
  3. Elle fait ses courses où?
  4. Elle va où pour acheter du pain?
  5. Si elle veut de la viande, elle va où?
  6. Si elle veut du poisson, elle peut aller où?
  7. Qu'est-ce qu'elle achète à l'épicerie?
  8. Quand est-ce que les petits magasins sont fermés?

B Stratégie de lecture Reread the Reading Strategy on page 206. You don't know the meaning of the word **commerçants.** Using the suggestion given in the Reading Strategy, can you figure out the meaning of this word?

C Les petits commerçants Expliquez. *(Explain.)*
  1. Qui sont les petits commerçants du quartier?
  2. Comment est la qualité de leurs produits?
  3. En général, comment sont leurs prix?
  4. Qu'est-ce que les Français aiment faire avec les commerçants?

La Suisse

La Belgique

La Tunisie

Le Maroc

Le Mali

Le Sénégal

FL.B.1.1.2 (I)

Les grandes surfaces

Beaucoup de Français font leurs courses dans les petits magasins de leur quartier. Mais beaucoup d'autres Français—surtout les gens[1] qui travaillent ou qui n'habitent pas en ville—font leurs courses dans les grandes surfaces.

Les grandes surfaces sont de grands supermarchés ou hypermarchés. Ils sont généralement situés à la périphérie des villes. Il y a toujours un grand parking parce que les clients y vont en voiture.

Dans un hypermarché on peut tout acheter: de la nourriture, mais aussi des vêtements[2], des bicyclettes, des livres, des disques et même des ordinateurs[3]. Les clients prennent des chariots pour transporter leurs achats[4]. Les grandes chaînes ont pour nom Leclerc et Carrefour.

[1] gens *people*
[2] vêtements *clothes*
[3] ordinateurs *computers*
[4] achats *purchases*

Un hypermarché, Nantes

L'intérieur d'un hypermarché

Vous avez compris?

Les courses Vrai ou faux? (*True or false?*)
1. Les supermarchés et les hypermarchés sont des grandes surfaces.
2. Les grandes surfaces sont situées surtout au centre des villes.
3. Les clients vont presque toujours à pied dans les grandes surfaces.
4. Dans un hypermarché on peut acheter toutes sortes de marchandises.

Les marchés

Sarlat-la-Canéda, Dordogne

Dans les villes et les villages de France, il y a toujours un marché. Dans les grandes villes, il y a des marchés permanents et temporaires. Les marchés temporaires ont lieu[1] en général deux fois par semaine, le mercredi ou le jeudi et le samedi. Ils ont lieu dans la rue ou sur une place.

Les marchés existent dans les autres pays francophones. Voici un très joli marché à Dakar. Et voici un marché à Fort-de-France. Les fruits et les légumes ont l'air[2] très bons, n'est-ce pas? Ils sont délicieux!

[1] ont lieu *take place*   [2] ont l'air *look*

Dakar, Sénégal

Fort-de-France, Martinique

La Belgique

Le Mali

Vous avez compris?

Les marchés Complétez. *(Complete.)*

1. Dans les villes et les villages de France, il y a toujours un _____.
2. Les marchés peuvent être temporaires ou _____.
3. Ils peuvent avoir lieu dans _____ ou _____.
4. Ils ont lieu le _____ ou le _____ et le _____.
5. Il y a aussi des marchés dans _____.

CONNEXIONS

🔍 FL.C.1.1.1 (I)   🔍 FL.D.2.2.2 (I)

Les mathématiques

Les conversions

When you travel in many of the French-speaking countries, or almost anywhere in Europe, you need to make many mathematical conversions. The metric system, rather than the English system, is used for distance, weights, and measures.

soupe d'été

Je trouve sympa de présenter la soupe avec tous ces petits morceaux de légumes. Parfois, je la sers accompagnée de croûtons de pain à l'ail et de gruyère coupé en dés. On se régale tous. Au menu, j'ai prévu une salade crue (pour la vitamine C) avec un œuf dur (pour les éléments bâtisseurs: les protéines). 1 œuf, cela peut remplacer 50 g de viande ou de poisson.

LES USTENSILES
- 1 planche à découper
- 1 cocotte
- 1 couteau de cuisine en acier inoxydable
- 1 cuillère à soupe
- 1 cuillère en bois

LES INGREDIENTS POUR 4 PERSONNES
- Pommes de terre : 250 g — 3 moyennes
- Courgettes : 250 g — 2 moyennes
- Tomates : 3 moyennes
- Oignons : 2
- Huile : 1 cuillerée à soupe
- Eau : 1 litre

Le système métrique

Le système métrique est un système décimal: il a pour base 10. Les mesures ont pour base le mètre et les poids ont pour base le gramme. Pour les liquides, la base est le litre. Les unités supérieures et inférieures sont formées avec les préfixes suivants:

kilo = × 1 000	un kilogramme = 1 000 grammes
hecto = × 100	un hectomètre = 100 mètres
déca = × 10	un décalitre = 10 litres
déci = ÷ 10	un décimètre = 1 mètre ÷ 10
centi = ÷ 100	un centilitre = 1 litre ÷ 100
milli = ÷ 1 000	un milligramme = 1 gramme ÷ 1 000

Un kilogramme (un kilo) est équivalent à environ[1] deux livres[2]. Une livre est équivalente à un peu moins[3] d'un demi-kilo. Un mile américain est équivalent à environ un kilomètre et demi. Un litre est équivalent à environ un quart américain.

[1] environ *about*
[2] livres *pounds*
[3] un peu moins *a little less*

Vous avez compris?

Poids et mesures

Vrai ou faux? *(True or false?)*

1. Le système anglais de poids et mesures a pour base 10.
2. Les poids ont comme unité de base le litre.
3. Il y a 1 000 grammes dans un kilo.
4. Un kilo est l'équivalent d'environ deux livres anglaises.
5. Une livre américaine est l'équivalent de 500 grammes.
6. On mesure les liquides en quarts en France.
7. En France, on mesure les liquides en litres.

C'est à vous

Use what you have learned

FL.A.1.2.2 (I)

1

Au marché
✔ *Buy food from a vendor at the market*

Work with a classmate. You are spending a semester studying in Belgium. You are going to prepare a dinner for your Belgian family. Decide what you need to buy at the market and in what quantities. Then have a conversation with your classmate, who will be the vendor at the market.

FL.A.3.1.1 (I)

2

Je veux bien, mais je ne peux pas parce que...
✔ *Talk about what you want to do but can't*

Work in groups of three or four. Tell some things you want to do but can't do because you are going to do something else. Tell what you are going to do.

3

PARLER
ÉCRIRE

Jeu   Une compétition
✔ *Express quantities*

Compete with a classmate. You each have two minutes. See which one of you can make up the most phrases using the following words.

un kilo de   une livre de   un litre de   une bouteille de

une boîte de   six tranches de   un paquet de

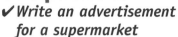

4 Une publicité

✔ *Write an advertisement for a supermarket*

Using these French supermarket ads as a guide, write similar food advertisements in French for your local supermarket. Choose any four foods you like to advertise.

Lait 1/2 écrémé
AUCHAN
Origine France,
bouteille de 1 L

0 € 53

Pain
d'Autrefois
aux raisins
Fabriqué en France,
500 g

1 € 01

Jambon LE FUMAY
Origine France, le kg

6 € 08

EAU MINÉRALE
NATURELLE

c'est un
produit
cora

Le lot

€ 1,52

EAU MINÉRALE
NATURELLE "CORA"
Le lot de 6 bouteilles
de 1,5 litre

Writing Strategy

Ordering ideas You can order ideas in a variety of ways when writing. Therefore, you must be aware of the purpose of your writing in order to choose the best way to organize your material. When describing an event, it is logical to put the events in the order in which they happen. Using a sensible and logical approach helps readers develop a picture in their minds.

FL.A.1.2.2 (I)

5 On fait les courses.

Your class is planning a French meal. Describe the trip you take with your class to the local market or supermarket to buy the ingredients. Tell what you buy, whom you buy it from, and how much everything costs.

Un supermarché, Dakar, Sénégal

Assessment

Vocabulaire

1 Identifiez. *(Identify each item.)*

*To review **Mots 1**, turn to pages 186–187.*

1.

2.

3.

4.

2 Choisissez. *(Choose.)*

*To review **Mots 2**, turn to pages 190–191.*

5. Une pomme et une poire sont des _____.
   a. fraises **b.** légumes **c.** fruits
6. C'est _____, un kilo de carottes?
   a. comment **b.** combien **c.** un marchand
7. Il va acheter _____ de moutarde.
   a. un paquet **b.** une boîte **c.** un pot
8. Je voudrais six _____ de jambon, s'il vous plaît.
   a. bouteilles **b.** tranches **c.** litres

Structure

*To review the verb **faire**, turn to page 194.*

3 Complétez avec «faire». *(Complete with* faire.*)*

9. Je _____ les courses le matin.
10. Mon frère _____ du latin.
11. Vous _____ vos devoirs?
12. Les élèves ne _____ pas la cuisine.

For more Chapter 6 test preparation, go to the Chapter 6 **Self-Check Quiz** on the Glencoe French Web site at glencoe.com.

4 Choisissez. *(Choose.)*

13. Moi, j'aime beaucoup ____ lait.
   a. le   **b.** du   **c.** de
14. Je voudrais ____ eau.
   a. d'   **b.** de l'   **c.** du
15. Il va acheter ____ fruits et ____ légumes.
   a. des   **b.** de   **c.** les

To review the partitive and the definite article, turn to pages 196, 198.

5 Récrivez au négatif. *(Rewrite the sentences in the negative.)*

16. Je vais acheter du pain.
17. Je voudrais de la crème.

6 Récrivez les phrases. *(Rewrite the sentences.)*

18. Les carottes sont très bonnes.
   Le poisson ____.
19. Tu veux quel sandwich?
   Tu veux ____ salade?

To review these special adjectives, turn to page 201.

7 Complétez. *(Complete.)*

20. Je ____ faire le travail. (pouvoir)
21. Vous ____ aller au restaurant? (vouloir)
22. Tu ____ aller au marché. (pouvoir)
23. Ils ____ parler au prof. (vouloir)

*To review the verbs **pouvoir** and **vouloir**, turn to page 201.*

Culture

8 Répondez. *(Answer.)*

24. Beaucoup de magasins sont fermés quel jour en France?
25. On peut aller où pour acheter un pot de confiture ou une bouteille d'eau minérale?

To review this cultural information, turn to pages 206–207.

Do these practice activities to help you succeed on your FCAT through the study of a foreign language.

Read the passage below. Then answer the questions that follow.

En général les Américains font les courses dans un supermarché. Et les Français? Les supermarchés existent en France, mais les gens préfèrent aller d'un petit magasin à un autre pour faire les courses. Par exemple, on achète du pain à la boulangerie, de la viande à la boucherie et du lait et du beurre à la crémerie. À l'épicerie on peut acheter des fruits et des légumes mais les Français aiment mieux aller au marché. Il y a aussi en France les hypermarchés ou les grandes surfaces où on peut trouver toutes sortes de choses. Aujourd'hui les marchands français donnent des sacs à leurs clients. Les sacs sont en plastique ou en papier. Mais beaucoup de gens ont leur propre sac pour leurs achats.

Il y a d'autres différences aussi entre les courses en France et les courses aux États-Unis. Quand les Français vont au marché, ils ne parlent pas de *pounds*. En France on utilise le système métrique. On parle de «kilos» dans le système métrique. Le pain français est très célèbre. Tout le monde adore une baguette bien croustillante avec son odeur délicieuse. Les Français mangent du pain à tous les repas. Tous les quartiers ont une ou deux boulangeries où on achète du pain tous les matins. En France, il y a beaucoup de variétés de pain. Dans certaines boulangeries, faire du pain, c'est un art.

1 Quelle phrase est correcte?
- **A.** En France on peut acheter des tomates, des pommes de terre et des haricots verts dans une boulangerie.
- **B.** En France on préfère faire les courses dans les grandes surfaces.
- **C.** Aux États-Unis on utilise le système métrique.
- **D.** Au marché on peut acheter des fruits et des légumes.

2 Que signifie «Aujourd'hui les marchands français donnent des sacs à leurs clients»?

    F. Donner des sacs aux clients est une chose assez nouvelle en France.

    G. Maintenant on force les marchands à donner des sacs aux clients.

    H. Demain les marchands français ne vont pas donner de sacs aux clients.

    I. Les marchands français veulent imiter les marchands américains.

3 Pourquoi les Français préfèrent-ils aller au marché pour acheter des fruits et des légumes?

    A. parce qu'on ne vend pas de fruits et de légumes aux épiceries

    B. parce que les fruits et les légumes sont généralement plus frais au marché

    C. parce que les fruits et les légumes sont trop chers à l'épicerie

    D. parce qu'ils détestent faire des courses au supermarché

4 Quelle phrase signifie la même chose?
Dans certaines boulangeries, faire du pain, c'est un art.

    F. Les boulangeries en France sont artistiques.

    G. On considère que faire du pain est une chose très importante.

    H. Il y a beaucoup de variétés de pain dans les boulangeries.

    I. On peut apprendre à faire du pain dans une boulangerie.

5 READ THINK EXPLAIN   Comparez et contrastez les courses en France et aux États-Unis.

6 READ THINK EXPLAIN   Écrivez une liste des magasins différents où les Français font les courses.

> **FCAT Tip**
>
> Plan your writing by organizing your ideas. Use a variety of sentence structures. Review and edit your writing.

FL.A.2.1.2 (I)

Tell all you can about this illustration.

Shopping for food

faire les courses *(f. pl.)*	une poissonnerie	le/la marchand(e)
une boulangerie	une charcuterie	un sac
une pâtisserie	une épicerie	surgelé(e)
une crémerie	un marché	
une boucherie	un supermarché	

Identifying some food

du pain	de la viande	de l'eau minérale	un légume
un pain complet	du bœuf	de la moutarde	une salade
un croissant	de l'agneau *(m.)*	un fruit	une carotte
une baguette	du porc	une banane	une pomme de terre
une tarte aux pommes	du jambon	une pomme	des haricots verts
de la crème	du saucisson	une orange	des épinards *(m. pl.)*
du lait	du poisson	une poire	des petits pois *(m. pl.)*
du beurre	une crevette	une fraise	un oignon
du fromage	un crabe	un melon	
de la confiture	du sel	une tomate	
un œuf	du poivre		
un yaourt	de l'huile *(f.)*		
un poulet	du vinaigre		

Identifying quantities

un paquet	un litre
un pot	une douzaine
un gramme	une boîte
un kilo(gramme)	une bouteille
une livre	une tranche

> **How well do you know your vocabulary?**
> - Choose two foods that you like from the list.
> - Tell how you buy each, for example, *une douzaine, une bouteille,* etc.

Other useful words and expressions

aller chercher	C'est combien?	Vous voulez autre chose?	C'est tout.
il n'y a plus de	Ça fait combien?	Et avec ça?	Pourquoi?
je regrette	bon(ne)		parce que

VIDÉOTOUR

Épisode 6

In this video episode, you will join Manu and Vincent as they do their food shopping. See page 531 for more information.

CHAPITRE 7

Les vêtements

Objectifs

In this chapter you will learn to:

- ✔ *identify and describe articles of clothing*
- ✔ *state color and size preferences*
- ✔ *shop for clothing*
- ✔ *describe people's activities*
- ✔ *compare people and things*
- ✔ *express opinions and make observations*
- ✔ *discuss clothes and clothes shopping in the French-speaking world*

Un tissu de la Côte d'Ivoire

French Online
To interact with your online edition of
Bon voyage! go to: glencoe.com.

Les vêtements

SUNSHINE STATE STANDARDS

This chapter is all about clothing. The material in the chapter will address the Sunshine State Standards listed below.

FL.A.1.1.1	express likes and dislikes when asked simple questions (e.g., about toys or other objects).
FL.A.1.2.1	express likes or dislikes regarding various objects, categories, people, and events present in the everyday environment.
FL.A.1.2.2	exchange information necessary to plan events or activities (e.g., picnics, birthday parties, science projects, and crafts).
FL.A.2.1.2	restate and rephrase simple information from materials presented orally, visually, and graphically in class.
FL.A.2.1.3	understand oral messages that are based on familiar themes and vocabulary (e.g., short conversations between familiar persons on familiar topics such as everyday school and home activities).
FL.A.2.2.3	organize information in spoken or written form about a variety of topics of academic and cultural interest (e.g., by making lists, categorizing objects, or organizing concepts).
FL.A.2.2.5	comprehend and respond to oral messages (e.g., personal anecdotes or narratives) based on familiar themes and vocabulary.
FL.A.3.1.1	provide simple information in spoken form (e.g., descriptions of family members, friends, objects present in his or her everyday environment, or common school and home activities).
FL.A.3.2.1	describe important people (e.g., family members and friends) and objects present in his or her everyday environment and in school.
FL.A.3.2.3	give responses in spoken or written form (e.g., answering simple questions, formulating questions, and making simple statements) to age-appropriate stories, poems or other literature, songs, films, or visual works.
FL.B.1.1.1	participate in age-appropriate cultural activities (e.g., games, songs, birthday celebrations, storytelling, dramatizations, and role playing).

St. Augustine, Florida

FL.B.1.1.3 recognize various familiar objects and norms of the target culture (e.g., toys, dresses, and typical foods).

FL.C.1.2.1 participate in activities in the language class designed to integrate content-area concepts (e.g., mathematical calculations or cause-and-effect relationships) into target-language instruction (e.g., about countries or cultures).

FL.D.1.1.2 use simple vocabulary and short phrases in the target language.

FL.D.2.2.2 recognize forms of the target language evident in the local culture (e.g., signs, symbols, advertisements, packages, displays, murals, songs, and rhymes).

TIPS FOR SUCCESS

Review the Study Tips below to help you succeed on the Sunshine State Standards identified.

Alligator, Everglades National Park

Vocabulaire Mots 1 Mots 2 *(pages 220–227)*

- Look at illustrations in **Mots 1** and repeat each word aloud.

- Write each word for additional reinforcement.

- When you have finished studying the vocabulary, determine how much you remember. Say to yourself or aloud all the items you know for boy's clothing, girl's clothing, and unisex clothing. When you get dressed in the morning for school, notice how many words you know in French for those items you are wearing.

- After studying the vocabulary in **Mots 2**, make a list of the things that you would most probably want to say in French to a salesperson when shopping for clothes. **FL.D.1.1.2; FL.A.2.2.3; FL.B.1.1.1**

Review These vocabulary activities contain many adjectives, or descriptive words. Remember that many adjectives have an **e** when used with a feminine noun. They drop the **e** when used with a masculine noun.

	verte.		vert.
	grise.		gris.
La jupe est	petite.	Le blouson est	petit.
	grande.		grand.
	bleue		bleu.
	jolie.		joli.

Structure Le comparatif des adjectifs *(pages 230–231)*

- Remember to make the association that **plus** (+) is more; **moins** (−) is less, and **aussi** (=) is the same. All three words are followed by **que**.

- As you do these activities, pay particular attention to each adjective. **FL.D.1.2.2**

Conversation *(page 234)*

This conversation should be very easy for you. You have already learned all the French that is used in the conversation. When practicing this conversation with a classmate, feel free to make as many changes as you want, as long as they make sense. **FL.A.2.1.2**

> **For other tips to help you address the Sunshine State Standards in Chapter 7, see pages H61 and H62 at the back of your textbook.**

Vocabulaire

FLORIDA
Use your StudentWorks Plus
CD for more practice.

Les vêtements sport 🎧

un short

une casquette

un sweat-shirt

un anorak

un pull

un blouson

un t-shirt

un polo
(à manches courtes)

un jean

un survêtement

des sandales

une basket

une paire de
chaussures

une chaussette

un manteau

Les vêtements pour hommes 🎧

un centre commercial

une boutique

une chemise (à manches longues)

un complet

une veste

une cravate

un pantalon

Marc porte des sandales.
Il voit des chaussures
    dans la vitrine.
Il entre dans la boutique.

plus cher

le prix

35€

20€

moins cher

Les prix sont moins chers
    quand il y a des soldes.

Les vêtements pour femmes 🎧

Johanne va au grand magasin.
Elle voit beaucoup de chemisiers.
Elle voit des chemisiers au rayon des
    vêtements pour femmes.
Tous les chemisiers sont en solde!

Qu'est-ce que je vais
mettre samedi?

une robe sport

un chemisier

un tailleur

une jupe plissée

une
vendeuse

une robe
habillée

Quel est le mot?

1 FL.A.3.2.3 (I)

Chloé et Adrien Répondez d'après les photos. *(Answer according to the photos.)*

1. Qu'est-ce que Chloé porte?
2. Et Adrien? Qu'est-ce qu'il porte?

2 FL.D.1.1.2 (I)

Qu'est-ce qu'on va mettre?
Répondez. *(Answer.)*

1. Ce soir M. Ben Azar va aller dans un restaurant chic. Qu'est-ce qu'il va mettre?
2. Qu'est-ce que sa femme va mettre?
3. Qu'est-ce que tu portes à l'école?
4. Qu'est-ce que tu portes à la maison?
5. Qu'est-ce qu'on porte en juillet et en août?
6. Qu'est-ce qu'on porte en décembre et janvier?
7. Qu'est-ce qu'une femme porte quand elle va travailler?
8. Qu'est-ce qu'un homme porte quand il va au travail?

Chloé

Adrien

La vitrine d'une boutique, Paris

3 **Sport ou habillé?** Identifiez. *(Tell whether each item is casual or formal.)*

1. des baskets
2. un tailleur
3. un jean
4. un complet
5. un blouson
6. une cravate
7. un polo à manches courtes
8. une chemise à manches longues
9. un survêtement
10. une jupe plissée

4 **Historiette** **Au rayon des chemisiers** Inventez une histoire.
(Make up a story.)

1. Mélanie entre dans un grand magasin ou dans une boutique?
2. La boutique est dans une rue ou dans un centre commercial?
3. Il y a des soldes aujourd'hui?
4. Il y a des chemisiers dans la vitrine?
5. Elle va au rayon des chemisiers?
6. Elle voit beaucoup de chemisiers?
7. Elle parle à la vendeuse?
8. Elle veut un chemisier à manches courtes ou à manches longues?
9. Elle veut un chemisier habillé ou sport?
10. Les chemisiers sont en solde?
11. Les vêtements sont moins chers quand ils sont en solde?

FL.A.2.2.5 (I)

5 **C'est qui?** Work with a classmate. One of you describes what someone in the class is wearing and the other has to guess who it is. Take turns.

French Online
For a fun way to review this vocabulary, go to the Chapter 7 **eGame** on the Glencoe French Web site at glencoe.com.

FL.A.1.2.1 (I)

6 **Mon ensemble favori** Work with a classmate. Discuss what you consider an ideal outfit for school. Tell what you like to wear and what you don't like to wear. See if you are on the same wavelength.

Des jeunes habillés sport

*For more practice using words from **Mots 1**, do Activity 20 on page H21 at the end of this book.*

Vocabulaire

On fait des courses. 🎧

le shopping

une cabine d'essayage

essayer

Julien essaie le pantalon.

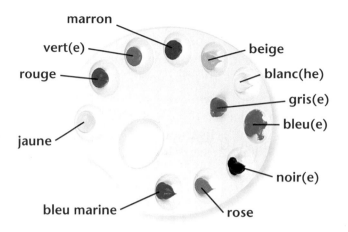

marron
vert(e)
rouge
jaune
bleu marine
beige
blanc(he)
gris(e)
bleu(e)
noir(e)
rose

De quelle couleur est la jupe?
Elle est verte.

Et les chaussures?
Elles sont marron.

Note
The following colors are invariable. They do not change to agree with the noun they modify.

bleu marine   **marron**   **orange**

À mon avis, la robe rouge est plus jolie que la (robe) verte.

Moi, je crois que j'aime mieux la (robe) verte.

Moi, le rouge, c'est ma couleur favorite.

Quel est le mot?

7 **Historiette** **Olivier fait des courses.** Inventez une histoire.
(Make up a story.)

1. Olivier fait des courses?
2. Il veut acheter un blue jean?
3. Il voit un jean qu'il aime dans la vitrine?
4. Il entre dans le grand magasin?
5. Il fait quelle taille?
6. Il va essayer le jean?
7. Il est comment, le pantalon—grand, petit, juste à sa taille?
8. Il veut la taille au-dessus ou la taille au-dessous?
9. Les jeans sont en solde?
10. Ils sont moins chers quand ils sont en solde?
11. Olivier trouve que les jeans sont chers?
12. Olivier va acheter le jean?

Rayon des vêtements pour hommes, Galeries Lafayette, Paris

FL.A.1.1.1 (I)

8 **Ta couleur favorite** Donnez des réponses personnelles.
(Give your own answers.)

1. De quelle couleur est ton blouson favori?
2. De quelle couleur est ton jean favori?
3. De quelle couleur est ta chemise favorite ou ton chemisier favori?
4. Qu'est-ce que tu portes aujourd'hui? De quelle couleur sont tes vêtements?

FL.A.1.1.1 (I)

9 **Mes préférences** Donnez des réponses personnelles.
(Give your own answers.)

1. Tu aimes mieux les vêtements sport ou habillés?
2. Les baskets ou les chaussures?
3. Les chemises ou les chemisiers à manches longues ou à manches courtes?
4. Les vêtements un peu serrés ou larges?
5. Les couleurs sombres ou les couleurs claires?
6. Les vêtements chers ou pas chers?

10 De petits problèmes Répondez. *(Answer.)*

1. Les chaussures sont trop petites ou trop grandes?

2. La jupe est trop longue ou trop courte?

3. Le pantalon est un peu serré ou un peu large?

4. Les manches sont trop longues ou trop courtes?

5. Le tailleur est joli ou pas?

11 Les couleurs Complétez d'après la couleur. *(Complete with the color.)*

1. Aurélien va acheter un pantalon ____.

2. Anne va acheter un chemisier ____.

3. Fred va acheter une chemise ____.

4. Justine va acheter une robe ____.

5. Mélodie va acheter une jupe ____.

6. Cyril va acheter des chaussures ____.

12 Jeu

FL.A.2.2.5 (I) FL.A.3.1.1 (I)

Qui porte une jupe bleue? Study the clothing of all the students in the next row for several minutes. Then turn your back to that row. One of your classmates will mention an item of clothing and ask you who is wearing it. If you don't remember, your classmates can help you out by giving hints such as: **La personne est blonde. Elle est très amusante.**

 *For more practice using words from **Mots 2**, do Activity 21 on page H22 at the end of this book.*

Structure

Le verbe mettre au présent
Describing people's activities

FLORIDA
Use your **StudentWorks** *Plus*
CD for more practice.

1. Study the forms of the verb **mettre** *(to put, to put on)* in the present tense.

METTRE			
je	mets	nous	mettons
tu	mets	vous	mettez
il/elle/on	met	ils/elles	mettent

2. Note that **mettre** has various meanings.

> Il **met** une chemise et une cravate pour aller au travail.
> Les serveurs **mettent** la table au restaurant.
> On **met** la télévision pour regarder un film.

French Online
To investigate French clothing fashions and French designers, do the **WebQuest** activity on the Glencoe French Web site at glencoe.com.

Comment dit-on?

13 **Qu'est-ce qu'on met?**
Répondez. *(Answer.)*

1. Tu mets un survêtement quand tu fais du jogging?
2. Tu mets la table pour le dîner?
3. Ton père met la télé le matin pendant le petit déjeuner?
4. Ta mère met la radio pour écouter les informations?
5. Tes copains mettent une cravate pour aller à l'école?
6. Tes copines mettent une jupe plissée pour aller à l'école?

Des amis devant l'école

14 **Dans le sac à dos** Complétez avec **mettre** d'après les dessins.
(Complete with mettre *according to the illustrations.)*

1. Qu'est-ce qu'ils _____ dans
   leur sac à dos?
   Ils _____.

2. Qu'est-ce que tu _____ dans
   ton sac à dos?
   Je _____.

3. Qu'est-ce que vous _____ dans votre sac à dos?
   On _____.

FL.A.3.1.1 (I)

15 **Qu'est-ce que vous mettez?** Work with a
classmate. Compare what you wear on different occasions.

- pour aller à l'école
- quand vous allez dîner chez des amis
  de vos parents
- pour aller au cinéma le samedi soir
- pour aller à un mariage
- pour aller dans un restaurant chic

Complétez et prononcez.
(Complete and pronounce aloud.)

1. sérieux
   un élève _____ et une élève _____

2. long
   une jupe _____ et un manteau _____

3. favori
   mon pull _____ et ma robe _____

4. blanc
   une chemise _____ et un chemisier _____

5. long
   des pantalons _____ et des manches _____

Attention!

Pay particular attention to the spelling
and pronunciation of the following
adjectives. Note that the final consonant
sound is pronounced in the feminine
forms but not in the masculine forms.

FÉMININ	MASCULIN
sérieuse(s)	sérieux
longue(s)	long(s)
favorite(s)	favori(s)
blanche(s)	blanc(s)

Note that all forms of **cher—chère(s)**,
cher(s)—sound alike.

For more practice using the verb
***mettre,** do Activity 22 on page H23*
at the end of this book.

Le comparatif des adjectifs
Comparing people and things

1. When you compare two or more people or things, you use **plus (+)… que, moins (−)… que,** and **aussi (=)… que.** Study the following chart.

> Le jean est plus   cher que le pantalon.
> Le jean est aussi   cher que le pantalon.
> Le jean est moins cher que le pantalon.

Les sandales sont moins confortables que les baskets.
Mais elles sont plus confortables que les chaussures.

Attention!

Note the liaison with **plus** and **moins.**
plus‿intéressant(e)
moins‿élégant(e)

2. You use the stress pronouns **moi, toi, lui, elle, nous, vous, eux,** and **elles** after **que (qu')** when comparing people.

> Elle est plus   sympa que moi.
> Elle est aussi   sympa que lui.
> Elle est moins sympa que vous.

Il est aussi intelligent que moi.
Mais il est plus intelligent qu'eux.

Comment dit-on?

FL.A.1.2.1 (M)

16 **À mon avis** Donnez des réponses personnelles. *(Give your own answers.)*

1. Le français, c'est plus difficile ou plus facile que les maths?
2. Le professeur de français est plus strict, moins strict ou aussi strict que les autres professeurs?
3. Le football américain est plus amusant ou moins amusant que le basket-ball?
4. Ton école secondaire est plus grande ou moins grande que ton école primaire?
5. Ta classe de français est aussi grande ou plus petite que ta classe de sciences?

17 **Plus ou moins que l'autre** Répondez d'après les dessins.
Suivez le modèle. *(Answer according to the illustrations.)*

—Le blouson bleu est aussi grand que le blouson noir?
—Oui, le blouson bleu est aussi grand que le blouson noir.
1. Le blouson bleu est aussi cher que le blouson noir?
2. Le blouson bleu est moins beau que le blouson noir?
3. La jupe jaune est moins chère que la jupe grise?
4. La jupe grise est plus courte que la jupe jaune?

18 **Ma famille et mes copains** Donnez des réponses personnelles. *(Give your own answers.)*

1. Ta sœur, elle est plus petite ou plus grande que toi?
   Tu es plus grand(e) ou plus petit(e) qu'elle?
2. Tu es plus patient(e) ou moins patient(e) que ton frère?
   Il est plus patient ou moins patient que toi?
3. Tes grands-parents sont aussi stricts que tes parents?
   Ils sont vraiment moins stricts qu'eux?
4. Tes copains sont plus sociables que toi?
   Tu es plus timide qu'eux?

FL.A.3.1.1 (I)

19 **Comparaisons** Work with a classmate. Compare people you know. You may want to use the following words.

grand   petit   sociable   intéressant   dynamique

amusant   beau   sympa   sérieux

deux cent trente et un ❖ 231

Les verbes voir et croire
Seeing and believing

Study the forms of the verbs **voir** (*to see*) and **croire** (*to believe*).

VOIR	CROIRE
je vois	je crois
tu vois	tu crois
il/elle/on voit	il/elle/on croit
nous voyons	nous croyons
vous voyez	vous croyez
ils/elles voient	ils/elles croient

Savez-vous que... ?

When **voir** and **croire** are followed by a clause, you must use **que (qu')**.
Je vois que vous êtes content.
Je crois qu'il est content aussi.

Comment dit-on?

20 **À votre avis** Répondez que oui. (*Answer* yes.)

1. Vos parents croient que vous êtes intelligents?
2. Votre professeur de français croit que vous travaillez bien?
3. Vos camarades de classe croient que vous êtes sympathiques?
4. Vos grands-parents croient que vous êtes adorables?

21 **Dans une boutique**
Répondez que oui. (*Answer* yes.)

1. Tu vois des choses que tu aimes dans la vitrine?
2. Tu crois qu'on peut entrer dans la boutique?
3. Tu crois que tu vas acheter le pantalon noir?
4. Tu crois qu'ils vont avoir ta taille?
5. Tu vois le prix?

22 **Vraiment?** Conversez d'après le modèle.
(*Make up a conversation according to the model.*)

—**Il va bientôt arriver.**
—**Vous croyez?**

1. Il va bientôt téléphoner.
2. Il va bientôt payer.
3. Il va bientôt rentrer.
4. Il va bientôt acheter une maison.

23 **Des opinions différentes!** Complétez avec **croire**.
(Complete with croire.*)*

1. Il _____ que tout est moins cher pendant les soldes. Et vous, vous _____ ça aussi?

2. Julien _____ que l'examen va être facile, mais nous, on _____ qu'il va être difficile.

3. Tu _____ que les chats sont plus intelligents que les chiens, mais moi, je _____ que les chiens sont plus intelligents que les chats.

4. Alice _____ que Paris est près de Nice, mais nous, nous _____ que c'est loin de Nice.

5. Moi, je _____ que la cousine de Sandra est française, mais mes copains _____ qu'elle est italienne.

Attention!

Pay particular attention to the spelling of verbs that end in **–yer**.

ESSAYER	j'essaie	nous essayons
	tu essaies	vous essayez
	il essaie	ils essaient
PAYER	je paie	nous payons
	tu paies	vous payez
	il paie	ils paient

Complétez. *(Complete.)*

1. Vous _____ où? (payer)

2. On _____ à la caisse. (payer)

3. Je _____ parce que j'invite. (payer)

4. Il va _____ la chemise? (essayer)

5. Non, mais il _____ le pantalon. (essayer)

ENCORE PLUS

*For more practice using the verbs **voir** and **croire**, do Activity 23 on page H24 at the end of this book.*

Vous êtes sur le bon chemin. Allez-y!

Conversation

FL.A.2.1.3 (I)

Dans une petite boutique

Vendeur: Bonjour, monsieur. Vous voulez voir quelque chose?

Fabien: Bonjour. Oui, je voudrais un jean, s'il vous plaît.

Vendeur: Oui, vous faites quelle taille?

Fabien: Je fais du 36.

Vendeur: Voilà un 36. La cabine d'essayage est juste là.
(Fabien essaie le jean dans la cabine d'essayage.)

Vendeur: Ça va, la taille?

Fabien: Pas vraiment. Je crois que c'est un peu petit.

Vendeur: Vous voulez la taille au-dessus?

Fabien: Oui, je veux bien.
(Fabien essaie l'autre jean.)

Fabien: Ah oui, c'est bien.

Vendeur: Vous désirez autre chose?

Fabien: Oui, un polo bleu marine ou blanc.

Vendeur: Vous avez de la chance. Ils sont en solde.

Vous avez compris?

Répondez. *(Answer.)*

1. À qui parle Fabien?
2. Qu'est-ce qu'il veut voir?
3. Il fait quelle taille?
4. Où est-ce qu'il essaie son jean?
5. Le jean est trop grand ou trop petit?
6. Il veut la taille au-dessus ou la taille au-dessous?
7. Il veut acheter autre chose?

Parlons un peu plus

A **Au magasin** Work with a classmate. Take turns playing the role of the salesperson and the customer in the following situations.

- **Au rayon des vêtements pour hommes** You want to buy a shirt as a gift for your father or a friend. They have his size but not the color you want.

- **Au rayon des chaussures** You are looking for a pair of brown shoes. The ones the salesperson shows you are quite expensive.

B **Jeu** **Qu'est-ce qu'il/elle porte?** Have one student leave the room while others choose a classmate to describe. The student who left comes back in and has to guess which classmate the others have chosen by asking questions about his or her clothes.

Prononciation

Les sons /sh/ et /zh/ 🎧

It is important to make a distinction between the sounds /sh/ as in **chat** and /zh/ as in **joli.** Put your fingers on your throat. When you say the sound /zh/ as in **joli,** you should feel a vibration, but not when you say /sh/ as in **chat.** Repeat the following words with the sound /sh/.

acheter	chaussure	chemise
chemisier	achat	short

Now repeat the following words with the sound /zh/.

large	jupe	orange
beige	joli	

Now repeat the following sentences that combine both sounds.

J'achète toujours mes chaussures au marché.
Le t-shirt jaune est joli, mais le short orange est moins cher.

chemise orange

Lectures culturelles

FL.B.1.1.3 (I)

On fait des courses où, à Paris?

Chez les grands couturiers[1]

Les noms des grands couturiers français—Yves Saint-Laurent, Dior, Cardin, Givenchy, Coco Chanel—sont célèbres dans le monde entier. On peut voir les boutiques élégantes des grands couturiers dans l'avenue Montaigne ou dans la rue du Faubourg-Saint-Honoré. C'est là que les gens aisés (riches) vont acheter leurs vêtements et accessoires.

Rue du Faubourg-Saint-Honoré, Paris

Magasin de la Samaritaine, Paris

Les petites boutiques et les grands magasins

Mais la plupart (la majorité) des Parisiens ne font pas leurs achats chez les grands couturiers. Partout à Paris, il y a de petites boutiques qui sont beaucoup moins chères que les boutiques des grands couturiers. Il y a aussi des grands magasins. À Paris, les grands magasins du Printemps et des Galeries Lafayette sont les plus renommés (célèbres). Il y a aussi des chaînes de magasins bon marché[2] comme le Prisunic.

Dans les grands magasins, on peut aller d'un rayon à un autre. Il y a souvent des articles en promotion[3] et deux fois par an il y a des soldes—début janvier et début juillet.

[1] grands couturiers *designers*
[2] bon marché *inexpensive*
[3] en promotion *on special*

Haïti

La Martinique

FLORIDA
Use your **StudentWorks** Plus™
CD for more practice.

Les marchés aux puces[4]

Les adolescents aiment bien aller aux puces. Ils y vont pendant le week-end parce que les marchés aux puces sont fermés[5] pendant la semaine.

Les marchés aux puces sont de grands marchés où on trouve de tout—des vêtements, de la nourriture, des tables, des chaises, etc. On peut trouver un vêtement ou un accessoire avec la griffe[6] d'un grand couturier très bon marché… ou très cher!

[4] marchés aux puces *flea markets*
[5] fermés *closed*
[6] griffe *label*

Marché aux puces, Saint-Ouen, Paris

Vous avez compris?

A Des informations Donnez les informations suivantes. *(Give the following information.)*

1. les noms de quelques grands couturiers français
2. les noms de quelques rues très élégantes à Paris
3. là où la plupart des Parisiens vont faire leurs achats
4. le nom d'un grand magasin parisien assez élégant
5. le nom d'une chaîne de magasins aux prix plus modestes
6. là où les adolescents aiment faire leurs achats

B Les achats Vrai ou faux? *(True or false?)*

1. La plupart des Parisiens font leurs achats chez les grands couturiers.
2. Les petites boutiques sont plus chères que les boutiques des grands couturiers.
3. Les Galeries Lafayette, c'est le nom d'un grand magasin à Paris.
4. Les grands magasins n'ont pas de soldes.
5. On va souvent au marché aux puces le lundi.
6. On peut acheter beaucoup de marchandises différentes dans un marché aux puces.

Marché aux puces, Nice

FL.B.1.1.3 (I)

Les vêtements

En Afrique du Nord

Dans les pays du Maghreb (le Maroc, l'Algérie et la Tunisie), beaucoup de gens[1] vont dans les souks pour acheter leurs vêtements. Un souk est un grand marché, souvent situé dans la médina, le vieux quartier d'une ville arabe. Dans les pays du Maghreb, beaucoup d'hommes portent un pull et un jean. Beaucoup de femmes portent une jupe et un chemisier. Mais on voit souvent des vêtements plus traditionnels. On voit des hommes qui portent une djellaba, par exemple. En Tunisie, beaucoup de femmes ont un sifsari. Le sifsari est un type de voile[2]. Le sifsari n'a pas de signification religieuse.

Deux hommes en djellaba, Tunisie

Un souk, Marrakech, Maroc

En Afrique Occidentale

Dans les pays d'Afrique Occidentale, les femmes portent souvent un boubou. Un boubou est une longue tunique ample. Les boubous sont très jolis. Les hommes aussi portent un boubou. Ils portent un boubou par-dessus[3] un pantalon et une chemise.

[1] gens *people*
[2] voile *veil*
[3] par-dessus *on top of, over*

Deux femmes en boubou, Sénégal

Vous avez compris?

Quel est le mot? Identifiez le mot.
(Identify the word.)
1. un marché arabe
2. le vieux quartier d'une ville arabe
3. un vêtement masculin des pays du Maghreb
4. un type de voile tunisien
5. un vêtement porté par les hommes et les femmes en Afrique Occidentale

FL.A.2.1.2 (I)

Les tailles

En France et dans les autres pays d'Europe, les pointures et les tailles ne sont pas les mêmes qu'aux États-Unis. Voici des tableaux qui indiquent les correspondances.

FEMMES				
Chaussures				
États-Unis	6	7	8	9
France	36	37	38	39
Robes, Tailleurs, Pulls, Chemisiers				
États-Unis	6	8	10	12	14
France	38	40	42	44	46

HOMMES				
Chaussures				
États-Unis	9	10	11	12
France	40	41	42	43
Chemises				
États-Unis	$14\frac{1}{2}$	15	$15\frac{1}{2}$	16	$16\frac{1}{2}$
France	37	38	39	40	41

Si vous trouvez des chaussures que vous aimez et que vous voulez acheter, vous allez demander quelle pointure?

Si vous voyez une chemise ou un chemisier que vous voulez acheter, vous allez demander quelle taille?

Vous avez compris?

Moi Donnez des réponses personnelles.
(*Give your own answers.*)
1. Vous êtes en France. Vous voulez des chaussures. Vous faites quelle pointure?
2. Vous voulez une chemise ou un chemisier. Quelle est votre taille?

La Belgique

La Tunisie

Le Maroc

Le Mali

CONNEXIONS

Les lettres

La poésie

A poem is a literary piece most often written in verse. The poet uses images, meter, rhythm, and sounds to evoke or suggest ideas, sensations, and emotions in the reader. Many poets say a great deal in very few words. The poem we are about to read by the French poet Apollinaire is an example.

Apollinaire (1880–1918)

Guillaume Apollinaire a une vie[1] bohème. Sa poésie reflète sa vie. Il visite beaucoup de pays européens. Les mouvements intellectuels et artistiques de son époque intéressent Apollinaire. C'est une période (avant la guerre[2] de 1914) très riche en idées. Les poètes et les artistes peintres échangent leurs nouvelles idées. Apollinaire discute ses idées avec son bon ami, le peintre Picasso.

Apollinaire est un des premiers grands poètes modernes français. Certains de ses poèmes sont des calligrammes. Le poème a la forme de l'objet que le poète décrit[3]. Le poème «La cravate» est un exemple de calligramme.

[1] vie *life*
[2] guerre *war*
[3] décrit *describes*

Pablo Picasso

Giorgio de Chirico *Guillaume Apollinaire*

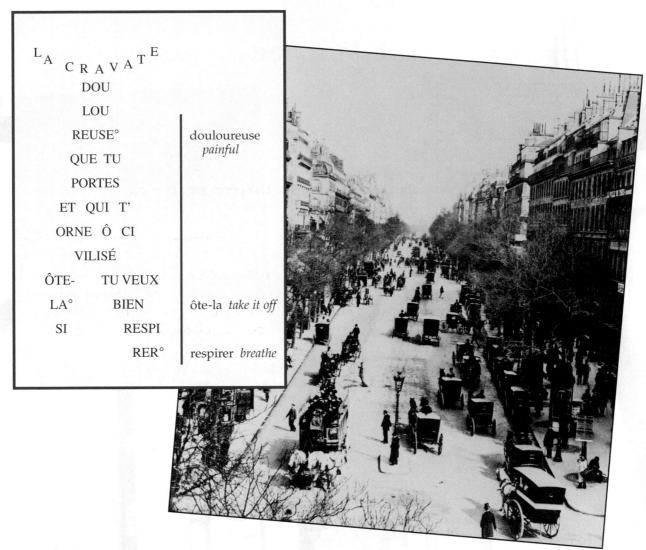

```
L A       T E
  A  C R A V A
      DOU
      LOU
      REUSE°           douloureuse
                       painful
      QUE TU
      PORTES
    ET  QUI  T'
  ORNE  Ô  CI
      VILISÉ
  ÔTE-      TU VEUX
  LA°       BIEN        ôte-la take it off
  SI        RESPI
            RER°        respirer breathe
```

Paris vers 1900

Vous avez compris?

A Mes idées Répondez. *(Answer.)*

1. Si tu es un garçon, tu aimes mettre une cravate?
2. Si tu es une fille, tu trouves que c'est une bonne idée d'obliger un garçon à porter une cravate?
3. Apollinaire aime les cravates?
4. Il croit qu'on peut bien respirer si on porte une cravate?

B Explication du texte Explain in English
Apollinaire's ideas and tell whether you agree with him.

Use what you have learned

PARLER

1

FL.A.3.1.1 (I)

Une fête

✔ *Identify and describe articles of clothing*

You are talking with a friend after school. You are both invited to a party, but you don't know what to wear. Discuss what kind of a party it is and what would be appropriate.

PARLER

2

FL.A.1.2.1 (I)

Un nouveau look

✔ *State your color and style preferences in clothes*

You and your partner have decided that you are going to change your style of clothes. Discuss what the new "you" is going to look like.

Des amies à Ouagadougou, Burkina Faso

PARLER

3

ÉCRIRE

FL.B.1.1.1 (I)

Des cadeaux

✔ *Shop for clothing*

You have just spent a few weeks in France and want to buy some gifts for family and friends back home. Make a list of what you want to buy. Go to different stores to buy the items you want. With a classmate, take turns being the customer and salesperson at the stores where you are purchasing the items on your list.

ÉCRIRE

4 FL.D.1.1.2 (I)   FL.D.2.2.2 (I)

On commande des vêtements.
✔ *Order clothing from a catalogue and give color preferences and size*

You want to order from the catalogue to the right. Write a letter stating which items you want, what color, what size.

ÉCRIRE

5 FL.D.1.1.2 (I)

Le catalogue
✔ *Write descriptions of clothing*

Write five descriptions for an online clothing catalogue. Describe the items, tell the sizes they come in, the colors, the occasions they could be worn for, and the prices.

REVUE DE DETAILS
NEWS MODE Repéré aux quatre coins de la mode, tout ce qui nous plaît. De la tête aux pieds.

Coloris: noir, beige.
Tailles: du 36 au 40 pour la femme; du 40 au 45 pour l'homme.

modèle femme
du 36 au 40   76,07 €
modèle homme
du 40 au 45   76,07 €

l'une
15,23 €   **Chemise**
77% viscose, 23% polyester.
Coloris assortis.
Du 37/38 au 43/44.

l'une
15,23 €   **Cravate**
100% soie.
Coloris assortis.

(1) Robe en velours (150 €, 5 tailles, 8 coloris).
(2) Veste sur jupe en taffetas de soie (75 €, 3 tailles, 5 coloris (veste) et 150 €, du 36 au 42, en noir ou bronze (jupe)).

Writing Strategy

Clustering   Most writers brainstorm ideas before they begin to write. The next logical step is to "cluster" these ideas. This is done by writing down your main ideas and drawing a box around each one. Then draw a line indicating which ideas are connected to each other. Once you do this, it is easy to add other details to each cluster of ideas. When beginning to write, sort out your clusters and present each in a logical and organized paragraph.

Quel est leur look?

ÉCRIRE

6 FL.A.3.2.1 (I)

Le look de ton école

Write a note to your French friend describing **le look** at your school. Tell him or her what boys and girls usually wear to school and what types of clothing and colors are "in" (**à la mode**).

Assessment

Vocabulaire

To review **Mots 1**, turn to pages 220–221.

1 Identifiez. *(Identify.)*

1.
2.
3.
4.

To review **Mots 2**, turn to pages 224–225.

2 Complétez. *(Complete.)*

5. —_____, le pantalon?
   —Non, il est trop grand.
6. —Vous faites quelle ____?
   —Je fais du 38, pour les chemises.
7. —De quelle ____ est la jupe?
   —Elle est grise.
8. —Le jean est trop petit.
   —Je voudrais la taille ____.

Structure

To review the verb **mettre**, turn to page 228.

3 Complétez avec «mettre». *(Complete with* mettre.*)*

9. Les garçons ne ____ pas de cravate pour aller à l'école.
10. Après le dîner je ____ la télé.
11. Qu'est-ce que vous ____ quand vous faites du jogging?
12. Qu'est-ce que tu ____ dans ton sac à dos?

To review the forms of these adjectives, turn to page 229.

4 Complétez. *(Complete.)*

13. C'est ma boutique ____. (favori)
14–15. La chemise est ____ et le pantalon est ____ aussi. (blanc)
16. Elle met une robe ____. (long)

5 Complétez. *(Complete.)*

17. —Jean est très sympa.
    —Oui. Mais il n'est pas ____ sympa ____ toi.
18. —Ce jean ne coûte pas cher.
    —Non, il est ____ cher ____ les autres.
19. —Les deux frères sont très intelligents.
    —C'est vrai. Paul est ____ intelligent ____ Loïc.

To review the comparative of adjectives, turn to page 230.

6 Récrivez chaque phrase. *(Rewrite each sentence.)*

20. Je crois que oui.
    Vous ____.
21. Elle voit de jolies chaussures dans la vitrine.
    Elles ____.
22. Vous voyez ça?
    Tu ____?

To review the verbs **voir** and **croire**, turn to page 232.

Culture

7 Vrai ou faux? *(True or false?)*

23. Les boutiques des grands couturiers sont très chères.
24. Un grand magasin a beaucoup de rayons différents.
25. On trouve les marchés aux puces dans les quartiers élégants de Paris.

To review this cultural information, turn to pages 236–237.

La boutique d'un grand couturier, Paris

French Online
For more Chapter 7 test preparation, go to the Chapter 7 **Self-Check Quiz** on the Glencoe French Web site at glencoe.com.

Do these practice activities to help you succeed on your FCAT through the study of a foreign language.

Read the story below. Then answer the questions that follow.

C'est le mois de septembre et tous les élèves veulent acheter de nouveaux vêtements pour l'école. Annie va au centre commercial. Elle veut acheter une jupe. Dans la vitrine d'un grand magasin elle voit une jupe rouge qu'elle aime. Elle entre dans le magasin et essaie la jupe. Annie fait quelle taille? Elle fait du 36. Mais la jupe est trop serrée. Elle cherche une autre jupe mais elle ne trouve pas la couleur qu'elle préfère. Le rouge est sa couleur favorite. Elle décide d'acheter un chemisier. Elle met le chemisier mais les manches sont trop courtes. Elle voit une robe sport qui est très jolie mais c'est trop chère.

Pauvre Annie! Elle est découragée. Enfin elle va dans un magasin de chaussures. Il y a des chaussures marron qu'elle trouve jolies. La vendeuse demande: «Vous faites quelle pointure?» Annie fait du 38. La vendeuse apporte les chaussures à Annie.

—Ça va?

—Oui! Je veux acheter ces chaussures.

Annie a de la chance. Les chaussures sont en solde!

LA.A.2.4.1 (M)

1 Quel est un bon titre pour cette histoire?
- **A.** Dans une petite boutique
- **B.** Annie fait du shopping
- **C.** Des vêtements pour l'école
- **D.** Les vêtements et les chaussures

2 Pourquoi Annie va-t-elle dans un grand magasin?
- **F.** parce qu'on peut y trouver beaucoup de vêtements différents
- **G.** parce qu'elle n'aime pas les boutiques
- **H.** parce qu'on y vend des chaussures
- **I.** parce qu'il n'y a pas de boutiques dans un centre commercial

3 Quelle phrase est correcte?

    A. Annie aime la jupe mais elle veut la taille au-dessus.

    B. Annie aime la jupe mais elle veut la taille au-dessous.

    C. Les chaussures sont chères mais Annie les achète.

    D. Annie n'achète pas la robe sport parce qu'elle n'aime pas la couleur.

4 Quelle phrase veut dire la même chose?
La jupe est trop serrée.

    F. La jupe est trop chère.

    G. La jupe est trop petite.

    H. La jupe est trop large.

    I. La taille de la jupe est au-dessus de la taille d'Annie.

5 Pourquoi Annie n'achète-t-elle pas une jupe verte?

    A. parce qu'il n'y a pas de jupes de cette couleur dans le magasin

    B. parce qu'elle préfère le rouge

    C. parce qu'elle décide d'acheter un chemisier

    D. parce qu'elle ne trouve pas sa taille

6 READ THINK EXPLAIN Expliquez pourquoi Annie est découragée.

7 Finalement Annie est contente. Pourquoi?

    F. Elle paie moins d'argent pour les chaussures.

    G. La vendeuse est très gentille.

    H. Elle trouve des chaussures rouges.

    I. Les chaussures sont chères.

FCAT Tip

Relax. Some people get nervous about tests. It's natural. Just do your best.

On parle super bien!

FL.A.2.1.2 (I)   FL.A.3.2.1 (I)

Tell all you can about this illustration.

Identifying articles of clothing

les vêtements *(m. pl.)*	une veste	un polo	une basket
un jean	un pantalon	un manteau	une chaussure
un short	un t-shirt	un anorak	une chaussette
une casquette	une sandale	un blouson	
un pull	un sweat-shirt	un survêtement	

Identifying men's clothing

une chemise
une cravate
un complet

Identifying women's clothing

une jupe plissée	une robe
un chemisier	un tailleur

How well do you know your vocabulary?

- Choose words that describe an outfit you would like to have.
- Describe your shopping trip to look for the outfit.

Shopping

une boutique	un vendeur	cher (chère)	trouver
un centre commercial	une vendeuse	faire des courses	mettre
un grand magasin	un rayon	essayer	
une vitrine	des soldes *(m. pl.)*	entrer (dans)	
une cabine d'essayage	le prix	porter	

Describing clothes

large	sport	à manches	la pointure
serré(e)	joli(e)	longues	la taille
habillé(e)	favori(te)	courtes	au-dessus
			au-dessous

Identifying colors

De quelle couleur?	noir(e)	rouge	marron
blanc(he)	gris(e)	beige	orange
brun(e)	bleu(e)	rose	
vert(e)	jaune	bleu marine	

Other useful words and expressions

Vous faites quelle taille?	en solde	voir
Je fais du 40.	à mon avis	croire

VIDÉOTOUR

Épisode 7

In this video episode, you will visit a boutique with Chloé and Christine. See page 532 for more information.

Conversation

Faire la cuisine!

Julie: Tu vas préparer le déjeuner?

Miéna: Moi? Préparer le déjeuner? Tu rigoles!
Je déteste faire la cuisine.

Julie: Tu veux aller au resto, alors?

Miéna: Non, je ne peux pas. Je n'ai pas le
temps. Je vais manger une tranche de
pizza.

Julie: Tu n'as pas le temps d'aller au resto?
Pourquoi?

Miéna: Je veux acheter quelque chose pour
samedi. Je vais à une fête chez une amie.

Julie: Qu'est-ce que tu vas acheter?

Miéna: Je crois que je vais acheter une robe.

Julie: Près de chez moi, il y a des soldes dans
une petite boutique sympa.

Miéna: Merci, mais je vais aller aux Galeries.
Je trouve toujours quelque chose là.

Galeries Lafayette, Paris

Vous avez compris?

Répondez. (*Answer.*)

1. Miéna va préparer le déjeuner?
2. Elle aime faire la cuisine?
3. Elle veut aller déjeuner au restaurant?
4. Elle ne peut pas aller au restaurant?
5. Qu'est-ce qu'elle va manger?
6. Qu'est-ce qu'elle veut acheter?
7. Elle va où samedi?
8. Elle va aller dans quel magasin?

CHAPITRES 5 – 7

Structure

Les verbes irréguliers au présent

1. Review the following irregular verbs.

ALLER	je vais, tu vas, il/elle/on va, nous‿allons, vous‿allez, ils/elles vont
PRENDRE	je prends, tu prends, il/elle/on prend, nous prenons, vous prenez, ils/elles prennent
FAIRE	je fais, tu fais, il/elle/on fait, nous faisons, vous faites, ils/elles font
POUVOIR	je peux, tu peux, il/elle/on peut, nous pouvons, vous pouvez, ils/elles peuvent
VOULOIR	je veux, tu veux, il/elle/on veut, nous voulons, vous voulez, ils/elles veulent
METTRE	je mets, tu mets, il/elle/on met, nous mettons, vous mettez, ils/elles mettent
CROIRE	je crois, tu crois, il/elle/on croit, nous croyons, vous croyez, ils/elles croient
VOIR	je vois, tu vois, il/elle/on voit, nous voyons, vous voyez, ils/elles voient

2. Note that for all the preceding verbs except **aller,** the three singular forms sound alike. For all these verbs except **faire,** the **nous** and **vous** stems are the same.

1 **Historiette** **On fait des courses.** Répondez d'après les indications. *(Answer according to the cues.)*

1. Tu vas aller où? (aux Galeries Lafayette)
2. Qu'est-ce que tu vas faire? (acheter un cadeau)
3. Qu'est-ce que tu veux acheter? (une chemise blanche)
4. C'est pour qui, la chemise? (mon père)
5. Il fait quelle taille? (du 39)
6. Tu vois un chemisier pour ta mère? (oui)
7. Qui met le chemisier dans un sac? (le vendeur)

2 **Historiette** **À l'école** Mettez au pluriel. *(Make the sentences plural.)*

1. Je vais à l'école.
2. Je prends le car pour aller à l'école.
3. Je veux poser une question.
4. L'élève peut poser des questions.
5. Sandrine croit qu'elle a la bonne réponse.
6. Elle prend ses cahiers.

Galeries Lafayette, Paris

Des pâtisseries

Les contractions au et du

The prepositions **à** and **de** contract with **le** to form **au** and **du,** and with **les** to form **aux** and **des.**

à + le = au	Il va au collège.
à + les = aux	Le prof parle aux élèves.
de + le = du	Il rentre du collège.
de + les = des	Il parle des élèves.

3 **Où?** Répondez d'après les indications. *(Answer according to the cues.)*

1. On achète des tartes où? (pâtisserie)
2. Et du saucisson? (charcuterie)
3. Et de l'eau minérale? (épicerie)
4. Et du poisson? (marché)
5. On parle à qui au marché? (marchands)

4 **D'où?** Complétez en utilisant **de** + un article défini. *(Answer with* de *+ a definite article.)*

1. Mon frère rentre _____ lycée.
2. Mon autre frère rentre _____ collège.
3. Ma sœur rentre _____ école.
4. Mon autre sœur rentre _____ cantine.
5. Nous parlons tous _____ professeurs.

 # Le partitif

1. Remember that the partitive, "some," "any," is expressed in French by **de** + the definite article. **De** contracts with **le** to form **du** and with **les** to form **des**. In the negative, **du, de la, de l'**, and **des** all become **de** or **d'**.

Je veux de l'argent.	Je ne veux pas d'argent.
J'ai des croissants.	Je n'ai pas de croissants.

2. Remember that **un** and **une** also become **de** or **d'** after a negative expression.

Tu veux un couteau?	Tu ne veux pas de couteau?
J'ai une serviette.	Je n'ai pas de serviette.

 FL.B.1.1.3 (M)

5 **Dans le chariot** Dites ce qu'il y a dans le chariot. *(Tell what is in the cart.)*

6 **Pas dans le chariot** Dites ce qu'il n'y a pas dans le chariot de l'Activité 5. *(Tell what is not in the cart in Activity 5.)*

FL.A.1.1.1 (M)

7 **J'ai faim.** Répondez d'après le modèle.
(*Answer according to the model.*)

—**Tu veux du poisson?**

—**Non, je ne veux pas de poisson. Je n'aime pas le poisson!**

1. Tu veux du bœuf?
2. Tu veux des œufs?
3. Tu veux des carottes à la crème?
4. Tu veux du poulet?
5. Tu veux de la salade?
6. Tu veux du gâteau au chocolat?

Le comparatif

1. You use the comparative to compare two people or two items.

> **Aurélie est plus (aussi, moins) sportive que son frère.**
> **Le pantalon est plus (aussi, moins) cher que le jean.**

2. You use the stress pronouns **moi, toi, lui, elle, nous, vous, eux,** and **elles** after **que (qu')** when comparing people.

> **Il est moins sympa qu'elle (que toi, qu'eux).**

Marie est plus fatiguée que sa sœur.

8 **Cyril et moi** Répondez d'après le modèle.
(*Answer according to the model.*)

Cyril est très sérieux. ⟶
—**Il est plus sérieux que moi?**
—**Non, il est aussi sérieux que toi.**

1. Cyril est très timide.
2. Cyril est très grand.
3. Cyril est très amusant.
4. Cyril est très patient.
5. Cyril est très beau.
6. Cyril est très sympathique.

9 **Christelle et moi** Remplacez Cyril par Christelle dans l'Activité 8. *(Replace* Cyril *with* Christelle *in Activity 8.)*

FL.B.1.1.1 (I)

10 **Au restaurant** With a classmate, make up a conversation between a server and a customer.

Un restaurant, Paris

11 **Qu'est-ce que tu fais?** Work with a classmate. Ask each other questions about the things you do or want to do. Use the following words in the conversation.

prendre   vouloir   pouvoir   croire   faire   aller

FL.A.1.2.2 (I) **FL.A.2.2.3 (M)**

12 **Des courses** Work with a classmate. Each of you will make up a grocery list. Exchange lists. Then tell each other where you are going to go and what you are going to do.

 LITERARY COMPANION *You may wish to read the poem «Dors mon enfant» by Elolongué Epanya Yondo, on pages 510–511. The activities for this reading will help you continue to practice your reading comprehension skills.*

Florida

Qui habite en Floride?

Il n'y a pas de doute que la population de la Floride est en hausse. Des milliers de nouveaux résidents arrivent chaque jour. Le climat doux et agréable de la Floride les attire[1].

La population de la Floride comprend dix-sept millions de personnes et elle est très hétérogène. La plupart habitent la côte. Il y a beaucoup d'ethnies différentes—des gens d'origine indigène, européenne, africaine, latino-américaine, antillaise et asiatique. Dans les écoles publiques de la Floride il y a des élèves de 280 pays différents qui parlent plus de 260 langues.

Le groupe minoritaire le plus grand, c'est bien sûr les Latino-Américains. À Miami même, il y a beaucoup de personnes d'origine cubaine, mais dans l'état toutes les nations latino-américaines sont représentées.

Le troisième groupe minoritaire des résidents nés hors des[2] États-Unis sont les Haïtiens. En 1991 il y a en Haïti un coup d'État militaire qui renverse[3] le gouvernement du Président Jean-Bertrand Aristide. Des sanctions économiques sont imposées parce que, dans le pays, il y a des abus graves contre les droits de l'homme[4]. Les Haïtiens commencent à fuir[5] leur pays et beaucoup d'entre eux arrivent à Miami où ils établissent un quartier qui s'appelle le Petit Haïti. C'est là où se trouve[6] le Centre des Réfugiés Haïtiens qui donne beaucoup de renseignements[7] sur la vie en Haïti et la vie des Haïtiens en Floride. Il faut signaler qu'il y a des Haïtiens partout en Floride, mais la plupart habitent dans le sud de l'état.

[1]attire *attracts, draws*
[2]nés hors des *born outside of*
[3]renverse *takes down*
[4]droits de l'homme
    human rights
[5]fuir *flee*
[6]se trouve *is located*
[7]renseignements *information*

Un enfant hondurien en Floride

Une cérémonie de naturalisation, le conté Broward

Les Haïtiens parlent créole. Le créole est dérivé du français mais il y a aussi beaucoup d'éléments africains avec quelques mots empruntés à[8] l'anglais et à l'espagnol.

Il y a beaucoup d'émissions de radio haïtiennes. De temps en temps les présentateurs parlent français, la langue officielle d'Haïti, mais le plus souvent, ils parlent créole. Même si vous ne comprenez pas très bien le créole il faut écouter les émissions haïtiennes parce que la musique est magnifique.

Si le troisième groupe de résidents nés hors des États-Unis sont les Haïtiens, quel est le deuxième groupe? Ce sont les Canadiens qui viennent passer les mois d'hiver en Floride. Beaucoup d'entre eux sont des Canadiens français qui fuient le froid de l'hiver québécois. Il est très facile de parler français sur la plage ou dans les supermarchés en Floride.

Les Afro-Américains représentent 16 pour cent de la population totale de l'état, les Asiatiques 2 pour cent et les indigènes 0,4 pour cent.

Il n'y a aucun doute qu'un citoyen de la Floride fait partie d'une communauté très cosmopolite.

[8]empruntés à *borrowed from*

Une petite fille haïtienne, Miami

Florida

Étude de mots

A. Cherchez un mot apparenté.

1. le peuple
2. l'Europe
3. l'Afrique
4. l'Asie
5. la différence
6. gouverner
7. abuser
8. le Canada

B. Choisissez le contraire.

1. en hausse	a. dans
2. doux	b. privé
3. hétérogène	c. en baisse
4. public	d. homogène
5. la minorité	e. sévère
6. hors de	f. la majorité, la plupart

Une maison créole, Pensacola

Compréhension

A. Répondez.

1. Quelle est la population de la Floride?
2. Où habitent la plupart des gens?
3. Quel est le plus grand groupe minoritaire en Floride?
4. Quel pourcentage de la population est d'origine africaine?

La Petite Havane, Miami

B. Vrai ou faux?

1. C'est le centre de l'état qui est le plus peuplé.
2. Les élèves des écoles en Floride parlent très peu de langues.
3. Il y a beaucoup d'Haïtiens qui habitent en Floride.
4. Les Haïtiens arrivent aux États-Unis pour des raisons religieuses.
5. La plupart des Haïtiens habitent dans le nord de la Floride.
6. Les Haïtiens parlent créole.
7. Le créole est dérivé du français.

C. Répondez.

1. Pourquoi la population de la Floride est-elle en hausse?
2. Pourquoi faut-il écouter les émissions haïtiennes à la radio même si on ne comprend pas bien le créole?
3. Pourquoi beaucoup de Canadiens, surtout les Canadiens français du Québec, visitent-ils la Floride?
4. Pourquoi un citoyen de la Floride est-il un citoyen d'une communauté très cosmopolite?

D. Discutez.

1. Dans la région de la Floride où vous habitez, il y a des gens de beaucoup d'ethnies? Quelles ethnies?
2. Dans votre école, il y a beaucoup d'élèves qui parlent d'autres langues? Quelles langues? Et vous? Vous parlez quelle(s) langue(s)?
3. Vous allez quelquefois à un restaurant latino-américain? Quel restaurant? Quand vous allez au restaurant, qu'est-ce que vous mangez?

Des réfugiés haïtiens, Miami, 1992

1. Maisons du pays Dogon au Mali
2. Masque sénoufo de la Côte d'Ivoire
3. Danse rituelle et tambourinaires du Burundi
4. Une petite fille du Mali
5. Dakar, la capitale du Sénégal
6. Youssou N'Dour, le célèbre chanteur pop du Sénégal
7. Un griot raconte aux jeunes du village l'histoire de leurs ancêtres

1

3

2

4

5

6

NATIONAL
GEOGRAPHIC

REFLETS
de l'Afrique

7

8

10

9

11

12

NATIONAL GEOGRAPHIC

REFLETS
de l'Afrique

CHAPITRE 8

L'aéroport et l'avion

Objectifs

In this chapter you will learn to:

✔ *check in for a flight*

✔ *talk about some services aboard the plane*

✔ *talk about more activities*

✔ *ask more questions*

✔ *talk about people and things as a group*

✔ *discuss air travel in France*

René Magritte *La grande famille*

⑧ L'aéroport et l'avion

SUNSHINE STATE STANDARDS

This chapter is all about the airport and plane travel. The material in the chapter will address the Sunshine State Standards listed below.

FL.A.1.1.1 express likes and dislikes when asked simple questions (e.g., about toys or other objects).

FL.A.1.2.2 exchange information necessary to plan events or activities (e.g., picnics, birthday parties, science projects, and crafts).

FL.A.2.1.2 restate and rephrase simple information from materials presented orally, visually, and graphically in class.

FL.A.2.1.3 understand oral messages that are based on familiar themes and vocabulary (e.g., short conversations between familiar persons on familiar topics such as everyday school and home activities).

FL.A.2.2.1 give and understand written and verbal instructions, using known, verbal patterns in the target language.

FL.A.2.2.3 organize information in spoken or written form about a variety of topics of academic and cultural interest (e.g., by making lists, categorizing objects, or organizing concepts).

FL.A.2.2.5 comprehend and respond to oral messages (e.g., personal anecdotes or narratives) based on familiar themes and vocabulary.

FL.A.3.1.1 provide simple information in spoken form (e.g., descriptions of family members, friends, objects present in his or her everyday environment, or common school and home activities).

FL.A.3.2.1 describe important people (e.g., family members and friends) and objects present in his or her everyday environment and in school.

FL.A.3.2.3 give responses in spoken or written form (e.g., answering simple questions, formulating questions, and making simple statements) to age-appropriate stories, poems or other literature, songs, films, or visual works.

FL.B.1.1.1 participate in age-appropriate cultural activities (e.g., games, songs, birthday celebrations, storytelling, dramatizations, and role playing).

FL.C.1.2.1 participate in activities in the language class designed to integrate content-area concepts (e.g., mathematical calculations or cause-and-effect relationships) into target-language instruction (e.g., about countries or cultures).

FL.C.1.2.2 use target-language vocabulary or concepts to reinforce knowledge of a related topic studied in another class (e.g., geographical place names, parts of the body, or basic mathematical operations).

Florida wetlands

FL.C.2.1.1   use the target language to gain access to information that is only available through the target language or within the target culture (listen to a story told in the target language).

FL.D.1.1.2   use simple vocabulary and short phrases in the target language.

FL.D.1.2.2   recognize the similarities and differences between his or her native language and the target language in terms of the pronunciation, alphabet, and forms of written expression.

FL.D.2.2.2   recognize forms of the target language evident in the local culture (e.g., signs, symbols, advertisements, packages, displays, murals, songs, and rhymes).

FL.E.1.2.2   demonstrate an awareness of employment possibilities (and other applications) for those who are able to master the target language.

TIPS FOR SUCCESS

Review the Study Tips below to help you succeed on the Sunshine State Standards identified.

Surfboards

Vocabulaire | **Mots 1** | **Mots 2** | *(pages 260–267)*

- Repeat each new word in the **Mots** sections several times. Look at the photo or illustration as you pronounce the word.

- Listen carefully to what your classmates say when they respond in class. The more you hear people use the new words, the more likely you are to remember them. **FL.A.2.1.2**

Conversation   *(page 276)*

- Listen carefully to the native speaker's intonation or melody on the audio CD or Interactive Conversation video. Then, imitate the native's intonation as closely as you can when you repeat. **FL.D.1.2.2**

 Lectures culturelles   **On va en France.** *(pages 278–279)*

- To figure out the organization of this reading, scan the passage and look for the following information:
  - Who's going where and how?
  - What do they do when they arrive?

- *Sequencing events* is an important reading comprehension skill. Sequence the events in this reading selection. Then see if you came up with a sequence similar to the following:
  - **La classe de Madame Cadet est dans le hall de l'aérogare.**
  - **Les élèves sont dans l'avion.**
  - **Ils arrivent à l'aéroport à Paris.**
  - **Ils visitent la belle ville de Paris. FL.A.2.2.3**

> **For other tips to help you address the Sunshine State Standards in Chapter 8, see pages H62 and H63 at the back of your textbook.**

Vocabulaire

À l'aéroport

le hall de l'aérogare

un agent

le comptoir de la compagnie aérienne

une passagère

un bagage à main

Maintenant Justine est dans le hall de l'aéroport.
Elle fait enregistrer ses bagages.
L'agent vérifie son billet.

Justine choisit une place dans l'avion.
Elle demande une place côté couloir.

une valise

les arrivées

le numéro du vol

un écran

une carte d'embarquement

un passeport

L'avion a du retard.
L'avion n'est pas à l'heure.

un billet

passer par le contrôle
de sécurité

la porte
d'embarquement

F32

le départ

L'avion part de la porte 32.

L'avion atterrit.

la piste

L'avion décolle.

Justine aime voyager.
Elle fait un voyage à Montréal.
Avant le voyage elle fait sa valise.

un vol à destination de Paris = un vol qui va à Paris
un vol en provenance de Lyon = un vol qui arrive de Lyon
un vol intérieur = un vol entre deux villes du même pays (Paris–Lyon)
un vol international = un vol entre deux villes de pays différents (Paris–Rome)

Quel est le mot?

1 **Historiette** **Un voyage à Genève**
Inventez une histoire.

1. Laurence aime voyager?
2. Elle fait un voyage à Genève?
3. Elle fait ses valises avant de partir pour l'aéroport?
4. Elle est au comptoir de la compagnie aérienne?
5. L'agent vérifie son billet et son passeport?
6. Laurence a beaucoup de bagages à main?
7. Elle fait enregistrer ses bagages?
8. Elle choisit une place dans l'avion?
9. Elle veut une place côté couloir ou côté fenêtre?
10. Elle a sa carte d'embarquement?
11. Elle va à la porte d'embarquement?

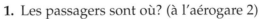

French Online
For a fun way to review this vocabulary, go to the Chapter 8 **eGame** on the Glencoe French Web site at glencoe.com.

Laurence part pour Genève.

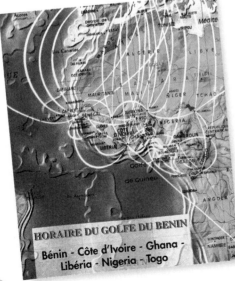

2 **Historiette** **À l'aéroport**
Répondez d'après les indications.

1. Les passagers sont où? (à l'aérogare 2)
2. Leur avion part à quelle heure? (à onze heures trente)
3. Il part de quelle porte? (trente-deux)
4. Qu'est-ce que les passagers regardent pour vérifier la porte et l'heure du départ? (l'écran)
5. Leur avion va partir à l'heure ou va avoir du retard? (va partir à l'heure)
6. Les passagers vont passer par où? (le contrôle de sécurité)
7. Qu'est-ce qu'on annonce? (le départ du vol)
8. Les passagers vont d'Abidjan à Dakar. Ils prennent un vol intérieur? (non, international)
9. L'avion est sur la piste? (oui)
10. Il va décoller ou atterrir? (décoller)
11. L'avion va atterrir à Paris? (non, à Dakar)
12. C'est un vol à destination ou en provenance de Dakar? (à destination)

FL.B.1.1.1 (I)

3

À l'aéroport Work with a classmate. You're checking in at the airport for your flight to Fort-de-France in Martinique. Have a conversation with the airline agent (your partner) at the ticket counter.

Aéroport Charles-de-Gaulle, Roissy

FL.A.2.1.2 (I)

4

Un vol Work with a classmate. Look at the illustration. You are a passenger on this flight. Tell as much as you can about your experience at the airport.

For more practice using words from Mots 1, do Activity 24 on page H25 at the end of this book.

L'AÉROPORT ET L'AVION

Vocabulaire

Mots 2

À bord

un pilote

Le personnel de bord:
le pilote
le steward
l'hôtesse de l'air

C'est un vol non-fumeurs.

la cabine

un coffre à bagages

un siège

un steward

sous le siège

Il faut mettre vos bagages sous le siège devant
vous ou dans le coffre à bagages.

une ceinture de sécurité

Il faut attacher votre
ceinture de sécurité.

une hôtesse de l'air

L'hôtesse de l'air fait une annonce.

Le steward sert des boissons à bord.
On sert un repas.

Vous ne finissez pas votre repas?

Non, merci. Je n'ai plus faim.

On ramasse les plateaux.

Un passager sort ses bagages du coffre à bagages.
Une passagère dort.
Une autre remplit sa carte de débarquement.

Quel est le mot?

5 **Historiette** **À bord de l'avion**

Inventez une histoire.

1. Les passagers sont à bord?
2. Le personnel de bord fait des annonces?
3. Il faut attacher sa ceinture de sécurité avant le décollage?
4. Il faut mettre ses bagages à main sous le siège?
5. On peut mettre des bagages dans le coffre à bagages?
6. Après le décollage, on sert le dîner?
7. Qui sert le dîner, le steward ou le pilote?
8. On peut fumer pendant le vol?

AIR FRAN

LES BAGAGES EN CABINE

Prenez quelques instants
pour lire
cette information

Pour des raisons de **sécurité et de confort**, Air France vous demande de limiter le nombre et le volume des bagages que vous emporterez avec vous en cabine.

Ces bagages doivent être placés dans les coffres au-dessus de vous ou sous les sièges devant vous.

L'avion décolle.

6 **Antonymes** Trouvez le contraire.

1. atterrir   a. mettre
2. l'embarquement   b. à destination de
3. une hôtesse de l'air   c. l'atterrissage
4. en provenance de   d. le débarquement
5. un vol intérieur   e. un steward
6. embarquer   f. un vol international
7. l'arrivée   g. décoller
8. sortir   h. débarquer
9. le décollage   i. le départ

7 **À bord** Vrai ou faux?

1. Il faut passer par le contrôle de sécurité avant le vol.
2. On peut laisser ses bagages à main dans le couloir pendant le vol.
3. Il faut attacher sa ceinture de sécurité avant le décollage et l'atterrissage.
4. Il faut faire ses valises après le vol.
5. L'hôtesse de l'air ou le steward ramasse les plateaux après le repas.
6. Le pilote sert un repas et des boissons pendant le vol.
7. L'hôtesse de l'air fait une annonce.
8. Le steward dort pendant le vol.
9. Il faut remplir sa carte de débarquement.

FL.A.3.1.1 (I) **FL.D.2.2.2 (I)**

8

Une carte d'embarquement
This is a boarding card for a flight you are about to take. Tell a classmate (your partner) all you can about your flight based on the information on the card.

 FL.A.2.2.5 (I) **FL.D.2.2.2 (I)**

9

Arrivées Work with a classmate. Look at this arrival screen at Charles-de-Gaulle airport. Give as much information about the flights as you can. Then ask each other questions about them.

Aéroport Charles-de-Gaulle, Roissy

For more practice using words from **Mots 2**, *do Activity 25 on page H26 at the end of this book.*

Structure

Les verbes en -ir au présent
Describing people's activities

1. A second group of regular verbs in French has infinitives that end in **-ir.** Verbs like **finir** *(to finish)* and **choisir** *(to choose)* are regular **-ir** verbs. They have two different stems, one for the singular and one for the plural. Study the following chart.

			FINIR		CHOISIR	
je	fin	-is	je	finis	je	choisis
tu	fin	-is	tu	finis	tu	choisis
il/elle/on	fin	-it	il/elle/on	finit	il/elle/on	choisit
nous	fin + iss	-ons	nous	finissons	nous	choisissons
vous	fin + iss	-ez	vous	finissez	vous	choisissez
ils/elles	fin + iss	-ent	ils/elles	finissent	ils/elles	choisissent

2. Other verbs that belong to this group are **atterrir** and **remplir.**

Ils remplissent une carte de débarquement.
L'avion atterrit à l'heure.

Comment dit-on?

10 **Historiette** **Un vol pour Paris**
Répondez d'après les indications.

1. Madame Lauzier choisit quelle compagnie? (Air France)
2. Elle choisit quelle classe? (la classe économique)
3. Elle choisit une place côté couloir ou côté fenêtre? (côté fenêtre)
4. Elle finit tout son repas? (non)
5. Son avion atterrit à quelle heure? (à midi)
6. Il atterrit à quel aéroport? (à Charles-de-Gaulle)
7. Qu'est-ce qu'elle remplit avant l'arrivée? (une carte de débarquement)

VOL N° AF 007   DATE Nov. 7
CARTE INTERNATIONALE
D'EMBARQUEMENT/DEBARQUEMENT

- En caractère d'imprimerie
- Nom   Rodgers
- Prénoms   Amy
- Nom de jeune fille
- Date de naissance   5 May 1985
- Lieu de naissance   Michigan
- Nationalité   American
- Profession   Student
- Adresse à l'étranger
- Adresse dans le pays   8901 66th St. New York, NY
- Venant de   New York
- Allant à   Paris
- Passeport n°   013424386
- Émis par   New York

Visa n°
Par
Délivré le
DURÉE DE VALIDITÉ

11 **Historiette** **Au restaurant** Donnez des réponses personnelles.

1. En général, tu choisis des restaurants chers ou pas chers?
2. Tu choisis la spécialité de la maison?
3. Tu choisis de la viande ou du poisson?
4. Tu finis ton repas par un dessert ou du fromage?
5. Tu choisis un gâteau ou une glace?
6. Tu finis toujours tout sur ton assiette?

12 **Un bon dîner** Mettez au pluriel d'après le modèle.

> Je choisis du bœuf et tu choisis du poisson.

> Nous choisissons du bœuf et vous choisissez du poisson.

1. Je choisis un petit restaurant et tu choisis un restaurant gastronomique.
2. Je choisis un steak bien cuit et tu choisis un steak à point.
3. Je remplis mon assiette et tu remplis ton assiette.
4. Je finis mon repas par une tarte et tu finis ton repas par des crêpes Suzette.
5. Je finis mon repas par un crème et tu finis ton repas par un express.

AIR FRANCE

DÉJEUNER

SAUMON FROID PARISIENNE

SAUTÉ DE VEAU MARENGO

BOUQUETIÈRE CALIFORNIENNE

SALADE DE SAISON

FROMAGE

GATEAU CASINO

CAFÉ DE COLOMBIE

13 **Un autre vol** Complétez avec **choisir** ou **remplir**.

1. Les passagers _____ un vol Air France?
2. Ils _____ une place côté fenêtre ou côté couloir?
3. Ils _____ le poulet ou le poisson pour le dîner à bord?
4. Ils _____ leur carte de débarquement pendant le vol?

 ENCORE PLUS

*For more practice using -**ir** verbs, do Activity 26 on page H27 at the end of this book.*

Quel et tout
Describing people and things as a group

1. You use the interrogative adjective **quel** with a noun when you want to ask "what" or "which." Note that all forms of **quel** are pronounced the same even though they are spelled differently.

	Masculin	Féminin
Singulier	quel vol quel avion	quelle compagnie quelle hôtesse
Pluriel	quels vols quels‿avions	quelles compagnies quelles‿hôtesses

2. You use **tout(e)** with the definite articles **le, la,** and **l'** to express "the whole" or "the entire." You use **tous** and **toutes** with **les** to express "all" or "every."

	Masculin	Féminin
Singulier	tout le personnel	toute la compagnie
Pluriel	tous les stewards	toutes les hôtesses

Toute la classe fait le voyage.   *The whole class is taking the trip.*
Tous les élèves prennent le même vol.   *All the students are taking the same flight.*
Il y a un vol tous les jours.   *There is a flight every day.*

Rappelez-vous que...

The expression **tout le monde** means "everyone."
Tout le monde veut aller en France.

Comment dit-on?

FL.A.1.1.1 (M)

14 **Quels cours?** Répondez d'après le modèle.

—**Tu aimes quels cours?**
—**Moi? J'aime tous les cours.**

1. Tu aimes quelles matières?
2. Tu aimes quelles langues?
3. Tu aimes quelles sciences?
4. Tu aimes quels livres?
5. Tu aimes quels CD?
6. Tu aimes quels profs?

15 **Quel vol?** Complétez avec **quel** et puis répondez.

1. Tu fais un voyage? _____ voyage?
2. Ton avion part à _____ heure?
3. Ton avion part de _____ porte?
4. Pendant le vol, tu vas regarder _____ film?
5. Tu vas lire _____ livres?
6. Tu aimes _____ compagnies?

16 **Tous les vols pour quelle ville?**
Complétez avec **tout.**

1. _____ les places sont occupées.
2. _____ l'avion est classe économique. Il n'y a pas de première classe.
3. _____ la cabine est non-fumeurs.
4. C'est vrai. Maintenant _____ les vols sont non-fumeurs.

17 **Dans l'avion** Complétez et puis répondez.

1. _____ le personnel parle _____ langues? (tout, quel)
2. _____ les stewards servent _____ boissons et _____ repas? (tout, quel, quel)
3. _____ les hôtesses font _____ annonces? (tout, quel)
4. _____ les passagers font enregistrer _____ bagages? (tout, quel)
5. _____ les vols ont _____ destination? (tout, quel)

FL.A.3.1.1 (I)

18 **Toute la famille** Get together with a classmate. Tell each other some things that your whole family often does together. Compare notes and see if both your families do many of the same things.

AIR FRANCE

faire du ciel le plus bel endroit de la terre

le billet électronique
si simple, si pratique

Les verbes sortir, partir, dormir et servir
Describing more activities

The verbs **sortir**, **partir**, **dormir**, and **servir** all follow the same pattern—the consonant sound in the infinitive is heard in the plural forms but not in the singular forms. Study the following.

SORTIR		PARTIR		DORMIR		SERVIR	
je	sors	je	pars	je	dors	je	sers
tu	sors	tu	pars	tu	dors	tu	sers
il/elle/on	sort	il/elle/on	part	il/elle/on	dort	il/elle/on	sert
nous	sortons	nous	partons	nous	dormons	nous	servons
vous	sortez	vous	partez	vous	dormez	vous	servez
ils/elles	sortent	ils/elles	partent	ils/elles	dorment	ils/elles	servent

Savez-vous que... ?

Sortir means "to go out" or "to leave."

Je sors de l'école à trois heures.

With a direct object, it means "to take out."

Je sors mes livres de mon sac à dos.

Comment dit-on?

19 **Historiette** **Un vol Paris–Abidjan**

Inventez une histoire.

1. M. Kuti va prendre l'avion. Il sort son billet?
2. Il sort son passeport?
3. Son avion part de quelle porte?
4. Son avion part à quelle heure?
5. À bord, on sert des boissons?
6. On sert un repas?
7. M. Kuti dort un peu pendant le vol?

FL.A.3.2.1 (I)

20 **Historiette** **Qui part?**

Donnez des réponses personnelles.

1. Tu pars pour l'école à quelle heure le matin?
2. Tu sors de la maison à quelle heure le matin?
3. Quand tu arrives à l'école, qu'est-ce que tu sors de ton sac à dos?
4. Quelquefois, tu dors un peu en classe?
5. Le week-end, tu sors avec tes copains? Qu'est-ce que vous faites?

M. Kuti part pour Abidjan.

French Online

For more information on air travel in the Francophone world, go to **Web Explore** on the Glencoe French Web site at glencoe.com. You may also want to do the **WebQuest** activity at this site.

21 **On part demain.** Répétez la conversation.

Valérie: Demain, on part pour Tunis, Marie et moi!

Philippe: Vous partez à quelle heure?

Valérie: On part à onze heures.

Philippe: Et vous partez de quel aéroport?

Valérie: D'Orly. C'est la première fois que je pars d'Orly.

Philippe: Ah oui?

Valérie: Oui, en général, nous partons toujours de Charles-de-Gaulle.

22 **Après la conversation** Complétez d'après la conversation.

1. Valérie et Marie _____ pour Tunis.
2. Elles _____ en avion.
3. Leur avion _____ à onze heures.
4. Il _____ d'Orly.
5. En général, Valérie _____ d'Orly ou de Charles-de-Gaulle?

Port El Kantaoui, Tunisie

23 **Historiette** **Un petit voyage** Complétez.

1. Vous _____ quand? (partir)
2. Votre avion _____ à quelle heure? (partir)
3. Vous _____ pendant le vol? (dormir)
4. Vos copains _____? (dormir)
5. Après votre arrivée à Paris, vous _____ tout de suite? (sortir)
6. Et vos amis, ils _____ aussi ou ils _____? (sortir, dormir)

FL.A.2.2.5 (I)   **FL.E.1.2.2 (I)**

24 **Un travail** Work with a classmate. You've got a part-time job working at your local airport because you speak French. Help each of the following passengers.

- A passenger is leaving on flight 125 for Chicago. He doesn't know if it's leaving on time. Help him out.
- Another passenger is confused. He doesn't know his flight number to New York. Let him know what it is and also what time it leaves.
- An older passenger doesn't have his glasses. They are in his suitcase. He asks you to tell him what his seat number is.
- Another passenger is in a real hurry. She wants to know what gate to go to for her flight to Los Angeles. Tell her.

Fort-de-France, Martinique

Attention!

A masculine adjective or noun that ends in -al changes to -aux in the plural.

un journal ⟶
des journaux

un vol international ⟶
des vols internationaux

but

une ville internationale ⟶
des villes internationales

Complétez.

La Martinique est une île __1__ (tropical) dans la mer des Caraïbes. Sa ville __2__ (principal) est Fort-de-France. À Fort-de-France, il y a plusieurs petits parcs __3__ (municipal). L'aéroport __4__ (international) est près de la ville. Tous les jours, il y a des vols __5__ (international) qui décollent et atterrissent. Il y a des vols __6__ (international) à destination de Paris et de beaucoup de villes des États-Unis comme Miami et New York.

Vous êtes sur le bon chemin. Allez-y!

Conversation

On part pour Toulouse.

> Départ à destination de Toulouse, vol Air France numéro 6106. Embarquement immédiat, porte 24.

Cécile: C'est notre vol. On y va?

Pierre: D'accord. Tu sors les cartes d'embarquement?

Cécile: Mais moi, je n'ai pas les cartes d'embarquement!

Pierre: Tu n'as pas les cartes d'embarquement! Ben, elles sont où alors?

Cécile: Dans ton sac?

Pierre: Ah, oui. Voilà! On part de la porte 24.

Cécile: On a quelles places?

Pierre: 10A et 10B.

Cécile: Ah, c'est bien. C'est à l'avant de la cabine. On va pouvoir sortir vite.

Vous avez compris?

Répondez.

1. Où sont Cécile et Pierre?
2. Qu'est-ce qu'on annonce?
3. Quel est le numéro de leur vol?
4. Ils vont où?
5. Ils partent de quelle porte?
6. Qui a les cartes d'embarquement?
7. Ils ont quelles places?
8. Pourquoi c'est bien d'avoir des places à l'avant de la cabine?

Parlons un peu plus

A FL.A.2.2.5 (I)

Tu vas où? You're at the airport waiting for your flight. You strike up a conversation with the person sitting next to you (your partner). Find out information about each other's flight.

B FL.B.1.1.1 (I)

Un billet pour Nice Work with a classmate. You want to fly from New York to Nice. Call the airline to get a reservation. Your partner will be the reservation agent. Before you call, think about the information you will need to give or get from the agent: date of departure, departure time, arrival time in Nice, flight number, price.

Cap Ferrat, près de Nice, France

Prononciation
FL.D.1.2.2 (I)

Le son /l/ final 🎧

1. The names Michelle and Nicole were originally French names, but today many American girls also have these names. When you hear French people say the names Michelle and Nicole, the final /l/ sound is much softer than in English. Say "Michelle" and "Nicole" in French. Repeat the following words.

il	vol	animal	elle	école
salle	décolle	journal	quel	ville

2. Now repeat the following sentences.

   C'est un vol international spécial.
   Quelle est la ville principale?
   Mademoiselle Michelle, elle est très belle.

Il décolle.

Lectures culturelles

On va en France. FL.A.3.2.3 (I)

FL.A.3.2.3 (I)

Reading Strategy

Recognizing text organization

Before you read a passage, try to figure out how the text is organized. If you can follow the organization of a text, you will understand the main ideas more quickly and be able to look for certain ideas and information more easily.

C'est le mois d'avril et toute la classe de Madame Cadet va passer les vacances de Pâques[1] en France. Ils sont maintenant dans le hall de l'aérogare 1 de l'aéroport international JFK à New York. Ils sont au comptoir d'Air France. Ils vont prendre le vol 007. L'agent vérifie leurs billets et leurs passeports. Il donne toutes les cartes d'embarquement à Madame Cadet.

Les falaises d'Étretat, Normandie

Mont-Saint-Michel, Normandie

Les élèves passent par le contrôle de sécurité. Leur avion part de la porte A. Il part à l'heure. Il ne va pas avoir de retard. Après le décollage, le personnel de bord sert des boissons et un repas. Après le repas, il y a un film. Beaucoup de personnes ne regardent pas le film; elles dorment. Mais pas les élèves de Madame Cadet. Ils ne dorment pas. Ils parlent de leur voyage. Ils vont passer quelques jours à Paris et ensuite[2] ils vont en Normandie. Là, ils vont visiter le Mont-Saint-Michel. Avant l'arrivée à Paris, tout le monde remplit une carte de débarquement.

[1] Pâques *Easter*   [2] ensuite *then*

NÉSIE FR
Bonne Fête Maman
La Polynésie française
Tahiti
FUTUNA RF
Haïti
La Martinique

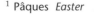

À huit heures du matin, après un vol agréable, l'avion atterrit à l'aéroport Charles-de-Gaulle à Roissy. Charles-de-Gaulle est un des deux aéroports de Paris. D'abord, il faut passer au contrôle des passeports. Ensuite les formalités de douane[3] sont très simples et quarante minutes après l'atterrissage, les élèves de Madame Cadet sont dans l'autocar (le bus) qui fait la navette[4] entre l'aéroport et Paris. Tout le monde est très fatigué après le long vol. Vous croyez qu'ils vont dormir? Pas question! Le premier jour à Paris, on ne dort pas. On va visiter la belle ville de Paris.

[3] douane *customs*
[4] fait la navette *makes the run*

L'île de la Cité, Paris

Un car Air France, aéroport Charles-de-Gaulle

Tunisie

Le Maroc

Vous avez compris?

A Un voyage en France Vrai ou faux?
1. Toute la classe de Madame Cadet va à Montréal.
2. À l'aéroport, l'agent de la compagnie aérienne donne toutes les cartes d'embarquement à un des élèves de Madame Cadet.
3. L'avion pour Paris va avoir du retard.
4. Les passagers servent un bon repas après le décollage.
5. Beaucoup de passagers dorment pendant le vol.
6. Le Mont-Saint-Michel est à Paris.
7. Les formalités de douane sont très compliquées en France.
8. Quand les élèves de Madame Cadet arrivent à Paris, ils vont dormir.

B Des informations Cherchez les informations.
1. Quel est le nom d'un aéroport à New York?
2. Quel est le nom d'un des aéroports de Paris?
3. Quel est le numéro du vol des élèves de Madame Cadet?
4. Leur avion part de quelle porte?
5. Quelle est la destination de leur vol?
6. Ils arrivent à Paris à quelle heure?

Le Mali

Le Sénégal

RÉPUBLIQUE DE CÔTE D'IVOIRE

FL.A.2.1.2 (I)   **FL.C.1.2.2 (I)**

Le décalage horaire

Les gens qui voyagent beaucoup souffrent souvent du décalage horaire. Le décalage horaire, qu'est-ce que c'est? C'est la différence entre l'heure d'une ville—New York, par exemple—et une autre ville comme Paris. Quand il est minuit à New York, il est six heures du matin à Paris. Les voyageurs souffrent du décalage horaire parce que quand c'est l'heure de dormir dans une ville, c'est l'heure de travailler dans une autre.

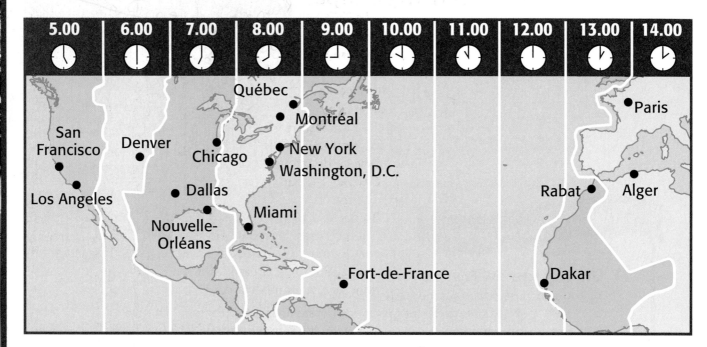

Vous avez compris?

Le décalage horaire Regardez la carte et répondez.
1. Quand il est midi à Washington, D.C., il est quelle heure à Paris?
2. Et à Dakar?
3. Et à Alger?
4. Et à Québec?
5. Et à Los Angeles?
6. Et à la Nouvelle-Orléans?

FL.C.2.1.1 (I)

Un pilote écrivain

Antoine de Saint-Exupéry (1900–1944) est un écrivain (un auteur) français célèbre. Mais c'est aussi un homme d'action. Il est né[1] à Lyon en 1900. Pendant son service militaire, il apprend à piloter un avion. Il est pilote de ligne entre Toulouse et Dakar en Afrique. Il est aussi chef de l'Aéropostale (la poste par avion) à Buenos Aires. Il participe aux premiers vols France-Amérique.

Antoine de Saint-Exupéry

Le Petit Prince est son livre le plus connu[2]. Il est connu dans le monde entier. Ses autres romans[3] reflètent sa carrière de pilote. *Courrier sud* parle de ses vols Toulouse–Dakar. *Vol de nuit* parle de trois pilotes basés à Buenos Aires. L'un d'eux est en difficulté dans le ciel[4] noir d'Amérique du Sud. *Terre des hommes* évoque le souvenir[5] de ses camarades disparus, comme Jean Mermoz, le grand aviateur français.

Le 13 juillet 1944, Saint-Exupéry disparaît aussi. Il disparaît dans une mission aérienne militaire au-dessus de la mer Méditerranée. Il reste[6] pour la légende le courageux, le charmant, l'exceptionnel «Saint-Ex».

[1] est né *was born*
[2] le plus connu *best-known*
[3] romans *novels*
[4] ciel *sky*
[5] souvenir *memory*
[6] reste *remains*

Vous avez compris?

Saint-Exupéry Identifiez.
1. le nom de l'écrivain
2. la ville où il est né
3. une ville d'Amérique du Sud où il travaille
4. le nom d'un grand aviateur français

La Belgique

La Tunisie

Le Maroc

Le Mali

CONNEXIONS

FL.C.1.2.1 (I)

Les sciences physiques

Le climat et le temps

We often speak about the weather, especially when we are traveling. Weather can have a very positive or negative effect on our trip. When planning a vacation, for example, it's a good idea to take into account the climate of the area we are going to visit. When we talk about weather or climate, we must remember that there is a big difference between the two. Weather is the condition of the atmosphere for a short period of time. Climate refers to the weather that prevails in one area over a long period of time.

Aujourd'hui

19 °
16 ° 18 °
20 °
17 ° 19 °
21 ° 20 ° 19 °
21 ° 21 °
24 ° 22 ° 23 °
25 °
25 ° 24 °
27 °
27 °
27 °

☀	Soleil	☔	Averses
⛅	Eclaircies Peu nuageux	🌧	Pluies ou bruines
☁	Nuageux Courtes éclaircies	⛈	Orages
☁	Très nuageux ou couvert	≈	Brumes et brouillard
⇨	Vent faible	🌨	Neige
⇨	Vent modéré		
⇨	Vent fort	**23°**	Température

Demain

20 °
21 °
20 °
19 °
24 ° 24 °
28 ° 22 °
26 ° 27 °
27 ° 24 °

Différence entre climat et temps[1]

Il y a une grande différence entre le climat et le temps. Le temps est la condition de l'atmosphère pendant une courte période. Le temps peut changer très vite. Il peut changer plusieurs fois dans une seule journée.

Le climat, c'est le temps qu'il fait chaque année dans le même endroit[2], dans la même région.

[1] temps *weather*   [2] endroit *place*

Des champs de lavande, Digne, Provence

Zones climatiques

Dans le monde francophone, il y a beaucoup de zones climatiques. La France, par exemple, a un climat tempéré. Dans une région où le climat est tempéré, il y a quatre saisons: l'été, l'automne, l'hiver, le printemps. Le temps change à chaque saison.

Beaucoup de pays francophones en Afrique sont dans des zones tropicales. Le Bénin et la Côte d'Ivoire, par exemple, sont des pays tropicaux. Ils sont tout près de l'équateur. Là il fait chaud[3] toute l'année et les pluies[4] sont abondantes. Il y a deux saisons—la saison des pluies et la saison sèche[5]. Les saisons varient d'une région à l'autre.

[3] il fait chaud *it's hot*   [4] pluies *rains*   [5] sèche *dry*

Val-d'Isère, France

Un village de la brousse, Bénin

Vous avez compris?

Explication du texte
Expliquez en anglais.

1. What's the difference between weather and climate?
2. What is a characteristic of an area with a temperate climate?
3. What is a characteristic of a tropical climate?

C'est à vous

Use what you have learned

PARLER

1

 FL.A.2.2.5 (I)

Tu vas où?
✔ *Talk about a plane trip*

You just got to the airport and unexpectedly ran into a friend (your partner). Exchange information about the trip and flight each of you is about to take.

Musées, lieux et loisirs touristiques

PARLER

2

ÉCRIRE

 FL.A.1.2.2 (I)

On fait un voyage?
✔ *Plan a plane trip to a French-speaking destination*

Go to a travel agency in your community. Get some travel brochures and plan a plane trip. Tell all about your trip.

ÉCRIRE

3

 FL.A.2.2.1 (I)

Un voyage en avion
✔ *Write about airport activities and services aboard the plane*

You have a French key pal who is going to visit you this winter. This will be his or her first flight. Write your key pal an e-mail and explain all the things he or she is going to experience before and during the flight.

Writing Strategy

Answering an essay question When writing an answer to an essay question, first read the question carefully and determine how to structure your answer. Then restate the essay question in a single statement in your introduction. Next, support the statement with facts, details, and reasons. Finally, close with a conclusion that summarizes your answer.

ÉCRIRE

4

FL.A.2.2.3 (I)

Un concours

In order to win an all-expense-paid trip to the French-speaking country of your choice, you have to write an essay in French and send it to the company sponsoring the trip. Read the following essay questions and then write your answers. You really want to go, so be sure to plan your answers carefully and check your work.

Tu veux aller dans quel pays?
Tu vas y aller comment?
Qu'est-ce que tu veux faire là-bas?
Qu'est-ce que tu veux apprendre?

Lac Léman, Genève, Suisse

Fès, Maroc

Paris, France

Assessment

Vocabulaire

To review **Mots 1,** turn to pages 260–261.

1 Vrai ou faux?

1. Un bagage à main est une très grande valise.
2. Avant un voyage on fait ses valises.
3. Un vol intérieur est un vol entre deux pays.
4. Les passagers partent d'une porte d'embarquement.
5. L'avion atterrit dans le hall de l'aéroport.

2 Identifiez.

To review **Mots 2,** turn to pages 264–265.

8.

9.
10.

7.

6.

Structure

To review **-ir** verbs, turn to page 268.

3 Complétez.

11. Je ____ mon dîner. (finir)
12. Les passagers ____ leur carte de débarquement. (remplir)
13. Vous ____ votre place dans l'avion. (choisir)
14. Nous ____ nos devoirs. (finir)
15. L'avion ____ à l'heure. (atterrir)

To review **quel,** turn to page 270.

4 Complétez avec «quel».

16. —C'est ____ vol?
    —C'est le vol pour Paris.
17. —Tu voyages avec ____ compagnie aérienne?
    —Air France.
18. —Il parle de ____ hôtesses?
    —Des hôtesses d'Air France.

5 **Complétez pour indiquer** *the whole* **ou** *every.*

19. _____ classe va faire le voyage.

20. _____ vols n'arrivent pas à la même heure.

6 **Récrivez chaque phrase.**

21. Je sers le dîner.
    Ils _____.

22. Vous sortez?
    Tu _____?

23. Ils partent demain.
    Elle _____.

To review the use of **tout** *with definite articles, turn to page 270.*

To review these **-ir** *verbs, turn to page 272.*

Culture

7 **Vrai ou faux?**

24. Charles-de-Gaulle est le nom d'un aéroport près de Paris.

25. Le Mont-Saint-Michel est un monument célèbre à Paris.

To review this cultural information, turn to pages 278–279.

For more Chapter 8 test preparation, go to the Chapter 8 **Self-Check Quiz** on the Glencoe French Web site at glencoe.com.

Mont-Saint-Michel

Do these practice activities to help you succeed on your FCAT through the study of a foreign language.

Read the story below. Then answer the questions that follow.

Toute la classe de Madame Gagnier va passer les vacances de printemps en France. Ils sont devant le comptoir d'Air France à l'aéroport JFK à New York. Ils enregistrent leurs bagages. L'agent vérifie leurs billets et leurs passeports et donne toutes les cartes d'embarquement à Madame Gagnier. Ensuite ils passent par le contrôle de sécurité. Leur avion part de la porte C. Il ne va pas avoir de retard. Après le décollage un steward sert des boissons et un repas. Après le repas il y a un film, mais si on préfère, on peut dormir. Les élèves ne veulent pas dormir; ils sont trop excités. Ils parlent de leur voyage. Ils vont passer une semaine dans la capitale et ensuite ils vont aller en Normandie pour visiter le Mont-Saint-Michel.

Après un vol agréable, l'avion atterrit à l'aéroport Charles-de-Gaulle à Roissy. C'est un des deux aéroports de Paris. On passe au contrôle des passeports. Ensuite on passe par la douane. Quarante-cinq minutes après l'atterrissage, les élèves sont dans l'autocar qui les transporte à Paris. Tout le monde est très fatigué après le long voyage mais ils ne vont pas dormir. Absolument pas! Ils vont explorer la belle ville de Paris!

❶ Quelle est la profession de Madame Gagnier?

    A. guide touristique

    B. agent de voyages

    C. professeur

    D. agent d'Air France

❷ L'agent qui vérifie les billets travaille pour qui?

    F. l'aéroport JFK

    G. la compagnie aérienne

    H. le personnel de bord

    I. la douane

❸ Quelle phrase signifie la même chose? **Il ne va pas avoir de retard.**

    A. Il va partir à l'heure.

    B. Il va être en retard.

    C. Il ne va pas partir à l'heure.

    D. Il ne va pas partir.

❹ Quelle est la phrase correcte?

    F. Leur vol est un vol à destination de New York.

    G. Leur vol est un vol en provenance de Paris.

    H. Leur vol est un vol intérieur.

    I. Leur vol est un vol international.

5 Dans quel ordre est-ce qu'on fait les choses dans cette histoire?

A. On passe par le contrôle des passeports, on va à la porte d'embarquement, l'avion décolle, on mange un repas dans l'avion, on arrive à sa destination.

B. On passe par le contrôle de sécurité, on va au comptoir de la compagnie aérienne, on regarde un film dans l'avion, l'avion atterrit.

C. L'avion décolle, on mange dans l'avion, l'avion atterrit, on passe au contrôle des passeports et à la douane.

D. L'avion décolle, on passe par le contrôle de sécurité, on dort dans l'avion, on arrive à sa destination, on passe à la douane.

6 Quel est l'itinéraire des élèves de Madame Gagnier?

F. Ils vont en province et ensuite à Paris.

G. Ils vont à Paris et ensuite en Normandie.

H. Ils vont au Mont-Saint-Michel et ensuite à Paris.

I. Ils vont d'abord à Roissy et ensuite au Mont-Saint-Michel.

7 Pourquoi les élèves veulent-ils visiter tout de suite Paris quand ils arrivent?

A. parce que Paris est une belle ville

B. parce qu'ils ne sont absolument pas fatigués

C. parce qu'ils vont partir pour la Normandie

D. parce qu'ils préfèrent dormir dans l'avion

8 READ THINK EXPLAIN Qu'est-ce qu'on fait quand on arrive à l'aéroport pour prendre un vol international?

9 À votre avis, quel temps fait-il quand la classe de Mme Gagnier est en France?

F. Il neige.

G. Il fait très chaud.

H. Il fait frais.

I. Il fait très froid.

FCAT Tip

Check each answer to make sure it is the best answer for the question asked.

On parle super bien!

FL.A.2.1.2 (I) FL.A.3.2.1 (I)

Tell all you can about this illustration.

Getting around an airport

un aéroport	le numéro du vol	un vol
une aérogare	une porte d'embarquement	intérieur
un avion	une carte d'embarquement	international
un hall	une place	non-fumeurs
un comptoir	côté couloir	à destination de
une compagnie aérienne	côté fenêtre	en provenance de
un passager	un départ	une annonce
une passagère	une arrivée	un pays
un bagage à main	une piste	une ville
une valise	le contrôle de sécurité	
un billet		
un passeport		

Aboard the plane

à bord	une ceinture de sécurité
la cabine	un coffre à bagages
un siège	un plateau
le couloir	une carte de débarquement

How well do you know your vocabulary?

- Choose a word from the list.
- Have a classmate give a related word: **annonce, annoncer.**

Identifying airline personnel

un agent	un steward
le personnel de bord	une hôtesse de l'air
un pilote	

Describing activities at the airport and aboard the plane

voyager	partir	passer par	ramasser
faire un voyage	sortir	vérifier	être à l'heure
faire une annonce	dormir	décoller	avoir du retard
finir	servir	attacher	(faire) enregistrer
choisir			
remplir			
atterrir			

Other useful words and expressions

sous
il faut
faire ses valises

VIDÉOTOUR

Épisode 8

In this video episode, Christine has an unusual "adventure" at the airport. See page 533 for more information.

La gare et le train

Objectifs

In this chapter you will learn to:

✔ *purchase a train ticket and request information about arrival and departure*

✔ *use expressions related to train travel*

✔ *talk about people's activities*

✔ *point out people or things*

✔ *discuss an interesting train trip in French-speaking Africa*

Claude Monet *La locomotive*

French Online
To interact with your online edition of
Bon voyage! go to: glencoe.com.

SUNSHINE STATE STANDARDS

This chapter is all about trains and travel by rail. The material in the chapter will address the Sunshine State Standards listed below.

FL.A.1.2.1   express likes or dislikes regarding various objects, categories, people, and events present in the everyday environment.

FL.A.1.2.2   exchange information necessary to plan events or activities (e.g., picnics, birthday parties, science projects, and crafts).

FL.A.2.1.2   restate and rephrase simple information from materials presented orally, visually, and graphically in class.

FL.A.2.1.3   understand oral messages that are based on familiar themes and vocabulary (e.g., short conversations between familiar persons on familiar topics such as everyday school and home activities).

FL.A.2.2.1   give and understand written and verbal instructions, using known, verbal patterns in the target language.

FL.A.2.2.3   organize information in spoken or written form about a variety of topics of academic and cultural interest (e.g., by making lists, categorizing objects, or organizing concepts).

FL.A.2.2.5   comprehend and respond to oral messages (e.g., personal anecdotes or narratives) based on familiar themes and vocabulary.

FL.A.3.2.1   describe important people (e.g., family members and friends) and objects present in his or her everyday environment and in school.

FL.A.3.2.3   give responses in spoken or written form (e.g., answering simple questions, formulating questions, and making simple statements) to age-appropriate stories, poems or other literature, songs, films, or visual works.

FL.B.1.1.1   participate in age-appropriate cultural activities (e.g., games, songs, birthday celebrations, storytelling, dramatizations, and role playing).

FL.C.1.2.1   participate in activities in the language class designed to integrate content-area concepts (e.g., mathematical calculations or cause-and-effect relationships) into target-language instruction (e.g., about countries or cultures).

Orlando, Florida

Especially for Florida Students

FL.C.1.2.2   use target-language vocabulary or concepts to reinforce knowledge of a related topic studied in another class (e.g., geographical place names, parts of the body, or basic mathematical operations).

FL.C.2.1.1   use the target language to gain access to information that is only available through the target language or within the target culture (listen to a story told in the target language).

FL.D.1.1.2   use simple vocabulary and short phrases in the target language.

FL.D.2.2.2   recognize forms of the target language evident in the local culture (e.g., signs, symbols, advertisements, packages, displays, murals, songs, and rhymes).

TIPS FOR SUCCESS

Review the Study Tips below to help you succeed on the Sunshine State Standards identified.

Vocabulaire   *Mots 1*   *Mots 2*   (pages 292–299)

Hermit crab

- A good way to remember vocabulary is to group words in some meaningful way. For example, you can group cognates, synonyms, or antonyms. An antonym is a word that means the exact opposite of another. There are quite a few words in **Mots 2** for which you know the antonyms.
  Match the following antonyms.

1. **monter**	poser une question
2. **assis**	descendre
3. **lit**	terminer, finir
4. **répondre à la question**	debout
5. **commencer**	écrit

  FL.A.2.2.3

Conversation   (page 308)

- You have not learned the expression **tarif étudiant**, but it's easy to guess its meaning through association with other words. **Tarif** is a word that also exists in English. **Étudiant**, a word that is related to the verb **étudier**, is a close cognate of *student*. **FL.D.1.2.1**

Lectures culturelles   **Un voyage intéressant**   (pages 310–311)

- Always locate the area of the world you are reading about. Look at the map on page 310. Locate the countries of Mali and Sénégal. Locate the cities of Bamako and Dakar. **FL.C.1.2.2**

Vocabulaire   (page 321)

- After going over the vocabulary you need when traveling by train, think about a plane trip in French to review the words you already know about this topic. **FL.A.2.2.3**

> **For other tips to help you address the Sunshine State Standards in Chapter 9, see pages H63 and H64 at the back of your textbook.**

Vocabulaire

Mots 1

À la gare 🎧

la salle d'attente

le kiosque

un journal

le buffet

une carte postale

L'EXPRESS
SPÉCIAL
Et si on parlait de la France...

Les plus fascinantes baies du monde

un magazine

On vend des journaux et des magazines au kiosque.

le guichet

Un aller-retour en seconde pour Avignon, s'il vous plaît.

la queue

On vend les billets au guichet.
Les passagers font la queue au guichet.

un aller (simple)

SNCF BILLET
Départ: PARIS → LYON

un billet aller (et) retour

SNCF BILLET
Départ: PARIS → LYON → PARIS

un horaire

Numéro de train Notes à consulter	5792 1		57100 2		3	54		
Marseille-St-Charles	D							
Arles	D							
Avignon	D							
Valence-Ville	D		00.21					
Vienne	D	00.36	01.40			03.19		
Lyon-Perrache	D				04.28	04.44		
Lyon-Part Dieu	A	01.31	02.35		05.15	05.28		
Satolas-TGV	A				05.36			
Mâcon-Ville	A					05.50		06.28
Dijon-Ville	A							06.36
Laroche-Migennes	A	03.24	04.24	04.45				
Sens	A	04.57		06.25				
Melun	A						06.34	
Paris-Gare-de-Lyon	A	06.27					07.05	
							07.58	
							08.29	

1. Circule: jusqu'au 6 juil : les lun, mar, sam et dim sauf le 30 mai;Circule du 7 juil au 7 sept : tous les jours;à partir du 11 sept : les lun, mar, sam et dim et le 3 nov-2ᵉ CL certains jours. 🚲 1ʳᵉ 2ᵉ temporaire certains jours.

2. Circule : les 5, 12 et 19 juin; du 26 juin au 1er août : tous les jours sauf les lun; Circule à partir du 28 août : les sam sauf le 13 nov;Circule les 29 août et 11 nov- Conditions spéciales d'admission pour ce train 2ᵉ temporaire certains jours.

3. Circule : les lun sauf le 1er nov;Circule 15 juil, 2 et 12 nov.🚲

4. Circule : tous les jours sauf les 30 mai, 6 juin, 12 et 19 sept-🚲

5. Circule : tous les jours sauf les sam, dim et fêtes.

6. Circule : tous les jours sauf les dim et sauf le 1er nov-🚲

un voyageur

une voyageuse

la voie

le quai

Les voyageurs attendent le train.
On attend le train sur le quai.

composter
son billet

un chariot

On annonce le départ du train.
Un voyageur n'arrive pas à
    entendre l'annonce.

Marie est en retard.
Elle n'est pas en avance.

Quel est le mot?

1 **Historiette** **Un voyage en train**
Inventez une histoire.

1. Les voyageurs sont à la gare?
2. Ils attendent le train dans la salle d'attente?
3. On vend des billets où?
4. Où est-ce que M. Merlin prend son billet?
5. Il va faire Paris–Lyon–Paris. Il veut un billet aller-retour ou un aller simple?
6. Avant de prendre son billet, il fait la queue au guichet?
7. Les voyageurs peuvent consulter l'horaire pour vérifier l'heure du départ de leur train?
8. On annonce les départs à la gare?
9. M. Merlin arrive à comprendre l'annonce?
10. Il prend un chariot?
11. Il met ses bagages sur le chariot?
12. Son train part à l'heure ou en retard?

Gare de Lyon, Paris

2 **Historiette** **Ton voyage en train** Donnez des réponses personnelles.

1. Tu fais un voyage en train? Tu vas où?
2. Tu arrives à la gare en avance?
3. Tu prends ton billet?
4. Tu achètes un billet aller-retour ou un aller simple?
5. Tu voyages en première ou en seconde?
6. Tu consultes l'horaire?
7. Ton train part à quelle heure?
8. Ton train part de quelle voie?
9. Tu vas acheter un journal ou un magazine? Où?
10. Tu vas prendre un café au buffet de la gare?

Gare de Lyon, Paris

3 **On attend le train.** Choisissez la bonne réponse.

1. On vend des journaux, des magazines et des cartes postales _____.
   a. au guichet   b. au kiosque   c. sur le quai

2. On _____ le train dans la salle d'attente.
   a. attend   b. prend   c. entend

3. Les voyageurs _____ l'annonce du départ de leur train.
   a. mettent   b. entendent   c. font

4. On fait _____ au guichet pour prendre son billet.
   a. l'annonce   b. le quai   c. la queue

5. Le train part _____.
   a. de la voie   b. du chariot   c. du kiosque

6. Il faut _____ son billet avant d'aller sur le quai.
   a. vendre   b. faire   c. composter

 FL.A.2.2.5 (I)

4 **La SNCF (La Société nationale des chemins de fer français)** You're in France and you want to visit one of the cities on the map. A classmate will be the ticket agent. Get yourself a ticket and ask the agent any questions you have about your train trip.

lignes à grande vitesse
autres lignes
gares

For more information on the SNCF, go to **Web Explore** on the Glencoe French Web site at glencoe.com. You may also want to do the **WebQuest** activity at this site.

For more practice using words from Mots 1, do Activity 27 on page H28 at the end of this book.

Vocabulaire

Mots 2

Un voyage en train 🎧

BORDEAUX

une voiture, un wagon

changer de train

descendre du train

monter en voiture

VOIE A

DEPART	MISSION	VOIE
10h11	RIPA	01
10h26	ZORA	03
12h14	NICE	05
12h28	BERN	02

VOIE B

DEPART	MISSION	VOIE
10h36	LYON	02
10h45	TORI	07
11h10	VENI	05
11h40	GLEN	08
12h13	MONT	09

Les voyageurs vont changer de train.
Ils attendent la correspondance.
Ils ont une correspondance à Bordeaux.

Dans le train 🎧

debout

assis

La plupart des voyageurs sont assis.
Il y a quelques voyageurs debout.
Sylvain lit un livre.
Sa copine Christine écrit des cartes (postales).

Le contrôleur contrôle les billets.
Romain a une question.
Le contrôleur répond à sa question.

Jean et Thouria attendent un ami
   devant la gare.
Ils vont tous les trois à La Rochelle.
Jean et Thouria attendent depuis
   quarante-cinq minutes!
Jean dit qu'il commence à perdre
   patience.

Quel est le mot?

5 **Historiette** **De Paris à Avignon** Répondez d'après les indications.

1. Pour aller à Avignon, on change de train? (non)
2. Qui monte en voiture? (les voyageurs)
3. Qui contrôle les billets? (le contrôleur)
4. Presque toutes les places sont occupées? (oui)
5. La plupart des voyageurs sont assis? (oui)
6. Il y a quelques voyageurs debout? (oui)
7. Qu'est-ce que le contrôleur contrôle? (les billets)
8. Les voyageurs descendent où? (à Avignon)

6 **Historiette** **Aïcha prend le train.** Complétez avec le mot ou l'expression qui convient.

descend	lit	écrit	monte	attendre
contrôle	rater	dit	snack-bar	arrêt

1. Aïcha fait un voyage en train. Elle _____ en voiture.
2. Le contrôleur _____ son billet.
3. Elle _____ un article dans un magazine.
4. Elle n'_____ pas de cartes postales.
5. Elle a faim. Elle va au _____.
6. Aïcha _____ au contrôleur qu'elle va à Aix-en-Provence.
7. Il répond: «Il faut changer de train à Marseille. C'est le prochain _____.»
8. Elle _____ du train à Marseille.
9. À Marseille, elle va _____ sa correspondance pour Aix-en-Provence.
10. Elle ne va pas _____ le train pour Aix-en-Provence.

Aix-en-Provence, France

For more practice using words from **Mots 2**, *do Activity 28 on page H29 at the end of this book.*

7 **Toujours des questions!** Répondez.

Nantes, France

1. Le train pour Lyon part de la voie numéro 5
   à six heures trente.
   > C'est le train ou l'avion qui part pour Lyon?
   > Le train va où?
   > Il part de quelle voie?
   > Il part à quelle heure?
2. Sandrine va à Nantes et elle ne trouve pas
   sa place dans le train.
   > Qui va à Nantes?
   > Où est Sandrine?
   > Qu'est-ce qu'elle ne trouve pas?

FL.A.2.1.2 (I)

8 **L'horaire** Look at the information on this schedule. Take turns
with a classmate asking and answering questions about it.

MARSEILLE - ARLES - TARASCON - AVIGNON

SEMAINE

	•	⊙ CAR	•	⊙	⊙	•	⊙	⊙	•	•		⊙	⊙	⊙	⊙	⊙	⊙	⊙	⊙	•	⊙	⊙	⊙ CAR		⊙	⊙	•	⊙	⊙	•	⊙
				TGV																					TGV						TGV
			28	3		29		30		31	32						12								33	34			14	35		36
Marseille-St-Charles		05.29		06.12	06.31	06.35	06.51			08.27	08.36	08.47	09.08	10.59		11.36	12.09			13.18	14.03	14.36		15.24			16.12			16.26	16.40	16.57
Miramas		06.00			07.04	07.15	•	07.40		09.11	09.11	•	•	11.33		•	12.42			14.04	•	•		15.59			16.51			•	17.27	•
Arles		06.05	06.17		06.57	07.21	07.32	07.39	08.00		09.28	09.28	09.35	•	11.51		•	12.59	13.23		14.24	14.52	15.21	15.30	16.17	16.45		17.08			•	17.49	•
Arles (Le Trébon)		•	•		•	•	•	•	•		•	•	•	•	•		•	•	•		•	•	•	•	•	•		•			•	•	•
Arles (Car. St-Gabriel)		•	•		•	•	•	•	•		•	•	•	•	•		•	•	•		•	•	•	•	•	•		•			•	•	•
Tarascon	05.06	06.25		•	07.25	•	07.31	•	07.48	•	08.42	•	•	09.44	•		•	12.16	•	13.08	•	13.52	•	•	15.50		•	•	16.54	17.21	18.02	•	•
Tarascon (Pl.Condamine)	•	•		•	•	•	•	•	•		•	•	•	•	•		•	•	•		•	•	•	•	•	•		•			•	•	•
Graveson (Maillane)	•	•		•	•	•	•	•	•		•	•	•	•	•		•	•	•		•	•	•	•	•	•		•			•	•	•
Graveson (Bon-Accueil)	•	•		•	•	•	•	•	•		•	•	•	•	•		•	•	•		•	•	•	•	•	•		•			•	•	•
Graveson (La Roque)	•	•		•	•	•	•	•	•		•	•	•	•	•		•	•	•		•	•	•	•	•	•		•			•	•	•
Rognonas (Emb.Gare)	•	•		•	•	•	•	•	•		•	•	•	•	•		•	•	•		•	•	•	•	•	•		•			•	•	•
Rognonas (Pl.Mairie)	•	•		•	•	•	•	•	•		•	•	•	•	•		•	•	•		•	•	•	•	•	•		•			•	•	•
Avignon (Gambetta)	•	•		•	•	•	•	•	•		•	•	•	•	•		•	•	•		•	•	•	•	•	•		•			•	•	•
Avignon	05.18	06.55		06.33	07.40	07.13		07.50		08.16	08.55	09.45	09.45		10.11	12.09	12.29	12.41		13.42	14.04	14.42	15.10		16.20	16.34	17.03	17.10		18.14	17.30	18.07	17.57

La desserte détaillée entre Marseille et Miramas figure sur la
fiche horaire Marseille - Miramas
via Rognac et Port de Bouc.

Voir aussi Fiche horaire Marseille - Salon - Cavaillon - Avignon.

• Du lundi au vendredi.
⊙ Du lundi au samedi.

Ⓘ Certains trains périodiques ne figurent pas sur ce document horaire.

CAR Desserte assurée par autocar. Tarification SNCF.

Ⓘ TGV : réservation obligatoire.

Ⓘ Horaires en italiques : train soumis à des conditions d'emprunt,
ou à supplément; renseignements dans les gares.

Ⓘ Ces horaires sont donnés sous réserve de toute modification.

3 Ne circule
12 Ne circule
14 Ne circule
17 Circule les
   circule aus
24 Circule du
26 Ne circule
27 Circule les

FL.D.1.1.2 (I)

9 **Jeu**
Les phrases Play a game with a classmate. See who can make
up the most sentences using the following words. The time limit is two minutes.

 le quai

 aller-retour

 le contrôleur

 l'annonce

 assis

 debout

 le train

 le billet

 la correspondance

LA GARE ET LE TRAIN

Structure

Les verbes en -re au présent
Describing more activities

1. Another group of regular verbs in French has infinitives that end in **-re.** Some verbs that belong to this group are: **vendre, attendre, descendre, répondre, entendre, perdre.**

	VENDRE	ATTENDRE
je **vend** -s	je vends	j' attends
tu **vend** -s	tu vends	tu attends
il/elle/on **vend** —	il/elle/on vend	il/elle/on ₙattend
nous **vend** -ons	nous vendons	nous ᵤattendons
vous **vend** -ez	vous vendez	vous ᵤattendez
ils/elles **vend** -ent	ils/elles vendent	ils ᵤ/elles ᵤattendent

2. Descendre can have several meanings. When used alone, it means "to go down" or "to get off." When used with a direct object, it means "to take down."

> **Ils descendent du train.**
> **Ils descendent les bagages sur le quai.**

Savez-vous que... ?

The verb **répondre** is followed by **à.**

Il répond à la question du contrôleur.

Il répond à l'employé.

La gare, Dakar, Sénégal

Comment dit-on?

10 **Historiette** **Les voyageurs** Répondez que oui.

1. Les voyageurs attendent le train?
2. Ils attendent le train dans la salle d'attente?
3. Ils perdent patience?
4. Ils entendent l'annonce du départ de leur train?
5. Ils descendent du train?

La gare Windsor, Montréal

11 **Historiette** **Un voyage à Montréal**
Répondez que oui.

1. Tu es à la gare de Grand Central à New York?
2. Tu attends le train pour Montréal?
3. Tu attends depuis une heure?
4. Tu perds patience?
5. Tu entends l'annonce du départ de ton train?
6. Tu vas sur le quai?
7. Quand tu descends du train à Montréal, tu es fatigué(e)?

12 **Le train** Complétez.

1. —Vous _____ depuis combien de temps? (attendre)
   —Nous _____ depuis cinq minutes. C'est tout! (attendre)
2. —Vous allez à Rennes?
   —Oui.
   —Vous _____ au prochain arrêt, alors. (descendre)
   —Ah bon? Merci.
   —Hé, les copains! On _____ au prochain arrêt! (descendre)

13 **Historiette** **Dans la salle d'attente** Complétez.

Les voyageurs __1__ (attendre) le train dans la salle d'attente. Marc __2__ (attendre) le train pour Saint-Malo. Ah, voilà son ami, Luc.

Marc: Salut, Luc! Quelle surprise! Tu __3__ (attendre) un train?

Luc: Oui, j'__4__ (attendre) le train pour Saint-Malo.

Marc: Pas vrai? Moi aussi je vais à Saint-Malo.

Les deux garçons __5__ (entendre) l'annonce du départ de leur train. Il part de la voie numéro 5. Ils vont sur le quai. Les voyageurs qui arrivent __6__ (descendre) leurs bagages du train. Ils __7__ (descendre) leurs bagages sur le quai. Le contrôleur crie: «En voiture, s'il vous plaît!» et tout le monde qui part monte dans le train. Le contrôleur demande aux garçons où ils vont. Luc __8__ (répondre) au contrôleur. Il __9__ (répondre): «À Saint-Malo».

Saint-Malo, Bretagne, France

FL.A.2.2.5 (I)

14 **À la gare** Work with a classmate. Pretend you are at a train station somewhere in France. Take turns asking and answering questions about your wait at the train station. You may want to use the following expressions: **attendre le train, entendre l'annonce du départ, prendre un billet, faire la queue, aller au kiosque, prendre un café au buffet de la gare.**

Les adjectifs démonstratifs
Pointing out people and things

1. You use the demonstrative adjectives to point out people or things. In English, the demonstrative adjectives are "this," "these," "that," and "those." However, in French there is only one set of demonstrative adjectives. Study the following forms.

	Masculin		Féminin	
	Consonne	Voyelle	Consonne	Voyelle
Singulier	ce train	cet_t horaire	cette voiture	cette annonce
Pluriel	ces trains	ces_z horaires	ces voitures	ces_z annonces

2. The word **-là** is often attached to the noun following the demonstrative adjectives for emphasis.

—**C'est un magazine super.**
—**Ce magazine-là! Tu rigoles! Il est horrible!**

Un ancien wagon-restaurant

Comment dit-on?

15 **Tu parles de qui ou de quoi?** Suivez le modèle.

> Tu parles d'une fille?
> De quelle fille?

> De cette fille-là.

1. Tu parles d'un garçon? De quel garçon?
2. Tu parles d'une copine? De quelle copine?
3. Tu parles d'un copain? De quel copain?
4. Tu parles des élèves? De quels élèves?
5. Tu parles des filles? De quelles filles?
6. Tu parles d'un train? De quel train?
7. Tu parles d'un horaire? De quel horaire?
8. Tu parles des journaux? De quels journaux?
9. Tu parles d'un arrêt? De quel arrêt?
10. Tu parles d'une carte? De quelle carte?

16 **À Grenoble ou à Chamonix?** Complétez avec **ce, cet, cette** ou **ces**.

Christine: __1__ train va à Grenoble?

Contrôleur: Non, il va à Chamonix.

Christine: Et tous __2__ voyageurs, alors, ils ne prennent pas __3__ train?

Contrôleur: Non, ils attendent le train pour Grenoble.

Christine: Il va partir de __4__ quai aussi?

Contrôleur: Oui, mais pas de __5__ voie.
De la voie numéro 2.

Chamonix-Mont-Blanc,
France

17 **Historiette Au kiosque** Répondez d'après les photos.

1. Ce kiosque est dans une gare ou dans la rue?
2. Qu'est-ce qu'on vend dans ce kiosque?
3. Combien coûtent ces cartes postales?
4. Ces journaux sont français ou américains?

Gare de l'Est, Paris

FL.B.1.1.1 (I)   FL.C.1.2.1 (M)

 18

Au kiosque You want to buy several items but you don't know how much they cost. Ask the vendor (your partner) how much they cost. Then make sure the addition is correct when he or she asks you for the sum you owe. You may want to use the following words.

 du chewing-gum   un livre   un journal

 un magazine   une carte postale   des kleenex

Les verbes dire, écrire et lire
Describing more activities

Study the forms of the irregular verbs **dire** *(to say)*, **écrire** *(to write)*, and **lire** *(to read)*.

DIRE	ÉCRIRE	LIRE
je dis	j' écris	je lis
tu dis	tu écris	tu lis
il/elle/on dit	il/elle/on écrit	il/elle/on lit
nous disons	nous écrivons	nous lisons
vous dites	vous écrivez	vous lisez
ils/elles disent	ils/elles écrivent	ils/elles lisent

Comment dit-on?

19 **Historiette Christine et Juliette** Remplacez **Christine** par **Christine et Juliette**.

Christine est dans le train. Elle lit. Elle dit que le livre qu'elle lit est très intéressant. Christine a aussi des cartes postales à écrire. Elle écrit ses cartes postales. Elle dit que ses amis, eux, n'écrivent pas. Ils lisent les cartes postales de Christine? Bien sûr qu'ils lisent ses cartes postales!

20 **Petites conversations** Suivez le modèle.

 lire des journaux →
—Tu lis des journaux?
—Oui, je lis des journaux.

1. lire le journal local
2. lire beaucoup de livres
3. lire des magazines
4. écrire des lettres aux copains
5. écrire des cartes
6. dire toujours que oui

 For more practice using these verbs, do Activity 29 on page H30 at the end of this book.

FL.A.3.2.1 (I)

21 Oui ou non? Répondez.

1. Tes amis et toi, vous dites toujours des choses sérieuses?
2. Vous dites quelquefois des choses stupides?
3. Vous dites des choses amusantes?
4. Vous lisez beaucoup de livres?
5. Vous lisez beaucoup de poèmes?
6. Vous écrivez beaucoup de lettres?

La Conciergerie, Paris, France

Une jolie baie, Tahiti

22 Tout le monde Complétez.

1. (dire) Lui, il ____ toujours des choses stupides. Il ____ des bêtises. Ses amis ____ des bêtises aussi. Et vous, vous ____ quelquefois des bêtises aussi?
2. (dire) Lui, il ____ que oui. Ses amis ____ que oui. Et vous, qu'est-ce que vous ____?
3. (écrire) Lui, il ____ toujours des lettres. Mais ses amis n'____ pas de lettres. Ils ____ quelquefois des cartes postales. Et vous, vous ____ des lettres ou des cartes postales?
4. (lire) Lui, il ____ toujours des magazines. Ses amis ne ____ pas de magazines. Ils ____ des livres. Et vous? Vous ____ des magazines ou des livres?

Vous êtes sur le bon chemin. Allez-y!

Conversation

Au guichet

Employé: Bonjour.

Voyageuse: Bonjour, monsieur. Un billet pour Nice, s'il vous plaît.

Employé: Aller-retour ou aller simple?

Voyageuse: Aller-retour en seconde, tarif étudiant, s'il vous plaît.

Employé: Vous avez votre carte?

Voyageuse: Oui, voilà… C'est combien?

Employé: Alors, tarif étudiant, c'est trente euros.

Voyageuse: Le prochain train part à quelle heure?

Employé: À dix heures trente, voie numéro 12.

Voyageuse: Merci, monsieur. Au revoir.

Vous avez compris?

Répondez.

1. La voyageuse est à la gare?
2. Elle parle à un employé de la gare?
3. Elle veut aller où?
4. Elle prend un billet aller-retour ou aller simple?
5. Elle est étudiante?
6. Elle a sa carte d'étudiante?
7. Elle a une réduction?
8. Le billet coûte combien?
9. Le prochain train part à quelle heure?
10. Il part de quelle voie?

Parlons un peu plus

Réservation: 3615 3616 AF
-www.airfrance.fr

Jours	Dép.	Arr.	N° Vol		Corr. Validité
PARIS					
→ Madison (WI)					-6:00
1234567	**16.00** C **21.05**		AF380/AF8737(DL)		CVG 29/10-23
→ Madrid					+1:00
1234567	**07.15** F **09.15** 1		AF1000		→ 29/10-24
1234567	**09.40** F **11.40** 1		AF1300		→ 29/10-24
1234567	**10.45** F **12.45** 1		AF1500		→ 29/10-24
1234567	**12.45** F **14.45** 1		AF1600		→ 29/10-24
1234567	**14.15** F **16.15** 1		AF1700		→ 29/10-24
1234567	**15.30** F **17.30** 1		AF1800		→ 29/10-24
1234567	**16.30** F **18.30** 1		AF1900		→ 29/10-24
1234567	**17.35** F **19.35** 1		AF2000		→ 29/10-24
1234567	**19.20** F **21.20** 1		AF2100		→ 29/10-24
12345-7	**20.00** F **22.00** 1		AF2200		→ 29/10-23
→ Malaga					+1:00
1234567	**10.25** W **12.45**		AF3408		→ 29/10-24

A

On va à Madrid. You and a classmate are spending a semester in Paris. You will be going to Madrid for a couple of days. One of you is going to fly, and the other is going to take the train. Compare your trips: time of departure, how long the trip takes, and what you have to do the day you leave.

FL.A.1.2.2 (I)

TRAIN HOTEL — Francisco de Goya
HORAIRES

	TRAIN 409		TRAIN 407
PARIS-AUSTERLITZ	19.47	MADRID-CHAMARTIN	19.00
POITIERS	22.18	VALLADOLID	21.20
VITORIA/GASTEIZ	04.12	BURGOS	22.19
BURGOS	05.21	VITORIA/GASTEIZ	23.29
VALLADOLID	06.19	POITIERS	05.45
MADRID-CHAMARTIN	08.58	PARIS-AUSTERLITZ	08.29

Circulation quotidienne

B

Renseignements You're at the information desk at one of the Paris train stations. You need some information. Have a conversation with the SNCF agent (your partner). You may wish to use the following expressions: **à quelle heure, le prochain train, quelle voie, quel quai, voyager en seconde, c'est combien, changer de train, attendre la correspondance.**

FL.A.2.2.1 (I)

Prononciation

Les sons /õ/ et /ẽ/

1. Listen to the difference between the nasal sound /ã/ as in **cent** and the two other nasal sounds, /õ/ as in **son** and /ẽ/ as in **cinq: cent / son / cinq.** Repeat the following words with the sounds /õ/ and /ẽ/.

annonce	non	bon	son	correspondance
cinq	copain	train	pain	vingt

2. Now repeat the following sentences.

   On annonce le train dans combien de temps?
   Nous attendons des copains.

son train

Lectures culturelles

Un voyage intéressant

Reading Strategy

Thinking while reading

Good readers always think as they read. They read the title and look at the visuals to determine the topic of the passage. They predict, create visual images, check for understanding, and pay close attention to each sentence in the reading.

Vous dites que vous voulez faire un voyage intéressant en train. J'ai une bonne idée. Vous pouvez prendre le train de Bamako à Dakar. Deux fois par semaine, il y a un train entre ces deux villes. Les trains partent dans les deux sens (directions) tous les mercredis et les samedis matins.

Vous aimez lire? Pas de problème! Vous avez beaucoup de cartes postales à écrire à vos amis? Pas de problème non plus! Vous avez trente heures pour lire tous les livres que vous voulez et écrire beaucoup de cartes postales! Quand je dis trente heures, c'est d'après l'horaire. En réalité, le train est toujours en retard et c'est plutôt[1] un voyage de trente-cinq heures.

Si vous voulez dormir pendant le voyage, vous pouvez louer une couchette[2]. Il y a des wagons-couchettes et un wagon-restaurant. Le train fait beaucoup d'arrêts et les voyageurs peuvent descendre sur le quai et acheter quelque chose à manger ou à boire. Quand on entend l'annonce du départ du train, on remonte vite en voiture avec sa nourriture et le voyage continue.

[1] plutôt *more*
[2] louer une couchette *reserve a berth*

Le train qui fait Bamako–Dakar

Haïti   La Martinique

Le Sahara, Mali

La France

La Belgique

Où sont Bamako et Dakar? Bamako est la capitale du Mali. Le Mali est le pays francophone le plus grand d'Afrique Occidentale. Le Sahara couvre 60 pour cent du pays et il y a très peu de pluie[3]. Dakar est la capitale du Sénégal. Dakar est une très grande ville moderne sur l'océan Atlantique. C'est aussi un port important.

[3] pluie *rain*

Un marché, Mali

Vous avez compris?

A Bamako–Dakar Choisissez la bonne réponse.

1. Il y a un train entre Bamako et Dakar _____.
   a. une fois par semaine
   b. deux fois par semaine
2. Les trains partent _____.
   a. le matin
   b. l'après-midi
3. Les trains partent _____.
   a. le mardi et le dimanche
   b. le mercredi et le samedi
4. Le voyage entre Bamako et Dakar dure trente heures d'après _____.
   a. les contrôleurs
   b. l'horaire
5. Le train arrive presque toujours _____.
   a. en retard
   b. à l'heure
6. Beaucoup de voyageurs achètent quelque chose à manger _____.
   a. dans les gares
   b. au wagon-couchette

FL.C.1.2.2 (M)

B Un peu de géographie Choisissez la bonne réponse.

1. a. Le Sahara est un grand lac.
   b. Le Sahara est un grand désert.
2. a. Le Sénégal est un pays désertique.
   b. Le Mali est un pays désertique.
3. a. Bamako est la capitale du Mali.
   b. Bamako est la capitale du Sénégal.
4. a. Il y a très peu de pluie à Dakar.
   b. Il y a très peu de pluie à Bamako.

Le Maroc

Le Mali

Le Sénégal

FL.C.2.1.1 (I)

La SNCF
(La Société¹ nationale des chemins de fer français)

   Erica Saunders est une élève américaine. Elle passe ses vacances d'été en France. En ce moment elle est à la gare de Lyon à Paris. Elle va prendre le train pour Avignon. Tous les trains qui partent de cette gare vont vers le sud. Le train est un moyen de transport très populaire en France. Il y a six gares à Paris. Erica va au guichet et prend son billet. Elle veut un aller-retour en seconde. Elle a de la chance parce qu'il n'y a pas de queue.

   Munie de² son billet, Erica va sur le quai et monte dans le train. Avant d'aller sur le quai, elle composte son billet—elle passe son billet dans une machine. Ça indique où elle commence son voyage. C'est très important. Si on ne composte pas son billet, on paie une amende³. Erica n'attend pas longtemps. Il est 10 h 11 et le train part. Comme toujours le train part exactement à l'heure. En France, le service de la SNCF est excellent. Il y a très peu de retards.

¹ société *company*
² Munie de *With*
³ amende *fine*

Gare de Lyon, Paris

Si Erica a faim pendant le voyage, elle peut aller au snack-bar. Là on offre de la restauration rapide—un sandwich, une pizza ou une boisson, par exemple.

Pendant le voyage, Erica lit un guide sur Avignon. Le guide répond à toutes ses questions. Elle apprend qu'Avignon est une ville de culture et de fête. Elle va visiter le célèbre palais des Papes. Elle a de la chance, parce qu'en juillet, il y a un grand festival de théâtre qui a lieu[4] dans la cour du palais… et dans toute la ville. Elle veut voir aussi le pont d'Avignon qui traverse le Rhône. Ce pont célèbre date du douzième siècle. Là, elle va chanter «Sur le pont d'Avignon». Tous les élèves américains qui font du français apprennent cette chanson.

[4] a lieu *takes place*

Palais des Papes, Avignon, France

Le Maroc

Le Mali

Vous avez compris?

On va à Avignon. Répondez.

1. Qui est Erica Saunders?
2. Elle est où, en ce moment?
3. Elle va aller où?
4. Elle prend quel type de billet?
5. Le train part à quelle heure?
6. Comment est le service de la SNCF?
7. Si Erica a faim, elle peut manger où?
8. Qu'est-ce qu'elle lit pendant le voyage?
9. Qu'est-ce qu'elle veut voir à Avignon?
10. Qu'est-ce qu'il y a à Avignon pendant le mois de juillet?

CONNEXIONS

Le _____Samedi 25/1_____ à _11h 45_
Le _____ à _____
Le _____ à _____
Le _____ à _____
Le _____ à _____
Le _____ à _____
Le _____

Docteur Marcel BEGIN
CHIRURGIEN-DENTISTE   Tel: 45-48-18-27
Maître de Conférences des Universités

71, Rue de Rennes
75006 PARIS

M lle _____Annette Renaud_____

Votre prochain rendez-vous est fixé le ➡

FL.C.1.2.1 (I)

Les mathématiques

Des conversions—les horaires

When traveling through the French-speaking countries, you will need to make some mathematical conversions. The metric system is used for weights and measures rather than the English system, which we use in the United States. For schedules, the twenty-four-hour clock is used, rather than our A.M./P.M. system of indicating time. Let's learn to make some of these conversions.

Arman *L'heure de tous*

L'heure

Il y a deux façons[1] de dire l'heure. Il y a l'heure de la conversation normale: la journée est divisée[2] en deux fois douze heures—de une heure du matin à midi et de une heure de l'après-midi à minuit. Mais il y a aussi l'heure officielle. C'est l'heure des horaires de train, d'avion, de manifestations culturelles. C'est aussi l'heure qu'on utilise quand on prend rendez-vous[3] chez le dentiste, par exemple.

[1] façons *ways*   [3] prend rendez-vous *make an appointment*
[2] divisée *divided*

Pour l'heure officielle, la journée est divisée en 24 heures, de zéro heure à 23 heures. Étudiez le tableau suivant.

HORAIRES		CONVERSATION
0.25	zéro heure vingt-cinq	minuit vingt-cinq
8.15	huit heures quinze	huit heures et quart du matin
12.00	douze heures	midi
14.00	quatorze heures	deux heures de l'après-midi
16.40	seize heures quarante	cinq heures moins vingt de l'après-midi
22.00	vingt-deux heures	dix heures du soir
23.50	vingt-trois heures cinquante	minuit moins dix

Vous voulez prendre rendez-vous chez le dentiste pour 3 h de l'après-midi. C'est quelle heure en langage officiel? Votre train part à 21 h 35. C'est quelle heure en langage courant?

Les distances

Pour mesurer la distance, le système métrique utilise le mètre et non le *yard* ni le *mile* comme en anglais. Le mètre est un peu plus d'un *yard.* Un kilomètre (1 000 mètres) est équivalent à 0,621 *mile*—un peu plus d'un demi-*mile.*

Vous avez compris?

FL.D.2.2.2 (I)

A L'heure Read the departure board on page 314 and give the departure times of the trains in conversational French.

FL.D.2.2.2 (I)

B Les distances Read these road signs. Give the approximate distance in miles to each town.

C'est à vous

Use what you have learned

PARLER **1** **FL.A.1.2.1 (I)**

Le train, l'autocar ou l'avion?
✔ *Discuss train, bus, and plane travel*

 Work in groups of three or four. Discuss the advantages **(les avantages)** and disadvantages **(les inconvénients)** of train, bus **(autocar),** or plane travel. In your discussion, include such things as speed, price, location of terminals, and anything else you consider important.

Le bus, Dakar

L'aéroport, Saint-Barthélemy, les Antilles

La gare, Québec

Un bouchon, place d'Italie, Paris

PARLER **2** **FL.A.2.2.5 (I)**

Qu'est-ce qu'on va faire?
✔ *Discuss what to do if you miss your train*

 You and a classmate are on a bus on the way to **la gare de l'Est** in Paris. There's an awful traffic jam **(un bouchon).** You know you are going to miss your train. Discuss your predicament and decide what you are going to do.

ÉCRIRE

3

FL.A.3.2.3 (I)

Dans la gare

✔ *Write a paragraph using expressions related to train travel*

Look at the photograph and use it as a basis for writing a paragraph about a train station.

La gare Saint-Charles, Marseille

Writing Strategy

Writing a descriptive paragraph Your goal in writing a descriptive paragraph is to enable the reader to visualize a scene. To achieve this, you must select and organize details that create an impression. Using a greater number of specific nouns and vivid, descriptive adjectives will make your writing livelier.

ÉCRIRE

4

FL.A.2.2.3 (I)

Un voyage fabuleux

Write about a trip you want to take. It can be a real or imaginary trip. Describe how you'll go and when. Describe in great detail how you'll get there. Describe all the things you have to do. Continue by writing about what you are going to see and do when you get there. Try to make your readers understand what it is about the place that makes you like it so much.

À NOUS DE VOUS FAIRE PRÉFÉRER LE TRAIN.

SNCF

Voyagez avec
AIR FRANCE

Assessment

Vocabulaire

1 Répondez.

To review **Mots 1,** turn to pages 292–293.

1. Qu'est-ce qu'on vend au kiosque?
2. Les voyageurs attendent le train où?
3. Qu'est-ce qu'on regarde pour vérifier l'heure du départ ou de l'arrivée d'un train?
4. On vend les billets de train où?

2 Complétez d'après le dessin.

To review **Mots 2,** turn to pages 296–297.

5. La plupart des voyageurs sont _____.
6. Trois voyageurs sont _____.
7. Une passagère écrit _____.
8. Un autre passager lit _____.

For more Chapter 9 test preparation, go to the Chapter 9 **Self-Check Quiz** on the Glencoe French Web site at glencoe.com.

Structure

3 Récrivez chaque phrase.

To review **-re** verbs in the present, turn to page 300.

9. Ils attendent le train.
   Il _____.
10. Tu entends l'annonce?
    Vous _____?
11. Tout le monde perd patience.
    Je _____.
12. Qu'est-ce qu'elle vend?
    Qu'est-ce qu'elles _____?
13. On descend au prochain arrêt.
    Tu _____.

4 **Complétez avec «ce».**

14. _____ train va à Bordeaux.

15. _____ carte postale est très jolie.

16. Notre train part de _____ voie ou de la voie 5?

17. _____ voitures sont assez vieilles.

To review demonstrative adjectives, turn to page 303.

5 **Complétez.**

18. J'_____ des cartes postales. (écrire)

19. Ils _____ beaucoup. (lire)

20. Vous _____ que oui ou que non? (dire)

21. Vous _____ beaucoup de lettres. (écrire)

22. Tu _____ quel livre? (lire)

To review **dire**, **écrire**, and **lire**, turn to page 306.

Culture

6 **Vrai ou faux?**

23. Il y a un train deux fois par semaine entre Bamako et Dakar.

24. Ce train arrive toujours à l'heure.

25. Dakar, la capitale du Sénégal, est une très grande ville moderne sur la mer Mediterranée.

To review this cultural information, turn to pages 310–311.

La gare, Dakar, Sénégal

LA GARE ET LE TRAIN

Do these practice activities to help you succeed on your FCAT through the study of a foreign language.

Read the passage below. Then answer the questions that follow.

À Paris il y a six grandes gares. Les trains qui partent de chaque gare vont dans des directions différentes. Le train est un moyen de transport important et populaire en France. Et en Amérique? Le train est important? Populaire? Les trains en France partent presque toujours à l'heure. Les retards ne sont pas du tout fréquents. Et les trains en France sont très propres. Le TGV (le train à grande vitesse) est extrêmement rapide. Ce train va à beaucoup de villes.

Aujourd'hui c'est le 3 juillet et Maryse prend le train pour Avignon. Elle va à la gare de Lyon. Tous les trains qui partent de cette gare vont vers le sud. Maryse va au guichet pour prendre son billet. Elle n'attend pas longtemps. Elle demande un aller-retour en seconde. Puis elle composte son billet parce qu'elle ne veut pas payer d'amende! Elle va ensuite sur le quai pour attendre le train. On annonce le départ du train. Dans le train il y a un snack-bar où elle peut prendre un sandwich ou une boisson. Maryse lit un guide sur Avignon, une ville de culture et de fête. Elle a l'intention de visiter le célèbre Palais des Papes à Avignon où il y a un grand festival de théâtre en juillet. Et comme tous les touristes, elle veut voir le célèbre pont d'Avignon qui traverse le Rhône et qui date du douzième siècle. Tous les élèves américains qui font du français apprennent la chanson «Sur le pont d'Avignon».

1  Comparez et contrastez le train en France et en Amérique.

2 Pourquoi Maryse va-t-elle à la gare de Lyon?
   A. parce qu'elle va à Lyon
   B. parce que les trains qui partent de cette gare partent toujours à l'heure
   C. parce qu'elle veut prendre un billet aller-retour
   D. parce que le train pour Avignon part de cette gare

3 READ THINK EXPLAIN À votre avis, pourquoi les trains en France sont-ils plus populaires que les trains aux États-Unis?

4 Quelle phrase signifie la même chose? **Elle n'attend pas longtemps.**

    F.   Elle est à l'heure.

    G. Elle fait la queue pendant quelques minutes seulement.

    H. Elle est obligée de faire la queue pendant une demi-heure.

    I.   Son train n'est pas en retard.

5 Pourquoi Maryse prend-elle un billet aller-retour?

    A. parce qu'elle veut passer ses vacances à Avignon

    B. parce qu'elle va retourner à Paris après son voyage

    C. parce que c'est moins cher qu'un aller simple

    D. parce qu'elle ne veut pas prendre l'avion

6 Quand est-ce qu'on paie une amende?

    F.   quand on ne composte pas son billet

    G. quand on n'a pas assez d'argent pour payer son billet

    H. quand on veut aller sur le quai

    I.   quand on achète un billet aller-retour

7 Pourquoi Maryse voyage-t-elle en juillet?

    A. parce que voyager en été, c'est moins cher

    B. parce qu'on peut voir le pont d'Avignon seulement en été

    C. parce que les trains partent toujours à l'heure en juillet

    D. parce qu'il y a un festival de théâtre à Avignon en juillet

8 Pourquoi le pont d'Avignon est-il célèbre?

    F.   C'est un pont très moderne qui traverse le Rhône.

    G. Tous les touristes veulent le voir.

    H. Il est très vieux et il y a une chanson qui parle de ce pont.

    I.   Les élèves américains qui font du français apprennent «Sur le pont d'Avignon».

> **FCAT Tip**
>
> Allow about five minutes to answer the short-response questions and about ten to fifteen minutes to answer the extended-response questions.

FL.A.2.1.2 (I)

Tell all you can about this illustration.

Vocabulaire

Getting around a train station

une gare	un guichet	un chariot	une salle d'attente
un train	un billet	un kiosque	un buffet
un quai	un aller simple	un journal	
une voie	un aller (et) retour	un magazine	
la correspondance	en seconde	une carte (postale)	
un horaire	en première		

Describing activities at a train station

faire la queue	vendre	partir
attendre	monter (en voiture)	changer (de)
descendre	composter	rater

On board the train

une voiture	lire
un wagon	dire
assis(e)	écrire
debout	répondre
un voyageur	un snack-bar
une voyageuse	un arrêt
un contrôleur	au prochain arrêt
contrôler les billets	

How well do you know your vocabulary?
- Choose five words from the vocabulary list.
- Use the words in original sentences to tell a story.

Other useful words and expressions

arriver à + infinitif
être en avance
être en retard
perdre patience
la plupart des
quelques
depuis

VIDÉOTOUR

Épisode 9

In this video episode, Amadou and Chloé set out on a train trip to Lille. Or at least they try to. See page 534 for more information.

CHAPITRE
10

1998 France championne du monde

Les sports

Objectifs

In this chapter you will learn to:

✓ *talk about team sports and other physical activities*

✓ *describe past actions and events*

✓ *ask people questions*

✓ *discuss sports in Canada and in French-speaking Africa*

Robert Delaunay *Les coureurs*

French Online
To interact with your online edition of **Bon voyage!** go to: glencoe.com.

SUNSHINE STATE STANDARDS

This chapter is all about sports. The material in the chapter will address the Sunshine State Standards listed below.

FL.A.1.2.1 express likes or dislikes regarding various objects, categories, people, and events present in the everyday environment.

FL.A.1.2.2 exchange information necessary to plan events or activities (e.g., picnics, birthday parties, science projects, and crafts).

FL.A.1.3.4 use repetition, rephrasing, and gestures effectively to assist in communicating spoken messages.

FL.A.2.1.2 restate and rephrase simple information from materials presented orally, visually, and graphically in class.

FL.A.2.1.3 understand oral messages that are based on familiar themes and vocabulary (e.g., short conversations between familiar persons on familiar topics such as everyday school and home activities).

FL.A.2.2.3 organize information in spoken or written form about a variety of topics of academic and cultural interest (e.g., by making lists, categorizing objects, or organizing concepts).

FL.A.2.2.5 comprehend and respond to oral messages (e.g., personal anecdotes or narratives) based on familiar themes and vocabulary.

FL.A.3.1.1 provide simple information in spoken form (e.g., descriptions of family members, friends, objects present in his or her everyday environment, or common school and home activities).

FL.A.3.2.1 describe important people (e.g., family members and friends) and objects present in his or her everyday environment and in school.

FL.A.3.2.3 give responses in spoken or written form (e.g., answering simple questions, formulating questions, and making simple statements) to age-appropriate stories, poems or other literature, songs, films, or visual works.

FL.B.1.1.1 participate in age-appropriate cultural activities (e.g., games, songs, birthday celebrations, storytelling, dramatizations, and role playing).

FL.B.1.1.3 recognize various familiar objects and norms of the target culture (e.g., toys, dresses, and typical foods).

Delray Beach, Florida

FL.C.1.2.2 use target-language vocabulary or concepts to reinforce knowledge of a related topic studied in another class (e.g., geographical place names, parts of the body, or basic mathematical operations).

FL.C.2.1.1 use the target language to gain access to information that is only available through the target language or within the target culture (listen to a story told in the target language).

FL.D.1.1.2 use simple vocabulary and short phrases in the target language.

FL.D.1.2.1 identify examples and understand the significance of true and false cognates (i.e., words derived from a common original form).

FL.D.2.1.1 know the similarities and differences between the patterns of behavior of the target culture related to recreation, celebration, holidays, customs, and the patterns of behavior of the local culture.

FL.D.2.2.1 distinguish the similarities and differences between the patterns of behavior of the target culture related to recreation, holidays, celebrations, and the patterns of behavior of the local culture.

 TIPS FOR SUCCESS
Review the Study Tips below to help you succeed on the Sunshine State Standards identified.

Kayak in shallow waters of reef

Vocabulaire Mots 1 Mots 2 *(pages 324–331)*

- Look at each photo or illustration carefully.
- Read the labels. What does each word refer to?
- The words are then used in a meaningful context in a complete sentence. Repeat the sentence aloud as you look at the illustration.
- To help you learn vocabulary, work with a friend or classmate. Have a contest. See who can say the most about each illustration or photo. **FL.A.2.1.2; FL.A.3.1.1**

Conversation *(page 340)*

- The activity **Vous avez compris?** enables you to practice question words. **FL.D.1.1.2**

 Lectures culturelles **Le hockey et le basket-ball** *(pages 342–343)*

- Before reading this selection, sit back and think for a moment about what you know concerning hockey and basketball. Get a mental picture of the game. This will help you understand the reading selection. **FL.D.2.1.1**

Vocabulaire *(page 353)*
- Look at each word and see if you can use it in a short sentence. **FL.D.1.1.2**

> **For other tips to help you address the Sunshine State Standards in Chapter 10, see page H64 at the back of your textbook.**

Vocabulaire

Le foot(ball)

une joueuse

un ballon

Le gardien arrête le ballon.
Il bloque le ballon.
Le ballon n'entre pas dans le but.

Une équipe de foot a onze joueurs.

Pour jouer au football, on a besoin d'un ballon.
Et c'est tout!

un stade
les gradins
les deux camps
le camp adverse
un terrain (de football)
une spectatrice
un spectateur

Le stade est comble.
Il y a beaucoup de monde.
Les gradins sont pleins.

un arbitre
siffler
la tête
le pied

Une joueuse passe le ballon à l'autre.

hier — 2 AVRIL | 3 AVRIL — aujourd'hui
MATCH AUXERRE-LYON

AUXERRE 3 LYON 2

You're going to hit the guy!!!

Hier Auxerre a joué contre Lyon.
Le match a opposé Lyon et Auxerre.
Ils ont joué au foot(ball).
Lafitte a donné un coup de pied dans le ballon.
Auxerre a gagné par 3 à 2.
Lyon a perdu.

Sissoko a envoyé le ballon dans le but.
Il a marqué un but.
Il a égalisé le score—2 à 2.

Quel est le mot?

1 **Historiette** **Un match de foot** Répondez d'après les indications.

1. On a besoin de quoi pour jouer au foot? (un ballon)
2. Dans un match de foot, il y a combien d'équipes? (deux)
3. Chaque équipe a combien de joueurs? (onze)
4. Il y a combien de joueurs sur le terrain? (vingt-deux)
5. Dans un match, il y a combien de camps? (deux)
6. Le match est divisé en quoi? (en deux mi-temps)
7. Chaque mi-temps dure combien de minutes? (quarante-cinq minutes)
8. Qui garde le but? (le gardien de but)
9. Qu'est-ce que chaque équipe veut faire? (marquer des buts)
10. Qui bloque ou arrête le ballon? (le gardien de but)

CHAMPIONNAT D'EUROPE DES NATIONS

LE LIVRE D'OR

la victoire est en bleu

SOLAR

DOMINIQUE GRIMAULT

Des fanas de foot

2 **Historiette** **Le stade est comble.** Inventez une histoire.

1. Il y a beaucoup de spectateurs dans le stade aujourd'hui?
2. Les gradins sont pleins ou il y a beaucoup de places libres?
3. Le stade est comble?
4. Il y a beaucoup de monde dans le stade?
5. Le foot, c'est un sport d'équipe ou un sport individuel?

3 **Auxerre contre Lyon** Répondez que oui.

1. Hier, Lyon a joué contre Auxerre?
2. Lafitte a donné un coup de tête dans le ballon?
3. Lafitte a passé le ballon à Sissoko?
4. Sissoko a marqué un but?
5. Sissoko a égalisé le score?
6. L'arbitre a sifflé?
7. Il a déclaré un penalty contre Lyon?
8. Auxerre a gagné le match?
9. Lyon a perdu le match?

Hors manifestations, le Stade de France® se visite tous les jours

Départ visites : Porte H

Le parcours "Premiers regards" vous permet d'explorer à votre rythme 500m² d'exposition ludique et interactive avant de découvrir l'arène grandeur nature. Confortablement assis en tribune, vous êtes alors rejoint par un guide du Stade de France qui vous présente l'arène et répond à vos questions. Visite de 10H00 à 18H00. Fermeture des caisses à 17H30. Adultes : 5,79 €. Enfants *(jusqu'à 18 ans)* : 4,57 €.

http://www.stadefrance.com

FL.A.2.1.2 (I)   FL.B.1.1.3 (I)

4 **Un match de foot** Work with a classmate. Take turns describing the soccer game in the illustration.

Boys against girls!!!

For more practice using words from **Mots 1**, do Activity 30 on page H31 at the end of this book.

Vocabulaire

D'autres sports d'équipe 🎧

Le basket(-ball)

lancer

un joueur
de basket

le panier

dribbler

le demi-cercle

Une joueuse a dribblé le ballon.
Elle a dribblé le ballon jusqu'au
demi-cercle.

Le volley(-ball)

le filet

Un joueur a servi.

par-dessus le filet

le sol

Un autre joueur a renvoyé le ballon.
Le ballon ne doit pas toucher le sol.

Le joueur a lancé le ballon dans
le panier.
Il a réussi un beau panier.

Le cyclisme

des coureurs cyclistes

un vélo, une bicyclette

une course cycliste

Le coureur roule vite.
Pendant la course, les coureurs boivent
de l'eau.

L'athlétisme

une coureuse

une piste

un gagnant

la coupe

Khalil (Numéro 27) a gagné la course.
Leblanc (Nº 10) a perdu la course.

Khalil a reçu la coupe.
C'est la première fois qu'il reçoit la coupe.

Note 🎧
The following expressions are
often used to express past
events:

hier
avant-hier
la semaine dernière
l'année dernière

Quel est le mot?

5 **Historiette** **Un match de basket**
Répondez.

1. Le basket-ball est un sport individuel ou collectif (d'équipe)?
2. Il y a cinq ou onze joueurs dans une équipe de basket?
3. Pendant un match de basket, les joueurs dribblent le ballon ou donnent un coup de pied dans le ballon?
4. Un joueur dribble le ballon jusqu'au demi-cercle ou jusqu'au sol?
5. Un joueur de basket lance le ballon dans le panier ou dans le filet?

Un match de basket

6 **Historiette** **Le volley-ball** Vrai ou faux?

1. Une équipe de volley-ball a onze joueurs.
2. Un joueur sert.
3. Un joueur du camp adverse renvoie le ballon.
4. Quand il renvoie le ballon, le ballon peut toucher le filet.
5. On renvoie le ballon par-dessus le filet.
6. Le ballon doit toucher le sol.

7 **Historiette** **Une course cycliste** Choisissez.

1. Un vélo est _____.
   a. une bicyclette   **b.** une voiture   **c.** un stade
2. _____ roule à vélo.
   a. Un spectateur   **b.** Un coureur cycliste   **c.** Un joueur
3. Dans une course internationale, chaque équipe _____.
   a. reçoit une coupe   **b.** représente son pays   **c.** roule
4. Le gagnant de la course est _____.
   a. la coupe   **b.** le champion   **c.** le coureur
5. Dans une course cycliste, les coureurs roulent sur _____.
   a. des gradins   **b.** un terrain   **c.** une piste
6. Pendant la course les coureurs boivent _____.
   a. du vinaigre   **b.** du café   **c.** de l'eau

8 C'est quel sport? Choisissez.

1. Le joueur a dribblé le ballon très vite.
2. Le joueur a donné un coup de tête dans le ballon.
3. La joueuse a réussi un beau panier.
4. La coureuse française a gagné.
5. Le gardien de but a arrêté le ballon.
6. La joueuse américaine a renvoyé le ballon par-dessus le filet.
7. Un joueur a servi.

  9 Jeu FL.A.3.2.1 (I) **C'est quel sport?** Work with a classmate. Use complete sentences to give him or her some information about a sport. He or she has to guess the sport you're talking about. Take turns.

FrenchOnline

For a fun way to review this vocabulary, go to the Chapter 10 **eGame** on the Glencoe French Web site at glencoe.com.

Fabien Barthez, gardien de but de l'équipe de France

FrenchOnline

To learn more about sports in the Francophone world, go to **Web Explore** on the Glencoe French Web site at glencoe.com. The **WebQuest** activity also includes links to French sports Web sites.

 FL.A.1.2.1 (I) FL.D.1.2.1 (M)

  10 Mon équipe favorite Work with a classmate. Find out each other's favorite team. Explain why it is your favorite team. You may like to know that "baseball" is the same word in French: **le base-ball.**

For more practice using words from **Mots 2,** *do Activity 31 on page H32 at the end of this book.*

Structure

Le passé composé des verbes réguliers
Describing past actions

1. You use the **passé composé** to express an action that began and was completed in the past. To form the **passé composé,** you use the present tense of the verb **avoir** and the past participle. Study the forms of the past participle of regular verbs.

-er → é		-ir → i		-re → u	
parler	parlé	finir	fini	perdre	perdu
jouer	joué	choisir	choisi	vendre	vendu

2. Study the forms of the **passé composé.**

JOUER	CHOISIR	PERDRE
j' ai joué	j' ai choisi	j' ai perdu
tu as joué	tu as choisi	tu as perdu
il/elle/on a joué	il/elle/on a choisi	il/elle/on a perdu
nous avons joué	nous avons choisi	nous avons perdu
vous avez joué	vous avez choisi	vous avez perdu
ils/elles ont joué	ils/elles ont choisi	ils/elles ont perdu

Hier soir, j'ai téléphoné à un copain.
Après j'ai regardé un match de foot.
Mon copain aussi a regardé le match.
Malheureusement, notre équipe a perdu.

3. In the **passé composé, n'… pas** goes around the verb **avoir.**

Tu n'as pas regardé la télé?
Non, parce que je n'ai pas fini mes devoirs.

Savez-vous que... ?

When you talk about playing a sport, you use **jouer à.**

Ils ont joué au football.
Mais moi, j'ai joué au base-ball.

Comment dit-on?

11 **Participes passés** Donnez le participe passé des verbes suivants.

1. habiter
2. parler
3. écouter
4. travailler
5. remplir
6. réussir
7. servir
8. dormir
9. perdre
10. vendre
11. attendre
12. répondre

FL.D.1.1.2 (I)

12 **Historiette** **Hier** Donnez des réponses personnelles.

1. Hier matin, tu as quitté la maison à quelle heure?
2. Tu as rigolé un peu avec les copains avant les cours?
3. Tu as parlé au prof de français?
4. Tu as passé un examen?
5. Tu as répondu à toutes les questions?
6. Tu as quitté l'école à quelle heure?
7. Tu as attendu le bus pour rentrer à la maison?

13 **Historiette** **La fête de Chloé** Complétez au passé composé.

Samedi dernier, Chloé __1__ (donner) une fête. Elle __2__ (téléphoner) à tous ses copains. Tous ses copains __3__ (répondre) au téléphone. Chloé __4__ (inviter) tous ses amis à la fête. Tous, ils __5__ (accepter) son invitation. Yves et moi, nous __6__ (préparer) des sandwichs, mais c'est Chloé qui __7__ (acheter) la nourriture et les boissons. À la fête, on __8__ (écouter) de la musique, on __9__ (danser). On __10__ bien __11__ (rigoler).

14 **Historiette** **Un match de foot**
Inventez des réponses.

1. Tu as regardé un match de foot à la télé hier soir?
2. Auxerre a joué contre Lyon?
3. L'année dernière, qui a gagné la coupe? Lyon?
4. Mais hier soir, Lyon a perdu?
5. L'arbitre a puni un joueur lyonnais?
6. Il a déclaré un penalty contre Lyon?
7. Les spectateurs ont applaudi?

Paris-Saint-Germain contre Metz

15 **Un voyage en avion** Répondez que non.

1. Tu as voyagé l'année dernière?
2. Tu as voyagé sur Air France?
3. Tu as choisi classe économique?
4. Tu as choisi une place côté couloir?
5. L'avion a décollé à l'heure?
6. Et il a atterri à l'heure?

7. Tu as voyagé avec un copain ou une copine?
8. Tu as attendu longtemps tes bagages?
9. La compagnie aérienne a perdu tes bagages?

FL.A.2.1.3 (I)

16 **Historiette** **Un voyage en train** Mettez au passé composé.

J'attends le train. Ma copine Alice et moi, nous voyageons ensemble. Nous attendons le train dans la salle d'attente. J'achète un magazine au kiosque. Ma copine choisit un livre. Nous entendons l'annonce du départ de notre train. Nous trouvons la voiture numéro 11. Nous montons nos bagages dans le train. Nous trouvons nos places réservées occupées par deux personnes très désagréables! Que faire? Nous laissons nos places à ces personnes!

FL.A.2.1.3 (I)

17 **Le voyage d'Alice** Relisez l'Activité 16 et posez des questions à Alice et sa copine sur leur voyage. Suivez le modèle.

Vous avez voyagé ensemble?

FL.A.2.2.5 (I)

18 **La semaine dernière** Work with a classmate. Ask each other what you did last week. Answer each other's questions. Talk about the things you both did. You can also talk about some things your friends did. Here are some words you may wish to use: **regarder, parler, jouer, quitter, étudier, acheter, voyager, écouter, travailler, préparer, gagner, servir, dormir, attendre, perdre, répondre à.**

For more practice using regular verbs in the **passé composé**, do Activity 32 on page H33 at the end of this book.

Stade de France, Paris

Qui, qu'est-ce que, quoi
Asking questions

1. You use **qui** in questions when asking about a person.

> **Qui va gagner?**   Paul.
> **Tu as invité qui?**   Nathalie.

2. You use **qu'est-ce que (qu')** or **quoi** to ask "what." **Qu'est-ce que (qu')** goes at the beginning of a sentence and **quoi** at the end.

> **Qu'est-ce que tu regardes?**
> **Tu regardes quoi?**   }   **Un match de foot.**

3. After a preposition, you use **qui** for people and **quoi** for things.

> **Tu vas aller au match avec qui?**   Avec Loïc.
> **On joue au foot avec quoi?**   Avec un ballon.
> **Tu as besoin de quoi?**   D'un ballon.

Savez-vous que... ?

Qu'est-ce que tu as? can mean "What's the matter (with you)?"

Comment dit-on?

19   **Qui ça?**   Posez des questions avec **qui**.

1. *Marie* parle au téléphone.
2. Elle parle à *son copain Julien*.
3. Elle invite *Julien* à un match de football.
4. *Julien* veut aller au match.
5. *Ézédine* va jouer.
6. *Ézédine* est un très bon joueur.
7. Julien parle souvent d'*Ézédine*.

 FL.A.1.3.4 (I)

20   **Comment? Qu'est-ce que tu fais?**   Posez des questions d'après le modèle.

J'écoute la radio.

Comment? Qu'est-ce que tu écoutes?

1. Je lis le journal.
2. Je regarde la télé.
3. Je fais des exercices.
4. J'écris une carte postale.
5. Nous voulons le journal.
6. Nous mettons la table.
7. Nous préparons le petit déjeuner.

21 Mini-conversations Posez des questions et répondez d'après le modèle.

marquer un but →

—Qu'est-ce que les joueurs ont marqué?

—Ils ont marqué un but.

1. lancer le ballon
2. dribbler le ballon
3. envoyer le ballon
4. perdre le match
5. gagner la coupe
6. égaliser le score

Le garçon dribble le ballon.

FL.A.1.3.4 (I)

22 On a besoin de quoi? Conversez d'après le modèle.

—J'ai besoin d'un verre pour boire de l'eau.

—Qu'est-ce que tu dis? Tu as besoin de quoi?

1. J'ai besoin d'une télé pour regarder des vidéos.
2. J'ai besoin d'un ballon pour jouer au basket.
3. J'ai besoin d'un billet pour prendre le train.
4. J'ai besoin d'un stylo-bille pour écrire des cartes postales.
5. J'ai besoin d'un oignon pour faire la salade.

I need an onion for my fairy salad.

23 Je n'ai pas bien entendu. Posez des questions.

1. Il aime bien *Marie*.
2. Il parle souvent de *Marie*.
3. Il parle à *Marie* maintenant.
4. Il invite Marie à *une fête*.
5. Il parle à Marie de *la fête*.

FL.A.2.2.5 (I)

24 Jeu **Beaucoup de questions** Work with a classmate. Play a guessing game. Ask as many questions as you can. See who can answer the most questions.

Les verbes boire, devoir et recevoir
Describing more activities

Study the forms of the irregular verbs **boire** *(to drink)*, **devoir** *(to owe)*, and **recevoir** *(to receive)*.

BOIRE	DEVOIR	RECEVOIR
je bois	je dois	je reçois
tu bois	tu dois	tu reçois
il/elle/on boit	il/elle/on doit	il/elle/on reçoit
nous buvons	nous devons	nous recevons
vous buvez	vous devez	vous recevez
ils/elles boivent	ils/elles doivent	ils/elles reçoivent

Vous buvez de l'eau ou de la limonade?
Je dois beaucoup d'argent à mes parents.
Cet enfant reçoit toujours trop de cadeaux.

Savez-vous que... ?

When **devoir** is followed by another verb, it means "must" or "to have to."
Elle doit étudier parce qu'elle doit passer un examen demain.

Comment dit-on?

25 **Historiette** **Un match de volley-ball** Répondez.

1. Pendant un match de volley-ball, les joueurs reçoivent le ballon?
2. Ils doivent renvoyer le ballon?
3. Le ballon doit toucher le sol?
4. Il doit passer par-dessus le filet?
5. Après le match, les joueurs boivent de l'eau?

Elles jouent au volley-ball.

26 **Moi** Donnez des réponses personnelles.

1. Tu dois boire beaucoup d'eau?
2. Tu bois de l'eau?
3. Qu'est-ce que tu bois quand tu as soif?
4. Tu dois de l'argent à tes amis?
5. Tu dois de l'argent à tes parents?
6. Tu reçois de l'argent pour ton anniversaire?
7. Tu reçois des cadeaux?

À CONSOMMER SANS MODÉRATION

C'est au cours des repas que nous consommons près de 70% de ce que nous buvons. Mais où placer les autres pauses boisson? L'idéal est de commencer par boire un verre d'eau avant le petit déjeuner pour bien drainer notre organisme. Un autre avant de passer à table remet à neuf le palais et permet de mieux jouir du goût des aliments. Enfin, un petit dernier avant de se coucher évite la trop grande concentration des urines. C'est tout? Mais non! Un verre toutes les deux heures, même sans avoir spécialement soif, cela fait du bien.

FL.A.1.3.4 (I)

27 **Pardon?** Suivez le modèle.

 Je bois beaucoup d'eau.

Pardon? Je n'ai pas bien entendu. Qu'est-ce que vous buvez?

1. Je bois beaucoup d'eau minérale.
2. Je dois boire beaucoup d'eau.
3. Je reçois le ballon.
4. Je dois renvoyer le ballon.

FL.A.3.1.1 (I)

28 **Qu'est-ce que je dois faire?** Work with a classmate. Discuss some things you should or must do. Tell if you can do them or not. If you can't, try to explain why.

Le marathon de Paris

For more practice using **boire, devoir,** and **recevoir,** do Activity 33 on page H34 at the end of this book.

Vous êtes sur le bon chemin. Allez-y!

Conversation

On a gagné!

Jean: Tu as regardé la télé hier soir?

Rémi: Ben, bien sûr. J'ai regardé France–Brésil, comme tout le monde!

Jean: On a gagné, mais tout juste, hein! Un–zéro.

Rémi: Oui, heureusement que Lafitte a marqué à la dernière minute.

Jean: Les Brésiliens ne doivent pas être contents!

Rémi: Ça, c'est sûr! Marcos a bien arrêté tous les ballons mais…

Jean: Il n'a pas bloqué le dernier!

Rémi: Remarque, le match d'avant, les Brésiliens ont réussi à égaliser à deux secondes de la fin!

Vous avez compris?

Répondez.

1. À qui parle Rémi?
2. Qu'est-ce qu'ils ont regardé hier?
3. Qui a gagné le match?
4. Qui a marqué le but pour la France?
5. Qui est Marcos?
6. Qu'est-ce qu'il n'a pas bloqué?
7. Dans le match précédent qui a égalisé le score?

Parlons un peu plus

FL.A.1.2.1 (I)

A **Je ne suis pas très fana de...**
Work with a classmate. Tell him or her what sport you don't like to play. Tell what sport or sports you like. Then ask your classmate questions to find out what sports he or she does or doesn't like.

FL.B.1.1.3 (I)

B **Un match de foot** You are at a soccer game with a friend (your classmate). He or she has never been to a soccer game before and doesn't understand the game. Your friend has a lot of questions. Answer his or her questions and explain the game. You may want to use some of the following words: **jouer, recevoir, donner un coup de pied, donner un coup de tête, marquer, perdre, gagner, devoir, passer, arrêter, bloquer.**

Prononciation

Liaison et élision

- You know that liaison or elision occurs when certain words are followed by a vowel. Some liaisons are obligatory, some are optional.

- Liaison is obligatory with plural subject pronouns, plural articles, plural possessive and demonstrative adjectives, and plural adjectives preceding the noun. Repeat the following.

  ils‿ont   les‿équipes   des‿amateurs
  mes‿amis   ces‿arbitres   de bonnes‿équipes

- Elision is always obligatory. It occurs with **le** and **la**, with **je,** the negative **ne,** and **que.** Repeat the following.

  l'arbitre   Je n'aime pas ça.   Qu'est-ce qu'il fait?
  l'équipe   j'attends

des‿arbitres

- Now repeat the following pairs of sentences.

  Vous‿avez perdu. / Vous n'avez pas perdu.
  J'ai fini. / Je n'ai pas fini.

Lectures culturelles

Le hockey et le basket-ball

Au Québec

Le hockey est un sport très apprécié au Québec. Le hockey ressemble un peu au football, sauf[1] qu'on joue sur de la glace. Il y a deux équipes de cinq joueurs et deux gardiens de but. Un match de hockey est divisé en trois périodes de vingt minutes. Chaque joueur pousse le palet avec une crosse et essaie de mettre le palet dans le but de l'équipe adverse. Comme au football, on fait des passes à ses coéquipiers[2] pour essayer de marquer des buts.

[1] sauf *except*
[2] coéquipiers *teammates*

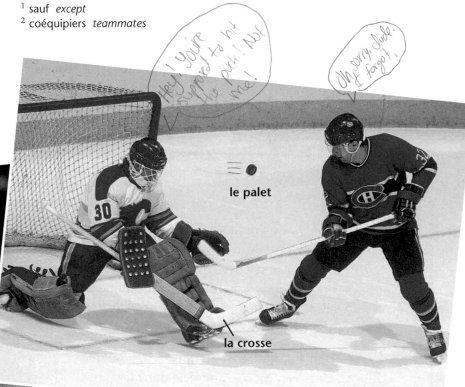

le palet

la crosse

la glace

Les Canadiens de Montréal contre les Calgary Flames

Turner Stevenson, les Canadiens de Montréal

Haïti

La Martinique

En Afrique

Dans les pays d'Afrique Occidentale, le sport numéro un, c'est le football, comme en France. Mais le deuxième sport, c'est le basket-ball. Une équipe de basket-ball est composée de cinq joueurs. Chaque joueur veut prendre possession du ballon. Il essaie de lancer le ballon dans le panier de l'équipe adverse. On joue au basket-ball avec les mains uniquement. On ne peut pas marcher[3] avec le ballon dans les mains.

Il faut dribbler le ballon.

Et toi, quel est ton sport favori? Tu es fana de foot, de basket ou de hockey? Tu aimes mieux les sports d'équipe ou les sports individuels?

Tu préfères participer ou être spectateur (spectatrice)?

[3] marcher *walk*

Un match de basket: Sénégal contre Canada

Vous avez compris?

A Le hockey Répondez.

1. Quel est un sport très apprécié au Québec?
2. On joue au hockey sur quoi?
3. On joue au hockey avec quoi?
4. Il y a combien de joueurs dans une équipe de hockey?
5. Qu'est-ce qu'un joueur de hockey essaie de faire?
6. Qu'est-ce qu'il fait à ses coéquipiers?

B Le basket-ball Vrai ou faux?

1. Le basket-ball est très apprécié dans les pays d'Afrique Occidentale.
2. C'est le sport le plus populaire.
3. Une équipe de basket-ball a onze joueurs.
4. Un joueur de basket-ball essaie de lancer le ballon dans le panier de l'équipe adverse.
5. On joue au basket avec les mains et les pieds.

Un joueur de basket du Cameroun

FL.A.3.2.3 (I)   **FL.C.2.1.1 (I)**

Le Tour de France

Un sport très apprécié

Un des sports les plus appréciés en France, c'est le cyclisme. Et l'événement sportif le plus populaire, c'est le Tour de France. Le Tour de France a lieu[1] tous les ans au mois de juillet. C'est une course cycliste sur un long circuit de routes françaises, tout autour du pays et quelquefois dans d'autres pays. Des coureurs cyclistes de tous les pays du monde participent au Tour de France.

Qu'est-ce que le Tour de France?

Le Tour de France est divisé en plusieurs étapes[2]. On va d'une ville à l'autre. On part le matin et on arrive le soir. Le Tour de France dure trois semaines. On donne au gagnant une coupe et le droit[3] de porter le maillot[4] jaune. Il reçoit aussi une somme d'argent.

On a organisé le premier Tour de France en 1903. C'est Maurice Garin qui a gagné le premier Tour de France. Il a fait 2 397 kilomètres en six étapes. Depuis 1903, 21 Français ont gagné le Tour de France.

Lance Armstrong a gagné!

En 1999, il y a un miracle. Un Américain, Lance Armstrong, gagne le Tour de France. Le miracle, ce n'est pas qu'un Américain gagne le Tour de France. Non, un autre Américain, Greg LeMond, a gagné le Tour de France trois fois. Pourquoi un miracle? Parce que trois ans avant, à l'âge de 25 ans, Lance Armstrong a

Tour de France

[1] a lieu *takes place*
[2] étapes *laps*
[3] droit *right*
[4] maillot *jersey*

le cancer. Après deux opérations et quatre traitements de chimiothérapie et beaucoup de courage et de volonté[5] de sa part, le jeune Armstrong est guéri[6] et il recommence sa carrière de coureur cycliste.

Depuis cent ans, les Français appellent le vélo, «la petite reine»[7]. Ils disent que c'est la petite reine qui choisit toujours le nouveau roi du Tour de France. Pour sept années, de 1999 jusqu'à 2005, elle a choisi son roi—Lance Armstrong. Et pour lui, comme pour tout le monde, c'est un vrai miracle!

[5] volonté *willpower*   [7] reine *queen*
[6] guéri *cured*

Tour de France

Lance Armstrong

↑Lance the Beaver

Le Maroc

Vous avez compris?

A Une course cycliste Vrai ou faux?
1. Le cyclisme n'est pas très apprécié en France.
2. Le Tour de France est une course cycliste.
3. Le Tour de France a lieu au mois de décembre.
4. Tous les cyclistes qui participent au Tour de France sont français.
5. Le Tour de France est divisé en deux mi-temps.
6. Pendant le Tour de France, les cyclistes roulent la nuit—de minuit à six heures.
7. Le gagnant du Tour de France reçoit une coupe et une somme d'argent.

B Un miracle Répondez.
1. Qui a gagné le Tour de France trois fois?
2. Il est de quelle nationalité?
3. Qui est le deuxième Américain qui a gagné le Tour de France?
4. Il a quel âge quand il apprend qu'il a le cancer?
5. Armstrong a recommencé à faire du vélo après combien d'opérations?
6. Quelles sont les qualités de Lance Armstrong?
7. D'après les Français, qui est la petite reine qui choisit le gagnant du Tour de France?
8. C'est une personne?
9. Elle a choisi qui de 1999 jusqu'à 2005?

CONNEXIONS

Les sciences naturelles

L'anatomie

Staying in good physical condition is important for all athletes. To do so, they have to know how to care for their bodies. They also have to know something about their bone structure to avoid injuries. Athletes should have some basic knowledge of anatomy. Anatomy is the branch of science that studies the structures of humans and animals.

Before reading this selection on anatomy, study the diagrams of the human body.

le squelette

la poitrine

une jambe

Le corps humain

Le squelette

Le squelette humain a en tout 206 os. Il y a 32 os dans chaque bras et 31 os dans chaque jambe. Il y a plus de 600 muscles dans le corps humain. Certains muscles sont attachés à un os. Ils peuvent être attachés directement à l'os ou par l'intermédiaire d'un tendon.

En plus des muscles squelettiques, il y a de nombreux muscles internes. Le cœur, par exemple, est un muscle.

Le cerveau et le système nerveux

Le cerveau est bien protégé par la boîte crânienne[1]. Le cerveau est

le cerveau

la moelle épinière

[1] boîte crânienne *skull*

composé de deux hémisphères. Le tronc cérébral[2] relie[3] le cerveau à la moelle épinière. Le tronc cérébral contient les centres nerveux qui contrôlent les fonctions automatiques telles que le rythme cardiaque et la respiration[4].

Le cœur et les poumons

Le cœur est un organe musculaire. C'est le principal organe de la circulation du sang. Le cœur est situé plus ou moins au centre de la poitrine. Les poumons sont situés de part et d'autre[5] du cœur. Le poumon est le principal organe de l'appareil respiratoire. L'air arrive dans chaque poumon par une bronche. Le sang arrive par l'artère pulmonaire. Quand il arrive, l'air est chargé de gaz carbonique. Quand le sang ressort[6] par les veines pulmonaires, il est purifié et enrichi en oxygène.

Il n'y a pas de doute, le corps humain est une machine extraordinaire!

[2] tronc cérébral *medulla oblongata*
[3] relie *connects*
[4] respiration *breathing*

[5] de part et d'autre *on each side*
[6] ressort *leaves*

les vaisseaux sanguins

le cœur

les poumons

le bras

un os

un muscle

un tendon

Vous avez compris?

FL.D.1.2.1 (I)

A Les mots apparentés Trouvez les mots apparentés dans la lecture.

B Des informations Identifiez.

1. le nombre d'os dans chaque bras
2. le nombre de muscles dans le corps humain
3. ce qui attache un muscle à un os
4. un muscle interne très important, un muscle vital
5. ce qui protège le cerveau
6. ce qui relie le cerveau à la moelle épinière
7. ce qui contrôle les fonctions automatiques du corps humain
8. l'organe vital situé au centre de la poitrine
9. l'organe principal de l'appareil respiratoire
10. là où le sang est purifié et enrichi en oxygène

C'est à vous

Use what you have learned

PARLER

1 Je suis fana de...
✔ *Describe your favorite sport*

Work with a classmate. Each of you will name a sport you really like and give a description of that sport.

La France est victorieuse.

Elles jouent au foot.

PARLER

2 Une interview du capitaine
✔ *Ask someone questions about his or her team*

You have to interview the captain of one of the school's sports teams (your classmate) for a French television station. Find out as much information as possible from him or her. Then reverse roles.

PARLER

3 Jeu Devinette
✔ *Describe your favorite sports hero and ask questions about your classmates' favorites*

Think of your favorite sports hero. Tell a classmate something about him or her. Your classmate will ask you three questions about your hero before guessing who it is. Then reverse roles and guess who your classmate's hero is.

ÉCRIRE

4 FL.A.2.1.3 (I) FL.A.2.2.3 (I)

Reportage
✔ *Write a description of a sporting event*

Work in groups of three. One of you is the captain of one of the school's teams. The other two are sports reporters for a French newspaper. The two reporters will prepare an interview with the captain about the team's last game. The reporters will edit the information they get from the interview and write their report for tomorrow's paper. The report can be in the present tense.

ÉCRIRE

5 FL.A.1.2.2 (M)

Calendrier sportif
✔ *Post a schedule of sporting events*

Your French class has a Web site. Prepare your school's schedule of sporting events for the coming month in French to post at your site.

Writing Strategy

Gathering information If your writing projects deal with a subject you are not familiar with, you may need to gather information before you begin to write. Some of your best sources are the library, the Internet, and people who know something about the topic. Even if you plan to interview people about the topic, it may be necessary to do some research in the library or on the Internet to acquire enough knowledge to prepare good interview questions.

ÉCRIRE

6 FL.D.2.2.1 (I)

La Coupe du Monde
Many of you already know that the World Cup is a soccer championship. Try to give a description of the World Cup as best you can in French. If you are not familiar with it, you will need to do some research. It might be interesting to take what you know or find out about the World Cup and compare it to the World Series in baseball. Gather information about both these championships and write a report in French.

Assessment

Vocabulaire

To review **Mots 1,** *turn to pages 324–325.*

1 Complétez.

1–2. Il y a onze _____ dans une _____ de foot.

3. Le gardien veut arrêter ou _____ le ballon.

4. Le stade est comble. Les _____ sont pleins.

5. Le joueur peut donner un coup de _____ ou un coup de tête dans le ballon.

2 Identifiez.

6.

7.

8.

9.

10.

To review **Mots 2,** *turn to pages 328–329.*

Structure

To review the **passé composé** *of regular verbs, turn to page 332.*

3 Récrivez au passé composé.

11. Je joue au foot.

12. Ils regardent le match à la télé.

13. Elle réussit un beau panier.

14. Notre équipe ne perd pas.

15. Vous finissez la course?

4 Complétez.

16. —Tu as invité _____?
    —Nathalie.
17. —_____ tu as regardé à la télé?
    —La course cycliste.
18. —Pour jouer, tu as besoin de _____?
    —D'un ballon et d'un filet.

To review asking questions, turn to page 335.

5 Complétez au présent.

19. Tu _____ des cadeaux. (recevoir)
20. Je _____ beaucoup d'eau. (boire)
21. Elle _____ passer l'examen. (devoir)
22. Vous _____ combien d'argent? (recevoir)
23. Ils _____ faire attention. (devoir)

To review *boire*, *devoir*, and *recevoir* in the present, turn to page 337.

Culture

6 Identifiez.

24. un sport populaire qui est très apprécié au Québec
25. le deuxième sport dans les pays d'Afrique Occidentale

To review this cultural information, turn to pages 342–343.

Un match de hockey

Do these practice activities to help you succeed on your FCAT through the study of a foreign language.

Read the story below. Then answer the questions that follow.

Hier soir mes amis et moi __1__ un match à la télé. Lyon __2__ Marseille. À __3__ ont-ils joué? Au foot, bien entendu! __4__ a gagné la coupe l'année dernière? Lyon. Et hier Lyon __5__ trois buts. Mais les joueurs de Marseille ont égalisé le score. Un joueur de Lyon a passé le ballon à l'autre, mais __6__ l'arbitre a déclaré? Un penalty! Mes amis ont rigolé parce qu'ils adorent l'équipe de Marseille. Enfin, Lyon __7__ le match. Après un match de foot, les joueurs __8__ toujours de l'eau. On __9__ toujours boire après avoir joué. Mes amis et moi, nous __10__ toute une pizza pendant le match!

1 Quelle est la forme du verbe qui complète le numéro (1)?

    A. regardons

    B. avons regardé

    C. ont regardé

2 Quelle est la forme du verbe qui complète le numéro (2)?

    F. a opposé

    G. as opposé

    H. opposent

3 Quel est le mot qui complète le numéro (3)?

    A. qui

    B. quoi

    C. qu'est-ce qu'

4 Quel est le mot qui complète le numéro (4)?

    F. Quoi

    G. Qu'est-ce que

    H. Qui

5 Quelle est la forme du verbe qui complète le numéro (5)?

    A. ont marqué

    B. marquent

    C. a marqué

6 Quel est le mot qui complète le numéro (6)?

    F. qui

    G. qu'est-ce que

    H. quoi

7 Quelle est la forme du verbe qui complète le numéro (7)?

    A. ont perdu

    B. a perdu

    C. avons perdu

8 Quelle est la forme du verbe qui complète le numéro (8)?

    F. boit

    G. buvons

    H. boivent

9 Quelle est la forme du verbe qui complète le numéro (9)?

    A. doivent

    B. doit

    C. dois

10 Quelle est la forme du verbe qui complète le numéro (10)?

    F. ai fini

    G. avez fini

    H. avons fini

FCAT Tip

Be sure to fill in the answer bubbles correctly. Do not make any stray marks around answer spaces.

FL.A.2.1.2 (I)   FL.A.3.2.1 (I)

Tell all you can about this illustration.

Describing a sports event

un stade	une joueuse	jouer (à)	gagner
des gradins (m. pl.)	une équipe	lancer	perdre
un spectateur	le camp (adverse)	servir	siffler
une spectatrice	un arbitre	envoyer	beaucoup de monde
un terrain	un penalty	renvoyer	comble
une piste	le score	passer	plein
un match	un(e) gagnant(e)	recevoir	contre
un joueur	une coupe	égaliser	

Describing a soccer game

le foot(ball)	un coup	bloquer
un ballon	de pied	arrêter
marquer un but	de tête	
un gardien de but	un but	

Describing a basketball game

le basket(-ball)	dribbler
un panier	réussir un beau panier
un demi-cercle	

Describing a volleyball game

le volley(-ball)	le sol
un filet	

How well do you know your vocabulary?

- Choose a sport from the list.
- Ask classmates to give a word associated with the sport you chose.

Describing a bicycle race

un vélo	un coureur cycliste	le cyclisme	rouler vite
une bicyclette	une coureuse cycliste	une course	

Describing a track event

l'athlétisme (m.)	un coureur
une piste	une coureuse

Expressing the past

hier	avant-hier	une fois
hier matin	la semaine dernière	
hier soir	l'année dernière	

VIDÉOTOUR

Épisode 10

In this video episode, Manu entertains the crowd with his narration of an exciting game. See page 535 for more information.

Other useful words and expresssions

par-dessus

L'été et l'hiver

Objectifs

In this chapter you will learn to:

- ✓ *describe summer and winter weather*
- ✓ *talk about summer activities and sports*
- ✓ *talk about winter sports*
- ✓ *discuss past actions and events*
- ✓ *make negative statements*
- ✓ *talk about a ski trip in Quebec*

Maurice Utrillo *Montmartre sous la neige*

SUNSHINE STATE STANDARDS

This chapter is all about summer and winter activities. The material in the chapter will address the Sunshine State Standards listed below.

FL.A.1.1.1 express likes and dislikes when asked simple questions (e.g., about toys or other objects).

FL.A.1.2.1 express likes or dislikes regarding various objects, categories, people, and events present in the everyday environment.

FL.A.1.2.2 exchange information necessary to plan events or activities (e.g., picnics, birthday parties, science projects, and crafts).

FL.A.2.1.2 restate and rephrase simple information from materials presented orally, visually, and graphically in class.

FL.A.2.1.3 understand oral messages that are based on familiar themes and vocabulary (e.g., short conversations between familiar persons on familiar topics such as everyday school and home activities).

FL.A.2.2.3 organize information in spoken or written form about a variety of topics of academic and cultural interest (e.g., by making lists, categorizing objects, or organizing concepts).

FL.A.2.2.5 comprehend and respond to oral messages (e.g., personal anecdotes or narratives) based on familiar themes and vocabulary.

FL.A.3.1.1 provide simple information in spoken form (e.g., descriptions of family members, friends, objects present in his or her everyday environment, or common school and home activities).

FL.A.3.2.1 describe important people (e.g., family members and friends) and objects present in his or her everyday environment and in school.

FL.A.3.2.3 give responses in spoken or written form (e.g., answering simple questions, formulating questions, and making simple statements) to age-appropriate stories, poems or other literature, songs, films, or visual works.

FL.B.1.1.1 participate in age-appropriate cultural activities (e.g., games, songs, birthday celebrations, storytelling, dramatizations, and role playing).

FL.B.1.1.3 recognize various familiar objects and norms of the target culture (e.g., toys, dresses, and typical foods).

Miami Marina

FL.B.1.2.1   recognize various activities and celebrations in which children participate in the target culture (e.g., games, songs, birthday celebrations, storytelling, dramatizations, and role playing).

FL.C.1.2.2   use target-language vocabulary or concepts to reinforce knowledge of a related topic studied in another class (e.g., geographical place names, parts of the body, or basic mathematical operations).

FL.C.2.1.1   use the target language to gain access to information that is only available through the target language or within the target culture (listen to a story told in the target language).

FL.D.1.2.2   recognize the similarities and differences between his or her native language and the target language in terms of the pronunciation, alphabet, and forms of written expression.

TIPS FOR SUCCESS

Review the Study Tips below to help you succeed on the Sunshine State Standards identified.

Vocabulaire   Mots 1   Mots 2   *(pages 356–363)*

- For **Mots 1**, after going over the new vocabulary, review immediately. Sit back for a moment and say aloud or to yourself five words or expressions associated with the beach. **FL.A.2.2.3**

- Pretend you are on the beach. Think of three things you would like to do while on the beach. Start your sentences with **Je voudrais**… **FL.A.1.2.1**

Structure   Les mots négatifs   *(pages 367–368)*

Sea turtle

- To learn the meaning of the negative words, pay particular attention to the opposites.

Oui, quelque chose.	Non, rien.
Oui, quelqu'un.	Non, personne.
Oui, toujours.	Non, jamais.
Oui, souvent.	Non, jamais.
Oui, quelquefois.	Non, jamais.

FL.A.2.2.3

Le passé composé avec être   *(pages 369–371)*

- **Hints for speaking and writing** Past participles that end in a vowel (**é, i, u**) sound the same in all forms. Even though all forms are pronounced the same, you must pay particular attention to the spelling of these past participles when writing. They add **e** for the feminine and **s** for the plural.

- In the activities on pages 370–371, pay particular attention to the spelling of the past participle. **FL.D.1.2.2**

> **For other tips to help you address the Sunshine State Standards in Chapter 11, see pages H64 through H66 at the back of your textbook.**

Vocabulaire

Mots 1

À la plage 🎧

au bord de la mer
une station balnéaire

la plage

une vague

la mer

une serviette

un maillot de bain

de la crème solaire

Fabien a passé la journée à la plage.
Il a apporté sa crème solaire et sa serviette.
À la plage, il faut faire attention.
Il faut mettre de la crème solaire.
Il ne faut pas rester trop longtemps au soleil.

des lunettes de soleil

Caroline a pris un bain de soleil.
Elle a bronzé.
Elle a mis de la crème solaire.
Elle n'a pas attrapé de coup de soleil.

Des activités d'été 🎧

faire de la planche
à voile

faire du ski nautique

faire du surf

faire une promenade

Cécile a plongé dans la piscine.
Laure a pris des leçons de natation.
Elle a appris à nager.

Le printemps 🎧

Il fait quel temps au printemps?

L'été 🎧

Il fait beau.
De temps en temps,
   il y a des nuages.

Il y a du vent.
Il pleut.
Il fait mauvais.

En été il fait chaud.
Il fait du soleil.

Vocabulaire

Quel est le mot?

1 Historiette À la plage
Inventez une histoire.

1. Juliette a passé la journée à la plage?
2. Elle a beaucoup nagé?
3. Elle a pris un bain de soleil?
4. Elle a apporté de la crème solaire?
5. Elle a fait attention? Elle a mis de la crème solaire?
6. Elle a mis aussi des lunettes de soleil?
7. Elle a bronzé?
8. Elle a fait du ski nautique?
9. Elle a fait une promenade sur la plage?
10. Elle a fait de la planche à voile aussi?

FrenchOnline
To investigate summer camps in the Francophone world, do the Chapter 11 **WebQuest** activity on the Glencoe French Web site at glencoe.com.

Nice, France

De la crème solaire et des lunettes de soleil

2 Historiette En été Donnez des réponses personnelles.

1. En été, tu aimes aller à la plage?
2. Tu vas dans quelle station balnéaire?
3. Tu vas à la plage quand il pleut?
4. Tu aimes nager dans la mer ou dans une piscine?
5. Tu aimes plonger?
6. Qu'est-ce que tu mets pour nager?
7. Il faut mettre de la crème solaire quand on va à la plage?
8. Et toi, tu mets de la crème solaire?
9. Tu bronzes facilement ou tu attrapes des coups de soleil?
10. Tu mets des lunettes de soleil quand tu vas à la plage?
11. Tu apportes ta serviette?

3 **Historiette** **Au bord de la mer** Complétez.

1. Au bord de la mer, on va à la ____ pour nager et bronzer.
2. Il y a beaucoup de plages et de stations balnéaires sur la ____ Méditerranée.
3. Il y a de grandes ____ sur la mer ou sur l'océan, surtout quand il y a du ____.
4. Beaucoup de gens aiment prendre un ____ de soleil sur la plage.
5. Il faut mettre de la ____ si on ne veut pas attraper de coup de soleil.
6. Quand on va nager, on met un ____.
7. Quand il fait chaud à la plage, il ne faut pas ____ trop longtemps au soleil.
8. On peut faire du ____ ou du ____ sur la mer quand il fait beau.
9. Quand il fait mauvais, il y a souvent des ____ dans le ciel.
10. À Biarritz, sur l'océan Atlantique, il y a souvent des ____ qui font du surf.

 Marie, interpretive dance teacher.

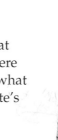 Look! I'm a BIRD!

Une leçon de natation

4 **Qu'est-ce qu'elle a appris?**
Répondez d'après la photo.

1. Jeanne a appris à nager?
2. Elle a pris des leçons de natation?
3. Elle a appris à nager dans la mer ou dans une piscine?
4. Elle a compris toutes les instructions de la monitrice?

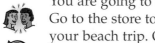 FL.B.1.1.1 (I)

5 **On va à la plage.** Work with a classmate. You are going to spend a day or two at the beach. Go to the store to buy some things you need for your beach trip. One of you will be the salesperson and the other will be the shopper. Take turns.

FL.A.1.2.2 (I)

6 **Des vacances parfaites** Plan a great summer vacation. Tell your classmate where you want to go and why. Tell him or her what you do there. Then find out your classmate's summer plans.

Une jolie baie, Tahiti

FL.A.1.2.1 (I)

7 **Le temps au printemps ou en été**
With a classmate describe the spring or summer weather where you live. Which season do you prefer? Tell why.

 ENCORE PLUS *For more practice using words from* **Mots 1,** *do Activity 34 on page H35 at the end of this book.*

Vocabulaire

Mots 2

Une station de sports d'hiver

un sommet

une montagne

la neige

un télésiège

une skieuse

un bonnet

une écharpe

un gant

un anorak

une piste

une bosse

un skieur

le ski de fond

le ski alpin

un ski

un bâton

une chaussure de ski

Les skieurs ont descendu la piste verte.
La piste verte, c'est pour les débutants.

Marie est débutante.
Elle n'a jamais fait de ski.
Elle tombe tout le temps.

Ce matin, elle a pris sa première leçon.
Elle a eu un très bon moniteur.

une patinoire

la glace

un patin

Les filles font du patin à glace avec leur mère.

L'automne 🎧

En automne il ne fait pas froid.
Il fait frais.

L'hiver 🎧

Il fait quel temps en hiver?

Il fait froid.

Il neige.

Il gèle.

Quel est le mot?

8 **Historiette** **Dans une station de sports d'hiver**
Répondez d'après les indications.

1. Les stations de sports d'hiver sont très fréquentées en quelle saison? (en hiver)
2. Quel temps fait-il en hiver à la montagne? (froid)
3. Il y a quelles catégories de pistes dans une station de sports d'hiver? (pour les skieurs débutants, pour les skieurs moyens et pour les skieurs experts)
4. Les skieurs ont fait du ski où? (sur la piste verte)
5. Qu'est-ce qu'ils ont pris pour monter au sommet de la montagne? (un télésiège)
6. Ils ont descendu quelle piste? (la piste noire)
7. Qu'est-ce qu'il y a sur les pistes noires? (beaucoup de bosses)
8. Les bosses, c'est dangereux pour les débutants? (oui, très)
9. Après le ski, ils ont mis leurs patins? (oui)
10. Ils ont fait du patin à glace où? (à la patinoire)

FL.A.2.1.2 (I)

9 **On fait du ski.** Répondez d'après les dessins.

1. C'est une station balnéaire ou une station de sports d'hiver?
2. C'est une plage ou une montagne?
3. C'est la neige ou la mer?
4. C'est le sommet de la montagne ou la vallée?
5. C'est quelle saison? L'automne ou l'hiver?
6. C'est une piste ou une piscine?
7. C'est une skieuse ou une nageuse?
8. Elle fait du ski alpin ou du ski de fond?
9. Elle skie bien ou elle tombe souvent?

10 Historiette Leçons de ski
Inventez une histoire.

1. Christine a appris à faire du ski?
2. Qui a appris à Christine à faire du ski?
3. Elle a eu un très bon moniteur?
4. Christine a mis un anorak de quelle couleur?
5. Elle a mis des gants, une écharpe et un bonnet?
6. Elle a mis ses chaussures de ski et ses skis?
7. Elle a pris le télésiège?
8. Elle a descendu quelle piste?
9. Il a fait très froid? Il a neigé? Il a gelé?

FL.A.3.1.1 (I)

11 Qu'est-ce qu'on fait? A French exchange student (a classmate) asks you what the weather is like in your town in the summer and in the winter and what people do during these seasons. Answer his or her questions, giving as much information as possible.

French Online

For a fun way to review this vocabulary, go to the Chapter 11 **eGame** on the Glencoe French Web site at glencoe.com.

FL.A.2.2.5 (I)

12 Dans une station de sports d'hiver Have a conversation with a classmate. Tell as much as you can about what people do at a ski resort. Find out which one of you knows more about skiing. If skiing is a sport that is new to you, tell whether you think you would like to ski.

FL.A.1.2.1 (I)

13 Dans quelle ville?
With a classmate, look at this weather map that appeared in a Paris newspaper. You are both in Paris and you want to take a short side trip. Since you both have definite preferences concerning weather, use the map to help make a decision. Choose what city you want to go to, tell why, and explain what you are going to do there.

For more practice using words from Mots 2, do Activity 35 on page H36 at the end of this book.

Structure

Le passé composé des verbes irréguliers
Describing more past actions

1. You have already learned that the past participles of regular verbs end in the sounds /é/, /i/, and /ü/. The past participles of most irregular verbs also end in the sounds /i/ or /ü/, even though they are not spelled the same way.

Infinitif → participe passé /i/		Infinitif → participe passé /ü/	
dire	dit	avoir	eu
écrire	écrit	croire	cru
		voir	vu
mettre	mis	boire	bu
permettre	permis	devoir	dû
		pouvoir	pu
prendre	pris	lire	lu
apprendre	appris	recevoir	reçu
comprendre	compris	vouloir	voulu

J'ai pris des leçons de natation.
J'ai appris à nager.
J'ai eu un bon moniteur.

Tu as lu son livre?
Il a écrit un livre?
Tu as compris ce qu'il a dit?

2. The verbs **être** and **faire** have irregular past participles.

être → été   faire → fait

J'ai fait un voyage à Megève l'année dernière.
J'ai été content d'apprendre à faire du ski.

Une classe de ski

Comment dit-on?

14 **Historiette** Gilles a fait du ski.
Répondez que oui.

1. Gilles a mis son anorak?
2. Son ami a dit «Bonne chance» à Gilles?
3. Son ami a déjà fait du ski aujourd'hui?
4. Gilles a bien fait du ski?
5. Il a eu un accident?
6. Après l'accident, il a lu un livre pour les débutants?

15 Ce matin
Donnez des réponses personnelles.

1. Tu as pris ton petit déjeuner à quelle heure ce matin?
2. Qu'est-ce que tu as bu au petit déjeuner?
3. Est-ce que tu as lu le journal ce matin? Et tes parents?
4. Est-ce que tu as reçu une lettre?
5. Est-ce que tu as vu tes copains avant les cours?
6. Est-ce que tu as dit bonjour à ton prof de français?

Une vue de la ville de Québec

16 Qu'est-ce que tu as dit?
Complétez d'après le modèle.

—J'_____ que j'_____ ce que j'_____.
—J'ai dit que j'ai lu ce que j'ai écrit.

1. Il _____ qu'il _____ ce qu'il _____.
2. Nous _____ que nous _____ ce que nous _____.
3. Tu _____ que tu _____ ce que tu _____.
4. J'_____ que j'_____ ce que j'_____.
5. Vous _____ que vous _____ ce que vous _____.
6. Elles _____ qu'elles _____ ce qu'elles _____.

17 **Historiette** À Chamonix

Complétez au passé composé.

Laurent aime beaucoup le ski. Son ami Étienne et lui __1__ (décider) d'aller faire du ski. Ils __2__ (prendre) le Guide Michelin et __3__ (lire) la description de plusieurs stations. Finalement, ils __4__ (choisir) Chamonix. Ils __5__ (avoir) de la chance. Les parents de Laurent __6__ (permettre) aux deux garçons de prendre leur voiture. La voiture, c'est plus pratique que le train! Alors les deux copains __7__ (mettre) leurs skis sur la voiture et… en route! Mais la voiture, ça n'est pas toujours plus pratique que le train: il y __8__ (avoir) une avalanche et la route __9__ (être) bloquée pendant dix heures!

Chamonix, France

FL.A.3.1.1 (I)

18 **L'été dernier** Your classmate wants to know what you did last summer. Tell him or her several things you did, using some of the verbs below. Then reverse roles.

recevoir

voir

prendre

écrire

lire

pouvoir

bronzer

nager

boire

mettre

faire

For more practice using irregular verbs in the **passé composé***, do Activity 36 on page H37 at the end of this book.*

Les mots négatifs
Making negative statements

1. You already know the negative expressions **ne… pas** and **ne… plus**. Study the following negative expressions that function the same way as **ne… pas** and **ne… plus**.

Affirmatif	Négatif
Elle voit quelque chose.	Elle ne voit rien.
Elle voit quelqu'un.	Elle ne voit personne.
Il lit toujours.	Il ne lit jamais.
Il lit souvent.	Il ne lit jamais.
Il lit quelquefois.	Il ne lit jamais.
Il lit encore.	Il ne lit plus.

Rappelez-vous que…

Un, une, des, du, de la, de l' change to **de (d')** after **pas** and other negative expressions.

Il n'a pas d'amis.
Il ne fait jamais de sport.
Elle n'écrit plus de lettres.

2. With the exception of **personne**, the negative words go around the verb **avoir** in the **passé composé**. **Personne** goes after the past participle.

Je n'ai jamais dit ça!
On n'a plus parlé de ça.   *mais*
On n'a rien dit.

Je n'ai vu personne.
Et je n'ai parlé à personne!

Comment dit-on?

19 **Le matin, en haut de la montagne** Répondez que non.

Il voit quelque chose?

Non, il ne voit rien.

1. Il dit quelque chose?
2. Il entend quelque chose?
3. Il regarde quelque chose?
4. Il voit quelqu'un?
5. Il regarde quelqu'un?
6. Il parle à quelqu'un?
7. Il attend quelqu'un?

De la planche à voile à la Martinique

20 **Elle ne fait jamais de sport.**
Répondez d'après le modèle.

—**Jeanne adore nager.**
—**Elle dit ça, mais elle ne nage jamais!**

1. Jeanne adore faire du surf.
2. Elle adore aller à la plage.
3. Elle adore faire de la planche à voile.
4. Elle adore faire du sport.
5. Elle adore jouer au tennis.
6. Elle adore faire du ski nautique.

21 **C'est fini!** Répondez que non.

1. Ta grand-mère travaille encore?
2. Ta sœur joue encore au foot?
3. Tu écris encore à ton amie Marie?
4. Tes amis et toi, vous allez encore en vacances à Chamonix?
5. Tes amis sont encore à Paris?

22 **Non, non et non!**
Répondez que non.

1. Tu as dit quelque chose?
2. Il a vu quelque chose?
3. Ils ont acheté quelque chose?
4. Ils ont appris quelque chose?
5. Ils ont toujours fait du sport?
6. Il a vu quelqu'un?
7. Ils ont entendu quelqu'un?
8. Tu as téléphoné à quelqu'un?

FL.A.3.1.1 (I)

23 **L'été** Work with a classmate. Tell him or her some things you like to do in the summer. For some reason, you didn't get to do these things last summer. Tell what you didn't do.

Une piscine, Paris

Le passé composé avec être
Describing more past actions

1. Certain verbs form their **passé composé** with **être** instead of **avoir**. Many verbs that are conjugated with **être** express motion to or from a place.

arriver	Il est arrivé.
entrer	Il est entré.
monter	Il est monté.
descendre	Il est descendu.
aller	Il est allé.
partir	Il est parti.
sortir	Il est sorti.
rentrer	Il est rentré.

> **Rappelez-vous que...**
>
> **Ne... pas** goes around the verb **avoir** in the **passé composé.** It also goes around the verb **être** in the **passé composé.**
> **Il n'est pas arrivé.**

2. The past participle of verbs conjugated with **être** must agree with the subject in number (singular and plural) and in gender (masculine and feminine). Note that when **on** means **nous,** the past participle agreement is the same as for **nous.** Study the following forms.

Masculin	Féminin
je suis parti	je suis partie
tu es parti	tu es partie
il est parti	elle est partie
on est parti(s)	on est partie(s)
nous sommes partis	nous sommes parties
vous êtes parti(s)	vous êtes partie(s)
ils sont partis	elles sont parties

Note that since all the past participles of the verbs above end in a vowel, there is no difference in sound.

3. Although the following verbs do not express motion to or from a place, they are also conjugated with **être.**

rester	Il est resté huit jours.	*He stayed a week.*
tomber	Il est tombé.	*He fell.*
naître	Elle est née en France.	*She was born in France.*
mourir	Elle est morte en 2003.	*She died in 2003.*

Comment dit-on?

Un téléphérique, Grenoble

24 **Historiette** **Un voyage à Grenoble**
Répondez que oui.

1. Carine est allée à Grenoble?
2. Elle est arrivée à la gare de Lyon à 10 h?
3. Elle est allée sur le quai?
4. Elle est montée dans le train?
5. Le train est parti à l'heure?
6. Le train est arrivé à Grenoble à l'heure?
7. Carine est descendue du train à Grenoble?
8. Elle est sortie de la gare?

25 **Historiette** **À l'école** Donnez des réponses personnelles.

1. Tu es allé(e) à l'école ce matin?
2. Tu es arrivé(e) à quelle heure?
3. Tu es entré(e) immédiatement?
4. Tu es sorti(e) de l'école à quelle heure hier?
5. Tu es rentré(e) chez toi à quelle heure?

Villefranche, Côte d'Azur

26 **Historiette** **Au bord de la mer**
Mettez au passé composé.

Michel et sa sœur vont au bord de la mer. Ils partent à l'heure. Ils montent dans l'autocar. Ils arrivent à Villefranche. Ils descendent de l'autocar. Ils vont à la plage. La sœur de Michel va nager. Elle sort de l'eau. Tous les deux, ils vont au café. Ils rentrent chez eux très tard.

27 **Qui est sorti?** Donnez des réponses personnelles.

1. Le mois dernier, vous êtes allés au cinéma, tes copains et toi?
2. Vous y êtes allés comment? En voiture? En bus?
3. Qu'est-ce que vous avez vu comme film?
4. Vous êtes partis tous ensemble?
5. Vous êtes arrivés en retard?
6. Vous êtes allés manger et boire quelque chose après le film?
7. À quelle heure est-ce que vous êtes rentrés chez vous?

Mont-Saint-Michel, Normandie

28 **Une excursion** Complétez en utilisant le passé composé.

Mathieu: Tu __1__ (aller) en Normandie avec Laure. C'est ça?

Thérèse: C'est ça. Nous __2__ (aller) au Mont-Saint-Michel.

Mathieu: Vous avez aimé?

Thérèse: Nous avons adoré! Nous __3__ (monter) à la basilique. Heureusement, nous __4__ (arriver) avant tous les touristes!

Mathieu: Vous __5__ (sortir) sur la terrasse?

Thérèse: Oui. Superbe, la vue! Mais des cars entiers de touristes __6__ (arriver), alors nous __7__ (partir). Nous __8__ (rentrer) à l'hôtel.

FL.A.3.2.1 (M)

29 **Être ou ne pas être**
Donnez des réponses personnelles.

1. Tu es né(e) quel jour?
2. Tu es né(e) à l'hôpital? Dans quel hôpital?
3. Ta mère est restée combien de jours à l'hôpital?
4. Tes parents sont nés où?
5. Et tes grands-parents, ils sont nés où?
6. Ta grand-mère est morte? Et ton grand-père?

FL.A.2.2.5 (I) **FL.B.1.1.1 (I)**

30 **À Saint-Jean-de-Luz** Work with a classmate. You both went to Saint-Jean-de-Luz, on the Atlantic Ocean, near the Spanish border, but you did not go together. Ask each other what you did there. Find out as much as you can about each other's trip.

Saint-Jean-de-Luz, Pays Basque

ENCORE PLUS

*For more practice using the **passé composé** with **être**, do Activity 37 on page H38 at the end of this book.*

Vous êtes sur le bon chemin. Allez-y!

Conversation

FL.A.2.1.3 (I)

À la plage

Laurène: Qu'est-ce que tu as fait hier?

Marine: Je suis allée à la plage.

Laurène: Tu as eu de la chance. Il a fait très beau hier!

Marine: Oui, mais je suis arrivée à la plage, j'ai regardé dans mon sac et… pas de maillot!

Laurène: Ben, qu'est-ce que tu as fait, alors?

Marine: Je suis allée dans l'eau.

Laurène: Sans maillot!

Marine: Oui, mais en blue-jean! Et toi, qu'est-ce que tu as fait?

Laurène: Absolument rien. Je n'ai rien fait et je n'ai vu personne.

Vous avez compris?

Répondez.

1. Marine est allée où hier?
2. Il a fait beau?
3. Elle a pris son maillot?
4. Elle a nagé?
5. Elle est allée dans l'eau sans maillot?
6. Elle est allée dans l'eau comment?
7. Et Laurène, qu'est-ce qu'elle a fait hier?
8. Elle a vu quelqu'un?

Parlons un peu plus

FL.B.1.1.1 (I)

A **Quel temps fait-il?** Work with a classmate. Pretend that one of you lives in Montreal and the other lives in Fort-de-France in Martinique. Compare what it's like on a typical day in February. Tell some things you do in February.

FL.A.2.2.5 (I)

B **À Tahiti** Work with a classmate. Pretend you spent a week on the beach in Tahiti. Tell your partner about your vacation and answer any questions he or she may have.

Martinique
Les Plages

Vauclin / Plage de Macabou : Entrée payante, plage aménagée, sable blanc et raisiniers bord de mer, tables pour pique-nique.

Plage du Diamant / Plage de la Dizac : Plage sauvage, très ventilée, beaucoup de vagues. Littoral ombragé et aménagé. Baignade avec prudence.

Anses d'Arlets / Plage de Grande Anse et Petite Anse : Jolies plages de sable blanc, très ensoleillées. Mer très calme, peu ventée, restaurants à proximité.

Sainte-Luce : Plage de Corps de Garde et de Gros Raisin, plages animées et aménagées, tables et bancs, sable blanc.

L'Anse Céron / L'Anse Couleuvre : Belle plage aménagée et typique. Sable noir. En continuant le petit chemin pittoresque, à un kilomètre de marche, vous arriverez à l'Anse Couleuvre, plage déserte de dable noir. Eaux profondes.

Plage du Carbet / Anse Turin : Grande plage de sable noir, eaux profondes.

Prononciation

Le son /y/ 🎧

1. The sound /y/ occurs in two positions: final, and between two vowel sounds. Repeat the following.

fille	soleil	travaille	taille
bouteille	maillot	travailler	billet

2. Now repeat the following sentences.

J'ai un vieux maillot.
On ne travaille pas bien au soleil.

un soleil en maillot

Lectures culturelles

FL.A.3.2.3 (I)

Un petit voyage au Canada

En février, pendant les huit jours de vacances d'hiver, les élèves de Madame Lebrun sont allés au Canada, avec Madame Lebrun, bien sûr. Ils ont pris le train à New York et sont descendus à Montréal. Ils ont passé trois jours à Montréal. Montréal est la deuxième ville francophone après Paris. Les élèves de Madame Lebrun ont été très contents parce qu'ils ont pu pratiquer leur français. Et ils ont tout compris!

Après trois jours à Montréal, ils sont partis pour le parc du Mont-Tremblant. Le Mont-Tremblant est une station de sports d'hiver tout près de la jolie ville de Québec. Ils sont arrivés au parc à midi. Ils ont mis leurs skis et sont montés au sommet de la montagne en télésiège. De là-haut, quelle vue superbe on a sur les montagnes et les vallées couvertes de neige! Tu n'as jamais vu de montagnes couvertes de neige? Il n'y a rien de plus beau!

Une rue résidentielle, Montréal

Vieux-Port à Montréal

Mont-Tremblant, Québec

Haïti

La Martinique

Skis aux pieds et bâtons en mains, ils ont commencé à descendre la piste. Ils ont choisi une piste verte. Au Québec, les pistes vertes sont les pistes faciles pour débutants. Après trois heures sur les pistes, ils sont allés à la patinoire où ils ont fait du patin à glace.

À neuf heures du soir, un des élèves a dit: «Moi, je n'ai jamais été aussi fatigué!» Ça a été le signal de la retraite vers les dortoirs[1]. Ils ont tous dormi comme des souches[2]!

[1] dortoirs *dormitories*
[2] souches *tree stumps*

Vous avez compris?

A Au Canada Répondez.

1. La classe de Madame Lebrun est allée où?
2. Ils y sont allés quand?
3. Ils y sont allés comment?
4. Ils ont pratiqué leur français où?
5. Après trois jours à Montréal, ils sont partis pour où?
6. Qu'est-ce que le Mont-Tremblant?
7. C'est près de quelle ville?
8. Ils y sont arrivés à quelle heure?
9. Ils sont montés jusqu'où?
10. Qu'est-ce qu'ils ont vu du sommet?

B Les vacances d'hiver Vrai ou faux?

1. Les élèves ont eu un mois de vacances.
2. Ils ont pris le train pour aller à Montréal.
3. Montréal est une petite ville.
4. Les élèves sont montés à skis au sommet de la montagne.
5. Pour faire du ski, ils ont mis des patins.
6. Ils ont pris la piste rouge pour les très bons skieurs.
7. Ils ont fait aussi du patin à glace.

FL.B.1.1.3 (I)

Les grandes vacances

Le mois d'août, c'est le mois des grandes vacances en France. Beaucoup de Français quittent la ville et vont à la montagne, à la campagne[1] ou au bord de la mer.

En été, quand le soleil brille dans le ciel bleu, il est fabuleux de passer la journée à la plage. La France est un pays de plages merveilleuses. Il y a plus de mille kilomètres de côtes et des stations balnéaires tout le long de ces côtes—sur la Manche au nord; sur l'océan Atlantique à l'ouest; sur la mer Méditerranée au sud.

Étretat, Normandie

Biarritz, Pays Basque

Cannes, Côte d'Azur

Vous avez compris?

Vous voulez passer une petite semaine sur une belle plage en France? Vous voulez rentrer chez vous bien bronzé(e)(s)? Vous allez aller où?

Au bord de la mer Identifiez.
1. le mois des grandes vacances en France
2. la mer qui sépare l'Angleterre de la France
3. l'océan à l'ouest de la France
4. la mer au sud de la France

[1] campagne *countryside*

Lecture supplémentaire 2

Le carnaval

La neige arrive au Québec fin novembre et reste jusqu'au mois d'avril. Les jours sont courts, froids, mais très beaux. Le soleil brille souvent dans le ciel bleu et la neige scintille[1].

En février, les Québécois sortent de chez eux pour célébrer le carnaval. Des milliers de visiteurs vont à Québec à cette époque pour célébrer le carnaval. Pendant les dix jours de festivités, il y a un grand défilé de chars[2]. On construit un magnifique palais de glace et il y a un concours[3] de sculptures de glace.

Toutes ces festivités sont orchestrées par un gigantesque bonhomme de neige appelé «Bonhomme Carnaval».

[1] scintille *sparkles*
[2] défilé de chars *float parade*
[3] concours *contest*

«Bonhomme Carnaval», Québec

Le palais de glace, Québec

Vous avez compris?

Au Québec et à Québec Décrivez.
1. un jour d'hiver au Québec
2. le carnaval de Québec
3. «Bonhomme Carnaval»

La Belgique

Le Maroc

Le Mali

L'ÉTÉ ET L'HIVER

CONNEXIONS

FL.C.1.2.2 (I)   FL.C.2.1.1 (I)

Les Beaux-Arts

La peinture

One may know a great deal or just a little about art. But almost everyone has at least some interest in art. How often have we heard, "I may not know anything about art, but I certainly know what I like"?

There is no doubt that France has produced many of the world's greatest artists. Do you recognize the names of these famous French artists: Renoir, Monet, Manet, Degas, Seurat, Boudin, Gauguin?

In 1874, two of these painters, Monet and Renoir, were among a group of artists who held a famous exhibition of their works in Paris. The critics laughed at their works and called the artists "Impressionists" to mock one of Monet's paintings entitled *Impression, soleil levant*. Today, paintings by the Impressionists are among the most admired works in the history of art.

Claude Monet *La pie*

Claude Monet *La route sous la neige à Honfleur*

Les impressionnistes

On dit que les impressionnistes sont les peintres de la vie moderne. Ils ont peint la vie quotidienne[1] des gens (personnes) simples. Pour eux, tous les sujets sont bons. Ils ont peint des parcs, des gares, des usines[2]. Beaucoup de peintres impressionnistes ont préféré quitter leur atelier[3] pour aller peindre en plein air. Les scènes d'été et les scènes d'hiver sont des sujets favoris de plusieurs impressionnistes.

Voici deux tableaux de paysages d'hiver de Claude Monet—*La pie* et *La route sous la neige à Honfleur*.

[1] vie quotidienne *daily life*
[2] usines *factories*
[3] atelier *studio*

Voici maintenant des scènes de plage. Eugène Boudin a peint *La plage de Trouville*.

Ce tableau *Sur la plage* a été peint par l'ami de Monet, Édouard Manet.

Georges Seurat a peint *Les baigneurs à Asnières*. Asnières est dans la banlieue[4] parisienne sur la Seine. Au fond, on voit les cheminées des usines de Clichy. Il fait très chaud et les ouvriers[5] font un petit plongeon dans la Seine.

[4] banlieue *suburbs*
[5] ouvriers *workers*

Édouard Manet *Sur la plage*

Georges Seurat *Les baigneurs à Asnières*

Vous avez compris?

A **Un peu de géographie**
Find all the places mentioned where these artists painted.

FL.A.3.2.3 (I)

B **Mon tableau favori** Pick your favorite painting, describe it, and explain why it is your favorite.

C'est à vous

Use what you have learned

PARLER
1

 FL.A.1.2.1 (I)

La mer ou la montagne?
✔ *Talk about summer or winter vacations*

Work with a classmate. Tell him or her where you like to go on vacation. Tell what you do there and some of the reasons you enjoy it so much. Take turns.

Mont-Blanc, Chamonix

Dans les Alpes

PARLER
2

Des vacances merveilleuses
✔ *Talk about vacation activities*

Work with a classmate. Pretend you each had a million dollars. You went on a dream vacation. Take turns describing what you did.

PARLER
3

 FL.A.2.2.5 (I)

Le ski
✔ *Talk about skiing*

You're having a hot chocolate on the terrace of a chalet near the slopes of Pralognan-la-Vanoise in the French Alps. You make friends with a French skier (your classmate). Find out as much as you can about each other's skiing habits and abilities.

ÉCRIRE

4

Une carte postale

✔ *Write about a summer or winter vacation destination*

Look at these postcards. Choose one. Pretend you spent a week there. Write the postcard to a friend.

For more information on creating your own postcard, go to **Send a Postcard** on the Glencoe French Web site at glencoe.com.

Saint-Malo, Bretagne

Mont-Tremblant, Québec

FL.A.2.2.3 (I)

Writing Strategy

Comparing and contrasting Before you begin to write a comparison of people, places, or things, you must be aware of how they are alike or different. When you compare, you are emphasizing similarities; when you contrast, you are emphasizing differences. Making a diagram or a list of similarities and differences is a good way to organize your details before you begin to write.

ÉCRIRE

5

En été et en hiver

A summer day in most parts of the world is quite different from a winter day. Write a paragraph comparing how you spend a vacation day in the summer in comparison to the way you spend a vacation day in the winter. Because of the weather, many of your activities are probably quite different. Not everything is different, however. Describe some things you do whether it's summer or winter.

Assessment

Vocabulaire

1 Complétez.

To review Mots 1, turn to pages 356–357.

1. Au bord de la mer, on va à la _____.
2. Il faut mettre de la _____ quand on prend un bain de soleil.
3. Laure apprend à nager. Elle a un très bon _____.
4. Elle apprend à nager dans une _____.
5. Quand il fait mauvais, il y a souvent des nuages dans le _____.
6. Il y a beaucoup de stations balnéaires sur la _____ Méditerranée.

2 Identifiez.

To review Mots 2, turn to pages 360–361.

7.

8.

9.

10.

3 Répondez.

11. Il fait quel temps en hiver?
12. Qui tombe souvent—un skieur débutant ou un bon skieur?

Structure

4 Complétez au passé composé.

To review irregular verbs in the passé composé, turn to page 364.

13. Il _____ des leçons de natation. (prendre)
14. Il _____ un très bon moniteur. (avoir)
15. Elles _____ un maillot de bain. (mettre)
16. J'_____ une carte postale. (écrire)
17. Tu _____ le match? (voir)

5 Donnez le contraire.

18. Il joue toujours au foot.
19. Il entend quelque chose.
20. Il regarde quelqu'un.

French Online

For more Chapter 11 test preparation, go to the Chapter 11 **Self-Check Quiz** on the Glencoe French Web site at glencoe.com.

To review negative statements, turn to page 367.

6 Récrivez au passé composé.

21. Elles arrivent à la plage.
22. Il part.
23. Anne et Marie, vous sortez?

To review the **passé composé** with **être**, turn to page 369.

Culture

7 Vrai ou faux?

24. On peut pratiquer le français au Québec parce que les Québécois parlent français.
25. Il y a beaucoup de stations de sports d'hiver dans la ville de Montréal.

To review this cultural information, turn to pages 374–375.

Le ski alpin

Do these practice activities to help you succeed on your FCAT through the study of a foreign language.

Read the passage below. Then answer the questions that follow.

Les Français sont très travailleurs. Mais les vacances sont très importantes pour eux. Le Français typique a à peu près cinq semaines de vacances par an. Le mois favori pour les grandes vacances d'été, c'est le mois d'août. Le premier août il y a des bouchons partout. Tout le monde est enthousiaste d'arriver au bord de la mer pour commencer les vacances.

La mer—avec son complément naturel, le soleil—est la préférence des Français. Et 87 pour cent des Français restent fidèles à la France. Pourquoi? Surtout parce que la France est un pays de plages merveilleuses. Il y a plus de mille kilomètres de côtes et des stations balnéaires tout le long de ces côtes—sur la Manche au nord, sur l'océan Atlantique à l'ouest et sur la mer Méditerranée au sud. Les Français ne quittent pas la France pendant les grandes vacances à cause de ces plages, mais peut-être aussi parce qu'ils ne sont pas très aventureux ou ne veulent pas payer beaucoup d'argent pour un voyage à l'étranger.

1 Comparez et contrastez les vacances des Français et les vacances des Américains.

2 Selon le passage, comment sont les Français?
- **A.** Ils adorent le travail et travaillent même pendant les vacances.
- **B.** Ils considèrent que le travail est plus important que les vacances.
- **C.** Ils ont beaucoup de vacances mais ils préfèrent travailler.
- **D.** Ils travaillent beaucoup pendant l'année mais ils aiment partir en vacances.

3 Expliquez pourquoi il y a des bouchons partout le premier août.

4 Quelle phrase signifie la même chose?
Et 87 pour cent des Français restent fidèles à la France.

    F.   La majorité des Français aiment leur pays.

    G.   La majorité des Français quittent la France pendant les grandes vacances.

    H.   La majorité des Français sont heureux d'être Français.

    I.   La majorité des Français préfèrent voyager dans d'autres pays pendant les vacances.

5 Quelle phrase est correcte?

    A.   On trouve de jolies plages à l'est de la France.

    B.   La mer Méditerranée est au sud de la France.

    C.   L'océan qui sépare la France des États-Unis se trouve au sud de la France.

    D.   Il n'est pas facile de trouver une belle plage en France.

6 Quelles sont deux autres raisons que les Français passent les vacances dans leur pays?

    F.   leur caractère et l'argent

    G.   la mer et l'aventure

    H.   les bouchons

    I.   leur travail et pas assez de jours de vacances

7 **READ THINK EXPLAIN** Quelle est l'idée centrale de ce passage?

FCAT Tip

Practice. Remember that test-taking skills can improve with practice. If possible, take at least one practice test to familiarize yourself with the test format and instructions.

FL.A.2.1.2 (I)

Tell all you can about this illustration.

Going to the beach

une station balnéaire	des lunettes *(f. pl.)* de
au bord de la mer	soleil
la mer	de la crème solaire
une plage	un maillot de bain
une vague	une serviette

How well do you know your vocabulary?

• Choose one of the seasons from the list.

• Have a classmate make up a sentence that tells something about that season.

Describing summer activities

nager	faire du surf	la natation
plonger	faire du ski nautique	une leçon de natation
prendre un bain de soleil	faire de la planche à voile	un moniteur, une monitrice
bronzer	faire une promenade	une piscine
attraper un coup de soleil		un surfeur, une surfeuse

Going to a ski resort

une station de sports d'hiver	un télésiège	une chaussure de ski	un gant
une montagne	une piste	un bâton	un bonnet
un sommet	une bosse	une patinoire	une écharpe
un skieur, une skieuse	le ski alpin	la glace	un anorak
un(e) débutant(e)	le ski de fond	le patin à glace	
	un ski	un patin	

Describing winter activities

faire du ski	descendre une piste	faire du patin à glace
monter en télésiège	tomber	

Describing weather and seasons

le temps	Il fait quel temps… ?	Il fait beau.	Il pleut.	le ciel
le printemps	au printemps	Il fait mauvais.	Il neige.	le soleil
l'été *(m.)*	en été	Il fait chaud.	Il gèle.	un nuage
l'automne *(m.)*	en automne	Il fait froid.	le vent	
l'hiver *(m.)*	en hiver	Il fait frais.		
		Il fait du soleil.		

Other useful words and expressions

la journée	apporter	longtemps
passer	rester	de temps en temps
faire attention		tout le temps

VIDÉOTOUR

Épisode 11

In this video episode, Christine experiences "almost firsthand" the wonderful world of skiing. See page 536 for more information.

Conversation

En vacances

Anne: Tu es arrivé à Nice quand?

Loïc: Je suis arrivé ce matin.

Anne: Tu as pris le train ou l'avion?

Loïc: J'ai pris le train—le TGV.

Anne: Et maintenant qu'est-ce que tu vas faire?

Loïc: Absolument rien! Je ne vais rien faire. Je vais passer toute la journée à la plage et lire tous les magazines sportifs que je n'ai jamais le temps de lire.

Promenade des Anglais, Nice

Vous avez compris?

Répondez.

1. Loïc est arrivé à Nice quand?
2. Qu'est-ce qu'il a pris, le train ou l'avion?
3. Il a pris le TGV?
4. Qu'est-ce que Loïc va faire à Nice?
5. Il va passer toute la journée où?
6. Qu'est-ce qu'il veut lire?

Structure

Les verbes au présent

1. Review the following regular **-ir** and **-re** verbs.

FINIR	je finis, tu finis, il/elle/on finit, nous finissons, vous finissez, ils/elles finissent
VENDRE	je vends, tu vends, il/elle/on vend, nous vendons, vous vendez, ils/elles vendent

2. Review these other **-ir** verbs.

SORTIR	je sors, tu sors, il/elle/on sort, nous sortons, vous sortez, ils/elles sortent
PARTIR	je pars, tu pars, il/elle/on part, nous partons, vous partez, ils/elles partent
DORMIR	je dors, tu dors, il/elle/on dort, nous dormons, vous dormez, ils/elles dorment
SERVIR	je sers, tu sers, il/elle/on sert, nous servons, vous servez, ils/elles servent

3. Review the following irregular verbs.

ÉCRIRE	j'écris, tu écris, il/elle/on_n écrit, nous_z écrivons, vous_z écrivez, ils_z /elles_z écrivent
LIRE	je lis, tu lis, il/elle/on lit, nous lisons, vous lisez, ils/elles lisent
DIRE	je dis, tu dis, il/elle/on dit, nous disons, vous dites, ils/elles disent

RECEVOIR	je reçois, tu reçois, il/elle/on reçoit, nous recevons, vous recevez, ils/elles reçoivent
DEVOIR	je dois, tu dois, il/elle/on doit, nous devons, vous devez, ils/elles doivent
BOIRE	je bois, tu bois, il/elle/on boit, nous buvons, vous buvez, ils/elles boivent

1 **Historiette** **Un voyage en train** Complétez au présent.

Nous __1__ (partir) en voyage. Maman __2__ (attendre) devant le guichet. Elle __3__ (choisir) deux places en seconde. Maman __4__ (sortir) de l'argent et achète les billets. Nous __5__ (attendre) le train sur le quai. Le train __6__ (partir) à l'heure. Je __7__ (sortir) les billets de mon sac à dos. Je __8__ (donner) les billets au contrôleur. Nous __9__ (aller) au snack-bar. Je __10__ (choisir) un sandwich au jambon. Maman aussi __11__ (prendre) un sandwich au jambon. Le serveur __12__ (servir) Maman en premier. Nous __13__ (finir) notre sandwich. Nous commandons un express; nous __14__ (boire) notre express. Nous retournons à notre place. Nous __15__ (dormir) un peu… Et nous arrivons à Toulon. Tous les voyageurs __16__ (descendre) du train. Nous __17__ (descendre) aussi. Enfin, nous sommes en vacances!

2 **Qu'est-ce que tu fais?** Donnez des réponses personnelles.

1. Tu lis tous les magazines que tu reçois?
2. Tu écris des articles dans le journal de l'école?
3. Tu dis toujours quels sont tes projets à tes amis?
4. Tu reçois quelquefois des e-mails de tes amis?
5. Tu dois aller voir tes grands-parents de temps en temps?

3 **Qu'est-ce qu'il fait?**
Refaites l'Activité 2 en remplaçant **tu** par **il,** et puis répondez.

4 **Qu'est-ce que vous faites?**
Refaites l'Activité 2 en remplaçant **tu** par **vous,** et puis répondez.

Les adjectifs

1. Review the adjectives **quel, ce,** and **tout.**

Quel groupe?	Quels garçons?	Quelle classe?	Quelles filles?
Ce groupe?	Ces garçons?	Cette classe?	Ces filles?
Oui, tout le groupe.	Oui, tous les garçons.	Oui, toute la classe.	Oui, toutes les filles.

2. Remember that you use **cet** before a singular masculine noun that begins with a vowel or a silent **h: cet‿ami, cet‿horaire.**

FL.A.1.1.1 (I)

5

Quels sont tes favoris? Répondez.

1. Toutes les classes sont intéressantes?
   Tu aimes cette classe aussi?
   Quelle classe est vraiment ta favorite?
2. Tu trouves tous les sports intéressants?
   Tu aimes ce sport?
   Quel est ton sport favori?
3. Tous les joueurs de cette équipe sont bons?
   Cette équipe gagne tous les matchs?
   Tous les spectateurs aiment ce sport?
   On parle de quel sport?

Ils jouent au foot.

6

Les sports

Complétez d'après les indications.

1. Tu parles de _____ équipe et de _____ match? (quel)
2. Je parle de _____ équipe, de _____ match et de _____ arbitre. (ce)
3. J'aime _____ les sports, mais pas _____ les équipes. (tout)
4. Voilà _____ les joueurs de l'équipe. (tout)
5. _____ trois joueurs sont excellents. C'est pourquoi _____ équipe gagne toujours. (ce)

Les verbes au passé composé

1. The **passé composé** expresses an action begun and completed at a specific time in the past. You form the **passé composé** by using the present tense of **avoir** and the past participle. Review the regular **-er, -ir,** and **-re** verbs.

PARLER	CHOISIR	ATTENDRE
j' ai parlé	j' ai choisi	j' ai attendu
tu as parlé	tu as choisi	tu as attendu
il/elle/on a parlé	il/elle/on a choisi	il/elle/on a attendu
nous avons parlé	nous avons choisi	nous avons attendu
vous avez parlé	vous avez choisi	vous avez attendu
ils/elles ont parlé	ils/elles ont choisi	ils/elles ont attendu

2. Review the verbs that have an irregular past participle.

devoir	dû	recevoir	reçu	dire	dit
boire	bu	avoir	eu	écrire	écrit
croire	cru				
voir	vu	prendre	pris	être	été
lire	lu	apprendre	appris	faire	fait
pouvoir	pu	comprendre	compris		
vouloir	voulu	mettre	mis		

Aéroport Charles-de-Gaulle, Roissy

7 **Historiette** **En voyage** Répondez.

1. Tu as fait tes valises?
2. Tu as pris ton billet et ton passeport?
3. À l'aéroport, tu as fait enregistrer tes bagages?
4. Tu as choisi ta place?
5. Tu as fait bon voyage?

8 **Historiette** **C'est passé.** Complétez en utilisant le passé composé.

1. Ils ____ ce que vous ____. (croire, dire)
2. Elle ____ des leçons de natation et elle ____ toutes les instructions de son moniteur. (prendre, comprendre)
3. Nous ____ une lettre de Marianne mais nous n'____ pas ____ à sa lettre. (recevoir, répondre)
4. Il ____ des courses. Il ____ tout ce qu'il ____ dans un grand sac. (faire, mettre, acheter)
5. Chez elle, elle ____ un verre d'eau et elle ____ son journal. (boire, lire)
6. J'____ très contente de voir Sébastien, mais je n'____ pas ____ sortir avec lui. (être, vouloir)

Le passé composé avec être

1. Many verbs that express motion to or from a place are conjugated with **être** in the **passé composé.** Such verbs are: **aller, descendre, rentrer, entrer, sortir, monter, arriver,** and **partir.**

MASCULIN		FÉMININ	
ALLER	**DESCENDRE**	**ALLER**	**DESCENDRE**
je suis allé	je suis descendu	je suis allée	je suis descendue
tu es allé	tu es descendu	tu es allée	tu es descendue
il est allé	il est descendu	elle est allée	elle est descendue
on est allé(s)	on est descendu(s)	on est allée(s)	on est descendue(s)
nous sommes allés	nous sommes descendus	nous sommes allées	nous sommes descendues
vous êtes allé(s)	vous êtes descendu(s)	vous êtes allée(s)	vous êtes descendue(s)
ils sont allés	ils sont descendus	elles sont allées	elles sont descendues

Note that the past participle of verbs conjugated with **être** agrees with the subject.

2. The verbs **rester, tomber, naître,** and **mourir** are also conjugated with **être.**

Il est resté huit jours.	**Elle est née le 20 décembre.**
Elle est tombée.	**Son grand-père est mort le 2 janvier.**

9 **H**istoriette **À l'école** Répondez.

1. Tu es allé(e) à l'école à quelle heure ce matin?
2. Tu es sorti(e) de la maison à quelle heure?
3. Quand tu es entré(e) dans la classe de français, tu as dit bonjour au professeur?
4. Tu es resté(e) à l'école après les cours?
5. Tu es allé(e) où après les cours?
6. Tu es rentré(e) chez toi vers quelle heure?

10 **H**istoriette **En train** Refaites les phrases avec le sujet indiqué.

1. Ils sont allés à Genève. (elles)
2. Les voyageurs sont descendus du train. (la voyageuse)
3. Elle est sortie de la gare. (il)
4. Il a cherché un taxi. (elle)
5. Elles sont rentrées à neuf heures du soir. (nous)

Genève, Suisse

Les mots négatifs

Review the negative words. Pay particular attention to their placement.

Je ne vais pas au café.
Je ne vais jamais au café.
Je ne vais plus au café.

Je ne suis pas allé(e) au café.
Je ne suis jamais allé(e) au café.
Je ne suis plus allé(e) au café.

Je ne vois rien et je n'ai rien vu.
Je ne vois personne et je n'ai vu personne.

LITERARY COMPANION *You may wish to read the adaptation of* **La Chanson de Roland** *on pages 512–517. The activities for this reading will help you continue to practice your reading comprehension skills.*

11 **Non.** Répondez que non.

1. Tu vois quelqu'un?
2. Tu entends quelqu'un?
3. Tu vois quelque chose?
4. Tu veux quelque chose?
5. Tu vas encore au café?

6. Tu arrives toujours en retard?
7. Tu as vu quelque chose?
8. Tu as dit quelque chose?
9. Tu as vu quelqu'un?
10. Tu as attendu quelqu'un?

12

Enquête sur les saisons You want to know if your partner prefers summer or winter. On a separate sheet of paper, make a chart like the one to the right. Fill it out for both seasons. Compare your chart with your partner's and try to guess which season your partner prefers by asking questions about his or her choices.

	L'hiver	L'été
Vêtements		
Activités	le ski	le ski nautique
Équipement		
Nourriture		

13 FL.A.2.2.5 (I)

Un match Work with a classmate. Discuss the last sports event you saw.

14 FL.A.1.2.2 (I) FL.D.1.2.2 (M)

On y va comment? Look at this plane schedule. You want to go from Paris to London. With a classmate decide and discuss which flight you will take there and back. Then tell what you are going to do there.

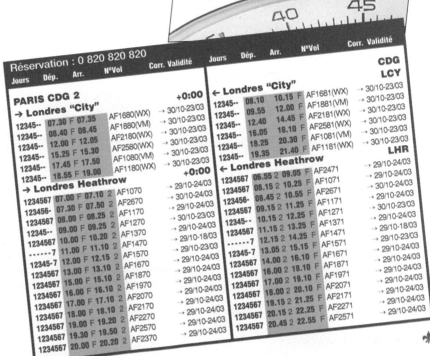

FOCUS ON Florida

Les plages de la Floride

Il est impossible de mentionner la Floride sans parler de ses plages. La Floride est très connue[1] pour ses plages et quelques-unes[2] sont parmi[3] les meilleures[4] du monde.

On va commencer notre petit voyage dans le sud-ouest de l'état—de Tampa à Naples. L'eau chaude et tranquille du golfe du Mexique baigne[5] les plages de sable blanc. Cette région a les plus belles plages de tout le pays—y compris[6] les plages de Hawaii. À Saint Petersburg Beach il y a même un musée dédié à la plage—le *Gulf Beaches Historical Museum*. Situé dans une ancienne église[7], le musée a une collection d'objets d'art et de photographies des plages qui date des années 1800.

Les plages du *panhandle* sont aussi très connues. Entre Tallahassee et Pensacola il y a plus de 300 kilomètres de jolies plages de fin sable blanc qui brille au soleil. L'eau du golfe a une couleur vert-émeraude. Si on veut avoir une expérience merveilleuse, il faut observer le coucher du soleil de la plage de Pensacola.

[1]connue *known*
[2]quelques-unes *some*
[3]parmi *among*
[4]meilleures *best*
[5]baigne *bathes*
[6]compris *including*
[7]ancienne église *former church*

Un pont à Saint Petersburg

L'île de Santa Rosa dans le golfe du Mexique

Tout le long de la côte, la plongée sous-marine ou simplement nager avec un masque et un tuba sont des sports populaires. L'eau claire permet d'observer la vie sous-marine des récifs de corail[8] qui se trouvent tout le long de la côte du golfe.

Si on aime la ville autant que la plage, il faut aller à Miami qui est renommée pour ses plages. Miami Beach a 40 kilomètres de plages. Comme l'eau de l'océan est plus agitée[9] que l'eau du golfe et comme les vagues sont plus grandes, beaucoup de gens font du surf et de la planche à voile à Miami et sur les autres plages de la côte atlantique.

Les plages de la Floride ont beaucoup d'importance dans l'économie de l'état. Chaque année des milliers de touristes visitent la Floride. Le tourisme est l'industrie la plus importante de l'état. En effet, un très fort désir de beaucoup de touristes, c'est de passer quelques journées agréables sur une jolie plage, nager et prendre des bains de soleil pour rentrer ensuite chez eux très bronzés.

[8]récifs de corail *barrier coral reefs*
[9]agitée *rough*

**La planche à voile,
Key Largo**

Miami

La vie sous-marine

Florida

Étude de mots

A. Cherchez un mot apparenté.

1. mondial
2. plonger
3. l'observation
4. désirer
5. le commencement

Compréhension

A. Répondez.

1. Où est Naples?
2. Comment est l'eau du golfe du Mexique?
3. Qu'est-ce qu'il y a à Saint Petersburg Beach?
4. Il y a combien de kilomètres de plages entre Tallahassee et Pensacola?
5. Quels sont des sports populaires sur les plages du golfe du Mexique?
6. Quelle grande ville a des plages où on peut surfer?
7. Quels sports est-ce qu'on pratique sur les plages de l'est de l'état?
8. Quelle est l'industrie la plus importante de la Floride?

B. Comparez.

Comparez l'eau du golfe du Mexique à l'eau de l'océan Atlantique.

La plage, Hollywood

Le coucher du soleil à la plage de Naples

C. Répondez.

1. Pourquoi la plongée sous-marine et nager avec un masque et un tuba sont-ils des sports populaires sur les plages du golfe?

2. Pourquoi le surf et la planche à voile sont-ils des sports populaires sur les plages de l'Atlantique?

3. Pourquoi les plages sont-elles très importantes pour l'état?

D. Décrivez.

1. le musée à Saint Petersburg Beach

2. une expérience merveilleuse sur la plage de Pensacola

E. Discutez.

Vous habitez le centre de l'état ou la côte? Vous allez à la plage? Vous y allez souvent ou simplement de temps en temps? Vous allez à quelle plage? Comment est la plage? Qu'est-ce que vous faites à la plage?

Florida Keys

Miami Beach

1. La ville de Québec vue du Saint-Laurent
2. La porte Saint-Louis à Québec
3. Le complexe Desjardins à Montréal
4. La chute Montmorency à l'est de la ville de Québec
5. Bateau de pêche dans la baie de Gaspé
6. Skieurs à Sainte-Agathe-des-Monts dans les Laurentides
7. Marionnettes sur le Vieux-Port à Montréal

6

REFLETS
du Canada

7

Merci

8

9

10

11

12

396

REFLETS
du Canada

13

14

La routine quotidienne

Objectifs

In this chapter you will learn to:

- describe your personal grooming habits
- talk about your daily routine
- talk about your family life
- tell some things you do for yourself
- talk about daily activities in the past
- discuss a French family's daily routine

Edgar Degas *Toilette matinale*

French Online
To interact with your online edition of
Bon voyage! go to: glencoe.com.

CHAPITRE 12
La routine quotidienne

SUNSHINE STATE STANDARDS

This chapter is all about daily routines. The material in the chapter will address the Sunshine State Standards listed below.

FL.A.2.1.2 restate and rephrase simple information from materials presented orally, visually, and graphically in class.

FL.A.2.1.3 understand oral messages that are based on familiar themes and vocabulary (e.g., short conversations between familiar persons on familiar topics such as everyday school and home activities).

FL.A.2.2.3 organize information in spoken or written form about a variety of topics of academic and cultural interest (e.g., by making lists, categorizing objects, or organizing concepts).

FL.A.2.2.5 comprehend and respond to oral messages (e.g., personal anecdotes or narratives) based on familiar themes and vocabulary.

FL.A.3.1.1 provide simple information in spoken form (e.g., descriptions of family members, friends, objects present in his or her everyday environment, or common school and home activities).

FL.A.3.2.1 describe important people (e.g., family members and friends) and objects present in his or her everyday environment and in school.

FL.A.3.2.3 give responses in spoken or written form (e.g., answering simple questions, formulating questions, and making simple statements) to age-appropriate stories, poems or other literature, songs, films, or visual works.

FL.B.1.1.2 recognize patterns of social behavior or social interaction in various settings (e.g., school, family, or immediate community).

FL.C.1.1.1 use simple vocabulary and phrases to identify familiar objects and concepts from other disciplines.

FL.D.1.2.1 identify examples and understand the significance of true and false cognates (i.e., words derived from a common original form).

FL.D.2.1.1 know the similarities and differences between the patterns of behavior of the target culture related to recreation, celebration, holidays, customs, and the patterns of behavior of the local culture.

Suwannee River

TIPS FOR SUCCESS
Review the Study Tips below to help you succeed on the Sunshine State Standards identified.

Vocabulaire Mots 1 Mots 2 *(pages 400–407)*

- In **Mots 1**, to make it easier to remember the meaning of the new words, they are put in a logical sequence of events:

  se réveiller, se lever, se laver (la figure, les cheveux), se peigner, se maquiller, s'habiller

- Matching synonyms and/or antonyms can often help you remember words.

  Match the antonyms *(opposites)* in **Mots 2**.

  1. **Il a mis la table.**   **Il a débarrassé la table.**
  2. **Il a allumé la télé.**   **Elle est rentrée.**
  3. **Elle est sortie.**   **Il a éteint la télé.**

  Match the synonyms.

  1. **un frigidaire**   **mettre la télé**
  2. **le salon**   **un réfrigérateur**
  3. **allumer la télé**   **changer de chaîne**
  4. **zapper**   **la salle de séjour**
  FL.A.2.2.3

Sand dollars

Structure Les verbes réfléchis au présent *(pages 408–412)*

- Remember that if a person is doing something to or for himself or herself, the verb in French is a reflexive verb, and you must use the additional pronoun.

- You have already learned all the verb endings that are used in these activities. The only new concept is the use of the reflexive pronoun. Pay particular attention to this pronoun as you do these activities. **FL.D.1.2.2**

> **For other tips to help you address the Sunshine State Standards in Chapter 12, see page H66 at the back of your textbook.**

Vocabulaire

La routine 🎧

se réveiller

se lever

Elle se lève tôt.
Elle ne se lève pas tard.

tôt   tard

se laver

un gant
de toilette

du savon

Il se lave la figure.

se laver
les cheveux

du shampooing

un peigne

une brosse

se laver (se brosser)
les dents

une brosse à dents

du dentifrice

une glace

se raser

un rasoir

Une fille se peigne.
L'autre se brosse les cheveux.

se maquiller

s'habiller

se coucher

prendre une douche

prendre un bain

Elle s'appelle Mélanie.
Mélanie se réveille.
Elle se lève tout de suite.

D'abord, elle se lave.

Ensuite elle se lave les dents.

Enfin elle prend son
petit déjeuner.

Elle se dépêche.

Quel est le mot?

1 **Historiette** **La matinée de Guillaume**

Inventez des réponses.

1. Le matin Guillaume se réveille à six heures? Il se lève tôt ou tard?
2. Il se lève tout de suite?
3. D'abord, il va dans la salle de bains pour se laver?
4. Il se lave la figure avec un gant de toilette?
5. Ensuite, il se lave les dents avec une brosse à dents et du dentifrice?
6. Il prend un bain ou une douche?
7. Il se regarde dans la glace quand il se rase?
8. Il s'habille dans sa chambre à coucher?
9. Enfin, il prend son petit déjeuner avant d'aller à l'école?
10. Il se dépêche? Pourquoi?

Guillaume se rase.

2 **Dans quelle pièce?** Complétez.

1. On se brosse les dents dans _____.
2. On se couche dans _____.
3. On prend une douche dans _____.
4. On se maquille dans _____.
5. On dort dans _____.
6. On prend son petit déjeuner dans _____.

3 **Qu'est-ce qu'il faut?** Choisissez la bonne réponse.

1. Pour se laver les dents il faut _____.
   a. de la crème   **b.** du dentifrice   **c.** du déodorant
2. Pour se laver la figure et les mains, il faut _____.
   a. du déodorant   **b.** du dentifrice   **c.** du savon
3. Pour se raser il faut _____.
   a. un rasoir   **b.** une brosse à dents   **c.** un peigne
4. Pour se peigner il faut _____.
   a. du shampooing   **b.** un peigne   **c.** du savon
5. Pour se laver les cheveux il faut _____.
   a. du déodorant   **b.** du shampooing   **c.** du savon
6. Pour se brosser les cheveux il faut _____.
   a. une brosse   **b.** un peigne   **c.** une brosse à dents

FL.A.3.1.1 (I)

4 **Pendant la journée** Work with a classmate. Each of you will choose a family member and tell each other about that person's daily activities.

 mon père

 mon cousin

 ma mère

 ma sœur

 ma cousine

 mon frère

Une famille fait les courses, Yerres, France.

French Online
For a fun way to review this vocabulary, go to the Chapter 12 **eGame** on the Glencoe French Web site at glencoe.com.

 ENCORE PLUS *For more practice using words from* **Mots 1,** *do Activity 38 on page H39 at the end of this book.*

Vocabulaire

Mots 2

Chez les Moulin 🎧

la cuisine

un évier

un frigidaire,
un réfrigérateur

un lave-vaisselle

Avant le dîner, Christophe met la table.

une télécommande

faire la vaisselle

débarrasser la table

Après le dîner, Mélanie débarrasse la table.
Et Maman fait la vaisselle.

M. Moulin a mis (a allumé) la télé.

la salle de séjour

faire ses devoirs

French Online
To learn about French TV programming,
do the Chapter 12 **WebQuest** activity on
the Glencoe French Web site at
glencoe.com.

M. Moulin a zappé pour éviter les publicités.
Il a changé de chaîne.
Il a regardé son émission favorite.
Mélanie a fait ses devoirs après le dîner.

un magnétoscope

une cassette vidéo

Mélanie a fait ses devoirs.
Elle n'a pas pu regarder le film à la télé.
Elle a enregistré le film.

Après l'émission M. Moulin a
éteint la télé.

Quel est le mot?

5 **Historiette** **Chez les Fauvet**

Répondez d'après les indications.

1. Qui a mis la table? (Paul)
2. Qui a servi le dîner? (Mme Fauvet)
3. Qui a débarrassé la table? (M. Fauvet)
4. Qui a fait la vaisselle? (Sophie)
5. Où est-ce qu'elle a mis les assiettes, les verres et les couverts? (dans le lave-vaisselle)
6. Après le dîner, qui a mis la télé? (M. Fauvet)
7. Qu'est-ce qu'ils ont regardé à la télé? (leur émission favorite)
8. Ils ont zappé pour éviter les publicités? (oui)
9. Qui a éteint la télé? (M. Fauvet)
10. Qui est sorti après le dîner? (Sophie)
11. Elle s'est bien amusée? (oui)
12. Elle a fait ses devoirs avant de sortir? (oui)

Ils regardent la télé.

6 **Quel est le mot?** Complétez.

1. L'évier, le frigidaire et le lave-vaisselle se trouvent dans la ____.
2. On rince la vaisselle dans l'____, et ensuite, on met les verres, les assiettes et les couverts dans le ____.
3. Avant le dîner, on ____ la table.
4. Après le dîner, on ____ la table.
5. Quand on veut regarder la télévision, on ____ la télévision.
6. M. Fauvet n'arrive pas à trouver une émission qu'il aime. Il change souvent de ____.
7. On peut changer de chaîne avec une ____.
8. Si on n'est pas à la maison pour regarder un film, on peut ____ le film sur une cassette vidéo.
9. Pour enregistrer un film à la télé il faut avoir un ____.

Pour 20€/MOIS*

découvrez les nouveaux pouvoirs de votre télécommande ...

LYONNAISE CABLE

7 **FL.A.3.2.1 (I)**

Historiette **Chez moi** Donnez des réponses personnelles.

1. Tu rentres à la maison vers quelle heure?
2. Qui prépare le dîner chez toi?
3. Qui met la table?
4. Qui sert le dîner?
5. Qui débarrasse la table?
6. Qui fait la vaisselle?
7. Qu'est-ce que vous faites après le dîner?
8. Tu fais tes devoirs avant de regarder la télévision?

8 **FL.A.3.1.1 (I)**

Chez nous Work with a classmate. Share information about what you usually do when you return home after school. Decide if much of your routine is the same.

9 **FL.A.2.1.2 (I)** **FL.A.3.2.3 (I)**

En famille Work with a classmate. Ask each other questions about the illustration. Answer each other's questions.

For more practice using words from **Mots 2,** *do Activity 39 on page H40 at the end of this book.*

Structure

Les verbes réfléchis au présent
Telling what people do for themselves

1. Compare the following pairs of sentences.

Paul regarde le bébé.

Paul se regarde.

Anne couche le bébé.

Anne se couche.

In the sentences on the left, one person performs the action and another receives the action. In the sentences on the right, the person performs the action and also receives the action. For this reason, the pronoun **se** must be used. **Se** refers to the subject or doer of the action and is called a "reflexive" pronoun. It indicates that the action of the verb is reflected back to the subject.

2. Each subject pronoun has its corresponding reflexive pronoun. Study the following.

SE LAVER		S'HABILLER	
je	me lave	je	m'habille
tu	te laves	tu	t'habilles
il/elle/on	se lave	il/elle/on	s'habille
nous	nous lavons	nous	nous_z habillons
vous	vous lavez	vous	vous_z habillez
ils/elles	se lavent	ils/elles	s'habillent

3. The reflexive pronoun cannot be separated from the verb. In the negative, **ne** comes before the reflexive pronoun and **pas** comes after the verb.

> **Je me réveille mais je ne me lève pas tout de suite.**
> **On ne se lave jamais les dents avant le dîner.**
> **Je ne me lave plus les cheveux tous les jours.**

4. When a reflexive verb follows another verb, the reflexive pronoun agrees with the subject.

> **Je ne veux pas me lever tôt.**
> **Vous allez vous coucher tard.**

Les lavages publics du Banco, Abidjan, Côte d'Ivoire

Harvesting Fresh clothes from the river.

LA ROUTINE QUOTIDIENNE

Comment dit-on?

FL.A.2.1.3 (I)

10 **La matinée de Jean-Marc** Répétez la conversation.

FL.A.2.1.3 (I)

11 **Historiette** **C'est malin!** Répondez d'après la conversation.

1. Jean-Marc se lève à quelle heure?
2. Il se lave?
3. Il se lave les dents?
4. Il se rase?
5. Il s'habille?
6. Qu'est-ce qu'il fait en une demi-heure?

12 **Historiette** **Caroline et Stéphanie** Remplacez **Caroline** par **Caroline et Stéphanie.**

1. Caroline se réveille à sept heures.
2. Caroline se lève tout de suite.
3. Caroline se lave les dents.
4. Caroline se lave les mains et la figure.
5. Caroline se brosse les cheveux.
6. Caroline s'habille.
7. Caroline se maquille.

Les deux sœurs se maquillent.

13 **Historiette** **Le matin** Donnez des réponses personnelles.

1. Tu te lèves à quelle heure le matin?
2. Tu vas dans la salle de bains?
3. Tu te laves?
4. Tu te laves les mains et la figure?
5. Tu prends une douche ou un bain?
6. Tu te laves les cheveux avec du shampooing?
7. Tu te peignes?
8. Tu te regardes dans la glace quand tu te peignes?

14 **Historiette** **Ma famille** Remplacez **on** par **nous.**

Je m'appelle Christian. Dans la famille on se réveille tôt. On ne se lave pas le matin parce qu'on se lave le soir. Ensuite on s'habille. On prend notre petit déjeuner tous ensemble. Après, on se lave les dents. Et on se dépêche d'aller, moi à l'école, mes parents au travail.

15 FL.A.3.2.3 (I)

Ta famille Posez des questions à Christian. Utilisez le paragraphe de l'Activité 14 comme guide. Vous pouvez utiliser les sujets suivants.

 tu **tes parents** **ta famille** **vous**

16 FL.A.3.2.3 (I)

Historiette **Dimanche** Donnez des réponses personnelles.

1. Tu vas te réveiller à quelle heure dimanche?
2. Tu vas t'habiller avant de prendre le petit déjeuner?
3. Tu vas sortir avec des amis?
4. Vous allez vous habiller comment?
5. Tu vas te coucher tard?

 For more practice using reflexive verbs, do Activity 40 on page H41 at the end of this book.

Structure

17 **Je me réveille et...** Work in groups of three or four. Tell the order of your daily activities from morning to night. Do you all do everything in the same order? What's the most common routine? Who has the oddest routine? Describe it.

18 **J'ai quelque chose.** You have something you use routinely. Tell a classmate what it is. He or she will guess what you use it for.

J'ai du dentifrice.   Tu te laves les dents.

Attention!

1. Note the changes in pronunciation and spelling of the following verbs.

SE LEVER
je me lève   nous nous levons
tu te lèves   vous vous levez
il se lève   ils se lèvent

S'APPELER
je m'appelle   nous nous appelons
tu t'appelles   vous vous appelez
il s'appelle   ils s'appellent

The verbs **se promener** and **acheter** have the same spelling changes as **se lever**.

2. Note the spelling of the **nous** form of verbs that end in **-ger** and **-cer: nous mangeons, nous nageons, nous voyageons, nous commençons.**

Répondez d'après le modèle.

— **Je me lève à six heures!**
— **Nous aussi, nous nous levons à six heures.**

1. Je me lève à cinq heures.

2. Je me promène un peu dans le parc.

3. Je nage dans la piscine.

4. J'achète un café et un croissant.

5. Je commence à manger mon croissant dans la rue.

6. Je mange tout mon croissant dans la rue.

Les verbes réfléchis au passé composé
Telling what people did for themselves

1. You form the **passé composé** of reflexive verbs with the verb **être.** Note the agreement of the past participle with reflexive verbs.

SE LAVER

Masculin	Féminin
je me suis lavé	je me suis lavée
tu t'es lavé	tu t'es lavée
il s'est lavé	elle s'est lavée
on s'est lavé(s)	on s'est lavée(s)
nous nous sommes lavés	nous nous sommes lavées
vous vous êtes lavé(s)	vous vous êtes lavée(s)
ils se sont lavés	elles se sont lavées

2. Note that when a part of the body follows a reflexive verb, there is no agreement.

Agreement	No agreement
Marie s'est lavée.	Marie s'est lavé les mains.
Nous nous sommes brossés.	Nous nous sommes brossé les cheveux.

3. In the negative sentence, you put the negative words around the reflexive pronoun and the verb **être.**

> **Je ne me suis pas levée tard.**
> **Mes amis ne se sont jamais amusés chez Paul.**

Comment dit-on?

 Papa va se réveiller? Il s'est déjà réveillé.

19 **Déjà fait** Répondez d'après le modèle.

1. Papa va se lever?
2. Papa va se laver?
3. Papa va se peigner?
4. Papa va s'habiller?

LA ROUTINE QUOTIDIENNE

20 **Maman** Refaites l'Activité 19 en remplaçant **Papa** par **Maman.**

21 **Historiette** **Tôt** Donnez des réponses personnelles.

1. Tu t'es réveillé(e) tôt ce matin?
2. Tu t'es levé(e) tout de suite ou tu t'es rendormi(e)?
3. Tu as pris une douche ou tu t'es lavé seulement la figure et les mains?
4. Tu t'es habillé(e) avant ou après le petit déjeuner?
5. Tu t'es peigné(e) ou tu t'es brossé les cheveux ce matin?
6. Tu t'es lavé les dents après le petit déjeuner?
7. Tu t'es bien amusé(e) à l'école?
8. Tu t'es couché(e) à quelle heure hier soir?

22 **Nous et vous** Complétez au passé composé.

1. Ce matin, ma sœur et moi, nous _____ à sept heures. Et vous, vous_____ à quelle heure? (se réveiller)
2. Nous _____ tard. Vous _____ tard? (se lever)
3. Nous _____. Vous _____ aussi? (se dépêcher)
4. Nous _____ très vite. Vous _____ vite aussi? (s'habiller)

Elles se dépêchent.

23 **Mes cousins** Mettez au pluriel.

1. Il s'est levé.
2. Il s'est lavé.
3. Il s'est rasé.
4. Il s'est habillé.
5. Elle s'est levée tard.
6. Elle s'est maquillée.
7. Elle s'est vite habillée.
8. Elle s'est dépêchée.

24 **Historiette** **Ce matin** Inventez une histoire.

1. Tu t'es levé(e) à quelle heure ce matin?
2. Et ton frère, il s'est levé à quelle heure?
3. Vous vous êtes tous habillés avant le petit déjeuner?
4. Vous vous êtes lavé les dents après le petit déjeuner?
5. Tes parents se sont dépêchés pour aller au travail?

25 **Qu'est-ce qu'elle a fait?** Complétez.

1. Elle s'est levé___ ce matin à six heures.
2. Elle s'est lavé___ la figure.
3. Elle s'est lavé___ les dents.
4. Elle s'est amusé___ à l'école.
5. Elle s'est couché___ de bonne heure.

FL.A.3.1.1 (I)

26 **Ce matin** Work with a classmate. Tell each other what you did this morning from the time you woke up until you left for school.

FL.A.2.2.5 (I)   **FL.A.3.2.3 (I)**

27 **On s'est bien amusé(e)s.** Choose one of the illustrations. Describe it. A classmate will tell which one you're describing and let you know whether the people had fun. Take turns.

1.

2.

3.

FL.A.2.1.3 (I)

28 **Une journée extraordinaire!** Work with a classmate. Imagine that yesterday was really a great day. Tell each other what happened.

ENCORE PLUS → *For more practice using reflexive verbs, do Activity 41 on page H42 at the end of this book.*

Vous êtes sur le bon chemin. Allez-y!

Conversation

Quelle interro?

Thomas: Tu n'as pas l'air très réveillée, ce matin.

Magali: Ben, non, je n'ai pas assez dormi.

Thomas: Tu t'es couchée à quelle heure?

Magali: À trois heures du matin.

Thomas: À trois heures du mat! Ça va pas, non? Qu'est-ce que tu as fait? Tu n'as pas pu éteindre la télé, c'est ça?

Magali: La télé? Tu rigoles! L'interrogation de maths, plutôt.

Thomas: L'interro de maths? Quelle interro de maths?

Vous avez compris?

Répondez.

1. Magali a assez dormi hier soir?
2. Elle s'est couchée à quelle heure?
3. Elle a regardé la télévision?
4. Qu'est-ce qu'elle a fait?
5. Et Thomas, il a étudié ses maths?

Parlons un peu plus

FL.A.3.1.1 (I)

A **Je suis fatigué(e)!** Neither you nor your classmate look too good this morning. You both got to bed really late. Tell each other why.

FL.A.3.1.1 (I)

B **Une journée horrible!** Work with a classmate. Imagine that yesterday was a really bad day. Tell each other what happened.

Prononciation

Les sons /s/ et /z/

1. It is important to make a distinction between the sounds /s/ and /z/. After all, you would not want to confuse **poisson** and **poison**! Repeat the following words with the sound /s/ as in **assez** and /z/ as in **raser**.

/s/		/z/	
assez	dessert	désert	télévision
classe	séjour	maison	zapper
vaisselle	boisson	raser	cousin
salle	savon	cousine	

2. Now repeat the following sentences.

Son cousin choisit le dessert et les boissons.
La télévision est dans la salle de séjour.
La salle de classe est assez grande.

poisson   poison

Lectures culturelles

Reading Strategy

Skimming

There are several ways to read an article or a passage—each one with its own purpose. Skimming means reading quickly in order to find out the general idea of a passage. To skim means to read without paying careful attention to small details, noting only information about the main theme or topic. Sometimes a reader will skim a passage only to decide whether it's interesting enough to read in detail.

FL.B.1.1.2 (I)

La famille Ben Amar

Les Ben Amar habitent à Saint-Quentin-en-Yvelines. C'est une ville nouvelle dans la banlieue[1] parisienne. Les Ben Amar sont des Français d'origine algérienne. En France, il y a beaucoup de gens originaires des pays du Maghreb, c'est-à-dire des trois pays francophones d'Afrique du Nord— le Maroc, l'Algérie et la Tunisie. Aujourd'hui, la deuxième religion en France, c'est la religion musulmane.

Le matin

Dans la famille Ben Amar, il y a six personnes: M. Ben Amar, sa femme et leurs quatre enfants. Ce matin, comme d'habitude, les Ben Amar se sont levés entre six heures et six heures et demie. Ils se sont lavés, peignés, habillés et ils ont pris leur petit déjeuner. Ils sont partis de chez eux vers sept heures et demie. M. Ben Amar est allé à l'usine[2] où il travaille comme contremaître[3]. Ahmed et Halima vont au collège et Aïcha est à l'école primaire. Le petit Jamal a deux ans. Il ne peut pas encore aller à l'école maternelle. Il passe la journée chez sa grand-mère qui habite dans le même immeuble. Comme beaucoup de femmes françaises, Mme Ben Amar travaille à l'extérieur. Tout est assez cher et la famille a besoin de deux salaires. Mme Ben Amar est assistante sociale[4]. Et Mima est toujours contente de garder son petit Jamal.

Les Ben Amar rentrent déjeuner? Non, ils ne rentrent pas chez eux à midi. M. et Mme Ben Amar déjeunent là où ils travaillent et les enfants déjeunent à la cantine de leur école. Le petit Jamal déjeune avec sa grand-mère.

Une famille d'origine algérienne

Mima avec son petit-fils

[1] banlieue *suburbs*
[2] usine *factory*
[3] contremaître *supervisor*
[4] assistante sociale *social worker*

Tahiti

Haïti

La Martinique

Le soir

Le soir, les enfants rentrent de l'école vers cinq heures. Ils vont chez leur grand-mère. Ils mangent une tartine de confiture ou des petits gâteaux faits par Mima et ils font leurs devoirs. Vers sept heures et demie, leurs parents rentrent. Ce soir, Mima a préparé un bon couscous pour toute la famille. Après le dîner, Ahmed débarrasse la table, Halima aide sa mère à faire la vaisselle et M. Ben Amar regarde la télévision. Ce soir, il y a un bon film égyptien à 22 h 30. Les films égyptiens sont excellents et M. et Mme Ben Amar aiment bien voir de temps en temps un film en arabe.

Saint-Quentin-en-Yvelines, près de Paris

La Tunisie

Le Maroc

Un bon couscous

Vous avez compris?

A **Les Ben Amar** Lisez rapidement le texte et trouvez les informations suivantes.
1. le nom de la petite ville où les Ben Amar habitent
2. les noms des pays du Maghreb
3. la deuxième religion en France
4. le nombre d'enfants dans la famille
5. leurs prénoms respectifs
6. l'heure où les Ben Amar se lèvent
7. comment les enfants appellent leur grand-mère

B **La journée des Ben Amar** Décrivez.
1. le travail de M. Ben Amar
2. le travail de Mme Ben Amar
3. le travail de la grand-mère
4. le dîner des Ben Amar
5. la soirée des Ben Amar

Le Mali

Lecture supplémentaire

FL.D.2.1.1 (I)

Le petit déjeuner

Tout le monde se réveille le matin, se lève, se lave, s'habille et… prend son petit déjeuner. On commence la journée par un bon petit déjeuner. Mais le petit déjeuner n'est pas le même partout[1].

Aux États-Unis

Aux États-Unis, on boit souvent un verre de jus de fruit—du jus d'orange, par exemple. Ensuite on mange des céréales ou des œufs— des œufs brouillés[2], des œufs sur le plat avec du bacon, des saucisses ou du jambon et du pain grillé. Avec ça, on boit du café ou du chocolat ou même un verre de lait. C'est un vrai petit déjeuner américain, mais ce n'est pas un petit déjeuner français. En France, on ne mange jamais d'œufs ni de bacon au petit déjeuner.

[1] partout *everywhere*
[2] brouillés *scrambled*

Un petit déjeuner américain—des œufs sur le plat

En France

Un petit déjeuner typiquement français, c'est du pain, des croissants ou des brioches avec un bol de café au lait (le lait est chaud.) Les enfants boivent souvent du chocolat chaud. On mange souvent des tartines. Une tartine, c'est une tranche de pain beurré avec de la confiture.

Une tartine

Un croissant et une brioche

Du droî

Des olives

Des figues et des raisins secs

Au Maghreb

En Tunisie, les enfants mangent souvent du droî pour le petit déjeuner. Le droî est de la farine de sorgho[3] cuite à l'eau bouillante[4]. On mange le droî chaud avec un peu de sucre. Les adultes mangent aussi quelquefois du droî, mais souvent ils mangent des tartines comme en France. À la campagne, on mange quelquefois des figues et des raisins secs blancs.

En Algérie, on mange des tartines et du café au lait comme en France, mais à la campagne, on mange quelquefois du fromage, des olives, du pain et de la soupe.

[3] farine de sorgho *sorghum flour*
[4] cuite à l'eau bouillante *cooked in boiling water*

Vous avez compris?

Un petit déjeuner excellent Décrivez.

1. un petit déjeuner américain
2. un petit déjeuner français
3. un petit déjeuner tunisien
4. un petit déjeuner algérien

La Belgique

La Tunisie

Le Maroc

Le Mali

CONNEXIONS

FL.C.1.1.1 (I)

Les sciences

L'écologie

Ecology is a subject of great interest to people around the world. No one wants to wake up each morning and breathe polluted air or drink contaminated water. Unfortunately, however, much of what we do in our daily life has a negative impact on our environment. The way we dispose of waste litters fields and pollutes waterways. Factories and vehicles belch smoke and fumes that pollute the air. We are all aware that urgent and dramatic steps must be taken to avert future disasters.

L'air pollué, Lyon

L'air pur, Pays Basque

L'écologie

L'écologie, c'est l'équilibre entre les êtres vivants[1] et la nature. Le terme est maintenant synonyme de survie[2] pour beaucoup d'êtres humains à cause de problèmes écologiques très graves.

La pollution de l'air

L'air que nous respirons est souvent pollué. Le plus souvent, il est pollué par des émissions de gaz qui s'échappent des voitures

[1] êtres vivants *living beings*
[2] survie *survival*

et des camions[3]. Il est pollué aussi par la fumée qui se dégage des cheminées des usines qui brûlent[4] des substances chimiques.

La pollution de l'eau

La contamination de l'eau de nos lacs, de nos rivières et de nos mers est catastrophique dans certaines régions. Les accidents de pétroliers font que des millions de litres de pétrole se déversent[5] dans les mers et les océans. Dans les zones industrielles les usines déversent des déchets[6] industriels dans les rivières. Beaucoup de ces déchets sont toxiques et peuvent causer des maladies[7] très graves.

Le recyclage

De nos jours, il y a de grandes campagnes de recyclage. Grâce au recyclage, nous pouvons utiliser à nouveau des déchets de verre, de papier, de métal et même de plastique.

[3] camions *trucks*
[4] brûlent *burn*
[5] se déversent *are spilled*
[6] déchets *wastes*
[7] maladies *illnesses*

Le naufrage d'un pétrolier, Bretagne

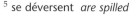
Conteneurs pour le recyclage

Vous avez compris?

FL.D.1.2.1 (I)

A En français, s'il vous plaît.
Trouvez l'équivalent des mots suivants dans la lecture.

1. ecology
2. ecological problems
3. chemical substances
4. air pollution
5. toxic wastes
6. recycling

FL.C.1.1.1 (I)

B Discussion Répondez.

1. L'air est pollué là où vous habitez?
2. Il y a beaucoup d'usines près de chez vous?
3. Il y a beaucoup de voitures, d'autocars et de camions qui passent?
4. Vous recyclez? Qu'est-ce que vous recyclez? Le papier, le carton (*cardboard*), le verre… ?

C'est à vous

Use what you have learned

PARLER

1

FL.A.2.2.5 (I)

Ma famille
✔ *Compare your family life to someone else's*

Work with a classmate. Find out about some family habits in your respective homes: who does what chores, what you do after dinner, etc. Compare your findings.

Vincent Van Gogh *La chambre de Vincent à Arles*

PARLER

2

Pas la même chose
✔ *Talk about your weekday and weekend routines*

Most people like a change of pace on the weekend. Talk with a classmate about things that students do or don't do during the week. Your partner will say how that differs on the weekend and why. Take turns.

> Pendant la semaine, on se lève tôt.

> Pendant le week-end, on se lève plus tard.

PARLER

3

FL.A.3.1.1 (I)

Quel jour!
✔ *Talk about an atypical day*

You have a set routine but sometimes you just can't stick to it. That was the case yesterday. Have a conversation with a friend. Use the model as a guide.

—**D'habitude je me lève à sept heures.**

—**Tu t'es levé(e) à quelle heure hier?**

—**Je me suis levé(e) à dix heures et demie.**

4 Une journée typique

✔ *Write about your daily routine*

Your Tunisian key pal is curious about your daily routine. Write him or her an e-mail describing all the activities you do on a typical day, from the time you wake up to the time you go to bed.

Halima est de Kairouan en Tunisie.

Writing Strategy

Taking notes Taking notes gives you a written record of important information you may need for later use. When taking notes from a lecture, write down key words and phrases as you continue to focus on what the speaker is saying. When the speaker has finished, go back over your notes as soon as possible, highlighting the most important points and adding details to make them as complete as possible. If necessary, rewrite your notes, organizing them so they will be of utmost use to you.

ÉCRIRE

 FL.A.2.1.3 (I) FL.A.2.2.3 (I)

5 Un job d'été

You are working in Quebec this summer. You are going to help take care of two small children. The children's parents give you many instructions about the children's routine and activities. Since you probably will not remember all they are telling you, you jot down notes. Take your notes and organize them to describe each child's day. Then write down your responsibilities—what it is you have to do.

Assessment

FrenchOnline

For more Chapter 12 test preparation, go to the Chapter 12 **Self-Check Quiz** on the Glencoe French Web site at glencoe.com.

Vocabulaire

1 Identifiez.

1.   2.   3.

4.   5.

To review **Mots 1**, turn to pages 400–401.

2 Mettez en ordre.

6. _____ **a.** se laver
7. _____ **b.** se réveiller
8. _____ **c.** se coucher
9. _____ **d.** se lever

3 Choisissez.

To review **Mots 2**, turn to pages 404–405.

10. Après le dîner, il _____ la table.
    a. met   **b.** débarrasse   **c.** fait

11. Il lave les assiettes, les verres, etc. Il fait _____.
    a. le lave-vaisselle   **b.** la vaisselle   **c.** l'évier

12. Il _____ pour éviter les publicités.
    a. allume la télé   **b.** fait ses devoirs   **c.** zappe

13. Après son émission favorite, il a _____ la télé.
    a. éteint   **b.** regardé   **c.** mis

Structure

To review reflexive verbs in the present, turn to pages 408–409.

4 Complétez au présent.

14. Il _____ la figure. (se laver)
15. Elles _____ les cheveux. (se brosser)
16. Nous _____ beaucoup. (s'amuser)
17. Je _____ à onze heures. (se coucher)
18. Éric, tu _____ tous les matins? (se raser)

5 **Récrivez.**

19. Tu t'appelles comment?
    Vous _____?
20. Nous nous levons tôt.
    Je _____.

6 **Complétez au passé composé.**

21. Elle _____. (se laver)
22. Elles _____ les cheveux. (se laver)
23. Mes amis _____. (s'amuser)

Culture

7 **Identifiez.**

24. les pays du Maghreb
25. la deuxième religion en France

To review verbs with spelling changes, turn to page 412.

To review reflexive verbs in the **passé composé,** turn to page 413.

To review this cultural information, turn to pages 418–419.

For more information on the Maghreb, go to **Web Explore** on the Glencoe French Web site at glencoe.com.

Un marché, Alger, Algérie

CHAPITRE ⑫ Florida

Do these practice activities to help you succeed on your FCAT through the study of a foreign language.

Read the story below. Then answer the questions that follow.

Caroline est souvent en retard. Hier matin, elle s'est __1__ à huit heures et ses cours ont commencé à 8 h 30. Donc, elle s'est __2__, s'est habillée et s'est __3__ les cheveux très rapidement. Elle ne __4__ pas maquillée. Normalement elle se lève à sept heures. Elle __5__ la figure, se brosse les dents et se maquille. Elle ne se dépêche pas!

❶ Quelle est la forme du verbe qui complète le numéro (1)?
- **A.** réveillée
- **B.** réveillé
- **C.** réveille

❷ Quelle est la forme du verbe qui complète le numéro (2)?
- **F.** lavé
- **G.** lavée
- **H.** laver

❸ Quelle est la forme du verbe qui complète le numéro (3)?
- **A.** brosse
- **B.** brossé
- **C.** brossée

❹ Quelle est le mot qui complète le numéro (4)?
- **F.** se
- **G.** est
- **H.** s'est

5 Quelle est la forme du verbe qui complète le numéro (5)?

    A. se laver

    B. s'est lavée

    C. se lave

ESSAY

Tout le monde a une routine quotidienne. Pour certaines personnes, la routine ne varie pas beaucoup d'un jour à l'autre. On fait la même chose à la même heure chaque jour. La majorité des gens qui suivent une routine fixe sont des gens très organisés. On peut même dire qu'ils sont un peu rigides. Mais il y a des gens qui ne suivent pas une routine fixe. Ils font quelque chose aujourd'hui mais cela ne veut pas dire qu'ils vont faire la même chose demain. Leur routine est assez flexible. En général, les gens qui ont une routine flexible sont de caractère docile et s'adaptent facilement à des situations différentes.

Écrivez une composition intitulée **Ma routine.** Pensez à votre routine. Qu'est-ce que vous faites tous les jours? Comment est votre routine? Fixe et rigide ou assez flexible? Écrivez quelques détails sur votre personnalité. Indiquez si votre personnalité a une influence sur votre routine.

FCAT Tip

Read the prompt carefully to be sure you understand what you are expected to do.

FL.A.2.1.2 (I)   FL.A.3.2.1 (I)

Tell all you can about this illustration.

Doing daily activities

la routine	se laver	s'habiller
prendre un bain	se brosser	s'amuser
prendre une douche	se raser	se dépêcher
se réveiller	se maquiller	se coucher
se lever	se peigner	

Identifying grooming articles

du savon	une brosse à dents	un rasoir
un gant de toilette	du dentifrice	un peigne
du shampooing	une glace	une brosse

Identifying more parts of the body

la figure
les cheveux (m. pl.)
les dents (f. pl.)

Identifying household appliances

un évier	une télé(vision)
un lave-vaisselle	une télécommande
un frigidaire, un	un magnétoscope
réfrigérateur	

How well do you know your vocabulary?

- Choose an expression from the list that describes something you do as part of your daily routine.
- Ask a classmate to give words related to that particular daily activity.

Discussing home activities

mettre la table	mettre la télévision	zapper	une émission
débarrasser la table	allumer	changer de chaîne	une publicité
faire la vaisselle	éteindre		une chaîne
faire ses devoirs	enregistrer		

Other useful words and expressions

s'appeler	d'abord	tout de suite
tôt	ensuite	
tard	enfin	

VIDÉOTOUR

Épisode 12

In this video episode, you will join Vincent as he "coaches" Manu through his morning routine. See page 537 for more information.

CHAPITRE 13

Les loisirs culturels

La Poste 2000
Camille Claudel 1,02 €
La Valse
RF

Objectifs

In this chapter you will learn to:

✔ *discuss movies, plays, and museums*

✔ *tell what you know and whom you know*

✔ *tell what happens to you or someone else*

✔ *refer to people and things already mentioned*

✔ *talk about some cultural activities in Paris*

Des statues béninoises du seizième siècle

French Online
To interact with your online edition of
Bon voyage! go to: glencoe.com.

SUNSHINE STATE STANDARDS

This chapter is all about cultural activities. The material in the chapter will address the Sunshine State Standards listed below.

FL.A.1.1.1   express likes and dislikes when asked simple questions (e.g., about toys or other objects).

FL.A.1.2.1   express likes or dislikes regarding various objects, categories, people, and events present in the everyday environment.

FL.A.1.2.2   exchange information necessary to plan events or activities (e.g., picnics, birthday parties, science projects, and crafts).

FL.A.2.1.2   restate and rephrase simple information from materials presented orally, visually, and graphically in class.

FL.A.2.1.3   understand oral messages that are based on familiar themes and vocabulary (e.g., short conversations between familiar persons on familiar topics such as everyday school and home activities).

FL.A.2.1.4   listen and read in the target language and respond through role playing, drawing, or singing.

FL.A.2.2.3   organize information in spoken or written form about a variety of topics of academic and cultural interest (e.g., by making lists, categorizing objects, or organizing concepts).

FL.A.2.2.5   comprehend and respond to oral messages (e.g., personal anecdotes or narratives) based on familiar themes and vocabulary.

FL.A.3.1.1   provide simple information in spoken form (e.g., descriptions of family members, friends, objects present in his or her everyday environment, or common school and home activities).

FL.A.3.2.1   describe important people (e.g., family members and friends) and objects present in his or her everyday environment and in school.

FL.A.3.2.3   give responses in spoken or written form (e.g., answering simple questions, formulating questions, and making simple statements) to age-appropriate stories, poems or other literature, songs, films, or visual works.

FL.B.1.1.2   recognize patterns of social behavior or social interaction in various settings (e.g., school, family, or immediate community).

FL.B.1.1.3   recognize various familiar objects and norms of the target culture (e.g., toys, dresses, and typical foods).

Horse farm in Ocala, Florida

FL.B.1.2.1   recognize various activities and celebrations in which children participate in the target culture (e.g., games, songs, birthday celebrations, storytelling, dramatizations, and role playing).

FL.C.1.1.1   use simple vocabulary and phrases to identify familiar objects and concepts from other disciplines.

FL.C.1.2.1   participate in activities in the language class designed to integrate content-area concepts (e.g., mathematical calculations or cause-and-effect relationships) into target-language instruction (e.g., about countries or cultures).

FL.C.1.2.2   use target-language vocabulary or concepts to reinforce knowledge of a related topic studied in another class (e.g., geographical place names, parts of the body, or basic mathematical operations).

FL.C.2.1.1   use the target language to gain access to information that is only available through the target language or within the target culture (listen to a story told in the target language).

FL.D.1.2.1   identify examples and understand the significance of true and false cognates (i.e., words derived from a common original form).

TIPS FOR SUCCESS

Review the Study Tips below to help you succeed on the Sunshine State Standards identified.

Vocabulaire   Mots 1   Mots 2   *(pages 432–439)*

- Remember to listen to the words and repeat them orally before reading them.
- After you have gone over the new vocabulary, see how many words you remember. Think of seven words about a movie. Think of five words about a play.
- Go over each activity orally before you write the answers. **FL.A.2.1.2; FL.A.2.2.3**

Structure Les verbes savoir et connaître   *(pages 440–441)*

- Simplify the grammatical rule: just remember that **savoir** means to know something simple, and **connaître** means to know or be familiar with something complex.
- When doing these activities, pay particular attention to the object of each verb to determine the use of **savoir** or **connaître**. **FL.D.1.2.2**

Les pronoms le, la, les   *(pages 444–447)*

- As you do these activities, determine which word is the direct object before trying to replace it with **le, la,** or **les.** Do each activity orally before you write it. **FL.D.1.2.2**

Mockingbird

Vocabulaire   *(page 461)*

- Read the list of words and determine how many you know. Many of these words are easy to remember because they are cognates. **FL.D.1.2.1**

> **For other tips to help you address the Sunshine State Standards in Chapter 13, see pages H66 and H67 at the back of your textbook.**

Vocabulaire

Mots 1

Au cinéma 🎧

un cinéma

Cinéma Rex
La Bataille des Samuraïs

une séance

SÉANCE 13h FILM 13h30

Une place, s'il vous plaît.

un guichet

Pierre est devant le guichet.
La prochaine séance est à treize heures.

une salle de cinéma

l'écran

un acteur célèbre (connu)

les sous-titres

une actrice

Qui joue dans ce film?
On joue un film étranger au Rex.
Le film est en V.O. (version originale).
On le voit avec des sous-titres.
Dans un autre cinéma, le film est doublé.
On peut le voir en français.

Qu'est-ce que tu veux voir?

Ça m'est égal.

Qu'est-ce qu'on joue au Rex?

Je ne sais pas. On peut regarder dans l'Officiel des Spectacles.

Les places coûtent combien?

un film de science-fiction

un film d'horreur

un film policier

un documentaire

un dessin animé

un film en vidéo

louer une vidéo
(un DVD)

un film d'amour

un film d'aventures

Au théâtre 🎧

chanter

un chanteur

une chanteuse

danser

une danseuse

Roméo et Juliette

ballet en trois actes
d'après William Shakespeare

musique
Sergueï Prokofiev

chorégraphie et mise en scène
Rudolf Noureev

réglées par
Patricia Ruanne
Frederick Jahn

choréologue
Kristin Johnson

décors
Ezio Frigerio
avec la collaboration de
Alexandre Beliaev

costumes
Ezio Frigerio et Mauro Pagano

lumières
Vinicio Cheli

production créée pour le Ballet
de l'Opéra en 1984

Orchestre de l'Opéra National de Paris

direction
Vello Pähn

fin du spectacle vers 22 h 40

Opéra NATIONAL DE PARIS

Roméo
et
Juliette

On va monter *Roméo et Juliette*.
C'est une pièce de théâtre en
trois actes.
Chaque acte a deux scènes.
Entre deux actes, il y a un entracte.
Roméo et Juliette est aussi un ballet.

Voici d'autres genres de
pièces:
une tragédie
une comédie
un drame
une comédie musicale

Quel est le mot?

1 **FL.A.1.1.1 (I)**

Fana de cinéma ou pas?
Donnez des réponses personnelles.

1. Tu vas souvent au cinéma?
2. Qu'est-ce que tu aimes comme films?
3. Quel est ton acteur préféré? Et ton actrice préférée? Il/Elle est très connu(e)?
4. Il y a un cinéma près de chez toi?
5. La première séance est à quelle heure?
6. Où est-ce que tu achètes les billets?
7. Tu fais souvent la queue devant le guichet?
8. Dans la salle de cinéma, tu aimes mieux une place près de l'écran ou loin de l'écran?
9. Si tu vas voir un film étranger, tu aimes mieux voir le film doublé ou en version originale avec des sous-titres?

Le cinéma Champollion, Paris

2 **Historiette** **Au cinéma** Complétez.

Ce soir, on __1__ un très bon film au Wepler. C'est un film étranger.
Il n'est pas doublé. Il y a des __2__. Le film est en __3__ originale. La
prochaine __4__ est à quelle heure? Les __5__ coûtent combien?

Les garçons louent un DVD.

3 **FL.A.1.1.1 (I)**

Tu aimes mieux quels genres de film?
Donnez des réponses personnelles.

1. Tu aimes mieux (préfères) les documentaires ou les westerns?
2. Tu aimes mieux les films policiers ou les films d'horreur?
3. Tu aimes mieux les films comiques ou les films d'amour?
4. Tu aimes mieux les films d'aventures ou les films de science-fiction?
5. Tu vas voir quelquefois des dessins animés?
6. Tu loues quelquefois des films en vidéo ou DVD? Quels genres de film?

4 **Des pièces et des films** Complétez.

1. Au lycée les élèves ____ une pièce tous les ans.
2. On voit un film au cinéma. On voit une pièce au ____.
3. Une ____ a des actes et les actes sont divisés en ____.
4. Entre deux actes, il y a un ____.
5. Un ____ joue le rôle de Roméo.
6. Une ____ joue le rôle de Juliette.
7. Dans une comédie musicale, les ____ chantent et les ____ dansent.

Comédie-Française

Molière
Le Malade imaginaire

 FL.A.1.1.1 (M)

5 **Historiette** **Au théâtre** Donnez des réponses personnelles.

1. Tu aimes le théâtre?
2. Tu vas souvent au théâtre?
3. Il y a un théâtre là où tu habites?
4. Ton école a un club d'art dramatique?
5. Tu es membre de ce club?
6. Le club monte combien de pièces par an?
7. Cette année, le club va monter quelle pièce?
8. C'est quel genre de pièce?
9. Il y a combien d'actes?
10. Il y a combien d'entractes?

 FL.A.1.2.1 (I)

6 **Mon film préféré** Find out what a classmate's favorite movies are and why. Then find out which movies he or she dislikes and why. Take turns.

French Online
To explore movie listings in France, do the Chapter 13 **WebQuest** activity on the Glencoe French Web site at glencoe.com.

ENCORE PLUS

For more practice using words from **Mots 1**, *do Activity 42 on page H43 at the end of this book.*

Vocabulaire

Mots 2

Au musée 🎧

Une exposition de peinture et sculpture

un tableau

une peintre

un sculpteur

une sculpture,
une statue

Le musée n'est pas ouvert le mardi.
Il est ouvert tous les jours sauf le mardi.

Quel est le mot?

FL.C.1.1.1 (M)

7 **Un peu de culture** Répondez d'après les dessins.

1. C'est un musée ou un théâtre?

2. Le musée est ouvert ou fermé?

3. Elle est peintre ou sculpteur?

4. C'est un tableau ou une statue?

8 **Historiette** **Au musée**

Inventez des réponses.

1. Michel sait comment s'appelle le peintre?
2. Il connaît le peintre personnellement?
3. Il connaît l'œuvre du peintre?
4. Annick sait dans quel musée il y a une exposition de Monet?
5. Elle trouve ses tableaux extraordinaires?
6. Elle connaît le musée de l'Orangerie?
7. Elle le visite souvent?
8. Elle sait que le musée est fermé le mardi?
9. Le musée de l'Orangerie est ouvert tous les jours sauf le mardi?

Claude Monet *Le bassin aux nymphéas*

9   FL.A.2.2.3 (I)   FL.C.1.2.1 (I)

L'art français Work with a classmate. Discuss together what you have learned so far about French art and French artists. Find out who appreciates art more and who knows more about art.

Paul Cézanne *Pommes et oranges*

Tours et crypte archéologique
de **Notre-Dame**   −12 ans : gratuit

Rue de Cloître, Paris 4ᵉ. **M°**: Cité, ou **RER C**: St. Michel. **Tours**: **tél**: 01 44 32 16 72, groupes: 01 44 32 16 72. **Horaires**: 9h30-19h30 du 1.04 au 30.09; 10h-17h du 1.10 au 31.03. Fermeture des caisses 45mn plus tôt. Crypte: **tél**: 01 43 29 83 51. **Horaires**: 9h30-18h du 1.04 au 30.09; 10h-16h30 du 1.10 au 31.03.
Du haut des tours: une vue exceptionnelle sur la cathédrale et la ville. . . Dans la crypte archéologique: l'histoire de Paris de l'époque gallo-romaine au XIXᵉ s.

Musée de l'**Ordre de la Libération**
                                 −12 ans : gratuit

Hôtel national des Invalides, 51 bis, boulevard de Latour-Maubourg, Paris 7ᵉ. **Tél**: 01 47 05 35 15. **M°**: Invalides. **Horaires**: 10h-17h.
Musée de la France Libre, de la Résistance et de la Déportation.

Musée d'**Orsay**
                                 − 18 ans : gratuit

1, rue de Bellechasse, Paris 7ᵉ. **Tél**: 01 40 49 48 14 . **M°**: Solférino, ou **RER C**: Musée d'Orsay. **Horaires**: 10h-18h, nocturne le jeudi jusqu' à 21h45. Le dimanche, et du 20.06 au 20.09: 9h-18h. Fermé le lundi.
Peintures impressionnistes et ensemble de la création artistique de 1848 à 1914.

10   FL.A.1.2.2 (I)   FL.A.2.1.4 (I)

Renseignements You're in Paris and you'd like to visit one of the museums listed in the brochure on the left. Call the museum and find out from the museum employee (your partner) where it's located, what time it opens and closes, what day it's closed, and how much a ticket costs. Your partner can use the information in the brochure to answer your questions.

For more practice using words from Mots 2, do Activity 43 on page H44 at the end of this book.

Structure

Les verbes savoir et connaître
Telling whom and what you know

1. Study the following present-tense forms of the verbs **savoir** and **connaître,** both of which mean "to know."

SAVOIR		CONNAÎTRE	
je	sais	je	connais
tu	sais	tu	connais
il/elle/on	sait	il/elle/on	connaît
nous	savons	nous	connaissons
vous	savez	vous	connaissez
ils/elles	savent	ils/elles	connaissent

Note the **passé composé** of these verbs: **j'ai su, j'ai connu.**

2. You use **savoir** to indicate that you know a fact or that you know something by heart.

Tu sais à quelle heure la séance commence?
Tu sais le numéro de téléphone de Philippe?

3. You use **savoir** + infinitive to indicate that you know how to do something.

Tu sais danser le tango?
Il ne sait pas nager.

4. **Connaître** means "to know" in the sense of "to be acquainted with." You can use **connaître** only with nouns—people, places, and things. Compare the meanings of **connaître** and **savoir** in the sentences below.

Je sais comment elle s'appelle. Nathalie.   **Je connais bien Nathalie.**
Je sais où elle habite. À Grenoble.   **Je connais bien Grenoble.**
Je sais le nom de l'auteur. Victor Hugo.   **Je connais son œuvre.**

Grenoble, France

Comment dit-on?

11 **Qu'est-ce que tu sais?** Donnez des réponses personnelles.

1. Tu sais où habite ton ami(e)? Il/Elle habite dans quelle ville?
2. Tu connais bien cette ville?
3. Tu sais où on peut bien manger pour pas cher?
4. Tu sais le nom de l'auteur de *Hamlet?*
5. Tu connais les pièces de Shakespeare?
6. Tu connais *Hamlet?*

12 **On sait tout!** Complétez.

1. Moi, je _____ où se trouve le théâtre.
2. Paul, tu _____ quel est le numéro de téléphone?
3. Nous ne _____ pas l'adresse exacte.
4. Nos amis _____ à quelle heure la pièce commence.
5. Vous _____ quelle pièce on joue en ce moment à la Comédie-Française?
6. Il faut demander à Julie. Elle _____ tout.

13 **Qu'est-ce que tu connais?** Complétez.

1. Je _____ bien la France.
2. Les élèves de Mme Benoît _____ bien la peinture française.
3. Mais ils ne _____ pas très bien la littérature française.
4. Tu _____ la culture française?
5. Et Paul, il _____ la peinture française contemporaine?
6. Vous _____ les sculptures de Rodin?
7. Nous _____ des impressionnistes comme Monet, Manet et Renoir.
8. Tu _____ l'œuvre du peintre Edgar Degas?
9. Oui, je _____ son œuvre. J'adore ses danseuses.

Edgar Degas *Deux danseuses en scène*

FL.A.2.2.5 (I)

14 **Tu le/la connais bien!** Work with a classmate. Think of someone in the class whom you know quite well. Tell your partner some things you know about this person. Don't say who it is. Your partner will guess. Take turns.

 *For more practice using **savoir** and **connaître**, do Activity 44 on page H45 at the end of this book.*

Les pronoms me, te, nous, vous
Telling who does what for whom

1. The pronouns **me, te, nous,** and **vous** are object pronouns.

Marie t'invite au théâtre?	Oui, elle m'invite au théâtre.
Elle te parle au téléphone?	Oui, elle me parle au téléphone.
Le prof vous regarde?	Oui, il nous regarde.
Il vous explique la leçon?	Oui, il nous explique la leçon.

2. The object pronoun **me, te, nous,** or **vous** always comes right before the verb it is linked to.

> Il me parle.
> Il ne me parle pas.
> Il veut me parler.
> Il ne veut pas me parler.

Comment dit-on?

15 **Historiette** **Une invitation**
Répondez que oui.

1. Jean te téléphone?
2. Il te parle longtemps?
3. Il t'invite au cinéma?
4. Il te demande quel film tu veux voir?
5. Il te paie la place?
6. Après le film il t'invite au café?

16 **Historiette** **En classe** Répondez que oui.

1. En classe, la prof vous parle, à toi et aux autres élèves?
2. Elle vous apprend à lire et écrire en français?
3. Elle vous explique la grammaire?
4. Elle vous présente le vocabulaire?
5. Elle vous donne beaucoup de devoirs?
6. Elle vous donne trop de devoirs?
7. Elle vous parle toujours en français?

Une conversation au café

17 Au rayon des chemisiers Complétez avec **me** ou **vous.**

Je suis au rayon des chemisiers des Galeries Lafayette. La vendeuse __1__ parle. Elle __2__ demande:

La vendeuse: Vous désirez?
Moi: Je voudrais ce chemisier, s'il __3__ plaît. Je fais du 40.
La vendeuse: Je __4__ donne quelle couleur?
Moi: Qu'est-ce que vous __5__ proposez?
La vendeuse: Je ne sais pas. En bleu marine, il __6__ plaît?
Moi: Oui, il __7__ plaît.
La vendeuse: Mais je __8__ suggère d'essayer un 38.
Moi: D'accord. Je peux __9__ payer par carte de crédit?
La vendeuse: Mais bien sûr, mademoiselle!

18 Pourquoi ça? Répondez d'après le modèle.

Il me regarde!

Il te regarde? Pourquoi?

1. Il me pose des questions!
2. Il me parle!
3. Il me téléphone!
4. Il me dit son numéro de téléphone!
5. Il me donne son adresse!

19 Historiette C'est ton anniversaire.
Inventez une histoire.

1. Tes copains vont te téléphoner le jour de ton anniversaire?
2. Ils vont te voir?
3. Ils vont t'inviter au cinéma ou au concert?
4. Ils vont te dire «Joyeux anniversaire!»?
5. Ils vont te faire un gâteau?
6. Ils vont te donner des cadeaux?

JOYEUX ANNIVERSAIRE!

Structure

Les pronoms le, la, les
Referring to people and things already mentioned

1. You have already learned to use **le, la, l',** and **les** as definite articles. These words are also used as direct object pronouns. A direct object receives the action of the verb. A direct object pronoun can replace either a person or a thing.

Singulier	Je connais ce film.	Je le connais.
	Je connais cet acteur.	Je le connais.
	J'admire cet acteur.	Je l'admire.
	Je connais cette pièce.	Je la connais.
	Je connais cette actrice.	Je la connais.
	J'admire cette actrice.	Je l'admire.
Pluriel	Je connais les tableaux de Monet.	Je les connais.
	Je connais les pièces de Molière.	Je les connais.
	Je connais ces actrices.	Je les connais.
	J'admire ces acteurs.	Je les_z admire.

2. Just as with the pronouns **me, te, nous, vous,** the pronouns **le, la, l',** and **les** come right before the verb they are linked to.

Attention!

Note the elision and liaison with the direct object pronouns.
Vous l'admirez.   **Vous les_z admirez.**

Je le vois.
Je ne le vois pas.
Je veux le voir.
Je ne veux pas le voir.

Opéra Garnier, Paris

Comment dit-on?

French Online
To learn more about the French film industry, go to **Web Explore** on the Glencoe French Web site at glencoe.com.

20 **Contacts** Répondez d'après le modèle.

Tu vois toujours Mélanie?

Oui, je la vois de temps en temps.

1. Tu vois toujours Sylvie?
2. Tu vois toujours tes copains tunisiens?
3. Tu vois toujours Marc?
4. Tu vois toujours tes cousines de Lyon?
5. Tu vois toujours tes professeurs de l'année dernière?

21 **En version originale** Complétez.

Paul: On va voir le film doublé ou en V.O.?
Annick: On va __1__ voir en V.O.
Paul: Tu connais l'actrice principale?
Annick: Tu rigoles! Bien sûr que je ne __2__ connais pas, mais je sais qui c'est!
Paul: Tu comprends l'espagnol?
Annick: Oui, je __3__ comprends un peu.
Paul: Tu __4__ comprends assez bien pour comprendre le film?
Annick: Non, mais il y a des sous-titres. Alors je __5__ lis quand je ne comprends pas les dialogues.

22 **Tout est très beau!**
Répondez d'après le modèle.

—Tu vois la statue?
—Oui, je la trouve très belle.
1. Tu vois le théâtre?
2. Tu vois les tableaux?
3. Tu vois l'acteur?
4. Tu vois l'actrice?
5. Tu vois les sculptures?

Jean-Antoine Houdon *Molière*

23 **Tout n'est pas très beau.** Refaites l'Activité 22
d'après le modèle.

—Tu vois la statue?
—Oui, mais je ne la trouve pas très belle.

Pierre Auguste Renoir *Bal du moulin de la Galette*

*For more practice using pronouns, do Activity
45 on page H46 at the end of this book.*

24 **Demain** Répondez d'après le modèle.

 —**Tu as vu ce film?**
—**Non, mais je vais le voir demain.**

 1. Tu as vu cette pièce?
2. Tu as vu cette exposition?
3. Tu as vu ces sculptures de Rodin?
4. Tu as vu ces tableaux?
5. Tu as vu l'exposition des tableaux de Gauguin?

Auguste Rodin *Le penseur*

 25 **Devinettes** Devinez ce que c'est.

 1. On le présente quand on va dans un pays étranger.
2. On le prend pour voyager très loin.
 3. On les lave avant de manger.
4. On les lave avec une brosse à dents.
5. On la remplit avant de débarquer.
6. On l'écoute attentivement en classe.

 26 **Jeu** **FL.A.3.1.1 (I)**
Encore des devinettes Work in groups and make up riddles similar to those in Activity 25. Ask other groups your riddles. The group that guesses the most riddles wins.

FL.A.3.2.3 (I)

27 **L'artiste** Have some fun. Pretend you are an artist. Draw something. Have a classmate give a critique of your artwork. Take turns.

 French Online
To learn more about museums in Paris, go to **Web Explore** on the Glencoe French Web site at glencoe.com.

Vous êtes sur le bon chemin. Allez-y!

Conversation

On va au cinéma? 🔁 🎧 💿 Interactive Conversations

Bruno: Qu'est-ce que tu veux faire?

Léa: Je ne sais pas, moi. Aller au cinéma.

Bruno: Qu'est-ce que tu veux voir?

Léa: Ça m'est égal. Comme tu veux. Qu'est-ce qu'il y a de bien?

Bruno: Attends. Je vais te dire… *(Il prend l'Officiel des Spectacles, il l'ouvre et il le lit…)* Il y a un film avec Ricki Dean.

Léa: Ah non, pas Ricki Dean. Je le déteste, ce type. Il est parfaitement ridicule et il ne le sait même pas!

Bruno: Il y a un film espagnol au Ciné-Élysées. Ça t'intéresse?

Léa: Oui, un film espagnol, ça me dit. On va pouvoir travailler notre espagnol.

Bruno: Alors, il faut se dépêcher. La prochaine séance est à seize heures.

Vous avez compris?

Répondez.

1. Qu'est-ce que Léa veut faire?
2. Qui a *l'Officiel des Spectacles*?
3. Qui le lit?
4. Léa aime Ricki Dean? Pour quelle raison?
5. Bruno et Léa vont voir quel film?
6. Pourquoi est-ce que Léa veut voir un film espagnol?
7. Ils vont aller à quelle séance?

Parlons un peu plus

FL.A.1.2.2 (I)   FL.A.2.1.4 (I)

On va au cinéma? Look at the movie guide. Decide which movie you'd like to see and invite a classmate to see it with you. Tell your partner when and where the movie is playing, whether it is dubbed or in the original language with subtitles. Discuss whether or not you both want to see the movie or figure out an alternative.

EXPLICATION — GENRE DES SIGNES — DES FILMS

● Films classés X
■ Interdits aux moins de 16 ans.
▲ Interdits aux moins de 12 ans.
◆ Recommendés aux très jeunes.
(vo) : version originale
(va) : version anglaise

Ⓔ Epouvante Horreur
Ⓕ Fantastique Science-Fiction
Ⓖ Guerre
Ⓗ Historique
Ⓙ Dessin animé Vie animaux
Ⓚ Karaté
Ⓜ Film musical
Ⓞ Comédie dramatique
Ⓟ Policier
Ⓢ Espionnage
Ⓢ Erotisme
Ⓦ Western
Ⓧ Divers

Ⓐ Aventure
Ⓑ Biographie
Ⓒ Comédie
Ⓓ Drame

Les Films dont le titre commence par un nombre sont classés en tête de liste.

Ⓙ ◆ **1001 PATTES** Amér., (1h35). Film d'animation, de John Lasseter, et Andrew Stanton: Aussi maladroit que sympathique, Tilt met en péril la colonie de fourmis à laquelle il appartient en détruisant la récolte de la saison et exposant les siens aux représailles des sauterelles. La réplique des studios Walt Disney à « Fourmiz ». **Studio Galande** 5ᵉ, **Cinoches** 6ᵉ, **5 Caumartin** 9ᵉ, **Denfert** 14ᵉ, **Grand Pavois** 15ᵉ, **Saint-Lambert** 15ᵉ.

Ⓟ **ARLINGTON ROAD** - Amér., (1h57). Thriller, de Mark Pellington: Dans une banlieue résidentielle de Washington, un professeur d'histoire spécialisé dans le terrorisme et ébranlé depuis la mort de sa femme, agent du FBI tué au cours d'une bavure, enquête sur les activités de ses nouveaux voisins. Avec Tim Robbins, Jeff Bridges, Joan Cusack, Hope Davis, Robert Gossett, Mason Gamble, Spencer Treat Clark, Stanley Anderson, Vivianne Vives, Lee Stringer. **Grand Pavois** 15ᵉ (vo).

Ⓞ **BARRIO** - Espagnol, (1h40). Comédie dramatique, de Fernando Leon de Aranoa : Un « barrio », une cité perdue quelque part en Espagne, l'été. Manu, Javi et Raï, trois copains, traînent entre les squares desséchés et les vitrines inaccessibles, rêvant d'ailleurs... Avec Crispulo Cabezas, Timy, Eloi Yebra, Marieta Orozco, Alicia Sanchez, Enrique Villen. **Latina** 4ᵉ (vo).

Ⓓ **CASABLANCA** - Amér., noir et blanc (1h42). Aventure dramatique, de Michael Curtiz: Traqué par la Gestapo, un couple de résistants se cache chez Rick, le propriétaire d'un bar de Casablanca, qui viendra en aide aux fugitifs à cause de la femme qu'il aima jadis à Paris. D'après une pièce de Murray Burnett. 3 Oscars en 1943. Avec Humphrey Bogart, Ingrid Bergman, Paul Henreid, Claude Rains, Conrad Veidt, Sydney Greenstreet, Peter Lorre, S.Z. Sakall, Madeleine Lebeau, Dooley Wilson, John Qualen, Marcel Dalio. **Action Ecoles** 5ᵉ (vo).

Prononciation

Le son /ü/

1. To say the sound /ü/, first say the sound /i/, then round your lips. Repeat the following words.

    une statue   **une sculpture**   **une peinture**
    une voiture   **un musée**

2. The sound /ü/ also occurs in combination with other vowels. Repeat the following words.

    aujourd'hui   **depuis**   **je suis**   **huit**

3. Now repeat the following sentences.

    Tu as vu ces statues?
    C'est une sculpture très connue?
    Le musée est rue Sully depuis huit ans.

une statue

Lectures culturelles

Reading Strategy

Identifying the main idea

When reading, it is important to identify the main idea the author is expressing. Each paragraph usually discusses a different idea. The main idea is often found in the first or second sentence in each paragraph. First, skim the passage. Once you know the main idea of the passage, go back and read it again more carefully.

FL.B.1.1.2 (I)   **FL.C.2.1.1 (I)**

Les loisirs culturels en France

Les musées

Les musées en France sont toujours très fréquentés par les Français et par les touristes qui visitent la France. Tu connais les impressionnistes? Tu apprécies leurs tableaux? Alors il faut aller au musée d'Orsay. Le musée d'Orsay est une ancienne gare qui a été transformée en musée. C'est le musée du dix-neuvième siècle[1]. On trouve des tableaux, des sculptures, des meubles[2], tout du dix-neuvième siècle. Il y a une exposition permanente de tableaux des impressionnistes.

Si tu es fana d'art moderne, tu vas beaucoup aimer le centre Pompidou. Là, il y a toujours des expositions d'art moderne. Il y a aussi une vue extraordinaire sur Paris.

Mais la perle des musées français, c'est le Louvre. Au Louvre, tu peux admirer des tableaux et des sculptures de grands artistes de tous les siècles.

Le premier dimanche de chaque mois, l'entrée des musées nationaux est gratuite. Les autres dimanches, elle est demi-tarif[3]. C'est pourquoi les musées sont toujours combles le dimanche.

[1] siècle *century*
[2] meubles *furniture*
[3] demi-tarif *half-price*

Centre Pompidou

Musée d'Orsay

Le ballet et l'opéra

Si tu aimes la danse classique, il faut aller voir un ballet à l'opéra Garnier.

Si tu aimes l'opéra, il faut aller à l'opéra Bastille. On a inauguré le nouvel opéra sur la place de la Bastille en 1989 pour commémorer le bicentenaire de la Révolution française de 1789. Tu préfères l'architecture de quel opéra? De l'ancien opéra Garnier ou du nouvel opéra Bastille? L'architecture, c'est un art aussi, tu sais.

Le théâtre

Tu connais les grands auteurs dramatiques du dix-septième siècle: Racine, Corneille, Molière? Si tu as envie[4] d'aller voir une de leurs pièces, tu peux aller à la Comédie-Française, le plus vieux théâtre national du monde.

[4] as envie *feel like*

Opéra Garnier

La Tunisie

Opéra Bastille

Comédie-Française

Vous avez compris?

A Les musées Répondez.

1. Qui fréquente les musées français?
2. Tu connais quelques peintres impressionnistes?
3. Tu apprécies leurs tableaux?
4. Tu connais leur œuvre?
5. Il y a une exposition permanente des impressionnistes dans quel musée?
6. Quel est le musée d'art moderne?
7. Quel est un autre musée très célèbre à Paris?
8. Qu'est-ce qu'il y a dans ce musée?
9. Les musées sont presque toujours combles le dimanche. Pourquoi?

B D'autres loisirs Répondez.

1. Tu es à Paris et tu veux voir un ballet. Tu vas où?
2. Tu veux voir un opéra. Tu vas où?
3. Tu veux voir une tragédie de Racine ou une comédie de Molière. Tu vas où?

Le Mali

Le Sénégal

🔊 **FL.B.1.1.3 (I)** 🔊 **FL.B.1.2.1 (I)**

La musique africaine

Quand on parle de musique africaine, on parle de deux sortes de musique—la musique traditionnelle et la musique moderne pop. Il y a une grande différence entre les deux.

La musique traditionnelle

La musique traditionnelle est la musique de la brousse[1], des villages ruraux. Cette musique traditionnelle accompagne toutes les activités de la vie quotidienne ainsi que[2] les événements mémorables de la vie sociale. Il y a de la musique pour les femmes, par exemple, de la musique pour les jeunes, pour les chasseurs[3], etc. À toutes ces festivités, les griots, des poètes musiciens, racontent des histoires et jouent de la musique. Tous les instruments de musique sont souvent faits à la main par les griots eux-mêmes[4].

Un griot

La musique moderne

La musique pop africaine est devenue[5] très populaire au-dehors des pays africains, surtout en Europe. La première fois que vous l'entendez, vous pensez que c'est un mélange de rythmes latins et afro-américains des États-Unis comme le rock et le jazz. C'est vrai. Pourquoi? Parce que la musique africaine est à l'origine de la musique latino-américaine et de la musique afro-américaine d'aujourd'hui.

[1] brousse *brush*
[2] ainsi que *as well as*
[3] chasseurs *hunters*
[4] eux-mêmes *themselves*
[5] est devenue *has become*

Un musicien joue du kora, Gambie

French Online
To learn more about music in the Francophone world, go to **Web Explore** on the Glencoe French Web site at glencoe.com.

Youssou N'Dour

    Le chanteur sénégalais Youssou N'Dour a un très grand succès. Il est né dans le quartier pauvre de la Médina à Dakar. Il est fils et petit-fils de griots, les poètes musiciens en Afrique. C'est lui le plus grand interprète de la musique «fusion pop». C'est une fusion d'un rythme africain, le m'balax, avec des rythmes de reggae, de rock et de jazz.

Vous avez compris?

La musique africaine Vrai ou faux?
1. La musique traditionnelle d'Afrique, c'est la musique des grandes villes cosmopolites.
2. La musique traditionnelle varie selon l'événement.
3. Les griots sont des poètes et des musiciens.
4. Les griots jouent toujours de la guitare électrique.
5. La musique moderne africaine est très populaire en Europe.
6. Le rock et le jazz ont influencé la musique africaine.
7. Youssou N'Dour est un chanteur sénégalais très connu.
8. La musique latino-américaine est une fusion de musique africaine avec du reggae, du rock et du jazz.

La Belgique

La Tunisie

Le Maroc

Le Mali

CONNEXIONS

FL.C.1.2.2 (I)

Les Beaux-Arts

La musique

Like painting and literature, music is a form of art. Think of all the times you hear music each day. Music has been an integral part of the daily lives of people since the beginning of recorded history.

Before reading some general information about music, let's take a look at some of the many cognates that exist in the language of music.

un ballet FL.D.1.2.1 (I)

un orchestre symphonique

un opéra

une fanfare

un chœur

The names of many musical instruments are also cognates.

un piano	**un saxophone**	**une trompette**
une guitare	**une flûte**	**une clarinette**
un accordéon	**un violon**	**une harpe**

La musique

Les instruments musicaux

On peut classifier les instruments musicaux en quatre groupes principaux—les instruments à cordes, les instruments à vent, les instruments à percussion et les instruments à clavier.

Un orchestre ou une fanfare

Quelle est la différence entre un orchestre et une fanfare? Une fanfare n'a pas d'instruments à cordes. Il n'y a pas de violons, par exemple. Et dans une fanfare, il n'y a pas de flûtes ni de hautbois[1]. Les fanfares qui jouent de la musique pendant les événements sportifs et qui participent aux défilés[2] sont plus populaires aux États-Unis qu'en France.

[1] hautbois *oboes*   [2] défilés *parades*

L'orchestre symphonique

Un orchestre symphonique est un grand orchestre composé d'instruments de tous les groupes musicaux. Une symphonie est une composition musicale pour orchestre. Une symphonie est en général une composition ambitieuse qui dure de vingt à quarante-cinq minutes.

L'opéra

Un opéra est une composition dramatique sans dialogue parlé. Dans un opéra, les acteurs chantent; ils ne parlent jamais. Ils chantent des airs d'une beauté extraordinaire. L'orchestre les accompagne. L'histoire est en général très tragique. Un opéra comique est un opéra avec des dialogues parlés. Un opéra comique n'est pas nécessairement très amusant. Un opéra bouffe est un opéra dont l'histoire est une comédie. *Carmen* de Georges Bizet et *Dialogue des Carmélites* de Francis Poulenc sont deux opéras français très célèbres.

La musique populaire

Il y a toutes sortes de musique populaire. Il y a des groupes de jazz, de rock et de rap, par exemple. De nos jours, le rap et la musique techno sont très populaires. Les chansons populaires ont souvent des thèmes romantiques. Il y a toujours une relation intime entre la musique populaire et la danse.

La chanteuse Céline Dion

Vous avez compris?

FL.A.2.2.3 (M)

A Des instruments Nommez.

1. un instrument à cordes
2. quelques instruments à vent

B Vous le savez? Répondez.

1. Quelle est la différence entre un orchestre et une fanfare?
2. Qu'est-ce qu'un opéra?
3. Quels sont quelques types de musique populaire?

C'est à vous

Use what you have learned

1 **FL.A.3.1.1 (I)**

Pour t'amuser

✔ *Discuss movies, plays, and museums*

Work with a classmate. Pretend you're on vacation in Brussels in Belgium. You meet a Belgian teenager (your partner) who's interested in what you do for fun in your free time. Tell him or her about your leisure activities. Then your partner will tell you about what he or she does.

Maison du Roi, Bruxelles, Belgique

2 **FL.A.2.2.5 (I)**

Une journée au musée

✔ *Ask and answer questions about a museum visit*

Work in groups of three or four. Pretend that one or two of you spent the day at a museum last Saturday. Other friends have some questions. Describe your museum visit and be sure to answer all their questions.

Musée du Louvre

3 **FL.A.1.2.2 (M)**

Une affiche

✔ *Make a poster for a play*

Prepare a poster in French for your school play. Give all the necessary information to advertise **le spectacle.**

ÉCRIRE

4

FL.A.2.2.3 (I)

Des renseignements, s'il vous plaît.

✔ *Write for information about cultural events*

You're going to spend a month in the French city of your choice. Write a letter or an e-mail to the tourist office **(le syndicat d'initiative)** asking for information about cultural events during your stay. Be sure to mention your age, what kind of cultural activities you like, and the dates of your stay.

Une colonne Morris, Paris

Les Grandes Heures du Parlement

L'Assemblée nationale présente dans l'aile du Midi du Château de Versailles un musée qui vous permet de découvrir la salle des séances du Congrès du Parlement, troisième hémicycle de la République, dans laquelle vous assisterez à un spectacle audiovisuel sur les grands débats de la Nation.

Sur le pourtour de cette salle, vous revivrez deux cents ans d'histoire parlementaire et vous vous familiariserez avec le travail au quotidien du député. Vous découvrirez l'activité internationale du Parlement français et ses liens avec les différents parlements du monde.

Prix d'entrée

Individuel : visite libre avec audioguide
Tarif normal : 4€ - Tarif réduit 3€ - Gratuit pour les scolaires

Group de 30 personnes au plus : visite commentée
Tarif normal : 40€ - Tarif réduit 30€ - Gratuit pour les scolaires

Visitez la salle
du Congrès du Parlement
au Château de Versailles

Découvrez

l'histoire du Parlement

le spectacle audiovisuel dans la salle des séances

" **Les grandes heures du Parlement** "

Musée présenté par l'Assemblée nationale
du mardi au samedi de 9h00 à 17h30

Writing Strategy

Persuasive writing Persuasive writing is writing that encourages a reader to do something or to accept an idea. Newspaper and magazine advertisements, as well as certain articles, are examples of persuasive writing. As you write, present a logical argument to encourage others to follow your line of thinking. Your writing should contain sufficient evidence to persuade readers to "buy into" what you are presenting. Explain how your evidence supports your argument; end by restating your argument.

ÉCRIRE

5

FL.A.3.2.3 (M)

Un reportage

Your local newspaper has asked you to write an article to attract French-speaking readers to a cultural event taking place in your community. You can write about a real or fictitious event. You have seen the event and you really liked it. Tell why as you try to convince or persuade your readers to go see it.

Assessment

French Online
For more Chapter 13 test preparation, go to the Chapter 13 **Self-Check Quiz** on the Glencoe French Web site at glencoe.com.

Vocabulaire

1 Choisissez.

To review **Mots 1**, turn to pages 432–433.

1. On joue des films où?
   - a. dans une séance
   - b. dans une salle de cinéma
   - c. dans un théâtre

2. Qui joue dans un film?
   - a. des acteurs et des actrices
   - b. des sous-titres
   - c. des joueurs

3. Une pièce de théâtre est divisée en quoi?
   - a. en version originale
   - b. en entractes
   - c. en actes et en scènes

4. Le film est doublé?
   - a. Oui, il y a deux films.
   - b. Non, il est en V.O.
   - c. Oui, il y a des sous-titres.

5. Qu'est-ce que *l'Officiel des Spectacles?*
   - a. un magazine
   - b. une place
   - c. un film

2 Identifiez.

To review **Mots 2**, turn to pages 436–437.

6.

7.

8.

9.

10.

Structure

3 **Récrivez.**

11. Je sais le numéro.
    Vous _____.

12. Vous connaissez mon ami?
    Il _____?

To review the verbs **savoir** and **connaître**, turn to page 440.

4 **Complétez avec «savoir» ou «connaître».**

13. Je ____ son numéro de téléphone.
14. Vous ____ où il habite, non?
15. Je ____ très bien l'œuvre de cet artiste.
16. Tu ____ Paris?
17. Ils ____ danser le tango.

5 **Répondez avec un pronom.**

18. Il <u>te</u> parle au téléphone? Oui, ____.
19. Tu invites <u>Jean</u>? Oui, ____.
20. Tu vas inviter <u>sa petite amie</u> aussi? Oui, ____.
21. Le prof <u>vous</u> donne beaucoup de devoirs? Oui, ____.
22. Tu vois <u>la petite fille</u>? Oui, ____.
23. Tu connais <u>les pièces de Molière</u>? Oui, ____.

To review the object pronouns, turn to pages 442–444.

Culture

6 **Identifiez.**

24. un musée à Paris
25. un auteur français dramatique du dix-septième siècle

To review this cultural information, turn to pages 450–451.

Musée du Louvre, Paris

Do these practice activities to help you succeed on your FCAT through the study of a foreign language.

Read the passage below. Then answer the questions that follow.

À Paris il y a beaucoup de musées. Tout le monde __1__ le musée du Louvre, qui est la perle des musées français. Mais il y a aussi le musée d'Orsay. C'est un musée extraordinaire où il y a une exposition permanente de peintres impressionnistes. Ces peintres, les touristes __2__ adorent! Ils visitent le musée d'Orsay pour voir les Impressionnistes mais ils ne __3__ pas toujours que le musée est une ancienne gare. Au centre Pompidou il y a toujours des expositions d'art moderne. Et au musée Picasso on peut voir les tableaux et sculptures de Picasso, bien entendu. Certaines personnes n'apprécient pas l'art moderne. Mais en général les touristes __4__ admirent beaucoup.

Et toi, est-ce que tu fréquentes les musées? Quand tes amis __5__ invitent à aller au musée, est-ce que tu dis oui? Tu __6__ accompagnes au musée pour voir les œuvres de tes artistes préférés? Moi, j'adore visiter les musées. Mes amis et moi y allons souvent le week-end. Mais ma sœur refuse de __7__ accompagner au musée. Elle préfère aller au cinéma avec ses copines. Elle me dit: « Tes amis et toi, vous parlez toujours de l'art moderne et cela ne __8__ intéresse pas!»

1 Quelle est la forme du verbe qui complète le numéro (1)?

   A. connaissez
   B. connaît
   C. sait

2 Quel est le mot qui complète le numéro (2)?

   F. le
   G. l'
   H. les

3 Quelle est la forme du verbe qui complète le numéro (3)?

    A. sait

    B. savent

    C. connaissent

4 Quel est le mot qui complète le numéro (4)?

    F. les

    G. le

    H. l'

5 Quel est le mot qui complète le numéro (5)?

    A. t'

    B. m'

    C. vous

6 Quel est le mot qui complète le numéro (6)?

    F. les

    G. l'

    H. nous

7 Quel est le mot qui complète le numéro (7)?

    A. les

    B. nous

    C. vous

8 Quel est le mot qui complète le numéro (8)?

    F. vous

    G. l'

    H. m'

FCAT Tip

Double-check your answers. When you have answered the questions, reread your answers to make sure they are reasonable and that they are the best answers to the questions.

FL.A.2.1.2 (I)　　FL.A.3.2.1 (I)

Tell all you can about this illustration.

Vocabulaire

Discussing a movie

un cinéma	un film comique	un documentaire	jouer un film
une salle de cinéma	policier	un dessin animé	louer une vidéo (un
un guichet	d'horreur	étranger	DVD)
une place	de science-fiction	en V.O.	
une séance	d'aventures	doublé	
un écran	d'amour	avec des sous-titres	

Describing a play

un théâtre	un danseur	une comédie
une pièce	une danseuse	un drame
un acteur	une scène	monter une pièce
une actrice	un acte	chanter
un chanteur	un entracte	danser
une chanteuse	une tragédie	

Describing a museum visit

un musée	une œuvre
une exposition	une peinture
un tableau	un(e) peintre
une sculpture	un sculpteur *(m. et f.)*
une statue	

How well do you know your vocabulary?

- Choose the name of a cultural event or artistic profession.
- Have a classmate tell you his or her favorite in the category you chose.

Other useful words and expressions

connaître	célèbre
savoir	connu
ouvert	sauf
fermé	ça (m')est égal

VIDÉOTOUR

Épisode 13

In this video episode, you will join Chloé and Vincent as they experience some cultural wonders. See page 538 for more information.

CHAPITRE 14

La santé et la médecine

Objectifs

In this chapter you will learn to:

✓ explain a minor illness to a doctor

✓ have a prescription filled at a pharmacy

✓ tell for whom something is done

✓ talk about some more activities

✓ give commands

✓ refer to people, places, and things already mentioned

✓ discuss medical services in France

Édouard Vuillard *Le docteur Viau dans son cabinet*

French Online
To interact with your online edition of **Bon voyage!** go to: glencoe.com.

CHAPITRE 14 La santé et la médecine

SUNSHINE STATE STANDARDS

This chapter is all about health and the medical world. The material in the chapter will address the Sunshine State Standards listed below.

FL.A.1.1.2 greet others and exchange essential personal information (e.g., home address, telephone number, place of origin, and general health).

FL.A.1.1.3 use appropriate gestures and expressions (i.e., body language) to complete or enhance verbal messages.

FL.A.1.2.2 exchange information necessary to plan events or activities (e.g., picnics, birthday parties, science projects, and crafts).

FL.A.2.1.2 restate and rephrase simple information from materials presented orally, visually, and graphically in class.

FL.A.2.1.3 understand oral messages that are based on familiar themes and vocabulary (e.g., short conversations between familiar persons on familiar topics such as everyday school and home activities).

FL.A.2.2.1 give and understand written and verbal instructions, using known, verbal patterns in the target language.

FL.A.2.2.5 comprehend and respond to oral messages (e.g., personal anecdotes or narratives) based on familiar themes and vocabulary.

FL.A.3.1.1 provide simple information in spoken form (e.g., descriptions of family members, friends, objects present in his or her everyday environment, or common school and home activities).

FL.A.3.2.3 give responses in spoken or written form (e.g., answering simple questions, formulating questions, and making simple statements) to age-appropriate stories, poems or other literature, songs, films, or visual works.

FL.B.1.1.2 recognize patterns of social behavior or social interaction in various settings (e.g., school, family, or immediate community).

FL.C.1.2.1 participate in activities in the language class designed to integrate content-area concepts (e.g., mathematical calculations or cause-and-effect relationships) into target-language instruction (e.g., about countries or cultures).

FL.C.1.2.2 use target-language vocabulary or concepts to reinforce knowledge of a related topic studied in another class (e.g., geographical place names, parts of the body, or basic mathematical operations).

FL.D.1.2.1 identify examples and understand the significance of true and false cognates (i.e., words derived from a common original form).

Everglades National Park

FL.D.1.2.2 recognize the similarities and differences between his or her native language and the target language in terms of the pronunciation, alphabet, and forms of written expression.

FL.D.2.2.1 distinguish the similarities and differences between the patterns of behavior of the target culture related to recreation, holidays, celebrations, and the patterns of behavior of the local culture.

FL.E.1.2.2 demonstrate an awareness of employment possibilities (and other applications) for those who are able to master the target language.

TIPS FOR SUCCESS

Review the Study Tips below to help you succeed on the Sunshine State Standards identified.

Orchid

Vocabulaire Mots 1 Mots 2 *(pages 464–471)*

- Whenever you have the chance to review, do so. As you do **Mots 1**, think of all the parts of the body you have learned in French. **FL.C.1.2.2**

- To determine if you know your new vocabulary from **Mots 2,** see whether you can do the following:
  - Tell three things a patient may do in a doctor's office.
  - Tell three things the doctor may do.
  - Tell three things a doctor may say to a patient.
  FL.A.2.2.3

Structure **Les pronoms lui, leur** *(pages 472–473)*

- Here's an easy way to tell the difference between a direct object and an indirect object. A direct object answers the question *who(m)* or *what*.

Who(m) did you see?	I saw the doctor.
What did you take?	I took the medicine.

- If it cannot answer the question *who(m)* or *what*, the object is indirect. **FL.D.1.2.2**

L'impératif *(pages 475–477)*

- Remember, you use the command (imperative) to tell someone what to do. You merely use the **tu** or **vous** form of the verb to form the command. Remember that you drop the final **s** from the **tu** form of regular -**er** verbs. **FL.D.1.2.2**

Le pronom en *(pages 478–479)*

- You will hear and use the word **en** quite frequently in French. Pay careful attention to the explanation of the use of this word.

For other tips to help you address the Sunshine State Standards in Chapter 14, see page H67 at the back of your textbook.

Vocabulaire

On est malade. 🎧

la tête

une oreille

un œil

le nez

la bouche

la gorge

le ventre

Les Misérables

avoir de la fièvre

Atchoum!

À tes souhaits!

un mouchoir

Paul a un rhume.
Il est enrhumé.
Il éternue.
Il a besoin d'un kleenex
   ou d'un mouchoir.

David tousse.

Christophe a très mal à la gorge.
Il a une angine.

La pauvre Miriam, qu'est-ce qu'elle a?
Elle a la grippe.
Elle a de la fièvre.
Elle a des frissons.

un médicament

Martin n'est pas en bonne santé.
Il est en mauvaise santé.
Il est très malade, le pauvre.
Il ne se sent pas bien. Il se sent très mal.

Elle a mal à la tête.

FL.D.1.2.1 (M)

Note 🎧

Study the following cognates related to health and medicine:

allergique
bactérien(ne)
viral(e)
une allergie
un antibiotique

un sirop
de l'aspirine
une infection
de la pénicilline
la température

Elle a mal au ventre.

Elle a mal aux oreilles.

Elle a le nez qui coule.

Elle a les yeux qui piquent.

Elle a la gorge qui gratte.

Quel est le mot?

1 **Qu'est-ce que c'est?**
Identifiez.

2 **Historiette** **Qu'est-ce qu'il a?**
Inventez une histoire.

1. David est malade?
2. Il ne se sent pas bien?
3. Qu'est-ce qu'il a?
4. Il a de la fièvre et des frissons?
5. Il a la gorge qui gratte?
6. Il a les yeux qui piquent et le nez qui coule?
7. Il a mal à la tête?
8. Il a mal au ventre?
9. Il a mal aux oreilles?

3 **Historiette** **La santé** Donnez des réponses personnelles.

1. Tu es en bonne santé ou en mauvaise santé?
2. Quand tu es enrhumé(e), tu as le nez qui coule?
3. Tu as les yeux qui piquent?
4. Tu as la gorge qui gratte?
5. Tu tousses?
6. Tu éternues?
7. Qu'est-ce qu'on te dit quand tu éternues?
8. Tu as mal à la tête?
9. Tu ne te sens pas bien?
10. Tu as de la fièvre quand tu as un rhume?
11. Et quand tu as la grippe, tu as de la fièvre?
12. Quand tu as de la fièvre, tu as quelquefois des frissons?

4 **On a mal.** Complétez.

1. On prend de l'aspirine quand on a mal à la ____.
2. Si on a très mal à la gorge, on a une ____.
3. La ____ est un antibiotique.
4. L'aspirine et les antibiotiques sont des ____.
5. On ne peut pas prendre de pénicilline quand on est ____ à la pénicilline.
6. Si on a une température de 40° Celsius, on a de la ____.
7. Quand on est toujours malade, on est en ____.
8. On donne des antibiotiques comme la pénicilline pour combattre des infections bactériennes, pas des infections ____.
9. Quand on a le nez qui coule, on a besoin d'un ____ ou d'un ____.
10. Quand on a un rhume, on ____ et on ____.
11. Quand on est enrhumé ou quand on écoute la musique trop fort, on a mal aux ____.

FL.A.2.2.5 (I)

5 **Qu'est-ce que tu as?** Work with a classmate. Ask him or her what the matter is. Your classmate will tell you. Then suggest something he or she can do to feel better. Take turns.

FL.D.1.2.2 (I)

6 **Devinette** Have some fun! Work with a classmate and look at the following illustrations and French sayings. Together come up with some English equivalents.

1.

Je ne suis pas dans mon assiette aujourd'hui.

2.

Tu vas vite être sur pied.

3.

Il a une fièvre de cheval.

4.

Ça fait mal. Aïe aïe aïe!

5.

J'ai un chat dans la gorge.

 For more practice using words from **Mots 1**, *do Activity 46 on page H47 at the end of this book.*

Vocabulaire

Chez le médecin 🎧

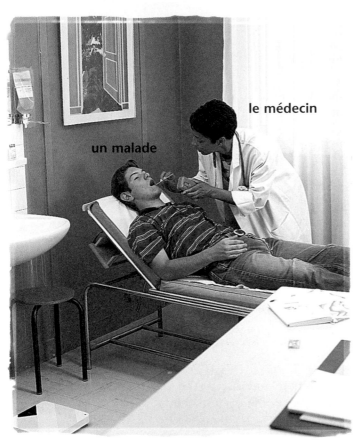

le médecin

un malade

Le médecin examine le malade.
Le malade ouvre la bouche.
Le médecin examine la gorge du malade.

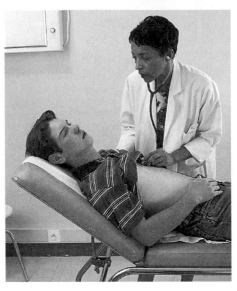

Elle ausculte le malade.
Il souffre, le pauvre.

Où avez-vous mal?

Là!

Le médecin parle.   Ouvrez la bouche!   Toussez!   Respirez à fond!

une ordonnance

Le médecin fait un diagnostic.
Sébastien a une sinusite aiguë.
Le médecin lui prescrit des antibiotiques.
Elle lui fait une ordonnance.

À la pharmacie

le pharmacien

la pharmacienne

un comprimé

avaler un comprimé

Sébastien prend les médicaments.
Il va mieux.

Qu'est-ce que la pharmacienne donne à Sébastien?
Elle lui donne des médicaments.

Quel est le mot?

7 **Il est malade.** Choisissez.

1. Où est le malade?
   - **a.** au travail
   - **b.** à la crémerie
   - **c.** chez le médecin

2. Qui souffre?
   - **a.** le médecin
   - **b.** le malade
   - **c.** le pharmacien

3. Qu'est-ce que le médecin examine?
   - **a.** la fièvre
   - **b.** la grippe
   - **c.** la gorge

4. Qu'est-ce que le malade ouvre?
   - **a.** le ventre
   - **b.** la bouche
   - **c.** l'oreille

5. Quand le médecin l'ausculte, comment respire le malade?
   - **a.** à fond
   - **b.** rien
   - **c.** bien

6. Qui est-ce que le médecin ausculte?
   - **a.** le malade
   - **b.** le pharmacien
   - **c.** la pharmacienne

7. Que fait le médecin?
   - **a.** des comprimés
   - **b.** des médicaments
   - **c.** des diagnostics

8. Qu'est-ce qu'il a, le malade?
   - **a.** une cassette
   - **b.** une sinusite aiguë
   - **c.** un grand nez

9. Qu'est-ce que le médecin lui fait?
   - **a.** un pharmacien
   - **b.** une ordonnance
   - **c.** des antibiotiques

10. Qu'est-ce qu'elle prescrit?
    - **a.** des yeux
    - **b.** des ordonnances
    - **c.** des comprimés

Une pharmacie

8 **Historiette** **Chez le médecin**
Donnez des réponses personnelles.

1. Tu vas chez le médecin quand tu es malade?
2. Le médecin te demande où tu as mal?
3. Qu'est-ce que tu réponds au médecin?
4. Quand tu as une angine, tu as mal où?
5. Qu'est-ce que le médecin te dit quand il t'ausculte?
6. Le médecin fait un diagnostic?
7. Il te prescrit des antibiotiques?
8. Tu vas à la pharmacie pour acheter des médicaments?
9. Tu prends quelquefois de l'aspirine? Quand?
10. Pour avaler des comprimés, qu'est-ce que tu bois?
11. Après quelques jours, tu vas mieux?

FL.A.3.1.1 (I)

9

Je ne suis pas dans mon assiette.
Work with a classmate. Yesterday you did something that made you feel ill today. Using the first list below, tell a classmate what you did. He or she has to guess what's wrong with you, choosing from the second list.

trop regarder la télé →
—Hier, j'ai trop regardé la télé.
—Tu as mal aux yeux.

French Online
For a fun way to review this vocabulary, go to the Chapter 14 **eGame** on the Glencoe French Web site at glencoe.com.

lire pendant six heures	être enrhumé(e)
manger trop de chocolat	avoir mal aux yeux
passer beaucoup d'examens	avoir mal aux pieds
faire une longue promenade	être fatigué(e)
étudier jusqu'à trois heures du matin	avoir mal aux oreilles
écouter de la musique trop fort	avoir mal à la tête
jouer dans la neige en T-shirt	avoir mal au ventre

FL.A.1.1.2 (I)

10

Qu'est-ce que tu as?
You were absent from school today. Your classmate, a French exchange student, is concerned about you and calls to find out how you are feeling. Let him or her know and tell all that you are doing to get better.

HÔPITAL SAINT-PIERRE

Dr Monique Dumas
Généraliste

01.43.25.31.96

Dr Paul Forêt
Oculiste

01.43.36.97.64

Dr André Simonet
Oto-rhino-laryngologiste

01.43.55.41.71

Dr Nicole Habib
Gastroentérologue

01.43.89.39.25

FL.A.1.2.2 (I)

11

Quel médecin?
While on a trip to France, you get sick. Describe your symptoms. A classmate will look at the list of doctors at the Hôpital Saint-Pierre and tell you which one to call and what the phone number is.

—J'ai mal à la gorge.
—On va appeler le docteur Simonet au 01.43.55.41.71.

FL.A.2.2.5 (I)

12

Au cabinet de consultation
Work with a classmate. You're sick. The doctor (your partner) will ask you questions about your symptoms. Answer the doctor's questions as completely as you can. Then reverse roles.

ENCORE PLUS

For more practice using words from Mots 2, do Activity 47 on page H48 at the end of this book.

$tructure

Les pronoms lui, leur
Telling what you do for others

1. You have already learned the direct object pronouns **le, la,** and **les.** Now, you will learn the indirect object pronouns **lui** and **leur.** Observe the difference between a direct and an indirect object in the following sentences.

Paul lance le ballon à Luc.

Paul lance ➝ le ballon.

Paul lance ➝ le ballon ➚ à Luc.

In the preceding sentence, **le ballon** is the direct object because it is the direct receiver of the action of the verb. What does Paul throw? The ball. The indirect object indicates to whom the ball is thrown. **Luc** is the indirect object of the verb. To whom does Paul throw the ball? To Luc. Note that the indirect object is preceded by the preposition **à**—**à Luc.**

2. The indirect object pronouns in French are **lui** and **leur.** Note that the masculine and feminine forms are the same. Study the following chart.

Singulier	Le médecin parle à Pierre. Le médecin parle à Marie.	} Il lui parle.
Pluriel	Le médecin parle à ses patients. Le médecin parle à ses patientes.	} Il leur parle.

Just like the direct object pronouns, the indirect object pronouns **lui** and **leur** come right before the verb they are linked to.

Rappelez-vous que...

The object pronouns **me, te, nous, vous** are both direct and indirect.
Je te vois.
Je te parle.

> Je **lui** parle.
> Je ne **lui** parle pas.
> Je veux **lui** parler.
> Je ne veux pas **lui** parler.

Comment dit-on?

13 **Historiette** **Une consultation**

Répondez en utilisant **lui**.

1. Le médecin parle à Paul?
2. Il demande à Paul s'il a de la fièvre?
3. Paul explique ses symptômes au médecin?
4. Le médecin dit à Paul qu'il a de la fièvre?
5. Il donne une ordonnance à Paul?
6. Paul téléphone à la pharmacienne?

14 **Un match de foot** Complétez avec **lui** ou **leur**.

1. Il lance le ballon à Marianne? Oui, il ____ lance le ballon.
2. Les joueurs parlent à l'arbitre? Oui, ils ____ parlent.
3. Et l'arbitre parle aux joueurs? Oui, il ____ parle.
4. L'arbitre explique les règles aux joueuses? Oui, il ____ explique les règles.
5. L'employée au guichet parle à un spectateur? Oui, elle ____ parle.

15 **Personnellement** Répondez en utilisant **lui** ou **leur**.

1. Tu parles souvent à tes professeurs?
2. Tu dis toujours bonjour à ton professeur de français?
3. Tu vas téléphoner à ton copain/ta copine ce week-end?
4. Tu aimes parler à tes copains au téléphone?
5. Tu parles souvent à tes copains?
6. Tu vas écrire à tes grands-parents?

FL.A.3.1.1 (I)

16 **Des cadeaux pour tout le monde?** Work with a classmate. Describe your favorite friends or relatives. Then tell what you buy or give to each one as a gift.

*For more practice using **lui** and **leur**, do Activity 48 on page H49 at the end of this book.*

Les verbes souffrir et ouvrir
Describing more activities

1. The verbs **souffrir** and **ouvrir** are conjugated the same way as regular **-er** verbs in the present.

SOUFFRIR	OUVRIR
je souffre	j' ouvre
tu souffres	tu ouvres
il/elle/on souffre	il/elle/on‿ouvre
nous souffrons	nous‿ouvrons
vous souffrez	vous‿ouvrez
ils /elles souffrent	ils‿/elles‿ouvrent

2. Note the past participles.

souffrir ⟶ souffert   **Ils ont beaucoup souffert.**
ouvrir ⟶ ouvert   **Il a ouvert la bouche.**

Comment dit-on?

17 **Historiette** **Elle est malade.**
Inventez des réponses.

1. Caroline souffre d'une angine?
2. Quand tu souffres d'une angine, tu as mal où?
3. Caroline va chez le médecin?
4. Quand le médecin lui examine la gorge, Caroline ouvre la bouche?
5. Le médecin lui donne une ordonnance?
6. Caroline va à la pharmacie?
7. Elle donne l'ordonnance au pharmacien?
8. Le pharmacien lui donne un paquet de comprimés?
9. Caroline ouvre le paquet?
10. Elle avale un comprimé?
11. Elle ne souffre plus?

À la pharmacie

L'impératif
Telling people what to do

1. You use the imperative to give commands and make suggestions. The forms are usually the same as the **tu, vous,** and **nous** forms. Note that the **nous** form means "Let's . . ."

PARLER	FINIR	ATTENDRE
Parle à ton prof!	Finis tes devoirs!	Attends ton ami.
Parlez à votre prof!	Finissez vos devoirs!	Attendez votre ami.
Parlons à notre prof!	Finissons nos devoirs!	Attendons notre ami.

2. Note that with **-er** verbs, you drop the final **s** of the **tu** form. The same is true for **aller** and verbs like **ouvrir.**

> **Regarde!**
> **Va voir le médecin!**
> **Ouvre la bouche!**

3. In negative commands, you put the **ne… pas** or any other negative expression around the verb.

> **Ne respirez plus!**
> **Ne dis rien.**

French Online
To investigate ways to practice a healthy lifestyle, do the **WebQuest** activity on the Glencoe French Web site at glencoe.com.

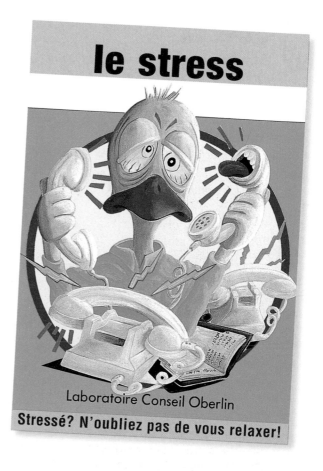

le stress

Laboratoire Conseil Oberlin

Stressé? N'oubliez pas de vous relaxer!

Comment dit-on?

FL.A.2.2.1 (I)

18 **La loi, c'est moi!** Donnez un ordre à un copain
ou à une copine d'après le modèle.

—regarder
—**Regarde!**
1. téléphoner à Jean
2. passer l'examen
3. parler français
4. travailler plus
5. préparer le dîner
6. ouvrir la porte
7. mettre la table
8. choisir un film
9. faire le travail
10. écrire l'exercice

FL.A.2.2.1 (I)

19 **Et vous aussi**
Donnez un ordre d'après le modèle.

—regarder
—**Regardez.**
1. téléphoner à Jean
2. passer l'examen
3. parler français
4. travailler plus
5. préparer le dîner
6. ouvrir la porte
7. mettre la table
8. choisir un film
9. faire le travail
10. écrire l'exercice

Hôpitaux de Toulouse

La Santé sans tabac

Avec l'aimable autorisation de la M.N.H.

*Afin de protéger votre santé
et par mesure de sécurité,
nous vous prions de ne pas fumer.
Merci de votre compréhension*

Décret n°92/478 du 29-5-92 Règlement intérieur du CHU de TOULOUSE

*For more practice using the commands, do
Activity 49 on page H50 at the end of this book.*

FL.A.2.2.1 (I)

20 Ne fais pas ça! Donnez un ordre à un copain ou à une copine d'après le modèle.

—regarder
—**Ne regarde pas!**
1. lire le journal
2. écrire une lettre
3. prendre le métro
4. attendre devant la porte
5. descendre
6. aller plus vite
7. faire attention
8. entrer
9. sortir

FL.A.2.2.1 (I)

21 Ne faites pas ça!
Refaites l'Activité 20 d'après le modèle.

—regarder
—**Ne regardez pas!**

FL.A.2.2.1 (I)

22 Allons-y! Répondez d'après le modèle.

On invite Marie?

D'accord, invitons Marie!

1. On va à la plage?
2. On nage?
3. On fait du ski nautique?
4. On prend notre petit déjeuner?
5. On dîne au restaurant?
6. On sort?

FL.A.2.2.1 (I)

23 Jeu Jacques a dit... This game is called "Simon Says" in English. Play in groups of five people or more. Give orders to your classmates. If you say **Jacques a dit** first, they have to obey the order. If you don't say **Jacques a dit** first, they should not obey your order. If they do, they are eliminated.

YEUX ROUGES, YEUX IRRITES

DÉCOUVREZ CE COLLYRE EN MONODOSES!

ANTALYRE

Une monodose stérile, pratique, évitant la contamination

Ceci est un médicament. Lire attentivement la notice. Pas en-dessous de 36 mois. Contre-indiqué en cas de glaucome. Demandez conseil à votre pharmacien.

ANTALYRE®
Collyre en monodoses

Le pronom en

Referring to people, places, and things already mentioned

1. The pronoun **en** is used to replace a noun that is introduced by **de** or any form of **de—du, de la, de l', des. En** refers mostly to things.

Tu as de l'aspirine?	Oui, j' en ai.
Il parle de sa santé?	Oui, il en parle.
Vous sortez de l'hôpital?	Oui, j' en sors.
Tu prends des médicaments?	Oui, j' en prends.

2. You also use the pronoun **en** with numbers or expressions of quantity. Note that in this case **en** refers not only to things but also to people.

Tu as des frères?	**Oui, j'en ai deux.**
Il prend combien de comprimés?	**Il en prend trois par jour.**
Il a combien de CD?	**Il en a beaucoup.**

3. Just like other pronouns, **en** comes directly before the verb whose meaning it is linked to.

Il en parle.
Il n'en parle pas.
Il veut en parler.
Il ne veut pas en parler.

Savez-vous que... ?

En comes after **y** in the expression **il y a.**
Il y en a deux.
Il y en a beaucoup.
Il n'y en a pas.

Comment dit-on?

24 **Historiette** **La fête de Laurence** Répondez d'après le modèle.

—**Laurence sert du coca?**
—**Oui, elle en sert.**

1. Elle sert de l'eau minérale?
2. Elle sert des sandwichs?
3. Elle sert de la pizza?
4. Elle sert de la salade?

5. Elle sert du fromage?
6. Elle sert des chocolats?
7. Elle sert de la glace?
8. Elle sert de la mousse au chocolat?

25 **Dans le frigo** Répondez d'après le modèle.

du coca →
—Il y a du coca dans ton frigo?
—Non, il n'y en a pas.

1. de l'eau minérale
2. de la glace
3. des légumes surgelés
4. du jambon
5. des tartes
6. de la viande

26 **Historiette** **Tu es malade?**
Répondez d'après le modèle.

1. Tu prends combien de comprimés? (trois)
2. Tu bois de l'eau? (un litre)
3. Tu manges des fruits? (beaucoup)
4. Tu lis des magazines? (deux ou trois)
5. Tu regardes des vidéos? (trop)

27 **Devinettes** Devinez ce que c'est.

1. On en prend quand on est malade.
2. On en boit beaucoup quand on a de la fièvre.
3. On en utilise pour se laver les mains.
4. On en met sur une brosse à dents pour se laver les dents.
5. On en donne au vendeur quand on achète quelque chose.

Vous êtes sur le bon chemin. Allez-y!

Conversation

Chez le médecin

Sylvie: Bonjour, docteur.

Médecin: Bonjour, Sylvie. Alors, qu'est-ce qui ne va pas?

Sylvie: Je ne sais pas… Je ne me sens pas bien du tout.

Médecin: Tu as mal où?

Sylvie: Ben, j'ai mal un peu partout, mais surtout à la gorge.

Médecin: Tu as mal à la tête?

Sylvie: Oui, à la tête aussi. Et j'ai froid, j'ai des frissons…

Médecin: Tu dois avoir de la fièvre. Ouvre la bouche, s'il te plaît. Dis «Aaa… »

Sylvie: Aaa…

Médecin: Tu as la gorge très rouge. C'est certainement une angine.

Sylvie: Une angine!

Médecin: Oui, mais ce n'est pas grave. Je vais te donner des antibiotiques. Tu vas en prendre trois par jour pendant une semaine.

Vous avez compris?

Répondez.

1. Qui est malade?
2. Quels sont ses symptômes?
3. Elle a mal où?
4. Sylvie ouvre la bouche. Pourquoi?
5. Qu'est-ce que le médecin lui donne?
6. Sylvie doit prendre combien de comprimés par jour?
7. Pendant combien de temps?

Parlons un peu plus

FL.A.2.1.3 (I)

A **Tu dois ou tu ne dois pas être médecin.** Work with a classmate. Interview each other and decide who would make a good doctor. Make a list of questions for your interview. One question you may want to ask is: **Tu as beaucoup de patience ou très peu de patience?**

FL.A.2.2.5 (I)

B **Je suis très malade.** Imagine you're sick with a cold, the flu, or a sore throat. Tell the doctor (your partner) what your symptoms are. He or she makes a diagnosis and tells you what to do to get better. Use the model as a guide.

> J'ai de la fièvre et des frissons.

> Vous avez la grippe. Restez au lit et prenez de l'aspirine.

Prononciation

Les sons /u/ et /ü/ 🎧

1. It is important to make a distinction between the sounds /u/ and /ü/, since many words differ only in these two sounds. Repeat the following pairs of words.

vous / vu	dessous / dessus	roux / rue
loue / lu	tout / tu	

2. Now repeat the following sentences.

Tu as beaucoup de température?
J'éternue toutes les deux minutes.

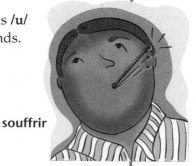

souffrir

température

Lectures culturelles

FL.B.1.1.2 (I)   FL.D.2.2.1 (I)

Une consultation

La pauvre Mélanie. Elle est très malade! Elle tousse. Elle éternue. Elle a mal à la tête. Elle a de la température. Elle a des frissons. Elle n'est pas du tout dans son assiette. Elle veut appeler le médecin, mais c'est le week-end et son médecin ne donne pas de consultations le week-end. La seule solution, c'est d'appeler S.O.S. Médecins.

S.O.S. Médecins est un service qui envoie des médecins à domicile[1]. Un médecin arrive chez Mélanie et l'examine. Elle l'ausculte, elle lui prend sa température. Elle lui dit qu'elle a la grippe. Mais ce n'est pas grave. Elle va être vite sur pied. Le médecin lui fait une ordonnance. Elle prescrit des

[1] à domicile *to the home*

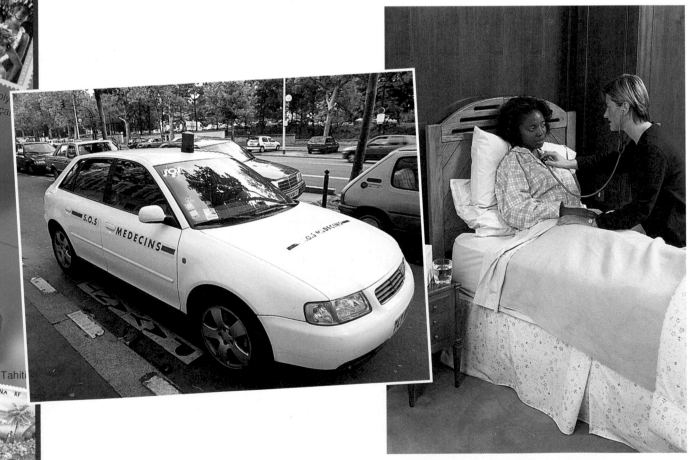

Le médecin ausculte la malade.

antibiotiques: trois comprimés par jour pendant une semaine. Mélanie va en prendre un à chaque repas.

Mélanie paie le médecin. Mais en France, la Sécurité Sociale rembourse les honoraires des médecins, c'est-à-dire l'argent qu'on donne aux médecins. Les honoraires et tous les frais[2] médicaux sont remboursés de 80 à 100% (pour cent) par la Sécurité Sociale.

[2] frais *expenses*

Vous avez compris?

A Autrement dit
Dites d'une autre façon.

1. Mélanie a *de la fièvre.*
2. Elle *ne se sent pas bien.*
3. Elle veut *téléphoner au* médecin.
4. Le médecin *ne voit pas de malades* le week-end.
5. S.O.S. Médecins envoie des médecins *chez les malades.*
6. Le médecin *écoute la respiration de* Mélanie.
7. La grippe n'est pas une maladie *alarmante.*
8. Mélanie va vite *se sentir mieux.*

B La pauvre Mélanie   Répondez.
1. Mélanie est très malade?
2. Elle a de la fièvre?
3. Elle a mal au ventre?
4. Elle veut appeler le médecin?
5. Son médecin donne des consultations tous les jours?
6. Mélanie téléphone à qui?
7. Le médecin lui prescrit de l'aspirine?
8. Les frais médicaux ne sont pas remboursés en France?

C En France   Qu'est-ce que vous avez appris sur les médecins et les services médicaux en France?

Lecture supplémentaire 1

FL.D.1.2.2 (M)

Culture et santé

La culture influence la santé et la médecine? Certainement. Par exemple, en France tout le monde parle de son foie[1]. Les Français disent souvent, «J'ai mal au foie». Aux États-Unis, on n'entend jamais dire ça. Pourquoi? Parce qu'aux États-Unis, une maladie du foie, c'est grave. Mais quand un Français dit qu'il a mal au foie, il veut dire tout simplement qu'il a un trouble digestif. Rien de grave. Il n'est peut-être pas dans son assiette aujourd'hui, mais il va vite être sur pied!

Aux États-Unis, par contre, on parle beaucoup d'allergies. De nombreux Américains souffrent d'une petite allergie. Les symptômes d'une allergie ressemblent aux symptômes d'un rhume. On éternue et on a souvent mal à la tête. Une allergie, c'est désagréable, mais d'habitude ce n'est pas grave. En France, on parle moins souvent d'allergies. Pourquoi? Qui sait? Vive la différence!

[1] foie *liver*

LES TROUBLES DIGESTIFS

Amis ou ennemis?

Vous avez compris?

Des différences Répondez.
1. On dit souvent qu'on a mal au foie dans quel pays?
2. Que veut dire un Français quand il dit qu'il a mal au foie?
3. Et pour un Américain, qu'est-ce que cela veut dire «J'ai mal au foie»?
4. Qui parle souvent d'allergies?
5. Quels sont les symptômes d'une allergie?

FL.B.1.1.2 (M)

Les services médicaux en France

En France, il y a de grands hôpitaux avec tout l'équipement haut de gamme[1] nécessaire à la pratique d'une médecine moderne. On compte plus de 3 500 établissements de soins polyvalents[2]. Il y a à peu près 900 établissements hospitaliers publics et plus de 2 500 cliniques privées. Beaucoup de ces cliniques ressemblent à des hôtels.

En France, on fait beaucoup de recherches médicales et pharmaceutiques. C'est à l'Institut Pasteur de Paris que le docteur Montagnier a isolé le virus du sida[3]. Aujourd'hui à l'Institut Pasteur on continue à faire des recherches contre cette terrible maladie.

[1] haut de gamme *state of the art*
[2] soins polyvalents *general care*
[3] sida *AIDS*

Un laboratoire de recherche à l'Institut Pasteur

L'Institut Pasteur, Paris

Vous avez compris?

FL.D.1.2.1 (I)

Des mots apparentés Trouvez les mots apparentés dans la lecture.

La Belgique

Tunisie

Le Maroc

Le Mali

CONNEXIONS

FL.C.1.2.2 (I)

Les sciences naturelles

La diététique

Good nutrition is very important. What we eat can determine if we will enjoy good health or poor health. For this reason, it is most important to have a balanced diet and avoid the temptation to eat "junk food."

Read the following information about nutrition in French. Before reading this selection, however, look at the following groups of related words. Often if you know the meaning of one word you can guess the meaning of several words related to it.

individuel, individu
actif, activité
consommation, consommer, consommateur
adolescent, adolescence
âge, âgé

Un bon régime[1]

Il est très important d'avoir une alimentation équilibrée[2] pour être en bonne santé. Un régime équilibré comporte une variété de légumes et de fruits, des céréales, de la viande et du poisson.

Tout le monde a besoin de calories, mais le nombre idéal dépend de l'individu—de son métabolisme, de sa taille, de son âge et de son activité physique. Les adolescents, par exemple, ont besoin de plus de calories que les personnes âgées. Ils ont besoin de plus de calories parce qu'ils sont plus actifs et ils sont en période de croissance[3].

Les protéines

Les protéines sont particulièrement importantes pour les enfants et les adolescents parce qu'ils sont en pleine croissance. Les protéines aident à fabriquer des cellules. La viande et les œufs contiennent des protéines.

[1] régime *diet*   [2] équilibrée *balanced*   [3] croissance *growth*

Les glucides (les hydrates de carbone)

Les glucides (les pommes de terre, les pâtes comme les spaghettis, le riz[4]) sont la source d'énergie la plus efficace pour le corps humain.

Les lipides (les graisses)

Les lipides sont aussi une bonne source d'énergie. Mais pour les personnes qui ont un taux de cholestérol élevé[5], les graisses ne sont pas bonnes. Il faut faire un régime sans graisse. Il faut les éliminer.

Les minéraux

Beaucoup de minéraux sont essentiels pour le corps humain. Le calcium est absolument nécessaire pour les os[6] et les dents.

L'eau

L'eau est absolument essentielle au corps humain qui est fait de 65% d'eau.

Les vitamines

Les vitamines sont indispensables au bon fonctionnement du corps humain. Ce tableau indique la source de quelques vitamines importantes.

[4] riz *rice*   [5] élevé *elevated, high*   [6] os *bones*

Vitamines	Sources
A	légumes, lait, quelques fruits
B	viande, œufs, céréales, légumes verts
C	fruits, tomates, salade verte
D	lait, œufs, poisson
E	huiles, légumes, œufs, céréales

Vous avez compris?

FL.C.1.2.2 (I)

A La diététique Répondez.

1. Qu'est-ce qu'on doit manger tous les jours?
2. Le nombre de calories pour chaque individu dépend de quoi?
3. Qui a particulièrement besoin de calories? Pourquoi?
4. Quelle est une source importante d'énergie?
5. Pourquoi faut-il contrôler la consommation de graisses?
6. Quel est un minéral important pour les os et les dents?
7. Qu'est-ce qui est indispensable au bon fonctionnement du corps humain?

FL.C.1.2.1 (I)

B Assez de vitamines? Faites une liste de tout ce que vous avez mangé hier. Vous avez eu toutes les vitamines nécessaires?

C'est à vous

Use what you have learned

PARLER

FL.A.3.2.3 (I)

1 Tout le monde est malade.
✔ *Describe cold symptoms and minor ailments*

Work with a classmate. Choose one of the people in the illustrations. Describe him or her. Your partner will guess which person you're talking about and say what's the matter with the person. Take turns.

1.

2.

3.

4.

PARLER

FL.A.2.2.1 (I)

2 Une ordonnance
✔ *Discuss a prescription with a pharmacist*

You are in a pharmacy in Bordeaux. Your classmate will be the pharmacist. Make up a conversation about your prescription. Explain why and how you have to take the medicine.

PARLER

FL.A.1.1.3 (I)

3 Jeu Je suis malade comme un chien!
✔ *Talk about how you are feeling*

Work with a partner. Make gestures to indicate how you're feeling today. Your partner will ask you why you feel that way. Tell him or her. Be as creative and humorous as possible.

4 Excusez-moi...

✔ *Write a note describing a minor illness*

You're supposed to take a French test today but you're not feeling well. Write a note to your French teacher explaining why you can't take the test, and mention some symptoms you have.

Une ambulance du SAMU

FL.E.1.2.2 (M)

5 Des bénévoles

Your French club has a community service requirement. You have decided to work in the emergency room **(le service des urgences)** at your local hospital. You serve as a translator or interpreter for patients who speak only French. Write a flyer for your French club. Tell about your experience with one or more patients. Give your feelings about the work you do and try to encourage other club members to volunteer their services, too.

Assessment

Vocabulaire

1 Choisissez.

To review **Mots 1**, turn to pages 464–465.

a.   b.   c.   d.

1. _____ Elle a mal à la tête.   3. _____ Elle tousse.
2. _____ Elle a mal au ventre.   4. _____ Elle est enrhumée.

2 Identifiez.

5. _____
6. _____
7. _____

French Online
For more Chapter 14 test preparation, go to the Chapter 14 **Self-Check Quiz** on the Glencoe French Web site at glencoe.com.

3 Complétez.

To review **Mots 2**, turn to pages 468–469.

8. Le médecin _____ le malade.
9. Le malade ouvre la _____ quand le médecin lui examine la gorge.
10. Le médecin fait un _____. Il dit que Nathalie a une sinusite aiguë.
11. Le médecin lui fait une _____ pour des antibiotiques.
12. Elle va à la _____ pour acheter ses médicaments.

Structure

4 **Complétez.**

13. Le médecin parle au malade?
    Oui, il _____ parle.
14. Le médecin donne une ordonnance à ses patients?
    Oui, il _____ donne une ordonnance.
15. Paul donne son ordonnance à la pharmacienne?
    Oui, il _____ donne son ordonnance.

To review **lui** and **leur**, turn to page 472.

5 **Complétez.**

16. Ils _____ beaucoup, les pauvres. (souffrir)
17. J'_____ le livre à la page 100. (ouvrir)
18. Vous _____ la bouche quand le médecin vous examine?
    (ouvrir)

To review **souffrir** and **ouvrir**, turn to page 474.

6 **Complétez avec l'impératif.**

19. (ouvrir) Paul, _____ ton livre.
    Luc et Louise, _____ vos livres aussi.
20. (attendre) Carole, _____ un moment.
    Sandrine et Maïa, _____ avec Carole.
21. (dire) Luc, _____ au médecin où tu as mal.
    Vous deux, _____ au médecin où vous avez mal.

To review commands, turn to page 475.

7 **Répondez avec un pronom.**

22. Tu as de l'aspirine?
    Oui, _____.
23. Tu as douze comprimés?
    Oui, _____.
24. Tu peux sortir de l'hôpital demain?
    Oui, _____.
25. Il a beaucoup d'argent?
    Oui, _____.

To review the use of **en**, turn to page 478.

Do these practice activities to help you succeed on your FCAT through the study of a foreign language.

Read the passage below. Then answer the questions that follow.

La culture influence la médecine? Certainement. Par exemple, en France tout le monde parle de son foie. Les Français disent souvent, «J'ai mal au foie». En Amérique on n'entend jamais «J'ai mal au foie». Pourquoi pas? Parce que, pour les Américains, une maladie du foie est quelque chose de grave. Mais quand un Français dit qu'il a mal au foie, il veut dire tout simplement qu'il a un trouble digestif. Ce n'est rien de grave. Il n'est peut-être pas dans son assiette aujourd'hui mais il va être vite sur pied.

Aux États-Unis on parle d'allergies. Beaucoup d'Américains souffrent d'une petite allergie. Les symptômes d'une allergie ressemblent aux symptômes d'un rhume. On éternue et on a souvent mal à la tête. Une allergie est désagréable mais d'habitude ce n'est pas grave. En France, on parle moins souvent d'allergies. Vive la différence!

1 Que pense l'auteur du passage de la différence entre la perspective médicale française et la perspective médicale américaine?
- **A.** C'est une question de culture.
- **B.** La culture n'est pas importante.
- **C.** C'est surtout une question médicale.
- **D.** Les Français ont raison et les Américains ont tort.

2 Pour les Français, que signifie «J'ai mal au foie»?
- **F.** On a un cancer du foie.
- **G.** On a une maladie assez grave.
- **H.** On a un problème de digestion.
- **I.** On a besoin de voir un médecin immédiatement.

3 READ THINK EXPLAIN Éternuer et avoir mal à la tête, qu'est-ce qu'ils ont en commun?

4 Quelle phrase signifie la même chose?

Il n'est peut-être pas dans son assiette aujourd'hui mais il va être vite sur pied.

  A. Le problème est temporaire.

  B. Il ne veut pas manger aujourd'hui mais demain il va manger normalement.

  C. Il a mangé quelque chose de mauvais mais demain il va faire une promenade et il se sentira mieux.

  D. Aujourd'hui il a un trouble digestif mais demain il va avoir mal aux pieds.

5 Laquelle des phrases suivantes est correcte?

  F. On parle beaucoup plus d'allergies en France qu'aux États-Unis.

  G. Les Américains considèrent qu'une allergie est une chose sérieuse.

  H. Les allergies, pour les Américains, ne sont pas agréables, mais d'habitude elles ne sont pas très graves.

  I. Une allergie est une maladie typiquement française.

6 Quelle est l'opinion de l'auteur de ce passage?

  A. Il n'est pas bon que la culture influence la perspective médicale.

  B. Il est bon que les Français et les Américains ont des perspectives médicales différentes.

  C. Il est certain que les Américains ont une perspective médicale plus optimiste que les Français.

  D. La différence entre la perspective médicale américaine et française n'est pas intéressante.

FCAT Tip

Do not "cram" the night before the test. It can confuse you and make you tired.

On parle super bien!

Tell all you can about this illustration.

Vocabulaire

Describing minor health problems

la santé	une sinusite aiguë	éternuer	avoir de la fièvre
en bonne santé	une allergie	avoir mal	le nez qui coule
en mauvaise santé	un mouchoir	à la tête	les yeux qui piquent
une infection	un kleenex	au ventre	la gorge qui gratte
un frisson	se sentir bien	aux oreilles	malade
la grippe	mal	à la gorge	viral(e)
un rhume	être enrhumé(e)		bactérien(ne)
une angine	tousser		allergique

Speaking with the doctor

le médecin	souffrir	respirer
le/la malade	ouvrir	prescrire
un diagnostic	examiner	
une ordonnance	ausculter	

Identifying more parts of the body

la tête	une oreille
un œil, des yeux	la gorge
le nez	le ventre
la bouche	

Speaking with a pharmacist

un(e) pharmacien(ne)	un sirop
une pharmacie	de la pénicilline
un médicament	de l'aspirine *(f.)*
un comprimé	avaler
un antibiotique	

Other useful words and expressions

À tes souhaits!	le/la pauvre
Qu'est-ce qu'il a?	à fond

> **How well do you know your vocabulary?**
> - Find as many cognates as you can in the list.
> - Use five cognates to write several sentences.

VIDÉOTOUR

Épisode 14

In this video episode, you will join Vincent as he experiences a strange nightmare. See page 539 for more information.

FL.A.2.1.3 (I)

Conversation

On va au cinéma?

Céline: Tu as déjà vu *Autant en emporte le vent* avec Clark Gable et Vivien Leigh?

Thomas: Non, mais c'est un classique.

Céline: Tu veux le voir? On le joue au Champollion en version originale.

Thomas: Je voudrais bien, mais je ne peux pas. Je dois me coucher de bonne heure ce soir.

Céline: Pourquoi? Tu ne te sens pas bien?

Thomas: Non, pas très bien. Je ne sais pas ce que j'ai… Je suis fatigué, j'ai mal à la tête… Je crois que j'ai la grippe.

Vous avez compris?

Répondez.

1. Céline parle à qui?
2. Elle lui parle de quoi?
3. Thomas a déjà vu *Autant en emporte le vent*?
4. Il croit que c'est un bon film?
5. On joue *Autant en emporte le vent* dans quel cinéma?
6. Pourquoi est-ce que Thomas ne peut pas aller au cinéma?
7. Qu'est-ce qu'il a?

Structure

Les verbes réfléchis

1. The subject of a reflexive verb both performs and receives the action of the verb. For this reason, an additional pronoun is used. It is called a reflexive pronoun. Review the following forms.

SE LAVER		S'HABILLER	
je	me lave	je	m'habille
tu	te laves	tu	t'habilles
il/elle/on	se lave	il/elle/on	s'habille
nous	nous lavons	nous	nous_z habillons
vous	vous lavez	vous	vous_z habillez
ils/elles	se lavent	ils/elles	s'habillent

2. Reflexive verbs are conjugated with **être** in the **passé composé.** Note that there is no agreement when the verb is followed by a noun referring to a part of the body.

Elle s'est brossée. **Elle s'est brossé les cheveux.**
Elles se sont maquillées. **Elles se sont maquillé les yeux.**
Ils se sont lavés. **Ils se sont lavé les dents.**

1 **Historiette** **Ce matin** Répondez que oui.

1. Il s'appelle Arnaud?
2. Qu'est-ce qu'il fait le matin? Il se dépêche?
3. Il se lève à sept heures?
4. Il s'habille vite?
5. Et toi, tu te lèves à sept heures?
6. Tu te laves les mains et la figure?
7. Tes parents se dépêchent le matin?

2 Historiette **La routine** Complétez en utilisant le passé composé.

Ce matin, je __1__ (se réveiller) tôt et je __2__ (se lever) tout de suite. Je __3__ (se laver) la figure et les mains et, après le petit déjeuner, je __4__ (se brosser) les dents.

Mes deux copains Sandrine et Sylvain __5__ (se lever) tard ce matin. Ils __6__ (se dépêcher) pour arriver à l'école à l'heure.

Et vous, vous __7__ (se lever) tard ou tôt ce matin? Vous __8__ (se dépêcher)?

Les pronoms

1. The pronouns **me, te, nous,** and **vous** can be either direct or indirect objects.

OBJET DIRECT:	Il me voit.	Elle t'invite à la fête.
	Ils nous regardent.	Je vous connais.
OBJET INDIRECT:	Tu me parles?	Elle te dit quoi?
	Il nous téléphone.	Je vous réponds que oui.

2. The pronouns **le, la,** and **les** are direct objects. They can replace either a person or a thing.

Jean? Je le connais.   Son collège? Je ne le connais pas.
Marie? Je la connais.   Sa voiture? Je la vois.
Tes copains? Je les connais.   Leurs billets? Je les ai.

3. **Lui** and **leur** are indirect objects. They replace **à** + a person.

Je téléphone à Jean.   Je lui téléphone.
Il lit la lettre à Anne.   Il lui lit la lettre.
Elle parle aux élèves.   Elle leur parle.

4. The pronoun **en** replaces **de (du, de la, de l', des)** + a thing.

Tu as de l'aspirine?   Oui, j'en ai.
Il prend des antibiotiques?   Non, il n'en prend pas.

Remember that with numbers and expressions of quantity **en** refers not only to things but also to people: **Tu as des frères? Oui, j'en ai deux.**

5. Object pronouns always come directly before the verb they are linked to.

Il me téléphone.   Il va lui téléphoner.
Elle en achète.   Il ne va pas leur parler.
Il ne la regarde pas.

3 **Vraiment?** Complétez avec **me, te, nous** ou **vous**.

1. —Je vous connais, vous deux.
   —Vraiment? Tu _____ connais?
2. —On va te téléphoner.
   —Vraiment? Vous allez _____ téléphoner?
3. —Je t'aime!
   —Vraiment? Tu _____ aimes?
4. —Elle nous invite, ma sœur et moi.
   —Vraiment? Elle _____ invite?
5. —Elle t'invite aussi.
   —Vraiment? Elle _____ invite aussi?
6. —Il vous regarde fixement, ta sœur et toi.
   —Vraiment? Il _____ regarde fixement?

Musée du Louvre, Paris

4 **Jean et ses amis** Refaites les phrases en utilisant des pronoms.

1. Je connais *Jean*, mais je ne connais pas *ses amis*.
2. Je ne vois pas souvent *Caroline*, mais je parle *à sa sœur* tous les jours.
3. Jean m'invite à sa fête et je veux apporter un cadeau *à ses parents*.
4. J'aime beaucoup *Virginie et ses amis*. Je vais téléphoner *à Virginie* pour les inviter tous.
5. J'aime beaucoup *ses CD*. Je vais acheter *trois CD*.

5 **Questions** Répondez en utilisant un pronom.

1. Tu lis ce magazine?
2. Tu achètes les billets?
3. Tu vas voir cette pièce de théâtre?
4. Tu veux voir ces deux films?
5. Tu aimes mieux voir les films en version originale ou doublés?
6. Tu vois beaucoup de films américains?

FL.A.3.1.1 (I)

6 **Une journée typique** Work with a classmate. Compare a typical day in your life with a typical day in your partner's life.

FL.A.3.1.1 (I)

7 **On s'amuse.** Work with a classmate. Discuss what you do when you have free time. Do you like to do the same activities?

LITERARY COMPANION *You may wish to read the adaptation of* Le Comte de Monte-Cristo *on pages 518–523. The activities for this reading will help you continue to practice your reading comprehension skills.*

Les animaux et les plantes de la Floride

Comme la Floride se trouve dans une région semi-tropicale on y trouve beaucoup d'animaux et de plantes intéressants.

Les animaux

En Floride il y a beaucoup d'alligators. Ce mot vient du mot espagnol «lagarto» qui veut dire *lizard* en anglais. Les alligators se trouvent surtout dans l'eau douce—les lacs, les marais, les fleuves, les ruisseaux[1] et les canaux. Les alligators aiment beaucoup le soleil et on les voit souvent en plein soleil sur les rives d'un fleuve[2]. Ils aiment beaucoup la chaleur et si la température baisse en dessous de 68 degrés Fahrenheit, ils cessent[3] de manger.

La Floride a aussi des crocodiles mais, heureusement, ils sont assez rares. Quelle chance pour nous! Les crocodiles sont en général plus petits que les alligators mais ils sont plus agressifs et dangereux.

[1]ruisseaux *brooks*
[2]rives d'un fleuve *riverbanks*
[3]cessent *stop*

Un crocodile

Un alligator

En Floride, il y a des tortues marines et des tortues terrestres. Ces deux espèces sont en voie d'extinction et donc, ce sont des espèces protégées. Les tortues marines pondent leurs œufs[4] sur la plage pendant la nuit entre les mois de mai et de septembre. Après avoir[5] pondu, les tortues rentrent tout de suite dans la mer. Elles ne restent pas pour garder le nid[6].

Les lamantins[7] comme les tortues sont en voie d'extinction. Les lamantins s'appellent aussi des vaches[8] de mer. Ils pèsent entre 450 et 800 kilos et consomment chaque jour entre 10 et 15 pour cent de leur poids.

Une autre espèce en voie d'extinction, c'est la panthère de Floride. On estime qu'il ne reste que de trente à cinquante de ces animaux. En 1982 la Floride déclare la panthère le mammifère officiel de l'état. Les panthères sont très gracieuses et élégantes. Elles peuvent peser jusqu'à 70 kilos. Les panthères vivent dans les Everglades.

[4]pondent leurs œufs *lay their eggs*
[5]Après avoir *After having*
[6]nid *nest*
[7]lamantins *manatees*
[8]vaches *cows*

Une panthère de Floride

Les tortues rentrent dans la mer après avoir pondu leurs œufs.

Les plantes

La Floride est très connue pour ses agrumes[9]. L'état exporte beaucoup de fruits—des oranges, des pamplemousses, des citrons et des mandarines. L'industrie des agrumes joue un rôle important dans l'économie de l'état.

En Floride on voit aussi une grande variété de plantes tropicales qui embellissent le paysage de notre état. En voici quelques exemples.

[9]agrumes *citrus fruit*

Les oranges sont des agrumes.

Des palmiers

La bougainvillée

L'hibiscus

497C ⚜

Étude de mots

A. Choisissez le contraire.

1. les animaux
2. l'eau douce
3. souvent
4. baisser
5. marine
6. cesser
7. exporter

a. rarement
b. continuer
c. terrestre
d. l'eau de mer
e. importer
f. les plantes
g. augmenter

Un dauphin

Compréhension

A. Identifiez.

1. trois types de masses d'eau douce
2. trois espèces en voie d'extinction
3. un animal plus agressif et plus dangereux que l'alligator
4. une industrie importante de la Floride
5. un arbre ou une fleur
6. une espèce de grand chat
7. des agrumes

B. Comparez.

Comparez un alligator à un crocodile.

C. Décrivez.

Donnez des détails sur la vie et les caractéristiques des animaux suivants.

1. l'alligator
2. la tortue marine
3. le lamantin
4. la panthère de Floride

Des aigrettes

D. Discutez.

Les animaux vous intéressent? Vous connaissez quels animaux de la Floride? Et quels animaux voyez-vous là où vous habitez? Donnez quelques-unes de leurs caractéristiques.

1. La cathédrale Notre-Dame de Paris sur l'île de la Cité
2. La tour Eiffel, symbole de Paris
3. Étudiants à la terrasse d'un café au Quartier latin
4. La fontaine Stravinski près du centre Georges-Pompidou
5. Entrée de la station de métro «Porte Dauphine»
6. La Grande Arche de la Défense, le quartier des affaires
7. Marché dans le quartier de Barbès-Rochechouart

BRASSERIE

METROPOLITAIN

6

NATIONAL GEOGRAPHIC

REFLETS
de Paris

7

8

9

10

11

12

REFLETS
de Paris

13

14

501

Literary Companion

These literary selections develop reading and cultural skills and introduce students to French literature.

La petite Fadette George Sand

Vocabulaire

Les jumeaux sont semblables.
Ils ont les yeux bleus.
Ils sont forts.

Il y a deux autres garçons dans la famille.
L'aîné a cinq ans.
Le cadet a deux ans.

Il est triste. Il pleure.

Le petit garçon a peur.

un paysan

un champ

Les paysans travaillent dans les champs.
La petite fille est très pauvre.

Elle est (tombe) malade.

 Activités

Le Berry, France

A **Historiette** **Les jumeaux**
Répondez.

1. Les deux frères sont jumeaux?
2. Ils sont très semblables?
3. Ils ont les yeux bleus?
4. Ils sont forts ou faibles?
5. Le cadet a cinq ans ou deux ans?
6. Et l'aîné, il a quel âge?

B **Quel est le mot?** Complétez.

1. Des _____ sont des frères qui ont le même âge.
2. Le petit garçon est triste. Il _____.
3. Il pleure aussi quand il a _____.
4. Les jumeaux sont blonds et ils ont les yeux bleus. Ils sont très _____.
5. M. et Mme Gaillard ont deux enfants. L'_____ a quinze ans et le _____ a huit ans.
6. M. et Mme Gaillard _____ dans les champs. M. et Mme Gaillard sont des _____.
7. La petite fille n'est pas riche. Elle est _____.
8. La petite fille est _____. Elle a la grippe.

INTRODUCTION Le vrai nom de George Sand (1804–1876) est Aurore Dupin. Elle est née[1] à Paris, mais elle passe son enfance à Nohant, dans le Berry. Le Berry est une région rurale.

George Sand a un mariage malheureux. Séparée de son mari, elle rentre à Paris avec ses deux enfants. Ses romans les plus connus[2] sont des romans champêtres[3]. Dans ses romans, elle montre un grand intérêt pour les paysans du Berry. *La petite Fadette* est un roman champêtre publié en 1849.

[1] née *born*
[2] romans les plus connus *best-known novels*
[3] champêtres *pastoral*

La petite Fadette

1

Le père Barbeau habite à la Cosse. Le père Barbeau est un homme important. Il a deux champs. Il cultive ses deux champs pour nourrir° sa famille. Il a aussi une maison avec un jardin. C'est un homme courageux et bon. Il aime beaucoup sa famille—sa femme, la mère Barbeau, et ses trois enfants.

C'est alors que le père Barbeau et la mère Barbeau ont deux garçons à la fois°: deux beaux jumeaux. Il est impossible de distinguer les jumeaux l'un de l'autre parce qu'ils° sont très semblables. Sylvinet est l'aîné et Landry est le cadet.

nourrir *to feed*

à la fois *at the same time*
parce qu'ils *because they*

2

Les deux garçons grandissent° sans problème. Ils sont blonds avec de grands yeux bleus. Ils parlent avec la même voix°. Ils sont très amis. Ils sont toujours ensemble.

Les enfants ont maintenant 14 ans. Le père Barbeau dit qu'ils ont l'âge de travailler. Mais il n'y a pas assez de travail pour les deux garçons chez les Barbeau. Le père décide d'envoyer° un des garçons chez un voisin, le père Caillaud. Le père Caillaud habite à la Priche.

grandissent *grow up*
voix *voice*

envoyer *to send*

Les jumeaux sont très tristes. Être séparés, c'est horrible. Sylvinet commence à pleurer et Landry pleure aussi.

—Mais, le père Caillaud n'habite pas très loin, dit Landry.

—C'est vrai. Je vais chez le père Caillaud…

—Non, Sylvinet. Pas toi, moi! Je vais chez le père Caillaud!

Donc Landry quitte la maison de son père… Maintenant, il travaille chez le père Caillaud. Le père Caillaud est content que Landry travaille pour lui. Landry est très fort.

Le père Caillaud aime beaucoup Landry. Il traite Landry comme un de ses enfants. Landry aussi aime beaucoup le père Caillaud. Il est content de travailler à la Priche. Mais Sylvinet n'est pas content. Il est jaloux de Landry.

3

Françoise Fadet est une petite fille très pauvre. Elle habite avec sa grand-mère et son petit frère handicapé. Ils habitent près de la rivière°, pas très loin de la Priche. On appelle Françoise «la petite Fadette». La petite Fadette est très solitaire. Elle n'est pas comme les autres enfants. Elle est assez différente des autres. Les autres enfants ont peur de la petite Fadette. Certains détestent la petite fille.

rivière *river*

Un jour, Landry rentre à la Priche et rencontre° la petite Fadette qui pleure.

—Pourquoi° tu pleures comme ça?

—Parce qu'on me déteste.

—C'est un peu ta faute°, Fadette.

—Ma faute? Pourquoi?

—Parce que tu es toujours très sale° et désagréable avec les autres.

rencontre *meets*
Pourquoi *Why*

faute *fault*

sale *dirty*

Émile Lambinet *Écouen, près de Paris*

Landry, lui, ne trouve° pas la petite Fadette désagréable. Il trouve même qu'elle est intelligente et intéressante. La petite Fadette trouve Landry très beau. Elle aime Landry. Landry et la petite Fadette sont souvent ensemble et Landry change la personnalité de la petite Fadette.

Le jumeau de Landry, Sylvinet, est très jaloux de Landry et la petite Fadette. Il tombe très malade. Sa famille est désespérée. Mais qui sauve Sylvinet? La petite Fadette, l'amie de son frère Landry. Maintenant, tout° est possible, même le mariage de Landry et de la petite Fadette.

trouve finds

tout everything

Vous avez compris?

 A **Recalling information** Répondez.

1. M. et Mme Barbeau ont des jumeaux?
2. L'aîné, c'est Sylvinet ou Landry?
3. Et le cadet?
4. Ils sont bruns ou blonds?
5. Ils ont les yeux de quelle couleur?
6. Ils ont la même voix?

 B **Describing**

1. Décrivez le père Barbeau.
2. Décrivez les jumeaux Barbeau.

William Bouguereau *Jeune fille au panier de fruits*

C **Scanning** Rapid reading to look for the answers to specific questions is called *scanning*. Scan Section 2 to find the words needed to complete the following sentences.

1. Quand les enfants ont ____ ans, le père Barbeau dit qu'ils ont l'âge de ____.
2. Le père Barbeau décide d'envoyer un enfant chez un ____, le père Caillaud.
3. Le père Caillaud ____ à la Priche.
4. Les jumeaux sont très ____ parce qu'ils vont être séparés.
5. Ils sont très tristes et ils ____.
6. ____ travaille chez le père Caillaud.
7. Le père Caillaud ____ beaucoup Landry. Il ____ Landry comme un de ses enfants.

D **Recalling information** Répondez.

1. Avec qui habite la petite Fadette?
2. Elle habite où?
3. Comment est la petite Fadette?
4. La petite Fadette pleure. Pourquoi?
5. Landry trouve la petite Fadette comment?
6. Qui change la personnalité de la petite Fadette?
7. Qui tombe malade?
8. Qui sauve Sylvinet?

E **Sequencing** The order in which thoughts are arranged is called *sequence*. One type of sequence is chronological order. That is, events take place in a logical time order. Write the following events from the story in chronological order.

Sylvinet tombe très malade.
Landry et la petite Fadette sont amis.
Le père Barbeau envoie Landry chez le père Caillaud.
Les Barbeau ont deux garçons à la fois.
La petite Fadette sauve Sylvinet.
Les petits jumeaux sont toujours ensemble.
Landry rencontre la petite Fadette qui pleure.
Sylvinet est jaloux de Landry et la petite Fadette.
Landry commence à travailler pour le père Caillaud.

Littérature 2

FL.A.3.2.3 (I)   FL.C.2.1.1 (I)

«Dors mon enfant» Elolongué Epanya Yondo

Vocabulaire

un écrivain

un oranger fleuri

une revue un magazine
l'avenir le futur

Gerard Sekoto *Jeune fille à l'orange*

Activité

Un oranger Répondez.

1. Un oranger, c'est un fruit ou un arbre?
2. L'orange, c'est le fruit de l'oranger?
3. Tu aimes les oranges?
4. Tu aimes le jus d'orange?
5. Il y a des orangers dans les régions tropicales?
6. C'est beau un oranger fleuri?

INTRODUCTION La poésie africaine francophone est la poésie écrite par des Africains de langue française. La poésie africaine francophone est riche et variée. Deux écrivains de langue française célèbres sont Léopold Sédar Senghor et Aimé Césaire. Ces deux écrivains créent dans les années 30 le mouvement de «la négritude». La négritude, c'est «l'ensemble des valeurs culturelles de l'Afrique noire».

En 1947, Alioune Diop fonde à Paris la revue *Présence Africaine*. La revue publie les œuvres[1] d'écrivains africains francophones et diffuse le concept de la négritude.

[1] œuvres *works*

510 ✤ *cinq cent dix*

Bridgeman Art Library, London

Étude de mots

A. Choisissez le contraire.

1. les animaux	a. rarement
2. l'eau douce	b. continuer
3. souvent	c. terrestre
4. baisser	d. l'eau de mer
5. marine	e. importer
6. cesser	f. les plantes
7. exporter	g. augmenter

Compréhension

A. Identifiez.

1. trois types de masses d'eau douce
2. trois espèces en voie d'extinction
3. un animal plus agressif et plus dangereux que l'alligator
4. une industrie importante de la Floride
5. un arbre ou une fleur
6. une espèce de grand chat
7. des agrumes

Un dauphin

B. Comparez.

Comparez un alligator à un crocodile.

C. Décrivez.

Donnez des détails sur la vie et les caractéristiques des animaux suivants.

1. l'alligator
2. la tortue marine
3. le lamantin
4. la panthère de Floride

Des aigrettes

D. Discutez.

Les animaux vous intéressent? Vous connaissez quels animaux de la Floride? Et quels animaux voyez-vous là où vous habitez? Donnez quelques-unes de leurs caractéristiques.

1. La cathédrale Notre-Dame de Paris sur l'île de la Cité
2. La tour Eiffel, symbole de Paris
3. Étudiants à la terrasse d'un café au Quartier latin
4. La fontaine Stravinski près du centre Georges-Pompidou
5. Entrée de la station de métro «Porte Dauphine»
6. La Grande Arche de la Défense, le quartier des affaires
7. Marché dans le quartier de Barbès-Rochechouart

1

2

3

BRASSERIE

4

METROPOLITAIN

6

NATIONAL
GEOGRAPHIC

REFLETS
de Paris

7

499

Literary Companion

Littérature 1

La petite Fadette George Sand

Vocabulaire

Les jumeaux sont semblables.
Ils ont les yeux bleus.
Ils sont forts.

Il y a deux autres garçons dans la famille.
L'aîné a cinq ans.
Le cadet a deux ans.

Il est triste. Il pleure.

Le petit garçon a peur.

504 ❖ *cinq cent quatre*

LITTÉRATURE 1

Aujourd'hui, *Présence Africaine* est une maison d'édition[2] qui publie les œuvres d'écrivains africains.

«Dors mon enfant» est tiré de[3] *Kamérun! Kamérun!* du poète Elolongué Epanya Yondo. Elolongué Epanya Yondo est né au Cameroun en 1930. Il va étudier à Paris où il habite chez Alioune Diop. Elolongué Epanya Yondo veut inspirer un esprit de solidarité chez ses compatriotes pour établir un avenir[4] solide sans oublier[5] les traditions passées.

[2] maison d'édition *publishing house*
[3] tiré de *taken from*
[4] avenir *future*
[5] sans oublier *without forgetting*

«Dors mon enfant»

Dors° mon enfant dors	**Dors**
Quand tu dors	*Sleep*
Tu es beau	
Comme un oranger fleuri…	
Dors mon enfant dors	
Tu es si° beau	**si** *so*
Quand tu dors…	
Mon beau bébé noir dors	

Elizabeth Barakah Hodges *Madone noire*

Vous avez compris?

A **Recalling information** Répondez.

1. La mère trouve son enfant beau?
2. Elle compare son enfant à quel arbre?
3. Un oranger est un bel arbre?
4. Un oranger est beau surtout quand il fleurit?
5. Le petit enfant est de quelle race?
6. C'est un bébé ou un petit garçon?

B **Making inferences**

An *inference* involves using your reason and experience to draw a conclusion based on what the author implies but does not directly state. Read the poem and figure out, or *infer*, the answer to the following question.

Qui parle dans le poème?

C **Identifying main ideas**

Quelle est l'idée principale de ce poème?

La Chanson de Roland   **Auteur anonyme**

Vocabulaire

un roi

une armée

C'est un champ de bataille.
Les deux armées ont une bataille.

un guerrier, un soldat

blessé

une ceinture

Les guerriers luttent.
Un guerrier est plus fort que l'autre.
Un guerrier est blessé.

un cor

une épée

Le guerrier sonne du cor.
Ça fait du bruit.

un rocher

Le guerrier frappe son épée contre le rocher.
Il veut briser son épée.

Il se couche sous un arbre.
Il cache l'épée sous lui.

une lutte une bataille, un combat
du bruit un son désagréable
la guerre Deux armées qui luttent font la guerre.
gagner la bataille être victorieux, sortir victorieux d'une bataille

Activités

A **Historiette** **Sur le champ de bataille** Répondez.

1. Il y a des guerriers sur le champ de bataille?
2. Ils luttent?
3. C'est l'armée du roi?
4. Un guerrier est plus fort que l'autre?
5. Un guerrier est blessé?
6. Il a une épée à la main?
7. Il a un cor à la ceinture?
8. Est-ce qu'un guerrier sonne du cor?
9. Ça fait du bruit quand il sonne du cor?
10. Un guerrier frappe son épée contre un rocher?
11. Il cache son épée?
12. Il cache son épée où?

B **Quel est le mot?** Complétez.

1. Un _____ est un ancien instrument musical.
2. Une _____ est une ancienne arme.
3. Une _____, c'est un groupe de guerriers ou de soldats.
4. Le guerrier qui _____ la bataille est victorieux.

La Chanson de Roland Auteur anonyme

INTRODUCTION *La Chanson de Roland* est un poème épique qui date de la fin du onzième siècle[1]. C'est le premier poème de ce genre qui est écrit en français et pas en latin. L'auteur est anonyme, c'est-à-dire qu'il est inconnu. Le poème raconte la guerre de Charlemagne en Espagne. Charlemagne passe sept années victorieuses en Espagne. Il reste une seule ville à prendre. C'est Saragosse. Roland est un chevalier[2] dans l'armée de Charlemagne. Il veut continuer la guerre pour prendre Saragosse. Mais un autre chevalier dans l'armée de Charlemagne, Ganelon, veut faire la paix[3] avec le roi de Saragosse. Il veut rentrer en France. On va voir ce qui arrive[4].

[1] siècle *century*
[2] chevalier *knight*

[3] faire la paix *make peace*
[4] ce qui arrive *what happens*

Roland et Durendal

1

Nous sommes en 771. Les Français s'appellent les Francs. Le roi des Francs, c'est Charlemagne. Il a une très grande armée composée de guerriers nobles et braves. Un de ces guerriers s'appelle Roland. Roland est le neveu de Charlemagne. Il est fort et grand comme un géant. Il est fier° et très courageux.

fier *proud*

Un jour Charlemagne donne à son neveu deux merveilleux cadeaux: un cor magique et une épée dorée°. Roland est très fier des cadeaux de son oncle. Partout où il va il garde avec lui le cor et l'épée. Il aime son épée comme une amie. Il donne un nom à son épée: «Durendal».

dorée *gilded*

Avec sa belle épée, Durendal, Roland lutte contre les ennemis de Charlemagne. Il est extraordinaire sur le champ de bataille avec son cor à la ceinture et son épée à la main. Sa belle épée dorée brille dans le soleil et protège Roland dans ses combats. Il est victorieux dans beaucoup de batailles.

Charlemagne et Roland

2

Un jour Roland est dans un pays étranger loin de la France. Il lutte contre un guerrier blond inconnu. Les deux guerriers sont forts et très braves. Ils luttent tous les deux avec beaucoup de courage. Leur combat commence le matin et continue toute la journée. Les deux hommes sont très fatigués. Ils sont épuisés mais ils continuent à lutter. Pendant la bataille l'épée du guerrier blond se brise°. Quand Roland voit que l'épée de son adversaire est brisée, il jette Durendal à terre°. Et la bataille continue. Les deux guerriers luttent toute la nuit. Mais le guerrier blond est blessé. Aussitôt° Roland arrête le combat et aide le guerrier blessé.

—Je m'appelle Roland et je suis le neveu de Charlemagne. On ne va pas continuer à lutter. Je veux être ton ami. Quel est ton nom?

—Olivier, répond le guerrier blond.

Les deux guerriers décident d'être amis. Désormais° ils vont toujours être ensemble. Ils ne sont plus ennemis. Ils sont comme deux frères.

778: Charlemagne et ses guerriers sont en Espagne où ils luttent victorieusement contre les Sarrasins. La bataille est presque finie. Il reste une seule ville à prendre, Saragosse. Roland veut aller à Saragosse pour prendre la ville mais un autre chevalier, Ganelon, ne veut pas y aller. Il veut faire la paix avec le roi de Saragosse, Marsile, et rentrer en France. La décision est prise. On va traverser les Pyrénées et rentrer en France. En fait, Ganelon est un traître qui veut la mort° de Roland. Il révèle aux Sarrasins le chemin° que Charlemagne va prendre pour traverser les Pyrénées.

Charlemagne s'engage dans° les montagnes à la tête de son armée. Ganelon l'accompagne. Roland et Olivier font partie de l'arrière-garde. Les soldats de Marsile sont cachés° dans les montagnes à Roncevaux. Ils laissent passer Charlemagne et les hommes qui sont avec lui. Mais quand Roland et ses hommes arrivent, ils attaquent. Ils jettent des rochers énormes sur les guerriers. Les Francs luttent avec grand courage, mais hélas, ils sont vingt mille contre cent mille. Olivier demande à Roland de sonner du cor pour appeler Charlemagne à l'aide. Mais Roland est fier, il veut lutter seul. Les Francs sont écrasés°. Seuls Olivier et Roland restent en vie°. Ils veulent continuer la bataille mais ils sont blessés et ils sont très faibles.

Roland sonne du cor.

se brise *breaks*
jette… à terre *throws . . . on the ground*
Aussitôt *Immediately*

Désormais *From then on*

mort *death*
chemin *route*
s'engage dans *heads into*

cachés *hiding*

écrasés *crushed*
en vie *alive*

Roland ne veut pas laisser Durendal aux mains de ses ennemis. Il essaie de briser son épée. Il frappe son épée contre un rocher. Le rocher est dur° mais l'épée est dure aussi. Roland frappe encore mais en vain. Il ne peut pas briser son épée.

Roland va mourir°. Il se couche sous un arbre et met sa belle épée sous lui. Là, ses ennemis ne peuvent pas trouver son amie Durendal. Enfin Roland prend son cor et sonne. Il appelle Charlemagne. Il sait qu'il va mourir.

Mais Charlemagne est très loin. Il est dans une plaine en France. Il croit entendre le cor de Roland.

—Écoute! dit-il à Ganelon. C'est Roland qui sonne du cor. Il demande notre aide.

—Mais non, ce sont des bergers° qui jouent de la flûte dans la montagne, répond Ganelon.

L'armée de Charlemagne continue son voyage. Roland sonne encore.

—Je suis sûr que c'est le cor de Roland. On fait demi-tour° et on va à son aide, dit Charlemagne.

—Mais Roland est brave, dit Ganelon. Il est fort et il a des hommes avec lui. Il n'a pas besoin de nous. Notre armée est fatiguée. On ne peut pas faire demi-tour.

Le pauvre Roland est désespéré et il sonne une dernière fois°.

—C'est Roland. C'est sûr. Il a besoin de notre aide. Demi-tour, immédiatement! crie Charlemagne.

Charlemagne et ses guerriers font demi-tour. Ils arrivent dans la vallée où est l'arrière-garde. Mais il est trop tard. Tous les guerriers francs sont morts. Charlemagne trouve les corps de Roland et d'Olivier l'un près de l'autre. Roland a sonné du cor si longtemps et si fort que les veines de ses tempes° ont éclaté°.

Charlemagne et son armée attaquent l'armée de Marsile. L'ennemi est finalement écrasé. Charlemagne sort victorieux et la mort de Roland et de ses hommes est vengée.

Voilà l'histoire de Roland, le noble guerrier.

dur *hard*

mourir *to die*

bergers *shepherds*

fait demi-tour *turn around*

dernière fois *last time*

tempes *temples*
ont éclaté *burst*

La mort de Roland

Vous avez compris?

Portrait de Charlemagne

A **Recalling information** Répondez.

1. Qui est le roi des Francs en 771?
2. Il a une grande armée?
3. Comment sont les soldats de Charlemagne?
4. Qui est Roland?
5. Qu'est-ce que Charlemagne donne à Roland?
6. Roland donne un nom à son épée? Quel nom?

Monument de Charlemagne à Roncevaux

B **Recalling information** Choisissez la bonne réponse.

1. Un jour Roland lutte contre _____.
   a. un ami brun   b. un étranger blond
2. Ils luttent _____.
   a. en France   b. dans un pays étranger
3. Pendant la bataille l'épée _____ se brise.
   a. de Roland   b. de l'étranger blond
4. _____ jette son épée à terre.
   a. L'inconnu blond   b. Roland
5. _____ est blessé.
   a. Roland   b. Le guerrier inconnu
6. Roland _____ le guerrier.
   a. n'aide pas   b. aide
7. Roland veut être _____ du guerrier blond.
   a. l'ami   b. l'ennemi
8. Les deux vont être _____.
   a. des neveux   b. comme des frères

C **Recalling information** Vrai ou faux?

1. Charlemagne et son armée luttent en Espagne.
2. Ils luttent contre les Romains.
3. Les soldats de Charlemagne prennent la ville de Saragosse.
4. Roland veut prendre la ville de Saragosse.
5. Charlemagne et ses guerriers décident de rentrer en France.
6. Ganelon est un ami de Roland.
7. Roland et Ganelon font partie de l'arrière-garde.
8. L'armée de Marsile attaque Roland et ses hommes.

D **Cause and effect** When an event or action causes other things to happen, it is called a *cause-and-effect* relationship. In English explain the cause and effect of Ganelon's actions.

E **Summarizing** Give a brief synopsis of the last section of the story in English.

Littérature 4

Le Comte de Monte-Cristo Alexandre Dumas

Vocabulaire

un marin

Le jeune marin va se marier.
Il regarde sa fiancée avec amour.
Ils célèbrent leurs fiançailles.

un gardien

une cellule

On emmène le criminel en prison.
On l'enferme dans une cellule.

un mur   un trou

creuser un tunnel

Le prisonnier est désespéré.
Il frappe sur la porte.
Il crie.

s'évader de prison

Il s'est évadé de prison.

une île

un bateau

Ils ont jeté le sac à la mer.

une grotte

des pierres précieuses

de l'or

un coffre

Il a trouvé un trésor.

Activités

A **Le marin** Répondez d'après les indications.

1. Le jeune homme est un soldat ou un marin? (un marin)
2. Il est marié? (non)
3. Il va se marier? (oui)
4. Il adore sa fiancée? (oui)
5. Qu'est-ce qu'il a pour sa fiancée? (de l'or)
6. Qu'est-ce qu'ils célèbrent? (leurs fiançailles)

B **La prison** Vrai ou faux?

1. Il y a des cellules dans une prison.
2. On emmène les criminels en prison.
3. Les cellules de prison sont très belles et agréables.
4. On enferme les gardiens dans des cellules.
5. Les gardiens travaillent dans une prison. Ils surveillent les prisonniers.
6. De temps en temps, un prisonnier complètement désespéré frappe sur la porte de sa cellule.
7. Les gardiens font des trous dans les murs.
8. Pour s'évader de prison, les prisonniers creusent un tunnel.

C **Un trésor** Répondez que oui.

1. C'est une île?
2. Il y a une grotte sur l'île?
3. Il y a un coffre à l'entrée de la grotte?
4. Le coffre est plein d'or et de pierres précieuses?
5. Il y a un bateau dans la mer?
6. Quelqu'un jette un sac à la mer?

FL.A.3.2.3 (I)   FL.C.2.1.1 (I)

INTRODUCTION Il y a deux Alexandre Dumas—Dumas père et Dumas fils. Les deux sont écrivains. Le père est connu surtout pour ses romans[1] d'aventures et le fils est connu surtout pour ses pièces de théâtre.

Alexandre Dumas (1802–1870) père est né à Villers-Cotterêts dans le nord de la France. Son père est général dans l'armée française et sa mère est de Saint-Domingue dans la mer des Caraïbes. Alexandre Dumas a écrit des centaines[2] de romans. Ses romans ont procuré du plaisir à des lecteurs[3] innombrables dans le monde entier. *Le Comte de Monte-Cristo* est un de ces romans.

[1] romans *novels*   [2] centaines *hundreds*   [3] lecteurs *readers*

Le Comte de Monte-Cristo

1

1815: Edmond Dantès est un jeune marin marseillais. Dantès est un jeune homme honnête et courageux. Il n'est pas riche, mais il est heureux°. Il a une fiancée, Mercédès. Il travaille pour M. Morrel, un homme bon et juste qui le traite comme son fils.

Mais il y a trois hommes qui n'aiment pas le jeune marin. Ces trois hommes, Fernand Mondego, Danglars et Villefort sont des ennemis dangereux. Fernand est jaloux de Dantès parce qu'il aime Mercédès. Danglars travaille aussi pour M. Morrel. Mais Danglars falsifie les comptes° de M. Morrel et Dantès le sait. Donc Danglars veut éliminer Dantès. Villefort lui aussi veut éliminer Dantès pour des raisons politiques. Les trois hommes conspirent contre Dantès. Ils l'accusent de comploter° contre le roi° et d'être pour le retour de Napoléon sur le trône. Leur accusation est totalement fausse. Le jeune Dantès est innocent, mais il est tout de même arrêté parce que ses ennemis— et Villefort en particulier—ont beaucoup d'influence. Il est arrêté pendant une fête en l'honneur de ses fiançailles avec Mercédès. Sans explication, on l'emmène en prison sur l'île du château d'If tout près de Marseille. Là on l'enferme dans une petite cellule froide et sombre. Le pauvre Dantès ne comprend pas. Il est désespéré. Il frappe contre la porte. «Pourquoi suis-je en prison?» crie-t-il. Mais il n'y a pas de réponse. Personne ne l'entend. Chaque jour, Dantès attend sa liberté, mais en vain. Le temps passe. Pendant quatre ans, Dantès reste seul dans sa cellule.

heureux *happy*

comptes *accounts*

comploter *conspiring*

contre le roi *against the king*

Dantès en prison

Château d'If

2

Un jour, il entend un bruit° de l'autre côté du mur de sa cellule. C'est un autre prisonnier qui creuse un tunnel. Cet homme arrive à faire un trou dans le mur de la cellule de Dantès et à entrer dans sa cellule. Les deux hommes sont fous° de joie. Le nouvel ami de Dantès est un abbé°, l'abbé Faria. L'abbé Faria est un intellectuel italien d'environ soixante ans. Il raconte à Dantès ses occupations en Italie et Dantès lui raconte ses voyages. Les deux amis font le projet° de s'évader de prison. Mais l'abbé n'est pas en bonne santé. Il sait qu'il ne va pas avoir la force de s'évader avec Dantès. Il lui révèle alors l'existence d'un trésor fabuleux caché° sur une petite île de la mer Méditerranée. Cette île s'appelle l'île de Monte-Cristo. Il donne un document à Dantès qui explique comment trouver le trésor.

bruit *noise*

fous *crazy*
abbé *abbot*

projet *plan*

caché *hidden*

3

Peu de temps après les gardiens de la prison trouvent l'abbé Faria mort° dans sa cellule. Ils mettent son corps dans un sac. Il vont le jeter à la mer. Mais pendant la nuit, Dantès prend la place de Faria et se met dans le sac. Les gardiens jettent le sac à la mer et Dantès est libre! Il ouvre le sac et commence à nager. Il nage longtemps dans une mer très agitée. Finalement, il est recueilli° par un bateau. Il est sauvé!

Maintenant Dantès est un homme libre! Il part à la recherche du trésor. Après de nombreuses aventures, il arrive enfin sur l'île de Monte-Cristo. Il a quelques difficultés à trouver le trésor qui est bien caché. Finalement il découvre dans une grotte un coffre avec de l'or et des pierres précieuses—des diamants, des rubis et des perles de toute beauté. Edmond Dantès est très riche! Il change de nom. Il prend le nom de l'île où il a trouvé le trésor. Le comte de Monte-Cristo est né.

mort *dead*

recueilli *picked up*

Ils jettent le sac à la mer.

Le Comte de Monte-Cristo va à Paris où il achète une maison splendide. Il voyage à Rome et en Grèce. Il est invité à toutes les fêtes. Il devient° vite célèbre. Tout le monde veut faire la connaissance de cet homme mystérieux et fabuleusement riche. Mais le Comte de Monte-Cristo n'a qu'une° idée. Il veut se venger°. Il retrouve Fernand qui s'est marié avec Mercédès. Fernand est devenu très riche, lui aussi. Il a pris le nom de Comte de Morcerf. Il retrouve Danglars et Villefort. Évidemment personne ne le reconnaît. Un à un, le comte de Monte-Cristo se venge de ses ennemis. Mercédès quitte Fernand et va dans un couvent. Fernand meurt°. Danglars est ruiné et Villefort devient fou°. Mais la vengeance ne satisfait pas le comte de Monte-Cristo. Il ne se sent pas libre. Au contraire, il se sent angoissé et plein de doutes. Il décide de tout abandonner. Il laisse sa fortune à Maximilien Morrel, le fils de son ancien patron°. Puis il s'embarque sur un bateau pour une destination inconnue en compagnie d'Haydée, une très belle jeune fille.

devient *becomes*

n'a qu'une *has only one*
se venger *to get revenge*

meurt *dies*
devient fou *goes crazy*

ancien patron *former boss*

Château d'If

Vous avez compris?

A   **Recalling information**   Vrai ou faux?

1. Edmond Dantès est un jeune soldat parisien.
2. Il est très riche.
3. Il va se marier avec sa fiancée Mercédès.
4. Il n'a pas d'ennemis.
5. Il y a des hommes qui sont jaloux de Dantès.
6. Ils l'accusent d'un crime.
7. Dantès n'est pas un criminel.
8. Les gardiens savent qu'ils libèrent Dantès.
9. Dantès reste longtemps en prison.

B Recalling information Répondez.

1. Un jour, qu'est-ce que Dantès entend?
2. Quel est ce bruit?
3. Qui est le nouvel ami de Dantès?
4. Quel projet font les deux amis?
5. Qui est malade?
6. Qu'est-ce que l'abbé révèle à Dantès?
7. Où est caché le trésor?
8. Qu'est-ce que le document de l'abbé Faria explique?

C Recalling information Choisissez.

1. Les gardiens trouvent _____ mort.
   a. Dantès   b. l'abbé Faria   c. M. Morrel
2. Ils le trouvent dans _____.
   a. un tunnel   b. un trou   c. sa cellule
3. Les gardiens mettent _____ dans un sac.
   a. le document   b. l'abbé Faria   c. Dantès
4. Les gardiens jettent le sac _____.
   a. dans le tunnel   b. à la mer   c. dans une grotte
5. Dantès est sauvé par _____.
   a. un homme libre   b. un bateau   c. une île
6. Quand Dantès arrive sur l'île de Monte-Cristo, il cherche _____.
   a. l'abbé Faria   b. le trésor   c. le document
7. Il découvre le trésor _____.
   a. dans la mer   b. dans le bateau   c. dans une grotte
8. Des diamants et des rubis sont _____.
   a. de l'or   b. des perles   c. des pierres précieuses

Une cellule au château d'If

D Describing Décrivez tout ce que Dantès fait à Paris.

E Comparing and contrasting
When you describe how two or more things are similiar, you are *comparing* them. When you describe how they are different, you are *contrasting* them. Compare and contrast the life of Edmond Dantès with the life of the Count of Monte-Cristo.

Video Companion

Using video in the classroom

The use of video in the classroom can be a wonderful asset to the World Languages teacher and a most beneficial learning tool for the language student. Video enables students to experience whatever it is they are learning in their textbook in a real-life setting. With each lesson, they are able to take a vicarious field trip. They see people interacting at home, at school, at the market, etc., in an authentic milieu. Students sitting in a classroom can see real people going about their real life in real places. They may experience the target culture in many countries. The cultural benefits are limitless.

Developing listening and viewing skills In addition to its tremendous cultural value, video, when properly used, gives students much needed practice in developing good listening and viewing skills. Video allows students to look for numerous clues that are evident in a tone of voice, facial expressions, and gestures. Through video students can see and hear the diversity of the target culture and, as discerning viewers and listeners, compare and contrast the French-speaking cultures to each other and to their own culture. Video introduces a dimension into classroom instruction that no other medium—teachers, overhead, text, Audio CDs—can provide.

Reinforcing learned language Video that is properly developed for classroom use has speakers reincorporate the language students have learned in a given lesson. In keeping with reality, however, speakers introduce some new words, expressions, and structures because students

functioning in a real-life situation would not know every word native speakers use with them in a live conversation. The lively and interactive nature of video allows students to use their listening and viewing skills to comprehend new language in addition to seeing and hearing the language they have learned come to life.

Getting the most out of video The intrinsic benefit of video is often lost when students are allowed to read the scripted material before viewing. In many cases, students will have come to understand language used by the speakers in the video by means of reading comprehension, thus negating the inherent benefits of video as a tool to develop listening and viewing skills. Because today's students are so accustomed to the medium of video as a tool for entertainment and learning, a well-written and well-produced video program will help them develop real-life language skills and confidence in those skills in an enjoyable way.

On Location!

Je suis Christine. Je suis de Fort-de-France, à la Martinique.

Je suis Vincent. Je suis de Paris.

Je suis Chloé. Je suis de Lyon, en France.

Je suis Manu. Je suis algérien.

Je suis Amadou. Je suis malien.

Vidéotour

Bon voyage!

Épisode 1: Une amie et un ami

Vincent et Chloé à Montmartre

Une vue splendide sur Paris

Avant de regarder

Can you spot the following?

1. un garçon brun
2. une fille brune
3. une vue splendide sur Paris
4. une caméra
5. une fille enthousiaste

Après avoir regardé

Expansion You will be taking a video tour of Paris. As you watch, look for similarities you notice between Paris and the city or town where you live. What differences do you notice? Choose several places in Paris that you would like to visit. Do some research to find out more about Paris. Why do you find it interesting?

Vidéotour

Bon voyage!

Épisode 2: Les cours et les profs

Vincent et une amie, Élodie, au lycée Louis-le-Grand

Manu et Vincent en cours de chimie

Avant de regarder

Make an educated guess!

1. In the first photograph, what do you think Vincent is doing?

2. In the second photo, does Manu look as if he knows what he is doing?

3. How does Vincent look as he watches Manu?

4. Do you think the experiment is going to be successful?

Après avoir regardé

Expansion   As you watch the video, think about whether there are any similarities between the school you see in the video and the one you attend. Do you notice any differences? Which might you prefer? Why? Do some research about schedules in French schools. Are the schedules for French students like yours?

Vidéotour

Bon voyage!

Épisode 3: Pendant et après les cours

Amadou et Christine dans la rue après les cours

Amadou et Christine dans la papeterie

Avant de regarder

Can you spot the following?

1. une papeterie
2. une calculatrice
3. une rue
4. des fournitures scolaires
5. deux amis

Après avoir regardé

Expansion You will see something in the video that Christine enjoys doing after school. Compare her likes to some of those that you may have. See whether or not you have anything in common with your new French friends. Think about the other people in the video. Knowing what you know about them, what might they enjoy doing after school?

Vidéotour
Bon voyage!

Épisode 4: La famille et la maison

Christine a une surprise pour Mme Séguin.

Christine et Mme Séguin dans la cuisine de la maison de Monet

Avant de regarder

Can you spot the following? If so, give an adjective to describe each.

1. un jardin
2. un immeuble
3. une cuisine
4. une fleur
5. une voiture

Après avoir regardé

Expansion   Giverny, a charming village northwest of Paris, is a beautiful spot. Can you think of any place near where you live that could compare to Giverny? Do some research to find out more about this famous place where Monet lived and write a paragraph about it or discuss with a friend what you found out that is of interest to you.

Vidéotour
Bon voyage!

Épisode 5: Au café et au restaurant

Chloé et Christine vont dans un café.

Elles commandent une boisson.

Avant de regarder

Invent the following.

1. le nom du café
2. ce que Chloé commande
3. ce que Christine commande
4. ce que dit le serveur

Après avoir regardé

Expansion   As you can imagine from what you saw in the video, café life is an important part of French culture. Do you have any cafés near where you live? If you do, do you and your friends go there often? If not, do you think you might enjoy them based on what you viewed in the video?

Vidéotour

Bon voyage!

Épisode 6: La nourriture et les courses

Vincent et Manu font les courses.

Manu «prépare» un repas fabuleux.

Avant de regarder

Answer the questions.

1. Où sont Vincent et Manu?
2. Qu'est-ce qu'ils font?
3. Qu'est-ce qu'ils achètent, d'après vous?
4. Qui va payer, d'après vous?
5. Qu'est-ce qu'ils vont manger?

Après avoir regardé

Expansion What foods that you saw in the French supermarket are similar to those found in your supermarket? Do some research on the Internet to find a French recipe that you and your family might enjoy. Then make a list of all the ingredients you need from the supermarket to prepare this recipe.

Vidéotour

Bon voyage!

Épisode 7: Les vêtements

Christine et Chloé veulent acheter une robe.

Chloé essaie une robe.

Avant de regarder

Describe the following.

1. ce que porte Christine
2. ce que porte Chloé
3. ce que porte la vendeuse
4. la robe que Christine essaie

Après avoir regardé

Expansion The world of fashion is significant in Paris and in other parts of the French-speaking world. Do some research on a famous French designer. Tell whether or not you might enjoy wearing his or her clothing. If you are artistic, draw a fashion that your designer might design.

Vidéotour

Bon voyage!

Épisode 8: L'aéroport et l'avion

Où est Christine en réalité?

Manu est à l'aéroport avec Christine?

Avant de regarder

Can you spot the following? How many of each do you see?

1. une valise
2. un passager
3. une carte d'embarquement
4. un comptoir
5. un bagage à main

Après avoir regardé

Expansion   You have been exposed to many parts of the French-speaking world. Choose a place that you would most like to visit. Do some research on the Internet to plan your itinerary. Include the places you would like to visit in the city or town of your choice and explain how you would get there.

Vidéotour

Bon voyage!

Épisode 9: La gare et le train

Amadou et Chloé partent pour Lille. Ils prennent leurs billets.

Leur train part d'où?

Avant de regarder

Answer the questions.

1. Où sont Amadou et Chloé?
2. Qu'est-ce qu'ils font?
3. D'après vous, qui est l'homme avec eux?
4. D'après vous, qu'est-ce que nos amis demandent à cet homme?

Après avoir regardé

Expansion What is your favorite means of transportation for long trips? Why? Do you think most Americans would make the same choice? Survey your friends to find out their preferences.

Vidéotour
Bon voyage!

Épisode 10: Les sports

Manu joue bien au basket.

Manu est fana de basket-ball. C'est son sport favori.

Avant de regarder

Make an educated guess!

1. Où est Manu?
2. Qui joue au basket-ball?
3. Ce sont des amies de Manu?
4. Quel est le score?
5. Que fait Manu à la fin du match?

Après avoir regardé

Expansion Think of some famous French athletes and do some research to find out about them. Choose one you think is particularly good and research his or her career.

Vidéotour

Bon voyage!

Épisode 11: L'été et l'hiver

Christine «apprend» à faire du ski.

Manu est un très bon moniteur.

Avant de regarder

Can you spot the following? If so, describe each one.

1. une montagne
2. un skieur
3. une piste
4. un sommet
5. un anorak

Après avoir regardé

Expansion   What fun activity do you do in the winter? And in the summer? Are video games a big part of your life?

Vidéotour
Bon voyage!

Épisode 12: La routine quotidienne

Manu se réveille.

Manu prend son petit déjeuner.

Avant de regarder

Answer the questions.

1. Que fait Manu?
2. Que lui donne Vincent dans la salle de bains?
3. Que va faire Manu avec ça?
4. Qu'est-ce que Vincent donne à Manu dans sa chambre?
5. Qu'est-ce que Manu va faire?

Après avoir regardé

Expansion Is it easy for you to get up in the morning or not? Do you go to bed early or late? Do you sleep well at night? Compare Manu's day with a typical day in your life.

Vidéotour

Bon voyage!

Épisode 13: Les loisirs culturels

Chloé visite le musée d'Orsay. Elle trouve les tableaux fabuleux.

Chloé et Vincent sur la place Igor Stravinsky

Avant de regarder

Can you spot the following?

1. une exposition
2. une danseuse
3. un tableau
4. une peinture
5. une statue

Après avoir regardé

Expansion Are you aware of your cultural heritage? Can you name some famous American painters, musicians, architects? Do some research on the Internet about the musée d'Orsay. Who are some of the artists whose art is shown there? Can you find out what special exhibitions there are currently?

Vidéotour

Bon voyage!

Épisode 14: La santé et la médecine

Le docteur Nguyen est très sympa.

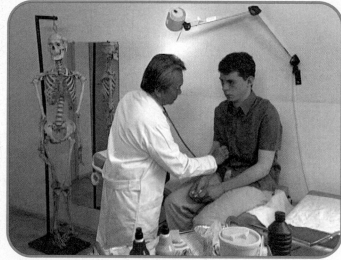

Vincent n'est pas en bonne santé.

Avant de regarder

Answer the questions.

1. Où est Vincent?
2. Pourquoi, d'après vous?
3. Vincent a un mouchoir dans la main. Pourquoi?
4. D'après vous, Vincent est très malade?
5. Que lui dit le médecin?

Après avoir regardé

Expansion   Do you go to the doctor every time something is wrong with you? Why or why not? Does your doctor make house calls? Do some research online about medical achievements and famous doctors in France. You may want to begin with an online visit to **l'Institut Pasteur**.

Activity 1

Luc / Lyon   Olivier / Nice

Sylvie / Montréal   Sophie / Paris

Élève A Answer your partner's questions based on the pictures below.

Élève A Ask your partner the following questions. Correct answers are in parentheses.

1. Comment est Sophie, petite ou grande?
   (*Sophie est petite.*)

2. Comment est Sylvie?
   (*Elle est grande.*)

3. Il est d'où, Olivier?
   (*Il est de Nice.*)

4. Luc est américain ou français?
   (*Il est français.*)

5. Comment est Olivier, brun ou blond?
   (*Il est brun.*)

6. Qui est de Montréal?
   (*Sylvie est de Montréal.*)

Élève B Answer your partner's questions based on the pictures below.

Sophie / Paris   Sylvie / Montréal

Olivier / Nice   Luc / Lyon

Élève B Ask your partner the following questions. Correct answers are in parentheses.

1. Comment est Olivier, petit ou grand?
   (*Olivier est petit.*)

2. Comment est Luc?
   (*Luc est grand.*)

3. Elle est d'où, Sophie?
   (*Elle est de Paris.*)

4. Qui est de Lyon?
   (*Luc est de Lyon.*)

5. Sophie est française ou américaine?
   (*Elle est française.*)

6. Comment est Luc, brun ou blond?
   (*Il est blond.*)

Activity 2

Élève A Ask your partner the following questions. Correct answers are in parentheses.

Élève A Answer your partner's questions based on the pictures below.

1. Qui est Luc?
(Luc est le frère de Nathalie.)

2. Qui est Philippe?
(Philippe est l'ami de Nathalie.)

3. Carol est élève dans une école américaine?
(Oui, Carol est élève dans une école américaine.)

4. Bruno est élève dans un collège français?
(Oui, Bruno est élève dans un collège français.)

Carol Smith

Bruno Lapierre

Nathalie et
Luc Simonet

Nathalie Simonet et
Philippe Latour

Élève B Answer your partner's questions based on the pictures below.

Élève B Ask your partner the following questions. Correct answers are in parentheses.

Nathalie et
Luc Simonet

Nathalie Simonet et
Philippe Latour

Carol Smith

Bruno Lapierre

1. Qui est Nathalie?
(Nathalie est la sœur de Luc.)

2. Nathalie est sympathique?
(Oui, Nathalie est très sympathique.)

3. Carol est américaine?
(Oui, Carol est américaine.)

4. Bruno est français?
(Oui, Bruno est français.)

Activity 3

Napoléon Bonaparte

Oprah Winfrey

4. Napoléon est très grand.
   (Non, il n'est pas très grand. Il est assez petit.)

3. Oprah Winfrey est timide.
   (Non, elle n'est pas timide. Elle est sociable.)

2. Charles de Gaulle est américain.
   (Non, il n'est pas américain. Il est français.)

1. Meg Ryan est brune.
   (Non, elle n'est pas brune. Elle est blonde.)

Charles de Gaulle

Meg Ryan

Élève A Correct your partner's statements based on the pictures below.

Élève A Read your partner the following false statements. Correct answers are in parentheses.

Élève B Correct your partner's statements based on the pictures below.

Meg Ryan

Charles de Gaulle

Oprah Winfrey

Napoléon Bonaparte

Élève B Read your partner the following false statements. Correct answers are in parentheses.

1. Meg Ryan est timide.
   (Non, elle n'est pas timide. Elle est dynamique.)

2. Charles de Gaulle est petit.
   (Non, il n'est pas petit. Il est grand.)

3. Oprah Winfrey est française.
   (Non, elle n'est pas française. Elle est américaine.)

4. Napoléon est américain.
   (Non, il n'est pas américain. Il est français.)

Activity 4

Élève A Answer your partner's questions based on the picture below.

Élève A Ask your partner the following questions. Correct answers are in parentheses.

1. Le cours de français est facile?
   (Oui, le cours de français est facile.)

2. Le prof est très sympathique?
   (Oui, le prof est très sympathique.)

3. Les élèves sont françaises ou américaines?
   (Les élèves sont françaises.)

4. Les élèves sont amies?
   (Oui, les élèves sont amies.)

Élève B Answer your partner's questions based on the picture below.

Élève B Ask your partner the following questions. Correct answers are in parentheses.

1. Les élèves sont dans le même lycée?
   (Oui, les élèves sont dans le même lycée.)

2. Les élèves sont dans la salle de classe?
   (Oui, les élèves sont dans la salle de classe.)

3. Les élèves sont sympathiques?
   (Oui, les élèves sont sympathiques.)

4. Le cours de français est difficile?
   (Non, le cours de français n'est pas difficile.) or
   (Non, le cours de français est facile.)

Activity 5

Élève A Answer your partner's questions based on the report card below.

Marie Newall

Les langues:	
Le français	A–
L'anglais	B+
Les sciences sociales:	
L'histoire	D
La géographie	C+
D'autres matières:	
La musique	A

Élève A Ask your partner the following questions. Correct answers are in parentheses.

1. Guy est fort en mathématiques?
   (Oui, il est fort en mathématiques.)

2. Guy est très fort en sciences naturelles?
   (Non, il n'est pas fort en sciences naturelles.)
   or *(Non, il est mauvais en sciences naturelles.)*

3. Il est mauvais en géométrie?
   (Non, il n'est pas mauvais en géométrie.)
   or *(Non, il est fort en géométrie.)*

4. L'économie est une science naturelle?
   (Non, l'économie n'est pas une science naturelle.) or *(Non, l'économie est une science sociale.)*

Élève B Answer your partner's questions based on the report card below.

Guy Peters

Les sciences naturelles:	
La biologie	C−
La chimie	D
Les mathématiques:	
La géométrie	A
Le calcul	B+
Les sciences sociales:	
L'économie	B

Élève B Ask your partner the following questions. Correct answers are in parentheses.

1. Marie est très forte en sciences sociales?
   (Non, elle est mauvaise en sciences sociales.) or *(Elle n'est pas forte en sciences sociales.)*

2. Le cours de français est très difficile?
   (Non, le cours de français est très facile.)
   or *(Non, le cours de français n'est pas difficile.)*

3. Marie est mauvaise en histoire?
   (Oui, Marie est mauvaise en histoire.)

4. L'anglais est une science sociale?
   (Non, l'anglais est une langue.) or
   (Non, l'anglais n'est pas une science sociale.)

Activity 6

Élève A Answer your partner's questions in complete sentences, using either **Oui** or **Non.**

Élève A Ask your partner the following questions. Correct answers are in parentheses.

1. La salle de classe est petite?
   (Oui, la salle de classe est petite.) or *(Non, la salle de classe n'est pas petite.)*

2. Les élèves sont intelligents?
   (Oui, les élèves sont intelligents.) or *(Non, les élèves ne sont pas intelligents.)*

3. Le lycée est grand?
   (Oui, le lycée est grand.) or *(Non, le lycée n'est pas grand.)*

4. Vous deux, vous êtes élèves dans un lycée français?
   (Oui, nous sommes élèves dans un lycée français.) or *(Non, nous ne sommes pas élèves dans un lycée français.)*

5. Tu es fort(e) en maths?
   (Oui, je suis fort[e] en maths.) or *(Non, je ne suis pas fort[e] en maths.)*

Élève B Answer your partner's questions in complete sentences, using either **Oui** or **Non.**

Élève B Ask your partner the following questions. Correct answers are in parentheses.

1. La prof est patiente?
   (Oui, la prof est patiente.) or *(Non, la prof n'est pas patiente.)*

2. Les élèves sont sympas?
   (Oui, les élèves sont sympas.) or *(Non, les élèves ne sont pas sympas.)*

3. Le prof est intéressant?
   (Oui, le prof est intéressant.) or *(Non, le prof n'est pas intéressant.)*

4. Vous êtes copains?
   (Oui, nous sommes copains.) or *(Non, nous ne sommes pas copains.)*

5. Tu es fort(e) en histoire?
   (Oui, je suis fort[e] en histoire.) or *(Non, je ne suis pas fort[e] en histoire.)*

Activity 7

Élève A Answer your partner's questions based on the picture below.

Élève A Ask your partner the following questions. Correct answers are in parentheses.

1. Les élèves sont où?
   (Les élèves sont dans la cour.)

2. Ils parlent entre les cours?
   (Oui, ils parlent entre les cours.)

3. Ils étudient dans la cour?
   (Non, ils n'étudient pas dans la cour.)

4. Les copains rigolent?
   (Oui, ils rigolent.)

Élève B Answer your partner's questions based on the picture below.

Élève B Ask your partner the following questions. Correct answers are in parentheses.

1. Les élèves passent la journée à l'école?
   (Oui, ils passent la journée à l'école.)

2. Ils regardent la prof?
   (Oui, ils regardent la prof.)

3. Un élève pose une question?
   (Oui, il pose une question.)

4. Les élèves déjeunent pendant le cours?
   (Non, ils ne déjeunent pas pendant le cours.)

Activity 8

Élève A Ask your partner the following questions. Correct answers are in parentheses.

Élève A Answer your partner's questions based on the picture below.

1. Camille est à la papeterie?
   (Oui, elle est à la papeterie.)

2. Elle achète des fournitures scolaires?
   (Oui, elle achète des fournitures scolaires.)

3. Elle achète un classeur et une calculatrice?
   (Oui, elle achète un classeur et une calculatrice.)

4. Elle paie où?
   (Elle paie à la caisse.)

Marc

Sophie

Élève B Answer your partner's questions based on the picture below.

Camille

Élève B Ask your partner the following questions. Correct answers are in parentheses.

1. Sophie travaille après les cours?
   (Oui, elle travaille après les cours.)

2. Elle travaille où?
   (Elle travaille dans une papeterie.)

3. Marc achète un sac à dos?
   (Oui, il achète un sac à dos.)

4. Il achète un classeur?
   (Oui, il achète un classeur.)

Activity 9

Élève A Answer your partner's questions using the correct form of the verb below.

1. arriver

2. poser

3. rigoler

4. parler

5. travailler

Élève A Ask your partner the following questions. Possible responses are in parentheses.

1. Tu quittes la maison à quelle heure le matin?
(Je quitte la maison à sept heures et demie.)

2. Qui écoute quand le prof parle?
(Les élèves écoutent quand le prof parle.)

3. On parle français en Belgique?
(Oui, on parle français en Belgique.)

4. Vous étudiez quelle langue?
(Nous étudions le français.)

5. Vous détestez les examens?
(Oui, nous détestons les examens.) or
(Non, nous ne détestons pas les examens.)

Élève B Answer your partner's questions using the correct form of the verb below.

1. quitter

2. écouter

3. parler

4. étudier

5. détester

Élève B Ask your partner the following questions. Possible responses are in parentheses.

1. On arrive à l'école à quelle heure?
(On arrive à l'école à huit heures.)

2. Qui pose des questions?
(Les élèves posent des questions.) or
(Le prof pose des questions.)

3. Vous rigolez dans la cour?
(Oui, nous rigolons dans la cour.) or
(Non, nous ne rigolons pas dans la cour.)

4. Tu parles beaucoup au téléphone?
(Oui, je parle beaucoup au téléphone.) or
(Non, je ne parle pas beaucoup au téléphone.)

5. Tu travailles après les cours?
(Oui, je travaille après les cours.) or
(Non, je ne travaille pas après les cours.)

Élève A Read your partner the following statements. He or she will fill in the blank. Correct answers are in parentheses.

1. Le frère de mon père est mon ———.
   (oncle)

2. La mère de mon cousin est ma ———.
   (tante)

3. Le mari de ma mère est mon ———.
   (père)

4. La mère de mon père est ma ———.
   (grand-mère)

5. Le fils de ma tante est mon ———.
   (cousin)

Élève A Complete your partner's statements with the name of the relative.

Élève B Complete your partner's statements with the name of the relative.

Élève B Read your partner the following statements. He or she will fill in the blank. Correct answers are in parentheses.

1. La sœur de ma mère est ma ———.
   (tante)

2. La femme de mon père est ma ———.
   (mère)

3. La fille de mes parents est ma ———.
   (sœur)

4. Les parents de ma mère sont mes ———.
   (grands-parents)

5. Les enfants de mon oncle sont mes ———.
   (cousins)

Activity 11

Élève A Ask your partner the following questions. Correct answers are in parentheses.

Élève A Now answer your partner's questions.

1. On regarde la télé dans la salle de bains ou la salle de séjour?
   (On regarde la télé dans la salle de séjour.)

2. On dîne dans la chambre à coucher ou la salle à manger?
   (On dîne dans la salle à manger.)

3. Le balcon donne sur la cour ou sur la cuisine?
   (Le balcon donne sur la cour.)

4. On habite au troisième étage d'un immeuble ou d'une maison?
   (On habite au troisième étage d'un immeuble.)

5. La voiture est dans la cuisine ou le garage?
   (La voiture est dans le garage.)

Élève B Answer your partner's questions.

Élève B Ask your partner the following questions. Correct answers are in parentheses.

1. On parle avec les voisins dans la cour ou la salle de bains?
   (On parle avec les voisins dans la cour.)

2. On prépare le dîner dans l'ascenseur ou la cuisine?
   (On prépare le dîner dans la cuisine.)

3. On monte à l'appartement dans le métro ou l'ascenseur?
   (On monte à l'appartement dans l'ascenseur.)

4. Les toilettes sont dans l'appartement ou dans la cour?
   (Les toilettes sont dans l'appartement.)

5. On habite dans un quartier ou dans une entrée?
   (On habite dans un quartier.)

Activity 12

CHAPITRE 4, Structure, pages 120–125

Élève A Ask your partner the following questions. Correct answers are in parentheses.

1. Marc a quel âge?
   (Il a quinze ans.)

2. Tes grands-parents ont une maison?
   (Non, ils ont un joli appartement.)

3. Tu as quel âge, toi?
   (J'ai ——— ans.)

4. Qui a deux chiens?
   (La prof de maths a deux chiens.)

5. Quel âge ont tes grands-parents?
   (Ils ont quatre-vingts ans.)

Élève A Use the chart below to answer your partner's questions. Reminder: **toi** is you.

Paul	15 ans	Une sœur
Tes grands-parents	75 ans	Un chien
Toi	?	Des profs intéressants
Tes cousines	16 ans	Deux chats
Marie	14	Une petite famille

Élève B Use the chart below to answer your partner's questions. Reminder: **toi** is you.

Marc	15 ans	Une sœur
Tes grands-parents	80 ans	Un joli appartement
Toi	?	Des profs intéressants
La prof de maths	35	Deux chiens
Sophie	14	Une petite famille

Élève B Ask your partner the following questions. Correct answers are in parentheses.

1. Qui a des profs intéressants?
   (Moi, j'ai des profs intéressants.)

2. Tes cousines ont combien de chats?
   (Mes cousines ont deux chats.)

3. Tes grands-parents ont quel âge?
   (Mes grands-parents ont soixante-quinze ans.)

4. Qui a une petite famille?
   (Marie a une petite famille.)

5. Paul a un frère ou une sœur?
   (Paul a une sœur.)

Activity 13

Élève A Now your partner is the server. Use the following picture menu to give your order.

Élève A You are the server in a French café. Ask your partner what he or she wants to order. Correct answers are in parentheses.

1. Vous désirez?
   (Un citron pressé, s'il vous plaît.)

2. Vous désirez?
   (Un croissant, s'il vous plaît.)

3. Vous désirez?
   (Une salade verte, s'il vous plaît.)

4. Vous désirez?
   (Un café, s'il vous plaît.) or *(Un express, s'il vous plaît.)*

5. Vous désirez?
   (Une tartine de pain beurré, s'il vous plaît.)

Élève B Your partner is the server in a French café. Use the following picture menu to give your order.

1.

2.

3.

4.

5.

Élève B Now you are the server. Ask your partner what he or she wants to order. Correct answers are in parentheses.

1. Vous désirez?
   (Un jus d'orange, s'il vous plaît.)

2. Vous désirez?
   (Une saucisse de Francfort, s'il vous plaît.) or *(Un hot-dog, s'il vous plaît.)*

3. Vous désirez?
   (Un croque-monsieur, s'il vous plaît.)

4. Vous désirez?
   (Une soupe à l'oignon, s'il vous plaît.)

5. Vous désirez?
   (Une omelette nature, s'il vous plaît.)

Activity 14

Élève A Use the pictures below to answer your partner's questions.

Élève A Ask your partner the following questions. Correct answers are in parentheses.

1. Un couteau, c'est pour la soupe?
   (Non, une cuillère, c'est pour la soupe.)

2. Un verre, c'est pour le café?
   (Non, une tasse, c'est pour le café.)

3. Une soupe à l'oignon, c'est pour le dessert?
   (Non, une glace au chocolat, c'est pour le dessert.)

4. Un couteau, c'est pour le steak?
   (Oui, un couteau, c'est pour le steak.)

5. Un verre, c'est pour la limonade?
   (Oui, un verre, c'est pour la limonade.)

Élève B Use the pictures below to answer your partner's questions.

1.

2.

3.

4.

5.

Élève B Now ask your partner the following questions. Correct answers are in parentheses.

1. On prend un croissant pour le dîner?
   (Non, on prend une omelette pour le dîner.)

2. On prend une crêpe pour le déjeuner?
   (Non, on prend un sandwich au jambon pour le déjeuner.)

3. C'est un pourboire ou une fourchette?
   (C'est un pourboire.)

4. C'est un steak saignant ou bien cuit?
   (C'est un steak bien cuit.)

5. C'est une assiette ou une serviette?
   (C'est une serviette.)

Activity 15

Élève A Ask your partner the following questions. Correct answers are in parentheses.

1. Les copains vont où?
   (*Ils vont à l'école.*)

2. Ils y vont comment?
   (*Ils y vont en voiture.*)

3. Tu vas où?
   (*Je vais à la papeterie.*)

4. Tu y vas à pied?
   (*Non, j'y vais en bus.*)

Élève A Answer your partner's questions based on the cues below.

1. l'école

2. à pied

3. le café

4. le métro

Élève B Answer your partner's questions based on the cues below.

1. l'école

2. en voiture

3. la papeterie

4. en bus

Élève B Ask your partner the following questions. Correct answers are in parentheses.

1. Vous allez où?
   (*Nous allons à l'école.*)

2. Vous y allez comment?
   (*Nous y allons à pied.*)

3. Tu vas où?
   (*Je vais au café.*)

4. Tu prends le bus pour aller au café?
   (*Non, je prends le métro.*)

Activity 16

Élève A Ask your partner the following questions. Correct answers are in parentheses.

Élève A Use the following pictures to answer your partner's questions.

1. Pour acheter du pain, on va où?
   (On va à la boulangerie-pâtisserie.)

2. Pour acheter du lait, on va où?
   (On va à la crémerie.)

3. Pour acheter une tarte aux pommes, on va où?
   (On va à la boulangerie-pâtisserie.)

4. Pour acheter du jambon, on va où?
   (On va à la charcuterie.)

5. Pour acheter de la crème, on va où?
   (On va à la crémerie.)

Élève B Answer your partner's questions based on the pictures below.

Élève B Ask your partner the following questions. Correct answers are in parentheses.

1. Pour acheter de la viande, on va où?
   (On va à la boucherie.)

2. Pour acheter du poisson, on va où?
   (On va à la poissonnerie.)

3. Pour acheter du poivre, on va où?
   (On va à l'épicerie.)

4. Pour acheter du porc, on va où?
   (On va à la boucherie.)

5. Pour acheter des crevettes, on va où?
   (On va à la poissonnerie.)

Activity 17

(The upper half of the activity is printed upside-down.)

une bouteille

une boîte

une douzaine

250 grammes

un pot

Élève A Answer your partner's questions based on the information below.

Élève A You play the part of the vendor. Ask your partner the following questions. Correct answers are in parentheses.

1. Vous voulez de la confiture?
   (*Oui, je voudrais un pot de confiture, s'il vous plaît.*)

2. Vous voulez des légumes surgelés?
   (*Oui, je voudrais un paquet de légumes surgelés, s'il vous plaît.*)

3. Vous voulez des petits pois?
   (*Oui, je voudrais une boîte de petits pois, s'il vous plaît.*)

4. Vous voulez du lait?
   (*Oui, je voudrais un litre de lait, s'il vous plaît.*)

5. Vous voulez du jambon?
   (*Oui, je voudrais une tranche de jambon, s'il vous plaît.*)

Élève B Answer your partner's questions based on the information below.

Élève B Now you are the vendor. Ask your partner the following questions. Correct answers are in parentheses.

un pot

un paquet

une boîte

un litre

une tranche

1. Vous voulez de la moutarde?
   (*Oui, je voudrais un pot de moutarde, s'il vous plaît.*)

2. Vous voulez du beurre?
   (*Oui, je voudrais deux cent cinquante grammes de beurre, s'il vous plaît.*)

3. Vous voulez des œufs?
   (*Oui, je voudrais une douzaine d'œufs, s'il vous plaît.*)

4. Vous voulez des petits pois?
   (*Oui, je voudrais une boîte de petits pois, s'il vous plaît.*)

5. Vous voulez de l'eau minérale?
   (*Oui, je voudrais une bouteille d'eau minérale, s'il vous plaît.*)

Activity 18

Élève A Ask your partner the following questions. Correct answers are in parentheses.

1. Qui fait le déjeuner?
   (Moi, je fais le déjeuner.)

2. Qui fait du français?
   (Nous faisons du français.)

3. Qui fait des études?
   (Tu fais des études.)

4. Qui fait les exercices?
   (Alain et Eric font les exercices.)

5. Qui fait le gâteau?
   (Vous faites le gâteau.)

Élève A Use the information in the chart below to answer your partner's questions.

Qui?	Activité
Moi, je	(faire) les courses
Hugo et Marie	(faire) un pique-nique
Nous	(faire) de l'allemand
Vous	(faire) la cuisine
Tu	(faire) les devoirs

Élève B Use the information in the chart below to answer your partner's questions.

Qui?	Activité
Moi, je	(faire) le déjeuner
Nous	(faire) du français
Tu	(faire) des études
Alain et Eric	(faire) les exercices
Vous	(faire) le gâteau

Élève B Ask your partner the following questions. Correct answers are in parentheses.

1. Qui fait les courses?
   (Moi, je fais les courses.)

2. Qui fait un pique-nique?
   (Hugo et Marie font un pique-nique.)

3. Qui fait de l'allemand?
   (Nous faisons de l'allemand.)

4. Qui fait la cuisine?
   (Vous faites la cuisine.)

5. Qui fait les devoirs?
   (Tu fais les devoirs.)

Activity 19

Élève A Ask your partner the following questions. Correct answers are in parentheses.

1. Qui veut aller au restaurant?
   (*Moi, je veux aller au restaurant.*)

2. Qui peut travailler après l'école?
   (*Il peut travailler après l'école.*)

3. Qui veut inviter des amis?
   (*Tu veux inviter des amis.*)

4. Qui veut manger maintenant?
   (*Nous voulons manger maintenant.*)

5. Qui peut regarder le film?
   (*Vous pouvez regarder le film.*)

6. Qui veut aller au marché?
   (*Pierre veut aller au marché.*)

7. Qui veut écouter des CD?
   (*Eric et Michel veulent écouter des CD.*)

Élève A Use the information in the chart below to answer your partner's questions.

Qui?	Activité
Moi, je	(pouvoir) regarder le film
Elle	(vouloir) aller au restaurant
Nous	(pouvoir) faire des sandwichs
Ils	(vouloir) écouter des CD
Tu	(pouvoir) manger maintenant
Alain	(pouvoir) aller au marché
Hugo et Marie	(pouvoir) inviter des amis

Élève B Use the information in the chart below to answer your partner's questions.

Qui?	Activité
Moi, je	(vouloir) aller au restaurant
Il	(pouvoir) travailler après l'école
Tu	(vouloir) inviter des amis
Nous	(vouloir) manger maintenant
Vous	(pouvoir) regarder le film
Pierre	(vouloir) aller au marché
Eric et Michel	(vouloir) écouter des CD

Élève B Ask your partner the following questions. Correct answers are in parentheses.

1. Qui peut regarder le film?
   (*Moi, je peux regarder le film.*)

2. Qui veut aller au restaurant?
   (*Elle veut aller au restaurant.*)

3. Qui peut faire des sandwichs?
   (*Nous pouvons faire des sandwichs.*)

4. Qui veut écouter des CD?
   (*Ils veulent écouter des CD.*)

5. Qui peut manger maintenant?
   (*Tu peux manger maintenant.*)

6. Qui peut aller au marché?
   (*Alain peut aller au marché.*)

7. Qui peut inviter des amis?
   (*Hugo et Marie peuvent inviter des amis.*)

Activity 20

Élève A Use the information in the chart below to answer your partner's questions.

Elle porte…	Elle voit… dans la vitrine.

Élève A Ask your partner the following questions. Correct answers are in parentheses.

1. Marc porte un anorak?
   (Oui, il porte un anorak.)

2. Marc porte un blouson?
   (Non, il voit un blouson dans la vitrine.)

3. Marc porte un pull?
   (Oui, il porte un pull.)

4. Marc porte un t-shirt?
   (Non, il voit un t-shirt dans la vitrine.)

5. Marc porte une paire de chaussures?
   (Oui, il porte une paire de chaussures.)

6. Marc porte un survêtement?
   (Non, il voit un survêtement dans la vitrine.)

Élève B Use the information in the chart below to answer your partner's questions.

Il porte…	Il voit… dans la vitrine.

Élève B Ask your partner the following questions. Correct answers are in parentheses.

1. Chloé porte des sandales?
   (Oui, elle porte des sandales.)

2. Chloé porte un anorak?
   (Non, elle voit un anorak dans la vitrine.)

3. Chloé porte un blouson?
   (Oui, elle porte un blouson.)

4. Chloé porte une paire de chaussures?
   (Non, elle voit une paire de chaussures dans la vitrine.)

5. Chloé porte un t-shirt?
   (Oui, elle porte un t-shirt.)

6. Chloé porte un manteau?
   (Non, elle voit un manteau dans la vitrine.)

Activity 21

Élève A Find out your partner's opinion of different clothing items. Correct answers are in parentheses.

1. Il est joli, le pull bleu. Tu ne trouves pas?
   (Non, il est trop serré.)

2. Il est joli, le manteau gris. Tu ne trouves pas?
   (Non, il est trop long.)

3. Il est joli, l'anorak rouge. Tu ne trouves pas?
   (Non, il est trop cher.)

4. Elle est jolie, la jupe verte. Tu ne trouves pas?
   (Non, elle est un peu courte.)

5. Elles sont jolies, les chaussures marron. Tu ne trouves pas?
   (Oui, c'est ma couleur favorite.)

Élève A Use the information below to answer your partner's questions.

un peu large

Oui, c'est ma couleur favorite.

trop grand

trop petit

trop chères

Élève B Use the information below to answer your partner's questions.

trop serré

trop long

trop cher

un peu courte

Oui, c'est ma couleur favorite.

Élève B Find out your partner's opinion of different clothing items. Correct answers are in parentheses.

1. Il est joli, le short vert. Tu ne trouves pas?
   (Non, il est trop grand.)

2. Il est joli, le t-shirt orange. Tu ne trouves pas?
   (Non, il est trop petit.)

3. Elles sont jolies, les sandales bleues. Tu ne trouves pas?
   (Non, elles sont trop chères.)

4. Il est joli, le survêtement jaune. Tu ne trouves pas?
   (Non, il est un peu large.)

5. Il est joli, le blouson bleu. Tu ne trouves pas?
   (Oui, c'est ma couleur favorite.)

Activity 22

Élève A Use the information in the chart below to answer your partner's questions.

Qui?	Activité
Moi, je	(mettre) la télé le matin
Les serveurs	(mettre) la table au restaurant
Ma mère	(mettre) une jupe pour aller au marché
Nous	(mettre) des chaussettes rouges
Tu	(mettre) des baskets pour faire du jogging
Vous	(mettre) un pantalon pour aller à l'école

Élève A Ask your partner the following questions. Correct answers are in parentheses.

1. Qui met un short?
   (Moi, je mets un short pour faire du jogging.)

2. Qui met la radio le matin?
   (Mes copains mettent la radio le matin.)

3. Qui met une cravate?
   (Mon père met une cravate pour aller au travail.)

4. Qui met la table?
   (Vous mettez la table pour le dîner.)

5. Qui met un jean?
   (Tu mets un jean pour aller au cinéma.)

6. Qui met un complet?
   (Nous mettons un complet pour aller à un mariage.)

Élève B Use the information in the chart below to answer your partner's questions.

Qui?	Activité
Moi, je	(mettre) un short pour faire du jogging
Mes copains	(mettre) la radio le matin
Mon père	(mettre) une cravate pour aller au travail
Vous	(mettre) la table pour le dîner
Tu	(mettre) un jean pour aller au cinéma
Nous	(mettre) un complet pour aller à un mariage

Élève B Ask your partner the following questions. Correct answers are in parentheses.

1. Qui met la télé?
   (Moi, je mets la télé le matin.)

2. Qui met la table?
   (Les serveurs mettent la table au restaurant.)

3. Qui met une jupe?
   (Ma mère met une jupe pour aller au marché.)

4. Qui met des chaussettes rouges?
   (Nous mettons des chaussettes rouges.)

5. Qui met des baskets?
   (Tu mets des baskets pour faire du jogging.)

6. Qui met un pantalon?
   (Vous mettez un pantalon pour aller à l'école.)

Activity 23

Élève A Read the statements about clothing to your partner. Your partner does not agree with what you believe to be true. Correct answers are in parentheses.

1. Moi, je crois que le polo est plus grand que le t-shirt.
(Non, je vois que le t-shirt est plus grand que le polo.) or *(Non, je vois que le polo est plus petit que le t-shirt.)*

2. Moi, je crois que la chemise est plus grande que le polo.
(Non, je vois que la chemise est aussi grande que le polo.)

3. Moi, je crois que la jupe plissée est moins élégante que le chemisier.
(Non, je vois que la jupe plissée est aussi élégante que le chemisier.)

Élève A Your partner tells you what he or she thinks about articles of clothing. Use the chart below to give your partner the correct information. Begin your response with **Non, je vois que...**

cher	l'anorak $ $ $	le blouson $	le manteau $ $ $ $ $ $
confortables	les baskets + +		les chaussures + +

Élève B Your partner tells you what he or she thinks about articles of clothing. Use the chart below to give your partner the correct information. Begin your response with **Non, je vois que...**

grand(e)	le t-shirt + + + + +	la chemise + + +	le polo + + +
élégant(e)	la jupe plissée + +		le chemisier + +

Élève B Read the statements about clothing to your partner. Your partner does not agree with what you believe to be true. Correct answers are in parentheses.

1. Moi, je crois que les chaussures sont moins confortables que les baskets.
(Non, je vois que les chaussures sont aussi confortables que les baskets.)

2. Moi, je crois que le blouson est aussi cher que l'anorak.
(Non, je vois que le blouson est moins cher que l'anorak.) or *(Non, je vois que l'anorak est plus cher que le blouson.)*

3. Moi, je crois que l'anorak est plus cher que le manteau.
(Non, je vois que le manteau est plus cher que l'anorak.) or *(Non, je vois que l'anorak est moins cher que le manteau.)*

Activity 24

Élève A Make the following statements to your partner. He or she will add the location where the activity takes place. Correct answers are in parentheses.

1. Le passager vérifie la carte d'embarquement.
   (*Le passager vérifie la carte d'embarquement à la porte d'embarquement.*)

2. Le passager demande une place.
   (*Le passager demande une place côté couloir.*)

3. Le passager vérifie son billet.
   (*Le passager vérifie son billet au comptoir de la compagnie aérienne.*)

4. Le passager va passer par le contrôle de sécurité.
   (*Le passager va passer par le contrôle de sécurité dans l'aérogare.*)

Élève A Your partner will make a statement about an activity. Tell where each activity takes place according to the chart below.

Activité	Où
prendre un vol	à l'aéroport
vérifier l'heure du départ	sur l'écran
décoller	sur la piste
faire enregistrer ses bagages	au comptoir de la compagnie aérienne

Élève B Your partner will make a statement about an activity. Tell where each activity takes place according to the chart below.

Activité	Où
vérifier la carte d'embarquement	à la porte d'embarquement
demander une place	côté couloir
vérifier son billet	au comptoir de la compagnie aérienne
passer par le contrôle de sécurité	dans l'aérogare

Élève B Make the following statements to your partner. He or she will add the location where the activity takes place. Correct answers are in parentheses.

1. Le passager va prendre un vol.
   (*Oui, le passager va prendre un vol à l'aéroport.*)

2. Le passager vérifie l'heure du départ.
   (*Oui, le passager vérifie l'heure du départ sur l'écran.*)

3. L'avion décolle.
   (*Oui, l'avion décolle sur la piste.*)

4. Le passager fait enregistrer ses bagages.
   (*Oui, le passager fait enregistrer ses bagages au comptoir de la compagnie aérienne.*)

Activity 25

Élève A Ask your partner the following questions. Correct answers are in parentheses.

1. Il faut attacher sa ceinture de sécurité quand?
   (avant le décollage)
2. Qui sert les boissons?
   (le steward)
3. On peut fumer quand?
   (après le vol)
4. On ramasse les plateaux quand?
   (après le repas)
5. Il faut un passeport quand?
   (pour un vol international)
6. Il faut mettre vos bagages à main où?
   (sous le siège devant vous)

Élève A Answer your partner's questions. Choose from the answers below.

1. avant le vol / après le vol
2. le passager / le pilote
3. avant le vol / pendant le vol
4. avant le décollage / pendant le décollage
5. dans la cabine / dans le coffre à bagages
6. le pilote / le passager

Élève B Answer your partner's questions. Choose from the answers below.

1. avant le décollage / après le décollage
2. le steward / le pilote
3. pendant le vol / après le vol
4. après le repas / pendant le repas
5. pour un vol intérieur / pour un vol international
6. sous le siège devant vous / dans le couloir

Élève B Ask your partner the following questions. Correct answers are in parentheses.

1. Il faut faire ses valises quand?
   (avant le vol)
2. Qui remplit sa carte de débarquement?
   (le passager)
3. On sert un repas quand?
   (pendant le vol)
4. Il faut mettre ses bagages sous le siège quand?
   (avant le décollage)
5. Les toilettes sont où?
   (dans la cabine)
6. Qui dort pendant le vol?
   (le passager)

Activity 26

3.

2.

1.

Élève A Answer your partner's questions according to the illustrations.

Élève A Ask your partner the following questions. Correct answers are in parentheses.

1. Qu'est-ce que vous faites?
   (Nous remplissons la carte de débarquement.)

2. Qu'est-ce-que l'hôtesse fait?
   (Elle sert le dîner.)

3. Qu'est-ce que l'avion fait?
   (L'avion atterrit.)

Élève B Answer your partner's questions according to the illustrations.

1.

2.

3.

Élève B Ask your partner the following questions. Correct answers are in parentheses.

1. Qu'est-ce que le steward fait?
   (Il sert des boissons.)

2. Qu'est-ce que le passager fait?
   (Il sort ses bagages du coffre à bagages.)

3. Qu'est-ce que tu fais pendant le vol?
   (Je dors pendant le vol.)

Activity 27

Élève A Look at the picture below; then choose the best response from the options given to answer your partner's questions.

1. un journal / un billet

2. le guichet / la voie

3. au buffet / au kiosque

4. sur le quai / dans la salle d'attente

5. au buffet de la gare / au guichet

Élève A Ask your partner the following questions. Correct answers are in parentheses.

1. Que font les passagers?
   (Ils font la queue.)

2. Qu'est-ce que Ahmed achète?
   (un billet)

3. Il achète son billet où?
   (au guichet)

4. Tu achètes un billet Paris-Lyon-Paris?
   (Oui, un aller-retour.)

5. Tu achètes un billet Paris-Lyon?
   (Oui, un aller simple.)

Élève B Look at the pictures below; then choose the best response from the options given to answer your partner's questions.

1. Ils attendent le train. / Ils font la queue.

2. un billet / une carte postale

3. au kiosque / au guichet

4. Oui, un aller simple. / Oui, un aller-retour.

5. Oui, un aller simple. / Oui, un aller-retour.

Élève B Ask your partner the following questions. Correct answers are in parentheses.

1. Qu'est-ce que Monsieur Roget achète?
   (un journal)

2. Qu'est-ce que Monsieur Laporte regarde?
   (la voie)

3. Monsieur Boucher fait la queue où?
   (au kiosque)

4. Monsieur Longtemps attend le train où?
   (dans la salle d'attente)

5. Paul prend une boisson où?
   (au buffet de la gare)

Activity 28

Pierre

Madame Renoir

Élève A Answer your partner's questions based on the pictures below.

Élève A Ask your partner the following questions. Correct answers are in parentheses.

1–2.

1. Les voyageurs sont debout dans le wagon?
   (Non, ils sont assis.)

2. Anne lit le journal?
   (Non, elle écrit une carte postale.)

3. Paul et Sylvie sont où?
   (Ils sont devant la gare.)

4. Ils attendent une amie?
   (Oui, ils attendent une amie.)

3–5.

5. Paul commence à perdre patience?
   (Oui, il commence à perdre patience.)

Élève B Answer your partner's questions based on the pictures below.

1–2.

Anne

3–5.

Paul et Sylvie

Élève B Ask your partner the following questions. Correct answers are in parentheses.

1. Madame Renoir est assise?
   (Non, elle est debout.)

2. Pierre écrit des cartes postales?
   (Non, il lit le journal.)

3. Le passager est debout?
   (Non, il est assis.)

4. Le contrôleur contrôle les boissons?
   (Non, il contrôle les billets.)

5. Toutes les places sont occupées?
   (Non, toutes les places ne sont pas occupées.)

Activity 29

Élève A Say each of the following words to your partner. He or she will make a sentence using the word and one of the verbs listed. Possible answers are in parentheses.

1. un voyageur
   (J'attends un voyageur.)

2. les annonces
   (J'entends les annonces.)

3. un ami
   (J'attends un ami.) or
   (J'écris à un ami.)

4. des choses amusantes
   (Je dis des choses amusantes.) or
   (J'écris des choses amusantes.)

5. les bagages
   (Je descends les bagages.) or
   (J'attends les bagages.)

Élève A Your partner will say a word or phrase. Use the word with one of the verbs below to make a statement about what you do.

Example: You hear: **Le journal.**
You respond: **Je lis le journal.** *or*
Je vends le journal.

vendre	descendre	répondre	perdre	lire

Élève B Your partner will say a word or phrase. Use the word with one of the verbs below to make a statement about what you do.

Example: You hear: **Le train.**
You respond: **J'attends le train.** *or*
Je descends du train.

attendre	descendre	entendre	écrire	dire

Élève B Say each of the following words to your partner. He or she will make a sentence using the word and one of the verbs listed. Possible answers are in parentheses.

1. des cartes postales
   (Je vends des cartes postales.) or
   (Je lis des cartes postales.)

2. la voiture
   (Je descends de la voiture.) or
   (Je vends la voiture.)

3. la question
   (Je réponds à la question.) or
   (Je lis la question.)

4. patience (Je perds patience.)

5. des magazines
   (Je lis des magazines.) or
   (Je vends des magazines.)

Activity 30

InfoGap

Élève A Ask your partner the following questions. Correct responses are in parentheses.

1. Est-ce que Rennes joue contre Auxerre?
   (Non, Rennes joue contre Lille.)

2. Il y a beaucoup de spectateurs dans le stade?
   (Oui, il y a beaucoup de spectateurs dans le stade.)

3. Le gardien de but, il bloque le ballon?
   (Non, il ne bloque pas le ballon.)

4. Le ballon entre dans le but?
   (Oui, le ballon entre dans le but.)

Élève A Answer your partner's questions based on the illustration.

Élève B Answer your partner's questions based on the illustration.

Élève B Ask your partner the following questions. Correct responses are in parentheses.

1. Un joueur a donné un coup de tête dans le ballon?
   (Non, un joueur a donné un coup de pied dans le ballon.)

2. Il y a beaucoup de places libres dans les gradins?
   (Non, les gradins sont pleins.)

3. Le gardien arrête le ballon?
   (Non, le gardien n'arrête pas le ballon.)

4. Le joueur a marqué un but?
   (Oui, le joueur a marqué un but.)

Activity 31

CHAPITRE 10, Mots 2, pages 328–329

Élève A Read the following statements to your partner, some of which are false. Your partner will correct them. The correct answers are in parentheses.

1. Le basket-ball est un sport individuel.
   (*Non, le basket-ball est un sport d'équipe.*)
2. Un joueur de basket sert le ballon.
   (*Non, un joueur de basket ne sert pas le ballon.*)
3. Les joueurs dribblent le ballon pendant un match de basket.
   (*Oui, …*)
4. Une joueuse lance le ballon dans le panier pendant un match de basket.
   (*Oui, …*)
5. Les joueurs de basket donnent un coup de pied au ballon.
   (*Non, les joueurs de basket dribblent le ballon.*)

Élève A Listen to the statements made by your partner, some of which are false. Correct the false statements.

Élève B Listen to the statements made by your partner, some of which are false. Correct the false statements.

Élève B Read the following statements to your partner, some of which are false. Your partner will correct them. The correct answers are in parentheses.

1. Le volley-ball est un sport individuel.
   (*Non, le volley-ball est un sport d'équipe.*)
2. Les joueurs dribblent le ballon pendant un match de volley-ball.
   (*Non, les joueurs ne dribblent pas le ballon pendant un match de volley-ball.*)
3. Une joueuse de volley-ball sert le ballon.
   (*Oui, … *)
4. Une joueuse de volley-ball renvoie le ballon par-dessus le filet.
   (*Oui, … *)
5. Le ballon doit toucher le sol pendant un match de volley-ball.
   (*Non, le ballon ne doit pas toucher le sol.*)

Activity 32

Élève A Ask your partner who did the following activities. Correct answers are in parentheses.

1. Qui a joué au foot?
   (*Chloé a joué au foot.*)

2. Qui a perdu le match?
   (*Tu as perdu le match.*)

3. Qui a regardé le match?
   (*Les spectateurs ont regardé le match.*)

4. Qui a choisi une place?
   (*Moi, j'ai choisi une place.*)

5. Qui a dansé?
   (*Nous avons dansé.*)

Élève A Your partner wants to know who did the activities below. Answer based on the information in the chart.

Qui?	Activité
Les spectateurs	attendre longtemps
L'arbitre	voyager
Nous	gagner la coupe
Tu	finir le match
Julien	lancer le ballon

Élève B Your partner wants to know who did the activities below. Answer based on the information in the chart.

Qui?	Activité
Chloé	jouer au foot
Tu	perdre le match
Les spectateurs	regarder le match
Moi, je	choisir une place
Nous	danser

Élève B Ask your partner who did the following activities. Correct answers are in parentheses.

1. Qui a attendu longtemps?
   (*Les spectateurs ont attendu longtemps.*)

2. Qui a voyagé?
   (*L'arbitre a voyagé.*)

3. Qui a gagné la coupe.
   (*Nous avons gagné la coupe.*)

4. Qui a fini le match?
   (*Tu as fini le match.*)

5. Qui a lancé le ballon?
   (*Julien a lancé le ballon.*)

Activity 33

Élève A Ask your partner who does the following activities. Correct answers are in parentheses.

1. Qui doit passer un examen?
(*Nathalie doit passer un examen.*)

2. Qui reçoit le ballon?
(*Tu reçois le ballon.*)

3. Qui boit de la limonade?
(*Les enfants boivent de la limonade.*)

4. Qui doit être content?
(*Vous devez être contents.*)

5. Qui boit du lait?
(*Moi, je bois du lait.*)

Élève A Your partner wants to know who does the following. Answer based on the information in the chart.

Qui?	Activité
Rémi	boire du coca
Tu	devoir étudier
Les copains	recevoir un cadeau
Moi, je	boire de l'eau
Nous	devoir travailler

Élève B Your partner wants to know who does the following. Answer based on the information in the chart.

Qui?	Activité
Nathalie	devoir passer un examen
Tu	recevoir le ballon
Les enfants	boire de la limonade
Vous	devoir être contents
Moi, je	boire du lait

Élève B Ask your partner who does the following activities. Correct answers are in parentheses.

1. Qui boit du coca?
(*Rémi boit du coca.*)

2. Qui doit étudier?
(*Tu dois étudier.*)

3. Qui reçoit un cadeau?
(*Les copains reçoivent un cadeau.*)

4. Qui boit de l'eau?
(*Moi, je bois de l'eau.*)

5. Qui doit travailler?
(*Nous devons travailler.*)

Activity 34

Élève A Ask your partner the following questions. Correct answers are in parentheses.

Élève A Answer your partner's questions based on the picture below.

1. Marc fait de la planche à voile?
   (Oui, Marc fait de la planche à voile.)

2. Il pleut?
   (Non, il fait beau.) or
   (Non, il ne pleut pas.)

3. Sandrine fait une promenade?
   (Non, elle fait du ski nautique.)

4. Les amis sont où?
   (Les amis sont à la plage.)

5. Ils vont faire du surf?
   (Oui, ils vont faire du surf.)

Élève B Answer your partner's questions based on the pictures below.

1–2.

3.

4–5.

Élève B Ask your partner the following questions. Correct answers are in parentheses.

1. Jeanne a passé la journée à la piscine?
   (Non, elle a passé la journée à la plage.)

2. Elle a mis un maillot de bain?
   (Oui, elle a mis un maillot de bain.)

3. Elle a mis de la crème solaire?
   (Oui, elle a mis de la crème solaire.)

4. Il a fait mauvais temps?
   (Non, il a fait beau.)

5. Elle a pris un bain de soleil?
   (Oui, elle a pris un bain de soleil.)

Activity 35

Élève A Answer your partner's questions based on the picture below.

Élève A Ask your partner the following questions. Correct answers are in parentheses.

1. Qu'est-ce qu'on prend pour monter au sommet?
   (On prend un télésiège.)

2. Quel temps fait-il à la montagne?
   (Il fait froid.)

3. Il y a beaucoup de neige?
   (Oui, il y a beaucoup de neige.)

4. On fait du ski à la montagne?
   (Oui, on fait du ski à la montagne.)

Pauline

Élève B Answer your partner's questions based on the picture below.

Élève B Ask your partner the following questions. Correct answers are in parentheses.

1. Pauline a mis un anorak de quelle couleur?
   (Elle a mis un anorak bleu.)

2. Elle est bonne en ski?
   (Non, elle est débutante.)

3. Elle apprend à faire du ski?
   (Oui, elle apprend à faire du ski.)

4. Elle a eu un bon moniteur?
   (Oui, elle a eu un bon moniteur.)

Activity 36

CHAPITRE 11, Structure, pages 364–366

Élève A Read your partner the following statements. Correct responses are in parentheses.

1. Je fais un voyage en hiver.
(J'ai fait un voyage en hiver l'année dernière.)

2. Je prends des leçons de ski alpin.
(J'ai pris des leçons de ski alpin l'année dernière.)

3. J'apprends à faire du patin à glace.
(J'ai appris à faire du patin à glace l'année dernière.)

4. Je dis "Merci" au moniteur.
(J'ai dit "Merci" au moniteur l'année dernière.)

5. Je mets un bonnet.
(J'ai mis un bonnet l'année dernière.)

6. Je lis un livre pour les débutants.
(J'ai lu un livre pour les débutants l'année dernière.)

Élève A Your partner will tell you what he or she is doing today. Use the **passé composé** of the verb below to tell him or her you did the same thing last year (**l'année dernière**).

1. apprendre
2. prendre
3. mettre
4. faire
5. avoir
6. boire

Élève B Your partner will tell you what he or she is doing today. Use the **passé composé** of the verb below to tell him or her you did the same thing last year (**l'année dernière**).

1. faire
2. prendre
3. apprendre
4. dire
5. mettre
6. lire

Élève B Read your partner the following statements. Correct responses are in parentheses.

1. J'apprends à faire du ski.
(J'ai appris à faire du ski l'année dernière.)

2. Je prends le télésiège.
(J'ai pris le télésiège l'année dernière.)

3. Je mets un anorak.
(J'ai mis un anorak l'année dernière.)

4. Je fais du ski de fond.
(J'ai fait du ski de fond l'année dernière.)

5. J'ai un bon moniteur.
(J'ai eu un bon moniteur l'année dernière.)

6. Je bois du chocolat chaud.
(J'ai bu du chocolat chaud l'année dernière.)

InfoGap ❖ H37

Activity 37

Élève A Read your partner the following statements. Correct responses are in parentheses.

1. J'arrive au bord de la mer.
   (Hier, je suis arrivé[e] au bord de la mer.)

2. Je monte dans le train.
   (Hier, je suis monté[e] dans le train.)

3. Je vais à la montagne.
   (Hier, je suis allé[e] à la montagne.)

4. Je sors de la gare.
   (Hier, je suis sorti[e] de la gare.)

5. Je tombe sur la glace.
   (Hier, je suis tombé[e] sur la glace.)

Élève A Your partner will tell you what he or she is doing today. Use the **passé composé** of the verb below to tell him or her you did the same thing yesterday **(hier).**

1. partir
2. descendre
3. rentrer
4. entrer
5. aller

Élève B Your partner will tell you what he or she is doing today. Use the **passé composé** of the verb below to tell him or her you did the same thing yesterday **(hier).**

1. arriver
2. monter
3. aller
4. sortir
5. tomber

Élève B Read your partner the following statements. Correct responses are in parentheses.

1. Je pars à l'heure.
   (Hier, je suis parti[e] à l'heure.)

2. Je descends du train.
   (Hier, je suis descendu[e] du train.)

3. Je rentre à l'hôtel.
   (Hier, je suis rentré[e] à l'hôtel.)

4. J'entre dans la classe de français.
   (Hier, je suis entré[e] dans la classe de français.)

5. Je vais à la plage.
   (Hier, je suis allé[e] à la plage.)

Activity 38

Élève A Your partner will read you a statement about daily routine. Use the picture cues to tell him or her which products or equipment are needed.

Élève A Read your partner the following statements. He or she will tell you how people use the items in the daily routine. Correct responses are in parentheses.

1. Il faut une brosse à dents. Il faut du dentifrice.
   (*Elle se brosse les dents.*)

2. Il faut un peigne.
   (*Elle se peigne.*)

3. Il faut un rasoir. Il faut une glace.
   (*Il se rase.*)

Élève B Your partner will tell you which products or equipment are needed in a daily routine. Use the picture cues to tell him or her what people use the items for.

1.

2.

3.

Élève B Read your partner the following statements about daily routine. He or she will tell you what products or equipment are needed. Correct responses are in parentheses.

1. Elle se brosse les cheveux.
   (*Il faut une brosse.*)

2. Il se lave.
   (*Il faut du savon. Il faut un gant de toilette.*)

3. Il se lave les cheveux.
   (*Il faut du shampooing.*)

Élève A Answer your partner's questions based on the pictures below.

Élève A Ask your partner the following questions. Correct answers are in parentheses.

1. Qui regarde la télé?
   (Christophe et Julie regardent la télé.)

2. Qui regarde son émission favorite?
   (Christophe regarde son émission favorite.)

3. Qui peut changer de chaîne?
   (Christophe peut changer de chaîne.)

4. Julie fait ses devoirs?
   (Non, Julie ne fait pas ses devoirs.)

5. Christophe s'est bien amusé?
   (Oui, il s'est bien amusé.)

Élève B Answer your partner's questions based on the picture below.

Élève B Ask your partner the following questions. Correct answers are in parentheses.

1. Qui débarrasse la table après le dîner?
   (Mme Fauvet débarrasse la table après le dîner.)

2. Qui fait la vaisselle?
   (M. Fauvet et Jean font la vaisselle.)

3. Qui fait ses devoirs?
   (Paul fait ses devoirs.)

4. Qui est sorti?
   (Sophie est sortie.)

5. Sophie s'est bien amusée?
   (Oui, elle s'est bien amusée.)

Élève A — (top right, inverted)

Élève A Ask your partner the following questions. Correct answers are in parentheses.

1. Qui se maquille?
   (Sophie se maquille.)

2. Qui se réveille tôt?
   (Vous vous réveillez tôt.)

3. Qui se regarde dans la glace?
   (Moi, je me regarde dans la glace.)

4. Qui s'habille?
   (Les enfants s'habillent.)

5. Qui se promène dans le parc?
   (Nous nous promenons dans le parc.)

Élève A Answer your partner's questions based on the information in the chart below.

Qui?	Activité
Moi, je	se lever tôt
Les étudiants	se coucher tard
Paul	se raser
Nous	se brosser les dents
Tu	se peigner

Élève B

Élève B Answer your partner's questions based on the information in the chart below.

Qui?	Activité
Sophie	se maquiller
Vous	se réveiller tôt
Moi, je	se regarder dans la glace
Les enfants	s'habiller
Nous	se promener dans le parc

Élève B Ask your partner the following questions. Correct answers are in parentheses.

1. Qui se lève tôt?
   (Moi, je me lève tôt.)

2. Qui se couche tard?
   (Les étudiants se couchent tard.)

3. Qui se rase?
   (Paul se rase.)

4. Qui se brosse les dents?
   (Nous nous brossons les dents.)

5. Qui se peigne?
   (Tu te peignes.)

Activity 41

Élève A Ask your partner the following questions. Correct answers are in parentheses.

1. Qui s'est maquillé?
   (Sophie s'est maquillée.)

2. Qui s'est réveillé tôt?
   (Vous vous êtes réveillé[s] tôt.)

3. Qui s'est regardé dans la glace?
   (Moi, je me suis regardé[e] dans la glace.)

4. Qui s'est habillé?
   (Les enfants se sont habillés.)

5. Qui s'est promené dans le parc?
   (Nous nous sommes promenés dans le parc.)

Élève A Answer your partner's questions based on the information in the chart below.

Qui?	Activité
Moi, je	se lever tôt
Les étudiants	se coucher tard
Paul	se raser
Nous	se brosser les dents
Tu	se peigner

Élève B Answer your partner's questions based on the information in the chart below.

Qui?	Activité
Sophie	se maquiller
Vous	se réveiller tôt
Moi, je	se regarder dans la glace
Les enfants	s'habiller
Nous	se promener dans le parc

Élève B Ask your partner the following questions. Correct answers are in parentheses.

1. Qui s'est levé tôt?
   (Moi, je me suis levé[e] tôt.)

2. Qui s'est couché tard?
   (Les étudiants se sont couchés tard.)

3. Qui s'est rasé?
   (Paul s'est rasé.)

4. Qui s'est brossé les dents?
   (Nous nous sommes brossé les dents.)

5. Qui s'est peigné?
   (Tu t'es peigné[e].)

Activity 42

Élève A Answer your partner's questions according to the illustrations.

Élève A Ask your partner the following questions. Correct answers are in parentheses.

1. Qu'est-ce que tu aimes comme film?
   (J'aime les documentaires.)

2. Qu'est-ce qu'on monte?
   (On monte Roméo et Juliette.)

3. Tu aimes mieux aller au cinéma ou louer des vidéos ou des DVD?
   (J'aime mieux louer des vidéos ou des DVD.)

Élève B Answer your partner's questions according to the illustrations.

1.

2.
Roméo
et
Juliette

ballet en trois actes
d'après William Shakespeare

musique
Sergueï Prokofiev

chorégraphie et mise en scène
Rudolf Noureev

réglées par
**Patricia Ruanne
Frederick Jahn**

choréologue
Kristin Johnson

décors
Ezio Frigerio
avec la collaboration de
Alexandre Beliaev

costumes
Ezio Frigerio et Mauro Pagano

lumières
Vinicio Cheli

production créée pour le Ballet
de l'Opéra en 1984

Orchestre de l'Opéra National de Paris

direction
Vello Pähn

fin du spectacle vers 22 h 40

3.

Élève B Ask your partner the following questions. Correct answers are in parentheses.

1. Qu'est-ce que tu aimes comme film?
   (J'aime les dessins animés.)

2. Tu as déjà vu le chanteur?
   (Non, mais j'ai déjà vu la danseuse.)

3. Tu vas voir une pièce de théâtre?
   (Non, je vais voir un film au cinéma.)

Activity 43

Élève A Answer your partner's questions according to the illustration.

Élève A Ask your partner the following questions. Correct answers are in parentheses.

1. C'est un musée ou un théâtre?
   (C'est un musée.)

2. Le musée est ouvert ou fermé?
   (Le musée est ouvert.)

3. Il y a beaucoup de tableaux ou de statues au musée?
   (Il y a beaucoup de tableaux.)

Élève B Answer your partner's questions according to the photograph.

Élève B Ask your partner the following questions. Correct answers are in parentheses.

1. Elle est peintre ou sculpteur?
   (Elle est peintre.)

2. Il est peintre ou sculpteur?
   (Il est sculpteur.)

3. Qu'est-ce qu'il y a au musée?
   (Il y a une exposition de peinture et sculpture au musée.)

Activity 44

Élève A You are familiar with some people, places, and things, but your partner knows some facts or information he or she wants to share with you about them. Make your statement and your partner will respond. Correct responses are in parentheses.

1. Je connais Nathalie.
   (Je sais qu'elle habite à Grenoble.)
2. Je connais Hamlet.
   (Je sais que c'est une pièce de Shakespeare.)
3. Je connais Paris.
   (Je sais que c'est la capitale de la France.)
4. Je connais l'œuvre de Degas.
   (Je sais que Degas est un peintre français.)
5. Je connais Paul.
   (Je sais quel est son numéro de téléphone.)

Élève A Your partner and some of his or her friends are familiar with certain people, places, and things, but you and your friends have some facts or information to share. Add your comment according to the cues. Begin your statements with **Nous savons…**

1. …qu'ils sont très beaux.
2. …quelle pièce on joue en ce moment.
3. …où se trouve le théâtre.
4. …qu'elles savent danser le tango.
5. …qu'elles sont célèbres.

Élève B Your partner and some of his or her friends are familiar with certain people, places, and things, but you and your friends have some facts or information to share. Add your comment according to the cues. Begin your statements with **Je sais…**

1. …qu'elle habite à Grenoble.
2. …que c'est une pièce de Shakespeare.
3. …que c'est la capitale de la France.
4. …que Degas est un peintre français.
5. …quel est son numéro de téléphone.

Élève B You are familiar with some people, places, and things, but your partner knows some facts or information he or she wants to share with you about them. Make your statement and your partner will respond. Correct responses are in parentheses.

1. Nous connaissons les tableaux de Monet, Manet et Renoir.
   (Nous savons qu'ils sont très beaux.)
2. Nous connaissons les pièces de Molière.
   (Nous savons quelle pièce on joue en ce moment.)
3. Nous connaissons la Comédie-Française.
   (Nous savons où se trouve le théâtre.)
4. Nous connaissons des danseuses.
   (Nous savons qu'elles savent danser le tango.)
5. Nous connaissons les sculptures de Rodin.
   (Nous savons qu'elles sont célèbres.)

Activity 45

Élève A Ask your partner the following questions. Correct answers are in parentheses.

1. Tu connais les tableaux de Monet?
   (Oui, je les connais.)

2. Tu vois la sculpture moderne?
   (Non, je ne la vois pas.)

3. Tu sais le nom du film?
   (Oui, je le sais.)

4. Tu lis les sous-titres?
   (Non, je ne les lis pas.)

5. Tu veux voir la pièce?
   (Oui, je veux la voir.)

Élève A Your partner will ask a question. Respond according to the cues, using the correct object pronoun.

1. Oui…

2. Non…

3. Oui…

4. Oui…

5. Oui…

Élève B Your partner will ask a question. Respond according to the cues, using the correct object pronoun.

1. Oui…

2. Non…

3. Oui…

4. Non…

5. Oui…

Élève B Ask your partner the following questions. Correct answers are in parentheses.

1. Tu m'invites au cinéma?
   (Oui, je t'invite.)

2. Ce film te plaît?
   (Non, ce film ne me plaît pas.)

3. Je te parle au téléphone avant le film?
   (Oui, tu me parles au téléphone avant le film.)

4. Le prof nous donne beaucoup de devoirs?
   (Oui, le prof nous donne beaucoup de devoirs.)
   or
   (Oui, le prof vous donne beaucoup de devoirs.)

5. Julie vous dit quand le musée est fermé?
   (Oui, Julie nous dit quand le musée est fermé.)
   or
   (Oui, Julie me dit quand le musée est fermé.)

Activity 46

Élève A Use the pictures below to tell your partner about each person's symptoms.

Élève A Read your partner the following statements. He or she will tell you each person's symptoms. Possible responses are in parentheses.

1. Miriam n'est pas en bonne santé.
   (Elle a mal aux oreilles.)

2. Elle a besoin d'un mouchoir.
   (Elle a le nez qui coule.) or *(Elle a un rhume.)*

3. Anne est très malade, la pauvre.
   (Elle a des frissons.) or *(Elle a de la fièvre.)*

4. David ne se sent pas bien.
   (Il tousse.)

Élève B Use the pictures below to tell your partner about each person's symptoms.

1.

2.

3.

4.

Élève B Read your partner the following statements. He or she will tell you each person's symptoms. Possible responses are in parentheses.

1. Pauline est malade.
   (Elle est enrhumée.) or *(Elle éternue.)*

2. Martine est en mauvaise santé.
   (Elle a un rhume.) or *(Elle tousse.)*

3. Juliette ne se sent pas bien.
   (Elle a mal à la tête.)

4. Jeanne est très malade, la pauvre.
   (Elle a mal au ventre.)

Activity 47

Élève A You are the doctor and your partner, the patient, needs help. Ask him or her the following questions.

1. Où avez-vous mal?
   (J'ai mal au ventre.)

2. Qu'est-ce que vous avez?
   (J'ai une angine.)

3. Qu'est-ce que vous avez?
   (J'ai une sinusite aiguë.)

4. Qu'est-ce que vous avez?
   (J'ai un chat dans la gorge.)

5. Où avez-vous mal?
   (J'ai mal à la tête.)

Élève A Answer your partner's questions according to the cues below.

1. des frissons
2. aux oreilles
3. une allergie
4. une fièvre de cheval
5. une infection

Élève B Answer your partner's questions according to the cues below.

1. au ventre
2. une angine
3. une sinusite aiguë
4. un chat dans la gorge
5. à la tête

Élève B You are the doctor and your partner, the patient, needs help. Ask him or her the following questions.

1. Qu'est-ce que vous avez?
   (J'ai des frissons.)

2. Où avez-vous mal?
   (J'ai mal aux oreilles.)

3. Qu'est-ce que vous avez?
   (J'ai une allergie.)

4. Qu'est-ce que vous avez?
   (J'ai une fièvre de cheval.)

5. Qu'est-ce que vous avez?
   (J'ai une infection.)

Activity 48

InfoGap

Élève A — Ask your partner the following questions. Correct answers are in parentheses.

1. Tu parles souvent à ta copine?
   (Oui, je lui parle souvent.)

2. Les joueurs lancent le ballon à l'arbitre?
   (Oui, ils lui lancent le ballon.)

3. Le médecin prescrit des antibiotiques aux malades?
   (Oui, il leur prescrit des antibiotiques.)

4. Tu vas acheter un cadeau à ton frère?
   (Oui, je vais lui acheter un cadeau.)

5. Le pharmacien donne des médicaments à ta mère?
   (Oui, il lui donne des médicaments.)

Élève A — Answer your partner's questions using **lui** or **leur**.

1. Oui, je _____ dis bonjour.

2. Oui, il _____ vend des billets.

3. Oui, il _____ fait une ordonnance.

4. Oui, ils _____ téléphonent.

5. Oui, elle _____ dit qu'il a de la fièvre.

Élève B — Answer your partner's questions using **lui** or **leur**.

1. Oui, je _____ parle souvent.

2. Oui, ils _____ lancent le ballon.

3. Oui, il _____ prescrit des antibiotiques.

4. Oui, je vais _____ acheter un cadeau.

5. Oui, il _____ donne des médicaments.

Élève B — Ask your partner the following questions. Correct answers are in parentheses.

1. Tu dis bonjour à tes amis?
   (Oui, je leur dis bonjour.)

2. L'employé vend des billets à ton père?
   (Oui, il lui vend des billets.)

3. Le médecin fait une ordonnance à Marie?
   (Oui, il lui fait une ordonnance.)

4. Les malades téléphonent au professeur?
   (Oui, ils lui téléphonent.)

5. Sa mère dit à Paul qu'il a de la fièvre?
   (Oui, elle lui dit qu'il a de la fièvre.)

Activity 49

Élève A Use the imperative to answer your partner's question based on the information in the chart below.

Personne(s)	Activité
tu	prendre le métro
vous	attendre devant la porte
tu	faire du ski
tu	sortir ce soir
vous	regarder le film

Élève A Ask your partner the following questions. Correct answers are in parentheses.

1. Finir les devoirs?
   (Finis tes devoirs!)

2. Préparer le dîner?
   (Prépare le dîner!)

3. Choisir un film?
   (Choisissons un film!)

4. Travailler plus?
   (Travaille plus!)

5. Dîner au restaurant?
   (Dînons au restaurant!)

Élève B Use the imperative to answer your partner's questions based on the information in the chart below.

Personne(s)	Activité
tu	finir les devoirs
tu	préparer le dîner
nous	choisir un film
tu	travailler plus
nous	dîner au restaurant

Élève B Ask your partner the following questions. Correct answers are in parentheses.

1. Prendre le métro?
   (Prends le métro!)

2. Attendre devant la porte?
   (Attendez devant la porte!)

3. Faire du ski?
   (Fais du ski!)

4. Sortir ce soir?
   (Sors ce soir!)

5. Regardez le film?
   (Regardez le film!)

For students and parents/guardians

This guide is designed to help you as students achieve success as you embark on the adventure of learning another language and to enable your parents or guardians to help you on this exciting journey. There are many ways to learn new information. You may find some of these suggestions more useful than others, depending upon which style of learning works best for you. Before you begin, it is important to understand how we acquire language.

Receptive Skills

Each day of your life you receive a great deal of information through the use of language. In order to obtain (get, receive) this information, it is necessary to understand the language being used. It is necessary to understand the language in two different ways. First you must be able to understand what people are saying when they speak to you. This is referred to as oral or listening comprehension. Oral comprehension or listening comprehension is the ability to understand the spoken language.

You must also be able to understand what you read. This is referred to as reading comprehension. Reading comprehension is the ability to understand the written language.

Listening comprehension and reading comprehension are called the *receptive skills.* They are receptive skills because as you listen to what someone else says or read what someone else has written you receive information without having to produce any language yourself.

It is usually very easy to understand your native language. It is a bit more problematic to understand a second language that is new to you. As a beginner, you are still learning the sounds of the new language, and you recognize only a few words. Throughout **Bon voyage!** we will give you hints or suggestions to help you understand when people are speaking to you in

French or when you are reading in French. Following are some general hints to keep in mind.

HINTS FOR LISTENING COMPREHENSION
When you are listening to a person speaking French, don't try to understand every word. It is not necessary to understand everything to get the idea of what someone is saying. Listen for the general message. If some details escape you, it doesn't matter. Also, never try to translate what people are saying in French into English. It takes a great deal of experience and expertise to be a translator. Trying to translate will hinder your ability to understand.

HINTS FOR READING COMPREHENSION
Just as you will not always understand every word you hear in a conversation, you will not necessarily understand every word you encounter in a reading selection, either. In **Bon voyage!,** we have used only words you know or can easily figure out in the reading selections. This will make reading comprehension much easier for you. However, if at some time you wish to read a newspaper or magazine article in French, you will most certainly come across some unfamiliar words. Do not stop reading. Continue to read to get the "gist" of the selection. Try to guess the meanings of words you do not know.

Productive Skills

There are two productive skills in language. These two skills are speaking and writing. They are called productive skills because it is you who has to produce the language when you say or write something. When you speak or write, you have control over the language and which words you use. If you don't know how to say something, you don't have to say it. With the receptive skills, on the other hand, someone else produces the language that you listen to or read, and you have no control over the words they use.

There's no doubt that you can easily speak your native language. You can write, too, even though you may sometimes make errors in spelling or punctuation. In French, there's not a lot you can say or write as a beginner. You can only talk or write about those topics you have learned in French class.

HINTS FOR SPEAKING Try to be as accurate as possible when speaking. Try not to make mistakes. However, if you do, it's not the end of the world. French people will understand you. You're not expected to speak a language perfectly after a limited time. You have probably spoken with people from other countries who do not speak English perfectly, but you can understand them. Remember:

* Keep talking! Don't become inhibited for fear of making a mistake.
* Say what you know how to say. Don't try to branch out in the early stages and attempt to talk about topics or situations you have not yet learned in French.

HINTS FOR WRITING There are many activities in each lesson of **Bon voyage!** that will help you speak and write in French. When you have to write something on your own, however, without the guidance or assistance of an activity in your book, be sure to choose a topic for which you know the vocabulary in French. Never attempt to write about a topic you have not yet studied in French. Write down the topic you are going to write about. Then think of the words you know that are related to the topic. Be sure to include some action words (verbs) that you will need.

From your list of words, write as many sentences as you can. Read them and organize them into a logical order. Fill in any gaps. Then proof your paragraph(s) to see if you made any errors. Correct any that you find.

When writing on your own, be careful not to rely heavily, if at all, on a bilingual dictionary. It's not that bilingual dictionaries are bad, but when you look up a word you will very often find that there are several translations for the same word. As a beginning language student, you do not know which translation to choose; the chances are great that you will pick the wrong one.

As a final hint, never prepare your paragraph(s) in English and attempt to translate word for word. Always write from scratch in French.

*In each chapter of **Bon voyage!**, you will learn how to say and write new words. In Chapter 1, you learn how to describe a person. It won't be long before you'll be able to talk about many things in French. **Bon voyage!***

CHAPITRE 1

Vocabulaire

Mots 1 & 2 *(pages 18–25)*

1. Repeat each new word in the **Mots** sections as many times as possible. The more you use a word, the more apt you are to remember it and keep it as part of your active vocabulary.
2. Read the words as you look at the illustrations.
3. If you're the type who has to write something down in order to remember it, copy each word once or twice.
4. Do these activities diligently. They provide you with the opportunity to use your new words many times.
5. This may sound strange, but it's a good idea to read these exercises aloud at home or when using the CD-ROM.
6. When doing the vocabulary activities by yourself or for homework, try to do each item orally before writing the answer.
7. After doing any activity that says **Historiette,** read all the answers aloud. Each time you do this, you will be telling a story in French. It's an excellent way to keep using the material you are learning.

CLASSROOM SUGGESTION Listen to what your classmates say when they respond in class. Do not tune them out. Paying attention to them allows you additional opportunities to hear your new words. The more you hear them, the more likely you are to learn and retain them.

Structure

L'accord des adjectifs *(pages 28–30)*
Pay particular attention to the final sound of many of the descriptive words you are learning. Remind yourself that you hear the final consonant sound of many descriptive words when you are describing a girl. You do not hear the sound when describing a boy.

HINT FOR SPELLING What letter do you delete from the feminine form? Remember that you delete the **e** that follows the consonant when referring to a male.

Le verbe être *au singulier* *(pages 30–32)*
1. **Être** is the first verb you are learning in French. Throughout your study of French, you will continue to learn many more verbs. Verbs are extremely important in French. At this point, you know three verb forms:
   je suis when talking about yourself
   tu es when talking to someone
   il/elle est when talking about someone

Get off to a good start! Learn these three simple forms and remember them.

2. As you do the activities, don't try to use words you don't know in French. For example, you may want to talk about someone who is very outgoing, but you don't know a French equivalent for "outgoing." Give the message using what you do know. For example, you can say: **Jean n'est pas timide, pas du tout.** You can also say: **Marie, elle est timide? Non, pas du tout. Marie n'est pas timide.** Using **ne… pas** with a word you know, you can convey the meaning you wish even though you do not know the precise word.

CLASSROOM SUGGESTION Listen to your classmates as they respond to the structure activities. Remember, the more you hear a form, the more readily you will be able to use it.

3. After doing any activity that says **Historiette,** read all the answers aloud. Each time you do this, you will be telling a story in French. It's an excellent way to keep using the material you are learning.

Lecture culturelle
Un garçon et une fille *(pages 36–37)*

1. Always read the Reading Strategy at the beginning of the **Lecture culturelle.** Practice these strategies and try applying them to other selections you read in French. The Reading Strategy on page 36 talks about cognates and how they help you guess the meanings of words you do not know. For example, you read: **Jean est un garçon français. Il est très intelligent, très capable.** You have probably never seen or used the word **capable** in French. However, you can guess its meaning because it is a cognate of the English word *capable.*

   In addition, it is used in apposition to **intelligent.** When you see a word or expression followed by a comma and then another word (in apposition), the word in apposition almost always clarifies the precise word and has the same or similar meaning.

2. Let's look at another way to guess meaning: **Jean est intelligent et il est aussi très sage. Il est prudent.** You don't know the word **sage,** but its meaning is clarified by **prudent.** Which of the following do you think **sage** means? *Talented? Wise, smart? Nice?* Hopefully you chose *wise, smart.* Think about how and why you arrived at this correct answer.

HINTS FOR WRITING As you complete your first chapter in French, you are able to write a description of a person. At this point, you cannot tell what the person does because you don't have the necessary vocabulary. So avoid this. However, you are able to tell what he or she is like. Write down the words you know in order to write your description. Do not think of words in English. Try to think only of the words you know in French. Begin to write your description. Remember what you learned about **e** if your description is of a female.

VOCABULAIRE *(page 47)*
As you complete the chapter, look at the reference vocabulary list. If there are several words you don't remember, go back to the **Mots 1** and **Mots 2** sections and review. If there are only one or two, you can choose to look them up in the dictionaries beginning on page H72 at the end of this book.

CHAPITRE 2
Get off to a good start! Do your French homework diligently and study for a short period of time each day. Do not skip some days and then try to cram. It doesn't work when studying a foreign language.

   In each lesson of **Bon voyage!** you will learn a very manageable amount of new material. Since French is a romance language, much of the new material will involve word endings. Study each small set of new endings on a daily basis, and you'll have no problem. Don't wait until you have lots of them and try to cram them in all at once.

Vocabulaire
Mots 1 & 2 *(pages 50–57)*

1. In Chapter 1, you learned that adjectives describing something feminine end in **e.** The final consonant is pronounced. The **e** is dropped and the consonant is not pronounced when describing something masculine. In Chapter 2, you have four new words that reinforce the same concept: **fort, mauvais, strict,** and **intéressant.**

   Elle est forte en maths.
   Il est fort en maths.
   La classe est intéressante.
   Le cours est intéressant.

HINT FOR PRONOUNCING NEW WORDS
Imitate the pronunciation of your teacher or the CDs to the best of your ability. Try to acquire the best pronunciation possible.

However, don't be worried if you have a slight American accent. There are three levels of pronunciation.

* **Near-native** Try to pronounce like a native. Strive for a near-native pronunciation.
* **Accented but comprehensible** Many people have an accent when they speak a foreign language. You can tell they are not native speakers, but in spite of their accent, you can understand them. If you have such an accent, don't be concerned.
* **Very accented and incomprehensible** Some people have such a strong accent that it's impossible to understand what they're saying. If you have such a strong accent, it will be necessary to repeat and imitate more carefully.

Always remember to listen carefully, repeating as accurately as possible, and you'll succeed in acquiring acceptable pronunciation.

HINT FOR SPEAKING Listen to your teacher pronounce new words or phrases and then repeat them several times. Once you know how to pronounce the words, read the words in your book. If you try to read a word in French before ever having pronounced it, the spelling will most probably interfere with your pronunciation. Always try to listen, repeat, and then read.

2. The vocabulary in **Mots 2** should be very easy to recognize and learn because many words are cognates. A cognate is a word that looks alike in both English and French and has the same meaning in both languages. In the early lessons of **Bon voyage!** we have used many cognates to help you acquire a substantial vocabulary quickly and easily. However, be careful with the pronunciation of cognates. Even though they look alike and mean the same thing in both languages, they can be pronounced very differently.

Structure
Le pluriel: articles, noms et adjectifs
(pages 58–60)
When listening, you will not hear the **s** ending for the plural of a descriptive word. When speaking, you will not pronounce the **s**. However, when writing, you have to remember to write the **s** for plural words.

> **Les garçons intelligents**
> **Les filles intelligentes**

Le verbe être au pluriel (pages 60–63)
In this lesson, you learn three new verb forms:

> **nous sommes** when talking about yourself and someone else
> **vous êtes** when talking to two or more people
> **ils/elles sont** when talking about two or more people or things

Go over these three forms until you feel confident that you know them.

Conversation
(page 66)
When you listen to people speak, you will notice that they often use little words or expressions that you will never see in written form. *Yeah* and *ya' know* are examples in English. You can often guess the meaning of these expressions by the speaker's tone of voice. In this conversation, listen to the tone of voice when the young woman says **Ben oui.** Do you think **Ben oui** means *No* or *Yeah?*

Lecture culturelle
Le français aux États-Unis (pages 68–69)
1. Read the Reading Strategy at the beginning of the **Lecture culturelle.** Look at the title of the reading on page 68. It lets you know immediately the general topic you'll be reading about.
2. Read the three subtitles or heads in the passage. They give you a more specific idea of what you'll be reading. Without having read

the reading selection, you now have some understanding of what the reading is about. This will make comprehension much easier.

3. After looking at the title and subtitles, you may very quickly skim the reading. Rather than trying to remember all the information, look at the comprehension questions that follow it. Then go back to the reading and look for the specific factual information called for.

CHAPITRE 3

Vocabulaire

Mots 1 & 2 *(pages 82–89)*

1. Look at each photo or illustration carefully.
2. Read the labels. What does each word refer to?
3. Each word is then used in a meaningful context in a complete sentence. Repeat the individual words and then the sentences.
4. Note that in Activity 4 on page 85, the answer to the question word **qu'est-ce que (qu')** is always a thing. Therefore you should be able to guess the meaning of this question word. Does it mean *who* or *what?*
5. On page 86, after you have practiced your new words, cover up the words as you look at the drawing or photo of each classroom item. See how many you remember. If you don't remember many, you'll have to practice the words some more.

HINT Always pay careful attention to both the pronunciation and the spelling of your new words. You have now seen more than one form of certain verbs. For example: **Ils jouent. Il joue. Ils regardent. Il regarde.** Have you noticed that there is no difference in pronunciation between **regardent** and **regarde** even though they are written differently?

HINT FOR SPEAKING Whenever possible, read all the answers aloud to any activity labeled **Historiette.** Every time you do, you'll be telling a story on your own with the guidance of the activity in the text. This is an easy and useful way to get yourself speaking lots of French.

Structure

Les verbes réguliers en -er au présent
(pages 90–93)

1. Now that you know the word **on,** which often replaces **nous,** you will see that you really only have to pronounce two forms of a regular **-er** verb. When speaking, whether the subject of the sentence is **je, tu, il, on, elle, ils,** or **elles,** the verb sounds the same. Only the **vous** form has a different pronunciation. This makes spoken French quite easy.

1	2
je parle	
tu parles	vous parlez
il/elle/on parle	
ils/elles parlent	

2. However, when you write, remember that there are spelling changes.
   je parle
   tu parles
   il/elle/on parle
   ils/elles parlent

HINT Note that the structure activities in your book build from easy to more complex. In the beginning activities, you very often have to use only one verb form. For example, in Activity 13 on page 91, you use only the **il** form. However, in Activity 20 on page 93, you have to use all forms of the verb.

3. When doing Activity 21 on page 93, remember to use only French that you know. Refer to the list of words given here. This list will prevent you from thinking about things you cannot yet say in French.

La négation des articles indéfinis *(page 94)*
Try to condense a grammatical rule into one
easy sentence that you can remember easily:
Un, une, and **des** all become **de** after **ne… pas.**

Verbe + infinitif *(page 95)*
Note that the infinitive form of the verb used
after a verb is pronounced the same as the **vous**
form: **Vous travaillez.**
         J'aime travailler.
Travaillez and **travailler** are pronounced the
same. When writing, remember the difference
in spelling:
    Vous travaillez? Moi, j'aime travailler.
    Vous rigolez? Moi, j'aime rigoler.

Conversation
(page 96)
1. This conversation should be very easy for
   you. You have already learned all the French
   that is used in the conversation. When
   practicing this conversation with a classmate,
   feel free to make as many changes as you
   want, as long as they make sense.
2. In the conversation, you hear Carol say, **C'est
   pas vrai.** In spoken French, **ne** is often
   dropped from the expression **ne… pas.**
3. Note also that Cedric says **Si, c'est vrai.** When
   someone tells you **no** in French and you want
   to contradict, you say **si** rather than **oui.**

Lecture culturelle
Une journée avec Jacqueline *(pages 98–99)*
1. Look at the photos on pages 98–99. These
   photos let you know the reading is about:
   a. shopping for clothes
   b. going to school
   c. making a meal
2. Skim the reading selection and look for the
   important information such as:
   ✤ Who's the story about?
   ✤ Where does she live and go to school?
   ✤ What are her school hours?

3. Factual recall is an important reading skill.
   First, find the facts in the reading and then
   commit them to memory. Activity B tells you
   what factual information to look for.

VOCABULAIRE *(page 109)*
As you complete the chapter, look at the
reference vocabulary list. If there are several
words you don't remember, go back to the
Mots 1 and **Mots 2** sections and review. If there
are only one or two, you can choose to look
them up in the dictionaries beginning on page
H72 at the end of this book.

CHAPITRE 4
Vocabulaire
Mots 1 & 2 *(pages 112–119)*

1. In **Mots 1**, remember to listen to the words
   and repeat orally before reading them. Many
   names for family members are cognates. Be
   careful to repeat them correctly.

HINT If you're the type of learner who has to
write something before you can remember, copy
the words in the **Mots** section once or twice.
Use the following learning sequence: *listen,
repeat, read, write.*

2. Activity 2 on page 114 helps you review
   several important question words. The answer
   in parentheses tells you the meaning of the
   question word for that sentence. Look at the
   following question words and answers:
Quand?	**aujourd'hui**
Qu'est-ce que?	**une fête, des cadeaux**
Qui?	**ses cousins, ses cousines**

   Decide which question words mean *who,
   what,* and *when.*

3. Activity 4 on page 115 helps you with
   productive skills. Remember that when you
   speak or write about yourself, you must
   always use the masculine form if you are a
   male and the feminine form if you are a
   female.

4. After you have learned the new words in **Mots 2,** look at each illustration, cover up the sentences, and say as much as you can about the illustration. If you can describe the illustration, you know your vocabulary. If you cannot describe it, you have to study some more.

HINT Read or say aloud all the answers to the **Historiette** activities to give you practice in telling coherent stories in French.

Structure

Le verbe avoir *au présent (pages 120–122)*
So far, you have learned one irregular verb in French, the verb **être.** All forms of **être** are different. You will now learn your second irregular verb, **avoir.** All forms of **avoir** are also different.
1. Familiarize yourself with the forms of **avoir** as you go over the explanation in class.
2. Do the activities diligently. They give you the opportunity to use and learn the new verb forms without having to memorize them one by one.
3. Do the activities orally and in writing.
4. After doing the activities, reread the grammar explanation. See if you can give the forms of **avoir** on your own without reading them.

REVIEW You know that **un, une,** and **des** all change to **de** after **ne… pas.** The activities on pages 120–122 will help you review this point as you talk about your own home and family.

Conversation

(page 128)
Pay careful attention when you listen to the conversation on the CD-ROM or when other students are repeating it in class. The more you hear spoken French, the easier it will be for you to understand.

Lecture culturelle
Où habitent les Français? (pages 130–131)
1. Read the title. When you finish this reading, what will you be able to tell?
   a. where France is
   b. who the French are
   c. where the French people live
2. As you read each paragraph, draw a mental picture of what you're reading. To help you draw your mental picture, look at the photographs, too.

C'est à vous
(pages 136–137)
In Activity 5 on page 137, you are going to write about your house or a house of your dreams.
1. Picture the house.
2. In French, think of or write a list of words you can use to identify parts of the house.
3. In French, think about or write a list of words you can use to describe a house or rooms of a house.
4. Organize your story. Divide the house into parts, such as living area, sleeping area, first floor, second floor. You may even want to make a drawing of your house. Write a few sentences about each area.
5. Put the sentences in a logical order.
6. Add a few sentences to describe the area around your house.

CHAPITRE 5
Vocabulaire
Mots 1 & 2 *(pages 154–161)*
1. It can be fun to study with a classmate. You can do the following.
   ✤ Ask one another questions in French about the illustrations.
   ✤ Have a contest. See who can give more French words describing the illustrations in a three-minute period.
   ✤ Tell your friend which of the items you would order if you were at a café.

2. Activity 1 on page 156 helps you reinforce the meaning of the important question words:

où	au café
qui	Chantal, le serveur
qu'est-ce que	une table libre, une boisson
quand	après les cours

3. Act out Activity 4 on page 157 with a classmate. The more you practice speaking French together, the better you'll be able to communicate.

Structure

Le verbe aller *au présent* (pages 162–164)

You will now learn your third irregular verb. Make an association with another irregular verb you have already learned. Repeat the following aloud.

je vais ⟶ j'ai
tu vas ⟶ tu as
il va ⟶ il a
ils vont ⟶ ils ont

The forms of **aller** almost sound like the forms of **avoir** with a **v** sound.

HINT The more you practice speaking French, the better. When doing your homework, go over all the activities aloud. Don't just do your French homework silently.

Aller + *infinitif* (page 165)

1. The concept of an infinitive after a verb is not new to you. You already know how to express what you like to do:

J'aime manger.
J'aime aller au restaurant.

2. Now, using the same type of construction, you will be able to tell what you are going to do.

J'aime manger et je vais manger quelque chose.
J'aime aller au restaurant et je vais aller au restaurant vendredi.

Conversation

(page 170)

Listen carefully to the conversation. You can listen to your teacher or use the CD-ROM. Listen more than once. Each time listen for a different bit of information.

* Where are Claire and Loïc?
* What do they order?
* Why is there a possible disagreement?

Lecture culturelle

Au restaurant? Vraiment? (pages 172–173)

1. Making comparisons while reading is an important reading comprehension skill. In this reading, you learned about a cultural difference that's quite interesting. What is it? You may want to share this information with family or friends who don't know any French.

2. Finding the main idea is another important reading comprehension skill. As you read, look for the main idea in the second paragraph. What is it? What is the main idea in the third paragraph?

C'est à vous

(pages 178–179)

In Activity 4 on page 179, you're going to write about a restaurant in French.

1. Get a mental picture of the restaurant.
2. Write words you know in French to describe a restaurant and restaurant activities.
3. List items that people may order.
4. Put these words into sentences. Your first paragraph will describe the restaurant. Your second paragraph will tell what your "characters" order and how they pay.

CHAPITRE 6

Vocabulaire

Mots 1 & 2 *(pages 186–193)*

1. Try to use your French as often as possible. When you see a food item at home or in a

store that is labeled in French, say the French word to yourself. You'll learn to identify many more food items as you continue with your study of French.

2. As you complete the activities, answer each question orally before you write the answers for homework. Try reading your written responses aloud for Activities 2 and 3 on page 188. Activity 2 reviews the question words **qui, qu'est-ce que, quand, où.**

3. On your own, review the foods you have learned by putting them with an appropriate package or container. For example:

> **un paquet de fromage**
> **un paquet de six tranches de jambon**
> **un pot de confiture**
> **un paquet de légumes surgelés**

HINTS Note that Activity 10 on page 193 points out that in spoken French, you can omit the **ne** in the expression **ne… pas.**

Be sure you understand the meaning of **pourquoi** and **parce que** when you finish this activity.

Structure

Le verbe faire au présent (pages 194–195)

1. Look at the forms of the verb **faire.** Repeat them aloud, then copy them.

2. When you complete homework activities, go back to the verb chart. Cover the verb forms and see if you can say the forms without looking at them.

Le partitif et l'article défini (pages 196–197)

1. Always try to make what you are learning as simple as possible. If you're talking about something in general, you use **le, la, les.** If you're talking about "some" or "any," you use **du, de la, des.**

2. When doing Activities 18 and 19 on page 197, pay particular attention to the contrast between the general sense and the partitive. You want to buy some (partitive) of the things you like (in general).

Le partitif au négatif (pages 198–200)

This concept of **de** is not new. Just remember **du, de la, de l',** and **des** all change to **de** after **ne… pas.** It's really simple, but you have to keep reminding yourself.

HINT Pay close attention as you and your classmates participate in each of these activities. The more you hear **j'ai du** (or **de la, des**) versus **je n'ai pas de,** the easier it will be for you to use the partitive.

HINTS FOR SPEAKING AND WRITING

Listen carefully for the difference in pronunciation between **bonne, bon,** and **gentille, gentil** as explained on page 201. Repeat the words carefully. Repeat the model sentences aloud, then copy them. Pay particular attention to the doubling of the consonant.

Les verbes pouvoir et vouloir
(pages 201–203)

Pay attention to the similarity between the forms of **pouvoir** and **vouloir.**

REVIEW Using the infinitive after a helping verb is not new. Remember:

> **J'aime dîner au restaurant.**
> **Je vais dîner au restaurant.**

Conversation
(page 204)

1. Intonation is the melody of a language. Intonation is produced by the rise and fall of the voice. Each language has its own intonation patterns. English intonation is very different from French intonation. Pay special attention to the rise and fall of the speakers' voices as you listen to the conversations on the CD or CD-ROM.

2. Try to imitate the native speakers' intonation as accurately as possible. If you do, you'll sound much more French. Don't be inhibited. Pretend you are acting while you imitate the intonation.

Lecture culturelle

Les courses *(pages 206–207)*

You may not know the meaning of a certain word you come across in a reading selection. However, you can often guess the meaning of the word by the way it is used in the context of the sentence. A new word in this reading is **les commerçants**. Guess what it means by the context of these sentences:

> **Les Français aiment bien aller chez les petits commerçants du quartier—l'épicier, le boucher, le boulanger, etc.**

The fact that the word **commerçants** is followed by the words **l'épicier, le boucher, le boulanger** helps you figure out the meaning of **commerçants**. What do you think the word **commerçants** means in this context?

    a. office workers
    b. shopkeepers
    c. commercials

CHAPITRE 7

Vocabulaire

Mots 1 & 2 *(pages 220–227)*

1. Look at the illustrations in **Mots 1** and repeat each word aloud.
2. Write each word for additional reinforcement.
3. When you have finished studying the vocabulary, determine how much you remember. Say to yourself or aloud all the items you know for boy's clothing, girl's clothing, and unisex clothing. When you get dressed in the morning for school, notice how many words you know in French for those items you are wearing.
4. Before you write the answers to the vocabulary activities, work with a friend. Go over each exercise together orally. Then, each of you can write your answers. If you wish, you can check each other's work.

5. After studying the vocabulary in **Mots 2**, make a list of the things that you would most probably want to say in French to a salesperson when shopping for clothes.

REVIEW These vocabulary activities contain many adjectives, or descriptive words. Remember that many adjectives have an **e** when used with a feminine noun. They drop the **e** when used with a masculine noun.

La jupe est		Le blouson est	
	verte.		vert.
	grise.		gris.
	petite.		petit.
	grande.		grand.
	bleue.		bleu.
	jolie.		joli.

Structure

Le verbe mettre *au présent* *(pages 228–229)*

1. Remember that you hear and pronounce the **t** in the plural forms of **mettre.** You do not hear or pronounce the **t** in the singular forms.
2. Do the **Attention** activity on page 229 aloud at least twice. As you do, pay very careful attention to pronunciation as well as spelling.

Le comparatif des adjectifs *(pages 230–231)*

1. Remember to make the association that **plus** (+) is more, **moins** (–) is less, and **aussi** (=) is the same. All three words are followed by **que.**
2. As you do these activities, pay particular attention to each adjective.

Les verbes voir *et* croire *(pages 232–233)*

Note that many forms of **voir** and **croire** are pronounced the same.

je crois	tu crois	il croit	ils croient
je vois	tu vois	il voit	ils voient

Conversation

(page 234)

This conversation should be very easy for you. You have already learned all the French that is used in the conversation. When practicing this conversation with a classmate, feel free to make as many changes as you want, as long as they make sense.

Lecture culturelle

On fait des courses où, à Paris?
(pages 236–237)

1. Look at the photos on pages 236–237. These photos let you know what the reading is about.
2. Look at the titles. They will give you an idea of what you'll be reading about.
3. Quickly scan the reading to get a general idea of what it's all about.
4. Activity A on page 237 will help you practice factual recall. To recall certain facts, it is often necessary to go back over the reading selection and look for details.
5. Drawing conclusions from a reading selection is another important reading comprehension skill. Based on what you read, draw a personal conclusion. Where would you shop in Paris? Why?

VOCABULAIRE *(page 247)*

As you complete the chapter, look at the reference vocabulary list. If there are quite a few words you don't know, go back to the **Mots 1** and **Mots 2** sections and review.

CHAPITRE 8

Vocabulaire

Mots 1 & 2 *(pages 260–267)*

1. Repeat each new word in the **Mots** sections several times. Look at the photo or illustration as you pronounce the word.
2. Some of you may remember information more easily after writing it down. Try copying each vocabulary word once or twice.
3. You may want to do the activities aloud with a friend as a paired activity. Then, individually write the answers and check each other's work.

4. Listen carefully to what your classmates say when they respond in class. The more you hear people use the new words, the more likely you are to remember them.

Structure

Les verbes en **-ir** *au présent (pages 268–269)*
The **je, tu,** and **il/elle/on** forms of many French verbs are all pronounced the same, even though they are spelled differently. The **-is** and **-it** endings are pronounced the same.

Quel *et* tout *(pages 270–271)*

In spoken French, **quel** is very easy. You pronounce all forms the same. Pay particular attention to the different spellings.

Les verbes sortir, partir, dormir *et* servir
(pages 272–275)

To learn the oral forms of many French verbs, pronounce the **ils/elles** form first. Then drop the final consonant sound and you have the pronunciation for the **je, tu, il/elle/on** forms.

ils sortent	je sors, tu sors, il sort
ils partent	je pars, tu pars, il part
ils dorment	je dors, tu dors, il dort
ils servent	je sers, tu sers, il sert

Conversation

(page 276)

Listen carefully to the native speakers' intonation or melody on the CD or CD-ROM. Then, imitate the natives' intonation as closely as you can when you repeat.

Lecture culturelle

On va en France. (pages 278–279)

1. To figure out the organization of this reading, scan the passage and look for the following information:
   * Who's going where and how?
   * What do they do when they arrive?
2. Sequencing events is an important reading comprehension skill. Sequence the events in this reading selection. Then see if you came up with a sequence similar to the following:

✤ **La classe de Madame Cadet est dans le hall de l'aérogare.**

✤ **Les élèves sont dans l'avion.**

✤ **Ils arrivent à l'aéroport à Paris.**

✤ **Ils visitent la belle ville de Paris.**

3. See if you can do all of Activity A on page 279 without referring to the reading for answers.

4. Activity B deals with factual recall. See how many of the facts you remember. Go back to the reading selection and find those you do not remember.

CHAPITRE 9

Vocabulaire

Mots 1 & 2 *(pages 292–299)*

1. Listen to the new words in **Mots 1** and repeat them orally before reading them.

2. Answer Activities 1 and 2 on page 294 however you wish. The more information you can give the better.

3. A good way to remember vocabulary is to group words in some meaningful way. For example, you can group cognates, synonyms, or antonyms. An antonym is a word that means the exact opposite of another. There are quite a few words in **Mots 2** for which you know the antonyms.

   Match the following antonyms.

1. monter	poser une question
2. assis	descendre
3. lit	terminer, finir
4. répondre à la question	debout
5. commencer	écrit

4. Activity 7 on page 299 helps you review the following question words: **qui, qu'est-ce que, où, quel.**

Structure

Les verbes en -re au présent *(pages 300–302)*
Remember to drop the final sound of the **ils/elles** form to get the pronunciation for the **je, tu, il/elle/on** forms of the verb.

ils ven~~dent~~	je vends, tu vends, il/elle/on vend
ils atten~~dent~~	j'attends, tu attends, il/elle/on attend
ils descen~~dent~~	je descends, tu descends, il/elle/on descend
ils enten~~dent~~	j'entends, tu entends, il/elle/on entend

Remember the **je, tu, il/elle/on** forms of these verbs are all pronounced the same.

HINT When doing these activities on your own, go over them first orally. Then write the answers.

Les adjectifs démonstratifs *(pages 303–305)*
Pronounce the following forms aloud and note how the final **t** sound becomes softer when used before a masculine noun that begins with a vowel sound.

cette announe	cet horaire	ce train
cette gare	cet aéroport	ce billet

Les verbes **dire, écrire, lire** *(pages 306–307)*

1. Again remember to drop the final sound of the **ils/elles** form to get the pronunciation for **je, tu, il/elle/on.**

ils di~~sent~~	je dis, tu dis, il dit
ils li~~sent~~	je lis, tu lis, il lit
ils écri~~vent~~	j'écris, tu écris, il écrit

2. Pay particular attention to **vous dites.** Other similar verb forms you have learned are:

   vous faites

   vous êtes

Conversation

(page 308)
You have not learned the expression **tarif étudiant,** but it's easy to guess its meaning through association with other words. **Tarif** is a word that also exists in English. **Étudiant,** a word that is related to the verb **étudier,** is a close cognate of *student.*

Lecture culturelle
Un voyage intéressant (*pages 310–311*)
Always locate the area of the world you are reading about. Look at the map on page 310. Locate the countries of Mali and Sénégal. Locate the cities of Bamako and Dakar.

VOCABULAIRE (*page 321*)
After going over the vocabulary you need when traveling by train, think about a plane trip in French to review the words you already know about this topic.

CHAPITRE 10
Vocabulaire
Mots 1 & 2 (*pages 324–331*)

1. Look at each photo or illustration carefully.
2. Read the labels. What does each word refer to?
3. The words are then used in a meaningful context in a complete sentence. Repeat the sentence aloud as you look at the illustration.
4. To help you learn vocabulary, work with a friend or classmate. Have a contest. See who can say the most about each illustration or photo.
5. It is important to review the question words in French often. Activity 1 on page 326 reviews the following question words: **quoi, combien, qui, qu'est-ce que.**

Structure
Le passé composé des verbes réguliers
(*pages 332–334*)
1. The formation of the past tense, the **passé composé,** in French is very easy.
   ✣ Review the forms of the verb **avoir.**
   ✣ To form the past participle of all regular verbs, you only have to remember three vowel sounds: /é/, /i/, /ü/
2. Using the **passé composé** in the negative is simple. Think of **ne… pas** as the bread of a sandwich. The filling for the sandwich is the verb **avoir.**

Les verbes **boire, devoir** et **recevoir**
(*pages 337–339*)
Remember once again to drop the final sound of the **ils/elles** form of these verbs to get the pronunciation of the **je, tu, il/elle/on** forms.

ils boi~~vent~~	je bois, tu bois, il/elle/on boit
ils doi~~vent~~	je dois, tu dois, il/elle/on doit
ils reçoi~~vent~~	je reçois, tu reçois, il/elle/on reçoit

Conversation
(*page 340*)
The activity **Vous avez compris?** enables you to practice question words.

Lecture culturelle
Le hockey et le basket-ball (*pages 342–343*)
Before reading this selection, sit back and think for a moment about what you know concerning hockey and basketball. Make a mental picture of each game. This will help you understand the reading selection.

VOCABULAIRE (*page 353*)
Look at each word and see if you can use it in a short sentence.

CHAPITRE 11
Vocabulaire
Mots 1 & 2 (*pages 356–363*)

1. For **Mots 1**, after going over the new vocabulary, review immediately. Sit back for a moment and say aloud or to yourself five words or expressions associated with the beach.
2. Pretend you are on the beach. Think of three things you would like to do while on the beach. Start your sentences with **Je voudrais…**
3. After completing each activity on pages 358–359, read all the answers aloud or

silently. You're not only reading a story with words you know; you're also having another opportunity to use your new words.

4. In **Mots 2,** when learning the winter weather expressions, review the summer expressions on pages 356–357.

5. As you do the activities on pages 362–363, work with a classmate. Take turns asking and answering the questions orally. Then write your answers individually. Correct each other's work.

Structure

Le passé composé des verbes irréguliers (pages 364–366)

1. Past participles of regular verbs have only three sounds:

-er	/é/
-ir	/i/
-re	/ü/

2. Remember that participles of all irregular verbs, except **être** and **faire,** have only two of these sounds: /i/ and /ü/. /Ü/ is always spelled the same, but **i** is sometimes spelled **-is** and sometimes **-it.**

3. When reading or writing the activities on pages 365–366, pay particular attention to the spelling of past participles with the /i/ sound.

Les mots négatifs (pages 367–368)

To learn the meaning of the negative words, pay particular attention to the opposites.

Oui, quelque chose.	Non, rien.
Oui, quelqu'un.	Non, personne.
Oui, toujours.	Non, jamais.
Oui, souvent.	Non, jamais.
Oui, quelquefois.	Non, jamais.

Le passé composé avec **être** (pages 369–371)

1. If necessary, quickly review the verb **être.**

je suis	nous sommes
tu es	vous êtes
il/elle/on est	ils/elles sont

HINTS FOR SPEAKING AND WRITING Past participles that end in a vowel (**/é/, /i/, /ü/**) sound the same in all forms. Even though all forms are pronounced the same, you must pay particular attention to the spelling of these past participles when writing. They add **e** for the feminine and **s** for the plural.

parti /i/
partis /i/
partie /i/
parties /i/

2. In the activities on pages 370–371, pay particular attention to the spelling of the past participle.

Lecture culturelle

Un petit voyage au Canada (pages 374–375)

1. Skim the selection quickly to get a very general idea of what it's about.

2. Scan the selection to look for specific information.
   * Who went where? When? How?
   * What did they see and do?

3. Which statement best summarizes the first paragraph?
   a. C'est le mois de février.
   b. La classe de Madame Lebrun a pris le train.
   c. La classe de Madame Lebrun est allée au Canada.

4. Which statement best summarizes the second paragraph?
   a. Ils ont passé trois jours à Montréal.
   b. Ils sont allés à une très belle station de sports d'hiver.
   c. Ils ont mis leurs skis.

Inference is an important reading comprehension skill. In this selection, we learn the students are really tired and they sleep like logs. The reading doesn't actually tell us why they are so tired, but you can figure it out from the information you read.

5. Why are the students so tired?
   a. They didn't sleep the night before the trip.
   b. They were anxious to get back to the dorms.
   c. They were worn out from all their activities.

CHAPITRE 12

Vocabulaire

Mots 1 & 2 *(pages 400–407)*

1. In **Mots 1,** to make it easier to remember the meaning of the new words, they are put in a logical sequence of events:

   se réveiller, se lever, se laver (la figure, les cheveux), se peigner, se maquiller, s'habiller

2. Activity 2 on page 402 helps you review the rooms of a house:

   la cuisine, la salle à manger, le salon, la chambre à coucher, la salle de bains

3. Matching synonyms and/or antonyms can often help you remember words.

   Match the antonyms *(opposites)* in **Mots 2.**
   1. **Il a mis la table.** **Il a débarrassé la table.**
   2. **Il a allumé la télé.** **Il a éteint la télé.**

   Match the synonyms.
   1. **un frigidaire**   **mettre la télé**
   2. **le salon**   **un réfrigérateur**
   3. **allumer la télé**   **changer de chaîne**
   4. **zapper**   **la salle de séjour**

Structure

Les verbes réfléchis au présent
(pages 408–412)

1. Remember that if a person is doing something to or for himself or herself, the verb in French is a reflexive verb, and you must use the additional pronoun.

2. You have already learned all the verb endings that are used in these activities. The only new concept is the use of the reflexive pronoun. Pay particular attention to this pronoun as you do these activities.

Les verbes réfléchis au passé composé
(pages 413–415)

Since the past participle of almost all reflexive verbs ends in a vowel, all forms are pronounced the same. However, in writing, the plural and feminine endings must be added.

CHAPITRE 13

Vocabulaire

Mots 1 & 2 *(pages 432–439)*

1. Remember to listen to the words and repeat them orally before reading them.
2. After you have gone over the new vocabulary, see how many words you remember. Think of seven words about a movie. Think of five words about a play.
3. Go over each activity orally before you write the answers.

Structure

Les verbes **savoir** et **connaître** *(pages 440–441)*

1. Simplify the grammatical rule: just remember that **savoir** means to know something simple, and **connaître** means to know or be familiar with something complex.
2. When doing these activities, pay particular attention to the object of each verb to determine the use of **savoir** or **connaître.**

Les pronoms **me, te, nous, vous**
(pages 442–443)

Remember that the pronouns **me, te, nous,** and **vous** are part of the "filling in the sandwich." **Ne... pas** is the bread that goes around the filling.

	me parle	
	te parle	
Il ne	**nous parle**	**pas.**
	vous parle	

Les pronoms **le, la, les** *(pages 444–447)*

As you do these activities, determine which word is the direct object before trying to replace it with **le, la,** or **les.** Do each activity orally before you write it.

Conversation
(page 448)

1. An important skill in understanding a foreign language is to guess the meaning of words from the context in which they occur. In this conversation, you will hear and use the expression **travailler notre espagnol.** This is new to you, but you can figure it out from the context.

   In this conversation, **travailler** means which of the following?
   a. **parler**
   b. **comprendre**
   c. **pratiquer**

2. Note how Léa says **ça me dit** in response to the question **ça t'intéresse?** Do you think **ça me dit** has the same meaning as the phrase **ça m'intéresse?**

Lecture culturelle

Les loisirs culturels en France *(pages 450–451)*
Identifying the main idea is an important comprehension skill. Read the title and subtitles. What do you think is the main idea of this reading?
   a. **Il y a des musées et des théâtres en France.**
   b. **Les Français apprécient les loisirs culturels.**
   c. **L'entrée des musées est gratuite le premier dimanche du mois.**

VOCABULAIRE *(page 461)*
Read the list of words and determine how many you know. Many of these words are easy to remember because they are cognates.

CHAPITRE 14
Vocabulaire
Mots 1 & 2 *(pages 464–471)*

1. Whenever you have the chance to review, do so. As you do **Mots 1,** think of all the parts of the body you have learned in French.

2. To determine if you know your new vocabulary from **Mots 2,** see whether you can do the following:
   * Tell three things a patient may do in a doctor's office.
   * Tell three things the doctor may do.
   * Tell three things a doctor may say to a patient.

Structure
***Les pronoms* lui, leur** *(pages 472–473)*
Here's an easy way to tell the difference between a direct object and an indirect object. A direct object answers the question *whom* or *what.*

Whom did you see?	I saw the doctor.
What did you take?	I took the medicine.

An indirect object answers the question *to (for) whom* or *to (for) what.*

   To whom did you give the CD?
   I gave the CD to Anne.
   I gave Anne the CD.

***Les verbes* souffrir *et* ouvrir** *(page 474)*
Review the forms of a regular **-er** verb. Compare them to the verb **ouvrir.**

j'écoute	j'ouvre
tu écoutes	tu ouvres
il écoute	il ouvre
nous écoutons	nous ouvrons
vous écoutez	vous ouvrez
ils écoutent	ils ouvrent

L'impératif *(pages 475–477)*
Remember, you use the command (imperative) to tell someone what to do. You merely use the **tu** or **vous** form of the verb to form the command. Just remember that you drop the final **s** from the **tu** form of regular **-er** verbs.

***Le pronom* en** *(pages 478–479)*
You will hear and use the word **en** quite frequently in French. Pay careful attention to the explanation of the use of this word.

Verb Charts

VERBES RÉGULIERS			
INFINITIF	**parler** *to speak*	**finir** *to finish*	**répondre** *to answer*
PRÉSENT	je parle tu parles il parle nous parlons vous parlez ils parlent	je finis tu finis il finit nous finissons vous finissez ils finissent	je réponds tu réponds il répond nous répondons vous répondez ils répondent
IMPÉRATIF	parle parlons parlez	finis finissons finissez	réponds répondons répondez
PASSÉ COMPOSÉ	j'ai parlé tu as parlé il a parlé nous avons parlé vous avez parlé ils ont parlé	j'ai fini tu as fini il a fini nous avons fini vous avez fini ils ont fini	j'ai répondu tu as répondu il a répondu nous avons répondu vous avez répondu ils ont répondu

VERBES AVEC CHANGEMENTS D'ORTHOGRAPHE			
INFINITIF	**acheter**[1] *to buy*	**appeler** *to call*	**commencer** *to begin*
PRÉSENT	j'achète tu achètes il achète nous achetons vous achetez ils achètent	j'appelle tu appelles il appelle nous appelons vous appelez ils appellent	je commence tu commences il commence nous commençons vous commencez ils commencent
INFINITIF	**manger**[2] *to eat*	**payer**[3] *to pay*	**préférer**[4] *to prefer*
PRÉSENT	je mange tu manges il mange nous mangeons vous mangez ils mangent	je paie tu paies il paie nous payons vous payez ils paient	je préfère tu préfères il préfère nous préférons vous préférez ils préfèrent

[1] *Verbes similaires:* **se lever, se promener**
[2] *Verbes similaires:* **nager, voyager**
[3] *Verbes similaires:* **essayer, renvoyer, employer, envoyer**
[4] *Verbes similaires:* **célébrer, espérer, suggérer**

VERBES IRRÉGULIERS

INFINITIF	aller *to go*	avoir *to have*	conduire *to drive*
PRÉSENT	je vais tu vas il va nous allons vous allez ils vont	j'ai tu as il a nous avons vous avez ils ont	je conduis tu conduis il conduit nous conduisons vous conduisez ils conduisent
PASSÉ COMPOSÉ	je suis allé(e)	j'ai eu	j'ai conduit

INFINITIF	connaître *to know*	croire *to believe*	devoir *to have to, to owe*
PRÉSENT	je connais tu connais il connaît nous connaissons vous connaissez ils connaissent	je crois tu crois il croit nous croyons vous croyez ils croient	je dois tu dois il doit nous devons vous devez ils doivent
PASSÉ COMPOSÉ	j'ai connu	j'ai cru	j'ai dû

INFINITIF	dire *to say*	dormir *to sleep*	écrire *to write*
PRÉSENT	je dis tu dis il dit nous disons vous dites ils disent	je dors tu dors il dort nous dormons vous dormez ils dorment	j'écris tu écris il écrit nous écrivons vous écrivez ils écrivent
PASSÉ COMPOSÉ	j'ai dit	j'ai dormi	j'ai écrit

INFINITIF	être *to be*	faire *to do, to make*	lire *to read*
PRÉSENT	je suis tu es il est nous sommes vous êtes ils sont	je fais tu fais il fait nous faisons vous faites ils font	je lis tu lis il lit nous lisons vous lisez ils lisent
PASSÉ COMPOSÉ	j'ai été	j'ai fait	j'ai lu

INFINITIF	mettre *to put*	ouvrir[5] *to open*	partir *to leave*
PRÉSENT	je mets tu mets il met nous mettons vous mettez ils mettent	j'ouvre tu ouvres il ouvre nous ouvrons vous ouvrez ils ouvrent	je pars tu pars il part nous partons vous partez ils partent
PASSÉ COMPOSÉ	j'ai mis	j'ai ouvert	je suis parti(e)

INFINITIF	pouvoir *to be able to*	prendre[6] *to take*	recevoir *to receive*
PRÉSENT	je peux tu peux il peut nous pouvons vous pouvez ils peuvent	je prends tu prends il prend nous prenons vous prenez ils prennent	je reçois tu reçois il reçoit nous recevons vous recevez ils reçoivent
PASSÉ COMPOSÉ	j'ai pu	j'ai pris	j'ai reçu

INFINITIF	savoir *to know*	servir *to serve*	sortir *to go out*
PRÉSENT	je sais tu sais il sait nous savons vous savez ils savent	je sers tu sers il sert nous servons vous servez ils servent	je sors tu sors il sort nous sortons vous sortez ils sortent
PASSÉ COMPOSÉ	j'ai su	j'ai servi	je suis sorti(e)

INFINITIF	venir[7] *to come*	voir *to see*	vouloir *to want*
PRÉSENT	je viens tu viens il vient nous venons vous venez ils viennent	je vois tu vois il voit nous voyons vous voyez ils voient	je veux tu veux il veut nous voulons vous voulez ils veulent
PASSÉ COMPOSÉ	je suis venu(e)	j'ai vu	j'ai voulu

[5] *Verbes similaires:* **couvrir, découvrir, offrir, souffrir**
[6] *Verbes similaires:* **apprendre, comprendre**
[7] *Verbes similaires:* **devenir, revenir**

VERBES AVEC ÊTRE AU PASSÉ COMPOSÉ

aller *(to go)*	je suis allé(e)
arriver *(to arrive)*	je suis arrivé(e)
descendre *(to go down, get off)*	je suis descendu(e)
entrer *(to enter)*	je suis entré(e)
monter *(to go up)*	je suis monté(e)
mourir *(to die)*	je suis mort(e)
naître *(to be born)*	je suis né(e)
partir *(to leave)*	je suis parti(e)
passer *(to go by)*	je suis passé(e)
rentrer *(to go home)*	je suis rentré(e)
rester *(to stay)*	je suis resté(e)
retourner *(to return)*	je suis retourné(e)
revenir *(to come back)*	je suis revenu(e)
sortir *(to go out)*	je suis sorti(e)
tomber *(to fall)*	je suis tombé(e)
venir *(to come)*	je suis venu(e)

This French-English Dictionary *contains all productive and receptive vocabulary from the text. The numbers following each productive entry indicate the chapter and vocabulary section in which the word is introduced. For example,* **2.2** *means that the word first appeared in* **Chapitre 2, Mots 2. BV** *refers to the introductory* **Bienvenue** *lessons.* **L** *refers to the optional literary readings. If there is no number or letter following an entry, this means that the word or expression is there for receptive purposes only.*

A

à at, in, to, **3.1**
  À bientôt! See you soon!, **BV**
  à bord (de) on board, **8.2**
  à cause de because of
  À demain. See you tomorrow., **BV**
  à destination de to (destination), **8.1**
  à domicile to the home
  à l'heure on time, **8.1**
  à mon (ton, son, etc.) avis in my (your, his, etc.) opinion, **7.2**
  à nouveau again
  à peu près about, approximately
  à pied on foot, **4.2**
  à point medium-rare (meat), **5.2**
  À tout à l'heure. See you later., **BV**
abandonner to abandon
l' **abbé** (m.) priest
abondant(e) plentiful
absolument absolutely
accessible accessible
l' **accessoire** (m.) accessory
l' **accident** (m.) accident
accompagner to accompany, to go with
l' **accordéon** (m.) accordion
l' **accusation** (f.) accusation
accuser to accuse
l' **achat** (m.) purchase

  faire des achats to shop
acheter to buy, **3.2**
l' **acte** (m.) act, **13.1**
l' **acteur** (m.) actor, **13.1**
actif, active active
l' **action** (f.) action
l' **activité** (f.) activity
l' **actrice** (f.) actress, **13.1**
l' **addition** (f.) check, bill (restaurant), **5.2**
additionner to add
admirer to admire
l' **adolescent(e)** adolescent, teenager
adorable adorable, **4.1**
adorer to love
l' **adresse** (f.) address
l' **adulte** (m. et f.) adult
l' **adversaire** (m. et f.) adversary, opponent
adverse opposing, **10.1**
aérien(ne) air, flight (adj.)
l' **aérogare** (f.) airport terminal, **8.1**
l' **aéroport** (m.) airport, **8.1**
l' **affiche** (f.) poster
africain(e) African
l' **Afrique** (f.) Africa
afro-américain(e) African-American
l' **âge** (m.) age, **4.1**
  Tu as quel âge? How old are you?, **4.1**
âgé(e) old
l' **agent** (m.) agent (m. and f.), **8.1**
agité(e) choppy, rough (sea)

l' **agneau** (m.) lamb, **6.1**
agréable pleasant
l' **aide** (f.) aid, help
  à l'aide de with the help of
aider to help
aigu(ë) acute, severe, **14.2**
aimer to like, love, **3.1**
  aimer mieux to prefer, **7.2**
l' **aîné(e)** older, **L1**
ainsi que as well as
l' **air** (m.) air; melody
  avoir l'air to look
aisé(e) well-to-do
l' **album** (m.) album
l' **algèbre** (f.) algebra, **2.2**
l' **Algérie** (f.) Algeria
algérien(ne) Algerian
l' **aliment** (m.) food
l' **alimentation** (f.) nutrition, diet
l' **Allemagne** (f.) Germany
l' **allemand** (m.) German (language), **2.2**
aller to go, **5.1**
  aller chercher to go (and) get, **6.1**
  aller mieux to feel better, **14.2**
  Allez! Come on!, **9.2**
  Qu'est-ce qui ne va pas? What's wrong?
l' **aller** (m.) going
  l'aller (simple) one-way ticket, **9.1**

le **billet aller (et) retour** round-trip ticket, **9.1**

l' **allergie** (f.) allergy, **14.1**

allergique allergic, **14.1**

allumer to turn on (*appliance*), **12.2**

alors so, then, well then, **BV**

ambitieux, ambitieuse ambitious

l' **amende** (f.) fine

américain(e) American, **1.1**

l' **Amérique** (f.) du Sud South America

l' **ami(e)** friend, **1.2**

l' **amour** (m.) love, **L4**

ample large, full

amusant(e) funny; fun, **1.1**

s' **amuser** to have fun, **12.2**

l' **an** (m.) year, **4.1**

avoir... ans to be . . . years old, **4.1**

l' **analyse** (f.) analysis

analyser to analyse

analytique analytical

l' **anatomie** (f.) anatomy

ancien(ne) old, ancient; former

l' **angine** (f.) throat infection, tonsillitis, **14.1**

l' **anglais** (m.) English (*language*), **2.2**

anglais(e) English

l' **Angleterre** (f.) England

l' **animal** (m.) animal

l' **année** (f.) year

l'année dernière last year

l' **anniversaire** (m.) birthday, **4.1**

Bon (Joyeux) anniversaire! Happy birthday!

l' **annonce** (f.) announcement, **8.2**

annoncer to announce, **9.1**

anonyme anonymous

l' **anorak** (m.) ski jacket, **7.1**

l' **antibiotique** (m.) antibiotic, **14.1**

Antilles: la mer des Antilles Caribbean Sea

l' **antonyme** (m.) antonym

l' **appareil** (m.) apparatus

apparenté: le mot apparenté cognate

l' **appartement** (m.) apartment, **4.2**

appeler to call

s' **appeler** to be called, be named, **12.1**

applaudir to applaud

apporter to bring, **11.1**

apprécier to appreciate

apprendre (à) to learn (to), **5;** to teach

apprendre à quelqu'un à faire quelque chose to teach someone to do something

après after, **3.2**

d'après according to

l' **après-midi** (m.) afternoon, **3.2**

arabe Arab

l' **arabe** (m.) Arabic (*language*)

l' **arbitre** (m.) referee, **10.1**

l' **arbre** (m.) tree, **L3**

l' **architecture** (f.) architecture

l' **argent** (m.) money, **5.2**

l' **arme** (f.) weapon

l' **armée** (f.) army, **L3**

l' **arrêt** (m.) stop, **9.2**

arrêté(e) arrested

s' **arrêter** to stop, **10.1;** to arrest

l' **arrière** (m.) rear, back, **8.2**

l' **arrière-garde** (f.) rear guard

l' **arrivée** (f.) arrival, **8.1**

arriver to arrive, **3.1;** to happen

arriver à (+ *inf.*) to manage to, to succeed in, **9.1**

l' **arrondissement** (m.) district (in Paris)

l' **artère** (f.) artery

l' **article** (m.) article

l' **artiste** (m. et f.) artiste

l'artiste peintre (m. et f.) painter

artistique artistic

l' **ascenseur** (m.) elevator, **4.2**

asiatique Asian

l' **aspirine** (f.) aspirin, **14.1**

assez fairly, quite; enough, **1.1**

l' **assiette** (f.) plate, **5.2**

ne pas être dans son assiette to be feeling out of sorts, **14.1**

assis(e) seated, **9.2**

l' **assistante sociale** (f.) social worker

l' **atelier** (m.) studio (*artist's*)

l' **athlétisme** (m.) track and field, **10.2**

l' **atmosphère** (f.) atmosphere

attaché(e) attached

attacher to fasten, **8.2**

attaquer to attack

attendre to wait (for), **9.1**

attente: la salle d'attente waiting room, **9.1**

l' **attention** (f.) attention

Attention! Careful! Watch out!, **4.2**

faire attention to pay attention; to be careful, **11.1**

atterrir to land, **8.1**

l' **atterrissage** (m.) landing (*plane*)

attraper un coup de soleil to get a sunburn, **11.1**

au bord de la mer by the ocean; seaside, **11.1**

au contraire on the contrary

au fond in the background

au revoir good-bye, **BV**

au-dessous (de) below

la taille au-dessous the next smaller size, **7.2**

au-dessus (de) above

la taille au-dessus the next larger size, **7.2**

aujourd'hui today, **BV**

auprès de with

ausculter to listen with a stethoscope, **14.2**

aussi also, too, **1.1;** as (*comparisons*), **7;** so

l' **auteur** (m.) author (m. and f.)

l'auteur dramatique playwright

l' **autocar** (m.) bus, coach

automatique automatic, autonomic

l' **automne** (m.) autumn, **11.2**

autour de around, **4.2**

autre other, **L1**

autre chose something else

Autre chose? Anything else? (shopping), **6.2**

d'autres some other, **2.2**

l'un… l'autre one . . . the other

autrement dit in other words

l' **avalanche** (f.) avalanche

avaler to swallow, **14.2**

avance: en avance early, ahead of time, **9.1**

avant before

avant de (+ inf.) before (+ verb)

l' **avant** (m.) front, **8.2**

avant-hier the day before yesterday, **10.2**

avec with, **3.2**

Avec ça? What else? (shopping), **6.1**

l' **avenir** (m.) future, **L2**

l' **aventure** (f.) adventure

l' **avenue** (f.) avenue

l' **aviateur, l'aviatrice** aviator

l' **avion** (m.) plane, **8.1**

en avion by plane

l' **avis** (m.) opinion, **7.2**

à mon avis in my opinion, **7.2**

avoir to have, **4.1**

avoir l'air to look

avoir… ans to be . . . years old, **4.1**

avoir besoin de to need, **10.1**

avoir de la chance to be lucky, to be in luck

avoir envie de to want (to), to feel like

avoir faim to be hungry, **5.1**

avoir une faim de loup to be very hungry

avoir lieu to take place

avoir mal à to have a(n) . . . -ache, to hurt, **14.1**

avoir peur to be afraid, **L1**

avoir du retard to be late (plane, train, etc.), **8.1**

avoir soif to be thirsty, **5.1**

B

le **baccalauréat** French high school exam

la **bactérie** bacterium

bactérien(ne) bacterial, **14.1**

les **bagages** (m. pl.) luggage, **8.1**

le bagage à main carry-on bag, **8.1**

le coffre à bagages baggage compartment, **8.2**

la **baguette** loaf of French bread, **6.1**

le **baigneur, la baigneuse** bather

le **bain** bath, **12.1**

prendre un bain to take a bath, **12.1**

prendre un bain de soleil to sunbathe, **11.1**

la salle de bains bathroom, **4.2**

le **balcon** balcony, **4.2**

le **ballet** ballet

le **ballon** ball (soccer, etc.), **10.1**

la **banane** banana, **6.2**

la **banlieue** suburbs

la **base** base; basis

à base de based on

le **base-ball** baseball

basé(e) based

la **basilique** basilica

la **basket** sneaker; running shoe, **7.1**

le **basket(-ball)** basketball, **10.2**

la **bataille** battle, **L3**

le champ de bataille battlefield, **L3**

le **bateau** boat, **L4**

le **bâton** ski pole, **11.2**

bavarder to chat

beau (bel), belle beautiful, handsome, **4.2**

Il fait beau. It's nice weather., **11.1**

beaucoup a lot, **3.1**

beaucoup de a lot of, many, **3.2**

le **beau-père** stepfather, **4.1**

la **beauté** beauty

de toute beauté of great beauty

le **bébé** baby

beige (inv.) beige, **7.2**

belge Belgian

la **Belgique** Belgium

la **belle-mère** stepmother, **4.1**

ben (slang) well

ben oui yeah

le/la **bénévole** volunteer

le **berger, la bergère** shepherd, shepherdess

le **besoin** need

avoir besoin de to need, **10.1**

la **bêtise** stupid thing, nonsense

le **beurre** butter, **6.1**

le **bicentenaire** bicentennial

la **bicyclette** bicycle, **10.2**

bien fine, well, **BV**

bien cuit(e) well-done (meat), **5.2**

bien élevé(e) well-behaved; well-mannered

bien sûr of course

eh bien well

bientôt soon

À bientôt! See you soon! **BV**

le/la **bienvenu(e)** welcome

le **billet** ticket, **8.1**
   le billet aller (et) retour
   round-trip ticket, **9.1**
la **biologie** biology, **2.2**
biologique biological
le/la **biologiste** biologist
blanc, blanche white, **7.2**
blessé(e) wounded, **L3**
bleu(e) blue, **7.2**
   bleu marine *(inv.)* navy
   blue, **7.2**
le **bloc-notes** notepad, **3.2**
blond(e) blond, **1.1**
bloquer to block, **10.1**
le **blouson** (waist-length)
   jacket, **7.1**
le **blue-jean** (pair of) jeans
le **bœuf** beef, **6.1**
bohème bohemian
boire to drink, **10.2**
   quelque chose à boire
   something to drink
le **bois** wood
la **boisson** beverage, drink,
   5.1
la **boîte: la boîte de conserve**
   can of food, **6.2**
   la boîte crânienne skull
boiteux, boiteuse lame
le **bol** bowl
bon(ne) correct; good, **6.2**
   Bon! Okay!, Right!, **6.1**
   bon marché *(inv.)*
   inexpensive
   de bonne heure early
le **bonhomme de neige**
   snowman
bonjour hello, **BV**
le **bonnet** ski cap, hat, **11.2**
le **bord: à bord (de)** aboard
   (plane, etc.), **8.2**
   au bord de la mer by the
   ocean, seaside, **11.1**
la **bosse** mogul *(ski)*, **11.2**
la **botanique** botany
le **boubou** boubou *(long,
   flowing garment)*
la **bouche** mouth, **14.1**
le **boucher, la bouchère**
   butcher
la **boucherie** butcher shop,
   6.1
la **bougie** candle, **4.1**

la **boulangerie-pâtisserie**
   bakery, **6.1**
la **bouteille** bottle, **6.2**
la **boutique** shop, boutique,
   7.1
le **bras** arm
le **Brésil** Brazil
le/la **Brésilien(ne)** Brazilian
   (person)
la **Bretagne** Brittany
breton(ne) Breton, from
   Brittany
le/la **Breton(ne)** Breton
   (person)
briller to shine
la **brioche** sweet roll
briser to break, **L3**
se **briser** to break
la **bronche** bronchial tube
bronzer to tan, **11.1**
la **brosse** brush, **12.1**
   la brosse à dents
   toothbrush, **12.1**
se **brosser** to brush, **12.1**
la **brousse** bush *(wilderness)*
le **bruit** noise, **L3**
brûler to burn
brun(e) brunette; dark-
   haired, **1.1**
le **buffet** train station
   restaurant, **9.1**
le **bungalow** bungalow
le **bus** bus, **5.2**
le **but** goal, **10.1**
   marquer un but to score
   a goal, **10.1**

ça that, **BV**
   Ça fait… euros. It's
   (That's) . . . euros., **6.2**
   Ça fait mal. It (That)
   hurts., **14.1**
   Ça va. Fine., Okay., **BV**
   Ça va? How's it going?,
   How are you? *(inform.)*,
   BV; How does it look?,
   7.2
   C'est ça. That's right.,
   That's it.
le **cabaret** cabaret

la **cabine** cabin *(plane)*, **8.1**
   la cabine d'essayage
   fitting room
cacher to hide, **L3**
le **cadeau** gift, present, **4.1**
le **cadet, la cadette**
   younger person, **L1**
le **café** café, **BV;** coffee, **5.1**
la **cafétéria** cafeteria
le **cahier** notebook, **3.2**
la **caisse** cash register,
   checkout counter, **3.2**
le **calcium** calcium
le **calcul** arithmetic, **2.2**
   le calcul différentiel
   differential calculus
   le calcul intégral
   integral calculus
la **calculatrice** calculator,
   3.2
le **calendrier** calendar,
   schedule
le **calligramme** picture-poem
calme quiet, calm
la **calorie** calorie
le/la **camarade** companion,
   friend
   le/la camarade de classe
   classmate
le **camembert** Camembert
   cheese
le **camion** truck
le **camp** side *(in a sport or
   game)*, **10.1**
   le camp adverse
   opponents, other side,
   10.1
la **campagne** country(side);
   campaign
   canadien(ne) Canadian, **6**
la **cantine** school dining hall,
   3.1
capable able
la **capitale** capital
le **car** bus *(coach)*
la **caractéristique**
   characteristic
   **Caraïbes: la mer des
   Caraïbes** Caribbean Sea
cardiaque cardiac
le **carnaval** carnival *(season)*
la **carotte** carrot, **6.2**
la **carrière** career

la **carte** menu, **5.1;** map; card
  la carte de crédit credit card
  la carte de débarquement landing card, **8.2**
  la carte d'embarquement boarding pass, **8.1**
  la carte postale postcard, **9.1**
le **carton** cardboard
la **casquette** cap, baseball cap, **7.1**
casse-pieds pain in the neck (*slang*)
la **cassette** cassette, tape **3.1**
  la cassette vidéo videocassette, **12.2**
le **catalogue** catalog
catastrophique catastrophic
la **catégorie** category
cause: à cause de because of
causer to cause
le **CD** CD, **3.1**
le **CD-ROM** CD-ROM
ce (cet), cette this, that, **9**
ce soir tonight
la **ceinture** belt, **L3**
  la ceinture de sécurité seat belt, **8.2**
célèbre famous
célébrer to celebrate, **L4**
la **cellule** cell, **L4**
celte Celtic
celtique Celtic
cent hundred, **2.2**
  pour cent percent
les **centaines** (*f. pl.*) hundreds
le **centilitre** centiliter
le **centre** center
  le centre commercial shopping center, mall, **7.1**
le **centre-ville** downtown
le **cercle** circle
les **céréales** (*f. pl.*) cereal, grains
certainement certainly
certains some
le **cerveau** brain

c'est it is, it's, **BV**
  C'est combien? How much is it?, **3.2**
  C'est quel jour? What day is it?, **BV**
  C'est tout. That's all., **6.1**
  c'est-à-dire that is
chacun(e) each (one), **5.2**
la **chaîne** chain; TV channel, **12.2**
la **chaise** chair
la **chambre à coucher** bedroom, **4.2**
le **champ** field, **L1**
  le champ de bataille battlefield, **L3**
champêtre pastoral
le/la **champion(ne)** champion
la **chance** luck
  avoir de la chance to be lucky, to be in luck
la **chanson** song
chanter to sing, **13.1**
le **chanteur, la chanteuse** singer, **13.1**
chaque each, every
le **char** float (*parade*)
la **charcuterie** deli(catessen), **6.1**
charger to load
le **chariot** shopping cart, **6.2;** baggage cart, **9.1**
charmant(e) charming
le **charme** charm
le **charpentier** carpenter
le **chasseur, la chasseuse** hunter
le **chat** cat, **4.1**
  avoir un chat dans la gorge to have a frog in one's throat, **14.1**
le **château** castle, mansion
chaud(e) warm, hot
  Il fait chaud. It's hot. (*weather*), **11.1**
la **chaussette** sock, **7.1**
la **chaussure** shoe, **7.1**
  les chaussures de ski ski boots, **11.2**
le **chef** head, boss
le **chemin** route; road; path
la **cheminée** chimney

la **chemise** shirt, **7.1**
le **chemisier** blouse, **7.1**
cher, chère dear; expensive, **7.1**
chercher to look for, seek
  aller chercher to go (and) get, **6.1**
le **chevalier** knight
les **cheveux** (*m. pl.*) hair, **12.1**
chez at (to) the home (business) of, **3.2**
le **chien** dog, **4.1**
la **chimie** chemistry, **2.2**
la **chimiothérapie** chemotherapy
chimique chemical
le/la **chimiste** chemist
chinois(e) Chinese
le **chœur** choir
choisir to choose, **8.1**
le **cholestérol** cholesterol
la **chose** thing
  ciao good-bye (*inform.*), **BV**
le **ciel** sky, **11.1**
le **cinéma** movie theater, movies, **13.1**
le **circuit** circuit
la **circulation** circulation
le **cirque** circus
  citer to cite, mention
le **citron pressé** lemonade, **5.1**
le/la **civilisé(e)** civilized person
clair(e) light (*color*)
la **clarinette** clarinet
la **classe** class, **2.1**
  la classe économique coach class (*plane*)
  la salle de classe classroom, **2.1**
le **classeur** loose-leaf binder, **3.2**
classifier to classify
classique classical
le **classique** classic
le **clavier** keyboard
le/la **client(e)** customer
le **climat** climate
climatique climatic
la **clinique** clinic
le **clown** clown

le **club d'art dramatique** drama club

le **coca** cola, **5.1**

le **code** code, **4.2**

le **coéquipier, la coéquipière** teammate

le **cœur** heart

le **coffre** (storage) chest, **L4**
le coffre à bagages (overhead) baggage compartment, **8.2**

le **coin: du coin** neighborhood (adj.)

la **collection** collection

le **collège** junior high, middle school, **1.2**

le/la **collégien(ne)** middle school/junior high student

le **combat** fight, battle, **L3**
combien (de) how much, how many, **3.2**
C'est combien? How much is it (that)?, **3.2**
comble packed (stadium), **10.1**

la **comédie** comedy, **13.1**
comique comic; funny, **13.1**
le film comique comedy, **13.1**
commander to order, **5.1**
comme like, as; for; since
comme ci, comme ça so-so
commémorer to commemorate
commencer to begin, **9.2**
comment how, what, **1.1**
Comment ça? How is that?

le/la **commerçant(e)** shopkeeper

la **compagnie** company
la compagnie aérienne airline, **8.1**
en compagnie de in the company of

la **comparaison** comparison
comparer to compare

le/la **compatriote** compatriot

la **compétition** contest

le **complet** suit (man's), **7.1**
complet, complète full, complete

le **pain complet** whole-wheat bread

complètement completely, totally

compléter to complete

compliqué(e) complicated

comploter to conspire

comporter to call for, require

composé(e) composed

le **compositeur, la compositrice** composer

la **composition** composition

composter to stamp, validate (a ticket), **9.1**

comprendre to understand, **5**

le **comprimé** pill, **14.2**

compris(e) included, **5.2**
Le service est compris. The tip is included., **5.2**

le **compte** account
compter to count

le **comptoir** counter, **8.1**

le **comte** count, **L4**

le **concept** concept

le **concert** concert

le **concert-bal** concert and ball

le **concours** competition, contest

la **condition** condition

la **confiture** jam, **6.2**
confortable comfortable

la **connaissance: faire la connaissance de** to meet

connaître to know, **13.2**

connecter to connect

connu(e) well-known; famous, **13.1**
le (la) plus connu(e) best-known

la **conserve: la boîte de conserve** can of food, **6.2**

la **consommation** drink, beverage, **5.1**

conspirer to plot

construire to build

la **consultation** medical visit
donner des consultations to have office hours (doctor)

consulter to consult

le **contact** contact

la **contamination** contamination

contenir to contain

content(e) happy, glad

le **continent** continent

continuer to continue

le **contraire** opposite

contre against, **10.1**
par contre on the other hand, however

le **contremaître, la contremaîtresse** foreman, forewoman

le **contrôle** check, control
le contrôle des passeports passport check
le contrôle de sécurité security (airport), **8.1**

contrôler to check; to control

le **contrôleur** conductor (train), **9.2**

la **conversation** conversation
converser to converse

la **conversion** conversion

convient: qui convient that is appropriate

le **copain** friend, pal (m.), **2.1**

la **copine** friend, pal (f.), **2.1**

le **cor** horn, **L3**
sonner du cor to blow a horn, **L3**

la **cornemuse** bagpipes

le **corps** body

la **correspondance** correspondence; connection (between trains), **9.2**

corriger to correct

cosmopolite cosmopolitan

la **côte** coast
la Côte d'Azur French Riviera
la Côte d'Ivoire Ivory Coast

le **côté** side
côté couloir aisle (seat), **8.1**
côté fenêtre window (seat), **8.1**

coucher to put (someone)
to bed, **12**

se **coucher** to go to bed, **12.1**

la **couchette** berth (on a train)

couler to flow

avoir le nez qui coule to
have a runny nose, **14.1**

la **couleur** color, **7.2**

le **couloir** aisle, corridor, **8.2**

le **coup: le coup de soleil**
sunburn, **11.1**

**donner un coup (de
pied, de tête, etc.)** to
kick, hit (with one's
foot, head, etc.), **10.1**

la **coupe** winner's cup, **10.2**

la **cour** courtyard, **3.2**; court

le **courage** courage

courageux, courageuse
courageous, brave

le **coureur, la coureuse**
runner, **10.2**

**le coureur (la coureuse)
cycliste** racing cyclist,
10.2

le **cours** course, class, **2.1**

**en cours de (français,
etc.)** in (French, etc.)
class

la **course** race (competition),
10.2

la course cycliste bicycle
race, **10.2**

les **courses** (f. pl.)**: faire des
courses** to go shopping,
6.1

court(e) short, **7.2**

le **couscous** couscous

le/la **cousin(e)** cousin, **4.1**

le **couteau** knife, **5.2**

coûter to cost, **3.2**

Ça coûte combien? How
much does this cost?, **3.1**

le **couturier** designer (of
clothes)

le **couvent** convent

couvert(e) covered

le **couvert** table setting;
silverware, **5.2**

couvrir to cover

le **crabe** crab, **6.1**

la **cravate** tie, **7.1**

le **crayon** pencil, **3.2**

créer to create

la **crème** cream

la crème solaire suntan
lotion, **11.1**

le **crème** coffee with cream
(in a café), **5.1**

la **crémerie** dairy store, **6.1**

le **créole** Creole (language)

la **crêpe** crepe, pancake, **BV**

creuser to dig, **L4**

crevé(e) exhausted

la **crevette** shrimp, **6.1**

crier to shout, **L4**

le/la **criminel(le)** criminal, **L4**

croire to believe, think,
7.2

la **croissance** growth

le **croissant** croissant,
crescent roll, **5.1**

le **croque-monsieur** grilled
ham and cheese
sandwich, **5.1**

la **crosse** hockey stick

la **cuillère** spoon, **5.2**

la **cuisine** kitchen, **4.2**;
cuisine (food)

faire la cuisine to cook, **6**

cuit(e) cooked

bien cuit(e) well-done
(meat), **5.2**

cultiver to cultivate

la **culture** culture

culturel(le) cultural

le **cyclisme** cycling, bicycle
riding, **10.2**

le/la **cycliste** cyclist, bicycle
rider

cycliste bicycle, cycling
(adj.), **10.2**

**le coureur (la coureuse)
cycliste** bicycle racer,
10.2

une course cycliste
bicycle race, **10.2**

d'abord first, **12.1**

d'accord okay, all right
(agreement)

être d'accord to agree, **2.1**

dangereux, dangereuse
dangerous

dans in, **1.2**

la **danse** dance

danser to dance, **13.1**

le **danseur, la danseuse**
dancer, **13.1**

la danseuse ballerina,
13.1

d'après according to

la **date** date

dater de to date from

d'autres some other, **2.2**

de from, **1.1**; of, belonging
to, **1.2**; about

de bonne heure early

de la, de l' some, any, **6**

De quelle couleur est... ?
What color is . . . ?, **7.2**

de temps en temps from
time to time,
occasionally

le **débarquement** landing,
deplaning

débarquer to get off
(plane)

débarrasser la table to
clear the table, **12.2**

debout standing, **9.2**

le **début** beginning

le/la **débutant(e)** beginner,
11.2

le **décalage horaire** time
difference

le **décalitre** dekaliter

le **déchet** waste

décider (de) to decide (to)

la **décision** decision

la décision est prise the
decision is made

déclarer to declare, call

le **décollage** takeoff (plane)

décoller to take off (plane),
8.1

découvrir to discover

décrire to describe

le **défilé** parade

définir to define

la **déformation** alteration

se **dégager** to be given off

dehors: au dehors de outside

déjà already; ever; yet, **BV**

déjeuner to eat lunch, **3.1**

le **déjeuner** lunch, **5.2**
  le petit déjeuner breakfast, **5.2**

délicieux, délicieuse delicious

demain tomorrow, **BV**
  À demain. See you tomorrow., **BV**

demander to ask (for), **3.2**

demi(e) half
  et demie half past *(time)*, **BV**

le **demi-cercle** semi-circle; top of the key *(on a basketball court)*, **10.2**

le **demi-frère** half brother, **4.1**

la **demi-heure** half hour

la **demi-sœur** half sister, **4.1**

le **demi-tarif** half price

le **demi-tour** about-face
  faire demi-tour to turn around

la **dent** tooth, **12.1**

le **dentifrice** toothpaste, **12.1**

le/la **dentiste** dentist

le **déodorant** deodorant

le **départ** departure, **8.1**

le **département d'outre-mer** French overseas department

se **dépêcher** to hurry, **12.1**

dépendre (de) to depend (on)

depuis since, for, **9.2**

dernier, dernière last, **10.2**

derrière behind

désagréable disagreeable, unpleasant

descendre to get off *(train, bus, etc.)*, **9.2**; to take down, **9**; to go down, **9**

désertique desert *(adj.)*

désespéré(e) desperate, **L4**

désirer to want, **5.1**

désormais from then on

le **dessert** dessert

le **dessin** art, **2.2**; drawing, illustration

le **dessin animé** cartoon, **13.1**

la **destination** destination
  à destination de to *(destination)*, **8.1**

la **destinée** destiny

détester to hate, **3.1**

déverser to spill
  se déverser to be spilled

deuxième second, **4.2**

devant in front of, **8.2**

devenir to become

deviner to guess

la **devinette** riddle

devoir to owe, **10**; must, to have to (+ *verb*), **10.2**

le **devoir** homework *(assignment)*
  faire ses devoirs to do homework, **12.2**

dévoué(e) devoted

d'habitude usually, **12.2**

le **diagnostic** diagnosis, **14.2**

le **dialecte** dialect

le **dialogue** dialog

le **diamant** diamond

dicter to dictate

la **différence** difference

différent(e) different, **8.1**

difficile difficult, **2.1**

la **difficulté** problem, difficulty
  être en difficulté to be in trouble

diffuser to spread, to propagate

dîner to eat dinner, **5.2**

le **dîner** dinner, **5.2**

le **diplôme** diploma

dire to say, tell, **9.2**
  Ça me dit! I'd like that!

directement directly

la **direction** direction

discuter to discuss

disparaître to disappear

disparu(e) disappeared, lost

la **disquette** diskette, floppy disk

distinguer to distinguish, to tell apart

divers(e) various

divisé(e) divided

diviser to divide

la **djellaba** djellaba *(long, loose garment)*

le **document** document

le **documentaire** documentary, **13.1**

le **doigt** finger

le **dollar** dollar, **3.2**

le **dolmen** dolmen

le **domaine** domain, field

le **domicile: à domicile** to the home

donc so, therefore

les **données** *(f. pl.)* data

donner to give, **4.1**
  donner un coup de pied to kick, **10.1**
  donner une fête to throw a party, **4.1**
  donner sur to face, overlook, **4.2**

dont of which

doré(e) golden

dormir to sleep, **8.2**

le **dortoir** dormitory

la **douane** customs

doublé(e) dubbed *(movies)*, **13.1**

la **douche** shower, **12.1**

douloureux, douloureuse painful

le **doute** doubt

la **douzaine** dozen, **6.2**

le **drame** drama, **13.1**

dribbler to dribble *(basketball)*, **10.2**

le **droit** right
  du coin neighborhood *(adj.)*

dur(e) hard

durer to last

dynamique dynamic, **1.2**

l' **eau** *(f.)* water, **6.2**
  l'eau bouillante boiling water
  l'eau minérale mineral water, **6.2**

l' **échange** *(m.)* exchange

échanger to exchange

s' **échapper** to escape
l' **écharpe** (*f.*) scarf, **11.2**
éclaté(e) burst
l' **école** (*f.*) school, **1.2**
 l'école primaire elementary school
 l'école secondaire junior high, high school, **1.2**
l' **écologie** (*f.*) ecology
écologique ecological
l' **économie** (*f.*) economics, **2.2**
 économique: la classe économique coach class (*plane*)
écouter to listen (to), **3.1**
l' **écran** (*m.*) screen, **8.1**
écrasé(e) crushed
écrire to write, **9.2**
l' **écrivain** (*m.*) writer (*m. and f.*), **L2**
efficace efficient
égal(e): Ça m'est égal. I don't care., It's all the same to me., **13.1**
égaliser to tie (*score*)
égoïste egotistical, **1.2**
égyptien(ne) Egyptian
l' **élément** (*m.*) element
l' **élève** (*m. et f.*) student, **1.2**
élevé(e) high
 bien élevé(e) well-behaved
éliminer to eliminate
l' **e-mail** (*m.*) e-mail
l' **embarquement** (*m.*) boarding, leaving
embarquer to board (*plane, etc.*)
l' **émission** (*f.*) program, show (*TV*), **12.2**
emmener to send, **L4**
l' **emploi** (*m.*) **du temps** schedule
l' **employé(e)** employee (*m. and f.*)
emprisonné(e) imprisoned
en in, **3.2**; by, **5.2**
 en avance early, ahead of time, **9.1**
 en avion plane (*adj.*), by plane, **8**

en ce moment right now
en classe in class
en fait in fact
en général in general
en l'honneur de in honor of
en particulier in particular
en plein air outdoors
en plus de besides, in addition
en première (seconde) in first (second) class, **9.1**
en provenance de arriving from (*flight, train*), **8.1**
en retard late, **9.1**
en solde on sale, **7.1**
en vain in vain
en ville in town, in the city
en voiture by car, **5.2**
encore still, **11**; another; again
s' **endormir** to fall asleep
l' **endroit** (*m.*) place
l' **énergie** (*f.*) energy
énergique energetic, **1.2**
l' **enfance** (*f.*) childhood
l' **enfant** (*m. et f.*) child, **4.1**
enfermer to shut up
enfin finally, at last, **12.1**
s' **engager dans** to head into
l' **ennemi(e)** (*m. et f.*) enemy
énorme enormous
l' **enquête** (*f.*) inquiry, survey
enregistrer to tape, **12.2**
 (faire) enregistrer to check (*baggage*), **8.1**
enrhumé(e): être enrhumé(e) to have a cold, **14.1**
enrichi(e) enriched
ensemble together, **5.1**
l' **ensemble** (*m.*) outfit; whole, entirety
ensuite then (*adv.*), **12.1**
entendre to hear, **9.1**
enthousiaste enthusiastic, **1.2**

entier, entière entire, whole
l' **entracte** (*m.*) intermission, **13.1**
entre between, among, **3.2**
l' **entrée** (*f.*) entrance, **4.2**; admission
l' **entreprise** (*f.*) firm
entrer to enter, **7.1**
environ about
envoyer to send, **10.1**
l' **épée** (*f.*) sword, **L3**
épicé(e) spicy
l' **épicerie** (*f.*) grocery store, **6.1**
les **épinards** (*m. pl.*) spinach, **6.2**
épique epic
l' **époque** (*f.*) period, times
épuisé(e) exhausted
l' **équateur** (*m.*) equator
l' **équilibre** (*m.*) balance
équilibré(e) balanced
l' **équipe** (*f.*) team, **10.1**
l' **équipement** (*m.*) equipment
l' **escalier** (*m.*) staircase, **4.2**
l' **espagnol** (*m.*) Spanish (*language*), **2.2**
l' **esprit** (*m.*) spirit
essayer to try on, **7.2**; to try
essentiel(le) essential
et and, **BV**
établir to establish
l' **établissement** (*m.*) establishment
l' **étage** (*m.*) floor (*of a building*), **4.2**
l' **étape** (*f.*) stage, lap
les **États-Unis** (*m. pl.*) United States
l' **été** (*m.*) summer, **11.1**
 en été in summer, **11.1**
éteindre to turn off (*appliance*), **12.2**
éternuer to sneeze, **14.1**
étranger, étrangère foreign, **13.1**
être to be, **1.1**
 être d'accord to agree, **2.1**
 être enrhumé(e) to have a cold, **14.1**

ne pas être dans son
assiette to be feeling
out of sorts, **14.1**
l' **être** *(m.)* being
l'**être humain** human
being
l' **étudiant(e)** *(university)*
student
l' **étude** *(f.)* study
étudier to study, **3.1**
l' **euro** *(m.)* euro, **6.2**
l' **Europe** *(f.)* Europe
européen(ne) European
s' **évader** to escape, **L4**
l' **événement** *(m.)* event
évidemment evidently
l' **évier** *(m.)* kitchen sink, **12.2**
éviter to avoid, **12.2**
évoquer to evoke
exact(e) exact
exactement exactly
l' **examen** *(m.)* test, exam, **3.1**
passer un examen to
take a test, **3.1**
réussir à un examen to
pass a test
examiner to examine, **14.2**
excellent(e) excellent
excepté(e) except
l' **exception** *(f.)* exception
exceptionnel(le)
exceptional
l' **excursion** *(f.)* excursion,
outing
exécuter to carry out
l' **exemple** *(m.)* example
par exemple for example
l' **exercice** *(m.)* exercise
l' **existence** *(f.)* existence
exister to exist, to be
expert(e) expert *(adj.)*
l' **explication** *(f.)*
explanation
expliquer to explain
l' **exposition** *(f.)* exhibit,
show, **13.2**
l' **express** *(m.)* espresso,
black coffee, **5.1**
l' **expression** *(f.)* expression
expulser to expel, banish
l' **extérieur** *(m.)* exterior,
outside

à l'**extérieur** outside,
outside the home
extraordinaire
extraordinary, **13.2**

la **fable** fable
fabriquer to build
fabuleusement fabulously
fabuleux, fabuleuse
fabulous
facile easy, **2.1**
la **façon** way, manner
faible weak, **L1**
faim: avoir faim to be
hungry, **5.1**
faire to do, make, **6.1**
Ça fait mal. It (That)
hurts., **14.1**
faire du (+ nombre) to
take size (+ number),
7.2
faire des achats to shop
faire attention to pay
attention, **6;** to be
careful, **11.1**
faire des courses to go
shopping, **7.2**
faire les courses to do the
grocery shopping, **6.1**
faire la cuisine to cook, **6**
faire ses devoirs to do
homework, **12.2**
faire enregistrer to check
(luggage), **8.1**
faire des études to study
**faire du français (des
maths, etc.)** to study
French (math, etc.), **6**
faire du jogging to jog
faire la navette to go
back and forth, make
the run
faire une ordonnance to
write a prescription, **14.2**
faire partie de to be a
part of
faire un pique-nique to
have a picnic

**faire de la planche à
voile** to windsurf, **11.1**
faire une promenade to
take a walk, **11.1**
faire la queue to wait in
line, **9.1**
faire du ski nautique to
water-ski, **11.1**
faire du surf to go
surfing, **11.1**
faire la vaisselle to do
the dishes, **12.2**
faire les valises to pack
(suitcases), **8.1**
faire un voyage to take a
trip, **8.1**
Il fait quel temps?
What's the weather
like?, **11.1**
**Vous faites quelle
pointure?** What size
shoe do you take?, **7.2**
Vous faites quelle taille?
What size do you take
(wear)?, **7.2**
fait(e) à la main
handmade
falsifier to falsify
la **famille** family, **4.1**
le nom de famille last
name
le/la **fana** fan
la **fanfare** brass band
fantastique fantastic
la **farine de sorgo** sorghum
flour
le **fast-food** fast-food
restaurant
fatigué(e) tired
faut: il faut one must, it is
necessary to, **8.2**
il ne faut pas one must
not, **11.1**
la **faute** fault, mistake
faux, fausse false
favori(te) favorite, **7.2**
la **femme** woman, **7.1;** wife,
4.1
la **fenêtre** window
côté fenêtre window
(seat) (adj.), **8.1**
fermé(e) closed, **13.2**

le **festival** festival

la **festivité** festivity

la **fête** party, **4.1**

  de fête festive

  donner une fête to throw a party, **4.1**

la **feuille de papier** sheet of paper, **3.2**

le **feutre** felt-tip pen, **3.2**

les **fiançailles** (*f. pl.*) engagement, **L4**

le/la **fiancé(e)** fiancé(e), **L4**

le **fichier** file (*computer*)

  fier, fière proud

la **fièvre** fever, **14.1**

  avoir de la fièvre to have a fever, **14.1**

  avoir une fièvre de cheval to have a high fever, **14.1**

la **figue** fig

la **figure** face, **12.1**

le **filet** net (*volleyball, etc.*), **10.2**

la **fille** girl, **1.1**; daughter, **4.1**

le **film** film, movie, **13.1**

  le film d'amour love story, **13.1**

  le film d'aventures adventure movie, **13.1**

  le film comique comedy, **13.1**

  le film étranger foreign film, **13.1**

  le film d'horreur horror film, **13.1**

  le film policier detective movie, **13.1**

  le film de science-fiction science-fiction movie, **13.1**

  le film en vidéo movie video, **13.1**

le **fils** son, **4.1**

la **fin** end

  finalement finally

  finir to finish, **8.2**

  fixement: regarder fixement to stare at

la **fleur** flower, **4.2**

  fleuri(e) in bloom, **L2**

  fleurir to bloom

le **fleuve** river

la **flûte** flute

le **foie** liver

  avoir mal au foie to have indigestion

la **fois** time (*in a series*), **10.2**

  à la fois at the same time

  deux fois twice

la **fonction** function

le **fonctionnement** functioning

  fond: au fond in the background

  respirer à fond to breathe deeply, **14.2**

  au fond de at the bottom of

  fonder to found

le **foot(ball)** soccer, **10.1**

  le football américain football

la **force** strength

la **formalité** formality

la **forme** form, shape

  former to form

  fort hard (*adv.*)

  fort(e) strong, **2.2**

  fort(e) en maths good in math, **2.2**

la **fortune** fortune

  fou, folle crazy; insane

la **fourchette** fork, **5.2**

la **fourniture** supply

  les fournitures scolaires school supplies, **3.2**

la **fracture** fracture (*of bone*)

  frais: Il fait frais. It's cool. (*weather*), **11.2**

les **frais** (*m. pl.*) expenses; charges

la **fraise** strawberry, **6.2**

le **français** French (*language*), **2.2**

le/la **Français(e)** Frenchman (-woman)

  français(e) French (*adj.*), **1.1**

la **France** France

  francophone French-speaking

  frapper to hit, **L3**; to knock, **L4**

  fréquenter to frequent, patronize

le **frère** brother, **1.2**

le **frigidaire** refrigerator, **12.2**

les **frissons** (*m. pl.*) chills, **14.1**

les **frites** (*f. pl.*) French fries, **5.1**

  froid(e) cold

  Il fait froid. It's cold. (*weather*), **11.2**

le **fromage** cheese, **5.1**

la **frontière** border

  frugal(e) light, simple

le **fruit** fruit, **6.2**

la **fumée** smoke

  fumer to smoke

la **fusion** fusion

le **futur** future, **L2**

le/la **gagnant(e)** winner, **10.2**

  gagner to earn; to win, **10.1**

le **gant** glove, **11.2**

  le gant de toilette washcloth, **12.1**

le **garage** garage, **4.2**

le **garçon** boy, **1.1**

  garder to guard, watch; to keep

le **gardien** guard, **L4**

  le gardien de but goalie, **10.1**

la **gare** train station, **9.1**

  gastronomique gastronomic, gourmet

le **gâteau** cake, **4.1**

le **gaz** gas

  le gaz carbonique carbon dioxide

le/la **géant(e)** giant

  geler to freeze

  Il gèle. It's freezing. (*weather*), **11.2**

le **général** general, **7**

  en général in general

  généralement generally

le **genre** type, kind, **13.1**

les **gens** (*m. pl.*) people

  gentil(le) nice (*person*), **6.2**

la **géographie** geography, **2.2**

la **géométrie** geometry, **2.2**
gigantesque gigantic
la **glace** ice cream, **5.1**; ice, **11.2**; mirror, **12.1**
le **glucide** carbohydrate
la **gomme** eraser, **3.2**
la **gorge** throat, **14.1**
  avoir un chat dans la gorge to have a frog in one's throat, **14.1**
  avoir la gorge qui gratte to have a scratchy throat, **14.1**
  avoir mal à la gorge to have a sore throat, **14.1**
le **gourmet** gourmet
grâce à thanks to
le **gradin** bleacher (stadium), **10.1**
la **graisse** fat
la **grammaire** grammar
le **gramme** gram, **6.2**
grand(e) tall, big, **1.1**; great
  le grand magasin department store, **7.1**
  de grand standing luxury (adj.)
  la grande surface large department store; large supermarket
grandir to grow (up) (children)
la **grand-mère** grandmother, **4.1**
le **grand-père** grandfather, **4.1**
les **grands-parents** (m. pl.) grandparents, **4.1**
gratter to scratch, **14.1**
gratuit(e) free
grave serious
la **Grèce** Greece
la **griffe** label
le **griot** griot (African musician-entertainer)
la **grippe** flu, **14.1**
gris(e) gray, **7.2**
la **grotte** cave, **L4**
le **groupe** group
guéri(e) cured
la **guerre** war, **L3**
le **guerrier** warrior, **L3**
le **guichet** ticket window, **9.1**; box office, **13.1**

le **guide** guidebook
guillotiné(e) guillotined
la **guitare** guitar
le/la **guitariste** guitarist
la **gymnastique** gymnastics, **2.2**

habillé(e) dressy, **7.1**
s' **habiller** to get dressed, **12.1**
habiter to live (in a city, house, etc.), **3.1**
haïtien(ne) Haitian
le **hall** lobby, **8.1**
le **hamburger** hamburger
le **hameau** hamlet
handicapé(e) handicapped
le **hardware** (computer) hardware
les **haricots** (m. pl.) **verts** green beans, **6.2**
la **harpe** harp
haut: en haut de la montagne at the top of the mountain
  haut de gamme state of the art
le **hautbois** oboe
l' **hectomètre** (m.) hectometer
l' **hémisphère** (m.) hemisphere
le **héros** hero
l' **heure** (f.) time (of day), **BV**; hour, **3.2**
  à l'heure on time, **8.1**
  à quelle heure? at what time?, **2**
  À tout à l'heure. See you later., **BV**
  de bonne heure early
  Il est quelle heure? What time is it?, **BV**
heureusement fortunately
heureux, heureuse happy
hier yesterday, **10.1**
  avant-hier the day before yesterday, **10.2**
  hier matin yesterday morning, **10.2**

  hier soir last night, **10.2**
l' **histoire** (f.) history, **2.2**; story
l' **hiver** (m.) winter, **11.2**
le/la **H.L.M.** low-income housing
le **hockey** hockey
l' **homme** (m.) man, **7.1**
honnête honest
les **honoraires** (m. pl.) fees (doctor)
l' **hôpital** (m.) hospital
l' **horaire** (m.) schedule, timetable, **9.1**
horrible horrible
hospitalier, hospitalière hospital (adj.)
le **hot-dog** hot dog, **5.1**
l' **hôtel** (m.) hotel
l' **hôtesse** (f.) **de l'air** flight attendant, **8.2**
l' **huile** (f.) oil, **6.1**
humain(e) human
l' **hydrate** (m.) **de carbone** carbohydrate
hyper: J'ai hyper faim. I'm super hungry.
l' **hypermarché** (m.) large department store/supermarket

I

idéal(e) ideal
l' **idée** (f.) idea
identifier to identify
il y a there is, there are, **4.1**
l' **île** (f.) island, **L4**
immédiat(e) immediate
immédiatement immediately
immense immense
l' **immeuble** (m.) apartment building, **4.2**
important(e) important
impossible impossible
les **impressionnistes** (m. pl.) Impressionists (painters)
l' **imprimante** (f.) printer
inaugurer to inaugurate
inconnu(e) unknown
l' **indication** (f.) cue

indiquer to indicate, show
indiscret, indiscrète indiscreet
indispensable indispensable
l' **individu** (m.) individual
individuel(le) individual
industriel(le) industrial
l' **infection** (f.) infection, **14.1**
inférieur(e) lower
infini(e) infinite
l' **influence** (f.) influence
influencer to influence
l' **information** (f.) information
les **informations** (f. pl.) news (TV)
l' **informatique** (f.) computer science, **2.2**
innocent(e) innocent
innombrable countless
insister to insist
inspirer to inspire
les **instructions** (f. pl.) instructions
l' **instrument** (m.) instrument
l'instrument à clavier keyboard instrument
l'instrument à cordes string instrument
l'instrument à percussion percussion instrument
l'instrument à vent wind instrument
intellectuel(le) intellectual
l' **intellectuel(le)** intellectual
intelligent(e) intelligent, **1.1**
intéressant(e) interesting, **1.1**
intéresser to interest
l' **intérêt** (m.) interest
intérieur(e) domestic (flight), **8.1**
international(e) international, **8.1**
interne internal
l' **interprète** (m. et f.) interpreter
l' **interro(gation)** (f.) quiz
intime intimate
inventer to make up

inviter to invite, **4.1;** to pay for someone's meal, **5.2**
isoler to isolate
l' **italien** (m.) Italian (language), **2.2**
italien(ne) Italian
l' **Ivoirien(ne)** (m. et f.) Ivorian (inhabitant of Côte d'Ivoire)

jaloux, jalouse jealous
jamais ever
ne… jamais never, **11.2**
la **jambe** leg
le **jambon** ham, **5.1**
janvier (m.) January, **BV**
le **jardin** garden, **4.2**
jaune yellow, **7.2**
le **jazz** jazz
je I, **1.2**
Je t'en prie. You're welcome. (fam.), **BV**
je voudrais I would like, **5.1**
Je vous en prie. You're welcome. (form.), **BV**
le **jean** jeans, **7.1**
jeter to throw, **L4**
le **jeu** game
jeune young
les **jeunes** (m. pl.) young people
le **jogging: faire du jogging** to jog
la **joie** joy
joli(e) pretty, **4.2**
jouer to play, **3.2;** to show (movie); to perform, **13.1**
jouer à to play a sport, **10.1**
jouer de to play a musical instrument
le **joueur, la joueuse** player, **10.1**
le **jour** day, **BV**
huit jours a week
de nos jours today, nowadays
tous les jours every day, **13.2**
le **journal** newspaper, **9.1**

la **journée** day, **3.1**
Belle journée! What a nice day!, **4.2**
Joyeux anniversaire! Happy birthday!
le **jumeau, la jumelle** twin, **L1**
la **jupe** skirt, **7.1**
le **jus** juice, **5.1**
le jus d'orange orange juice, **5.1**
le jus de pomme apple juice, **5.1**
jusqu'à (up) to, until, **10.2**
juste just, **2.1**
juste à sa taille fitting (him/her) just right
juste là right there
tout juste just barely

le **kilo(gramme)** kilogram, **6.2**
le **kilomètre** kilometer
le **kiosque** newsstand, **9.1**
le **kleenex** tissue, **14.1**

L

là there
là-haut up there
le **laboratoire** laboratory
le **lac** lake
laisser to leave (something behind), **5.2;** to let, allow
laisser un pourboire to leave a tip, **5.2**
le **lait** milk, **6.1**
lancer to throw, to shoot (ball), **10.2**
le **langage: en langage courant** commonly known as
la **langue** language, **2.2**
large loose, wide, **7.2**
le **latin** Latin, **2.2**
latin(e) Latin

latino-américain(e) Latin American
laver to wash, **12**
se **laver** to wash oneself, **12.1**
le **lave-vaisselle** dishwasher, **12.2**
la **leçon** lesson, **11.1**
le **lecteur, la lectrice** reader
la **lecture** reading
la **légende** legend
le **légume** vegetable, **6.2**
la **lettre** letter
lever to raise, **3.1**
    lever la main to raise one's hand, **3.1**
se **lever** to get up, **12.1**
la **liaison** liaison, linking
libérer to free
la **liberté** freedom
libre free, **5.1**
le **lieu** place
    avoir lieu to take place
la **ligne** line
la **limite** limit
la **limonade** lemon-lime drink, **BV**
le **lipide** fat
le **liquide** liquid
lire to read, **9.2**
le **litre** liter, **6.2**
la **littérature** literature, **2.2**
la **livre** pound, **6.2**
le **livre** book, **3.2**
local(e) local
le **logement** housing
le **logiciel** computer program
loin far (away)
    loin de far from, **4.2**
le **long: le long de** along
long(ue) long, **7.1**
longtemps (for) a long time, **11.1**
    trop longtemps (for) too long, **11.1**
le **look** style
louer to rent, **13.1**
les **lunettes** (f. pl.) **de soleil** sunglasses, **11.1**
la **lutte** fight, battle, **L3**
lutter to fight, **L3**

le **lycée** high school, **2.1**
le/la **lycéen(ne)** high school student

la **machine** machine
Madame (Mme) Mrs., Ms., **BV**
Mademoiselle (Mlle) Miss, Ms., **BV**
le **magasin** store, **3.2**
    le grand magasin department store, **7.1**
le **magazine** magazine, **9.1**
le **Maghreb** Maghreb
magique magic (adj.)
le **magnétoscope** VCR, **12.2**
magnifique magnificent
le **maillot** jersey
    le maillot de bain bathing suit, **11.1**
la **main** hand, **3.1**
    fait(e) à la main handmade
maintenant now, **2.2**
mais but, **2.1**
    Mais oui (non)! Of course (not)!
la **maison** house, **3.1**
    la maison d'édition publishing house
la **maisonnette** cottage
la **majorité** majority
mal badly, **14.1**
    avoir mal à to have a(n) . . . -ache, to hurt, **14.1**
    Ça fait mal. It (That) hurts., **14.1**
    Où avez-vous mal? Where does it hurt?, **14.2**
    Pas mal. Not bad., **BV**
malade ill, sick, **L1, 14.1**
le/la **malade** sick person, patient, **14.2**
la **maladie** illness, disease
malheureusement unfortunately
malheureux, malheureuse unhappy
malin (maligne): C'est malin! Very clever! (ironic)

la **maman** mom
la **Manche** English Channel
la **manche** sleeve, **7.1**
    à manches longues (courtes) long- (short-) sleeved, **7.1**
manger to eat, **5.1**
    la salle à manger dining room, **4.2**
la **manifestation culturelle** cultural event
le **manteau** coat, **7.1**
se **maquiller** to put on makeup, **12.1**
le/la **marchand(e) (de fruits et légumes)** (produce) seller, merchant, **6.2**
la **marchandise** merchandise
le **marché** market, **6.2**
    bon marché inexpensive
    le marché aux puces flea market
marcher to walk
le **mari** husband, **4.1**
le **mariage** marriage; wedding
marié(e) married
se **marier** to get married, **L4**
le **marin** sailor, **L4**
le **Maroc** Morocco
marocain(e) Moroccan
marquer un but to score a goal, **10.1**
marron (inv.) brown, **7.2**
marseillais(e) from Marseille
martiniquais(e) from or of Martinique
le **mat** (fam.) morning
le **match** game, **10.1**
les **mathématiques** (f. pl.) mathematics, **2.2**
les **maths** (f. pl.) math, **2.2**
la **matière** subject (school), **2.2**; matter
le **matin** morning, **BV**
    du matin A.M. (time), **BV**
mauvais(e) bad; wrong, **2.2**
    Il fait mauvais. It's bad weather., **11.1**
le **médecin** doctor (m. and f.), **14.2**

chez le médecin at (to) the doctor's office, **14.2**

la **médecine** medicine *(medical profession)*

médical(e) medical

le **médicament** medicine, **14.1**

la **médina** medina

le **mélange** mixture

le **melon** melon, **6.2**

même *(adj.)* same, **2.1;** *(adv.)* even

tout de même all the same, **5.2**

la **mer** sea, **11.1**

la mer des Antilles Caribbean Sea

la mer des Caraïbes Caribbean Sea

la mer Méditerranée Mediterranean Sea

merci thank you, thanks, **BV**

la **mère** mother, **4.1**

merveilleux, merveilleuse marvelous

le **message** message

la **mesure** measurement

mesurer to measure

le **métabolisme** metabolism

le **métal** metal

le **mètre** meter

le **métro** subway, **4.2**

la station de métro subway station, **4.2**

mettre to put (on), to place, **7.1;** to turn on *(appliance)*, **7**

mettre la table to set the table, **7**

les **meubles** *(m. pl.)* furniture

le **microbe** microbe, germ

microbien(ne) microbial

le **microprocesseur** microprocessor

le **microscope** microscope

midi *(m.)* noon, **BV**

mieux better, **7.2**

aimer mieux to prefer, **7.2**

aller mieux to feel better, **14.2**

militaire military

mille (one) thousand, **3.2**

le **milligramme** milligram

le **million** million

le **minéral** mineral

minuit *(m.)* midnight, **BV**

la **minute** minute, **9.2**

le **miracle** miracle

la **mi-temps** half *(sporting event)*

la **mode: à la mode** in style

le **modèle** model

le **modem** modem

moderne modern

modeste modest; reasonably priced

la **moelle épinière** spinal cord

moins less, **7.1;** minus

plus ou moins more or less

le **mois** month, **BV**

le **moment** moment, time

en ce moment right now

le **monde** world

beaucoup de monde a lot of people, **10.1**

tout le monde everyone, everybody, **1.2**

le **moniteur** *(computer)* monitor

le **moniteur, la monitrice** instructor, **11.1**

Monsieur *(m.)* Mr., sir, **BV**

le **mont** mount, mountain

la **montagne** mountain, **11.2**

monter to go up, **4.2;** to get on, get in, **9.2**

monter une pièce to put on a play, **13.1**

montrer to show

la **mort** death

le **mot** word

le mot apparenté cognate

le **mouchoir** handkerchief, **14.1**

la **moule** mussel

mourir to die, **11**

la **moutarde** mustard, **6.2**

le **mouvement** movement

moyen(ne) average, intermediate

le **moyen de transport** mode of transportation

multicolore multicolored

multiplier to multiply

muni(e) de with

municipal(e) municipal

le **mur** wall, **L4**

le **muscle** muscle

musculaire muscular

le **musée** museum, **13.2**

musical(e) musical

le/la **musicien(ne)** musician

la **musique** music, **2.2**

musulman(e) Muslim

mystérieux, mystérieuse mysterious

le **mythe** myth

nager to swim, **11.1**

naître to be born, **11**

la **nappe** tablecloth, **5.2**

la **natation** swimming, **11.1**

national(e) national

la **nationalité** nationality

la **nature** nature

nature plain *(adj.)*, **5.1**

naturel(le) natural

la **navette: faire la navette** to go back and forth, make the run

naviguer sur Internet to surf the Net

ne: ne… jamais never, **11.2**

ne… pas not, **1.2**

ne… personne no one, nobody, **11**

ne… plus no longer, no more, **6.1**

ne… que only

ne… rien nothing, **11**

né(e): elle est née she was born

nécessaire necessary

nécessairement necessarily

négatif, négative negative

la **négritude** black pride

la **neige** snow, **11.2**

neige *(inf.* **neiger***)***: Il neige.** It's snowing., **11.2**

nerveux, nerveuse
nervous
n'est-ce pas? isn't it?,
doesn't it (he, she, etc.)?,
2.2
le **neveu** nephew, **4.1**
le **nez** nose, **14.1**
avoir le nez qui coule to
have a runny nose, **14.1**
ni… ni neither . . . nor
la **nièce** niece, **4.1**
noir(e) black, **7.2**
le **nom** name; noun
le **nom de famille** last
name
le **nombre** number
nombreux, nombreuse
numerous
nommer to name, mention
non no
non plus either, neither
non-fumeurs non-
smoking (section), **8.1**
le **nord** north
nord-africain(e) North
African
normal(e) normal
la **note** note; grade
nourrir to feed
la **nourriture** food, nutrition
nouveau (nouvel),
nouvelle new, **4.2**
à nouveau again
la **Nouvelle-Angleterre** New
England
La **Nouvelle-Orléans** New
Orleans
le **nuage** cloud, **11.1**
la **nuit** night
nul(le) (slang) bad
le **numéro** number
le **numéro de téléphone**
telephone number

ô oh
l' **objet** (m.) object
obligatoire mandatory
obliger to oblige, force
observer to observe

occidental(e) western
occupé(e) occupied, taken,
5.1; busy
l' **océan** (m.) ocean
l'océan Atlantique
Atlantic Ocean
l' **œil** (m.) eye, **14.1**
l' **œuf** (m.) egg, **6.1**
l'œuf à la coque
poached egg
l'œuf brouillé scrambled
egg
l'œuf sur le plat fried egg
l' **œuvre** (f.) work(s) (of art or
literature), **13.1**
officiel(le) official
l' **oignon** (m.) onion, **5.1**
l' **oiseau** (m.) bird
l' **olive** (f.) olive
l' **omelette** (f.) omelette, **5.1**
l'omelette aux fines
herbes omelette with
herbs, **5.1**
l'omelette nature plain
omelette, **5.1**
on we, they, people, **3.2**
On y va? Let's go.; Shall
we go?
l' **oncle** (m.) uncle, **4.1**
l' **opéra** (m.) opera
l'opéra comique light
opera
l'opéra bouffe comic
light opera
l' **opération** (f.) operation
opposer to oppose, **10.1**
l' **or** (m.) gold, **L4**
l' **orange** (f.) orange, **6.2**
orange (inv.) orange
(color), **7.2**
l' **oranger** (m.) orange
tree, **L2**
l' **orchestre** (m.) orchestra
l'orchestre symphonique
symphony orchestra
orchestrer to orchestrate
ordinaire ordinary
l' **ordinateur** (m.) computer
l' **ordonnance** (f.)
prescription, **14.2**
faire une ordonnance to
write a prescription, **14.2**

l' **oreille** (f.) ear, **14.1**
avoir mal aux oreilles
to have an earache,
14.1
l' **organe** (m.) organ (of the
body)
organiser to organize
l' **organisme** (m.) organism
l' **orgue** (m.) organ (musical
instrument)
oriental(e) eastern
originaire de native of
l' **origine** (f.): **d'origine**
américaine (française,
etc.) from the U.S.
(France, etc.)
orner to decorate
l' **os** (m.) bone
ôter to take off (clothing)
ou or, **1.1**
où where, **1.1**
d'où from where, **1.1**
oublier to forget
l' **ouest** (m.) west
oui yes, **BV**
ouvert(e) open, **13.2**
l' **ouvrier, l'ouvrière** worker
ouvrir to open, **14.2**
l' **oxygène** (m.) oxygen

P

le **pain** bread, **6.1**
le pain complet whole-
wheat bread
le pain grillé toast
la tartine de pain beurré
slice of bread and butter
la **paire** pair, **7.1**
la **paix** peace
le **palais** palace
le **palet** puck
le **panier** basket, **10.2**
réussir un panier to
make a basket
(basketball), **10.2**
le **pantalon** pants, **7.1**
papa dad
la **papeterie** stationery store,
3.2
le **papier** paper, **3.2**

la **feuille de papier** sheet of paper, 3.2

Pâques Easter

le **paquet** package, 6.2

par by, through

par exemple for example

par semaine a (per) week, 3.2

le **parc** park

parce que because

par-dessus over (*prep.*), 10.2

pardon excuse me, pardon me

les **parents** (*m. pl.*) parents, 4.1

parfait(e) perfect

parfaitement perfectly

le **parfum** flavor

parisien(ne) Parisian

le **parking** parking lot

parler to speak, talk, 3.1

parler au téléphone to talk on the phone, 3.2

les **paroles** (*f. pl.*) words, lyrics

la **part: de part et d'autre** on each side

de sa part on his (her) part

participer (à) to participate (in)

particulièrement particularly

la **partie** part

faire partie de to be a part of

partir to leave, 8.1

partout everywhere

pas not, 2.1

pas du tout not at all, 3.1

Pas mal. Not bad., BV

Pas question! Out of the question! Not a chance!

le **passager, la passagère** passenger, 8.1

la **passe** pass

passé(e) past

le **passeport** passport, 8.1

passer to spend (*time*), 3.1; to go (through), 8.1; to pass, 10.1

passer un examen to

take an exam, 3.1

les **pâtes** (*f. pl.*) pasta

la **patience** patience, 9.2

le **patin** skate; skating, 11.2

faire du patin à glace to ice-skate, 11.1

la **patinoire** skating rink, 11.2

le/la **patron(ne)** boss

pauvre poor, 14.1, L1

Le/La pauvre! Poor thing!, 14.1

le **pavillon** small house, bungalow

payer to pay, 3.2

le **pays** country, 8.1

le **paysage** landscape

le/la **paysan(ne)** peasant, L1

le **peigne** comb, 12.1

se **peigner** to comb one's hair, 12.1

peindre to paint

le/la **peintre** painter, artist, 13.2

la **peinture** painting, 13.2

le **penalty** penalty (*soccer*)

pendant during, for (*time*), 3.2

la **pénicilline** penicillin, 14.1

penser to think

perdre to lose, 9.2

le **père** father, 4.1

la **période** period

la **périphérie** outskirts

la **perle** pearl

permanent(e) permanent

permettre to permit, allow

la **personnalité** personality

la **personne** person

ne… personne no one, nobody, 11

personnel(le) personal

le **personnel de bord** flight crew, 8.2

personnellement personally, 13.2

petit(e) short, small, 1.1

le **petit ami** boyfriend

la **petite amie** girlfriend

le **petit déjeuner** breakfast, 5.2

les **petits pois** (*m.*) peas, 6.2

la **petite-fille**

granddaughter, 4.1

le **petit-fils** grandson, 4.1

les **petits-enfants** (*m. pl.*) grandchildren, 4.1

le **pétrole** oil

le **pétrolier** oil tanker

peu (de) few, little

à peu près about, approximately

un peu a little, 2.1

un peu de a little

en très peu de temps in a short time

très peu seldom, 5.2

peur: avoir peur to be afraid, L1

pharmaceutique pharmaceutical

la **pharmacie** pharmacy, 14.2

le/la **pharmacien(ne)** pharmacist, 14.2

le **phénomène** phenomenon

la **photo** photograph

la **phrase** sentence

le/la **physicien(ne)** physicist

physique physical

la **physique** physics, 2.2

le **piano** piano

la **pie** magpie

la **pièce** room, 4.2; play, 13.1

la **pièce de théâtre** play, 13.1

le **pied** foot, 10.1

à pied on foot, 4.2

donner un coup de pied to kick, 10.1

être vite sur pied to be better soon, 14.1

la **pierre** stone

la **pierre précieuse** gem, L4

le/la **pilote** pilot, 8.2

piloter to pilot, to fly

piquer to sting, 14.1

la **piscine** pool, 11.1

la **piste** runway, 8.1; track, 10.2; ski trail, 11.2

pittoresque picturesque

la **pizza** pizza, BV

la **place** seat (*plane, train, movie, etc.*), 8.1; place; square

la **plage** beach, **11.1**
la **plaine** plain
le **plaisir** pleasure
la **planche à voile: faire de la planche à voile** to windsurf, **11.1**
la **plante** plant
le **plastique** plastic
le **plat** dish (food)
le **plateau** tray, **8.2**
plein(e) full, **10.1**
pleurer to cry, **L1**
pleut (inf. **pleuvoir**): Il **pleut.** It's raining., **11.1**
plissé(e) pleated, **7.1**
le **plongeon** dive
plonger to dive, **11.1**
la **pluie** rain
la **plupart (des)** most (of), **9.2**
le **pluriel** plural
plus plus; more, **7.1**
en plus de in addition to
ne... plus no longer, no more, **6.1**
plus ou moins more or less
plus tard later
plusieurs several
plutôt rather
le **poème** poem
la **poésie** poetry
le **poète** poet (m. and f.)
le **poids** weight
point: à point medium-rare (meat), **5.2**
la **pointure** size (shoes), **7.2**
Vous faites quelle pointure? What (shoe) size do you take?, **7.2**
la **poire** pear, **6.2**
le **poisson** fish, **6.1**
la **poissonnerie** fish store, **6.1**
la **poitrine** chest (body)
le **poivre** pepper, **6.1**
la **politesse** courtesy, politeness, **BV**
politique political
pollué(e) polluted
la **pollution** pollution
le **polo** polo shirt, **7.1**
la **pomme** apple, **6.2**
la tarte aux pommes

apple tart, **6.1**
la **pomme de terre** potato, **6.2**
le **pont** bridge
pop pop (music)
populaire popular, **1.2**
le **porc** pork, **6.1**
le **port** port, harbor
la **porte** gate (airport), **8.1;** door, **L4**
porter to wear, **7.1**
le/la **portraitiste** portraitist
portugais(e) Portuguese
poser une question to ask a question, **3.1**
la **position** position
posséder to possess, own
la **possession** possession
la **poste** mail
la poste par avion airmail
le **pot** jar, **6.2**
le **poulet** chicken, **6.1**
le **poumon** lung
pour for, **2.1;** in order to
pour cent percent
le **pourboire** tip (restaurant), **5.2**
pourquoi why, **6.2**
pourquoi pas? why not?
pousser to push
pouvoir to be able to, can, **6.1**
pratique practical
la **pratique** practice
pratiquer to practice
précédent(e) preceding
préféré(e) favorite
préférer to prefer, **6**
le **préfixe** prefix
premier, première first, **4.2**
en première in first class, **9.1**
prendre to have (to eat or drink, **5.1;** to take, **5.2;** to buy
prendre un bain (une douche) to take a bath (shower), **12.1**
prendre un bain de soleil to sunbathe, **11.1**
prendre le petit déjeuner to eat breakfast, **5.2**
prendre possession de

to take possession of
prendre rendez-vous to make an appointment
prendre le métro to take the subway, **5.2**
le **prénom** first name
préparer to prepare
près de near, **4.2**
prescrire to prescribe, **14.2**
présenter to present; to introduce
presque almost
prie: Je vous en prie. You're welcome., **BV**
primaire: l'école (f.) **primaire** elementary school
principal(e) main, principal
le **printemps** spring, **11.1**
au printemps in the spring
la **prison** prison, **L4**
le **prisonnier, la prisonnière** prisoner, **L4**
privé(e) private
le **prix** price, cost, **7.1**
le **problème** problem
prochain(e) next, **9.2**
procurer to provide
le **produit** product
le/la **prof** teacher (inform.), **2.1**
le **professeur** teacher (m. and f.), **2.1**
professionnel(le) professional
la **programmation** programming
le **programme** program
le **projet** plan
la **promenade: faire une promenade** to take a walk, **11.1**
promotion: en promotion on special, on sale
proposer to suggest
protéger to protect
la **protéine** protein
provenance: en provenance de arriving from (train, plane, etc.), **8.1**
les **provisions** (f. pl.) food

public, publique public
la **publicité** commercial (*TV*), **12.2**; advertisement
publier to publish
les **puces** (*f. pl.*): **le marché aux puces** flea market
le **pull** sweater, **7.1**
pulmonaire pulmonary
punir to punish
purifié(e) purified

le **quai** platform (*railroad*), **9.1**
la **qualité** quality
quand when, **4.1**
le **quart: et quart** a quarter past (*time*), **BV**
moins le quart a quarter to (*time*), **BV**
le **quartier** neighborhood, district, **4.2**
quatrième fourth
que as; that; than (*in comparisons*), **7.2**
québécois(e) from or of Quebec
quel(le) which, what
quelque some (*sing.*)
quelque chose something, **11**
quelque chose à manger something to eat, **5.1**
quelque chose de spécial something special
quelquefois sometimes, **5.2**
quelques some, a few (*pl.*), **9.2**
quelqu'un somebody, someone, **10.1**
la **question** question, **3.1**
Pas question! Out of the question! Not a chance!
poser une question to ask a question, **3.1**
la **queue** line, **9.1**
faire la queue to wait in line, **9.1**
qui who, **1.1**; whom, **10**; which, that

quitter to leave (*a room, etc.*), **3.1**
quoi what (*after prep.*)
quotidien(ne) daily, everyday

R

la **race** race (*human population*)
raconter to tell (about)
la **radio** radio, **3.2**
le **raisin sec** raisin
la **raison** reason
ramasser to pick up, **8.2**
le **rap** rap (*music*)
rapide quick, fast
rapidement rapidly, quickly
le **rapport** relationship; report
se **raser** to shave, **12.1**
le **rasoir** razor, shaver, **12.1**
rater to miss (*train, etc.*), **9.2**
le **rayon** department (*in a store*), **7.1**
le rayon des manteaux coat department, **7.1**
la **réalité** reality
recevoir to receive, **10.2**
la **recherche** research
à la recherche de in search of
recommencer to begin again
reconnaître to recognize
la **récré** recess, **3.2**
la **récréation** recess, **3.2**
récrire to rewrite
recueillir to pick up
le **recyclage** recycling
la **réduction** discount
refléter to reflect
le **réfrigérateur** refrigerator, **12.2**
regarder to look at, **3.1**
regarder fixement to stare at
le **reggae** reggae
le **régime** diet
faire un régime to follow a diet

la **région** region
la **règle** ruler, **3.2**; rule
regretter to be sorry, **6.1**
régulier, régulière regular
la **reine** queen
la **relation** relationship
relier to connect
religieux, religieuse religious
remarquer to notice
rembourser to pay back, reimburse
remonter to get back on
remplacer to replace
remplir to fill out, **8.2**
rencontrer to meet
le **rendez-vous: prendre rendez-vous** to make an appointment
se **rendormir** to fall asleep again
rendre to give back
rendre bien service to be a big help
renommé(e) renowned
les **renseignements** (*m. pl.*) information
rentrer to go home; to return, **3.2**
renvoyer to return (*volleyball*), **10.2**
le **repas** meal, **5.2**
répéter to repeat
répondre (à) to answer, **9.2**
le **reportage** news article
représenter to represent
réservé(e) reserved
respectif, respective respective
la **respiration** breathing; respiration
respiratoire respiratory
respirer to breathe, **14.2**
respirer à fond to breathe deeply, **14.2**
ressembler à to resemble
ressortir to leave
le **restaurant** restaurant, **5.2**
la **restauration** food service
la restauration rapide fast food
rester to stay, remain, **11.1**
il reste there remains

le **retard** delay
 avoir du retard to be late *(plane, train, etc.)*, **8.1**
 en retard late, **9.1**
le **retour** return
la **retraite** retreat; retirement
 retrouver to meet, get together with
 réussir to succeed
 réussir à un examen to pass an exam
 réussir un panier to make a basket *(basketball)*, **10.2**
 réveillé(e) awake
se **réveiller** to wake up, **12.1**
 révéler to reveal
la **révolution** revolution
 révolutionnaire revolutionary
la **revue** magazine, **L2**
le **rez-de-chaussée** ground floor, **4.2**
le **rhume** cold *(illness)*, **14.1**
 riche rich
 ridicule ridiculous
 rien nothing
 rigoler to joke around, **3.2**
 Tu rigoles! You're kidding!, **3.2**
 rigolo funny, **4.2**
 rincer to rinse
la **rivière** river
le **riz** rice
la **robe** dress, **7.1**
le **rocher** rock, boulder, **L3**
le **roi** king, **L3**
le **rôle** role
le **roman** novel
 romantique romantic
 rose pink, **7.2**
 rouge red, **7.2**
 rouler (vite) to go, drive, ride (fast), **10.2**
la **route** road
la **routine** routine, **12.1**
 royal(e) royal
le **rubis** ruby
la **rue** street, **3.1**
 ruiné(e) ruined
 rural(e) rural

le **russe** Russian *(language)*
le **rythme** rhythm

le **sac** bag, **6.1**
 le sac à dos backpack, **3.2**
 saignant(e) rare *(meat)*, **5.2**
la **saison** season
la **salade** salad, **5.1**; lettuce, **6.2**
le **salaire** salary
 sale dirty
la **salle** room
 la salle à manger dining room, **4.2**
 la salle d'attente waiting room, **9.1**
 la salle de bains bathroom, **4.2**
 la salle de cinéma movie theater, **13.1**
 la salle de classe classroom, **2.1**
 la salle de séjour living room, **4.2**
 Salut. Hi.; Bye., **BV**
la **salutation** greeting
les **sandales** *(f. pl.)* sandals, **7.1**
le **sandwich** sandwich, **BV**
le **sang** blood
 sans without
la **santé** health, **14.1**
la **sardine** sardine
 satisfaire to satisfy
la **sauce** sauce
la **saucisse** sausage
 la saucisse de Francfort hot dog, **BV**
le **saucisson** salami, **6.1**
 sauf except, **13.2**
 sauvegarder to safeguard, to save
 sauver to save
le **savant** scientist *(m. and f.)*,
 savoir to know *(information)*, **13.2**
le **savon** soap, **12.1**
le **saxophone** saxophone
la **scène** scene, **13.1**
les **sciences** *(f. pl.)* science, **2.1**

 les sciences naturelles natural sciences, **2.1**
 les sciences sociales social studies, **2.1**
 scientifique scientific
 scintiller to sparkle
 scolaire school *(adj.)*, **3.2**
le **sculpteur** sculptor *(m. and f.)*, **13.2**
la **sculpture** sculpture, **13.2**
la **séance** show(ing) *(movie)*, **13.1**
 sec, sèche dry
 second(e) second
 secondaire: l'école *(f.)* **secondaire** junior high, high school, **1.2**
 seconde: en seconde in second class, **9.1**
 secret, secrète secret
le **séjour** stay
 la salle de séjour living room, **4.2**
le **sel** salt, **6.1**
 selon according to
la **semaine** week, **3.2**; allowance
 la semaine dernière last week, **10.2**
 la semaine prochaine next week
 par semaine a (per) week, **3.2**
 semblable similar, **L1**
le/la **Sénégalais(e)** Senegalese *(person)*
le **sens** direction; meaning
se **sentir** to feel *(well, etc.)*, **14.1**
 séparer to separate
 sérieux, sérieuse serious, **7**
 serré(e) tight, **7.2**
le **serveur, la serveuse** waiter, waitress, **5.1**
le **service** service, **5.2**
 Le service est compris. The tip is included., **5.2**
la **serviette** napkin, **5.2**; towel, **11.1**
 servir to serve, **8.2**; **10.2**
 seul(e) alone, **5.2**; single; only *(adj.)*

tout(e) seul(e) all alone, by himself/herself, **5.2**

seulement only *(adv.)*

le **shampooing** shampoo, **12.1**

le **shopping** shopping, **7.2**

le **short** shorts, **7.1**

si if; yes *(after neg. question)*, **7.2;** so *(adv.)*

le **sida (syndrome immuno-déficitaire acquis)** AIDS

le **siècle** century

le **siège** seat, **8.2**

siffler to (blow a) whistle, **10.1**

le **sifsari** type of veil worn by North African women

le **signal** sign

la **signification** meaning, significance

signifier to mean

simple simple

l'**aller (simple)** one-way ticket, **9.1**

simplement simply

sinon or else, otherwise, **9.2**

la **sinusite** sinus infection, **14.2**

le **sirop** syrup, **14.1**

le **site** Web site

situé(e) located

le **ski** ski, skiing, **11.2**

faire du ski to ski, **11.2**

faire du ski nautique to water-ski, **11.1**

le **ski alpin** downhill skiing, **11.2**

le **ski de fond** cross-country skiing, **11.2**

le **skieur, la skieuse** skier, **11.2**

le **snack-bar** snack bar, **9.2**

sociable sociable, outgoing, **1.2**

social(e) social

la **société** company

la **sœur** sister, **1.2**

le **software** software

soi oneself, himself, herself

soif: avoir soif to be thirsty, **5.1**

le **soin** care

de soins polyvalents general care

le **soir** evening , **BV**

ce soir tonight

du soir in the evening, P.M., **BV**

le soir in the evening, **5.2**

le **sol** ground, **10.2**

le **soldat** soldier, **L3**

les **soldes** *(m. pl.)* sale *(in a store)*, **7.1**

le **soleil** sun, **11.1**

au soleil in the sun, **11.1**

Il fait du soleil. It's sunny., **11.1**

le soleil levant rising sun

la **solidarité** solidarity

solide solid

solitaire lonely

la **solution** solution

sombre dark

la **somme** sum

le **sommet** summit, mountaintop, **11.2**

le **son** sound, **L3**

le **sondage** survey, opinion poll

sonner du cor to blow a horn, **L3**

la **sorte** sort, kind, type

sortir to go out; to take out, **8.2**

sortir victorieux (victorieuse) to win (the battle)

la **souche** tree stump

dormir comme une souche to sleep like a log

souffrir to suffer, **14.2**

souhait *(m.)*: **À tes souhaits!** God bless you! Gesundheit!, **14.1**

le **souk** North African market

la **soupe** soup, **5.1**

la soupe à l'oignon onion soup, **5.1**

la **source** source

la **souris** mouse

sous under, **8.2**

les **sous-titres** *(m. pl.)* subtitles, **13.1**

soustraire to subtract

souterrain(e) underground

le **souvenir** memory

souvent often, **5.2**

les **spaghettis** *(m. pl.)* spaghetti

spécial(e) special

la **spécialité** specialty

le **spectateur, la spectatrice** spectator, **10.1**

splendide splendid

sport *(inv.)* casual *(clothes)*, **7.1**

le **sport** sport, **10.2**

le sport collectif team sport

le sport d'équipe team sport, **10.2**

les sports d'hiver winter sports, **11.2**

sportif, sportive athletic

le **squelette** skeleton

squelettique skeletal

le **stade** stadium, **10.1**

standing: de grand standing luxury

la **station** station, **4.2;** resort

la station balnéaire seaside resort, **11.1**

la station de métro subway station, **4.2**

la station de sports d'hiver ski resort, **11.2**

la **station-service** gas station

la **statue** statue, **13.2**

le **steak frites** steak and French fries, **5.2**

le **steward** flight attendant *(m.)*, **8.2**

stocker to store

la **stratégie** strategy

strict(e) strict, **2.1**

le **studio** studio (apartment)

stupide stupid

le **stylo-bille** ballpoint pen, **3.2**

la **substance** substance

le **succès** success

le **sucre** sugar

le **sud** south

suggérer to suggest

suite: tout de suite right away

suivant(e) following

suivre to follow

le **sujet** subject

super terrific, super

superbe superb

supérieur(e) higher

le **supermarché** supermarket, **6.2**

sur on, **4.2**

  donner sur to face, overlook, **4.2**

sûr(e) sure, certain

  bien sûr, of course

le **surf: faire du surf** to go surfing, **11.1**

le **surfeur, la surfeuse** surfer, **11.1**

surgelé(e) frozen, **6.2**

la **surprise** surprise

surtout especially, above all; mostly

surveiller to watch

le **survêtement** warmup suit, **7.1**

la **survie** survival

le **sweat-shirt** sweatshirt, **7.1**

sympa *(inv.)* nice *(abbrev. for* **sympathique***)*, **1.2**

sympathique nice *(person)*, **1.2**

la **symphonie** symphony

le **symptôme** symptom

le **synonyme** synonym

le **système** system

  le système métrique metric system

la **table** table, **5.1**

le **tableau** painting, **13.2**; chart

la **taille** size *(clothes)*, **7.2**

  juste à sa taille fitting (him/her) just right

  la taille au-dessous next smaller size, **7.2**

  la taille au-dessus next larger size, **7.2**

Vous faites quelle taille? What size do you take/wear?, **7.2**

le **tailleur** suit *(woman's)*, **7.1**

le **talent** talent

le **tango** tango

la **tante** aunt, **4.1**

tard late, **12.1**

  plus tard later

le **tarif** fare

la **tarte** pie, tart, **6.1**

  la tarte aux pommes apple tart, **6.1**

la **tartine** slice of bread with butter or jam

  la tartine de pain beurré slice of bread and butter, **5.1**

la **tasse** cup, **5.2**

le **taux** level

la **techno** techno *(music)*

la **télé** TV, **12.2**

  à la télé on TV, **12.2**

télécharger to download

la **télécommande** remote control, **12.2**

le **téléphone** telephone, **3.2**

  le numéro de téléphone telephone number

téléphoner to call (on the telephone)

téléphonique telephone *(adj.)*

le **télésiège** chairlift, **11.2**

la **tempe** temple

la **température** temperature, **14.1**

tempéré(e) temperate

temporaire temporary

le **temps** weather, **11.1**; time

  de temps en temps from time to time, **11.1**

  l'emploi *(m.)* **du temps** schedule

  en très peu de temps in a short time

  Il fait quel temps? What's the weather like?, **11.1**

le **tendon** tendon

le **terme** term

le **terrain de football** soccer field, **10.1**

la **terrasse** terrace, patio, **4.2**

  la terrasse d'un café sidewalk café, **5.1**

la **terre** earth, land

  à terre on the ground

terrible terrible

la **tête** head, **10.1**

  avoir mal à la tête to have a headache, **14.1**

le **texte** text

thaïlandais(e) Thai

le **thé** tea

le **théâtre** theater, **13.1**

  la pièce de théâtre play, **13.1**

le **thème** theme

timide shy, timid, **1.2**

tirer to take, to draw

les **toilettes** *(f. pl.)* bathroom, toilet, **4.2**

le **toit** roof

  le toit de chaume thatched roof

la **tomate** tomato, **6.2**

tomber to fall, **11.2**

  tomber malade to get sick, **L1**

tôt early, **12.1**

totalement totally

toucher to touch, **10.2**

toujours always, **4.2**; still

la **tour** tower

  la tour Eiffel Eiffel Tower

le **tour: à son tour** in turn

  À votre tour. (It's) your turn.

le/la **touriste** tourist

tous, toutes *(adj.)* all, every, **2.1, 8**

  tous (toutes) les deux both

  tous les jours every day, **13.2**

tousser to cough, **14.1**

tout *(pron.)* all, everything

  C'est tout. That's all., **6.1**

  en tout in all

  pas du tout not at all, **3.1**

tout(e) *(adj.)* the whole, the entire; all, any

tout le monde everyone, everybody, **1.2**

tout *(adv.)* very, completely, all, **4.2**

À tout à l'heure. See you later., **BV**

tout autour de all around *(prep.)*

tout de même all the same, **5.2**

tout près de very near, **4.2**

tout(e) seul(e) all alone, all by himself/herself, **5.2**

tout de suite right away

toxique toxic

la **tradition** tradition

traditionnel(le) traditional

la **tragédie** tragedy, **13.1**

tragique tragic

le **train** train, **9.1**

le **traitement** treatment

traiter to treat

le **traître, la traîtresse** traitor

la **tranche** slice, **6.2**

transformer to transform

transporter to transport

le **travail** work

travailler to work, **3.1**; to practice

traverser to cross

très very, **BV**

le **trésor** treasure, **L4**

la **trigonométrie** trigonometry, **2.2**

triste sad, **L1**

troisième third, **4.2**

la **trompette** trumpet

le **tronc cérébral** brain stem

le **trône** throne

trop too *(excessive)*, **2.1**

trop de too many, too much

tropical(e) tropical, **9**

le **trou** hole, **L4**

le **trouble digestif** indigestion, upset stomach

trouver to find, **5.1**; to think *(opinion)*, **7.2**

le **t-shirt** T-shirt, **7.1**

la **tunique** tunic

la **Tunisie** Tunisia

tunisien(ne) Tunisian

le **tunnel** tunnel, **L4**

le **type** type; guy *(inform.)*

typique typical

typiquement typically

l' **un(e)... l'autre** one . . . the other

un(e) à un(e) one by one

unique single, only one

l'enfant unique only child

uniquement solely

l' **unité** *(f.)* unit

l' **université** *(f.)* university

l' **usine** *(f.)* factory

utiliser to use

les **vacances** *(f. pl.)* vacation

en vacances on vacation

les grandes vacances summer vacation

la **vague** wave, **11.1**

le **vaisseau sanguin** blood vessel

la **vaisselle** dishes, **12.2**

faire la vaisselle to do the dishes, **12.2**

le **val** valley

la **valeur** value

la **valise** suitcase, **8.1**

faire les valises to pack, **8.1**

la **vallée** valley

la **vanille: à la vanille** vanilla *(adj.)*, **5.1**

varié(e) varied

varier to vary

la **variété** variety

la **veine** vein

le **vélo** bicycle, bike, **10.2**

le **vendeur, la vendeuse** salesperson, **7.1**

vendre to sell, **9.1**

vengé(e) avenged

la **vengeance** vengence

se **venger** to get revenge

le **vent** wind, **11.1**

Il y a du vent. It's windy., **11.1**

le **ventre** abdomen, stomach, **14.1**

avoir mal au ventre to have a stomachache, **14.1**

vérifier to check, verify, **8.1**

la **vérité** truth

le **verre** glass, **5.2**

vers toward

la **version originale** original language version *(of a movie)*, **13.1**

vert(e) green, **5.1**

la **veste** (sport) jacket, **7.1**

les **vêtements** *(m. pl.)* clothes, **7.1**

la **viande** meat, **6.1**

victorieux, victorieuse victorious

la **vidéo** video, **3.1**

la cassette vidéo videocassette, **12.2**

le film en vidéo movie video, **13.1**

la **vie** life

en vie alive

vieille old *(f.)*, **4.2**

vietnamien(ne) Vietnamese, **6**

vieux (vieil) old *(m.)*, **4.2**

la **villa** house

le **village** village, small town

la **ville** city, town, **8.1**

en ville in town, in the city

le **vinaigre** vinegar, **6.1**

violent(e) violent; rough

le **violon** violin

viral(e) viral, **14.1**

le **virus** virus

visionner to view

visiter to visit *(a place)*, **13.2**

vital(e) vital

la **vitamine** vitamin

vite fast *(adv.)*, **10.2**

la **vitrine** (store) window, **7.1**
vivant(e) living
Vive... ! Long live . . . !, Hooray for . . . !
voici here is, here are, **4.1**
la **voie** track *(railroad)*, **9.1**
voilà there is, there are; here is, here are *(emphatic)*, **1.2**
le **voile** veil
voir to see, **7.1**
le/la **voisin(e)** neighbor, **4.2**
la **voiture** car, **4.2**
en voiture by car, **5.2;** "All aboard!"
la **voix** voice
le **vol** flight, **8.1**
le vol intérieur domestic flight, **8.1**
le vol international international flight, **8.1**
le **volley(-ball)** volleyball, **10.2**

la **volonté** willpower
voudrais: je voudrais I would like, **5.1**
vouloir to want, **6.1**
le **voyage** trip, **8.1;** voyage
faire un voyage to take a trip, **8.1**
voyager to travel, **8.1**
le **voyageur, la voyageuse** traveler, passenger, **9.1**
vrai(e) true, real, **2.2**
vraiment really, **1.1**
la **vue** view, **4.2**

le **wagon** *(railroad)* car, **9.2**
le **wagon-couchette** sleeping car
le **wagon-restaurant** dining car

le **week-end** weekend
le **western** Western movie

le **yaourt** yogurt, **6.1**
les **yeux** *(m. pl; sing.* **œil***)* eyes, **14.1, L1**
avoir les yeux qui piquent to have itchy eyes, **14.1**

zapper to zap, to channel surf, **12.2**
la **zone** zone
la **zoologie** zoology
Zut! Darn!, **BV**

This English-French Dictionary *contains all productive vocabulary from the text. The numbers following each entry indicate the chapter and vocabulary section in which the word is introduced. For example,* **2.2** *means that the word first appeared in* **Chapitre 2, Mots 2.** **BV** *refers to the introductory* **Bienvenue** *lessons.* **L** *refers to the optional literary readings. If there is no number or letter following an entry, this means that the word or expression is there for receptive purposes only.*

a un, une, **1.1**
  a week par semaine, **3.2**
  a lot beaucoup, **3.1**
to **abandon** abandonner
abdomen le ventre, **14.1**
able capable
  to be able to pouvoir, **6.1**
aboard à bord (de), **8.2**
about *(on the subject of)* de; *(approximately)* à peu près
about-face le demi-tour
above au-dessus (de)
  above all surtout
absolutely absolument
accessible accessible
accessory l'accessoire *(m.)*
accident l'accident *(m.)*
to **accompany** accompagner
according to d'après; selon
accordion l'accordéon *(m.)*
account le compte
accusation l'accusation *(f.)*
to **accuse** accuser
act l'acte, *(m.)*, **13.1**
action l'action *(f.)*
active actif, active
activity l'activité *(f.)*
actor l'acteur *(m.)*, **13.1**
actress l'actrice *(f.)*, **13.1**
acute aigu(ë), **14.2**
to **add** additionner
address l'adresse *(f.)*
to **admire** admirer
admission l'entrée *(f.)*
adolescent l'adolescent(e)
adorable adorable, **4.1**

adult l'adulte *(m. et f.)*
adventure l'aventure *(f.)*
adversary l'adversaire *(m. et f.)*
advertisement la publicité
afraid: to be afraid avoir peur, **L1**
Africa l'Afrique *(f.)*
African africain(e)
African-American afro-américain(e)
after après, **3.2**
afternoon l'après-midi *(m.)*, **3.2**
  five o'clock in the afternoon cinq heures de l'après-midi, **BV**
again encore; à nouveau
against contre, **10.1**
age l'âge *(m.)*, **4.1**
agent *(m. and f.)* l'agent *(m.)*, **8.1**
to **agree** être d'accord, **2.1**
aid l'aide *(f.)*
AIDS le sida
air *(adj.)* aérien(ne)
air l'air *(m.)*
  air terminal l'aérogare *(f.)*, **8.1**
airline la compagnie aérienne, **8.1**
airmail la poste par avion
airplane l'avion *(m.)*, **8.1**
airport l'aéroport *(m.)*, **8.1**
  airport terminal l'aérogare *(f.)*, **8.1**
aisle le couloir, **8.2**
  aisle seat (une place) côté couloir, **8.1**

alas hélas
album l'album *(m.)*
algebra l'algèbre *(f.)*, **2.2**
Algeria l'Algérie *(f.)*
algerian algérien(ne)
alive en vie
all tout(e), tous, toutes, **2.1**
  All aboard! En voiture!
  all alone tout(e) seul(e), **5.2**
  all around tout autour de
  all right *(agreement)* d'accord, **2.1**
  all the same tout de même, **5.2**
  in all en tout
  not at all pas du tout
  That's all. C'est tout., **6.1**
allergic allergique, **14.1**
allergy l'allergie *(f.)*, **14.1**
to **allow** laisser; permettre
almost presque
alone seul(e), **5.2**
  all alone tout(e) seul(e), **5.2**
along le long de
already déjà, **BV**
also aussi, **1.1**
always toujours, **4.2**
a.m. du matin, **BV**
ambitious ambitieux, ambitieuse
American *(adj.)* américain(e), **1.1**
among entre, **3.2**
to **analyse** analyser
analysis l'analyse *(f.)*
analytical analytique

and et, **BV**
animal l'animal (*m.*)
to **announce** annoncer, **9.1**
announcement l'annonce, (*f.*), **8.2**
anonymous anonyme
another un(e) autre; encore
answer la réponse
to **answer** répondre (à), **9.2**
antibiotic l'antibiotique (*m.*), **14.1**
antonym l'antonyme (*m.*)
Anything else? Avec ça?, **6.1**; Autre chose?, **6.2**
apartment l'appartement (*m.*), **4.2**
  apartment building l'immeuble (*m.*), **4.2**
apparatus l'appareil (*m.*)
to **applaud** applaudir
apple la pomme, **6.2**
  apple tart la tarte aux pommes, **6.1**
appointment le rendez-vous
  to make an appointment prendre rendez-vous
to **appreciate** apprécier
April avril (*m.*), **BV**
Arab arabe
Arabic (*language*) l'arabe (*m.*)
architecture l'architecture (*f.*)
arithmetic le calcul
arm le bras
army l'armée (*f.*), **L3**
around autour de, **4.2**
to **arrest** arrêter
arrested arrêté(e)
arrival l'arrivée (*f.*), **8.1**
to **arrive** arriver, **3.1**
  arriving from (*flight*) en provenance de, **8.1**
art le dessin (*m.*), **2.2**
artery l'artère (*f.*)
article l'article (*m.*)
artist l'artiste (*m. et f.*); le/la peintre (*painter*)
artistic artistique
as aussi (*comparisons*), **7**; comme
  as . . . as aussi... que, **7**

as well as ainsi que
  the same . . . as le (la, les) même(s)... que
Asian asiatique
to **ask (for)** demander, **3.2**
  to ask a question poser une question, **3.1**
aspirin l'aspirine (*f.*), **14.1**
at à, **3.1;** chez, **3.2**
  at last enfin, **12.1**
  at the home (business) of chez, **3.2**
  at what time? à quelle heure?, **2**
athletic sportif, sportive
Atlantic Ocean l'océan Atlantique
atmosphere l'atmosphère (*f.*)
attached attaché(e)
to **attack** attaquer
attention l'attention (*f.*)
au pair au pair
August août, (*m.*), **BV**
aunt la tante, **4.1**
author l'auteur (*m.*)
automatic automatique
autumn l'automne (*m.*), **11.2**
avalanche l'avalanche (*f.*)
avenged vengé(e)
avenue l'avenue (*f.*)
average moyen(ne)
aviator l'aviateur (*m.*), l'aviatrice (*f.*)
to **avoid** éviter, **12.2**
awake réveillé(e)

baby le bébé
back l'arrière (*m.*), **8.2**
background le fond
backpack le sac à dos, **3.2**
bacon le bacon
bacterial bactérien(ne), **14.1**
bacterium la bactérie
bad mauvais(e), **2.2;** nul(le) (*slang*)
  It's bad weather. Il fait mauvais., **11.1**

Not bad. Pas mal., **BV**
badly mal, **14.1**
bag le sac, **6.1**
baggage les bagages (*m. pl.*), **8.1**
  baggage cart le chariot, **9.1**
  baggage compartment le coffre à bagages, **8.2**
bagpipes la cornemuse
bakery la boulangerie-pâtisserie, **6.1**
balance l'équilibre (*m.*)
balanced équilibré(e)
balcony le balcon, **4.2**
ball (*soccer, etc.*) le ballon, **10.1**
ballerina la danseuse, **13.1**
ballet le ballet
ballpoint pen le stylo-bille, **3.2**
banana la banane, **6.2**
base la base
baseball le base-ball
baseball cap la casquette, **7.1**
based basé(e)
  based on à base de
basilica la basilique
basis la base
basket le panier, **10.2**
basketball le basket (-ball), **10.2**
bath le bain, **12.1**
  to take a bath prendre un bain, **12.1**
bather le baigneur, la baigneuse
bathing suit le maillot (de bain), **11.1**
bathroom la salle de bains, les toilettes (*f. pl.*), **4.2**
battle la bataille, **L3**
battlefield le champ de bataille, **L3**
to **be** être, **1.1**
  to be able to pouvoir, **6.1**
  to be afraid avoir peur, **L1**
  to be better soon être vite sur pied, **14.1**

to be born naître, **11**
to be called s'appeler, **12.1**
to be careful faire attention, **11.1**
to be early être en avance, **9.1**
to be given off se dégager
to be hungry avoir faim, **5.1**
to be in luck avoir de la chance
to be late être en retard, **9.1;** avoir du retard *(plane, train, etc.)*, **8.1**
to be lucky avoir de la chance
to be named s'appeler, **12.1**
to be on time être à l'heure, **8.1**
to be part of faire partie de
to be sorry regretter, **6.1**
to be thirsty avoir soif, **5.1**
to be . . . years old avoir... ans, **4.1**
beach la plage, **11.1**
bean: green beans les haricots verts *(m. pl.)*, **6.2**
beautiful beau (bel), belle, **4.2**
beauty la beauté
because parce que
because of à cause de
to **become** devenir
bed: to go to bed se coucher, **12.1**
bedroom la chambre à coucher, **4.2**
beef le bœuf, **6.1**
before avant; avant de
to **begin** commencer, **9.2**
to begin again recommencer
beginner le/la débutant(e), **11.2**
beginning le début
beige beige *(inv.)*, **7.2**
being l'être *(m.)*

human being l'être humain *(m.)*
Belgian belge
Belgium la Belgique
to **believe** croire, **7.2**
below au-dessous (de)
belt la ceinture, **L3**
seat belt la ceinture de sécurité, **8.2**
berth (on a train) la couchette
better *(adv.)* mieux, **7.2**
to feel better aller mieux, **14.2**
between entre, **3.2**
beverage la boisson; la consommation, **5.1**
bicentennial le bicentenaire
bicycle la bicyclette, **10.2;** le vélo, **10.2**
bicycle race la course cycliste, **10.2**
bicycle racer le coureur (la coureuse) cycliste, **10.2**
big grand(e), **1.1**
bike le vélo, **10.2**
biological biologique
biologist le/la biologiste
biology la biologie, **2.2**
bird l'oiseau *(m.)*
birthday l'anniversaire *(m.)*, **4.1**
Happy birthday! Bon (Joyeux) anniversaire!
black noir(e), **7.2**
black pride la négritude
bleacher le gradin, **10.1**
to **block** bloquer, **10.1**
blond blond(e), **1.1**
blood le sang
blood vessel le vaisseau sanguin
bloom: in bloom fleuri(e), **L2**
to **bloom** fleurir
blouse le chemisier, **7.1**
to **blow a horn** sonner du cor, **L3**
to **blow a whistle** siffler, **10.1**
blue bleu(e), **7.2**
navy blue bleu marine *(inv.)*, **7.2**

to **board** *(plane)* embarquer
boarding l'embarquement *(m.)*
boarding pass la carte d'embarquement, **8.1**
boat le bateau, **L4**
body le corps
bohemian bohème
boiling bouillant(e)
bone l'os *(m.)*
book le livre, **3.2**
border la frontière
boss le chef; le/la patron(ne)
botany la botanique
both tous (toutes) les deux
bottle la bouteille, **6.2**
boulder le rocher, **L3**
boutique la boutique, **7.1**
bowl le bol
box office le guichet, **13.1**
boy le garçon, **1.1**
boyfriend le petit ami
brain le cerveau
brain stem le tronc cérébral
brass band la fanfare
brave courageux, courageuse; brave
Brazil le Brésil
Brazilian *(person)* le/la Brésilien(ne)
bread le pain, **6.1**
loaf of French bread la baguette, **6.1**
slice of bread and butter la tartine de pain beurré
whole-wheat bread le pain complet
to **break** briser
breakfast le petit déjeuner, **5.2**
to eat breakfast prendre le petit déjeuner, **5.2**
to **breathe** respirer, **14.2**
to breathe deeply respirer à fond, **14.2**
Breton breton(ne)
bridge le pont
to **bring** apporter, **11.1**
Brittany la Bretagne
bronchial tube la bronche
brother le frère, **1.2**

brown brun(e), marron (*inv.*), **7.2**
brunette brun(e), **1.1**
brush la brosse, **12.1**
to **brush** (*one's teeth, hair, etc.*) se brosser (les dents, les cheveux, etc.), **12.1**
to **build** construire; fabriquer
bungalow le bungalow
to **burn** brûler
burst éclaté(e)
bus le bus; l'autocar (*m.*)
  by bus en bus
bush (*wilderness*) la brousse
busy occupé(e)
but mais, **2.1**
butcher le boucher, la bouchère
butcher shop la boucherie, **6.1**
butter le beurre, **6.1**
to **buy** acheter, **3.2**
  by par
Bye. Salut., **BV**

cabaret le cabaret
cabin (*plane*) la cabine, **8.1**
café le café, **BV**
cafeteria la cafétéria
cake le gâteau, **4.1**
calcium le calcium
calculator la calculatrice, **3.2**
calculus: differential calculus le calcul différentiel
  integral calculus le calcul intégral
calendar le calendrier
to **call** appeler; (*on the telephone*) téléphoner
  to call a penalty déclarer un penalty
calm calme
calorie la calorie
Camembert cheese le camembert

campaign la campagne
can pouvoir, **6.1**
can of food la boîte de conserve, **6.2**
Canadian (*adj.*) canadien(ne), **6**
candle la bougie, **4.1**
cap la casquette, **7.1**
capital la capitale
car la voiture, **4.2**; (*railroad*) le wagon
  by car en voiture, **5.2**
  dining car le wagon-restaurant
  sleeping car le wagon-couchette
carbohydrate la glucide; l'hydrate (*m.*) de carbone
carbon dioxide le gaz carbonique
card la carte
cardboard le carton
cardiac cardiaque
care le soin
  general care (*adj.*) de soins polyvalents
to **care: I don't care.** Ça m'est égal., **13.1**
career la carrière
Careful! Attention!, **4.2**
Caribbean Sea la mer des Caraïbes, la mer des Antilles
carnival (*season*) le carnaval
carpenter le charpentier
carrot la carotte, **6.2**
carry-on bag le bagage à main, **8.1**
to **carry out** exécuter
cartoon le dessin animé, **13.1**
cash register la caisse, **3.2**
cassette la cassette, **3.1**
castle le château
casual (*clothes*) sport (*adj. inv.*), **7.1**
cat le chat, **4.1**
catalog le catalogue
catastrophic catastrophique
category la catégorie
to **cause** causer
cave la grotte, **L4**

CD le CD, **3.1**
CD-ROM le CD-ROM
to **celebrate** célébrer, **L4**
cell la cellule, **L4**
Celtic celte, celtique
center le centre
centiliter le centilitre
century le siècle
cereal les céréales (*f. pl.*)
certainly certainement
chain la chaîne
chairlift le télésiège, **11.2**
champion le/la champion(ne)
to **change** changer (de), **9.2**
channel (*TV*) la chaîne, **12.2**
  to channel surf zapper, **12.2**
characteristic la caractéristique
charges les frais (*m. pl.*)
charm le charme
charming charmant(e)
chart le tableau
to **chat** bavarder
check (*in restaurant*) l'addition (*f.*), **5.2**
to **check** vérifier, **8.1**; contrôler
  to check (*luggage*) (faire) enregistrer, **8.1**
checkout counter la caisse, **3.2**
cheese le fromage, **5.1**
chemical chimique
chemist le/la chimiste
chemistry la chimie, **2.2**
chemotherapy la chimiothérapie
chest (*storage*) le coffre, **L4**; (*body*) la poitrine
chewing gum le chewing-gum
chic chic (*inv.*)
chicken le poulet, **6.1**
child l'enfant (*m. et f.*), **4.1**
childhood l'enfance (*f.*)
chills les frissons (*m. pl.*), **14.1**
Chinese chinois(e)
chocolate le chocolat; (*adj.*) au chocolat, **5.1**

choir le chœur
cholesterol le cholestérol
to choose choisir, **8.1**
choppy *(sea)* agité(e)
circle le cercle
circuit le circuit
circulation la circulation
circus le cirque
to cite citer
city la ville, **8.1**
  in the city en ville
civilized civilisé(e)
clarinet la clarinette
class *(people)* la classe, **2.1**; *(course)* le cours, **2.1**
  in class en classe
  in (French, etc.) class en cours de (français, etc.)
  in first (second) class en première (seconde), **9.1**
classical classique
to classify classifier
classmate le/la camarade de classe
classroom la salle de classe, **2.1**
to clear the table débarrasser la table, **12.2**
clever: Very clever! *(ironic)* C'est malin!
climate le climat
climatic climatique
clinic la clinique
closed fermé(e), **13.2**
clothes les vêtements *(m. pl.)*, **7.1**
cloud le nuage, **11.1**
clown le clown
coach l'autocar *(m.)*
coast la côte
coat le manteau, **7.1**
code le code, **4.2**
coffee le café, **5.1**
  black coffee l'express *(m.)*, **5.1**
  coffee with cream le crème, **5.1**
cola le coca, **5.1**
cold froid(e) *(adj.)*; *(illness)* le rhume, **14.1**
  It's cold (weather). Il fait froid., **11.2**

to have a cold être enrhumé(e), **14.1**
collection la collection
color la couleur, **7.2**
  What color is . . . ? De quelle couleur est... ?, **7.2**
comb le peigne, **12.1**
to comb one's hair se peigner, **12.1**
Come on! Allez!, **9.2**
comedy la comédie, **13.1**; le film comique, **13.1**
  musical comedy la comédie musicale, **13.1**
comfortable confortable
comic comique, **13.1**
to commemorate commémorer
commercial *(TV)* la publicité, **12.2**
companion le/la camarade
company la société
  in the company of en compagnie de
to compare comparer
comparison la comparaison
compatriot le/la compatriote
complete complet, complète
to complete compléter
completely complètement
complicated compliqué(e)
composed of composé(e) de
composer le compositeur, la compositrice
composition la composition
computer l'ordinateur *(m.)*
  computer science l'informatique *(f.)*, **2.2**
concept le concept
concert le concert
condition la condition
conductor *(train)* le contrôleur, **9.2**
to connect connecter; relier
connection *(between trains)* la correspondance, **9.2**

to conspire comploter
to consult consulter
to contain contenir
contamination la contamination
contest la compétition, le concours
continent le continent
to continue continuer
contrary: on the contrary au contraire
to control contrôler
convent le couvent
conversation la conversation
to converse converser
conversion la conversion
to cook faire la cuisine, **6**
  cooked cuit(e)
  cool: It's cool (weather). Il fait frais., **11.2**
correct bon(ne), **6.2**
correspondence la correspondance
corridor le couloir, **8.2**
cosmopolitan cosmopolite
cost le prix, **7.1**
to cost coûter, **3.2**
cottage la maisonnette
to cough tousser, **14.1**
count le comte, **L4**
to count compter
counter le comptoir, **8.1**
countless innombrable
country le pays, **8.1**
country(side) la campagne
courage le courage
courageous courageux, courageuse
course le cours, **2.1**
  of course bien sûr; mais oui
  of course not mais non
court la cour
courtesy la politesse, **BV**
courtyard la cour, **3.2**
cousin le/la cousin(e), **4.1**
to cover couvrir
covered couvert(e)
crab le crabe, **6.1**
crazy fou, folle
cream la crème

coffee with cream le crème, **5.1**

to **create** créer

credit card la carte de crédit

Creole (*language*) le créole

crepe la crêpe, **BV**

criminal le/la criminel(le), **L4**

croissant le croissant, **5.1**

to **cross** traverser

crushed écrasé(e)

to **cry** pleurer, **L1**

cue l'indication (*f.*)

to **cultivate** cultiver

cultural culturel(le)

cultural event la manifestation culturelle

culture la culture

cup la tasse, **5.2**

winner's cup la coupe, **10.2**

cured guéri(e)

customer le/la client(e)

customs la douane

cycling le cyclisme, **10.2;** (*adj.*) cycliste

cyclist (*in race*) le coureur (la coureuse) cycliste, **10.2**

D

dad papa

daily quotidien(ne)

dairy store la crémerie, **6.1**

dance la danse

to **dance** danser, **13.1**

dancer le danseur, la danseuse, **13.1**

dangerous dangereux, dangereuse

dark sombre

dark haired brun(e), **1.1**

Darn! Zut!, **BV**

data les données (*f. pl.*)

date la date

What is today's date? Quelle est la date aujourd'hui?, **BV**

to **date from** dater de

daughter la fille, **4.1**

day le jour, **BV;** la journée, **3.1**

the day before yesterday avant-hier, **10.2**

every day tous les jours

What a nice day! Belle journée!, **4.2**

What day is it today? C'est quel jour aujourd'hui?, **BV**

dear cher, chère

death la mort

decaliter le décalitre

December décembre (*m.*), **BV**

to **decide (to)** décider de

decimal (*adj.*) décimal(e)

decision la décision

the decision is made la décision est prise

to **declare** déclarer

to **decorate** orner

delay le retard

delicatessen la charcuterie, **6.1**

delicious délicieux, délicieuse

dentist le/la dentiste

deodorant le déodorant

department (in a store) le rayon, **7.1**

coat department le rayon des manteaux, **7.1**

department store le grand magasin, **7.1**

large department store la grande surface

departure le départ, **8.1**

to **depend (on)** dépendre (de)

deplaning le débarquement

descendant le/la descendant(e)

to **describe** décrire

description la description

desert le désert; (*adj.*) désertique

designer (*clothes*) le couturier

desperate désespéré(e), **L4**

dessert le dessert

destination la destination

destiny la destinée

devoted dévoué(e)

diagnosis le diagnostic, **14.2**

dialect le dialecte

dialogue le dialogue

diamond le diamant

to **die** mourir, **11**

diet l'alimentation (*f.*); le régime

to follow a diet faire un régime

difference la différence

different différent(e), **8.1**

difficult difficile, **2.1**

difficulty la difficulté

to **dig** creuser, **L4**

dining car la voiture-restaurant

dining hall (*school*) la cantine, **3.1**

dining room la salle à manger, **4.2**

dinner le dîner, **5.2**

to eat dinner dîner, **5.2**

diploma le diplome

direction la direction; le sens

directly directement

dirty sale

disagreeable désagréable

to **disappear** disparaître

discount la réduction

to **discover** découvrir

to **discuss** discuter

disease la maladie

dish (*food*) le plat

dishes la vaisselle, **12.2**

to do the dishes faire la vaisselle, **12.2**

dishwasher le lave-vaisselle, **12.2**

diskette la disquette

to **distinguish** distinguer

district le quartier, **4.2;** (*Paris*) l'arrondissement (*m.*)

dive le plongeon

to **dive** plonger, **11.1**

to **divide** diviser

to **do** faire, **6.1**

to do the grocery shopping faire les courses, **6.1**

doctor le médecin
(*m. et f.*), **14.2**
at (to) the doctor's office
chez le médecin, **14.2**
document le document
documentary le
documentaire, **13.1**
dog le chien, **4.1**
dollar le dollar, **3.2**
domain le domaine
domestic (*flight*)
intérieur(e), **8.1**
door la porte, **L4**
dormitory le dortoir
doubt le doute
to **download** télécharger
downtown le centre-ville
dozen la douzaine, **6.2**
drama le drame, **13.1**
drama club le club d'art
dramatique
dramatic dramatique
drawing le dessin
dress la robe, **7.1**
dressed: to get dressed
s'habiller, **12.1**
dressy habillé(e), **7.1**
to **dribble** (*basketball*)
dribbler, **10.2**
drink la boisson; la
consommation, **5.1**
to **drink** boire, **10.2**
something to drink
quelque chose à boire
druid le druide
dry sec, sèche
dubbed (*movie*) doublé(e),
13.1
during pendant, **3.2**
dynamic dynamique, **1.2**

each (*adj.*) chaque
each (one) chacun(e), **5.2**
ear l'oreille (*f.*), **14.1**
earache: to have an
earache avoir mal aux
oreilles, **14.1**
early en avance, **9.1**; de
bonne heure; tôt, **12.1**
to **earn** gagner

Easter Pâques
eastern oriental(e)
easy facile, **2.1**
to **eat** manger, **5.1**
to eat breakfast prendre
le petit déjeuner,
5.2
to eat lunch déjeuner, **3.1**
ecological écologique
ecology l'écologie (*f.*)
economics l'économie (*f.*),
2.2
efficient efficace
egg l'œuf (*m.*), **6.1**
fried egg l'œuf sur le
plat
poached egg l'œuf à la
coque
scrambled egg l'œuf
brouillé
egotistical égoïste, **1.2**
Egyptian égyptien(ne)
electric électrique
electronic électronique
element l'élément (*m.*)
elevator l'ascenseur (*m.*),
4.2
to **eliminate** éliminer
else: something else autre
chose
Anything else? Avec ça?,
6.1; Autre chose?, **6.2**
e-mail l'e-mail (*m.*)
emission l'émission (*f.*)
employee
l'employé(e)
end la fin
enemy l'ennemi(e)
energetic énergique, **1.2**
energy l'énergie (*f.*)
engagement les fiançailles
(*f. pl.*), **L4**
England l'Angleterre (*f.*)
English anglais(e)
English (*language*)
l'anglais (*m.*), **2.2**
English Channel la
Manche
enormous énorme
enough assez, **1.1**
enriched enrichi(e)

to **enter** entrer, **7.1**
enthusiastic enthousiaste,
1.2
entire entier, entière
entrance l'entrée (*f.*), **4.2**
epic (*adj.*) épique
equation l'équation (*f.*)
equator l'équateur (*m.*)
equipment l'équipement
(*m.*)
equivalent l'équivalent
(*m.*)
eraser la gomme, **3.2**
to **escape** s'échapper;
s'évader, **L4**
especially surtout
espresso l'express (*m.*), **5.1**
essential essentiel(le)
to **establish** établir
establishment
l'établissement (*m.*)
euro l'euro (*m.*)
Europe l'Europe (*f.*)
European (*adj.*)
européen(ne)
evening le soir, **BV**
in the evening le soir, **5.2**
in the evening (P.M.) du
soir, **BV**
event l'événement (*m.*)
ever jamais
every tous, toutes, **2.1, 8**;
chaque
every day tous les jours,
13.2
everybody tout le monde,
1.2
everyday quotidien(ne)
everyone tout le monde,
1.2
everything tout
everywhere partout
evidently évidemment
to **evoke** évoquer
exact exact(e)
exactly exactement
exam l'examen (*m.*), **3.1**
to pass an exam réussir à
un examen
to take an exam passer
un examen, **3.1**
to **examine** examiner, **14.2**

example: for example par exemple
excellent excellent(e)
except excepté(e); sauf, **13.2**
exception l'exception (f.)
exceptional exceptionnel(le)
exchange l'échange (m.)
to **exchange** échanger
excursion l'excursion (f.)
excuse me pardon
to **execute** exécuter
exercise l'exercice (m.)
exhausted crevé(e); épuisé(e)
exhibit l'exposition (f.), **13.2**
to **exist** exister
existence l'existence (f.)
to **expel** expulser
expenses les frais (m. pl.)
expensive cher, chère, **7.1**
expert (adj.) expert(e)
to **explain** expliquer
explanation l'explication (f.)
expression l'expression (f.)
exterior l'extérieur (m.)
extraordinary extraordinaire
eye l'œil (m., pl. yeux), **14.1**
  to have itchy eyes avoir les yeux qui piquent, **14.1**
eyes les yeux (m. pl.), **L1**

fable la fable
fabulous fabuleux, fabuleuse
face la figure, **12.1**
to **face** donner sur, **4.2**
factory l'usine (f.)
fairly assez, **1.1**
fall (season) l'automne (m.), **11.2**
to **fall** tomber **11.2**
  to fall asleep s'endormir

to fall asleep again se rendormir
false faux, fausse
to **falsify** falsifier
family la famille, **4.1**
famous célèbre; connu(e), **13.1**
fan le/la fana
fantastic fantastique
far (away) loin
  far from loin de, **4.2**
fare le tarif
fast (adj.) rapide; (adv.) vite **10.2**
to **fasten** attacher, **8.2**
fast-food (adj.) de restauration rapide
  fast-food restaurant le fast-food
fat (n.) la graisse; le lipide
father le père, **4.1**
fault la faute
favorite favori(te); préféré(e)
February février (m.), **BV**
to **feed** nourrir
to **feel** (well, etc.) se sentir, **14.1**
  to feel better aller mieux, **14.2**
  to feel like avoir envie de
  to feel out of sorts ne pas être dans son assiette, **14.1**
fees (doctor) les honoraires (m. pl.)
felt-tip pen le feutre, **3.2**
festival le festival
festive de fête
festivity la festivité
fever la fièvre, **14.1**
  to have a fever avoir de la fièvre, **14.1**
  to have a high fever avoir une fièvre de cheval, **14.1**
few peu (de)
  a few quelques, **9.2**
fiancé(e) le/la fiancé(e), **L4**
field le champ, **L1**; le domaine
fig la figue

fight le combat, **L3**; la lutte, **L3**
to **fight** lutter, **L3**
file (computer) le fichier
to **fill out** remplir, **8.2**
film le film, **13.1**
  adventure film le film d'aventures, **13.1**
  detective film le film policier, **13.1**
  foreign film le film étranger, **13.1**
  horror film le film d'horreur, **13.1**
  science fiction film le film de science-fiction, **13.1**
finally enfin, **12.1**; finalement
to **find** trouver, **5.1**
fine ça va, bien, **BV**
fine l'amende (f.)
finger le doigt
to **finish** finir, **8.2**
firm l'entreprise (f.)
first premier, première (adj.), **4.2**; d'abord (adv.), **12.1**
  in first class en première, **9.1**
fish le poisson, **6.1**
  fish store la poissonnerie, **6.1**
fitting room la cabine d'essayage
flavor le parfum
flea market le marché aux puces
flight le vol, **8.1**
  domestic flight le vol intérieur, **8.1**
  flight attendant l'hôtesse (f.) de l'air, le steward, **8.2**
  flight crew le personnel de bord, **8.2**
  international flight le vol international, **8.1**
float (in a parade) le char
floor (of a building) l'étage (m.), **4.2**

ground floor le rez-de-chaussée, **4.2**
flower la fleur, **4.2**
flu la grippe, **14.1**
flute la flûte
to **fly** *(plane)* piloter
to **follow** suivre
  following suivant(e)
food la nourriture;
  l'aliment *(m.)*; les
  provisions *(f. pl.)*
  food service la
  restauration
foot le pied, **10.1**
  on foot à pied, **4.2**
football le football
  américain
for pour; *(time)* pendant,
  3.2; depuis, **9.2**
  for example par exemple
foreign étranger,
  étrangère, **13.1**
foreman, forewoman le
  contremaître, la
  contremaîtresse
to **forget** oublier
fork la fourchette, **5.2**
form la forme
to **form** former
formality la formalité
former ancien(ne)
fortunately heureusement
fortune la fortune
to **found** fonder
fourth quatrième
fracture la fracture
France la France
free libre, **5.1;** gratuit(e)
to **free** libérer
  freedom la liberté
  **freezing: It's freezing
  (weather).** Il gèle., **11.2**
French français(e) *(adj.),*
  1.1; *(language)* le français,
  2.2
  French fries les frites
  (f. pl.), **5.1**
Frenchman (-woman)
  le/la Français(e)
French-speaking
  francophone
to **frequent** fréquenter

Friday vendredi *(m.),* **BV**
friend l'ami(e), **1.2;** *(pal)* le
  copain, la copine, **2.1;**
  le/la camarade
from de, **1.1**
  from then on désormais
front l'avant *(m.),* **8.2**
  in front of devant, **8.2**
frozen surgelé(e), **6.2**
fruit le fruit, **6.2**
full plein(e), **10.1;**
  complet, complète
fun amusant(e), **1.1**
  to have fun s'amuser,
  12.2
function la fonction
functioning le
  fonctionnement
funny amusant(e), **1.1;**
  rigolo, **4.2;** comique, **13.1**
furniture les meubles
  (m. pl.)
fusion la fusion
future l'avenir *(m.),*
  le futur, **L2**

game le match, **10.1;** le jeu
garage le garage, **4.2**
garden le jardin, **4.2**
gas le gaz
  gas station la station-
  service
gate *(airport)* la porte, **8.1**
gem la pierre précieuse,
  L4
general le général
generally généralement
geography la géographie,
  2.2
geometry la géometrie, **2.2**
germ le microbe
German *(language)*
  l'allemand *(m.),* **2.2**
Germany l'Allemagne *(f.)*
Gesundheit! À tes
  souhaits!, **14.1**
to **get** recevoir, **10.2**
  to get back on remonter
  to get dressed s'habiller,
  12.1

to get married se marier,
  L4
to get sick tomber
  malade, **L1**
to get a sunburn
  attraper un coup de
  soleil, **11.1**
to get off *(bus, train)*
  descendre, **9.2**
  to get off *(plane)*
  débarquer
to get on (board)
  monter, **9.2**
to get up se lever, **12.1**
giant le/la géant(e)
gift le cadeau, **4.1**
gigantic gigantesque
girl la fille, **1.1**
girlfriend la petite amie
to **give** donner, **4.1**
  to give back rendre
glad content(e)
glass le verre, **5.2**
glove le gant, **11.2**
to **go** aller, **5.1**
  to go (in a car, etc.)
  rouler, **10.2**
  to go aboard
  s'embarquer sur
  to go down descendre, **9**
  to go fast rouler vite,
  10.2
  to go (and) get aller
  chercher, **6.1**
  to go home rentrer, **3.2**
  to go out sortir, **8.2**
  to go surfing faire du
  surf, **11.1**
  to go to bed se coucher,
  12.1
  to go through security
  (airport) passer par le
  contrôle de sécurité, **8.1**
  to go up monter, **4.2**
  to go windsurfing faire
  de la planche à voile,
  11.1
  to go with accompagner
  Should we go? On y va?
goal le but, **10.1**
  to score a goal marquer
  un but, **10.1**

goalie le gardien de but, **10.1**
God bless you! À tes souhaits!, **14.1**
gold l'or *(m.)*, **L4**
golden doré(e)
good bon(ne), **6.2**
  good in math fort(e) en maths, **2.2**
good-bye au revoir; ciao *(inform.)*, **BV**
gourmet le gourmet
grade la note
grains les céréales *(f. pl.)*
gram le gramme, **6.2**
grammar la grammaire
granddaughter la petite-fille, **4.1**
grandfather le grand-père, **4.1**
grandmother la grand-mère, **4.1**
grandparents les grands-parents *(m. pl.)*, **4.1**
grandson le petit-fils, **4.1**
gray gris(e), **7.2**
great grand(e)
Greece la Grèce
green vert(e), **5.1**
  green beans les haricots *(m. pl.)* verts, **6.2**
greeting la salutation
grilled ham and cheese sandwich le croque-monsieur, **5.1**
griot le griot
grocery store l'épicerie *(f.)*, **6.1**
ground le sol, **10.2**
  ground floor le rez-de-chaussée, **4.2**
  on the ground à terre
group le groupe
to **grow (up)** grandir
growth la croissance
guard le gardien, **L4**
to **guard** garder
to **guess** deviner
guide(book) le guide
guillotined guillotiné(e)
guitar la guitare
guitarist le/la guitariste
guy le type

gymnastics la gymnastique, **2.2**

hair les cheveux *(m. pl.)*, **12.1**
Haitian haïtien(ne)
half *(sporting event)* le mi-temps
half demi(e)
  half brother le demi-frère, **4.1**
  half hour la demi-heure
  half past *(time)* et demie, **BV**
  half price le demi-tarif
  half sister la demi-sœur, **4.1**
ham le jambon, **5.1**
hamburger le hamburger
hamlet le hameau
hand la main, **3.1**
handicapped handicapé(e)
handkerchief le mouchoir, **14.1**
handmade fait(e) à la main
handsome beau (bel), **4.2**
happy content(e); heureux, heureuse
  Happy birthday! Bon (Joyeux) anniversaire!
harbor le port
hard dur(e); *(adv.)* fort
hardware (computer) le hardware
harp la harpe
hat *(ski)* le bonnet, **11.2**
to **hate** détester, **3.1**
to **have** avoir, **4.1**; *(to eat or drink)* prendre, **5.1**
  to have a(n) . . . -ache avoir mal à (aux)... , **14.1**
  Have a nice day! Belle journée!, **4.2**
he il, **1.1**
head la tête, **10.1**; *(of department or company)* le chef
to **head into** s'engager dans

headache: to have a headache avoir mal à la tête, **14.1**
health la santé, **14.1**
  to be in good (poor) health être en bonne (mauvaise) santé, **14.1**
to **hear** entendre, **9.1**
heart le cœur
hello bonjour, **BV**
help l'aide *(f.)*
  to be a big help rendre bien service
  with the help of à l'aide de
to **help** aider
hemisphere l'hémisphère *(m.)*
here is, here are voici, **4.1**; *(emphatic)* voilà, **1.2**
hero le héros
hi salut, **BV**
to **hide** cacher, **L3**
  high élevé(e)
  high school le lycée, **2.1**
  higher supérieur
his sa, son, ses
history l'histoire *(f.)*, **2.2**
to **hit** frapper, **L3**; donner un coup (de pied, de tête, etc.), **10.1**
hockey le hockey
  hockey stick la crosse
hole le trou, **L4**
home: at (to) the home of chez, **3.2**
  to go home rentrer, **3.2**
homework *(assignment)* le devoir
  to do homework faire ses devoirs, **12.2**
honest honnête
horrible horrible
hospital l'hôpital *(m.)*; *(adj.)* hospitalier, hospitalière
hot chaud(e)
  hot chocolate le chocolat
  hot dog la saucisse de Francfort, **BV**
  It's hot (weather). Il fait chaud., **11.1**

hotel l'hôtel (*m.*)
house la maison, **3.1**; la villa
  publishing house la maison d'édition
  small house le pavillon
housing le logement
how comment, **1.1**
  How are you? Ça va? Comment vas-tu? Comment allez-vous?, **BV**
  How's it going? Ça va?, **BV**
  How long have you been waiting? Tu attends depuis combien de temps?
  how much, how many combien (de), **3.2**
  How much is it? C'est combien?, **3.2**
human humain(e)
  human being l'être humain (*m.*)
hundred cent, **2.2**
  hundreds les centaines (*f. pl.*)
hungry: to be hungry avoir faim, **5.1**
  I'm super hungry. J'ai hyper faim.
hunter le chasseur, la chasseuse
to **hurry** se dépêcher, **12.1**
to **hurt** avoir mal à, **14.1**
  It (That) hurts. Ça fait mal., **14.1**
husband le mari, **4.1**

I je, **1.2**
ice la glace, **11.2**
  ice cream la glace, **5.1**
idea l'idée (*f.*)
ideal idéal(e)
to **identify** identifier
if si
ill malade, **L1, 14.1**
illness la maladie

illustration le dessin
immediate immédiat(e)
immediately immédiatement
immense immense
important important(e)
impossible impossible
Impressionists les impressionnistes (*m. pl.*)
imprisoned emprisonné(e)
in dans, **1.2**; à, **3.1**; en, **3.2**
  in addition to en plus de
  in fact en fait
  in first (second) class en première (seconde), **9.1**
  in front of devant, **8.2**
  in general en général
  in particular en particulier
  in search of à la recherche de
  in vain en vain
  In what month? En quel mois?, **BV**
to **inaugurate** inaugurer
included compris(e), **5.2**
  The tip is included. Le service est compris., **5.2**
to **indicate** indiquer
indigestion le trouble digestif
  to have indigestion avoir mal au foie
indiscreet indiscret, indiscrète
indispensable indispensable
individual l'individu (*m.*); (*adj.*) individuel(le)
industrial industriel(le)
inexpensive bon marché (*inv.*)
infection l'infection (*f.*), **14.1**
infinite infini(e)
influence l'influence (*f.*)
to **influence** influencer
information l'information (*f.*)
innocent innocent(e)
inquiry l'enquête (*f.*)
insane fou, folle

to **insist** insister
to **inspire** inspirer
instructions les instructions (*f. pl.*)
instructor le moniteur, la monitrice, **11.1**
instrument l'instrument (*m.*)
  keyboard instrument l'instrument à clavier
  percussion instrument l'instrument à percussion
  string instrument l'instrument à cordes
  wind instrument l'instrument à vent
intellectual intellectuel(le)
intelligent intelligent(e), **1.1**
interest l'intérêt (*m.*)
interesting intéressant(e), **1.1**
intermediate moyen(ne)
intermission l'entracte (*m.*), **13.1**
internal interne
international international(e), **8.1**
interpreter l'interprète (*m. et f.*)
intimate intime
to **introduce** présenter
to **invite** inviter, **4.1**
island l'île (*f.*), **L4**
to **isolate** isoler
Italian (*adj.*) italien(ne)
Italian (*language*) l'italien (*m.*), **2.2**
to **itch** piquer **14.1**
  to have itchy eyes avoir les yeux qui piquent, **14.1**
Ivory Coast la Côte d'Ivoire

jacket le blouson, **7.1**
  (sport) jacket la veste, **7.1**
  ski jacket l'anorak (*m.*), **7.1**

jam la confiture, **6.2**
January janvier *(m.)*, **BV**
jar le pot, **6.2**
jazz le jazz
jealous jaloux, jalouse
jeans le jean, **7.1;** le blue-jean
jersey le maillot
to **jog** faire du jogging
to **joke around** rigoler, **3.2**
joy la joie
juice le jus, **5.1**
  apple juice le jus de pomme, **5.1**
  orange juice le jus d'orange, **5.1**
July juillet *(m.)*, **BV**
June juin *(m.)*, **BV**
junior high student le/la collégien(ne)
just juste, **2.1**
  fitting (him/her) just right juste à sa taille
  just barely tout juste

to **keep** garder
key la clé; le demi-cercle *(basketball)*, **10.2**
keyboard le clavier
to **kick** donner un coup de pied, **10.1**
to **kid: You're kidding!** Tu rigoles!, **3.2**
kilogram le kilo(gramme), **6.2**
kilometer le kilomètre
kind la sorte; le genre, **13.1**
king le roi, **L3**
kitchen la cuisine, **4.2**
  kitchen sink l'évier *(m.)*, **12.2**
knife le couteau, **5.2**
knight le chevalier
to **knock** frapper, **L4**
to **know** connaître *(be acquainted with)*; savoir *(information)*, **13.2**

label la griffe
laboratory le laboratoire
lake le lac
lamb l'agneau *(m.)*, **6.1**
lame boiteux, boiteuse
land la terre
to **land** atterrir, **8.1**
landing l'atterrissage *(m.)*; le débarquement
landing card la carte de débarquement, **8.2**
landscape le paysage
language la langue, **2.2**
lap *(race)* l'étape *(f.)*
large grand(e); ample
last dernier, dernière, **10.2**
  last name le nom de famille
  last night hier soir, **10.2**
  last week la semaine dernière, **10.2**
  last year l'année *(f.)* dernière
to **last** durer
  late en retard, **9.1;** *(adv.)* tard, **12.1**
  to be late être en retard, **9.1;** avoir du retard *(plane, train, etc.)*, **8.1**
later plus tard
  See you later. À tout à l'heure., **BV**
Latin le latin, **2.2**
Latin *(adj.)* latin(e)
  Latin American latino-américain(e)
to **learn (to)** apprendre (à), **5**
to **leave** partir, **8.1;** ressortir
  to leave (a room, etc.) quitter, **3.1**
  to leave (something behind) laisser, **5.2**
  to leave a tip laisser un pourboire, **5.2**
leg la jambe
legend la légende
lemonade le citron pressé, **5.1**
lemon-lime drink la limonade, **BV**

less moins, **7.1**
  less than moins de
  less . . . than moins... que, **7**
lesson la leçon, **11.1**
to **let** laisser
  Let's go. On y va.
lettuce la salade, **6.2**
level le taux
liaison la liaison
life la vie
light *(color)* clair(e)
like comme
to **like** aimer, **3.1**
  I'd like that! Ça me dit!
  I would like je voudrais, **5.1**
  What would you like? *(café, restaurant)* Vous désirez?, **5.1**
limit la limite
line la ligne; *(of people)* la queue, **9.1**
  to wait in line faire la queue, **9.1**
linked en liaison
linking la liaison
liquid le liquide
to **listen (to)** écouter, **3.1**
  to listen with a stethoscope ausculter, **14.2**
liter le litre, **6.2**
literature la littérature, **2.2**
little: a little un peu, **2.1;** un peu de
to **live** *(in a city, house, etc.)* habiter, **3.1**
liver le foie
living vivant(e)
  living room la salle de séjour, **4.2**
to **load** charger
lobby le hall, **8.1**
local local(e)
located situé(e)
lonely solitaire
long long(ue), **7.1**
  (for) a long time longtemps, **11.1**
  (for) too long trop longtemps, **11.1**

Long live . . . ! Vive... !
longer: no longer ne...
plus, **6.1**
to **look** *(seem)* avoir l'air
to **look at** regarder, **3.1**
to look at oneself se
regarder
to look at one another se
regarder
to **look for** chercher
loose *(clothing)* large, **7.2**
loose-leaf binder le
classeur, **3.2**
to **lose** perdre, **9.2**
to lose patience perdre
patience, **9.2**
lot: a lot beaucoup, **3.1**
a lot of beaucoup de, **3.2**
a lot of people beaucoup
de monde, **10.1**
to **love** aimer, **3.1;** adorer
love l'amour *(m.)*, **L4**
lower inférieur(e)
low-income housing
le/la H.L.M.
luck la chance
to be in luck avoir de la
chance
lucky: to be lucky avoir
de la chance
luggage les bagages
(m. pl.), **8.1**
lunch le déjeuner, **5.2**
to eat lunch déjeuner, **3.1**
lung le poumon
luxury *(adj.)* de grand
standing
lyrics les paroles *(f. pl.)*

M

ma'am madame, **BV**
machine la machine
magazine le magazine,
9.1, L2; la revue, **L2**
Maghreb le Maghreb
magic *(adj.)* magique
magnificent magnifique
magpie la pie
mail la poste
main principal(e)
majority la majorité

to **make** faire, **6.1;** fabriquer
to make a basket
(basketball) réussir un
panier, **10.2**
to make up inventer
mall le centre commercial,
7.1
man l'homme *(m.)*, **7.1**
to **manage to** arriver à, **9.1**
mandatory obligatoire
manner la façon
many beaucoup de, **3.2**
map la carte
March mars *(m.)*, **BV**
market le marché, **6.2**
flea market le marché
aux puces
marriage le mariage
married marié(e)
to get married se marier,
L4
marvelous merveilleux,
merveilleuse
masculine masculin(e)
math les maths *(f. pl.)*, **2.2**
mathematics les
mathématiques *(f. pl.)*, **2.2**
**matter: What's the matter
with you?** Qu'est-ce que
tu as?, **10**
May mai *(m.)*, **BV**
meal le repas, **5.2**
to **mean** signifier
meaning la signification;
le sens
to **measure** mesurer
measurement la mesure
meat la viande, **6.1**
medical médical(e)
medicine *(medical
profession)* la médecine;
(remedy) le médicament,
14.1
medina la médina
Mediterranean Sea la mer
Méditerranée
medium-rare *(meat)* à
point, **5.2**
to **meet** rencontrer; retrouver
(get together with); faire la
connaissance de
melody l'air *(m.)*
melon le melon, **6.2**

memorable mémorable
memory le souvenir
to **mention** citer
menu la carte, **5.1**
merchandise la
marchandise
merchant le/la
marchand(e), **6.2**
produce merchant le/la
marchand(e) de fruits et
légumes, **6.2**
message le message
metabolism le
métabolisme
metal le métal
meter le mètre
metric system le système
métrique
microbe le microbe
microbial microbien(ne)
microprocessor le
microprocesseur
microscope le microscope
middle school student
le/la collégien(ne)
midnight minuit *(m.)*, **BV**
military militaire
milk le lait, **6.1**
milligram le milligramme
million le million
mineral le minéral
mineral water l'eau *(f.)*
minérale, **6.2**
minus moins
minute la minute, **9.2**
miracle le miracle
mirror la glace, **12.1**
Miss (Ms.) Mademoiselle
(Mlle), **BV**
to **miss** *(train, etc.)* rater, **9.2**
mistake la faute
mixture le mélange
model le modèle
modem le modem
modern moderne
modest modeste
mogul la bosse, **11.2**
mom la maman
moment le moment
Monday lundi *(m.)*, **BV**
money l'argent *(m.)*, **5.2**
monitor *(computer)* le
moniteur

month le mois, **BV**
more *(comparative)* plus,
7.1
  more or less plus ou
    moins
  more . . . than plus...
    que, **7**
  no more ne... plus, **6.1**
morning le matin, **BV**; le
  mat *(fam.)*
  in the morning le matin
  in the morning (A.M.) du
    matin, **BV**
Moroccan marocain(e)
Morocco le Maroc
most (of) la plupart (des),
9.2
  the most . . . le (la, les)
    plus...
mother la mère, **4.1**
  mother tongue la langue
    maternelle
mount le mont
mountain le mont; la
  montagne, **11.2**
  to (in) the mountains à
    la montagne
mountaintop le sommet,
11.2
mouse la souris
mouth la bouche, **14.1**
movement le mouvement
movie le film, **13.1**
  detective movie le film
    policier, **13.1**
  movies le cinéma, **13.1**
  movie theater le cinéma,
    la salle de cinéma, **13.1**
  movie video le film en
    vidéo, **13.1**
  science-fiction movie le
    film de science-fiction,
    13.1
Mr. Monsieur (M.), **BV**
Mrs. (Ms.) Madame
  (Mme), **BV**
multicolored multicolore
to **multiply** multiplier
municipal municipal(e)
muscle le muscle
muscular musculaire
museum le musée, **13.2**

music la musique, **2.2**
musical musical(e)
  musical comedy la
    comédie musicale, **13.1**
musician le/la
  musicien(ne)
Muslim musulman(e)
mussel la moule
must devoir, **10.2**
  one must il faut, **8.2**
  one must not il ne faut
    pas, **8.2**
mustard la moutarde, **6.2**
my ma, mon, mes, **4**
mysterious mystérieux,
  mystérieuse
myth le mythe

name le nom
  first name le prénom
  last name le nom de
    famille
  My name is . . . Je
    m'appelle... , **BV**
  What's your name? Tu
    t'appelles comment?, **BV**
napkin la serviette, **5.2**
national national(e)
nationality la nationalité
native of originaire de
natural naturel(le)
  natural sciences les
    sciences naturelles
    (f. pl.), **2.1**
nature la nature
navy blue bleu marine
  (inv.), **7.2**
near près de, **4.2**
  very near tout près, **4.2**
necessarily
  nécessairement
necessary nécessaire
  it is necessary il faut, **8.2**
need le besoin
to **need** avoir besoin de, **10.1**
neighbor le/la voisin(e),
  4.2
neighborhood le quartier,
  4.2; *(adj.)* du coin

nephew le neveu, **4.1**
nervous nerveux,
  nerveuse
net le filet, **10.2**
never ne... jamais, **11.2**
new nouveau (nouvel),
  nouvelle, **4.2**
New England la
  Nouvelle-Angleterre
New Orleans La
  Nouvelle-Orléans
news *(TV)* les
  informations *(f. pl.)*
  news article le reportage
newspaper le journal, **9.1**
newsstand le kiosque, **9.1**
next prochain(e), **9.2**
nice *(person)* sympa, **1.2**;
  aimable; sympathique;
  gentil(le), **6.2**
  It's nice weather. Il fait
    beau., **11.1**
niece la nièce, **4.1**
night la nuit
  last night hier soir, **10.2**
no non
  no longer ne... plus, **6.1**
  no more ne... plus, **6.1**
  no one ne... personne, **11**;
    personne ne...
  no smoking (section) (la
    zone) non-fumeurs, **8.1**
noble noble
nobody ne... personne, **11**;
  personne ne...
noise le bruit
nonsmoking *(section)* non-
  fumeurs, **8.1**
noon midi *(m.)*, **BV**
north le nord
North African nord-
  africain(e)
nose le nez, **14.1**
  to have a runny nose
    avoir le nez qui coule,
    14.1
not ne... pas, **1.2**; pas, **2.1**
  **isn't it?, doesn't it (he,
    she, etc.)?,** n'est-ce pas?,
    2.2
  not at all pas du tout, **3.1**
  not bad pas mal, **BV**

note la note
notebook le cahier, **3.2**
notepad le bloc-notes, **3.2**
nothing ne... rien, **11**
to **notice** remarquer
noun le nom
novel le roman
November novembre *(m.)*, **BV**
now maintenant, **2.2**
  right now en ce moment
nowadays de nos jours
number le nombre; le numéro
  telephone number le numéro de téléphone
numerous nombreux, nombreuse
nutrition l'alimentation *(f.)*

object l'objet *(m.)*
to **oblige** obliger
oboe le hautbois
to **observe** observer
occupied occupé(e)
ocean l'océan *(m.)*
o'clock: It's . . . o'clock. Il est... heure(s)., **BV**
October octobre *(m.)*, **BV**
of *(belonging to)* de, **1.2**
  of course bien sûr
  Of course (not)! Mais oui (non)!
Off (they) go! En route!
office: to have office hours *(doctor)* donner des consultations
official officiel(le)
often souvent, **5.2**
oil l'huile *(f.)*, **6.1**; le pétrole
  oil tanker le pétrolier
okay *(health)* Ça va.; *(agreement)* d'accord, **BV**
  Okay! Bon!, **6.1**
old vieux (vieil), vieille, **4.2**; âgé(e); ancien(ne)
  How old are you? Tu as quel âge? *(fam.)*, **4.1**

older l'aîné(e), **L1**
omelette (with herbs/plain) l'omelette *(f.)* (aux fines herbes/nature), **5.1**
on sur, **4.2**
  on board à bord de, **8.2**
  on foot à pied, **4.2**
  on sale en solde, **7.1**
  on time à l'heure, **8.1**
  on Tuesdays le mardi, **13.2**
oneself soi
one-way ticket l'aller simple *(m.)*, **9.1**
onion l'oignon *(m.)*, **5.1**
only seulement; *(adj.)* seul(e)
open ouvert(e), **13.2**
to **open** ouvrir, **14.2**
opera l'opéra *(m.)*
  light opera l'opéra comique
operation l'opération *(f.)*
opinion l'avis *(m.)*, **7.2**
  in my opinion à mon avis, **7.2**
opponent l'adversaire *(m. et f.)*
  opponents le camp adverse, **10.1**
to **oppose** opposer, **10.1**
opposing adverse, **10.1**
opposite le contraire
or ou, **1.1**
  or else sinon, **9.2**
orange *(fruit)* l'orange *(f.)*, **6.2**; *(color)* orange *(inv.)*, **7.2**
  orange tree l'oranger *(m.)*, **L2**
orchestra l'orchestre *(m.)*
  symphony orchestra l'orchestre symphonique
to **orchestrate** orchestrer
order: in order to pour
to **order** commander, **5.1**
ordinary ordinaire
organ *(of the body)* l'organe *(m.)*; *(musical instrument)* l'orgue *(m.)*
organism l'organisme *(m.)*

to **organize** organiser
original language version *(of a film)* la version originale, **13.1**
other autre
  in other words autrement dit
  on the other hand par contre
  some other d'autres, **2.2**
otherwise sinon, **9.2**
our notre, nos, **4**
outdoors en plein air
outfit l'ensemble *(m.)*
outgoing sociable, **1.2**
outing l'excursion *(f.)*
outside *(n.)* l'extérieur *(m.)*; *(adv.)* à l'extérieur; *(prep.)* au dehors de
  to work outside the home travailler à l'extérieur
outskirts la périphérie
over *(prep.)* par-dessus, **10.2**
to **overlook** donner sur, **4.2**
overseas *(adj.)* d'outre-mer
to **owe** devoir, **10**
to **own** posséder
oxygen l'oxygène *(m.)*

to **pack** *(suitcases)* faire les valises, **8.1**
package le paquet, **6.2**
packed *(stadium)* comble, **10.1**
pain in the neck *(slang)* casse-pieds
painful douloureux, douloureuse
to **paint** peindre
  painter l'artiste peintre *(m. et f.)*, le/la peintre, **13.2**
painting la peinture, **13.2**; le tableau, **13.2**
pair la paire, **7.1**
pal le copain, la copine, **2.1**
palace le palais
pancake la crêpe, **BV**

pants le pantalon, **7.1**
paper le papier, **3.2**
  sheet of paper la feuille de papier, **3.2**
parade le défilé
pardon me pardon
parents les parents *(m. pl.)*, **4.1**
Parisian *(adj.)* parisien(ne)
park le parc
parking lot le parking
part la partie
  to be part of faire partie de
to **participate (in)** participer (à)
party la fête, **4.1**
  to throw a party donner une fête, **4.1**
pass la passe
to **pass** passer, **10.1**
  to pass an exam réussir à un examen
passenger le passager, la passagère, **8.1**; *(train)* le voyageur, la voyageuse, **9.1**
passport le passeport, **8.1**
  passport check le contrôle des passeports
past passé(e)
pasta les pâtes *(f. pl.)*
path le chemin
patience la patience, **9.2**
  to lose patience perdre patience, **9.2**
patient le/la malade, **14.2**; *(adj.)* patient(e), **1.1**
patio la terrasse, **4.2**
to **pay** payer, **3.2**
  to pay attention faire attention
  to pay back rembourser
peace la paix
pear la poire, **6.2**
pearl la perle
peas les petits pois *(m. pl.)*, **6.2**
peasant le/la paysan(ne), **L1**
pen: ballpoint pen le stylo-bille, **3.2**
  felt-tip pen le feutre, **3.2**

penalty *(soccer)* le penalty
pencil le crayon, **3.2**
penicillin la pénicilline, **14.1**
people les gens *(m. pl.)*
pepper le poivre, **6.1**
percent pour cent
perfect parfait(e)
perfectly parfaitement
to **perform** jouer, **13.1**
period l'époque *(f.)*; la période
permanent permanent(e)
to **permit** permettre
person la personne
personal personnel(le)
personality la personnalité
personally personnellement, **13.2**
pharmaceutical pharmaceutique
pharmacist le/la pharmacien(ne), **14.2**
pharmacy la pharmacie, **14.2**
phenomenon le phénomène
photograph la photo
physical physique
physicist le/la physicien(ne)
physics la physique, **2.2**
to **pick up** ramasser, **8.2**; recueillir
picnic le pique-nique
picturesque pittoresque
pie la tarte, **6.1**
pill le comprimé, **14.2**
pilot le/la pilote, **8.2**
  airline pilot le/la pilote de ligne
to **pilot** piloter
pink rose, **7.1**
pizza la pizza, **BV**
place l'endroit *(m.)*; la place
  to take place avoir lieu
to **place** mettre, **7.1**
plain la plaine
plan le projet
plane l'avion *(m.)*, **8.1**
  by plane en avion

plant la plante
plastic le plastique
plate l'assiette *(f.)*, **5.2**
platform *(railroad)* le quai, **9.1**
play la pièce (de théâtre), **13.1**
  to put on a play monter une pièce, **13.1**
to **play** jouer, **3.2**
  to play *(a sport)* jouer à, **10.1**
player le joueur, la joueuse, **10.1**
playwright l'auteur *(m.)* dramatique
pleasant agréable
please s'il vous plaît *(form.)*, s'il te plaît *(fam.)*, **BV**
pleasure le plaisir
pleated plissé(e), **7.1**
plentiful abondant(e)
to **plot** conspirer
plus plus
p.m. de l'après-midi; du soir, **BV**
poem le poème
poet *(m. and f.)* le poète
politeness la politesse, **BV**
political politique
polluted pollué(e)
pollution la pollution
polo shirt le polo, **7.1**
pool la piscine, **11.1**
poor pauvre, **L1, 14.1**
  Poor thing! Le/La pauvre!, **14.1**
pop *(music)* pop
popular populaire, **1.2**
pork le porc, **6.1**
port le port
Portuguese portugais(e)
position la position
to **possess** posséder
possession la possession
postcard la carte postale, **9.1**
poster l'affiche *(f.)*
potato la pomme de terre, **6.2**
pound la livre, **6.2**

practical pratique
practice la pratique
to practice pratiquer; travailler
preceding précédent(e)
to prefer préférer, 6
prefix le préfixe
to prepare préparer
to prescribe prescrire, 14.2
prescription l'ordonnance (f.), 14.2
  to write a prescription faire une ordonnance, 14.2
present le cadeau, 4.1
to present présenter
pretty joli(e), 4.2
price le prix, 7.1
priest l'abbé (m.)
principal principal(e)
printer l'imprimante (f.)
prison la prison, L4
prisoner le prisonnier, la prisonnière, L4
private individuel(le); privé(e)
problem le problème; la difficulté
product le produit
professional professionel(le)
program le programme; (TV) l'émission (f.), 12.2; (computer) le logiciel
programming la programmation
protein la protéine
proud fier, fière
public public, publique
to publish publier
to punish punir
purchase l'achat (m.)
purified purifié(e)
to push pousser
to put (on) mettre, 7.1
  to put on makeup se maquiller, 12.1
  to put (someone) to bed coucher, 12
  to put on a play monter une pièce, 13.1

Q

quality la qualité
quarter: quarter after (time) et quart, BV
  quarter to (time) moins le quart, BV
Quebec: from or of Quebec québécois
queen la reine
question la question, 3.1
  to ask a question poser une question, 3.1
quick rapide
quickly rapidement, vite
quite assez, 1.1
quiz l'interro(gation) (f.)

R

race (human population) la race; (competition) la course, 10.2
  bicycle race la course cycliste, 10.2
radio la radio, 3.2
rain la pluie
to rain: It's raining. Il pleut., 11.1
to raise lever
  to raise one's hand lever la main, 3.1
raisin le raisin sec
rap (music) le rap
rapidly rapidement, vite
rare (meat) saignant(e), 5.2
rather plutôt
razor le rasoir, 12.1
to read lire, 9.2
  reader le lecteur, la lectrice
  reading la lecture
real vrai(e), 2.2
reality la réalité
really vraiment, 1.1
rear l'arrière (m.), 8.2
  rear guard l'arrière-garde (f.)
reason la raison
to receive recevoir, 10.2

recess la récré(ation), 3.2
to recognize reconnaître
recycling le recyclage
red rouge, 7.1
referee l'arbitre (m.), 10.1
to reflect refléter
refrigerator le frigidaire, 12.2; le réfrigérateur, 12.2
reggae le reggae
region la région
to reimburse rembourser
relationship la relation
religious religieux, religieuse
to remain rester, 11.1
remote control la télécommande, 12.2
renowned renommé(e)
to rent louer, 13.1
to replace remplacer
to represent représenter
research la recherche
to resemble ressembler à
reserved réservé(e)
respective respectif, respective
respiration la respiration
respiratory respiratoire
restaurant le restaurant, 5.2
  train station restaurant le buffet, 9.1
retreat la retraite
return le retour
to return rentrer, 3.2; (volleyball) renvoyer, 10.2
revolution la révolution
revolutionary révolutionnaire
rhythm le rythme
rice le riz
rich riche
riddle la devinette
ridiculous ridicule
right le droit
right away tout de suite
right there juste là
to rinse rincer
river le fleuve; la rivière
Riviera (French) la Côte d'Azur
road la route; le chemin

rock le rocher, **L3;** *(music)* le rock
role le rôle
romantic romantique
roof le toit
  thatched roof le toit de chaume
room *(in house)* la pièce, **4.2;** la salle
  dining room la salle à manger, **4.2**
  living room la salle de séjour, **4.2**
round-trip ticket le billet aller-retour, **9.1**
route le chemin
routine la routine, **12.1**
royal royal(e)
ruby le rubis
ruined ruiné(e)
rule la règle
ruler la règle, **3.2**
runner le coureur, la coureuse, **10.2**
running shoe la basket, **7.1**
runny: to have a runny nose avoir le nez qui coule, **14.1**
runway la piste, **8.1**
rural rural(e)
Russian *(language)* le russe

sad triste, **L1**
to **safeguard** sauvegarder
sailor le marin, **L4**
salad la salade, **5.1**
salami le saucisson, **6.1**
salary le salaire
sale: on sale en solde, **7.1;** en promotion
sales les soldes *(m. pl.)*, **7.1**
salesperson le vendeur, la vendeuse, **7.1**
salt le sel, **6.1**
same même, **2.1**
  all the same tout de même, **5.2**
  It's all the same to me.

Ça m'est égal., **13.1**
sandals *(f. pl.)* les sandales, **7.1**
sandwich le sandwich, **BV**
  grilled ham and cheese sandwich le croque-monsieur, **5.1**
sardine la sardine
to **satisfy** satisfaire
Saturday samedi *(m.)*, **BV**
sauce la sauce
sausage la saucisse
to **save** sauver; sauvegarder
saxophone le saxophone
to **say** dire, **9.2**
scarf l'écharpe *(f.)*, **11.2**
scene la scène, **13.1**
schedule l'emploi *(m.)* du temps; l'horaire *(m.)*, **9.1**
  sports schedule le calendrier sportif
school l'école *(f.)*, **1.2;** *(adj.)* scolaire, **3.2**
  elementary school l'école primaire
  junior high/high school l'école secondaire, **1.2**
  high school le lycée, **2.1**
  school supplies la fourniture scolaire, **3.2**
science les sciences *(f. pl.)*, **2.1**
  natural sciences les sciences naturelles, **2.1**
  social sciences les sciences sociales, **2.1**
scientific scientifique
scientist le savant *(m. et f.)*
to **score a goal** marquer un but, **10.1**
to **scratch** gratter, **14.1**
screen l'écran *(m.)*, **8.1**
sculptor le sculpteur *(m. et f.)*, **13.2**
sculpture la sculpture, **13.2**
sea la mer, **11.1**
  by the sea au bord de la mer, **11.1**
  seashore le bord de la mer, **11.1**
  seaside resort la station balnéaire, **11.1**

season la saison
seat le siège, **8.2;** la place *(plane, train, movie, etc.)*, **8.1**
seated assis(e), **9.2**
second *(adj.)* deuxième, **4.2;** second(e)
  in second class en seconde, **9.1**
secret *(adj.)* secret, secrète
security (airport) le contrôle de sécurité, **8.1**
to **see** voir, **7.1**
  See you later. À tout à l'heure., **BV**
  See you soon! À bientôt!, **BV**
  See you tomorrow. À demain., **BV**
seldom très peu
to **sell** vendre, **9.1**
  seller le/la marchand(e), **6.2**
  produce seller le/la marchand(e) de fruits et légumes, **6.2**
semi-circle le demi-cercle, **10.2**
to **send** envoyer, **10.1;** emmener, **L4**
separate séparer
September septembre *(m.)*, **BV**
serious sérieux, sérieuse, **7;** grave
to **serve** servir, **8.2; 10.2**
service le service, **5.2**
to **set the table** mettre la table, **7**
several plusieurs
Shall we go? On y va?
shampoo le shampooing, **12.1**
shape la forme
to **shave** se raser, **12.1**
shaver le rasoir, **12.1**
she elle, **1.1**
sheet of paper la feuille de papier, **3.2**
shepherd le berger
shepherdess la bergère
to **shine** briller
shirt la chemise, **7.1**

shoe la chaussure, **7.1**
to **shoot** *(ball)* lancer, **10.2**
shop la boutique, **7.1**
to **shop** faire des achats
shopkeeper le/la commerçant(e)
shopping le shopping, **7.2**
  to do the grocery shopping faire les courses, **6.1**
  to go shopping faire des courses, **7.2**
  shopping cart le chariot, **6.2**
  shopping center le centre commercial, **7.1**
short petit(e), **1.1**; court(e), **7.1**
  in a short time en très peu de temps
shorts le short, **7.1**
to **shout** crier, **L4**
show *(TV)* l'émission *(f.)*, **12.2**
show(ing) *(movies)* la séance, **13.1**
to **show** montrer; *(movie)* jouer
shower la douche, **12.1**
  to take a shower prendre une douche, **12.1**
showing *(movies)* la séance, **13.1**
shrimp la crevette, **6.1**
shy timide, **1.2**
sick malade, **14.1, L1**
  to get sick tomber malade, **L1**
  sick person le/la malade, **14.2**
side le côté; *(in a sporting event)* le camp, **10.1**
sidewalk café la terrasse (d'un café), **5.1**
sign le signal
significance la signification
similar semblable, **L1**
simple simple
simply simplement
since *(time)* depuis, **9.2**
to **sing** chanter, **13.2**
  singer le chanteur,

la chanteuse, **13.1**
single unique; seul(e)
sink *(kitchen)* l'évier *(m.)*, **12.2**
sinus infection la sinusite, **14.2**
sir monsieur, **BV**
sister la sœur, **1.2**
to **sit: Where would you like to sit?** Qu'est-ce que vous voulez comme place?, **8.1**
size *(clothes)* la taille; *(shoes)* la pointure, **7.2**
  the next larger size la taille au-dessus, **7.2**
  the next smaller size la taille au-dessous, **7.2**
  to wear size (number) faire du (nombre), **7.2**
  What size do you wear? Vous faites quelle taille (pointure)?, **7.2**
skate le patin, **11.2**
to **skate (ice)** faire du patin (à glace), **11.1**
skating le patin
  to go skating faire du patin, **11.1**
  skating rink la patinoire, **11.2**
skeletal squelettique
skeleton le squelette
ski le ski, **11.2**
  ski boot la chaussure de ski, **11.2**
  ski cap le bonnet, **11.2**
  ski jacket l'anorak *(m.)*, **7.1**
  ski pole le bâton, **11.2**
  ski resort la station de sports d'hiver, **11.2**
  ski trail la piste, **11.2**
to **ski** faire du ski, **11.2**
skier le skieur, la skieuse, **11.2**
skiing le ski, **11.2**
  cross-country skiing le ski de fond, **11.2**
  downhill skiing le ski alpin, **11.2**
skirt la jupe, **7.1**
skull la boîte crânienne

sky le ciel, **11.1**
to **sleep** dormir, **8.2**
  to sleep like a log dormir comme une souche
  sleeping car le wagon-couchette
sleeve la manche, **7.1**
  long-(short-)sleeved à manches longues (courtes), **7.1**
slice la tranche, **6.2**
  slice of bread with butter or jam la tartine
  slice of bread and butter la tartine de pain beurré
small petit(e), **1.1**
smoke la fumée
to **smoke** fumer
snack bar *(train)* le snack-bar, **9.2**
sneaker la basket, **7.1**
to **sneeze** éternuer, **14.1**
snow la neige, **11.2**
to **snow: It's snowing.** Il neige., **11.2**
  snowman le bonhomme de neige
so alors, **BV**; donc; si *(adv.)*
soap le savon, **12.1**
soccer le foot(ball), **10.1**
  soccer field le terrain de football, **10.1**
sociable sociable, **1.2**
social social(e)
  social sciences les sciences sociales *(f. pl.)*, **2.1**
  social worker l'assistante sociale *(f.)*
sock la chaussette, **7.1**
software le software
soldier le soldat, **L3**
solely uniquement
solid solide
solidarity la solidarité
solution la solution
some du, de la, de l', des, **6**; *(adj.)* quelques *(pl.)*, **9.2**; *(pron.)* certains
  some other d'autres, **2.2**
somebody quelqu'un, **10.1**

someone quelqu'un, **10.1**
something quelque chose, **11**
  something else autre chose
  something special quelque chose de spécial
  something to drink quelque chose à boire
sometimes quelquefois, **5.2**
son le fils, **4.1**
song la chanson
soon bientôt
  See you soon. À bientôt., **BV**
sore throat: to have a sore throat avoir mal à la gorge, **14.1**
sorry: to be sorry regretter, **6.1**
so-so comme ci, comme ça
sound le son, **L3**
soup la soupe, **5.1**
source la source
south le sud
South America l'Amérique (f.) du Sud
spaghetti les spaghettis (m. pl.)
Spanish espagnol(e)
Spanish (language) l'espagnol (m.), **2.2**
to **sparkle** scintiller
to **speak** parler, **3.1**
  special spécial(e)
  specialty la spécialité
  spectator le spectateur, la spectatrice, **10.1**
to **spend** (time) passer, **3.1**
to **spill** déverser
  spinach les épinards (m. pl.), **6.2**
  spinal cord la moelle épinière
  spirit l'esprit (m.)
  splendid splendide
  spoon la cuillère, **5.2**
  sport le sport, **10.2**
  team sport le sport collectif; le sport d'équipe, **10.2**

winter sports les sports d'hiver, **11.2**
spring (season) le printemps, **11.1**
square la place
stadium le stade, **10.1**
stage (of a race) l'étape (f.)
staircase l'escalier (m.), **4.2**
to **stamp** (a ticket) composter, **9.1**
standing debout, **9.2**
to **stare at** regarder fixement
state of the art haut de gamme
station la station, **4.2**
  gas station la station-service
  subway station la station de métro, **4.2**
stationery store la papeterie, **3.2**
statue la statue, **13.2**
stay le séjour
to **stay** rester, **11.1**
  steak and French fries le steak frites, **5.2**
stepfather le beau-père, **4.1**
stepmother la belle-mère, **4.1**
still toujours; encore, **11**
stomach le ventre, **14.1**
stomachache: to have a stomachache avoir mal au ventre, **14.1**
stone la pierre
stop l'arrêt (m.), **9.2**
to **stop** s'arrêter, **10.1**
store le magasin, **3.2**
  department store le grand magasin, **7.1**
to **store** stocker
story l'histoire (f.)
strategy la stratégie
strawberry la fraise, **6.2**
street la rue, **3.1**
strength la force
strict strict(e), **2.1**
strong fort(e), **2.2**
student l'élève (m. et f.), **1.2;** (university) l'étudiant(e)
studio (artist's) l'atelier (m.)

studio (apartment) le studio
study l'étude (f.)
to **study** étudier, **3.1;** faire des études
  to study French (math, etc.) faire du français (des maths, etc.), **6**
stupid stupide
  stupid thing la bêtise
style le look
  in style à la mode
subject le sujet; (in school) la matière, **2.2**
substance la substance
subtitles les sous-titres (m. pl.), **13.1**
to **subtract** soustraire
subway le métro, **4.2**
  subway station la station de métro, **4.2**
to **succeed in** (doing) arriver à (+ inf.), **9.1**
success le succès
to **suffer** souffrir, **14.2**
sugar le sucre
to **suggest** proposer; suggérer
suit (men's) le complet; (women's) le tailleur, **7.1**
suitcase la valise, **8.1**
sum la somme
summer l'été (m.)
  in summer en été, **11.1**
summit le sommet, **11.2**
sun le soleil, **11.1**
  in the sun au soleil, **11.1**
to **sunbathe** prendre un bain de soleil, **11.1**
sunburn le coup de soleil, **11.1**
Sunday dimanche (m.), **BV**
sunglasses les lunettes (f. pl.) de soleil, **11.1**
sunny: It's sunny. Il fait du soleil., **11.1**
suntan lotion la crème solaire, **11.1**
super super
superbe superbe
supermarket le supermarché, **6.2**

supply la fourniture
  school supplies les
    fournitures scolaires, **3.2**
sure sûr(e)
to **surf the Net** naviguer sur
  Internet
surfer le surfeur, la
  surfeuse, **11.1**
surfing le surf, **11.1**
  to go surfing faire du
    surf, **11.1**
surprise la surprise
survey le sondage
survival la survie
to **swallow** avaler, **14.2**
sweater le pull, **7.1**
sweatshirt le sweat-shirt,
  7.1
to **swim** nager, **11.1**
swimming la natation,
  11.1
sword l'épée (f.), **L3**
symphony la symphonie
symptom le symptôme
syrup le sirop, **14.1**
system le système
  metric system le système
    métrique

table la table, **5.1**
  table setting le couvert,
    5.2
tablecloth la nappe, **5.2**
to **take** prendre, **5.2**
  What size do you take?
    Vous faites quelle taille
    (pointure)?, **7.2**
  to take down descendre,
    9
  to take an exam passer
    un examen, **3.1**
  to take off (airplane)
    décoller, **8.1**
  to take place avoir lieu
  to take possession of
    prendre possession de
  to take size (number)
    faire du (nombre), **7.2**
  to take the subway
    prendre le métro, **5.2**

to take a trip faire un
  voyage, **8.1**
  to take a walk faire une
    promenade, **11.1**
taken occupé(e)
to **talk** parler, **3.1**
  to talk on the phone
    parler au téléphone, **3.2**
tall grand(e), **1.1**
to **tan** bronzer, **11.1**
tango le tango
tape la cassette, **7.1**
to **tape** enregistrer
tart la tarte, **6.1**
  apple tart la tarte aux
    pommes, **6.1**
tea le thé
to **teach (someone to do**
  something) apprendre (à
  quelqu'un à faire quelque
  chose)
teacher le/la prof (inform.),
  2.1; le professeur, **2.1**
team l'équipe (f.)
teammate le coéquipier, la
  coéquipière
techno (music) la techno
teenager l'adolescent(e)
telephone le téléphone,
  3.2; (adj.) téléphonique
  telephone number le
    numéro de téléphone
television la télé, **12.2**
to **tell** dire, **9.2**
  to tell (about) raconter
temperate tempéré(e)
temperature la
  température
temple la tempe
temporary temporaire
ten dix, **BV**
tendon le tendon
term le terme
terrace la terrasse, **4.2**
terrible terrible
terrific super; terrible
test l'examen (m.), **3.1**
  to pass a test réussir à
    un examen
  to take a test passer un
    examen, **3.1**
Thai thaïlandais(e)

than (in comparisons) que,
  7.2
thank you merci, **BV**
thanks merci, **BV**
  thanks to grâce à
that ça; ce (cet), cette, **9**
  that is c'est-à-dire
  That's all. C'est tout., **6.1**
  That's it., That's right.
    C'est ça.
thatched roof le toit de
  chaume
the le, la, les, **1.1**
theater le théâtre, **13.1**
their leur(s), **4**
theme le thème
then alors, **BV**; ensuite,
  12.1
there là; y, **5.2**
  there are il y a, **4.1**
  there is il y a, **4.1**
therefore donc
they ils, elles, **2**; on, **3.2**
thing la chose
to **think** croire, **7.2**; (opinion)
  trouver, **7.2**
third troisième, **4.2**
thirsty: to be thirsty avoir
  soif, **5.1**
this ce (cet), cette
thousand mille, **3.2**
throat la gorge, **14.1**
  throat infection l'angine
    (f.), **14.1**
  to have a frog in one's
    throat avoir un chat
    dans la gorge, **14.1**
  to have a sore throat
    avoir mal à la gorge,
    14.1
throne le trône
through par
to **throw** lancer, **10.2**
  to throw a party donner
    une fête, **4.1**
Thursday jeudi (m.), **BV**
ticket le billet, **8.1**
  one-way ticket l'aller (m.)
    (simple), **9.1**
  round-trip ticket le billet
    aller (et) retour, **9.1**

ticket window le guichet, **9.1**
tie la cravate, **7.1**
to **tie** *(score)* égaliser
tight serré(e), **7.2**
time *(of day)* l'heure *(f.)*, **BV**; *(in a series)* la fois, **10.2**; le temps
  (for) a long time longtemps, **11.1**
  at the same time à la fois
  at what time? à quelle heure?, **2**
  in a short time en très peu de temps
  on time à l'heure, **8.1**
  time difference le décalage horaire
  times l'époque *(f.)*
  What time is it? Il est quelle heure?, **BV**
timetable l'horaire *(m.)*
tip *(restaurant)* le pourboire, **5.2**
  to leave a tip laisser un pourboire, **5.2**
  The tip is included. Le service est compris., **5.2**
tired fatigué(e)
tissue le kleenex, **14.1**
to à, **3.1**; à destination de *(plane, train, etc.)*, **8.1**; *(in order to)* pour
  (up) to jusqu'à
toast le pain grillé
today aujourd'hui, **BV**; de nos jours
together ensemble, **5.1**
tomato la tomate, **6.2**
tomorrow demain, **BV**
  See you tomorrow. À demain., **BV**
tonight ce soir
tonsillitis l'angine *(f.)*, **14.1**
too *(also)* aussi, **1.1**; *(excessive)* trop, **2.1**
  too many, too much trop de
tooth la dent
toothbrush la brosse à dents, **12.1**

toothpaste le dentifrice, **12.1**
totally complètement; totalement
to **touch** toucher, **10.2**
tourist le/la touriste
toward vers
towel la serviette, **11.1**
tower la tour
  Eiffel Tower la tour Eiffel
town la ville, **8.1**; le village
  in town en ville
  small town le village
toxic toxique
track la piste, **10.2**; *(railroad)* la voie, **9.1**
  track and field l'athlétisme *(m.)*, **10.2**
tradition la tradition
traditional traditionel(le)
tragedy la tragédie
tragic tragique
train le train, **9.1**
  train station la gare, **9.1**
  train station restaurant le buffet, **9.1**
traitor le traître, la traîtresse
to **transform** transformer
to **transport** transporter
traveler le voyageur, la voyageuse, **9.1**
tray le plateau, **8.2**
treasure le trésor, **L4**
to **treat** traiter
treatment le traitement
tree l'arbre *(m.)*, **L3**
trigonometry la trigonométrie, **2.2**
trip le voyage, **8.1**
  to take a trip faire un voyage, **8.1**
tropical tropical(e)
trouble: to be in trouble être en difficulté
truck le camion
true vrai(e), **2.2**
trumpet la trompette
truth la vérité
to **try on** essayer, **7.2**
  T-shirt le t-shirt, **7.1**

Tuesday mardi *(m.)*, **BV**
tunic la tunique
Tunisian tunisien(ne)
tunnel le tunnel
turn: It's your turn. À votre tour.
to **turn around** faire demi-tour
to **turn off** *(appliance)* éteindre, **12.2**
to **turn on** *(appliance)* mettre, **7**; allumer, **12.2**
  TV la télé, **12.2**
  on TV à la télé, **12.2**
twin le jumeau, la jumelle, **L1**
type le type, la sorte, le genre, **13.1**
typical typique
typically typiquement

uncle l'oncle *(m.)*, **4.1**
under sous, **8.2**
underground souterrain(e)
to **understand** comprendre, **5**
unfortunately malheureusement
unhappy malheureux, malheureuse
unit l'unité *(f.)*
United States les États-Unis *(m. pl.)*
university l'université *(f.)*
unknown inconnu(e)
until jusqu'à
up there là-haut
upset stomach le trouble digestif
to **use** utiliser
usually d'habitude, **12.2**

vacation les vacances *(f. pl.)*
  on vacation en vacances
  summer vacation les grandes vacances

valley la vallée; le val

value la valeur

vanilla *(adj.)* à la vanille, **5.1**

varied varié(e)

variety la variété

various divers(e)

to **vary** varier

VCR le magnétoscope, **12.2**

vegetable le légume, **6.2**

veil le voile

vein la veine

vengence la vengeance

to **verify** vérifier, **8.1**

very très, **BV;** tout

  very near tout près, **4.2**

  very well très bien, **BV**

victorious victorieux, victorieuse

video la vidéo, **3.1**

  movie video le film en vidéo, **13.1**

videocassette la cassette vidéo, **12.2**

Vietnamese vietnamien(ne), **6**

view la vue

village le village

vinegar le vinaigre, **6.1**

violent violent(e)

violin le violon

viral viral(e)

virus le virus

to **visit** *(a place)* visiter

vitamin la vitamine

voice la voix

volleyball le volley (-ball), **10.2**

volunteer le/la bénévole

voyage le voyage

to **wait (for)** attendre, **9.1**

  to wait in line faire la queue, **9.1**

waiter le serveur, **5.1**

waiting room la salle d'attente, **9.1**

waitress la serveuse, **5.1**

walk la promenade, **11.1**

  to take a walk faire une promenade, **11.1**

to **walk** marcher

wall le mur, **L4**

to **want** désirer, vouloir, avoir envie de

war la guerre, **L3**

warm chaud(e)

warmup suit le survêtement, **7.1**

warrior le guerrier, **L3**

to **wash** se laver, **12.1**

  to wash one's hair (face, etc.) se laver les cheveux (la figure, etc.), **12.1**

washcloth le gant de toilette, **12.1**

waste le déchet

to **watch** surveiller

  Watch out! Attention!, **4.2**

water l'eau *(f.)*, **6.2**

to **water-ski** faire du ski nautique, **11.1**

way la façon

we nous, **2;** on, **3.2**

weak faible, **L1**

weapon l'arme *(f.)*

to **wear** porter, **7.1**

  What size do you wear? Vous faites quelle taille?, **7.2**

weather le temps, **11.1**

  It's nice (bad) weather. Il fait beau (mauvais)., **11.1**

  What's the weather like? Il fait quel temps?, **11.1**

Web site le site

wedding le mariage

Wednesday mercredi *(m.)*, **BV**

week la semaine, **3.2**

  a week huit jours

  a (per) week par semaine, **3.2**

  last week la semaine dernière, **10.2**

  next week la semaine prochaine

weekend le week-end

weight le poids

welcome le/la bienvenu(e)

  Welcome! Bienvenue!

  You're welcome. Je t'en prie. *(fam.)*, **BV;** Je vous en prie. *(form.)*, **BV**

well bien, **BV;** eh bien; ben *(slang)*

  well then alors, **BV**

well-behaved bien élevé(e)

well-done *(meat)* bien cuit(e), **5.2**

well-known connu(e), **13.1**

well-to-do aisé(e)

west l'ouest *(m.)*

western occidental(e)

western *(movie)* le western

what qu'est-ce que, **3.2;** quel(le), **6;** quoi *(after prep.)*

  What color is . . . ? De quelle couleur est... ?, **7.2**

  What is . . . like? Comment est... ?, **1.1**

  What is it? Qu'est-ce que c'est?, **3.2**

  What is today's date? Quelle est la date aujourd'hui?, **BV**

  What's your name? Tu t'appelles comment?, **BV**

when quand, **4.1**

where où, **1.1**

  from where d'où, **1.1**

which quel(le), **6**

to **whistle** siffler, **10.1**

white blanc, blanche, **7.2**

who qui, **1.1**

whole *(adj.)* entier, entière; *(n.)* l'ensemble *(m.)*

whole-wheat bread le pain complet

whom qui, **10**

why pourquoi, **6.2**

  why not? pourquoi pas?

wide large, **7.2**

wife la femme, **4.1**

to **win** gagner, **10.1;** sortir victorieux (victorieuse)

wind le vent, **11.1**

window *(seat)* (une place) côté fenêtre, **8.1**

window *(store)* la vitrine, **7.1**

windsurfing la planche à voile, **11.1**

to go windsurfing faire de la planche à voile, **11.1**

windy: It's windy. Il y a du vent., **11.1**

winner le/la gagnant(e), **10.2**

winner's cup la coupe, **10.2**

winter l'hiver *(m.)*

with avec, **3.2;** auprès de; muni(e) de

without sans

woman la femme, **7.1**

wood le bois

word le mot

words *(of song, etc.)* les paroles *(f. pl.)*

work le travail; *(of art or literature)* l'œuvre *(f.)*, **13.1**

worker l'ouvrier, l'ouvrière

world le monde

wounded blessé(e)

to **write** écrire, **9.2**

to write a prescription faire une ordonnance, **14.2**

writer l'écrivain *(m.)*, **L2**

wrong mauvais(e), **2.2**

What's wrong? Qu'est-ce qui ne va pas?

What's wrong with him? Qu'est-ce qu'il a?, **14.1**

yeah ben oui

year l'an *(m.)*, **4.1;** l'année *(f.)*

to be . . . years old avoir... ans, **4.1**

yellow jaune, **7.2**

yes oui, **BV;** si *(after neg. question)*, **7.2**

yesterday hier, **10.1**

the day before yesterday avant-hier, **10.2**

yogurt la yaourt, **6.1**

you tu, **1;** vous, **2**

young jeune

young people les jeunes *(m. pl.)*

younger le cadet, la cadette, **L1**

your ton, ta, tes; votre, vos, **4**

to **zap** zapper, **12.2**

zero zéro

zone la zone

zoology la zoologie

Index

Credits